# Valuing Small Businesses and Professional Practices

# Valuing Small Businesses and Professional Practices

**Shannon P. Pratt**, D.B.A., C.F.A., C.F.P., A.S.A., C.R.A.
President
*Willamette Management Associates, Inc.*

BUSINESS ONE IRWIN   Homewood, Illinois   60430

© Richard D. Irwin, Inc., 1986

*All rights reserved.* No part of this publication may be
reproduced, stored in a retrieval system, or transmitted,
in any form or by any means, electronic, mechanical,
photocopying, recording, or otherwise, without the prior
written permission of the publisher.

This publication is designed to provide accurate and
authoritative information in regard to the subject matter
covered. It is sold with the understanding that the
publisher is not engaged in rendering legal, accounting, or
other professional service. If legal advice or other expert
assistance is required, the services of a competent
professional person should be sought.

*From a Declaration of Principles jointly adopted by a Committee
of the American Bar Association and a Committee of Publishers.*

ISBN 0-87094-598-X

Library of Congress Catalog Card No. 85–72255

*Printed in the United States of America*

7 8 9 0 E 3 2 1 0

*To Kathie*

# Preface

The purpose of this book is to provide objective guidance to anyone who may be involved in determining the value of a small business or professional practice. The intended audience includes:

- Owners and prospective owners of businesses and professional practices.
- Attorneys.
- CPAs.
- Financial and estate planners.
- Business brokers.
- Business appraisers.
- Bankers.
- Business consultants.

I have focused primarily on how to determine value for the following purposes:

- Buying or selling a business or practice.
- Buying or selling a partial interest in a business or practice.
- Merging with another business or practice.
- Property settlements in divorces.
- Buy/sell agreements.
- Estate planning.
- Determining the need for life insurance.
- Valuation for damage cases:
  - Breach of contract,
  - Condemnation,
  - Lost business opportunity,
  - Lost profits,
  - Antitrust,
  - Personal injury.
- "Squeeze-out" mergers and dissenting stockholder actions.
- Obtaining or providing financing.

My primary goal has been to present the topic as comprehensively as possible within a single volume. I have tried to discuss the valuation techniques and related issues clearly and nontechnically, so a reader needs no background in the topic in order to understand it. Also, since I find the topic intensely interesting, I have tried to share it in a manner that my readers, too, will find enjoyable as well as informative.

A secondary goal, which I found as challenging as it is interesting, has been to include discussions of several related and important subjects that have never before been dealt with in any detail in either books or articles. These subjects include the following:

- Definitions and appropriate applications of various commonly used standards of value.
- Differences between practices for valuing small businesses and those for valuing larger businesses.
- Comparisons in practices and terminology between business appraisal and real estate appraisal.
- How to convert a price that includes generous extended terms to a cash equivalent value, and vice versa.
- Understanding capitalization rates.
- An attempt to analyze objectively the highly controversial "excess earnings" method.
- Working with business brokers.
- The state of the art of the business appraisal profession.
- Using business appraisers to arbitrate disputed valuations.

The book is intended to be a handy reference tool as well as an instructive text. To this end, I have tried to organize the material so that it is easy to use, and have cross referenced extensively among chapters, as appropriate. Sources used in the text and exhibits, including citations to court cases, are referenced in footnotes. The bibliography includes both an extensive compendium of the most relevant books and articles related to the topic that are currently available and also an extensive listing of the most useful and widely used sources of information. Finally, the book is comprehensively indexed for convenient reference.

Many aspects of business appraisal are controversial, and I have tried to present all the most commonly encountered viewpoints on these issues. I have frequently offered my own opinion on matters that evoke controversy, based on my own experience and study of the subject, but I have intended to make it clear when such offerings represent my own views.

There are certain things a book such as this cannot do. Although the reader will gain a basic understanding of the valuation approaches applicable to almost any kind of business or practice valuation need, no book can make the reader an instant expert on the appraisal of businesses or professional practices. Real expertise requires not only a great deal of study, but also years of experience. Also, this book does not purport to offer either legal or investment advice.

Although the title of the book includes the word *small,* there is no clear-cut delineation between large and small businesses or practices. As a generalization, this book addresses businesses or practices worth up to about $1 million, although most of the principles and many of the related subjects addressed apply to larger businesses or practices as well. The larger the business or practice, the more likely it is that the reader would wish also to consult my earlier book, *Valuing a Business: The Analysis and Appraisal of Closely-Held Companies,* which is oriented more toward the valuation of medium-sized and larger companies. It is my intention that the two books will complement each other, together providing a reference source that covers the size spectrum from the smallest to the largest business or professional practice.

This book draws heavily on my own experience, as well as the experience of my associates. In addition, the unstinting cooperation from leading members of the business appraisal profession, the business brokerage community, and dozens of trade and professional associations has contributed immeasurably to the comprehensiveness of this effort. The following section acknowledges many of those who contributed most directly to the work. I sincerely hope that the experience and knowledge that so many people have shared through this book will be helpful to all our readers. I welcome all critiques, corrections, and suggestions for future printings and editions. Please address your comments or suggestions to me at Willamette Management Associates, Inc., 400 Southwest Sixth Avenue, Portland, Oregon 97204, or call me at (503) 222-0577.

**Shannon Pratt**

# Acknowledgments

This work has benefited from information and advice from literally hundreds of people. The entire manuscript was reviewed and critiqued by Jack Bakken, president of Business Appraisal Associates and chairman of the Business Valuation Committee of the American Society of Appraisers, 1981–85; Mike Hill, president of Business & Professional Associates, Inc., and chairman of the Business Valuation Committee of the American Society of Appraisers, 1985–86; Stan Deakin, a manager of appraisal and valuation for Arthur Andersen & Co. and a member of the American Society of Appraisers Business Valuation Committee, 1981–86; and Ralph Arnold, Marilyn Burr, Richard Dole, Kathryn Fisher, Warren Hastings, Robert Holman, Mary McCarter, Louis Paone, Jeffrey Patterson, Donna Walker, and Peter Wyckoff, all members of the professional staff of Willamette Management Associates, Inc.

People who reviewed one to several chapters related to their occupations or areas of specialization included John A. Bogdanski, Stoel, Rives, Boley, Fraser & Wyse; Joe Bowles, Arthur Young & Company; William T. Brooks, Campbell, Warburton, Britton, Fitzsimmons & Smith; Bruce Brown, Pocock-Brown & Associates; Robert Coulson, president, American Arbitration Association; Roger Giles, Pacific Business Brokers Co.; Alex W. Howard, Allied Capital Company; Bob Howard and Kit Lokey, both of Houlihan, Lokey, Howard & Zukin, Inc.; Ray Irving, Professional Practice Sales; D. Alan Jones, Revenue Canada Taxation and 1984–86 president of the Canadian Institute of Chartered Business Valuators; Kenneth Martin, Arthur Andersen & Co. and 1985–86 president of the American Society of Appraisers; Don R. McIver, First Main Capital Corp.; Scott G. McMullin, business and real estate appraiser; Joe Patchin, American Appraisal Co.; Paul O'Brien, executive director of the American Society of Appraisers; Steve Olson, the Consilium Company; James D. Pittman, Compensation Systems Northwest; David J. Scribner, UBI Business Brokers; Wally Stabbert, Institute of Certified Business Counselors; Bill Taylor, Bill Taylor & Associates; Sandy Weinstein, CLU Benefits West; and Tom West, Business Brokerage Press.

For permission to use material, I wish to thank The ESOP Association, *Estate Planning, Fair$hare,* Financial Research Associates, Gran-Tree Corporation, W.T. Grimm & Co., *Inc., Journal of Small Business Management,* Louisiana-Pacific Corporation, Robert Morris Associates, Petroleum Marketing Education Foundation, Prentice-Hall, Inc., *Real Estate Today, Small Business Reporter,* Standard & Poor's Corporation, Texas Instruments, Inc., John Wiley & Sons, and Wisconsin Legal Blank Co., Inc.

Several members of Willamette Management Associates, Inc., also made significant contributions to the development of the manuscript. Ralph Arnold drafted Part IV on valuing professional practices and Chapter 32 on valuing intangible assets. Mary McCarter created the John Dough Bakery case, as well as the suggested solution for it, and she also created the Annie's Apparel and Mary's Machinery & Equipment, Inc., examples used in several chapters. The bibliography was created by Marilyn Burr, who is Willamette's Information Manager, as well as a member of the professional staff. The bibliography also benefited from the kindness of Edgar Holton, of Edgar Holton Accountancy Corp., who made his library available to Marilyn Burr in the course of her collection of citations. Roger Shindell came aboard for three months' full-time temporary duty to assist with the development and analysis of the private company transaction data base.

The entire manuscript was edited by Jan Bear, appraisal report editor. Those who created input to the exhibits and word processing for tables and text included Carol Holla, Larry Trevarthen, and Tim Dollar. The coordinator for the overall project was Debbie Strickler, Willamette's office manager.

Pam Mastroleo, assistant librarian, was responsible for coordination with business brokers, trade and professional associations, and franchisers. On the following pages is a list of business brokers who responded to the survey of transaction prices for small businesses and professional practices, as well as a list of respondents to a general information survey among trade and professional associations, publications, and business franchisers.

Last, but not least, I thank my assistant, Kathie Martin, whose responsibilities include managing my schedule, for keeping her good humor while putting up with me during the entire project, and also for somehow succeeding in protecting enough of my time to get the job done.

My deep gratitude goes to all the above contributors of time, effort, and talent, and to many others who extended their help somewhere along the way. Final responsibility for all judgments and content rests, of course, with the author.

**S. P.**

### Business and Professional Practice Brokers

Oliver A. Gottschalk, *ABBEX of Sarasota, Inc.*, Sarasota, Florida
Richard Anthony, *Acquisition Catalyst*, Anaheim, California
Harvey P. Allan, *Allan Enterprises*, San Diego, California
Nick Clark, *ANI Business Brokers*, Jackson, Mississippi
C.R. Kip Kane, *Arizona Commercial Realty*, Phoenix, Arizona
Arthur R. Kara, *ARKCO Associates Incorporated*, Cleveland, Ohio
Joseph J. Brennan, *Baldwin Realty & Investments*, Gainesville, Florida
Marvin Barab, *BARBROOK, INC.*, Rolling Hills Estates, California
J.T. Barry, *James T. Barry Co., Inc.*, Milwaukee, Wisconsin
Gus N. Benakis, *Benakis, Inc.*, Minneapolis, Minnesota
Raymond R. Borgia, Erie, Pennsylvania
Daniel J. Leon, *Brokers Network & Realty*, Walnut Creek, California
Bruce Schirmers, *Bruce & Co.*, Soldotna, Alaska
Harold Lubbock, *Business Acquisition Consultants*, Walnut Creek, California
David C. Smith, *Business Brokerage, Inc.*, Laguna Beach, California
Robert F. Pierce, *Business Brokers International Corp.*, Braintree, Massachusetts
Murray E. Bronstein, *Business Brokers One*, Goldsboro, North Carolina
Kenneth M. Perry, *Business Opportunity Counselors, Inc.*, Auburn, Massachusetts
Brian J. Ollmert, *Business People Services, Inc.*, Bensenville, Illinois
Gregory Merrill, *Chapman Associates*, Logan, Utah
Richard S. Fleming, *Coast and Country Real Estate*, Brunswick, Maine
Wilbur M. Yegge, *Commercial Associates*, Wells, Maine
James A. Steffeck, *Cougill Gallagher*, Helena, Montana
Carlos O. Cuellar, *Cuellar Business Consultants, Inc.*, Corpus Christi, Texas
Donald E. Spangler, *D/R Incorporated*, Richmond, Virginia
Donald J. Dahlheimer, *Dahlheimer & Associates, Inc.*, Belmont, California
Mimi Bischoff, *Reel C. Davis & Co.*, Colorado Springs, Colorado
Louis V. Pellicore, *Era Olde Towne Re*, Richboro, Pennsylvania
Don R. McIver, *First Main Capital Corporation*, Dallas, Texas
Harry L. Peterson, *The Franchise Center*, Salt Lake City, Utah
Jerry Garner, *G.R. Bill Company, Inc.*, San Diego, California
Peter C. Geffers, *Geffers Realty*, Oshkosh, Wisconsin
Grant Gordon, *Gordon & Jenkins, Inc.*, Santa Monica, California
Paul G.W. Fetscher, *Great American Brokerage*, New York, New York
William D. White, *H.J. Carroll Agencies*, Port Townsend, Washington
Sandy Hansell, *Sandy Hansell & Associates*, Southfield, Michigan
Ronald L. Hammerle, *health resources*, Kansas City, Missouri
William H. Hill, *William H. Hill Associates, Inc.*, Jacksonville, Florida
A.G. "Al" Hocker, *Al Hocker & Associates*, Houston, Texas
James A. Hudkins, Alameda, California
Harvey Henjum, *IFS Investors Services, Inc.*, Bloomington, Minnesota
Bradford M. Johnson, *Johnson, Lane, Space, Smith & Co., Inc.*, Atlanta, Georgia
Dan Kemp, *Dan Kemp Real Estate, Inc.*, Indianapolis, Indiana
Donald A. Klassen, *Klassen Associates, Inc.*, Rochester, New York
Michael I. Brody and Anthony S. Lefco, *Lehigh Valley Financial Corporation*, Reading, Pennsylvania
Gary F. Turtle, *Lingate Financial Group, Inc.*, Minneapolis, Minnesota
Glen Cooper, *Maine Business Brokers, Inc.*, Auburn, Maine
Bradley L. Kaplan, *Mathurin & Kaplan Business Brokerage*, Portland, Maine
Michael M. Santomauro, *Metropolitan Business Finders*, New York, New York
Edwin O. Meyer, *Edwin O. Meyer Associates*, Richmond, Virginia
Ronald R. McCord, *Milmark Realty*, Milwaukee, Wisconsin
Roland Vance, *Motel, Hotel Sales and Management*, Sandy, Utah
T.H. McGuine, *N/C Automation, Inc.*, Turtle Lake, Wisconsin
L.C. "Jerry" Hall, *Nationwide Business Services*, Phoenix, Arizona
Homer J. Blalock, *National Lone Star Corporation*, El Paso, Texas
Jerry Marcy, *National Realty, Inc.*, Seattle, Washington

Murray V. Duffin, *The Opportunity Professionals, Inc.*, Plainview, New York

Harvey Osherenko, Bevery Hills, California

Roger Gileş and Al Irwin, *Pacific Business Brokers Co.*, Portland, Oregon

Robert A. Marcketti, *Palm Beach Business and Properties, Inc.*, Boca Raton, Florida

Tom Papadopoulos, *Papadopoulos Properties, Inc.*, Washington, D.C., and Bethesda, Maryland

Harry L. Parker, *Harry L. Parker & Associates, Inc.*, North Miami Beach, Florida

Dean Parkins, *Dean Parkins & Associates, Inc.*, Seattle, Washington

Gregory Swirtz, *Professional Investments*, Minneapolis, Minnesota

Raymond N. Irving, *Professional Practice Sales*, San Francisco, California

Leonard Pick, *Restaurant Sales and Acquisitions, Inc.*, McLean, Virginia

Thomas C. Roe, *Roe Investments*, Sacramento, California

David A. Rogier, *Rogier Associates*, Indianapolis, Indiana

Ernest A. Bigelow and Stephen Percy, *Soundview Associates, Inc.*, Waterford, Connecticut

Richard M. Frenkel, *Sunbelt Business Brokers*, Charleston, South Carolina

Bill Taylor, Orrin Granlund, and Charles S. Peck, Sr., *Bill Taylor Associates*, Portland, Oregon

T.W. Mobberley, *Transamerica Capital Corporation*, Dallas, Texas

Karen M. Lassen, *Turim/Winter/Associates, Ltd.*, Lake Forest, Illinois

David Scribner, *UBI Business Brokers*, Los Angeles, California

William D. Zantzinger, *W & Z Realty*, White Plains, Maryland

Atlee Kohl, *Woodland Capital Company*, Irving, Texas

Charles Ziegle, *Ziegle & Associates*, Lafayette, Louisiana

## Trade and Professional Associations, Trade and Professional Publications, and Franchisers

*Academy of Ambulatory Foot Surgery*, St. Louis, Missouri
*American Arbitration Association*, New York, New York
*American Automotive Leasing Association*, Milwaukee, Wisconsin
*American Coin-Op*, Chicago, Illinois
*American Collectors Association*, Minneapolis, Minnesota
*American College of Osteopathic Surgeons*, Coral Cables, Florida
*American Council of Independent Laboratories*, Washington, D.C.
*American Dental Association*, Chicago, Illinois
*American Home Sewing Association*, New York, New York
*American International Rent A Car Corporation*, Dallas, Texas
*American Nurseryman*, Chicago, Illinois
*American Traffic Safety Services Association*, Fredricksburg, Virginia
*Apparel Industry Magazine*, Atlanta, Georgia
*ASIA-ABT Service Corporation*, Salt Lake City, Utah
*Association of American Railroads/Bureau of Explosives*, Washington, D.C.
*Bailey Employment System, Inc.*, Monroe, Connecticut
*Best Resume'Service, Inc.*, Pittsburgh, Pennsylvania
*Building Products Digest*, Newport Beach, California
*Building Supply Home Centers*, Des Plaines, Illinois
*Business Exchange, Inc.*, North Hollywood, California
*Business Review*, Syracuse, New York
*Cable Television Business*, Englewood, Colorado
*Computer & Communications Industry Association*, Arlington, Virginia
*Concept III International, Inc.*, Louisville, Kentucky
*Consulting Engineer*, Barrington, Illinois
*Corporate Report Minnesota*, Minneapolis, Minnesota
*Dallas/Fort Worth Business Journal*, Dallas, Texas
*Delphi Stained Glass Centers, Inc.*, Lansing, Michigan
*Dip N Strip, Inc.*, Denver, Colorado
*The Director*, Minneapolis, Minnesota
*Flower News*, Chicago, Illinois
*Fluid Power Distributers Association*, Philadelphia, Pennsylvania
*Great Earth International*, Yorba Linda, California
*Hand Tools Institute*, Tarrytown, New York
*Home Call, Inc.*, Frederick, Maryland
*International Fabricare Institute*, Silver Spring, Maryland
*International Reprographic Association*, Franklin Park, Illinois
*Jobber Topics*, Lincolnwood, Illinois
*Journal of the American Optometric Association*, St. Louis, Missouri
*Kansas Business News*, Lindsborg, Kansas
*Lawn Care Industry*, Cleveland, Ohio
*Management Recruiters International, Inc.*, Cleveland, Ohio
*Marco's, Inc.*, Toledo, Ohio
*Memphis Business Journal*, Memphis, Tennessee
*Metal Treating Institute*, Tallahassee, Florida
*MicroAge, Inc.*, Tempe, Arizona
*National Association of Printing Ink Manufacturers*, Harrison, New York
*National Association of Television and Electronic Services of America*, Chicago, Illinois
*National Candy Brokers Association*, Washington, D.C.
*National Council of Investigation and Security Services*, Washington, D.C.
*National Equipment Servicing Dealers Association, Inc.*, Jefferson Valley, New York
*National Fertilizer Solutions Association*, Peoria, Illinois
*National Hairdressers*, St. Louis, Missouri
*National Handbag Association*, New York, New York

*National Newspaper Publishers Association*, Washington, D.C.
*National Satellite Cable Association*, Washington, D.C.
*Paper Trade Journal*, Prairie View, Illinois
*POP-INS, Inc.*, West Palm Beach, Florida
*Professional Carwashing*, Latham, New York
*Radio Shack*, Barrie, Ontario, Canada
*Rampart Industries, Inc.*, Longhorne, Pennsylvania
*Sir Speedy Printing, Inc.*, Newport Beach, California
*The Soap & Detergent Association*, New York, New York
*The Sporting Goods Dealer*, St. Louis, Missouri
*Spring-Green Lawn Care Corp.*, Naperville, Illinois
*Steel Tank Institute*, Northbrook, Illinois
*Taco Time International, Inc.*, Eugene, Oregon
*Teller Training Distributors, Inc.*, Seattle, Washington
*Towing and Recovery Association of America*, Winter Park, Florida
*Trophy Dealers & Manufacturers Association, Inc.*, Fresno, California
*Truck Renting and Leasing Association*, Washington, D.C.
*Vertiflite*, Alexandria, Virginia

# Contents

Capital Structure: *Classes of Corporate Stock. Treasury Stock. Limited Partnerships. General Partnerships.*

*Lease. Description of Facilities and Product Lines.* Financial Statements. Related Financial Data.

*and Respect. Dependence on Referral Sources. Education. Licensing and Certification.* Distinction between Practice Goodwill and Professional Goodwill: *Practice Goodwill. Professional Goodwill.* Buying and Selling a Practice—Elements of Goodwill: *Expected Future Earnings. Level of Competition. Referral Base. Types of Patients and Clients. Work Habits of the Practitioner. Fee Schedules. Practice Location. Employees of the Practice. Marketability of the Practice.* Divorce Valuation—Elements of Goodwill: *Practitioner's Age and Health. Demonstrated Past Earning Power. Reputation for Judgment, Skill, and Knowledge. Comparative Professional Success. Nature and Duration of Practice. Summary.*

# List of Exhibits

# Part I

Introduction: Understanding the
Valuation Problem

# Chapter 1

## Defining the Valuation Assignment

## First Things First

In order to have the valuation job on track from the very beginning, the first step is to define clearly and completely the valuation problem.

I make this the first chapter in this book for two reasons. First, defining the valuation assignment is the logical beginning of the valuation process, providing the focus for all the valuation considerations and efforts to be undertaken. Second, my experience has been that most people who approach the problem of valuing a business or professional practice infrequently or, especially, for the first time, either overlook or fail to specify adequately one or more of the key elements in the valuation situation. This often results in misdirected efforts and invalid conclusions.

*I highly recommend that the definition of the valuation assignment be written.* Writing valuation objectives and requirements forces those responsible for the valuation to think carefully through all of its essential elements. It also helps them avoid misdirecting the valuation process and helps the various parties involved, such as the principals, brokers, attorneys, and professional appraisers, avoid misunderstandings that otherwise may arise. If a professional appraiser is to be retained, the appraiser can draw on his experience to help define the appraisal assignment.

## Basic Elements of the Valuation Assignment

In simple terms, the first step in valuation is to make the following decisions and incorporate them into a "valuation assignment":

1. Exactly what is to be valued.
2. The use or uses to which the valuation exercise is expected to be put.
3. The valuation date.
4. The applicable standard of value.
5. Instructions to be given to a professional appraiser, if one is to be retained.

Exhibit 1–1 is a suggested checklist for use in defining the valuation assignment.

## Property to Be Valued

Much of the confusion and apparent disagreement among appraisers and appraisal writings arises simply because it is not clear exactly what property or interest is to be valued. In order to determine the applicable approach and steps to be taken, it must be made clear *exactly* what is to be valued. The most important single determination is

Exhibit 1–1

## VALUATION ASSIGNMENT CHECKLIST

Name of entity _____

Form of ownership

        □ Regular corporation             □ Limited partnership

        □ Subchapter S corporation     □ Sole proprietorship

        □ General partnership            □ Other (please specify)

State in which incorporated or registered _____

Valuation being done on     □ stock basis, or     □ asset basis

      (If asset basis, list assets to be included and liabilities to be assumed, if any)

Proportion of total entity being valued

Any restrictions on transfer?

Purpose or purposes of the valuation

Applicable standard of value

Valuation date

Is covenant not to compete involved?     □ Yes    □ No

Is employment agreement(s) involved?     □ Yes    □ No

If independent appraiser is retained:
    Name of appraiser

    Name of client

    Form and extent of appraisal report

    Expected completion date (specify due date of various phases)

    Fee arrangement

**SOURCE**: Willamette Management Associates, Inc., Portland, Oregon.

whether stock or assets are to be valued. More small businesses and professional practices are sold on the basis of an asset sale than on the basis of a stock sale.

Stock represents an indirect ownership interest in whatever bundle of assets and liabilities (actual or contingent) may exist in a corporation. Stock ownership is quite different from direct ownership of assets and direct obligation for liabilities. If stock is to be valued, then it must be identified in the appraisal assignment. If assets are to be valued, then those assets (and any liabilities to be assumed) must be specified. If it is a partial interest in an entity that is to be valued, then of obvious importance is the proportionate relationship of the partial interest to the whole.

## Valuation of Stock

**Identification of the Corporation.**   When valuing stock, the name of the corporation and the state of incorporation should be specified; this avoids the ambiguity frequently caused by the existence of many corporations with the same name, incorporated in different states. Also, most legal factors that have a bearing on valuation are matters of state laws, which, on some issues, vary considerably. So, for some valuation purposes, the state of incorporation has an important effect on certain valuation criteria. (State law is especially variable in regard to valuations of businesses and professional practices for property settlements in divorces, as discussed in Chapter 30.)

If the corporation has any special corporate registration, such as an S or a nonprofit corporation, that should be specified as part of the corporate identification, because it may have a bearing on the valuation process and conclusion.

**Specification of the Stock Interest to Be Valued.**   To preclude any uncertainty, specify if 100 percent of the stock is to be valued. If not, then the proportionate interest to be valued should be specified.

If there is only one class of common stock, it generally is sufficient to state the number of shares being valued out of the total number of shares outstanding. If there is more than one class of common stock, the appraisal assignment should specify the number of shares in each class being valued out of the total number of shares in that class. Where one or more classes of stock are outstanding but not subject to valuation, the assignment should nevertheless mention them. If the number of shares that may be involved in a contemplated transaction is unknown, then the assignment might contain general wording, such as "minority shares of common stock."

If there are any restrictions on transferring the shares of stock to be valued, it is a good idea to note them in the appraisal assignment, because restrictions on transfer usually affect the value of the shares to be appraised.

## Valuation on an Asset Sale Basis

Even if a business or practice is incorporated, it is quite common to transfer it on the basis of a sale of assets rather than a sale of stock. In such a case the assets to be transferred (and liabilities, if any) must be specified.

The following are commonly included in the sale of a small business or professional practice:

1. Inventory.
2. Fixed assets—leasehold improvements, furniture, fixtures, and equipment, etc.
3. Intangible assets—leasehold, trade name, patents, copyrights, customer lists, goodwill, advantageous financing arrangements, etc.

The seller frequently keeps the cash, collects the accounts receivable, and pays off all the existing liabilities. If the inventory is substantial and is financed by a manufacturer, the buyer may assume the liability for the inventory, subject, of course, to the manufacturer's approval.

Real estate may or may not be included in the sale. If it is, and is subject to a mortgage, the buyer may or may not assume the mortgage. (As discussed in later chapters, I generally prefer, if possible, to separate, or unbundle, the real estate value from the value of the business, at least if the real estate is multipurpose rather than an integral part of the business.)

Sometimes a buyer may purchase most or all of the receivables and assume most or all of the liabilities. If so, it must be determined whether these transfers are unconditional or if contingencies or recourses exist.

## Treatment of Covenants Not to Compete and Employment Agreements

Two types of intangible assets frequently are created specifically for the purpose of facilitating the sale of a business or professional practice. These are covenants not to compete and employment agreements. It is important to specify if either or both of these assets are to be included. Many small businesses and professional practices would have little or no value without such agreements.

If such contracts are included, the matter of how they are treated in the purchase agreement has tax consequences for both buyers and sellers. This matter is discussed in Chapter 28.

## The Purpose or Purposes of the Valuation

Although this book focuses primarily on valuation for the purpose of buying or selling a business or practice, it also addresses special aspects of valuations for many other needs: property settlements, taxes, damage cases, minority stockholder appraisal rights, and so on. Valuations for these different purposes are all affected by a mass of complex federal and state statutes and legal precedents. The result is that different standards of value, and different valuation criteria, must be applied in different cases, depending both on the purpose of the valuation and on the jurisdiction in which it is taking place. Consequently, the purpose of the valuation is an integral part of the valuation assignment, and the valuation process must meet the applicable standard of value and valuation criteria. The next two chapters are devoted to an overview of the different standards of value and how they may apply for different valuation purposes, and Part V contains chapters devoted to the peculiarities of the most important purposes for business and professional practice valuation.

# Valuation Date

The date or dates at which the business or practice is being valued is critically important, because changing circumstances can cause values to vary dramatically from one date to another, and the valuation date directly influences data available for valuation.

## Choosing an Applicable Valuation Date

It usually is easiest to arrive at the most precise valuation at the end of an entity's fiscal year, because most companies take physical inventories then and also analyze and adjust other accounts in the normal course of business. Consequently, it is common for sales of businesses and practices to close at the end of a fiscal year. The typical sale in this circumstance involves arriving at a value before the end of the fiscal year. This valuation is then subject to certain adjustments for physical inventory, accounts receivable, and/or certain other accounts, depending on exactly what is being transferred as part of the sale.

Valuations shortly after the end of a fiscal year often can rely on year-end data, in most cases with some minor adjustments. If the effective date of the closing is some other time, it may be necessary to go through a complete year-end closing of the books to arrive at the final price. More often, especially in smaller businesses and practices, a value can be arrived at without such a complete accounting exercise, but subject to adjustment for a physical inventory count if inventory is a significant item.

Valuations for Employee Stock Ownership Plans (ESOPs) usually are pegged to a fiscal year-end, and valuations for some other purposes, such as gifts, charitable contributions, and incentive stock options, can be pegged to any desirable dates.

## Valuation Dates Determined by Law

For many purposes, the effective date for valuation is out of the parties' hands. In most states, the valuation date for inheritance taxes is the date of death. For federal estate taxes, the taxpayer can elect the date of death or six months after, so the parties should determine which is more advantageous. For divorces, the most common valuation date is the effective date of the divorce, but it varies from state to state and from situation to situation (see Chapter 30, which addresses divorce litigation). For dissenting stockholder actions, the valuation date almost always is the date that the stockholders approved the action creating the dissenters' appraisal rights. Relevant valuation dates for damage cases must be determined case-by-case, and may themselves be a matter of dispute among the parties (Chapter 30 covers damage suits as well as divorces). If possible, the valuation date or alternate possible valuation dates should be specified.

# Applicable Standard of Value

As discussed in the following chapters, different standards of value govern valuations for different purposes. Some of these standards have fairly clear-cut definitions and interpretations that appraisers and courts widely accept; others do not.

Although fair market value is the most widely used standard of value, it does not apply to all valuation situations. Specify the standard of value applicable to the particular situation, if known. Where possible, this book attempts to identify the applicable standard of value for each common kind of valuation situation. If in doubt, consult a professional appraiser.

# Instructions to the Independent Professional Appraiser

If an outside appraiser is to be retained, discuss and agree to certain factors, such as extent and type of report expected, the time schedule, and the expected cost.

## Form and Extent of the Appraisal Report

The appraiser's report to the client can be oral, written, or a combination. An oral report can be anything from a quick phone call to lengthy meetings with the principals, attorneys, brokers, and/or other parties involved. The form and extent of a written report can range from a single-page letter report to a detailed, hundred-page-plus volume. Obviously, at least general expectations should be discussed and referenced in the assignment.

## Schedule

Most first-time, or infrequent, business appraisal clients tend to underestimate the amount of appraiser lead time needed for a thorough and professional job. My staff and I tell clients that our comfort zone is 60 days for a completely documented, written appraisal for a medium-sized company (as discussed more fully in Chapter 35). Often, however, it is necessary for the appraiser to act immediately and give a client at least minimal guidance about an imminent deal.

Perhaps the most serious lead-time problem that my staff and I encounter is a sudden attorney request for expert witness testimony, in court, on a disputed valuation issue. An attorney may jeopardize his client's position when he fails to allow enough lead time for an expert witness to prepare thoroughly for court testimony.

The best plan is to give the appraiser all the lead time possible, and agree at the beginning about the expected schedule.

## Fee Arrangements

An appraiser may work on a fixed fee, a range of estimated fees, hourly, or daily. The more clearly defined the appraisal assignment, the more likely it is that the appraiser will be able to quote a fixed fee or a very close estimate. For most types of appraisal assignments, an independent professional appraiser is legally and ethically prohibited from entering into an arrangement making the appraiser's fee contingent on completed settlement negotiations or the outcome of a court decision. More on all these points is discussed in Chapter 35.

# Chapter 2

## Defining Value

Fair Market Value
Effect of Terms on Value
Investment, Fundamental, or Intrinsic Value
Fair Value
Going-Concern Value
Liquidation Value
Book Value

*Value, like beauty, is in the mind of the beholder.*

Since the task of this book is to assist readers in reaching, understanding, or evaluating conclusions about value, its logical beginning is to identify and define different standards of value which may apply in different situations. Many terms are used to describe various notions of value; but, unfortunately, such terms mean different things to different people. As one experienced attorney put it:

> Many terms are used to define value, . . . Only a few of these terms have some definition. Others have the definition which the parties choose to place upon them.[1]

This chapter presents the concepts of value that are most widely encountered and most useful in business valuation.

# Fair Market Value

The most widely recognized and accepted standard of value is *fair market value*. It is the standard that applies to all federal and state tax matters, such as estate taxes, gift taxes, inheritance taxes, income taxes, and ad valorem taxes. It is also the legal standard of value in many other—though not all—valuation situations.

The definition of fair market value is almost universally accepted as the cash, or cash equivalent, price for which property would change hands between a willing buyer and a willing seller, both being adequately informed of the relevant facts, and neither being compelled to buy or to sell. There is also general agreement that the definition implies that the parties have the ability as well as the willingness to buy or to sell. The market in this definition can be thought of as all the potential buyers and sellers of like businesses or practices.

In legal interpretations of fair market value, the willing buyer and willing seller are hypothetical persons dealing at arm's length, rather than any "particular" buyer or seller. In other words, a price would not be considered representative of fair market value if influenced by special motivations not characteristic of a typical buyer or seller.

The concept of fair market value also assumes prevalent economic and market conditions at the date of the particular valuation. You probably have heard someone say many times, "I couldn't get anywhere near the value of my house if I put it on the market today," or, "The value of XYZ Company stock is really much more (or less) than the price it's selling for on the New York Stock Exchange today." The standard of value that those people have in mind is some standard *other than* fair market value, since the concept of fair market value means the cash equivalent price at which a transaction could be expected to take place under *conditions existing at the valuation date*. Also, one of

---

[1] John E. Moye, *Buying and Selling Businesses* (Minneapolis: National Practice Institute, 1983), p. 25.

the important aspects of the definition of fair market value is that it is denominated in cash or cash equivalents.

The terms *market value* and *cash value* frequently are used interchangeably with the term *fair market value*.[2]

# Effect of Terms on Value

*Most small businesses and professional practices do not sell for cash or cash equivalents*. The majority of small businesses and professional practice sales include a cash down payment, typically 20 to 35 percent of what we will call the *transaction price,* with the balance on a contract to be paid over some period of time, usually a few years.

The contracts for the balance of the transaction price usually are interest-bearing contracts, but the rate of interest almost always is below a *market rate*. In other words, third party lenders generally would charge higher rates on loans that have comparable collateral and the same terms as are in the contract for the balance of a transaction price. Consequently, the fair market values of such contracts accepted as part of the consideration in a sale usually are less than their face values. The procedure for converting the face value of such a contract to cash value is the subject of Chapter 17.

Some contracts may include a contingency clause, which makes the full expected amount that the seller will realize depend on certain future events; such an event could be the level of future earnings or retention for some time period of the clients who were doing business with the seller at the time of the transaction.

As discussed more fully in Chapter 17, I know of no other class of transactions whose prices diverge as far from a cash equivalent value or fair market value as the values of contracts arising from sales of small businesses and professional practices. It is not at all uncommon for the terms of the contract to be such that the cash equivalent value is 20 percent or more below the face value of the transaction.

# Investment, Fundamental, or Intrinsic Value

Most valuation terms, other than *fair market value* are not, unfortunately, defined with unanimous agreement by various writers and appraisers. For the purposes of this book, I use *investment value, fundamental value,* and *intrinsic value* interchangeably, because most people

---

[2] A leading authority on real estate appraisal terminology in the United States says that the definition of market value is synonymous with fair market value. (Byrl N. Boyce, ed., *Real Estate Appraisal Terminology* [Cambridge, Mass.: Ballinger Publishing Company, 1982], p. 98).

A prominent Canadian business appraiser draws a slight distinction between the two terms: "*Fair* in *fair market value* means that the market (and the price) must have some consistency and cannot be affected by a transient boom or sudden pause; that is, the word *fair* qualifies the market on which the valuation is based." (Richard M. Wise, "The CA's Role in Valuations: An Inside-Out Perspective," *CA Magazine,* [September 28, 1984], pp. 28–40.)

who use any of these three terms usually have the same general definition in mind, although some writers make certain distinctions among these standards of value.

In real estate terminology, investment value is defined as "Value to a particular investor, based on individual investment requirements, as distinguished from the concept of market value, which is impersonal and detached."[3] In real estate appraisal, calculations of *investment value* conventionally involve the discounting of an anticipated income stream.

The *Handbook for Financial Decision Makers* defines *intrinsic value* as follows:

> *Value, intrinsic of common stock.* The price that is justified for a share when the primary factors of value are considered. In other words, it is the real worth of the stock, as distinguished from the current market price of the stock. It is a subjective value in the sense that the analyst must apply his own individual background and skills to determine it, and estimates of intrinsic value will vary from one analyst to the next.
>
> The financial manager estimates intrinsic value by carefully appraising the following fundamental factors that affect common stock values:
>
> **1.** *Value of the Firm's Assets.* The physical assets held by the firm have some market value. In liquidation approaches to valuation, assets can be quite important. In techniques of going-concern valuation, assets are usually omitted.
> **2.** *Likely Future Earnings.* The expected future earnings of the firm are the most important single factor affecting the common stock's intrinsic value.
> **3.** *Likely Future Dividends.* The firm may pay out its earnings as dividends or may retain them to finance growth and expansion. The firm's policies with respect to dividends will affect the intrinsic value of its stock.
> **4.** *Likely Future Growth Rate.* A firm's prospects for future growth are carefully evaluated by investors and are a factor influencing intrinsic value."[4]

A prominent bank analyst defines *fundamental value* as follows: "The present value of the cash flows an investor will receive in the form of dividends and capital appreciation."[5]

As can be seen from the above, different people use the terms investment value, intrinsic value, and fundamental value to mean pretty much the same. Further evidence that the terms are used with similar meaning is found in the following definitions from an authority in the accounting field:

> **Intrinsic value.** The amount that an investor considers, on the basis of an evaluation of available facts, to be the "true" or "real" worth of an item, usually an *equity security*. The value that will become the market value when other investors reach the same conclusions. The various approaches to determining intrinsic value of the *finance* literature are

---
[3] *Real Estate Appraisal Terminology*, p. 140.
[4] John J. Hampton, *Handbook for Financial Decision Makers* (Reston, Va.: Reston Publishing Company, 1979), pp. 543–4.
[5] Bradford M. Johnson, "Valuing Community Bank Stocks," *Bank Administration* (September 1978), p. 1ff.

based on expectations and discounted cash flows. See *expected value; fundamental analysis; discounted cash flow method.*[6]

**Fundamental analysis.** An approach in security analysis which assumes that a security has an "intrinsic value" that can be determined through a rigorous evaluation of relevant variables. Expected earnings is usually the most important variable in this analysis, but many other variables, such as dividends, capital structure, management quality, and so on, may also be studied. An analyst estimates the "intrinsic value" of a security on the basis of those fundamental variables and compares this value with the current market price of this security to arrive at an investment decision.[7]

When I use the term *investment value* throughout this book, I mean the general notions described above.

There can be many valid reasons for the investment value to one particular owner or prospective owner to be different from the fair market value. These reasons include the following:

**1.** Differences in estimates of future earning power.
**2.** Differences in perception of the degree of risk.
**3.** Differences in tax status.
**4.** Synergies with other operations owned or controlled.

The discounted future earnings method (see Chapter 13) is oriented essentially toward developing an investment value. Whether or not the value thus developed also represents fair market value depends on whether the assumptions used would be accepted by a consensus of market participants.

If sound analysis leads to a valid conclusion that the investment value to a particular owner exceeded market value at a given time, then the rational economic decision for that owner would be not to sell at that time, unless a particular buyer could be found to whom investment value would be higher than the consensus of value among a broader group of typical buyers.

In the analysis of stocks, investment value is generally considered the appropriate price for a stock according to a security analyst who has completed his fundamental analysis of the company's assets, earning power, and other factors. If the market value is below what he concludes is the investment value, he considers the stock a "buy." If the market value is above what he considers to be the investment value, he suggests that the stock be sold.

# Fair Value

The expression *fair value* is an excellent example of ambiguous terminology used in the field of commercial appraisal. In order to understand

---

[6] W. W. Cooper and Yuji Ijiri, eds., *Kohler's Dictionary for Accountants*, 6th ed. (Englewood Cliffs, N.J.: Prentice-Hall, 1983), p. 285.

[7] Ibid., p. 228.

what the expression means, you have to know the context of its use. The accepted definition of fair value in real estate appraisal terminology is totally different from the interpretation the courts have given to fair value as a statutory standard of value applicable to a business appraisal.

A leading authority on real estate terminology states that fair value is synonymous with market value or fair market value.[8] However, in most states, fair value is the statutory standard of value applicable in cases of dissenting stockholders' appraisal rights. In these states, if a corporation merges, sells out, or takes certain other major actions, and the owner of a minority interest believes that he is being forced to receive less than adequate consideration for his stock, he has the right to have his shares appraised and to receive fair value in cash. There is no clearly recognized consensus about the definition of fair value in this context; but precedents established in the courts of the various states certainly have not equated it to fair market value. I have served as an advisor or expert witness for one side or the other in many dissenting stockholder suits, and I can say that when a situation arises of actual or potential stockholder dissent, it is necessary to research carefully the legal precedents applicable to each case.

# Going-Concern Value

The concept of *going-concern value* is not a standard of value, but an assumption about the status of the business. It merely means that the business or practice is being valued as a viable operating entity: It has its assets and inventory in place, its work force in place, and its doors open for business, with no imminent threat of discontinuance as a going concern.

As noted earlier, fair market value, fair value, and investment value are examples of standards of value. Thus, in many instances, it would be correct to characterize the value being estimated as "fair market value on a going-concern basis," "fair value on a going-concern basis," or "investment value on a going-concern basis." Unless otherwise noted, we will assume in this book that we are dealing with values of businesses or practices on a going-concern basis.

In most cases, the phrase going-concern value is used to mean the total value of the entity as a going concern. Sometimes, however, if the total value of the firm on a going-concern basis exceeds the net value of its tangible assets, the phrase *going-concern value* is used to refer to the difference between the two, that is, to the intangible value that exists over and above the net tangible asset value.[9]

---

[8] *Real Estate Appraisal Terminology*, p. 98.

[9] For a more complete discussion of the phrase *going-concern value* in this latter context, see Benjamin N. Henszley, "Going Concern Value after *Concord Control, Inc.*," *Taxes* (November 1983), p. 699.

# Liquidation Value

*Liquidation value* is, in essence, the antithesis of *going-concern value*. *Liquidation value* means the net amount that can be realized if the business is terminated and the assets sold off piecemeal. The term *orderly liquidation* means that the assets are sold over a reasonable period of time, attempting to get the best available price for each asset. The term *forced liquidation* means that the assets are sold as quickly as possible, frequently all at one time at an auction sale.

When computing liquidation value, it is essential to recognize all costs associated with the liquidation of the enterprise. These costs normally include commissions, the administrative cost of keeping the company alive until the liquidation is completed, taxes, and legal and accounting costs. Also, in computing the present value of a business on a liquidation basis, it is necessary to discount the estimated net proceeds, at a rate reflecting the risk involved, from the time the net proceeds are expected to be received back to the date of the valuation.

# Book Value

*Book value* is something of a misnomer because it *does not represent any standard of value at all. It is an accounting term, not an appraisal term.* Book value means the sum of the asset accounts, net of depreciation and amortization, less the liability accounts, as shown on a balance sheet.

Assets usually are accounted for at historical cost, less depreciation computed by one of various methods. Some assets may be completely written off the books. Liabilities are usually shown at face value. Intangible assets normally do not appear on the balance sheet unless they were purchased or the actual cost of development was recorded. Neither contingent assets nor contingent liabilities are recorded on the books.

The longer the time after an individual asset or liability item is placed on the books, the less likely is the book value of that item to bear any identifiable relationship to any standard of value for the individual item, much less for the entity as a whole.

# Chapter 3

## How Valuations Differ for Different Purposes

*Before you can value a company, you must know the purpose for which you need the valuation. Different purposes will provide different values and different valuation methods.*[1]

When I give speeches on valuing businesses and professional practices, I frequently tell the audience that the purpose of the valuation has an important bearing on the valuation process that should be undertaken, and, in some cases, on the conclusion that will be reached. This revelation usually shocks at least some of the members of the audience, who had never realized that different valuation considerations and conclusions can be appropriate for the same interest in a business or professional practice, depending on the purpose of the valuation.

While some people's first reaction is to think that there can be only one value for any given property at any one time, it simply isn't so. Different state and federal statutes, regulations, and legal precedents found in court cases impose different standards of value and different sets of criteria for valuations for different purposes. Also, apart from the valuation process and conclusion, the extent and form in which the valuation should be presented, oral and/or written, is influenced to a considerable extent by the purpose of the valuation.

# Buying or Selling a Business or Practice

A value for a purchase or sale is subject to all the forces that affect supply and demand, including all relevant economic factors prevalent at the time and all the vagaries of the market for the business or practice in question. As noted in the previous chapter, the *market* can be thought of as all the potential buyers and sellers of like businesses or practices.

It is logical for a potential seller to think of value in two ways. The first way is to identify what is acceptable to him, by whatever value criteria and parameters he chooses. This idea can be expressed as intrinsic value, sometimes also called fundamental value or investment value, as discussed in the previous chapter. The other way is to identify what potential buyers are willing to pay or what the market will bear, called market value.

There can be many reasons why the value of a business or practice to the present owner may be more than anyone else is willing to pay at any given time. In that case, the logical decision is to keep the business or practice. If the market value appears to be at, or above, the value acceptable to the prospective seller, the objective then becomes to find the buyer who is willing to pay the most.

It is logical for a potential buyer to think of value in the same two ways. He may first decide on his own valuation criteria and parameters, given his particular set of circumstances. He would use these criteria and parameters to determine his intrinsic, fundamental, or

---

[1] Paul B. Baron, *When You Buy or Sell a Company,* rev. ed. (Meriden Conn.: The Center for Business Information, Inc., 1983), pp. 8–9.

investment value for any given business or practice in which he might consider investing. He might also survey the prices at which businesses or practices that interest him would be available, and he could think of these prices as the market available to him.

If nothing is available at a price the prospective buyer would be willing to pay at the time, the logical decision is not to make an investment until a later time when market prices may be more appealing. If several investments do appear to be available at acceptable prices, then the objective is to find the one that represents the best value according to that buyer's criteria and parameters.

Market conditions for various types of businesses and practices vary considerably from time to time and from one locality to another. When many buyers are willing to pay prices at or above a typical seller's notion of fundamental value for a given type of business or practice, the condition is called a *seller's market*. When many sellers are willing to sell for an amount at or below a typical buyer's notion of fundamental value, the condition is called a *buyer's market*.

Partly because of these ever-changing market conditions, as well as because of the unique nature of each business and practice and other circumstances that may be unique to certain potential buyers, no formula can ever be devised that will produce a reliable conclusion about the market value of any particular business or practice at any given time. Chapter 28 discusses valuation factors that should be considered by prospective buyers or sellers that may differ from factors relevant for other valuation purposes or that deserve more emphasis than in valuations for other purposes.

# Buying or Selling a Partial Interest

A partial interest in a business or practice may or may not be worth a proportionate value of the total entity. Put another way, depending on the circumstances, the sum of the values of the various parts taken individually may or may not add up to the value of the business or practice if it were valued as one total entity.

Minority interests are typically worth something less than their proportion of the total entity value. This matter is discussed in some detail in the chapters on valuations for different purposes, and especially in the chapter on valuing minority interests.

# Obtaining or Providing Financing

A typical lending officer has no conception of the total value of the entity to which he is lending. He usually has some conception of the value of assets pledged as collateral, but neither has nor avails himself of expertise in the field of business appraisal. Many businesses and practices have far greater value than is indicated by their financial statements alone. If this value can be demonstrated convincingly, it may be helpful in obtaining desired financing.

There are many sources of *venture capital* today, including venture capital funds, insurance companies, and special venture capital departments or affiliates of some banks. Such sources almost always seek an equity participation, such as convertible debt or warrants. Owners who approach such sources should go in with a soundly based notion of the market value of their business, and, of course, the question of value will be of prime importance to the providers of the financing.

# Going Public

While the public market is composed mainly of the stocks of large companies, there were a few hundred successful public stock offerings in the $500,000 to $5,000,000 range in the first half of the 1980s. Most companies that succeeded in such offerings had innovative products or services offering the prospect of rapid growth and thus a high potential rate of return to the investor in the form of appreciation in the stock price. Most such offerings were sold to the public through small, regional, investment banking firms.

When appraising a company for the purpose of a public stock offering, the appraiser must pay special attention to other public offerings that may be considered comparable in some respect, and also to the receptiveness of the public market to the type of offering being considered. These factors are subject to constant change, sometimes changing dramatically in very short periods.

# Leveraged Buyouts

Leveraged buyouts have become increasingly popular in recent years. For businesses that have considerable unused borrowing capacity, prospective buyers may arrange to borrow a significant portion of the total purchase price by using the assets, and possibly also the stock, of the business as collateral, thus "cashing out" the seller. Both banks and insurance companies have become quite involved in leveraged buyouts in recent years.[2] They frequently want some equity participation. A well-documented appraisal of the fair market value of the business can be important to the implementation of a leveraged buyout.

# Employee Stock Ownership Plans

The Tax Reform Act of 1984 substantially enhanced the financial advantages of selling stock to employees through an Employee Stock Ownership Plan (ESOP). The stock to be sold through an ESOP can range from small minority interests to 100 percent of the company. The

---

[2] At this writing, banks are the primary source of funds for leveraged buyouts for small businesses, while most insurance companies are interested only in multimillion-dollar deals.

tax advantages of an ESOP make the vehicle attractive to use in conjunction with a leveraged buyout. The tax advantages of ESOPs are discussed in the chapter on estate planning considerations.

Valuations for ESOPs follow the guidelines of Revenue Ruling 59–60, used for gift and estate tax purposes, with certain special modifications necessary to accommodate the unique nature of ESOPs.[3]

# Estate, Gift, and Inheritance Taxes

The universal standard of value for estate, gift, and inheritance taxes is fair market value, which is defined and interpreted in the previous chapter. Guidelines for federal estate and gift taxes are found in Revenue Ruling 59–60, as modified by Revenue Ruling 68–609. Valuation guidelines for state inheritance taxes are generally consistent with federal estate and gift tax guidelines.

Although the standard of value for estate, gift, and inheritance taxes is fair market value, there can be many differences between a valuation for tax purposes and a valuation for the sale of a business or for other purposes. For example, estate and gift tax valuations are based on the value of a business to a hypothetical buyer who would have no special synergy with, or relationship to, the seller. In a normal tax valuation, the fact that the seller might be able to command a higher price because of some feature that might be uniquely valuable to a "particular" buyer would not be considered. According to legal precedents, items with intangible value are taxable only if the owner has the legal right to transfer them. However, a seller without the unequivocal legal right to transfer ownership to any buyer of his choice, as would be normal with an automobile dealership, would seek the necessary manufacturer's approval for a specific prospective buyer; with that approval obtained, the seller would expect to receive a price that would include whatever intangible value the operation may possess.

Another distinction between estate and gift tax valuations and valuations for the sale of a business is how much each relies on the historical record, as opposed to projections. Some buyers may be willing to pay for the opportunity for future profits that they envision; but such projections may not exist or may be considered too speculative to be relied on as a basis of value in a legal context, such as an estate or gift tax valuation.

Revenue Ruling 59–60 specifically recognizes that "valuation of securities is, in essence, a prophecy as to the future. . ."[4] Nevertheless, as a practical matter, valuations for tax purposes rely relatively more heavily on a company's historical record than do valuations for sales, which are more prone to rely on projections. This difference is a matter of emphasis rather than of concept.

---

[3] For detailed guidance on ESOP valuation procedures, see *Valuing ESOP Shares*, a 75-page booklet published by the ESOP Association, Washington, D.C.; and Shannon P. Pratt, *Valuing a Business: The Analysis and Appraisal of Closely Held Companies* (Homewood, Ill.: Dow Jones-Irwin, 1981), Chapter 20, "Employee Stock Ownership Plans," pp. 335–44.

[4] Revenue Ruling 59–60, (1959–1 C.B. 237) Section 3.

# Ad Valorem Taxes

*Ad valorem* is a Latin expression that has found its way into English dictionaries. It means "according to value," and is the basis for assessing property taxes in virtually all taxing jurisdictions.

Taxing authorities have been hard-pressed to raise adequate funds; sometimes assessing officers are pressured to be aggressive in their opinions of the values of taxable properties. There have been many sudden and huge increases in property taxes levied on such businesses as manufacturers, shopping centers, and motels. In many cases, the economics of the respective businesses have not justified the increases. Businesses have often been assessed for real estate values that exceeded the entire going concern value of the total business, *including* the real estate.

I believe that taxpayers can save millions of dollars by properly valuing businesses in which the business and the physical property are integrally interrelated. Fair market value is the legal standard of value in virtually all such cases. The real-world market values such properties on their ability to produce income, which is this book's primary valuation focus. Proper application of business valuation principles should be able to counteract some approaches used in many assessing jurisdictions. These approaches sometimes produce valuations well in excess of a sound estimate of value based on the applicable legal standard of fair market value.[5]

# Charitable Contributions

Revenue Ruling 59–60 is also the basic guideline for charitable contributions.

If the claimed value of securities donated is more than $10,000, the Tax Reform Act of 1984 makes it mandatory that the value be supported by a qualified appraisal attached to the return. The appraisal must be made by a "qualified appraiser" and must be received by the donor before the due date (including extensions) of the return on which the deduction is claimed.

# Incentive Stock Options

Incentive stock options may be granted in order to make it possible for employees to participate in the appreciation of the company's stock without any investment or risk, and pay income taxes at capital gains rates when they realize the gains from the appreciation. In order for the beneficiaries to qualify for this capital gains tax treatment, the exercise

---

[5] For further discussion of this concept, see Shannon P. Pratt, "Rates of Return as an Influence on Value," (*Third Annual Proceedings,* New York University, *Institute on State and Local Taxation,* 1985).

price of the options must be not less than the fair market value of the stock on the date the options are granted. The IRS regulations offer a "safe harbor" for the exercise price of the options if the company has stock appraisals done by two qualified independent appraisers at the time the options are granted and uses the average of the two.

# Buy/Sell Agreements

Valuations for buy/sell agreements can be based on whatever criteria the parties mutually agree to and may or may not bear any relationship to any recognized standard of value. Valuations for this purpose are discussed more fully in the chapter on estate planning.

# Property Settlements in Divorces

State laws govern disputed property settlements that involve marital dissolutions, and state statutes fail to specify what standard of value applies to businesses and professional practices in divorces. The law governing various aspects of the valuation of businesses and professional practices in divorces is established by case precedent in each state, and the cumulative result of such precedents varies greatly from state to state, and can vary from case to case within a state.

On some valuation issues, some state courts have established precedents that are diametrically opposed to those of courts of other states on the same issues.

For many valuation issues, many state courts have established no precedents at all. It is no wonder that the parties and their appraisers frequently find themselves far apart on the matter of valuation of a business or professional practice in a divorce! Added to the confusing and contradictory legal guidance is the acrimony and distrust that frequently accompany matrimonial dissolutions. Although we do far more appraisals of businesses and professional practices for other purposes than for divorces, my staff and I wind up presenting expert testimony in court more often for divorces than for any other single purpose.

Chapter 30 is devoted to valuations of businesses and professional practices in litigation or potential litigation situations, including divorces.

# Damage Cases

The most common damage situations that may require a business valuation to establish the amount of damages are the following:

Breach of contract.
Condemnation.

Lost business opportunity.

Lost profits.

Antitrust.

Personal injury.

Insurance casualty claims.

Each must be approached with as thorough an understanding as possible of the legal precedents that affect the valuation in the specific case, since the precedents vary considerably, not only from one type of damage situation to another, but also from one jurisdiction to another.

# Mergers

A merger involves the combination of two entities so that stock or partnership interests in one are exchanged for stock or assets of another. Some amount of cash may be offered in addition to stock or a partnership interest.

The situation usually requires the valuation of each entity, in order to establish an exchange ratio. Sometimes, however, an exchange ratio may be established by some criterion without actually valuing the entities. Mergers are discussed further in Chapter 28.

# Determining Life Insurance Needs

Life insurance can serve three important uses in a business or professional practice:

1. To fund the redemption of stock or a partnership interest from the estate of the deceased.
2. To pay estate and inheritance taxes.
3. To provide for the continuity of the business or practice for a period of time in the absence of a key person.

Valuation factors to determine the amount of life insurance needed to meet these objectives are discussed in Chapter 31.

# Squeeze-Out Mergers and Dissenting Stockholder Actions

In all, or virtually all, states, controlling stockholders have the right to effect certain actions which give rise to minority stockholders' appraisal rights. In general, these actions include a merger or sale of the company or the disposition of a major portion of its business or assets.

If controlling stockholders wish to eliminate minority stockholders, they can form a new corporation, sell the stock of the old corporation to the new corporation, and pay off the minority stockholders. This action gives rise to the term *squeeze-out merger,* since the result is to force out the minority stockholders.

If any minority stockholder believes that the consideration offered in the transaction is inadequate, he has the right to have his shares appraised and to be paid off, in cash, the amount finally determined. Almost all (but not all) state statutes specify that the standard of value for such actions is fair value, as discussed briefly in the previous chapter. A stockholder who exercises his dissenting stockholder rights may end up receiving more than, less than, or the same amount as was originally offered.

A study of the relevant legal precedents is extremely important in a valuation under dissenting stockholder rights. Such valuations are discussed in Chapter 30.

## Valuations for Multiple Purposes

The situation can become tricky when the same valuation is intended to be used for two or more different purposes. For example, a valuation for the purpose of selling the company or attracting outside investment capital may contain speculative elements based on future potential that may be acceptable to a risk-oriented investor, but not acceptable to a court charged with determining value under some set of statutory standards and legal precedents.

As noted earlier, valuations pursuant to buy/sell agreements can be just as arbitrary as the parties mutually agree to make them, but such valuations will not necessarily (or even usually) be appropriate for determining property settlements in divorces or estate and inheritance taxes.

Setting a value for a tender offer to buy out minority shareholders is quite a different matter from setting a price at which to effect a squeeze-out merger, in which all the stockholders are required to sell, whether they like it or not. A valuation for a tender offer may be at a lower price than a valuation for a squeeze-out merger. If so, and that valuation subsequently is used for a squeeze-out merger, a dissenting stockholder suit is likely to follow.

The material in this book should provide the reader with considerable guidance on when a certain valuation procedure will be suitable for two or more specific contemplated uses and when it will not. When in doubt, seek professional help.

## Considering Alternatives: Estate Planning and Other Types of Choices

It is not an uncommon need for an owner to find out a range of possible values for the business or practice in order to decide what to do. For example, the owner may be considering making charitable contributions, giving gifts within the family, selling stock to employees, and/or initiating an Employee Stock Ownership Plan, with all the possible choices depending to some extent on the values of the shares or interests to be transferred in each case. In such cases, the valuation process should proceed so that it encompasses whatever exercises are necessary to address all of the possible alternatives contemplated; it should note any differences in procedures and/or conclusions that may be applicable, depending on which of the possible alternatives are finally implemented.

# Chapter 4

## Differences between the Valuation of Large and Small Businesses

Status of Financial Statements
    Audited Statements
    Reviewed Statements
    Compiled Statements
    Tax Returns Only
    Records in a Shoe Box
Cash versus Accrual Accounting
Length of Track Record Available
Form of Business Ownership
Stock versus Asset Transaction
Consideration Offered by Purchaser
Comparative Transaction Data Available
Role of the Owner/Manager
Compensation to Owners
Accounting Policies for Financial Reporting
Earnings Analysis on Pretax or After-Tax Basis
Complexity of Capital Structure
    Classes of Corporate Stock
    Treasury Stock
    Limited Partnerships
    General Partnerships

Although the basic theory underlying the valuation is the same for any size business, there are many practical differences that dictate different valuation techniques. As noted in the preface, there is no clear-cut line of demarcation between small and large. Some businesses have some characteristics commonly associated with small businesses and other characteristics more commonly found in larger businesses. In general, even very large professional practices have characteristics that, for the purpose of determining applicable valuation techniques, fall more in line with the characteristics of small businesses than with large businesses.

The most important general categories of differences between small and large businesses, which determine the appropriate valuation techniques to be employed, are the following:

*Status of financial statements.* Larger companies are more likely to have statements that are audited, or at least reviewed, by outside CPAs, while smaller businesses are more likely to have statements that are merely compiled.

*Cash versus accrual accounting.* Most large companies use accrual accounting, while many small businesses use cash accounting.

*Length of "track record."* On the average, larger businesses have longer histories available for analysis by the appraiser.

*Form of business ownership.* Large operations are more likely to be regular corporations, while smaller operations are more likely to be sole proprietorships, partnerships, or S corporations.

*Stock versus asset transaction.* The larger the company, the more likely it is that stock is to be transferred in case of a sale, while a smaller entity is more likely to involve a transfer of assets.

*Consideration offered by purchaser.* The smaller the business, the more likely it is to be sold for a cash down payment and a term contract for the balance; the larger the business, the more likely it is to be sold for cash and/or stock in a public company.

*Comparative transaction data available.* The smaller the company, the fewer the comparative transaction data that are publicly available; while for valuations of larger companies, it is much more likely that useful, comparative, publicly traded stock data will be available.

*Role of owner/manager.* The smaller the company, the more important the role of one or a few owner(s)/manager(s).

*Compensation policies.* Larger companies are more likely to remunerate owners at something near a market rate of compensation, while small companies tend to pay owners what they can afford, which may be above or below a market rate.

*Accounting policies for financial reporting.* Smaller firms usually have a single set of financial statements, normally following whatever accounting policies minimize their tax liabilities. Larger companies are more likely to have a set of financial statements designed to present a truer picture for financial reporting than their tax statements would convey.

# Status of Financial Statements

## Audited Statements

If a company's financial statements are audited, it means that a CPA firm has done a complete audit and that the statements are presented in accordance with generally accepted accounting principles (GAAP), unless otherwise noted. Audited statements contain footnotes that explain accounting policies and provide some details beyond just the line items on the balance sheet and income statement. Audited statements are the most complete and reliable type of statements with which an appraiser works. An example of an auditor's "clean" audit opinion and an auditor's "qualified" opinion are shown as Exhibits 4–1 and 4–2.

## Reviewed Statements

From an appraiser's viewpoint, the next most preferred level of statement presentation after audited statements is reviewed statements. They also are prepared by independent, outside CPAs and usually contain the same footnote disclosures as audited statements. Although all the audit verification procedures are not done, the statements usually are prepared in accordance with generally accepted accounting principles. An example of a CPA firm's cover letter for reviewed statements is shown as Exhibit 4–3.

## Compiled Statements

A compilation involves merely putting together and presenting information supplied by management. Compiled statements may be prepared either by an outside CPA firm or by the company itself. They may include footnote disclosures similar to those found in audited or reviewed statements but usually do not. An example of a CPA firm's typical cover letter for compiled statements is shown as Exhibit 4–4.

Exhibit 4–1
"Clean" Auditor's Opinion

Independent Accountants' Report

The Board of Directors and Stockholders
GranTree Corporation

We have examined the consolidated balance sheets of GranTree Corporation and Subsidiaries as of November 1, 1984, and November 3, 1983, and the related consolidated statements of earnings, stockholders' equity and changes in financial position for each of the years in the three-year period ended November 1, 1984. Our examinations were made in accordance with generally accepted auditing standards and, accordingly, included such tests of the accounting records and such other auditing procedures as we considered necessary in the circumstances.

In our opinion, the aforementioned consolidated financial statements present fairly the financial position of GranTree Corporation and Subsidiaries at November 1, 1984 and November 3, 1983, and the results of their operations and the changes in their financial position for each of the years in the three-year period ended November 1, 1984, in conformity with generally accepted accounting principles applied on a consistent basis.

PEAT, MARWICK, MITCHELL & CO.

Portland, Oregon
December 7, 1984

Exhibit 4–2
"Qualified" Auditor's Opinion

**Report of Independent Public Accountants**
*To the Stockholders and Board of Directors of*
*Louisiana-Pacific Corporation:*

We have examined the consolidated balance sheets of Louisiana-Pacific Corporation (a Delaware corporation) and subsidiaries as of December 31, 1984, and 1983, and the related consolidated statements of income, stockholders' equity and changes in financial position for each of the three years in the period ended December 31, 1984. Our examinations were made in accordance with generally accepted auditing standards and, accordingly, included such tests of the accounting records and such other auditing procedures as we considered necessary in the circumstances.

As discussed further in the notes to the accompanying financial statements, an action by Louisiana-Pacific Corporation to recover the value of property taken by the U.S. Government in March 1978 for expansion of Redwood National Park is pending. The Company has recorded $330 million which management considers a conservative measure of the value of the land and timber taken. While management believes that its calculation is a conservative measure for financial reporting purposes, it is not possible for us to form an opinion as to the amount which will be eventually recovered through this action.

In our opinion, subject to the effect of any adjustments that might have been required had the final outcome of the Company's action against the U.S. Government mentioned in the preceding paragraph been known, the financial statements referred to above present fairly the financial position of Louisiana-Pacific Corporation and subsidiaries as of December 31, 1984, and 1983, and the results of their operations and the changes in their financial position for each of the three years in the period ended December 31, 1984, in conformity with generally accepted accounting principles which, except for the change made as of January 1, 1982 (with which we concur) in the method of computing depreciation on certain assets as described in the notes to the accompanying financial statements, were applied on a consistent basis.

**Arthur Andersen & Co.**

Portland, Oregon,
February 15, 1985.

Exhibit 4–3
Cover Letter to Reviewed Statements

The Shareholder and Board of Directors
Mary's Machinery & Equipment, Inc.

We have reviewed the accompanying balance sheet of Mary's Machinery & Equipment, Inc., as of December 31, 1985, and the related statements of income, retained earnings, and changes in financial position for the year then ended, in accordance with standards established by the American Institute of Certified Public Accountants. All information included in these financial statements is the representation of the management of Mary's Machinery & Equipment, Inc.

A review consists primarily of inquiries of company personnel and analytical procedures applied to financial data. It is substantially less in scope than an examination in accordance with generally accepted auditing standards, the objective of which is the expression of an opinion regarding the financial statements taken as a whole. Accordingly, we do not express such an opinion.

Based on our review, we are not aware of any material modifications that should be made to the accompanying financial statements in order for them to be in conformity with generally accepted accounting principles.

Green, Eye, Shade & Co.

# Tax Returns Only

Some small entities prepare no financial statements other than their tax returns. In such cases, the appraiser usually will want to recast the data from the tax returns into financial statement form. If the business is a sole proprietorship, the appraiser will have to separate business items from personal items.

# Records in a Shoe Box

Sometimes, there are no statements or tax returns, only journals and/or ledgers, or maybe even just invoices, vouchers, check stubs, and so on, in a shoe box. This form of recordkeeping usually will entail a fair amount of work even to create a semblance of a statement, which may or may not be reliable once it is done.

Exhibit 4–4
Cover Letter to Compiled Statements

Annie's Apparel Store

We have compiled the accompanying balance sheet of Annie's Apparel Store as of December 31, 1985, and the related statements of income, retained earnings, and changes in financial position for the year then ended, in accordance with standards established by the American Institute of Certified Public Accountants.

A compilation is limited to presenting in the form of financial statements information that is the representation of management. We have not audited or reviewed the accompanying financial statements and, accordingly, do not express an opinion or any other form of assurance on them.

Bean, Counter & Co.

# Cash versus Accrual Accounting

In accrual accounting, revenues are recognized when they are earned, and expenses are recognized when they are incurred. For example, if a dentist does work and bills it to his patient in January, it shows as revenue on the income statement for January, and the account receivable shows as an asset on the balance sheet at the end of January.

In cash accounting, revenues and expenses are recognized when the money is received or paid. In the dentist example, the work done and the bill would be reflected on cash-basis statements only when the money was received from the patient.

Valuations usually are based on accrual accounting information. Therefore, if an entity is on cash-basis accounting, conversion to an accrual basis usually needs to be made for valuation purposes.

# Length of Track Record Available

For most valuation purposes, it is useful to look at five years or so of comparative income and expense data, if it is available. For most small businesses, however, it is not. The business may not be that old; the business may have changed hands, and the prior owner's records are not available; or the business may have changed accounting procedures so that some of the data may not be comparable due to different accounting procedures. The more cyclical or variable the business, the more important it is to look at data over a period of years. The appraiser simply has to do the best he can with what he has to work with. Many valuations are based on only the latest year's data and/or a projection.

# Form of Business Ownership

In a corporation, all stockholders of a given class of stock share pro rata in earnings, at least on the books, because earnings are related to a retained earnings account which is part of stockholders' equity. In other words, each stockholder of a given stock class shares equally in the earnings and capital accounts, and each stockholder of the class shares equally in all distributions, whether in the form of dividends or sale of stock. If there is more than one class of stock, the appraiser must assess the relative rights of each class being appraised.

In a partnership, partners may share on different bases in earnings and in the capital accounts. Therefore, if appraising the interests of one or more partners, it is necessary to read the partnership agreement carefully and to analyze the distributions to each partner and the capital account balances.

# Stock versus Asset Transaction

Before one can determine a value, it is necessary to define precisely what is being valued, as noted in Chapter 1. In a stock valuation, the appraiser needs to determine whether there will be any major changes from the statements on which the valuation is based, such as any major cash withdrawal or any significant off-balance sheet liabilities or assets.

In an asset transaction, it is necessary to define just what assets are being transferred and what, if any, liabilities are being assumed by the buyer. Typically, in an asset transaction, the seller keeps the cash and receivables and pays off all liabilities. What is being transferred usually is the inventory, plant, and equipment, and whatever intangible values may exist, if any. What is typical in this respect varies from one industry to another and from deal to deal in any industry. This variability is one of the many problems with rule of thumb valuation approaches or valuations done on some "formula" basis. Such rules of thumb or formulas usually fail to specify exactly what is being transferred.

Since asset transfers typically do not include cash or accounts receivable, the buyer may have to provide some working capital in addition to the purchase price of the business. If the buyer has to invest additional cash for working capital, that should be regarded as an add-on to the purchase price of the total business on a going-concern basis. If the buyer is planning to borrow to meet working capital requirements, the cost of such borrowing should be considered in his projected earnings and cash flow. The seller, of course, may net out a considerable amount that is more or less than the transaction price, by collecting receivables and liquidating payables.

# Consideration Offered by Purchaser

In addition to determining just what is being sold, it is also necessary to think about the nature of the consideration being received. Most businesses are sold for some combination of cash, a contract balance, and/or stock of the acquiring company. In some cases, some portion of the contract balance may be contingent on certain future events.

It is simplest, of course, if the price is all in cash. However, as noted elsewhere, most small businesses and professional practices do not sell for 100 percent cash.

If a contract is involved, the strength of the commitment and all the terms must be evaluated. If the stock of the acquiror is part or all of the consideration, the stock of the acquiror must be valued. Various aspects of purchase terms are discussed in different places in this book.

# Comparative Transaction Data Available

Valuing a business or property by the "market approach" basically means finding actual transaction prices for similar businesses or practices and using those prices to guide in valuing the subject business or practice. (We shall discuss this in more detail in the chapter comparing real estate appraisal and business appraisal approaches.)

Large businesses, even ones privately held, usually can be valued by reference to transactions in stocks of publicly traded companies in the same or a similar industry. However, many small businesses and practices are in industries or professions in which there are no publicly traded companies. Even if publicly traded companies exist, there may be so many differences between the small business and its much larger, publicly traded counterpart that it would be very difficult to derive meaningful valuation parameters from the publicly traded big brother that will indicate the value of the small operation.

Until the present time, there has been no central bank containing reliable and generally useful data on prices of transactions in small businesses and professional practices. Willamette Management Associates has started such a data bank as part of the research for this book and will continue to add to it, but the data are very limited relative to the more than a million transactions that take place every year. If comparative transaction data are available, they should be very helpful. Otherwise, the appraiser can use the generalized approaches described in subsequent chapters, tempered by factors pointed out in later parts of the book that are applicable to certain industries and professions.

# Role of the Owner/Manager

The smaller the business or practice, the more important looms the role of the owner/manager. How much of the success of the operation is due to the talents and efforts of the owner/manager(s)? How much of that success can be transferred to new ownership? Is the seller including a noncompete agreement in the deal? Is the seller providing assistance in the transition? These are the types of questions that need to be addressed as part of the valuation process. Usually, in a small business or practice, growth will not be automatic, but will depend on continuing entrepreneurial skill and effort. In general, smaller businesses require much more personal involvement on the parts of their owners and are much less suitable for absentee ownership than medium-sized and larger businesses. In other words, the labor and ownership are much more difficult to separate.

In fact, not only is growth on its own less likely to occur in a smaller enterprise than in a medium-sized or larger one which has momentum, but considerable personal effort usually is required just to *maintain* the earnings stream. There is no point in paying a sizable sum for a business or practice from which the customers will disappear as soon as the new owner takes over, or which is dependent on a seller's talents that will not be available to the new owner. In other words, the buyer or appraiser must judge whether profit-contributing factors will persist or whether they are strictly attributable personally to the former owner.

Sometimes, profit factors attributable to the seller can stay with the business for a time, if the seller is willing to enter into an employment agreement, under which he will work for the new owner for some specified period.

# Compensation to Owners

Whenever a closely held business is appraised partly or entirely on the basis of profits, compensation to owners must be examined. The smaller the business or practice, the more important this factor becomes. Few small businesses or professional practices compensate their owners on the basis of what their services are worth. Large companies are more likely to remunerate officers at something near a market rate of compensation, while smaller entities tend to pay owners on the basis of what the business or practice has available in earnings and/or cash flow, which can be above or below a market rate of compensation.

In computing profits, it is necessary to figure out what a competent person who is not the owner would have to be paid to do the same job or jobs, and substitute that amount for the actual compensation paid to the owners. It is necessary to consider "all" the compensation, including benefits and perks of all kinds.

# Accounting Policies for Financial Reporting

The valuation analyst must determine the extent to which accounting policies conform either to economic reality or to the policies of other entities with which the subject is being compared, and make adjustments as necessary. Such adjustments are discussed in Part II, "Analyzing the Company."

# Earnings Analysis on Pretax or After-Tax Basis

When valuing a large corporation, you usually state earnings and cash flow figures on an after-tax basis. When valuing small businesses and professional practices, the opposite usually is true; that is, you usually state earnings and cash flow figures on a pretax basis.

In the final analysis, of course, what should be of greatest interest to an investor is what he can keep in his pocket after taxes. However, many small businesses are partnerships or sole proprietorships, and everybody's tax bracket is different. Also, accounting and compensation policies tend to greatly affect small corporations. Consequently, comparisons on a pretax basis tend to be more expedient for small businesses and professional practices.

Make sure that you compare any earnings or cash flow figures being used on an "apples-to-apples" basis. One valuation error I often encounter is a price/earnings multiple being taken from a group of public companies in an industry on an after-tax basis and then applied to a private company's pretax earnings to get a value. P/E multiples quoted for publicly traded stocks are always on an after-tax basis. If such a multiple is going to be used for valuation guidance for a private company, the subject company's earnings must also be on an after-tax basis. One way to make these bases comparable is simply to deduct taxes at statutory state and federal corporate rates from the subject company's pretax earnings, whether the subject company is actually a corporation or not, and regardless of the taxes it actually pays.

# Complexity of Capital Structure

*Capital structure* is generally defined as the equity (ownership interest) plus the long-term debt. Smaller entities tend to have simple capital structures; larger ones are likely to be more complex. The person doing the valuation should determine whether there are any complexities in the capital structure.

## Classes of Corporate Stock

Most corporations have only one class of common stock. Some corporations, however, have one or more classes of common and, in some cases, one or more classes of preferred. Classes of stock authorized in the articles of incorporation but never issued are of no concern in the valuation; it is the stock actually outstanding that matters.

## Treasury Stock

*Treasury stock* is stock that has been issued and subsequently reacquired by the corporation. Regarding the valuation of stock of a company, treat treasury stock as if it never had been issued. If the balance sheet shows that there is treasury stock, subtract the number of shares of treasury stock from the number of shares of stock shown issued to get the number of shares outstanding; this is the relevant number of shares to use to determine a value per share. The book value of the common stock should be net of any amounts shown on the balance sheet for the purchase of treasury stock.

## Limited Partnerships

A *limited partnership* has two or more classes of partners, each class usually with significantly different rights and obligations regarding partnership earnings, assets, and liabilities. It is called a limited partnership because the limited partners have only limited personal obligation for debts of the partnership (as is also true of a corporate stockholder); by contrast, general partners are personally liable for debts of the partnership. These differences obviously have a significant impact on the relative values of the respective partners' interests.

## General Partnerships

Even in general partnerships, however, every partner is not necessarily on the same footing. The most common differences among partners is that all partners may not have the same percentage interest in the partnership earnings as they do in the partnership capital account. Therefore, when valuing the interest of any particular partner, you must carefully study the articles of partnership (or the partnership agreement) and the statement of partners' capital accounts in order to determine exactly what the interest involves.

# Part II

## Analyzing the Company

# Chapter 5

## Adjusting the Balance Sheet

Accounts Receivable
Inventory
    Taking and Extending a Physical Inventory
    FIFO versus LIFO
    Write-Down and Write-Off Policies
    Tax Effect if Valuing Stock
Prepaid Expenses
Other Current Assets
Real Estate
Furniture, Fixtures, Equipment, and Leasehold Improvements
    Replacement or Reproduction Cost
    Used Replacement Cost
    Depreciated Replacement Cost
    Liquidation Value
    Making a S.W.A.G.
Intangible Assets
    Leaseholds
    Patents and Copyrights
Liabilities
    Interest-Bearing Debt
    Deferred Taxes
Contingent or Off-Balance Sheet Assets and Liabilities
    Product Liability
    Lawsuits
    Regulatory Compliance
    Past Service Liability
    Employment Agreements
    Unrecorded Obligations
    Liens
The Ultimate Adjusted Balance Sheet Analysis
Samples of Adjusted Balance Sheets
    Sole Proprietorship Example
    Corporation Example

*The process of determining the price begins with "normalizing" the company's financial records. Neither the balance sheets nor the income statements of smaller, privately held companies necessarily bear any relationship to reality.*[1]

The value of most businesses and practices generally depends on the assets being transferred and/or how much the business or practice can earn. The starting place, then, is to adjust the financial statements so that they reflect *a best estimate of economic reality*. Making these adjustments is often referred to as "normalizing" the financial statements.

This chapter deals with adjusting the balance sheet to get a realistic picture of the assets being transferred; the next chapter deals with adjusting the income statement to get a realistic picture of the entity's earning power. Many of the factors involved in these adjustments are interrelated; many of them have a bearing on both the balance sheet and the income statement.

# Accounts Receivable

When a small business or professional practice is sold, the seller typically collects his accounts receivable, and they are not part of the transaction. In other cases, a buyer may agree to collect the accounts on a contingent basis, paying the seller 85 percent or so of collections.

If accounts receivable are to be transferred on other than a contingent basis, it should be questioned whether they may be worth more or less than the net amount at which they are carried on the books. For companies using accrual accounting, accounts receivable usually are shown on the balance sheet as follows:

| | | |
|---|---|---|
| Accounts Receivable . . . . . | $100,000 | |
| Less: Allowance for Doubtful Accounts . . . . . . . . | 5,000 | $95,000 |

Some companies are extremely conservative, and allow more to accrue for doubtful accounts than will ultimately be necessary to offset uncollectible accounts. At the other extreme, some companies do not accrue any allowance for doubtful accounts. They just write off an account directly against accounts receivable when they determine it to be uncollectible.

An aged accounts receivable schedule (Exhibit 5–1) is the starting place to try to examine whether the net amount shown on the books is really a good estimate of the amount that actually will be collected.

Some buyers of businesses value accounts receivable by some arbitrary rule of thumb. For example, they may accept current accounts at face value, discount those over 30 days by 10 percent, those over 60

---

[1] Thomas P. Murphy, "What Price Independence?" *Forbes*, September 27, 1982, pp. 208–9.

Exhibit 5–1

**MARY'S MACHINERY & EQUIPMENT, INC.**
**AGED ACCOUNTS RECEIVABLE**
**AS OF DECEMBER 31, 1984**

| Account Name | Total $ | Current $ | 30-60 Days $ | 60-90 Days $ | 90-120 Days $ | Over 120 Days $ |
|---|---|---|---|---|---|---|
| Ace Widget Co. | 1,000 | 1,000 | | | | |
| A-1 Equipment | 20,000 | | | | | 20,000 |
| Best Rentals | 5,000 | | | | 5,000 | |
| Cascade Construction | 500 | | | 500 | | |
| Davidson Machine | 6,000 | | | 6,000 | | |
| E & F Transportation | 70,000 | 35,000 | 35,000 | | | |
| Frank Industries | 2,000 | 2,000 | | | | |
| General Equipment | 3,000 | | | | | 3,000 |
| Holt Industries | 1,500 | | | | 1,500 | |
| I.K. Industries | 12,000 | | | | | 12,000 |
| Jay Manufacturing | 500 | | | 500 | | |
| K Construction | 25,000 | 25,000 | | | | |
| Long's Machinery | 6,500 | | | | 6,500 | |
| Mountain Resources | 30,000 | 15,000 | 15,000 | | | |
| Nelson Excavating | 2,000 | | | | | 2,000 |
| Power Enterprises | 8,000 | | | | | 8,000 |
| Rolling Transportation | 25,000 | 20,000 | 5,000 | | | |
| Sam's Equipment | 40,000 | 12,000 | 20,000 | 8,000 | | |
| T. X. Resources | 2,000 | | | | 2,000 | |
| Vic's Manufacturing | 10,000 | 10,000 | | | | |
| Western Industries | 30,000 | | | | | 30,000 |
| TOTAL | 300,000 | 120,000 | 75,000 | 15,000 | 15,000 | 75,000 |
| | 100.0% | 40.0% | 25.0% | 5.0% | 5.0% | 25.0% |

days by 20 percent, those over 90 days by 30 percent, and allow little or nothing for accounts over 120 days. It is generally possible, however, to get a much more accurate estimate of net collectibility by analyzing each account, looking at the past payment history of any accounts that are sizable or that are more than 30 or 60 days old, taking into consideration the typical collection period for businesses in the particular industry. (Sources for average collection periods for different types of businesses are discussed in Chapter 7.)

A buyer may be willing to accept most of the accounts receivable, either at face value or at some discount, but will leave some for the seller to try to collect. In other cases, a buyer may accept accounts receivable on a contingent basis, reserving some portion to be paid to the seller when, and if, the accounts are collected.

# Inventory

Ideally, the inventory account would be adjusted by taking a physical inventory count and extending it at current costs. If the inventory account must be adjusted on the basis of the books and records, the two main questions to answer involve the basic accounting policy (generally either FIFO or LIFO) and the write-off and/or write-down policy.

# Taking and Extending a Physical Inventory

The most reliable way to get an accurate inventory value is to take a physical inventory count and price it out at current wholesale market prices, using suppliers' current effective price lists. Alternatively, and actually more commonly, the inventory may be priced out using the company's actual invoice costs. It may be appropriate to take discounts for slow-moving or overstocked items. Obsolete items may be accorded little or no value.

It is customary for retailers that have consistent gross margins, such as some clothing stores, to price the inventory at retail and then take a percentage discount that represents the gross margin on the retail price. The discount may be greater than the normal gross margin for older or out-of-season merchandise.

# FIFO versus LIFO

FIFO, or *first in, first out,* means that the first unit of an inventory item purchased is the first unit considered sold for accounting purposes. LIFO, or *last in, first out,* means that the unit of an inventory item purchased last is the first unit considered sold for accounting purposes. The difference between FIFO and LIFO accounting appears in the ending inventory on the balance sheet; this affects the cost of goods sold and thus the earnings on the income statement.

To the extent that prices go up, LIFO results in lower figures for ending inventory, a higher cost of goods sold, and therefore lower earnings than result with FIFO. Since LIFO accounting is acceptable for federal income tax purposes, there has been a widespread tendency for companies to adopt LIFO rather than FIFO inventory accounting in response to inflation.

Take a simple example of a company that started its accounting period with 30 widgets, purchased for $10 each, then purchased 60 more widgets for $15 each during the accounting period, and ended the period with an inventory of 40 widgets. Using FIFO versus LIFO accounting, compute the comparative inventory and cost of goods sold as follows:

|  | FIFO | | LIFO | |
|---|---|---|---|---|
| Beginning Inventory | 30 units @ $10 = | $300 | 30 units @ $10 = | $300 |
| Purchases | 60 units @ $15 = | 900 | 60 units @ $15 = | 900 |
| Goods Available for Sale | | $1,200 | | $1,200 |
| Ending Inventory | 40 units @ $15 = | $600 | 30 units @ $10 = | $300 |
| | | | 10 units @ $15 = | 150 |
| | | $600 | | $450 |
| Cost of Goods Sold | | $600 | | $750 |

In other words, under LIFO, the accounting perpetuates the fiction that the original units in the inventory are the ones still there. In the case above, under LIFO accounting, the ending inventory would be shown on the balance sheet at $450; under FIFO accounting, the same ending inventory would be shown on the balance sheet at $600.

Since the FIFO method results in showing more current values on the balance sheet, that method comes closer to portraying the inventory at an economically realistic current value. Therefore, if the subject company uses LIFO, you can adjust the balance sheet to a FIFO basis. If the company reporting on LIFO has audited statements, the footnotes usually provide the information necessary to adjust the inventory values from LIFO to FIFO. All that needs to be done is to add the amount shown as LIFO Reserve to the amount of the inventory account shown on the balance sheet. If the statements of a company reporting on LIFO are not audited, then the company's accountant should be able to provide the analyst with the necessary information to adjust to a FIFO basis.

Some companies account for inventory on some type of an average cost basis, but that practice is so uncommon that it does not warrant a discussion in this book.[2]

## Write-Down and Write-Off Policies

Regardless of whether the FIFO, LIFO, or average cost inventory method is used, most companies adhere to the "lower-of-cost-or-market" principle, which holds that the carrying value should be reduced if the market value is less than the cost. Market value for this purpose is defined as "current replacement cost except that market shall not be higher than net realizable value, nor should it be lower than net realizable value reduced by the normal profit margin."[3]

Implementation of the lower-of-cost-or-market principle varies tremendously—one company may have a stockroom full of obsolete inventory, while another company may have an aggressive program of automatic write-downs and write-offs of inventory on the basis of the number of months it has been in stock. Appropriate adjustments to inventory values may be necessary when a company goes to one extreme or the other in making, or not making, adjustments to inventory values in its implementation of the lower-of-cost-or-market principle. The more extreme the inventory accounting policies, the less the accounting records can be relied on to assist in obtaining an economically realistic inventory value.

## Tax Effect if Valuing Stock

If we are valuing a corporation as a going concern for the purpose of buying its stock, we must recognize that the cost basis of the inventory for income tax purposes still will be its book value, not our adjusted

[2] For a discussion of the average cost method, see Leopold A. Bernstein, *Financial Statement Analysis: Theory, Application, and Interpretation*, rev. ed. (Homewood, Ill.: Richard D. Irwin, 1978), pp. 125–26, 137–38.
[3] Ibid., p. 130.

value. Therefore, any adjustment made should net out the income tax effect.

For example, if we revalue inventory upward from a book value of $100,000 to an adjusted value of $150,000, the effect is that the $50,000 gain will be taxed to the corporation at the corporation's ordinary income tax rate when the inventory is sold. If the corporation is in the 30 percent tax bracket, the markup of $50,000 in the inventory account should be net of, or offset by, $15,000 in income taxes that eventually will come out of the $50,000 markup. Therefore, the net markup for the purpose of valuing the stock should be only $35,000.

# Prepaid Expenses

The components of the prepaid expense account shown on the balance sheet should be examined. The most common components are rent, insurance, and office supplies. If these items will be necessary on a going-concern basis, then no adjustment may be necessary. However, if they are not, the prepaid expense account should be adjusted accordingly. Such an item would be $10,000 worth of stationery and promotional materials that will not be used by a new buyer because he plans to change the name of the company. There could also be some valuable prepaid expenses that do not show up on the balance sheet because they were charged directly to expenses when paid.

# Other Current Assets

If other current assets are involved in the valuation, such as marketable securities or short-term notes or contracts receivable, they should be adjusted to market values. As with the inventory account adjustment, if stock in a corporation is being valued, any adjustment to current asset account values should net out the related income tax effect, that is, the income tax that will be incurred when the asset is sold.

# Real Estate

In valuing most small businesses and professional practices, my preference is to deal with real estate separately from the value of the business or practice. For one thing, many sellers who own the premises being occupied by the business are willing to sell the business or practice with or without the real estate. This means the business has to be valued separately. Also, since most small businesses and professional practices do not own the real estate they occupy, balance sheet and income statement data usually can best be compared from one entity to another and to industry averages without real estate on the balance sheet. Also, appraisal approaches appropriate for the real estate may be different from those appropriate for the operating entity, so an appraisal of the separate parts may be more accurate than an appraisal done as one package.

If the real estate is to be removed from the balance sheet, then items related to real estate must also be removed from the income statement and a reasonable rent included in the expenses. Examples of such items that may be included on the income statement would be interest, taxes, and insurance related to the property ownership. In some cases there could also be some rental income which may require an adjustment.

If real estate is to be left on the balance sheet, it may be adjusted to appraised fair market value if a current appraisal is available. If the appraisal available is outdated, or if the real estate changed hands a few years ago, the earlier value may be adjusted to an estimate of current value by using an index of real estate values for the subject property type and locale.

If no better approximation of current value is available, a tax-assessed value might be helpful. However, even in jurisdictions where tax-assessed values purportedly represent market value, they frequently do not. If there is a way of knowing the typical relationship between tax-assessed values and market values in a particular jurisdiction, the tax-assessed values can be adjusted accordingly. Incidentally, since Proposition 13, tax-assessed values are virtually worthless as indicators of market value in California; tax-assessed values there are limited by a formula ceiling, unless the property changes hands.

If stock is being valued, the question arises, should any tax effects of adjusting real estate values be taken into consideration on the balance sheet. If the real estate is likely to be sold, then tax effects certainly should be netted out of the real estate value adjustment. (Alternatively, the tax effects could be recognized by a Deferred Taxes Payable account in the liability section of the balance sheet.)

If a buyer would not be expected to sell the real estate, it is debatable whether implied taxes on the markup should be recognized on the adjusted balance sheet. I prefer recognizing the capital gains taxes implied in the markup with a deferred tax account. Alternatively, they could be footnoted as a contingent liability.

# Furniture, Fixtures, Equipment, and Leasehold Improvements

Generally speaking, to adjust a balance sheet on a going-concern basis, the furniture, fixtures, and equipment should be adjusted to their market values. Different people, however, have different ideas of what that means for this category of assets. The replacement cost for most used equipment is twice, or several times, as much as could be realized in a liquidation sale if the operation were closed. So what do people usually mean by market value, as applied to this category of assets?

# Replacement or Reproduction Cost

*Replacement cost* means the cost of replacing the item with one that performs the same function—an oven that bakes as many loaves per hour as the bakery is now baking.

*Reproduction cost* means the cost of exactly reproducing the same asset as the operation now has in place.

If these two terms are used without any qualifiers, they are usually understood to mean new replacement or reproduction cost. Although I have encountered at least one appraiser who says he uses a new replacement or reproduction cost for equipment when adjusting a balance sheet on a going-concern basis, that is not the common practice.

# Used Replacement Cost

The consensus is that *used replacement cost* best applies when adjusting the Furniture, Fixtures, and Equipment account on the balance sheet on a going-concern basis. This term generally is interpreted to mean the price at which used equipment in comparable condition could be purchased on the open market, plus the cost of transporting and installing it so it works. Estimates of such costs can be obtained from equipment appraisers or dealers. This is the concept of value usually meant when people use the term *market value* in reference to the Furniture, Fixtures, and Equipment account on an adjusted balance sheet. That is a reasonable way to look at the value of these assets on a going-concern basis, because in essence it represents an *opportunity cost,* an alternative that the buyers have available to them if they don't buy the entity being valued.

# Depreciated Replacement Cost

Perhaps because of the lack of readily available, reliable data on prices of comparable used equipment, one of the common approaches to valuing the furniture, fixtures, and equipment for an adjusted balance sheet on a going-concern basis is *depreciated replacement cost.* In simple terms, depreciated replacement cost means the current cost to replace the item new, less an allowance for the length of time it has been in service. For example, if a new, comparably productive machine would cost $1,000 and could be expected to have a useful economic life of 10 years, and the present machine had been in use for 4 years and could be expected to last 6 more years, the appraiser could estimate the depreciated replacement cost at $600 ($6/10 \times \$1,000 = \$600$).

This calculation assumes that the subject machine has been maintained in reasonably good operating order. If the condition of the equipment is exceptionally good or bad, an upward or downward adjustment would be in order. If the subject equipment suffers from obsolescence, a downward adjustment must be made to arrive at a proper value based on the depreciated replacement cost approach. For example, if the subject machine can do the same job as the new replacement machine, but only at a higher operating cost (perhaps because of a difference in energy efficiency, for example), a downward adjustment in value must be made to recognize this factor.

The depreciated replacement cost approach is commonly used by industrial appraisers analyzing asset values for manufacturing companies for ad valorem (property tax) appraisals. However, the older and/or more obsolete the subject assets are, the less applicable such a cost approach estimate of value will be, because the differences in operating efficiencies between the obsolete equipment and contemporary equipment will be very difficult to quantify, causing the appraiser to be more subjective than would be necessary for up-to-date equipment.

## Liquidation Value

*Liquidation value* is the net amount that could be expected to be received if the assets were sold off piecemeal in an orderly manner. Estimates of liquidation value can be obtained from equipment appraisers, wholesale dealers, or auctioneers. Although a creditor might focus heavily on a balance sheet adjusted to liquidation value, that is not normally the primary focus for an adjusted balance sheet on a going-concern basis. It should be kept in mind, however, that leasehold improvements usually are worthless in a liquidation sale, and most furniture, fixtures, and equipment bring prices in a liquidation sale that are heavily discounted even from used replacement cost.

## Making a S.W.A.G.

Having understood the generally accepted methods, the person making the appraisal may prefer to make a S.W.A.G. (a Scientific Wild Asset Guess), because, as a practical matter, detailed implementation of the generally accepted methods may be too expensive and/or too time-consuming for the purpose at hand.

In the majority of cases, net book value (cost less depreciation) is a lower limit of reasonable value for equipment on a going-concern basis, because most privately held companies write off depreciation at least as fast as the useful economic life of the equipment is used up. For some types of equipment, a reasonable approximation of current value would simply be the undepreciated original cost; the reasoning is, inflation in the cost of new equipment has proceeded at a pace at least fast enough to offset any physical deterioration and/or obsolescence in well-maintained used equipment. That was generally true for several years for equipment such as airplanes, trucks, and other rolling stock; on the other hand, for equipment such as computers, obsolescence rapidly takes its toll.

With a basic knowledge of the condition of the equipment and the general status of the market for equipment in the particular industry, a reasonable adjustment often can be made by adding back some portion of the depreciation account. Another possibility is to use personal property depreciation schedules available from most county assessors' offices. Such schedules give valuation factors as a percentage of cost for each of most major categories of equipment, depending on the age of the equipment.

# Intangible Assets

At this stage of the valuation process, balance sheet adjustments usually are limited to those necessary to arrive at an adjusted net tangible asset value. If the value of the business based on earning capacity is greater than the net tangible asset value, some intangible value is indicated. Frequently, this intangible value is simply called goodwill. However, that may be an improper characterization of the intangible value; and for tax and/or other reasons, it may be worthwhile to quantify the amount of value attributable to specific intangible assets such as patents, copyrights, customer lists, and many other possibilities. This concept is discussed more fully in Chapter 32.

## Leaseholds

A leasehold interest is one intangible asset that frequently is recognized and valued at this stage of the valuation process. If the operation has an especially favorable lease that can be assigned, the *leasehold estate* (the right to use the property as conveyed by a lease) may be valued.

The general method for valuing a leasehold estate is to calculate the net present value of the difference between the rent that the lease calls for over its remaining life and the market rent, that is, the rent that would have to be paid over the same period if a comparable new lease were entered into today on an arm's-length basis.

Let's say that the lease has 60 months to run at a rental of $800 per month, while a new lease today for comparable premises costs $1,000 per month. The lease represents a cost saving of $200 per month. If we discount the saving using a 15 percent annual discount (capitalization) rate (1.25 percent per month), the value of the lease can be computed as follows:

$$PV = \sum_{i=1}^{60} \frac{\$200}{(1.0125)^i} = \$8,406.92$$

Discussion of how to make present value calculations is included in Chapter 17.

## Patents and Copyrights

If there are identifiable cost savings or income streams attributable to patents and copyrights, they can be valued in the same manner as leaseholds: by discounting the cost saving or income stream to a present value by using an appropriate discount (capitalization) rate. More discussion of intangible asset valuation is included in Chapter 32.

# Liabilities

If stock is being valued, or if liabilities are to be assumed in conjunction with an asset sale, then the liability side of the balance sheet also should be examined for possible adjustments. Most liabilities, of course, would be left on an adjusted balance sheet at their face value. An adjustment can be made on an interest-bearing obligation with an interest rate significantly different from current market rates, or on a Deferred Taxes account.

## Interest-Bearing Debt

It is common to read or hear the phrase "assume favorable financing" as a selling point, to make a business more attractive to a potential buyer. Most people, however, fail to resolve this important question: in valuing the business in question, how many dollars' worth of difference does the favorable financing that is available really make?

For example, suppose that the buyer assumes a contract with a remaining principal balance of $500,000, payable in 84 equal monthly installments (seven years), including interest at 8 percent, when the current market rate for comparable debt financing is 14 percent. The payments on the obligation would be $7,793.21 per month. The present value of the contract can be computed as follows:

$$PV = \sum_{i=1}^{84} \frac{\$7,793.21}{(1.011667)^i} = \$415,834$$

In other words, the $500,000 face value of the obligation should be adjusted to a present value of $415,834 for the adjusted balance sheet under current economic conditions.

The procedures for computing the amounts of the payments and present values for such contracts are covered in Chapter 17.

Suppose an adjusted gross asset value is $700,000. Without adjusting the liability, the face amount of $500,000 would be deducted, resulting in an adjusted net asset value of $200,000. Applying the appropriate adjustment to the liability results in a deduction of only about $416,000, leaving an adjusted net asset value of $284,000. In other words, in this example, the ability to use favorable financing to control $700,000 worth of assets makes the business worth $84,000 more than it would if such financing were not available as part of the package.

## Deferred Taxes

An item called *Deferred Taxes* sometimes appears on the balance sheet because income taxes have been incurred but are not yet due to be paid. The analyst should inquire about the likely timing of such payments, or even whether they will have to be paid at all. It frequently is appropriate to reduce the Deferred Taxes item, or possibly eliminate it entirely, in constructing the adjusted balance sheet from an appraisal viewpoint.

# Contingent or Off-Balance Sheet Assets and Liabilities

Many items that do not actually appear on the balance sheet should be considered in the course of the balance sheet analysis. These are items for which it has not been established for certain whether or not a payment (complete or partial) actually will be made or received. The factors giving rise to such off-balance sheet items may already be in place: a lawsuit filed, accrued vacation or pension liabilities; or the item may be dependent on some future event—such as a change in taxation or some aspect of the regulatory environment. Whether or not such items warrant specific attention depends on their potential magnitude and the probability of their actually resulting in future payments or receipts.

Sometimes, when constructing the adjusted balance sheet, one or more of these contingencies should be added to the line items in the statement. More often, because of their uncertain nature, it would be appropriate to call attention to these items in a footnote. The following are a few fairly common examples of off-balance sheet liabilities and assets.

## Product Liability

If a company manufactures or sells widgets, it may have an obligation for repairs, replacements, or other restitution for defective widgets, through express warranty or otherwise. Many small manufacturing companies just charge the expense of such claims against earnings, as they occur. If a company is exposed, but has no reserve or liability account on its balance sheet to cover it, a good procedure is to estimate the probable cost of such future claims, perhaps from the history of such claims, and establish a liability account on the balance sheet to recognize these obligations.

In general, one of the reasons that many buyers prefer an asset purchase rather than a stock purchase is to avoid the obligation for any possible contingent liabilities of the selling corporation. However, under various states' bulk sales laws, this type of contingent liability is likely to be transferred to a new owner even through an asset transaction rather than a stock transaction. If that is a prospect, a buyer should seek his attorney's advice as to what his position will be on this matter.

# Lawsuits

Actual or potential lawsuits of all kinds are an area far too broad to treat in any detail; if such possibilities exist, they should be investigated as thoroughly as possible. It is also possible, of course, that the company could have a suit pending against someone else, which could be resolved with a great benefit to the company.

# Regulatory Compliance

In these days of extensive bureaucratic regulation, often administered with utter disregard for economic consequences to the individual business, community, or nation, the specter of the potential cost of complying with government mandates cannot be ignored.

Two of the most common sources of such mandatory expenditures are pollution control requirements and Occupational Safety & Health Administration (OSHA) requirements. A potential buyer should inquire into possible costs of compliance and should recognize a liability for incurring such costs.

A potential cost could be uncertain, perhaps pending the outcome of an administrative or legal proceeding that may require considerable time to resolve; therefore, a buyer might establish a reserve for the potential cost, with the seller entitled to any residual in the reserve not actually required to meet the final compliance mandate.

# Past Service Liability

There may be obligations to employees for past services, perhaps in the form of unfunded pension liabilities, accrued vacations, or arrangements with individual employees. These obligations should be quantified, if possible, and shown as a liability on the balance sheet.

# Employment Agreements

Some companies may have employment agreements or consulting agreements, under which regular payments are made to former owners or employees. In many cases, the payments are, in reality, part of the purchase price of a former owner's interest, or compensation for a former employee's past services, with little or no service being rendered currently for such payments. When that is the case, from an appraisal viewpoint, the obligations under such agreements should be viewed as liabilities.

# Unrecorded Obligations

The appraiser should investigate whether there may be any outstanding obligations, not recorded on the books, for goods or services. In one case, for example, a balance sheet on which a sale of a company was based showed accounts receivable for sales that had been made, but did not show the liability for the salesmen's commissions that would have to be paid out of the accounts receivable when collected.

## Liens

If the company has any of its assets pledged, either to secure its own indebtedness or because it is contingently liable for someone else's indebtedness, such facts should be noted.

# The Ultimate Adjusted Balance Sheet Analysis

One veteran business broker advises sellers that it is useful to inventory every item of furniture, fixtures, machinery, and equipment, including items that have been fully depreciated, and to develop four values for each item:

1. Book value ("cost less depreciation").
2. Liquidation value ("in an orderly sale, not in a crisis situation").
3. Replacement cost ("for a new item–similar function").
4. Fair market value ("to replace similar piece, similar condition from a dealer and set 'in place' ").[4]

# Samples of Adjusted Balance Sheets

The following are hypothetical examples of the procedures discussed in this chapter. These examples assume that the respective companies have done their accounting on an accrual basis. An example of how to handle balance sheet adjustments for companies accounting on a cash basis is included in Chapter 24.

## Sole Proprietorship Example

Annie was a good merchandiser and a shrewd businesswoman. When she decided to retire, the apparel shop she had bought a few years before was well maintained and operating profitably. Exhibit 5–2 is the adjusted balance sheet she prepared in connection with selling her business.

[4] Paul B. Baron, *When You Buy or Sell a Company*, rev. ed. (Meriden, Conn.: The Center for Business Information, Inc., 1983), pp. 6–12, 6–13.

Exhibit 5–2

**ANNIE'S APPAREL STORE**
**ADJUSTED BALANCE SHEET**
**AS OF DECEMBER 31, 1984**

| | Balance Sheet as Reported $ | % | Adjustments $ | Balance Sheet as Adjusted $ | % |
|---|---|---|---|---|---|
| **ASSETS** | | | | | |
| Current Assets: | | | | | |
| Cash | 5,000 | 2.2 | (5,000)[1] | — | — |
| Accounts Receivable | 30,000 | 13.2 | (3,000)[2] | 27,000 | 9.6 |
| Inventory | 180,000 | 78.9 | 40,000[3] | 220,000 | 78.6 |
| Prepaid Expenses | 3,000 | 1.3 | | 3,000 | 1.1 |
| Total Current Assets | 218,000 | 95.6 | | 250,000 | 89.3 |
| Fixed Assets: | | | | | |
| Fixtures & Equipment | 50,000 | 21.9 | | | |
| Less: Depreciation | 40,000 | 17.5 | | | |
| | 10,000 | 4.4 | 20,000[4] | 30,000 | 10.7 |
| TOTAL ASSETS | 228,000 | 100.0 | | 280,000 | 100.0 |
| **LIABILITIES & OWNER'S EQUITY** | | | | | |
| Current Liabilities: | | | | | |
| Accounts Payable | 110,000 | 48.2 | (110,000)[5] | — | — |
| Notes Payable | 1,000 | 0.4 | (1,000)[5] | — | — |
| Accrued Payroll | 2,000 | 0.9 | (2,000)[5] | — | — |
| Total Current Liabilities | 113,000 | 49.6 | | — | — |
| Long-Term Debt | | | | | |
| Contract Payable | 100,000 | 43.9 | (10,984)[6] | 89,016 | 31.8 |
| Total Liabilities | 213,000 | 93.4 | | 89,016 | 31.8 |
| Owner's Equity | 15,000 | 6.6 | | 190,984 | 68.2 |
| TOTAL LIABILITIES & EQUITY | 228,000 | 100.0 | | 280,000 | 100.0 |

[1] Cash to be retained by seller.
[2] It is easier for an ongoing operator to collect accounts receivable—accounts receivable discounted 10% for doubtful accounts and time to collect.
[3] Aggressive policy in inventory markdowns has been followed. This adjustment results from taking a physical inventory, extending at probable selling prices, and allowing a 45% gross margin, the store's average historical gross margin.
[4] Adjustment to furniture and fixtures based on talks with dealers—approximate cost to replace used furniture and fixtures delivered to store.
[5] Will pay out of proceeds of sale.
[6] Buyer will assume remaining balance of 7% contract from Annie's purchase of the store—60 payments of $1,980.12, discounted at 12% (See Chapter 17).

Exhibit 5–3

**MARY'S MACHINERY & EQUIPMENT, INC.**
**ADJUSTED BALANCE SHEET**
**AS OF DECEMBER 31, 1984**

| | Balance Sheet as Reported | | Adjustments | Balance Sheet as Adjusted | |
|---|---|---|---|---|---|
| | $ | % | $ | $ | % |
| **ASSETS** | | | | | |
| Current Assets: | | | | | |
|   Cash & Equivalents | 65,000 | 7.2 | | 65,000 | 6.3 |
|   Accounts Receivable | 300,000 | 33.3 | (70,000)[1] | 230,000 | 22.3 |
|   Inventory | 320,000 | 35.6 | 58,250[2] | 378,250 | 36.7 |
|   Prepaid Expenses | 15,000 | 1.7 | | 15,000 | 1.5 |
|   Marketable Securities | 10,000 | 1.1 | 10,530[3] | 20,530 | 2.0 |
|   Other | 5,000 | 0.6 | | 5,000 | 0.5 |
| Total Current Assets | 715,000 | 79.4 | (1,220) | 713,780 | 69.2 |
| Furniture, Fixtures, & Equip. | | | | | |
|   Equipment | 110,000 | 12.2 | | | |
|   Furnishings | 40,000 | 4.4 | | | |
|   Vehicles | 200,000 | 22.2 | | | |
| | 350,000 | 38.9 | | | |
|   Less: Accumulated Deprec. | 225,000 | 25.0 | | | |
| Net Furn., Fix., & Equip. | 125,000 | 13.9 | 125,000[4] | 250,000 | 24.2 |
| Leasehold Interest | — | — | 8,200[5] | 8,200 | 0.8 |
| Other Assets | 60,000 | 6.7 | | 60,000 | 5.8 |
| TOTAL ASSETS | 900,000 | 100.0 | 131,980 | 1,031,980 | 100.0 |
| | | | | | |
| **LIABILITIES & STOCKHOLDER'S EQUITY** | | | | | |
| Current Liabilities: | | | | | |
|   Notes Payable | 50,000 | 5.7 | | 50,000 | 4.8 |
|   Current Mat. Long-Term Debt | 40,000 | 4.4 | | 40,000 | 3.9 |
|   Accts & Notes Pay.—Trade | 120,000 | 13.3 | | 120,000 | 11.6 |
|   Accrued Expenses | 40,000 | 4.4 | | 40,000 | 3.9 |
|   Other | 30,000 | 3.3 | | 30,000 | 2.9 |
| Total Current Liabilities | 280,000 | 31.1 | | 280,000 | 27.1 |
| Long-Term Debt | 100,000 | 11.1 | (4,855)[6] | 95,145 | 9.2 |
| Other Liabilities | 20,000 | 2.2 | | 20,000 | 1.9 |
| Contingent Liabilities | — | — | 50,000[7] | 50,000 | 4.8 |
| Total Liabilities | 400,000 | 44.4 | 45,145 | 445,145 | 43.1 |
| Stockholder's Equity: | | | | | |
|   Common Stock | 25,000 | 2.8 | | 25,000 | 2.4 |
|   Paid-In Capital | 25,000 | 2.8 | | 25,000 | 2.4 |
|   Retained Earnings | 525,000 | 58.3 | 86,835[8] | 611,835 | 59.3 |
| | 575,000 | 68.9 | 86,835[8] | 661,835 | 64.1 |
|   Less: Treasury Stock | (75,000) | (8.3) | | (75,000) | (7.3) |
| Total Stockholder's Equity | 500,000 | 55.6 | 86,835[8] | 586,835 | 56.9 |
| **TOTAL LIABILITIES & STOCKHOLDER'S EQUITY** | 900,000 | 100.0 | 131,980 | 1,031,980 | 100.0 |

NOTE: Percentages may not total due to rounding.

Exhibit 5–3 (*concluded*)

[1] The following accounts are believed to be uncollectible (see Exhibit 5-1):

| | |
|---|---|
| A-1 Equipment | $20,000 |
| I. K. Industries | 12,000 |
| Power Enterprises | 8,000 |
| Western Industries | 30,000 |
| | $70,000 |

[2] Inventory needs to be adjusted to a FIFO basis as follows:

| | |
|---|---|
| LIFO Reserve | $110,000 |
| (1 – Marginal Tax Rate) | .575 |
| | $63,250 |

In addition, the inventory needs to be reduced by $5000 for obselete inventory.

[3] 200 shares of IBM common stock

| | | |
|---|---|---|
| | 200 | |
| (closing price 12/31/84) | X 123-1/8 | |
| | $24,625 | |
| | – 10,000 | Original Cost |
| | $14,625 | Implied Gain |
| | X .72 | 1 – Capital Gains Tax Rate |
| | 10,530 | Adjustment |

[4] Adjustment to Furnitures, Fixtures and Equipment based on talks with dealers—approximate cost to replace used, including delivery.

[5] Rent paid by Mary's is approximately $200 per month below fair market rent. Discount this amount at Mary's weighted cost of capital, computed as follows:

Balance sheet composition: 2/3 debt @ 12% cost = 8%
1/3 equity @ 24% cost = 8%
16% Cost of Capital

The lease has a five-year term. The present value of $200 discounted for 60 months at 16% annually is $8,200.

[6] $50,000 of the long-term debt is at current market interest rates. However, $50,000 is payable in 36 equal monthly installments (3 years) including interest at 6%, resulting in monthly payments of $1,521.10 per month. The current market rate for comparable debt financing is 13%. The present value of this contract is $45,144.51, or approximately $45,145.

[7] Mary's is currently involved in a lawsuit for which the probable judgment against the company will amount to $50,000.

[8] The net amount of adjustments 1 through 7.

# Corporation Example

Mary's Machinery & Equipment, Inc., distributes and services industrial machinery and equipment. Mary's is well known for its top-notch mechanics and rebuilding expertise. Mary wants to sell the business and move to Hawaii for rest and relaxation. The company felt the brunt of the recession in 1982 and 1983, but returned to profitability in 1984. Exhibit 5–3 is the adjusted balance sheet prepared by the company's accountants in connection with the sale of the business.

# Chapter 6

## Adjusting the Income Statement

The objective of adjusting the income statement to a "normalized" basis is to make the best possible estimate of the true economic earning power of the entity in question. The first set of income statement adjustments generally is done on the assumption that the entity will continue to remain independent and essentially in its present mode of operation. Adjustments under that assumption are the subject of this chapter. As one business appraiser explains it:

> In preparing the stabilized income account, you are attempting to show the most likely performance for the business over the ensuing 12-month period. It is not your own business plan projections, which may include a lot of changes you would make in the business, but rather a picture of the business with the strengths and weaknesses it has at present—that is what you pay for when you buy a business.[1]

If a particular buyer contemplates changes that will affect revenues and/or expenses, then it is a good idea for him to prepare an income statement as he would expect it to look with the change implemented. We will call this a *pro forma* income statement, or a *buyer's* income statement, to distinguish it from an *adjusted* income statement. The *pro forma* or *buyer's* income statement is discussed in Chapter 9.

In this chapter we will assume that the adjustments are being made in order to assist in valuing a controlling interest. Differences in procedures that might be appropriate for valuing minority interests are discussed in Chapter 23.

# Compensation to Owners

The item that most often begs adjustment on the income statements of a privately held entity is the compensation to the owners. Actual compensation tends to be based on what the entity can afford, or how the owners desire to be compensated, and may bear little or no relationship to the economic value of the services actually performed by the owners.

The general idea of the compensation adjustment is to substitute for the compensation actually paid the cost of hiring a nonowner outsider to perform the same function. Another way to look at it is to substitute for actual compensation paid some average amount that other people normally are compensated for performing similar services. For example, if we are valuing a small restaurant whose owner is being paid $50,000 per year, and a competent, full-charge manager could be hired for $30,000 to perform the same services, the owner's compensation would be adjusted downward by $20,000 on the adjusted income statement, resulting in a $20,000 addition to pretax profit.

---

[1] *Small Business Acquisitions Manual* (Brattleboro, Vt., Country Business Services, Inc., 1981), p. 55.

## Analyzing the Components of Compensation

The adjustment should reflect all components of compensation, many of which may be buried in various expense accounts. Expenses that would be considered discretionary on the owner's part normally should be adjusted. There are many types of expenses that are perfectly legitimate from an income tax viewpoint that would not be considered essential by an owner whose objective was to maximize bottom-line profits.

All salary, bonuses, and direct payments to owners are part of the compensation. Payments into pension, profit sharing, or other retirement accounts for the benefit of the owners also should be included. In some cases, there are substantial life insurance premiums that should be included.

Some of the most common expense items that may be considered discretionary are automobile expenses, travel and entertainment, and costs of maintaining boats, airplanes, various condominiums, and other residences. When analyzing compensation to owners, don't overlook the various kinfolk, in-laws, and outlaws who may be on the payroll or otherwise receiving benefit from the business.

## Sources of Comparative Compensation Data

Employment agencies are good sources of informal estimates of how much it would cost to fill a particular job. Some of the large CPA firms also maintain data on compensation levels for various positions in various locales. Many trade associations compile data on compensation in their respective industries.

Three sources that provide average levels of compensation to owners in various business and professional classifications are the Robert Morris Associates' *Annual Statement Studies*, the *Almanac of Business and Industrial Financial Ratios*, and *Financial Studies of the Small Business*. These sources are discussed more fully, with sample pages of each, in Chapter 7.

# Depreciation

Depreciation accounting policies differ greatly from one company to another. As noted in Chapter 4, large companies often account for depreciation in one way for tax purposes and in another way for financial reporting purposes; smaller businesses and professional practices tend to account for depreciation in whatever acceptable manner minimizes their income tax burdens. Exhibit 6–1 is a condensed primer on acceptable alternate depreciation methods currently in use.

Depreciation is a noncash charge against earnings; that is, the business makes no cash outlay at the time it charges the depreciation

Exhibit 6–1

## ALTERNATE DEPRECIATION METHODS

Data used for the following examples:
  Piece of equipment, purchased at beginning of Year 1
  Cost of equipment          $50,000
  Estimated useful life      5 years

### STRAIGHT-LINE METHOD

| Year | Computation | Year's Depreciation Charge | Balance Accumulated Depreciation | Book Value Year-End |
|---|---|---|---|---|
| 1 | 1/5 (20%) x $50,000 | $10,000 | $10,000 | $40,000 |
| 2 | 20% x  50,000 | 10,000 | 20,000 | 30,000 |
| 3 | 20% x  50,000 | 10,000 | 30,000 | 20,000 |
| 4 | 20% x  50,000 | 10,000 | 40,000 | 10,000 |
| 5 | 20% x  50,000 | 10,000 | 50,000 | — |

### 200% DECLINING BALANCE METHOD

| 1 | 40% x $50,000[a] | $20,000 | $20,000 | $30,000 |
|---|---|---|---|---|
| 2 | 40% x  30,000 | 12,000 | 32,000 | 18,000 |
| 3 | 40% x  18,000 | 7,200 | 39,200 | 10,800 |
| 4 | 40% x  10,800 | 4,320 | 43,520 | 6,480 |
| 5 | 40% x   6,480 | 2,592 | 46,112 | 3,888 |

[a] Based on double the straight-line rate of 20%, multiplied by the undepreciated book value.

### SUM OF THE YEARS' DIGITS METHOD

| 1 | 5/15 x $50,000[b] | $16,667 | $16,667 | $33,333 |
|---|---|---|---|---|
| 2 | 4/15 x  50,000 | 13,333 | 30,000 | 20,000 |
| 3 | 3/15 x  50,000 | 10,000 | 40,000 | 10,000 |
| 4 | 2/15 x  50,000 | 6,667 | 46,667 | 3,333 |
| 5 | 1/15 x  50,000 | 3,333 | 50,000 | — |

[b] Numerator is the remaining estimated useful life. Denominator is the sum of the years (5 + 4 + 3 + 2 + 1 = 15).

### THE ACCELERATED COST RECOVERY SYSTEM (ACRS)

| 1 | 15% x $50,000[c] | $ 7,500 | $ 7,500 | $42,500 |
|---|---|---|---|---|
| 2 | 22% x  50,000 | 11,000 | 18,500 | 31,500 |
| 3 | 21% x  50,000 | 10,500 | 29,000 | 21,000 |
| 4 | 21% x  50,000 | 10,500 | 39,500 | 10,500 |
| 5 | 21% x  50,000 | 10,500 | 50,000 | — |

[c] Statutory percentages for ACRS five-year property used for tax purposes.

The above are examples of the more popular depreciation methods now in use. Salvage value has not been considered in the examples. An introductory accounting text can be consulted for a thorough presentation of potential depreciation methods. ACRS was enacted as part of the Economic Recovery Tax Act of 1981 and is used for federal tax purposes. One of the periodic tax guides can be consulted for a thorough presentation of the provisions of the ACRS.

against earnings. (The cash outlay was made at the time the equipment was purchased.) Consequently, some people suggest that the entire amount of depreciation shown on the income statement be added back to earnings when adjusting the income statement in order to get a cash earnings or cash flow figure. If the assets are not really depreciating in value, even though they are being depreciated on the books, as is often the case with buildings, this procedure should result in adjusting the income statement so that it portrays a good approximation of economic reality. Consider, however, a construction company in Alaska, where equipment tends to wear out quickly as a result of hard use and the climate. In that case, pretending that physical depreciation does not occur contradicts economic reality.

If the objective of the income statement adjustment is to approximate true economic earnings, there are two ways to handle the typical situation, that is, one where some genuine economic depreciation is occurring, but not as much as is recorded on the books. One way is to adjust the amount of the depreciation charge so it approximates economic reality. For example, I know of a restaurant where the partners estimate that they are writing off their equipment about twice as fast as it actually will have to be replaced. In their buy/sell agreement, as part of a pricing formula based on earnings, they state that the earnings will be adjusted by adding back half the depreciation charged in any year that comes into play in the pricing formula.

An alternative approach is to add back all the depreciation to earnings, and then deduct a separate charge that is an estimate of the annual average cost to replace the equipment necessary to sustain the level of revenues that the income statement assumes.

# Cost of Goods Sold

For a merchandising or manufacturing business, the cost of goods obviously is a critical item. Like depreciation, it is an area where accounting practices differ significantly from one company to another. Moreover, it is an area where it is not uncommon to find accounting practices varying significantly from one year to another within the same company. It is desirable, if possible, to analyze statements for several years and to be able to explain any significant differences in the cost of goods sold as a percentage of sales from year to year, as well as any significant departures from the industry average.

## Adjustment for Companies Using LIFO Accounting

For companies using LIFO for their inventories, both the beginning and ending inventories shown on the income statement should be converted to a FIFO basis to get a good approximation of the true economic cost of goods sold. This adjustment can be done by adding back the LIFO reserve, as shown in the footnotes to the financial statements, as follows:

|  |  | Add LIFO Reserve | FIFO Basis |
|---|---|---|---|
| Beginning Inventory | $100,000 | $40,000 | $140,000 |
| Add: Purchases | 300,000 |  | 300,000 |
| Goods Available for Sale | $400,000 |  | $440,000 |
| Less: Ending Inventory | 120,000 | 50,000 | 170,000 |
| Cost of Goods Sold | $280,000 |  | $270,000 |

On a LIFO basis, the cost of goods sold was $10,000 more than it was on a FIFO basis, so the LIFO basis would have resulted in $10,000 less pretax earnings than the FIFO basis. (See also the example of the widgets in Chapter 5, where LIFO accounting produced a cost of goods sold of $750, versus $600 by the FIFO method. In that example, if the sales were $1,000, the gross margin would be $400 under FIFO accounting and $250 under LIFO accounting.)

# Unconventional but Not Uncommon Practices

When counting and pricing the inventory at the end of a particularly prosperous year, the owner(s) of a company may decide to be as aggressive as possible in taking write-offs or markdowns on slow or questionable inventory, in order to avoid paying an excessive amount of income tax. If the company counts and prices the inventory in a more conventional manner in the following year, there will be a pickup in inventory on a comparative basis and a commensurate reduction in cost of goods sold, resulting in an overstatement of gross margin and pretax earnings. One way to recognize and adjust for such erratic practices is to analyze income statements for several years, discounting an abnormally high gross margin in some years, unless there is evidence that such a higher-than-average margin is sustainable in future years.

The notion that unconventional inventory accounting practices exist is reinforced by the following quote:

> Understating year-end inventory is a simple and relatively safe—though improper—means of reducing a profitable concern's taxes. When goods are sold, their cost is deducted from sales revenue to determine taxable profit. Falsely reducing inventory has the effect of falsely increasing that deduction because the hidden goods are presumed to have been sold. . . . Cheating is the little guy's LIFO. . . . The New York garment maker who hides $500,000 of inventory at tax time uses a different fiscal period for financial statements to his bank. After writing down the inventory as of Dec. 31, he writes it up six months later when the financial statement year ends. In this way, he underpays the IRS and impresses his banker. Some describe that kind of inventory accounting as WIFL—Whatever I Feel Like.[2]

---

[2] *The Wall Street Journal*, August 4, 1981, quoted in Philip L. Cooley, *How to Value an Oil Jobbership for Purchase or Sale* (Bethesda, Md.: Petroleum Marketing Education Foundation, 1982), pp. 3–16.

# Occupancy Costs

By *occupancy costs,* we mean the cost of occupying the premises, primarily rent and utilities. If the premises are owned, the occupancy costs shown on the statements usually would include depreciation, insurance, property taxes, building repairs, and interest on any mortgage balance outstanding, as well as utilities.

## Rented or Leased Premises

If the premises are rented or leased, it should be determined whether rent or lease payments are on an arm's-length basis. If the premises are rented from the owner or his affiliates, kinfolk, or friends at something above or below a market rate of rent, an adjustment to a market rate should be made, unless the existing rate can be expected to prevail for a long period of time under a new, unrelated owner.

If a lease is about to expire, or if an existing month-to-month arrangement is tenuous, occupancy costs should be adjusted to the probable cost under a new lease or a new month-to-month arrangement. If the lessee is responsible for such variable items as taxes, common area maintenance, and/or insurance, the status and possible changes in those items should be investigated and adjusted as appropriate.

## Owner-Occupied Premises

As noted elsewhere, and except for certain kinds of special-use or single-use properties, my preference is to treat valuation of the business occupying the premises separately from the valuation of the premises themselves. To separate the real estate value from the business value, it is necessary to remove from the income statement all expenses associated with the property ownership and to substitute a market rate of rent for the premises occupied.

# Nonrecurring Items

Since the objective of the adjustment is to get a normalized income estimate, it is necessary to adjust any historical income statements for any items that would not be expected to recur in the future. Such items include a much broader spectrum than just those which would meet the narrow definition of extraordinary items under generally accepted accounting principles (GAAP). The following are a few examples of frequently encountered items that would call for an adjustment.

## Business Interruptions

Business interruptions may occur for any of a wide variety of reasons, such as strikes, storm or fire damage to premises, lack of access to premises due to street repair, extended closure for remodeling, interruption in availability of critical supplies, illness of a key person or owner, withdrawal of bank financing, loss of lease, or many other occurrences of a temporary but significant nature.

When such items are identified, their effect should be removed from the historical income stream being used as the basis for estimating a normalized income stream. If the amount of the effect can be reliably estimated, the income figures for that period of time can be adjusted accordingly. If not, then the period during which the business interruption occurred can be omitted from the historical income statement data being used to derive a normalized statement.

## Insurance Proceeds

A business may receive proceeds from life insurance on a key person, or from some type of property and casualty claim. The amount of such proceeds can be based on any of a number of factors, and the amount is not likely to be an exact offset to the amount of current earnings lost during the accounting period in which the proceeds are received. Consequently, such proceeds usually are removed from the normalized earnings stream calculations.

## Lawsuit Settlements

Sometimes, companies have substantial payments or receipts as a result of lawsuits, which can arise from a wide variety of circumstances, such as property and casualty losses, breach of contract, patent or copyright infringement, product liability, antitrust actions, income or property tax disputes, and many other situations. Usually the amounts of the settlements paid or received would be taken out for a normalized earnings calculation.

## Gains or Losses on Disposal of Assets

Gains or losses on the sale of assets should be adjusted out of the normalized income stream to the extent that they are nonrecurring in nature. If a company sells its only building or airplane, the gain or loss should be removed from computation of normalized earnings. On the other hand, if a construction company, for example, has $20,000 to $50,000 in gains from disposal of equipment almost every year, that would be recurring in nature. Be careful, however, not to "double count" earnings by adding back depreciation in excess of the actual economic decrement in value, but at the same time leaving in the earnings stream the gain on the depreciated asset that was sold.

## Discontinued Operations

If a company had earnings or losses in the past from operations that were discontinued, and consequently are not relevant to the company's current earning power, such earnings or losses should be adjusted out when computing a normalized earnings stream.

## Payments on Employment Contracts and Covenants Not to Compete

It is common to find included in expenses on the income statement payments to a former owner arising from an employment contract and/ or a covenant not to compete. An analysis should be made of the extent to which such payments were actually for services rendered to the company during the accounting periods in which they were paid. To the extent that such payments were actually for the purchase of the former owner's interest in the business, rather than for services rendered during the period of payment, they should be added back when computing the pretax normalized earnings stream. (If a new buyer is to assume such payments, the value of such future payments should be deducted from the value of the business as otherwise determined.)

## Abnormal Market Conditions

From time to time, businesses experience abnormally high or low profits (or losses) due to abnormal market conditions. For example, some service stations made unprecedented profits because of the very high gross margins they were able to achieve during periods of gasoline shortages. Some stations were sold at prices that were very high by historical standards, apparently to buyers who thought the high margins and lack of price competition at the retail level were here to stay. Buyers who paid high prices on the basis of that assumption never realized a good return on their investments, and many went broke because they couldn't service the debt they had incurred in the purchases.

During the early 1980s, when interest rates were high and automobile production and sales were low, many automobile dealerships sold at very low prices compared to prices for dealerships before and after that period. Those who bought dealerships during that period made handsome returns on their investments in the years not far ahead.

Some industries, such as sawmills, for example, are cyclical by nature and seem to have abnormally good or bad years from time to time; but for some companies, such so-called abnormalities keep recurring over the years. In cyclical industries, statements for several years should be examined to try to average out the especially good and bad years.

The problem, of course, if we are trying to estimate normalized earnings, is to identify what part of the historical record is abnormal. People tend to extrapolate future expectations on the basis of the most recent past, a practice which can be very misleading. Some informed and dispassionate judgment about the economy and the industry and its prospects should be brought to bear on the question of what adjustments, if any, should be made to the historical income statements for abnormal market conditions.

# Unrecognized Costs

Sometimes there are actual or potential expenses that have not been recognized on the income statement. If any such items exist, the statements should be adjusted to reflect them. The following are a few examples of such items that are frequently encountered.

## Accrued Expenses

Sometimes companies do not recognize incurred costs as expenses. In the last chapter, for example, I mentioned an occasion when salesmen's commissions, payable when the accounts were collected, were not recorded as expenses, even though the revenues were recorded when the sale was made. This oversight resulted in an overstatement of income, since the unrecorded commissions were really a cost of generating the revenue.

Sometimes invoices for purchases may not come in, or may not be recorded, until after the end of the accounting period, even though the merchandise was received and counted in the ending inventory. This lack of cost recognition would result in an understatement of cost of goods and an overstatement of profit.

The objective of accrual accounting is to match expenses with the associated revenues. Whenever revenues are recognized on the income statement, it is important also to recognize the expenses associated with those revenues, and vice versa.

## Bad Debts

Most companies and professionals who sell goods or services on credit have some accounts that don't get collected. Recommended accrual accounting practices call for recognizing some bad debt expense on the income statement at the time the revenues are recorded (and an allowance for doubtful accounts as a deduction from accounts receivable on the balance sheet). However, many small businesses and professional practices don't bother to accrue a deduction for bad debts; instead they write off bad debts against either accounts receivable (on the balance sheet) or sales (on the income statement) when the specific accounts are determined to be uncollectible.

Generally speaking, the appropriate amount of bad debt expense to be charged against revenues at the time the revenues are recognized can be determined by examining the company's historical amount of uncollectible accounts as a percentage of revenues. To the extent that the bad debt expense actually recorded for a period significantly differs from the company's historical bad debt experience, an adjustment to that expense item is indicated.

## Insurable Liabilities

Most companies exposed to product liabilities take out insurance to protect themselves against product liability claims. Similarly, most professional practitioners have some type of errors and omissions and/ or malpractice liability insurance. If a company or professional with such exposure lacks appropriate liability insurance, an additional expense in the amount of the premiums for the insurance that the company or practice "should" have is an appropriate adjustment.

# Imminent Changes

When normalizing the income statement, adjustment should be made to revenues and expenses for changes that are close at hand and predictable from the information available. For example, if the company has lost, or is about to lose, a major customer, with no replacement in sight, an adjustment to revenues would seem appropriate.

# Nonoperating Income and Expenses

When the business or practice has nonoperating items of income and/or expense, they usually should be removed when creating a normalized income statement. For example, if a company owns some property from which it is deriving income unrelated to the basic business or practice, such nonoperating income and any expenses associated with it should not be included in the normalized income statement. Then the entity can be valued on an operating basis, and the assets not part of the basic operations can be dealt with separately if they are to be a part of the total package being valued.

# Adjusting for Taxes, if Necessary

If it is desired to obtain an after-tax rather than a pretax earnings figure, each adjustment to pretax earnings must also be accompanied by an adjustment for the applicable income taxes. If the entity is incorporated, the appropriate rate to use is the corporation's marginal tax rate, that is, the tax rate applicable to its last dollar of taxable income. State and local income taxes should be included when applicable as well as federal income taxes.

If the entity is a sole proprietorship, a partnership, or an S corporation, the normalized income statement usually stops at pretax income, because each different owner may be subject to a different tax rate. If an estimated after-tax figure is desired, then one way to do it is to find out, or make an assumption about, the owner's tax bracket and use the

Exhibit 6–2

**ANNIE'S APPAREL STORE**
**ADJUSTED INCOME STATEMENT**
**FOR YEAR ENDED DECEMBER 31, 1984**

| | Income Statement as Reported $ | % | Adjustments $ | Adjusted Income Statement $ | % |
|---|---|---|---|---|---|
| Sales | 1,000,000 | 100.0 | | 1,000,000 | 100.0 |
| | | | | | |
| Cost of Goods Sold: | | | | | |
| Beginning Inventory | 170,000 | | 15,000[1] | 185,000 | |
| Plus: Purchases | 570,000 | | | 570,000 | |
| | 740,000 | | | 755,000 | |
| Less: Ending Inventory | 180,000 | | 40,000[2] | 220,000 | |
| Cost of Goods Sold | 560,000 | 56.0 | | 535,000 | 53.5 |
| Gross Margin | 440,000 | 44.0 | | 465,000 | 46.5 |
| | | | | | |
| Expenses: | | | | | |
| Owner's Salary | 70,000 | 7.0 | (20,000)[3] | 50,000 | 5.0 |
| Other Salaries | 150,000 | 15.0 | | 150,000 | 15.0 |
| Payroll Taxes | 30,000 | 3.0 | | 30,000 | 3.0 |
| Employee Benefits | 23,000 | 2.3 | | 23,000 | 2.3 |
| Rent | 65,000 | 6.5 | | 65,000 | 6.5 |
| Utilities | 3,000 | 0.3 | | 3,000 | 0.3 |
| Telephone | 3,000 | 0.3 | | 3,000 | 0.3 |
| Insurance | — | — | 2,000[4] | 2,000 | 0.2 |
| Supplies | 5,000 | 0.5 | | 5,000 | 0.5 |
| Advertising | 25,000 | 2.5 | | 25,000 | 2.5 |
| Travel & Entertainment | 25,000 | 2.5 | (20,000)[5] | 5,000 | 0.5 |
| Automobile Expense | 5,000 | 0.5 | | 5,000 | 0.5 |
| Outside Accountants | 5,000 | 0.5 | | 5,000 | 0.5 |
| Legal | 3,000 | 0.3 | | 3,000 | 0.3 |
| License, Registrations, etc. | 2,000 | 0.2 | | 2,000 | 0.2 |
| Dues & Subscriptions | 1,000 | 0.1 | | 1,000 | 0.1 |
| Allow. for Doubtful Accts. | — | — | 2,400[6] | 2,400 | 0.2 |
| Depreciation | 13,000 | 1.3 | | 13,000 | 1.3 |
| Interest | 7,000 | 0.7 | | 7,000 | 0.7 |
| Total Expenses | 435,000 | 43.5 | | 399,400 | 39.9 |
| | | | | | |
| Pretax Income | 5,000 | 0.5 | | 65,600 | 6.6 |

[1] In order to arrive at a realistic cost of goods sold, we have adjusted the beginning inventory to Annie's best estimate of what it would have been at the then-current market price.

[2] From inventory adjustment made in Exhibit 5-2.

[3] According to Robert Morris Associates *Annual Statement Studies*, the median officer's compensation/sales ratio for companies with assets of less than $1 million was 5.2%, or approximately $50,000 for a store the size of Annie's.

[4] Annie's should carry fire, casualty, and liability insurance at a cost of approximately $2,000 per year.

[5] Annie has had an above-average amount of travel and entertainment expenses through her business in an amount of approximately $20,000. In fact, a retail store the size of Annie's might not incur even $5,000 in travel and entertainment expense.

[6] About 24%, or $240,000, of Annie's sales are made on credit. Historically about 1%, or $2,400, has been uncollectible.

Exhibit 6–3

**MARY'S MACHINERY & EQUIPMENT, INC.**
**INCOME STATEMENTS**
(000s, except Per-Share Data)

| | Years Ended December 31 | | | | | | | | | |
|---|---|---|---|---|---|---|---|---|---|---|
| | 1984 | | 1983 | | 1982 | | 1981 | | 1980 | |
| | $ | % | $ | % | $ | % | $ | % | $ | % |
| Sales | 2,400 | 100.0 | 2,000 | 100.0 | 2,200 | 100.0 | 2,400 | 100.0 | 2,200 | 100.0 |
| Cost of Goods Sold: | | | | | | | | | | |
| Beg. Inventory | 300 | | 320 | | 340 | | 320 | | 320 | |
| Plus: Purchases | 1,620 | | 1,380 | | 1,480 | | 1,610 | | 1,450 | |
| | 1,920 | | 1,700 | | 1,820 | | 1,930 | | 1,770 | |
| Less: End. Inventory | 320 | | 300 | | 320 | | 340 | | 320 | |
| Cost of Goods Sold | 1,600 | 66.7 | 1,400 | 70.0 | 1,500 | 68.2 | 1,590 | 66.2 | 1,450 | 65.9 |
| Gross Margin | 800 | 33.3 | 600 | 30.0 | 700 | 31.8 | 810 | 33.8 | 750 | 34.1 |
| Operating Expenses: | | | | | | | | | | |
| Officers' Compensation | 120 | 5.0 | 100 | 5.0 | 110 | 5.0 | 120 | 5.0 | 110 | 5.0 |
| Salaries & Wages | 230 | 9.6 | 210 | 10.5 | 220 | 10.0 | 230 | 9.6 | 220 | 10.0 |
| Employee Benefits | 50 | 2.1 | 45 | 2.3 | 45 | 2.0 | 50 | 2.1 | 45 | 2.0 |
| Payroll Taxes | 50 | 2.1 | 40 | 2.0 | 45 | 2.0 | 50 | 2.1 | 45 | 2.0 |
| Rent | 24 | 1.0 | 24 | 1.2 | 24 | 1.1 | 24 | 1.0 | 24 | 1.1 |
| Depreciation | 33 | 1.4 | 35 | 1.8 | 37 | 1.7 | 39 | 1.6 | 41 | 1.9 |
| Insurance | 20 | 0.8 | 20 | 1.0 | 20 | 0.9 | 20 | 0.8 | 20 | 0.9 |
| Travel & Entertainment | 30 | 1.3 | 25 | 1.3 | 25 | 1.1 | 30 | 1.3 | 25 | 1.1 |
| Policy Adjustments | 26 | 1.1 | 32 | 1.6 | 30 | 1.4 | 24 | 1.0 | 35 | 1.6 |
| Transportation Vehicles | 24 | 1.0 | 28 | 1.4 | 30 | 1.4 | 26 | 1.1 | 25 | 1.1 |
| Prov. for Bad Debt | 13 | 0.5 | 21 | 1.1 | 15 | 0.7 | 13 | 0.5 | 10 | 0.5 |
| Other | 90 | 3.8 | 100 | 5.0 | 95 | 4.3 | 92 | 3.8 | 100 | 4.5 |
| Total Oper. Expenses | 710 | 29.6 | 680 | 34.0 | 696 | 31.6 | 718 | 29.9 | 700 | 31.8 |
| Operating Income | 90 | 3.3 | (80) | (4.0) | 4 | 0.2 | 92 | 3.8 | 50 | 2.3 |
| Other Income (Expense): | | | | | | | | | | |
| Interest Expense | (15) | (0.6) | (18) | (0.9) | (20) | (0.9) | (18) | (0.8) | (18) | (0.8) |
| Dividend Income | 1 | Nil | 1 | Nil | 1 | Nil | 1 | Nil | 1 | Nil |
| Gain (Loss) on | | | | | | | | | | |
| Sale of Assets | — | — | 10 | 0.5 | — | — | — | — | — | — |
| Fire Damage | — | — | — | — | (15) | (0.7) | — | — | — | — |
| Discont. Operations | — | — | — | — | — | — | (10) | (0.4) | 20 | 0.9 |
| Total Other Income (Expense) | (14) | (0.6) | (7) | (0.4) | (34) | (1.5) | (27) | (1.1) | 3 | 0.1 |
| Income Before Taxes | 76 | 3.2 | (87) | (4.4) | (30) | (1.4) | 65 | 2.7 | 53 | 2.4 |
| Income Taxes | 16 | 0.7 | — | — | — | — | 14 | 0.6 | 10 | 0.5 |
| Net Income | 60 | 2.5 | (87) | (4.4) | (30) | (1.4) | 51 | 2.1 | 43 | 1.9 |
| Average No. Shares Outstanding | 200 | | 200 | | 250 | | 250 | | 250 | |
| Earnings Per Share | $300 | | $(435) | | $(120) | | $204 | | $172 | |
| Dividends Per Share | $50 | | — | | — | | $50 | | $50 | |
| Effective Tax Rate | 21.2% | | — | | — | | 21.2% | | 19.1% | |

NOTE: Figures may not total due to rounding.
Nil = Inconsequential amount, greater (or less) than zero.
**SOURCE:** Company financial statements.

owner's marginal tax rate. Another method is to use what the corporate tax rate would be if it were a corporation, since incorporation almost always is an available option.

# Samples of Adjusted Income Statements

The accompanying examples illustrate the procedures discussed in this chapter. The two examples carry on with the same two hypothetical companies used in the last chapter.

Exhibit 6–4

**MARY'S MACHINERY & EQUIPMENT, INC.**
**ADJUSTED INCOME STATEMENTS**
(000s, except Per-Share Data)

| | 1984 $ | 1984 % | 1983 $ | 1983 % | 1982 $ | 1982 % | 1981 $ | 1981 % | 1980 $ | 1980 % |
|---|---|---|---|---|---|---|---|---|---|---|
| | | | | | Years Ended December 31 | | | | | |
| Sales | 2,400 | 100.0 | 2,000 | 100.0 | 2,200 | 100.0 | 2,400 | 100.0 | 2,200 | 100.0 |
| Cost of Goods Sold: | | | | | | | | | | |
| Beg. Inventory | 400[1] | | 430[1] | | 460[1] | | 425[1] | | 420[1] | |
| Plus: Purchases | 1,620 | | 1,380 | | 1,480 | | 1,610 | | 1,450 | |
| | 2,020 | | 1,810 | | 1,940 | | 2,035 | | 1,870 | |
| Less: End. Inventory | 430[1] | | 400[1] | | 430[1] | | 460[1] | | 425[1] | |
| Cost of Goods Sold | 1,590 | 66.2 | 1,410 | 70.5 | 1,510 | 68.6 | 1,575 | 65.6 | 1,445 | 65.7 |
| Gross Margin | 810 | 33.8 | 590 | 29.5 | 690 | 31.4 | 825 | 34.4 | 755 | 34.3 |
| Operating Expenses: | | | | | | | | | | |
| Officers' Compensation | 120 | 5.0 | 100 | 5.0 | 110 | 5.0 | 120 | 5.0 | 110 | 5.0 |
| Salaries & Wages | 230 | 9.6 | 210 | 10.5 | 220 | 10.0 | 230 | 9.6 | 220 | 10.0 |
| Employee Benefits | 50 | 2.1 | 45 | 2.3 | 45 | 2.0 | 50 | 2.1 | 45 | 2.0 |
| Payroll Taxes | 50 | 2.1 | 40 | 2.0 | 45 | 2.0 | 50 | 2.1 | 45 | 2.0 |
| Rent | 24 | 1.0 | 24 | 1.2 | 24 | 1.1 | 24 | 1.0 | 24 | 1.1 |
| Depreciation | 33 | 1.4 | 35 | 1.8 | 37 | 1.7 | 39 | 1.6 | 41 | 1.9 |
| Insurance | 20 | 0.8 | 20 | 1.0 | 20 | 0.9 | 20 | 0.8 | 20 | 0.9 |
| Travel & Entertainment | 30 | 1.3 | 25 | 1.3 | 25 | 1.1 | 30 | 1.3 | 25 | 1.1 |
| Policy Adjustments | 26 | 1.1 | 32 | 1.6 | 30 | 1.4 | 24 | 1.0 | 35 | 1.6 |
| Transportation Vehicles | 24 | 1.0 | 28 | 1.4 | 30 | 1.4 | 26 | 1.1 | 25 | 1.1 |
| Prov. for Bad Debt | 13 | 0.5 | 21 | 1.1 | 15 | 0.7 | 13 | 0.5 | 10 | 0.5 |
| Other | 90 | 3.8 | 100 | 5.0 | 95 | 4.3 | 92 | 3.8 | 100 | 4.5 |
| Total Oper. Expenses | 710 | 29.6 | 680 | 34.0 | 696 | 31.6 | 718 | 29.9 | 700 | 31.8 |
| Operating Income | 100 | 4.2 | (90) | (4.5) | (6) | (0.3) | 107 | 4.5 | 55 | 2.5 |
| Other Income (Expense): | | | | | | | | | | |
| Interest Expense | (15) | (0.6) | (18) | (0.9) | (20) | (0.9) | (18) | (0.8) | (18) | (0.8) |
| Dividend Income | 1 | Nil | 1 | Nil | 1 | Nil | 1 | Nil | 1 | Nil |
| Gain (Loss) on | | | | | | | | | | |
| Sale of Assets | — | — | — | —[2] | — | — | — | — | — | — |
| Fire Damage | — | — | — | — | —[3] | — | — | — | — | — |
| Discont. Operations | — | — | — | — | — | — | —[4] | — | —[4] | — |
| Total Other Income | | | | | | | | | | |
| (Expense) | (14) | (0.6) | (17) | (0.9) | (19) | (0.9) | (17) | (0.7) | (17) | (0.8) |
| Income before Taxes | 86 | 3.6 | (107) | (5.4) | (25) | (1.1) | 90 | 3.8 | 38 | 1.7 |
| Income Taxes | 20 | 0.8 | — | — | — | — | 23 | 1.0 | 7 | 0.3 |
| Net Income | 66 | 2.8 | (107) | (5.4) | (25) | (1.1) | 67 | 2.8 | 31 | 1.4 |

| | 1984 | 1983 | 1982 | 1981 | 1980 |
|---|---|---|---|---|---|
| Average No. Shares Outstanding | 200 | 200 | 250 | 250 | 250 |
| Earnings per Share | $330 | $(535) | $(100) | $268 | $124 |
| Dividends per Share | $50 | — | — | $50 | $50 |
| Effective Tax Rate | 23.3% | — | — | 25.6% | 18.4% |

NOTE: Figures may not total due to rounding.
Nil = Inconsequential amount, greater (or less) than zero.

| | As of December 31 (In 000s) | | | | | |
|---|---|---|---|---|---|---|
| | 1984 | 1983 | 1982 | 1981 | 1980 | 1979 |
| Inventory as Stated | $320 | $300 | $320 | $340 | $320 | $320 |
| Add: LIFO Reserve | 110 | 100 | 110 | 120 | 105 | 100 |
| Adjusted Inventory | $430 | $400 | $430 | $460 | $425 | $420 |

[2] The $10,000 gain was from the sale of the company's condominium. Since that was a nonrecurring item, the gain was eliminated in the adjusted income statement.

[3] The $45,000 loss was from a fire in the warehouse in 1982. That represented the amount of the loss not recovered from insurance proceeds. Since it was a nonrecurring item, it needed to be eliminated from the adjusted income statement.

[4] Mary's discontinued a retail parts store in 1981. Since we are interested only in Mary's current earning power, those gains were eliminated from the adjusted income statement.

## Sole Proprietorship Example

Exhibit 6–2 is an adjusted income statement for Annie's Apparel Store, a sole proprietorship, which she prepared when she was ready to sell her business.

## Corporation Example

Exhibit 6–3 shows the income statements as reported for Mary's Machinery & Equipment, Inc., for the years ended December 31, 1980 through 1984. Exhibit 6–4 shows the adjusted income statements for Mary's over the same time period. Both the reported and adjusted statements were prepared by Mary's accountants; the adjusted statements were prepared in connection with the sale of the business.

# Chapter 7

## Comparisons with Industry Averages

One of the benefits of having normalized the balance sheet and income statement is that it makes it possible to make valid comparisons between the entity being valued and others in the same business or profession. While comparison with peers is not an essential step in the valuation process, it can be helpful in several ways, especially for businesses and professional practices for which a good body of comparative data is available. However, care must be exercised in this process to be sure that comparison of income statement and balance sheet items are conducted under like accounting treatment and ratio definitions.

# Advantages of Comparative Analysis

Comparative analysis provides some insight into how the entity in which we are interested compares with its peers. This information is especially useful, of course, for those who do not have a great deal of financial experience with the business or profession in question, even though they may have considerable experience with it from other viewpoints. Even the veteran buyer, however, will sharpen his perspective on the entity at hand by going through a comparative analysis exercise.

## Identifying Errors

Comparative analysis makes it eminently apparent when the subject entity in some respect differs markedly from industry averages. This disparity could cause the valuator to recheck balance sheet and/or income statement data for possible errors.

## Identifying Strengths and Weaknesses

Comparative analysis points up the relative strengths and weaknesses of the subject entity compared to its peers, from both a balance sheet and an income statement point of view. It shows where the company shines compared with its peers, and what financial items need to be improved and by how much in order to bring it into line with industry averages.

## Identifying Opportunities

Comparative analysis can point out opportunities that become apparent from studying balance sheets, income statements, and ratios that use the two statements together.

For example, if a company has little or no debt compared with others in its line of business, its assets might be used as collateral for borrowing to help finance the purchase. That is the basic concept of the *leveraged buyout,* or using debt financing, supported by the company's assets, to pay a significant portion of the purchase price. If the bottom line profits fall below industry averages, this suggests room for improvement. The income statement comparisons may reveal specific categories of costs that might be reduced to improve profitability. If a retailer's gross margin is below the industry average, profits might be improved considerably by bringing the margin up to, or better than, standard. If the salary costs for a service business are out of line, it suggests that there should be room to generate the same revenue with less labor cost or to generate more revenue with the existing amount of labor.

Ratios that utilize both the balance sheet and the income statement include, for example, accounts receivable turnover (average collection period) and inventory turnover (average length of time merchandise is held in inventory). Improvements in these ratios would mean a reduction in working capital requirements, thus reducing interest costs if the company is borrowing money to finance receivables and inventory.

# Sources of Comparative Industry Data

Sources of comparative industry data can be classified into two broad groups: (1) general sources that provide data for a wide variety of businesses and professional practices; (2) specialized sources that provide data on some specific category of businesses or professional practices.

## General Sources

Three of the most widely used general sources for comparative financial data for small businesses are *RMA Annual Statement Studies,* the *Almanac of Business and Industrial Financial Ratios,* and *Financial Studies of the Small Business.* Each is published annually. The degree of usefulness of the data varies considerably from one type of business to another, depending largely on how many reasonably homogeneous businesses the publications are able to collect data for in each category.

**RMA Annual Statement Studies.**   Probably the most popular source is the *RMA Annual Statement Studies,* which is a product of a national association of bank loan and credit officers. The 1984 edition was based on financial statements of over 80,000 businesses and professional practices submitted by member banks. One reason for the broad appeal of the *Annual Statement Studies* is the over 330 classifications of businesses and professional practices it covers.

Exhibit 7–1 is a typical page from *RMA Annual Statement Studies,* in this case retailers of women's ready-to-wear. Note that each industry group is broken down into four size categories, based on total assets. (No figures are shown for the largest size category in this particular industry group because RMA considered that only four companies in

Exhibit 7–1

RETAILERS - WOMEN'S READY-TO-WEAR SIC# 5621

| Current Data | | | | | | ASSET SIZE<br>NUMBER OF STATEMENTS | Comparative Historical Data | | | | |
|---|---|---|---|---|---|---|---|---|---|---|---|
| 160(6/30-9/30/83) | | | 193(10/1/83-3/31/84) | | | | 6/30/79-<br>3/31/80 | 6/30/80-<br>3/31/81 | 6/30/81-<br>3/31/82 | 6/30/82-<br>3/31/83 | 6/30/83-<br>3/31/84 |
| 0-1MM<br>235 | 1-10MM<br>97 | 10-50MM<br>19 | 50-100MM<br>2 | | ALL<br>353 | | ALL<br>337 | ALL<br>334 | ALL<br>323 | ALL<br>349 | ALL<br>353 |
| % | % | % | % | | % | ASSETS | % | % | % | % | % |
| 9.8 | 9.9 | 16.1 | | | 10.1 | Cash & Equivalents | 12.0 | 11.1 | 10.9 | 10.1 | 10.1 |
| 13.3 | 20.9 | 15.2 | | | 15.5 | Accts. & Notes Rec.- Trade(net) | 17.5 | 17.0 | 16.3 | 16.1 | 15.5 |
| 54.4 | 40.7 | 37.2 | | | 49.6 | Inventory | 44.3 | 45.7 | 47.5 | 48.1 | 49.6 |
| 1.3 | 1.8 | 2.6 | | | 1.6 | All Other Current | 2.1 | 1.2 | 1.4 | 1.8 | 1.6 |
| 78.8 | 73.4 | 71.1 | | | 76.8 | Total Current | 75.9 | 75.1 | 76.0 | 76.1 | 76.8 |
| 15.6 | 18.5 | 23.2 | | | 16.9 | Fixed Assets (net) | 17.1 | 17.9 | 18.0 | 17.4 | 16.9 |
| .9 | 1.0 | .6 | | | .9 | Intangibles (net) | .8 | .6 | .7 | 1.1 | .9 |
| 4.6 | 7.1 | 5.2 | | | 5.3 | All Other Non-Current | 6.2 | 6.4 | 5.2 | 5.4 | 5.3 |
| 100.0 | 100.0 | 100.0 | | | 100.0 | Total | 100.0 | 100.0 | 100.0 | 100.0 | 100.0 |
| | | | | | | LIABILITIES | | | | | |
| 11.8 | 8.7 | 4.2 | | | 10.4 | Notes Payable-Short Term | 9.4 | 8.4 | 9.0 | 8.2 | 10.4 |
| 4.1 | 2.8 | .9 | | | 3.6 | Cur. Mat.-L/T/D | 3.1 | 3.1 | 3.4 | 3.2 | 3.6 |
| 17.9 | 22.6 | 18.4 | | | 19.2 | Accts. & Notes Payable - Trade | 19.1 | 19.1 | 19.5 | 19.0 | 19.2 |
| 4.4 | 8.2 | 10.0 | | | 5.8 | Accrued Expenses | 5.8 | 6.0 | 5.8 | 5.6 | 5.8 |
| 5.4 | 3.0 | 2.7 | | | 4.6 | All Other Current | 3.4 | 3.1 | 3.0 | 3.1 | 4.6 |
| 43.6 | 45.2 | 36.3 | | | 43.6 | Total Current | 40.7 | 39.6 | 40.6 | 39.1 | 43.6 |
| 14.3 | 12.9 | 8.3 | | | 13.5 | Long Term Debt | 12.8 | 12.8 | 15.1 | 14.8 | 13.5 |
| 2.7 | 2.7 | 3.5 | | | 2.8 | All Other Non-Current | 1.7 | 2.1 | 1.9 | 2.8 | 2.8 |
| 39.4 | 39.2 | 51.9 | | | 40.1 | Net Worth | 44.8 | 45.5 | 42.4 | 43.4 | 40.1 |
| 100.0 | 100.0 | 100.0 | | | 100.0 | Total Liabilities & Net Worth | 100.0 | 100.0 | 100.0 | 100.0 | 100.0 |
| | | | | | | INCOME DATA | | | | | |
| 100.0 | 100.0 | 100.0 | | | 100.0 | Net Sales | 100.0 | 100.0 | 100.0 | 100.0 | 100.0 |
| 59.2 | 60.1 | 65.7 | | | 59.8 | Cost Of Sales | 59.2 | 59.1 | 59.5 | 60.5 | 59.8 |
| 40.8 | 39.9 | 34.3 | | | 40.2 | Gross Profit | 40.8 | 40.9 | 40.5 | 39.5 | 40.2 |
| 37.8 | 37.8 | 27.1 | | | 37.2 | Operating Expenses | 38.1 | 38.4 | 37.4 | 37.0 | 37.2 |
| 3.0 | 2.1 | 7.2 | | | 3.0 | Operating Profit | 2.7 | 2.6 | 3.2 | 2.5 | 3.0 |
| .2 | -.1 | -.7 | | | .1 | All Other Expenses (net) | .0 | .0 | .7 | .3 | .1 |
| 2.8 | 2.2 | 7.9 | | | 2.9 | Profit Before Taxes | 2.7 | 2.6 | 2.5 | 2.3 | 2.9 |
| | | | | | | RATIOS | | | | | |
| 2.7 | 2.3 | 2.3 | | | 2.4 | | 2.8 | 2.9 | 2.9 | 3.2 | 2.4 |
| 1.8 | 1.6 | 2.1 | | | 1.8 | Current | 2.0 | 2.0 | 2.0 | 2.1 | 1.8 |
| 1.5 | 1.3 | 1.6 | | | 1.4 | | 1.5 | 1.5 | 1.4 | 1.5 | 1.4 |
| .9 | 1.1 | 1.4 | | | 1.1 | | 1.2 | 1.2 | 1.2 | 1.2 | 1.1 |
| (234) .5 | .7 | 1.0 | (352) | | .6 | Quick | (333) .7 | (322) .7 | (348) .7 | (352) .7 | .6 |
| .2 | .4 | .5 | | | .3 | | .4 | .4 | .3 | .3 | .3 |
| 2 228.0 | 3 108.6 | 1 279.9 | | | 2 198.0 | | 5 80.3 | 5 79.4 | 3 110.5 | 2 159.0 | 2 198.0 |
| 11 34.1 | 22 16.6 | 7 54.4 | | | 12 29.9 | Sales/Receivables | 20 18.0 | 19 19.6 | 17 21.8 | 15 24.3 | 12 29.9 |
| 32 11.4 | 55 6.6 | 41 8.8 | | | 40 9.1 | | 46 8.0 | 46 8.0 | 41 9.0 | 42 8.6 | 40 9.1 |
| 85 4.3 | 63 5.8 | 58 6.3 | | | 78 4.7 | | 72 5.1 | 74 4.9 | 73 5.0 | 74 4.9 | 78 4.7 |
| 126 2.9 | 87 4.2 | 79 4.6 | | | 107 3.4 | Cost of Sales/Inventory | 94 3.9 | 104 3.5 | 107 3.4 | 104 3.5 | 107 3.4 |
| 174 2.1 | 118 3.1 | 89 4.1 | | | 159 2.3 | | 135 2.7 | 152 2.4 | 152 2.4 | 152 2.4 | 159 2.3 |
| 22 16.3 | 28 13.1 | 26 13.8 | | | 24 15.1 | | 24 15.0 | 25 14.8 | 25 14.8 | 23 16.2 | 24 15.1 |
| 39 9.4 | 47 7.7 | 47 7.7 | | | 41 9.0 | Cost of Sales/Payables | 44 8.3 | 42 8.7 | 41 8.8 | 39 9.3 | 41 9.0 |
| 54 6.7 | 69 5.3 | 50 7.3 | | | 58 6.3 | | 62 5.9 | 62 5.9 | 62 5.9 | 59 6.2 | 58 6.3 |
| 5.0 | 6.4 | 5.6 | | | 5.3 | | 4.8 | 4.6 | 4.6 | 4.5 | 5.3 |
| 7.8 | 9.8 | 7.3 | | | 8.3 | Sales/Working Capital | 7.0 | 6.7 | 7.3 | 7.0 | 8.3 |
| 13.8 | 15.8 | 10.4 | | | 14.5 | | 12.7 | 14.8 | 13.8 | 12.3 | 14.5 |
| 6.5 | 7.2 | 15.4 | | | 6.6 | | 7.2 | 6.0 | 5.1 | 5.4 | 6.6 |
| (201) 2.7 | (79) 2.8 | (13) 7.0 | (294) | | 2.9 | EBIT/Interest | (268) 3.3 | (260) 2.4 | (264) 2.4 | (290) 2.0 | (294) 2.9 |
| 1.3 | 1.4 | 3.6 | | | 1.3 | | 1.3 | .9 | 1.1 | 1.0 | 1.3 |
| 5.2 | 7.7 | 111.7 | | | 7.7 | | 4.3 | 5.4 | 5.4 | 6.0 | 7.7 |
| (77) 1.3 | (56) 3.3 | (11) 12.1 | (145) | | 2.5 | Cash Flow/Cur. Mat. L/T/D | (133) 1.9 | (134) 2.2 | (129) 2.5 | (137) 2.2 | (145) 2.5 |
| .4 | 1.0 | 5.7 | | | .7 | | .8 | .7 | .8 | .9 | .7 |
| .1 | .3 | .2 | | | .2 | | .2 | .2 | .2 | .2 | .2 |
| .3 | .5 | .4 | | | .4 | Fixed/Worth | .3 | .4 | .4 | .4 | .4 |
| .8 | .8 | .7 | | | .7 | | .7 | .7 | .7 | .8 | .7 |
| .8 | 1.0 | .7 | | | .8 | | .6 | .6 | .7 | .6 | .8 |
| 1.4 | 1.7 | .9 | | | 1.4 | Debt/Worth | 1.2 | 1.2 | 1.4 | 1.3 | 1.4 |
| 2.9 | 3.1 | 1.4 | | | 2.7 | | 2.3 | 2.2 | 2.6 | 2.5 | 2.7 |
| 38.4 | 34.8 | 56.0 | | | 38.5 | % Profit Before Taxes/Tangible | 30.3 | 26.5 | 29.7 | 30.6 | 38.5 |
| (217) 15.4 | (96) 14.3 | 33.9 | (334) | | 15.3 | Net Worth | (326) 15.7 | (326) 13.3 | (306) 14.4 | (332) 12.2 | (334) 15.3 |
| 3.3 | 3.3 | 11.3 | | | 3.8 | | 4.7 | 1.5 | 2.6 | 1.8 | 3.8 |
| 14.9 | 14.0 | 23.5 | | | 15.0 | % Profit Before Taxes/Total | 13.7 | 12.5 | 12.6 | 12.6 | 15.0 |
| 5.8 | 5.4 | 16.2 | | | 6.1 | Assets | 6.3 | 5.6 | 5.8 | 4.9 | 6.1 |
| 1.0 | 1.4 | 7.2 | | | 1.3 | | 1.4 | .2 | .6 | 1.4 | 1.3 |
| 48.5 | 32.5 | 19.0 | | | 39.0 | | 37.2 | 35.2 | 36.1 | 42.9 | 39.0 |
| 23.4 | 17.1 | 13.5 | | | 20.2 | Sales/Net Fixed Assets | 19.3 | 17.5 | 18.8 | 19.9 | 20.2 |
| 11.4 | 10.6 | 7.7 | | | 10.6 | | 10.9 | 10.5 | 10.1 | 10.9 | 10.6 |
| 3.2 | 3.5 | 2.8 | | | 3.3 | | 3.3 | 3.2 | 3.2 | 3.3 | 3.3 |
| 2.6 | 2.7 | 2.6 | | | 2.6 | Sales/Total Assets | 2.6 | 2.5 | 2.6 | 2.6 | 2.6 |
| 2.0 | 2.0 | 2.3 | | | 2.0 | | 2.0 | 2.0 | 2.0 | 2.0 | 2.0 |
| .8 | .9 | .8 | | | .9 | | .7 | .8 | .8 | .8 | .9 |
| (196) 1.3 | (85) 1.4 | (18) 1.7 | (300) | | 1.4 | % Depr., Dep., Amort./Sales | (294) 1.2 | (294) 1.2 | (290) 1.2 | (305) 1.3 | (300) 1.4 |
| 2.0 | 1.9 | 2.3 | | | 2.0 | | 1.7 | 1.8 | 1.7 | 1.8 | 2.0 |
| 4.0 | 3.2 | | | | 3.8 | | 3.0 | 3.1 | 3.3 | 3.3 | 3.8 |
| (156) 5.1 | (59) 5.2 | | (224) | | 5.1 | % Lease & Rental Exp/Sales | (247) 4.9 | (243) 4.8 | (242) 4.8 | (250) 4.9 | (224) 5.1 |
| 7.1 | 6.9 | | | | 6.9 | | 6.1 | 6.2 | 6.2 | 6.6 | 6.9 |
| 3.5 | 1.7 | | | | 2.5 | | 3.0 | 2.9 | 2.7 | 2.4 | 2.5 |
| (118) 5.2 | (31) 2.5 | | (149) | | 4.6 | % Officers Comp/Sales | (171) 5.1 | (162) 4.6 | (165) 4.8 | (152) 3.8 | (149) 4.6 |
| 8.0 | 3.9 | | | | 7.3 | | 7.8 | 7.4 | 8.0 | 6.6 | 7.3 |
| 234721M | 763491M | 1283910M | 320931M | | 2603053M | Net Sales ($) | 1564064M | 1858191M | 1719478M | 2335781M | 2603053M |
| 85850M | 272027M | 490998M | 148530M | | 997405M | Total Assets ($) | 604409M | 785492M | 707747M | 992190M | 997405M |

© Robert Morris Associates 1984

M = $thousand    MM = $million
See Pages 1 through 13 for Explanation of Ratios and Data

SOURCE: *Annual Statement Studies*, 1984 edition (Philadelphia, Pennsylvania: Robert Morris Associates, 1984) (1616 Philadelphia National Bank Building, Philadelphia, Pennsylvania 19107).

that category constituted an insufficient sample.) Also, data are shown in the aggregate for five years, so that year-to-year comparisons can be made.

Each of the ratios given is defined in a section several pages long at the beginning of each RMA annual volume. Note that "all ratios computed by RMA are based on year-end statement data only." For example, the cost of sales/inventory (inventory turnover ratio) is computed by dividing the cost of goods sold for the year by the ending inventory. A truer picture of inventory would be derived by dividing cost of goods sold by average inventory, but the data on which the RMA ratios are based are insufficient to make that computation. I suggest that when using RMA as a basis for comparison, ratios be computed by the RMA definitions, even though it would be preferable to compute some ratios differently for other purposes.

**Almanac of Business and Industrial Financial Ratios.** The source of all data used in the *Almanac* is the data compiled from corporate tax returns by the U.S. Treasury and the Internal Revenue Service. It is broken down into slightly over 175 business and professional practice groups, a little more than half the number offered by RMA.

Exhibit 7–2 is a typical data presentation from the *Almanac*, in this case apparel and accessory stores. Each industry group is presented in two tables. One table includes corporations that reported a profit as well as those that did not; the second table includes only those that reported a profit.

For each group for which there are sufficient data, however, there are 12 breakdowns by asset size, compared with four in the RMA data. The *Almanac* gives more income statement line items than does RMA, while RMA gives more balance sheet line items and more ratios.

The various ratios used are defined in the front part of the *Almanac*. Computations of some of the ratios differ from computations used by RMA.

The biggest drawback to the *Almanac* is the degree to which the information is outdated. The 1985 edition covers tax returns for fiscal years ended July 1979 through June 1980. Nevertheless, operating figures for most industries have at least some degree of stability over time, and the *Almanac* offers some income statement items not found elsewhere.

**Financial Studies of the Small Business.** The *Financial Studies of the Small Business,* published by Financial Research Associates (FRA), is a compilation from over 25,000 financial statements submitted by over 1,000 independent certified public accountant firms, from all across the country. Slightly more than 50 small business and professional practice groups are included.

Exhibit 7–3 is a typical data presentation from *Financial Studies*, in this case, retail apparel stores with total assets of $150,000 to $250,000. *Financial Studies* differs particularly from *Annual Statement Studies* and the *Almanac* in that it focuses on especially small firms. Within each business or professional practice group for which sufficient data are available, four size breakdowns are presented by total assets: $10,000 to $50,000; $50,000 to $100,000; $100,000 to $150,000; and $150,000 to $250,000. A composite of the four size categories is also presented.

Median figures are used for financial statement line items, and it is necessary to read the explanation in order to interpret those figures correctly. Definitions of ratios are included in the front of the loose-leaf book, and most are similar, if not identical, to those used by RMA. As is the case with the RMA ratios, upper and lower quartile figures, as well as medians, are presented.

Exhibit 7-2

*TABLE I: CORPORATIONS WITH AND WITHOUT NET INCOME, 1983 EDITION*

RETAIL TRADE:

## Apparel and accessory stores

| Item Description For Accounting Period 7/78 Through 6/79 | A Total | B Zero Assets | C Under 100 | D 100 to 250 | E 250 to 500 | F 500 to 1,000 | G 1000 to 5,000 | H 5,000 to 10,000 | I 10,000 to 25,000 | J 25,000 to 50,000 | K 50,000 to 100,000 | L 100,000 to 250,000 | M 250,000 and over |
|---|---|---|---|---|---|---|---|---|---|---|---|---|---|
| | | | SIZE OF ASSETS IN THOUSANDS OF DOLLARS (000 OMITTED) | | | | | | | | | | |
| 1. Number of Enterprises | 42572 | 1416 | 22936 | 10422 | 4727 | 1734 | 1122 | 115 | 63 | 15 | 14 | 8 | - |
| 2. Total receipts (in millions of dollars) | 28968.0 | 105.9 | 3233.7 | 4092.0 | 3548.4 | 2787.8 | 5339.8 | 2186.2 | 2365.8 | 1096.3 | 1667.3 | 2544.9 | - |
| **Selected Operating Factors in Percent of Net Sales** | | | | | | | | | | | | | |
| 3. Cost of operations | 59.5 | 68.5 | 62.1 | 61.2 | 60.7 | 59.2 | 58.7 | 57.1 | 59.9 | 58.9 | 57.0 | 56.6 | - |
| 4. Compensation of officers | 3.3 | 2.4 | 6.6 | 5.0 | 5.3 | 4.1 | 2.6 | 1.5 | 1.0 | 1.0 | 0.8 | 0.3 | - |
| 5. Repairs | 0.4 | 5.8 | 0.3 | 0.3 | 0.4 | 0.4 | 0.4 | 0.3 | 0.3 | 0.6 | 0.5 | 0.3 | - |
| 6. Bad debts | 0.3 | 1.0 | 0.2 | 0.1 | 0.3 | 0.4 | 0.3 | 0.3 | 0.2 | 0.3 | 0.2 | 0.3 | - |
| 7. Rent on business property | 5.9 | 5.9 | 7.2 | 5.6 | 4.2 | 5.5 | 6.1 | 6.8 | 7.5 | 4.3 | 6.1 | 6.0 | - |
| 8. Taxes (excl Federal tax) | 2.3 | 3.1 | 2.4 | 2.0 | 2.2 | 2.2 | 2.5 | 2.3 | 2.2 | 2.5 | 2.7 | 2.4 | - |
| 9. Interest | 0.8 | 1.2 | 0.6 | 0.8 | 1.0 | 0.8 | 0.8 | 0.7 | 0.6 | 1.0 | 1.0 | 0.7 | - |
| 10. Deprec/Deplet/Amortiz† | 1.2 | 1.2 | 1.0 | 1.0 | 1.1 | 1.1 | 1.2 | 1.0 | 1.3 | 1.4 | 1.6 | 1.7 | - |
| 11. Advertising | 2.1 | 1.1 | 1.5 | 1.9 | 2.3 | 2.2 | 2.3 | 3.2 | 1.6 | 2.0 | 1.9 | 2.6 | - |
| 12. Pensions & other benef plans | 0.6 | 0.1 | 0.2 | 0.4 | 0.7 | 1.0 | 0.6 | 0.7 | 0.5 | 0.7 | 0.8 | 1.2 | - |
| 13. Other expenses | 21.5 | 25.1 | 18.5 | 19.3 | 20.6 | 22.2 | 23.0 | 23.4 | 22.6 | 23.4 | 22.6 | 21.7 | - |
| 14. Net profit before tax | 2.1 | * | * | 2.4 | 1.2 | 0.9 | 1.5 | 2.7 | 2.3 | 3.9 | 4.8 | 6.2 | - |
| **Selected Financial Ratios (number of times ratio is to one)** | | | | | | | | | | | | | |
| 15. Current ratio | 2.1 | - | 2.3 | 2.3 | 2.1 | 2.0 | 2.1 | 2.2 | 2.3 | 2.1 | 1.5 | 1.8 | - |
| 16. Quick ratio | 0.7 | - | 0.7 | 0.7 | 0.7 | 0.7 | 0.8 | 0.9 | 0.8 | 0.8 | 0.5 | 0.6 | - |
| 17. Net sls to net wkg capital | 6.1 | - | 6.3 | 5.5 | 5.4 | 5.9 | 6.0 | 6.3 | 5.9 | 6.6 | 9.1 | 6.4 | - |
| 18. Net sales to net worth | 4.8 | - | 7.6 | 5.7 | 4.7 | 4.7 | 4.8 | 4.9 | 4.3 | 4.4 | 4.3 | 3.2 | - |
| 19. Inventory turnover | 3.5 | - | 3.7 | 3.0 | 3.2 | 3.1 | 3.7 | 3.7 | 4.4 | 3.7 | 3.5 | 3.8 | - |
| 20. Total liab to net worth | 1.1 | - | 1.7 | 1.3 | 1.2 | 1.1 | 1.0 | 0.9 | 0.9 | 0.9 | 1.8 | 0.9 | - |
| **Selected Financial Factors in Percentages** | | | | | | | | | | | | | |
| 21. Current liab to net worth | 74.6 | - | 95.4 | 81.4 | 83.4 | 81.0 | 72.4 | 63.4 | 57.2 | 59.1 | 97.9 | 58.7 | - |
| 22. Inventory to curr assets | 59.0 | - | 64.5 | 63.6 | 62.4 | 60.3 | 54.5 | 53.1 | 54.9 | 53.4 | 56.0 | 60.1 | - |
| 23. Net income to net worth | 12.5 | - | 3.6 | 16.1 | 8.7 | 8.8 | 10.4 | 12.8 | 11.8 | 15.1 | 21.2 | 19.2 | - |
| 24. Retained earn to net inc | 65.9 | - | - | 56.5 | 75.2 | 71.7 | 75.8 | 76.1 | 78.0 | 79.3 | 56.7 | 84.9 | - |

†Depreciation largest factor

*Page 256*

Exhibit 7-2 (concluded)

TABLE II: CORPORATIONS WITH NET INCOME, 1983 EDITION

RETAIL TRADE:
## Apparel and accessory stores

| Item Description For Accounting Period 1/78 Through 6/79 | A Total | B Zero Assets | C Under 100 | D 100 to 250 | E 250 to 500 | F 500 to 1,000 | G 1,000 to 5,000 | H 5,000 to 10,000 | I 10,000 to 25,000 | J 25,000 to 50,000 | K 50,000 to 100,000 | L 100,000 to 250,000 | M 250,000 and over |
|---|---|---|---|---|---|---|---|---|---|---|---|---|---|
| | | | | | | | | | | SIZE OF ASSETS IN THOUSANDS OF DOLLARS (000 OMITTED) | | | |
| 1. Number of Enterprises | 28023 | 301 | 12935 | 8317 | 3799 | 1478 | *** | 111 | 56 | *** | 11 | 8 | - |
| 2. Total receipts (in millions of dollars) | 25309.2 | 56.5 | 2239.1 | 3379.3 | 2983.7 | 2485.7 | *** | 2111.2 | 2203.1 | *** | 1402.9 | 2544.9 | - |
| **Selected Operating Factors in Percent of Net Sales** | | | | | | | | | | | | | |
| 3. Cost of operations | 58.8 | 66.6 | 60.6 | 60.3 | 59.5 | 58.7 | *** | 57.0 | 60.2 | *** | 56.1 | 56.6 | - |
| 4. Compensation of officers | 3.2 | 2.0 | 6.6 | 5.1 | 5.6 | 4.2 | *** | 1.5 | 0.8 | *** | 0.7 | 0.3 | - |
| 5. Repairs | 0.3 | 1.9 | 0.3 | 0.3 | 0.4 | 0.3 | *** | 0.4 | 0.3 | *** | 0.4 | 0.3 | - |
| 6. Bad debts | 0.2 | 0.5 | 0.1 | 0.1 | 0.2 | 0.4 | *** | 0.3 | 0.2 | *** | 0.2 | 0.3 | - |
| 7. Rent on business property | 5.8 | 4.0 | 6.5 | 5.6 | 4.4 | 5.4 | *** | 6.8 | 7.6 | *** | 5.5 | 6.0 | - |
| 8. Taxes (excl Federal tax) | 2.3 | 2.5 | 2.3 | 2.0 | 2.3 | 2.2 | *** | 2.3 | 2.1 | *** | 2.7 | 2.4 | - |
| 9. Interest | 0.7 | 1.0 | 0.4 | 0.7 | 0.8 | 0.7 | *** | 0.7 | 0.6 | *** | 1.0 | 0.7 | - |
| 10. Deprec/Deplet/Amortiz† | 1.2 | 1.4 | 0.8 | 1.0 | 1.0 | 1.1 | *** | 1.0 | 1.3 | *** | 1.6 | 1.7 | - |
| 11. Advertising | 2.1 | 0.6 | 1.1 | 1.6 | 2.3 | 2.1 | *** | 3.2 | 1.5 | *** | 2.0 | 2.6 | - |
| 12. Pensions & other benef plans | 0.7 | - | 0.2 | 0.4 | 0.7 | 1.0 | *** | 0.7 | 0.4 | *** | 0.9 | 1.2 | - |
| 13. Other expenses | 20.9 | 25.7 | 17.4 | 18.3 | 19.8 | 21.2 | *** | 23.1 | 21.7 | *** | 22.0 | 21.7 | - |
| 14. Net profit before tax | 3.8 | # | 3.7 | 4.6 | 3.0 | 2.7 | *** | 3.0 | 3.3 | *** | 6.9 | 6.2 | - |
| **Selected Financial Ratios (number of times ratio is to one)** | | | | | | | | | | | | | |
| 15. Current ratio | 2.2 | - | 2.5 | 2.5 | 2.2 | 2.2 | *** | 2.3 | 2.4 | *** | 1.8 | 1.8 | - |
| 16. Quick ratio | 0.8 | - | 0.9 | 0.8 | 0.7 | 0.7 | *** | 0.9 | 0.9 | *** | 0.7 | 0.6 | - |
| 17. Net sls to net wkg capital | 5.9 | - | 6.2 | 5.3 | 5.3 | 5.6 | *** | 6.2 | 6.1 | *** | 7.0 | 6.4 | - |
| 18. Net sales to net worth | 4.5 | - | 6.5 | 5.2 | 4.5 | 4.7 | *** | 4.8 | 4.3 | *** | 4.0 | 3.2 | - |
| 19. Inventory turnover | 3.6 | - | 4.0 | 3.1 | 3.4 | 3.1 | *** | 3.7 | 4.5 | *** | 5.9 | 5.5 | - |
| 20. Total liab to net worth | 1.0 | - | 1.1 | 1.0 | 1.0 | 1.0 | *** | 0.9 | 0.8 | *** | 1.4 | 0.9 | - |
| **Selected Financial Factors in Percentages** | | | | | | | | | | | | | |
| 21. Current liab to net worth | 64.7 | - | 69.2 | 64.3 | 72.0 | 72.7 | *** | 62.3 | 52.3 | *** | 74.1 | 58.7 | - |
| 22. Inventory to curr assets | 58.2 | - | 62.3 | 64.8 | 60.0 | 58.6 | *** | 52.7 | 55.0 | *** | 57.7 | 60.1 | - |
| 23. Net income to net worth | 18.2 | - | 32.2 | 24.4 | 15.3 | 14.4 | *** | 13.8 | 13.6 | *** | 25.2 | 19.2 | - |
| 24. Retained earn to net inc | 76.0 | - | 65.7 | 70.0 | 84.5 | 81.6 | *** | 77.4 | 80.5 | *** | 60.5 | 84.9 | - |

†Depreciation largest factor

*Page 257*

SOURCE: Leo Troy, *Almanac of Business and Industrial Financial Ratios*, 1983 edition (Englewood Cliffs, New Jersey: Prentice-Hall, Inc., 1983).

# Exhibit 7-3

RETAIL
APPAREL                          TOTAL ASSETS $150000-$250000

## ASSETS

| CURRENT ASSETS | AS A PCT OF CURRENT ASSETS | AS A PCT OF TOTAL ASSETS |
|---|---|---|
| CASH | 13.06 | 11.56 |
| ACCOUNTS RECEIVABLES | 12.33 | 11.01 |
| INVENTORIES | 68.71 | 51.89 |
| OTHER CURRENT ASSETS | 0.0 | 0.0 |

| FIXED ASSETS | AS A PCT OF FIXED ASSETS | AS A PCT OF TOTAL ASSETS |
|---|---|---|
| LAND,BUILDINGS,LEASE-HOLD IMPROVEMENTS | 0.0 | 0.0 |
| EQUIPMENT | 100.00 | 4.86 |
| OTHER FIXED ASSETS | 0.0 | 0.0 |

## LIABILITIES & CAPITAL

| CURRENT LIABILITIES | AS A PCT OF CURRENT LIABILITIES | AS A PCT OF TOTAL LIABILITIES |
|---|---|---|
| ACCOUNTS PAYABLE/TRADE | 56.02 | 32.13 |
| SHORT TERM BANK LOANS | 10.17 | 6.71 |
| OTHER CURRENT DEBT | 18.28 | 10.00 |

| LONG TERM DEBT | AS A PCT OF LONG TERM DEBT | AS A PCT OF TOTAL LIABILITIES |
|---|---|---|
| MORTGAGES PAYABLE | 0.0 | 0.0 |
| LONG TERM BANK LOANS | 0.0 | 0.0 |
| STOCKHOLDER LOANS (DUE TO OWNERS) | 0.0 | 0.0 |
| OTHER LONG TERM DEBT | 0.0 | 0.0 |

RETAIL
APPAREL                          TOTAL ASSETS $150000-$250000

## INCOME DATA

| | AS A PCT OF NET SALES |
|---|---|
| NET SALES (GROSS INCOME) | 100.00 |
| COST OF SALES | 61.63 |
| GROSS PROFIT | 38.37 |
| OFFICER/EXECUTIVE SALARIES | 4.94 |
| OTHER GENERAL/ADMINISTRATIVE EXPENSES | 26.34 |
| OPERATING PROFIT | 6.09 |
| INTEREST EXPENSE | 0.56 |
| DEPRECIATION | 1.03 |
| PROFIT BEFORE TAXES | 2.85 |

## RATIOS

| | MEDIAN | UPPER QUARTILE | LOWER QUARTILE | UNITS |
|---|---|---|---|---|
| CURRENT | 2.7 | 5.2 | 1.5 | TIMES |
| QUICK | 0.8 | 1.9 | 0.3 | TIMES |
| CURRENT ASSETS/TOTAL ASSETS | 88.8 | 95.0 | 77.7 | PCT |
| SHORT TERM DEBT/TOTAL DEBT | 76.2 | 100.0 | 41.5 | PCT |
| SHORT TERM DEBT/NET WORTH | 56.0 | 137.0 | 12.4 | PCT |
| TOTAL DEBT/NET WORTH | 63.9 | 249.2 | 19.0 | PCT |
| SHORT TERM DEBT/TOTAL ASSETS | 33.5 | 56.3 | 15.7 | PCT |
| LONG TERM DEBT/TOTAL ASSETS | 12.4 | 39.4 | 0.0 | PCT |
| TOTAL DEBT/TOTAL ASSETS | 59.8 | 81.4 | 22.9 | PCT |
| SALES/RECEIVABLES | 11.2 | 35.9 | 5.5 | TIMES |
| AVERAGE COLLECTION PERIOD | 18. | 35. | 3. | DAYS |
| SALES/INVENTORY | 4.4 | 6.8 | 2.9 | TIMES |
| SALES/TOTAL ASSETS | 2.2 | 3.3 | 1.7 | TIMES |
| SALES/NET WORTH | 4.1 | 7.7 | 2.1 | TIMES |
| PROFIT (PRETAX)/TOTAL ASSETS | 6.8 | 17.1 | 0.3 | PCT |
| PROFIT (PRETAX)/NET WORTH | 27.1 | 45.1 | 3.3 | PCT |

SOURCE: *Financial Studies of the Small Business*, 7th edition (Washington, D.C.: Financial Research Associates, 1984) (P.O. Box 2502, Winter Haven, FL 33883).

I found it quite interesting to note that the 1984 edition offered the following statement:

> Again data has revealed noticeable differences when compared to studies including large firms in their sampling. FRA compared data on retail establishments to other studies containing a substantial number of firms with larger asset sizes. This comparison revealed the typical FRA firm to be more liquid, employing less debt, and earning a higher return on investment. These differences are significant and we would hope that one in an evaluating position would now be better able to make valid comparisons for the particularly small firm.[1]

## Specialized Sources

Many trade and professional associations compile and make available composite financial data on businesses or professions that are members. Also, some trade and professional publications offer financial data. Each issue of the *RMA Annual Statement Studies* now contains a bibliography listing over 100 sources of composite financial data for specific lines of business. One advantage of franchise operations is that most franchisers provide comparative financial data. Also, many manufacturers that sell through networks of retail outlets provide comparative financial data to their retailers. Certain CPA firms, and management consultants that specialize in particular lines of business, provide clients with comparative financial data.

# Interpretation of Financial Statement Ratios

Comparisons between financial statement ratios for the subject company and industry averages can indicate both specific opportunities for possible improvement and situations that could cause problems. Financial statement ratios fall into four broad categories:

**1.** Short-term liquidity measures.
**2.** Balance sheet leverage ratios.
**3.** Activity ratios.
**4.** Profitability ratios.

In addition to the traditional categories of ratios, each line item on the income statement can be compared with industry averages.

## Short-Term Liquidity Measures

The two primary short-term liquidity ratios are the *current ratio* and the *acid test ratio* (also called the *quick ratio*); both are discussed in

---

[1] *Financial Studies of the Small Business,* 7th ed. (Washington, D.C.: Financial Research Associates, 1984), p. i.

some detail in Chapter 9 in the section on analyzing working capital requirements. Their most important use is to indicate the extent to which a company may have either inadequate or excessive working capital.

# Balance Sheet Leverage Ratios

The primary balance sheet leverage ratios are the *equity ratio* (owner's equity as a percent of total assets) and the *long-term debt-to-equity ratio*. These ratios are one indicator of the degree of risk; the less the equity, relative to the total assets and to the long-term debt, the greater the degree of risk. For some companies, these ratios might also indicate borrowing power; leverage ratios well below industry averages may indicate unused borrowing power.

# Activity Ratios

The general idea of activity ratios is to measure how efficiently the assets are being employed. The primary activity ratios are *accounts receivable turnover, inventory turnover* (both discussed in Chapter 9 under working capital analysis), and *asset turnover* (sales divided by total assets).

# Profitability Ratios

Profitability ratios fall into two broad categories: income statement profitability ratios and rates of return on some level of investment. Income statement profitability ratios usually are expressed as a percent of sales. Rate of return ratios usually are expressed either as a percent of equity or as a percent of investment, with investment usually defined to mean either equity plus long-term debt, or equity plus all interest-bearing debt. The following measures of profitability are often expressed as a percentage of one or more of the four variables above:

1. *EBDIT*: Earnings before depreciation, interest, and taxes.
2. *EBIT:* Earnings before interest and taxes.
3. *EBT (pretax profit):* Net income before taxes.
4. *EBDT:* Earnings before depreciation and taxes.
5. *Net income:* Earnings after interest, depreciation, and taxes.

When comparing any ratios with industry averages, it is important to be sure that the comparison is on an apples-to-apples basis; that is, the industry average measures of comparison and the subject company ratios are being computed in exactly the same way. The following section offers some examples that compare company financial statement ratios with industry averages.

# Examples of Comparative Industry Analysis

The following hypothetical examples illustrate how the average industry data discussed in this chapter can be compared with data from the entity in which we are interested. The two examples continue to refer to the same two hypothetical companies used in the two previous chapters.

## Sole Proprietorship Example

Exhibit 7–4 shows how Annie's Apparel Store compares with other apparel and accessory stores. The *Almanac of Business and Industrial Financial Ratios* is used as the basis of comparison in this example, in order to compare as many expense items on the income statement as possible.

It is apparent that Annie's gross margin is far above the industry average, as is her return on equity. Her inventory does not turn over as fast as the industry average, but the slower-moving inventory may be

Exhibit 7–4

### ANNIE'S APPAREL STORE AND
### ALMANAC OF BUSINESS & INDUSTRIAL FINANCIAL RATIOS
### RETAIL TRADE: APPAREL AND ACCESSORY STORES
### COMPARATIVE ANALYSIS

| Asset Size | The Almanac $250,000 – $500,000 | Annie's Apparel[a] $280,000 |
|---|---|---|
| Revenues | $750,666[b] | $1,000,000 |
| Cost of Operations | 60.7% | 53.5% |
| Compensation of Officers | 5.3 | 5.0 |
| Bad Debts | 0.3 | 0.2 |
| Rent on Business Property | 4.2 | 6.5 |
| Interest | 1.0 | 0.7 |
| Depreciation | 1.1 | 1.3 |
| Advertising | 2.3 | 2.5 |
| Pension and Other Benefit Plans | 0.7 | 2.3 |
| Other Expenses | 23.2[c] | 21.4 |
| Net Profit before Taxes | 1.2 | 6.6 |
| **Ratios** | | |
| Net sales/Net worth | 4.7 | 5.2 |
| Inventory Turnover | 3.2 | 2.4 |
| Total Liabilities/Net Worth | 1.2 | 0.5 |
| Inventory/Current Assets | 62.4 | 88.0 |
| Net Income/Net Worth | 8.7% | 34.3 |

[a] Figures used are from the adjusted income statement and balance sheet (see Exhibits 5-2 and 6-1).

[b] Average revenues for the 4,727 companies in this asset size.

[c] Includes repairs and taxes (excluding federal income tax).

SOURCE: *Almanac of Business and Industrial Financial Ratios*, 1984 edition, Leo Troy, Ph.D. © 1984, Prentice-Hall, Inc. (Englewood Cliffs, NJ 07632).

Exhibit 7-5

**MARY'S MACHINERY & EQUIPMENT, INC., AND
RMA FINANCIAL STATEMENT STUDIES
COMPARATIVE ANALYSIS**

| | RMA | Mary's |
|---|---|---|
| Asset Size: | $0 — $1MM | |
| No. Statements: | 429 | |
| Statement Date: | 6/30/83 to 3/31/84 | 1984 |

**COMPOSITION OF THE BALANCE SHEET AND THE INCOME STATEMENT**

| | % | % |
|---|---|---|
| ASSETS: | | |
| Cash & Equivalents | 7.5 | 6.3 |
| Accnts. & Notes Rec. | 33.9 | 22.3 |
| Inventory | 35.9 | 36.7 |
| All Other Current | 1.8 | 2.5 |
| Total Current | 79.1 | 67.7 |
| Fixed Assets (Net) | 13.8 | 24.2 |
| Intangibles | 0.8 | 0.8 |
| All Other Noncurrent | 6.3 | 7.3 |
| Total Assets | 100.0 | 100.0 |
| | | |
| LIABILITIES AND NET WORTH: | | |
| Notes Pay.—Short Term | 14.6 | 4.8 |
| Current Mat. Long-Term Debt | 4.6 | 3.9 |
| Accnts. & Notes Pay.—Trade | 24.4 | 11.6 |
| Accrued Expenses | 4.6 | 3.9 |
| All Other Current | 4.9 | 2.9 |
| Total Current | 53.2 | 27.1 |
| Long-Term Debt | 10.9 | 9.2 |
| All Other Noncurrent | 1.7 | 6.8 |
| Net Worth | 34.3 | 56.9 |
| Total Liabilities & Net Worth | 100.0 | 100.0 |
| | | |
| INCOME STATEMENT DATA: | | |
| Net Sales | 100.0 | 100.0 |
| Cost of Sales | 68.7 | 66.2 |
| Gross Profit | 31.3 | 33.8 |
| Operating Expenses | 30.0 | 29.6 |
| Operating Profit | 1.2 | 4.2 |
| All Other Exp. (Net) | 0.4 | 0.6 |
| Profit Before Taxes | 0.8 | 3.6 |

**RATIOS**

| | Upper Quartile | Median | Lower Quartile | |
|---|---|---|---|---|
| Current Ratio | 2.2 | 1.5 | 1.2 | 2.5 |
| Quick Ratio | 1.2 | 0.8 | 0.5 | 1.1 |
| Sales/Receivables | 11.1 | 8.1 | 6.2 | 10.4 |
| Cost of Sales/Inventory | 9.4 | 5.4 | 3.3 | 4.2 |
| Cost of Sales/Payables | 14.9 | 8.6 | 5.4 | 13.3 |
| Sales/Working Capital | 5.7 | 10.6 | 26.8 | 5.7 |
| EBIT/Interest | 4.1 | 1.8 | 0.3 | 6.7 |
| Cash Flow/Cur. Mat. LTD | 3.3 | 1.2 | — | 2.5 |
| Fixed Assets/Net Worth | 0.1 | 0.3 | 0.8 | 0.4 |
| Debt/Net Worth | 0.9 | 1.9 | 4.7 | 0.8 |
| % Pretax Income/Tang. Net Worth | 29.2 | 9.5 | (3.8) | 14.9 |
| % Pretax Income/Total Assets | 10.0 | 3.0 | (2.5) | 8.3 |
| Sales/Net Fixed Assets | 61.9 | 32.2 | 12.9 | 9.6 |
| Sales/Total Assets | 3.5 | 2.7 | 2.0 | 2.3 |
| % Depr. Dep., Amort./Sales | 0.7 | 1.3 | 2.3 | 1.4 |
| % Lease & Rental Exp./Sales | 0.9 | 1.4 | 2.3 | 1.0 |
| % Officers' Comp./Sales | 3.2 | 5.4 | 8.3 | 5.0 |

[1] Mary's assets have been adjusted upward to reflect replacement cost, while RMA companies fixed assets are unadjusted; therefore, Mary's ratio would be higher in the case of fixed assets/net worth and lower in the case of sales/fixed assets if they were computed as the RMA ratios were.
LTD = long-term debt.
**SOURCE:** Robert Morris Associates, *Annual Statement Studies*, 1984 edition.

necessary to have a merchandise mix with an above-average gross margin. (Because the adjusted balance sheet eliminates the current liabilities for Annie's, several ratios that normally would be computed are omitted in this example.)

# Corporation Example

Exhibit 7–5 shows how Mary's Machinery and Equipment, Inc., compares with other wholesale machinery and equipment distributors. Robert Morris Associates' *Annual Statement Studies* is used as the basis of comparison in this example.

Many more comparisons are available by comparing Mary's with the industry averages, as shown in RMA data.

Mary's is well above the industry average short-term liquidity measures for both the current ratio and the quick ratio. She has much less balance sheet leverage, with a debt-to-equity ratio of only .8. This leverage position definitely suggests a very strong financial position and probable borrowing power, if she wanted to use it.

The activity ratios show that she is above the industry median for accounts receivable turnover, but her inventory turnover is between the industry median and the lower quartile. She is also between the industry median and lower quartile for sales to total assets. These statistics suggest that she might be able to use her assets a little more intensively to get a little more sales out of the assets in use.

Most importantly, however, Mary's is ahead of industry averages in all categories of profitability ratios. Her gross profit, operating profit, and pretax profit as a percent of sales are all above industry averages. Her pretax return on equity is between the industry median and the upper quartile.

Each of the various industry comparison services does not necessarily compute all the ratios of interest, but they offer enough to make very useful generalizations in many respects about how the subject company compares with its peers.

# Chapter 8

## Analyzing Qualitative Factors

Relevant Economic Data
 National Economic Data
 Regional and Local Economic Data
Industry Factors
 Markets
 Channels of Distribution
 Technology
 Sources of Industry Information
Competition
 Existing Competition
 Potential Competition
Regulation
 Present Regulations
 Potential Changes in Regulatory Environment
Product or Service Lines
 Existing Lines
 Opportunities for Related Lines
 Patents, Copyrights, Trademarks
 Relative Profitability of Lines
 Service or Warranty Obligations
Supplier Relationships
 Continuity
 Degree of Exclusivity
 Contractual Relationships
Market Position
 Reputation
 Geographic Scope
 Method of Marketing and Distribution
 Pricing Policies
 Customer Base
 Customer Relationships
 Market Continuity, Growth Opportunities, and Weaknesses
Management and Employees
 Size and Composition of Work Force
 Key Employees
 Other Employees
 Compensation
 Personnel Policies, Satisfaction, Conflict, and Turnover
Adequacy of Physical Facility
 Condition
 Heat, Light, Plumbing, and Other Systems
 Size
 Continuity of Occupancy

Qualitative factors are the characteristics of the business, industry, and the economy as a whole that affect the future of the company and whether its performance will be consistent with past results. Many of these factors are difficult or impossible to quantify, such as the effects of competition or anticipated upturns or downturns in the economy; others are more easily quantifiable, such as the expected cost of improvement to facilities and future compensation. A thorough analysis of these factors will assist the appraiser in assessing the company's ongoing earning power. It will also help him to estimate the degree of risk involved in the enterprise, which in turn will have an important bearing on the applicable capitalization rates. And it may bring to light additional capital investment that may be required in order to produce some expected level of income.

One good way of acquiring information on some of the factors discussed in this chapter is to visit the entity's operating facilities and talk with current owners, managers, and others, as well as outside sources. In some cases, the potential buyer may be wise to work in the operation for a day, a week, or even longer, to get a good look at the operation from the inside.

The relevance of the various factors will differ from one industry to another, and sometimes from one business to another within an industry. The following sections discuss the major categories of qualitative factors that should be considered in valuing a typical business or professional practice. For some companies, some of the factors discussed in this chapter obviously will not apply. For others, other factors, not discussed here, will be relevant.

# Relevant Economic Data

The importance of economic data varies greatly from one kind of business or practice to another. As a broad generality, businesses providing goods or services for which demand is highly elastic are more affected by changes in economic conditions than are businesses providing goods or services which people regard as daily necessities. The discretion available to buyers to avoid or postpone purchase of certain goods and services can determine how much broad economic influences affect the enterprise. The appraiser must use his judgment and experience when considering which economic factors will have a bearing on the fortunes of the business or practice being valued.

# National Economic Data

Relevant national economic data will provide clues to people's propensity to spend money for the goods or services offered by the business or practice being valued, along with anything else that might affect profit margins. Depending on the line of business, the following economic variables could have a bearing on the company's outlook:

1. *Gross national product (GNP):* A measure of the total market value of all "final product" goods and services produced during a specific period, usually a year.
2. *Disposable personal income:* The total income received by individuals, available for consumption and savings; this is total personal income less personal taxes.
3. *Business capital spending:* The total amount of business expenditures on durable assets, such as plant and equipment, during a specific time period.
4. *Consumer durable goods expenditures:* The total amount of consumer expenditures on such items as appliances and automobiles during a specific time period.
5. *Housing starts:* Total number of housing units started during a specific time period.
6. *Consumer price index (CPI):* The most common means of measuring the price changes of goods and services purchased by the typical household. The CPI indexes the cost of the typical market basket purchased by an urban family against its cost in a base year. The market basket includes such items as food, clothing, shelter, fuels, transportation fares, charges for doctors' and dentists' services, drugs, and other goods and services purchased for daily living.
7. *Producer price index (formerly known as the wholesale price index):* Designed to measure average changes in prices of all commodities at all stages of processing, produced or imported for sale in primary markets in the United States. It is based on approximately 3,400 commodity price series. All prices used in constructing the index are collected from sellers and generally apply to the first significant large-volume transaction for each commodity, for example, the manufacturer's or other producer's selling price.

Unfortunately, economists historically have not been able to predict relevant demand and other economic variables with enough accuracy to be very useful for this purpose. Nevertheless, the analyst must do the best he can with what is available. There are literally thousands of sources of such data. A few readily available ones are the following:

## 1. Government Publications

*The Federal Reserve Bulletin* (The Board of Governors of the Federal Reserve System in Washington, D.C.): Published monthly, the *Federal Reserve Bulletin* includes such data as employment, industrial production, housing and construction, consumer and producer prices, GNP, personal income and savings, and key interest rates. It is usually available at public and university libraries. However, the currency of the data usually lags four months or more.

*Survey of Current Business* (U.S. Department of Commerce): This monthly publication has two sections. The first deals with basic business trends, and starts with an article, "The Business Situation," which reviews business developments, pointing out relative strengths and weaknesses. The second section contains an extensive compilation of basic statistics on all phases of the economy. There is also a weekly supplement in which the indexes of business activity, prices, production, and so on, are kept up-to-date. It can be found in most major libraries.

## 2. Banks

*Manufacturers Hanover Financial Digest*: This weekly publication includes a commentary on various economic developments, as well as figures for GNP, CPI, unemployment, personal income, business capital expenditures, and housing starts on a monthly or quarterly basis. The financial digest is available in major libraries.

*Economic Trends* (Federal Reserve Bank of Cleveland): This monthly publication is an excellent source of economic variables, ranging from GNP and its components to money supply aggregates. The figures for such indicators as consumer income, business fixed investment, housing starts, producer and consumer prices, and so on, are usually given quarterly and monthly. In addition, most of the data are fairly timely, with only a two-month time lag. Most major libraries have *Economic Trends* on hand, along with publications of all the other Federal Reserve Bank Districts, which also contain economic information.

*Others*: *United States Economic Indicators* (Bank of New York) is a statistical tabulation of economic indicators, which provides the bank's forecast of prospective GNP, disposable personal income, index of industrial production, and corporate profits. Other major banks that publish some types of economic publications include Morgan Guaranty Trust Company and Chase Manhattan Bank.

## 3. Magazines

Perhaps one of the most comprehensive sources for economic indicator forecasts is *Fortune* magazine. In addition to monthly comments in each issue, the magazine makes quarterly and yearly forecasts for nearly all major economic indicators. Nearly all libraries subscribe to *Fortune*, making it easy to obtain.

# Regional and Local Economic Data

Obviously, the more a business or practice depends on the economy of some locality, the more relevant is the analysis of economic data about that area. An automobile dealership located in a town dependent on an economically troubled industry is not worth nearly as much as one with comparable sales and profits the prior year but located in a rapidly growing metropolis. Population, employment, and income forecasts are generally the most relevant types of local economic data. If a business depends on a certain industry, such as travel or construction, then estimates of such variables as the level of tourism or the number and dollar amounts of construction starts are relevant.

The primary sources for regional and local economic data are bank economics departments, public utilities, chambers of commerce, and various state agencies, such as departments of economic development and bureaus of labor statistics. Most major local banks publish statistical tabulations of economic indicators, although their availability is limited. Although major libraries usually subscribe to one or more bank economic publications, the selections at libraries are usually limited to those published nearest to the particular library. The best way to obtain regional bank publications is to write or call the particular bank's economic department.

Some universities publish regional and local economic data, sometimes focused on one or a few industries important to the region. Most states and multistate regions now have regular monthly business magazines that give economic statistics, and most metropolitan areas now have weekly newspapers that focus on business developments. I have found that the business sections of some metropolitan daily newspapers are offering more economic analysis and statistics, sometimes regularly in Sunday editions and sometimes irregularly in special features that focus on some specific part of the local economic scene.

Normally, I would think that a high level of local unemployment would have a negative impact on the value of local retail and service businesses. However, quite interestingly, one practicing attorney, who has handled over 2,000 business transactions as an attorney, broker, and consultant in his 20 years of experience, claims that that isn't necessarily so:

> Supply and demand . . . remains the first law of economics. The value of a business reflects the number of buyers available compared to businesses for sale. You must determine whether it's a buyer's or a seller's market. In periods of high unemployment, displaced workers seeking their own businesses can create a groundswell that increases business values by 10–20 percent. . . . Even local economic conditions can set the pace. When a Chevrolet plant in Framingham, Massachusetts, closed, laying off thousands of workers, hundred of businesses that barely attracted a nibble were sold quickly, and in many cases for more than the original asking price.[1]

# Industry Factors

Knowing something about the prospects and problems of the industry can provide a useful perspective for the valuation process. Quantitative comparisons between the subject company and industry-average operating figures were covered in the previous chapter. This section suggests some qualitative aspects to be considered, as well as some available information sources. The following sections on "Competition" and

---

[1] Arnold S. Goldstein, *The Complete Guide to Buying and Selling a Business* (New York: New American Library, 1984), p. 101.

"Regulation" also address some topics that may be industrywide matters, and some of the sources of information listed below will address those subjects.

# Markets

The industry factor most important to the value of most businesses and practices is the market outlook for the products or services being offered. For a given dollar amount of physical asset value, historical sales, or historical profits, a business or practice with a growing market for its products or services would be expected to be worth more than one facing a stagnant or declining market demand, all other things being equal.

# Channels of Distribution

For many industries, channels of distribution evolve over time. The most obvious and widespread trend is that of consolidation, which has at least three important aspects: 1) cutting out the middle man, 2) a trend toward larger business units, and 3) a trend toward more corporate chain and/or franchised units and fewer independent business units.

Independent wholesalers have been getting closer to extinction for many years in such fields as groceries, jewelry, and many, if not most, other consumer goods, as manufacturers more and more sell directly to retailers. Manufacturers' representative firms and brokerage firms, such as food brokers, have found the suppliers they represent to be a fickle lot, as accounts they have built successfully are taken away in favor of direct distribution by the manufacturer. Industrial distributors of all kinds are constantly in jeopardy of losing one or more of their leading lines because of the supplier's shift to a direct distribution policy.

Economic efficiencies of scale have been operating for years to increase the average size of such diverse entities as farms and ranches, motels and hotels, and grocery and discount merchandising stores. The effect, of course, has been a dramatic increase in the amount of investment required for such entities. In some cases, however, this trend toward bigness has opened up opportunities for businesses at the small end of the spectrum, the most outstanding example being the mercurial rise of what are now popularly called convenience stores.

The trend toward chain operations seems to be omnipresent. National chains have been actively buying up a variety of local merchandising, service, and professional entities, such as department stores, hotels, soft drink bottlers, funeral homes, cable TV operations, periodical publications of all kinds, insurance agencies, advertising agencies, medical testing laboratories, nursing homes, and accounting practices. Chains have increased their market shares in many industries by aggressively opening new outlets. Many lines of business and professional practices are moving in the direction of regional chains, with national chains seeming inevitable; even law firms are moving toward multicity operations. While the impact of chain operations increases the competitive pressure on independent operators, there also can be some advantages. One of the obvious ones is that national and regional acquirors provide an important group of prospective buyers for the owners of businesses and professional practices in lines in which such acquisitions are taking place. Another is that hundreds of chains are expanding through franchising. Some business owners may be able to benefit by becoming local franchise operators. In any case, some understanding of how the channels of distribution of an industry or profession are evolving should add perspective to the valuation of most businesses and professional practices.

# Technology

In today's dynamic environment, as economic philosopher Robert Heilbroner so aptly put it, the curve of technology is rising exponentially beneath our feet. Some products or services will be completely or nearly obsolete within a few years, while others will skyrocket in usage as technological advances make them more attractive because of such factors as lower costs, miniaturization, improved performance, and greater compatibility with other related products.

There is hardly a business or profession for which the dynamics of technological change do not have implications for the value of the entity. For some, technology will determine the very viability of the enterprise. For others, such as retail establishments, technological changes will merely mandate capital expenditures for new equipment, such as electronic bar code readers and reading and transmission equipment for the new generation of bank debit cards. The effects of technological change should be considered in terms of their impact on earnings potential, capital expenditure requirements, and risk for the entity being valued.

# Sources of Industry Information

Generally, the best sources of industry information are trade and professional associations and publications. The owners of the entity being appraised usually can direct the appraiser to the relevant associations and publications, although we have found that many small business owners are unaware of many of the sources of information relating to their own businesses. Several directories for such sources exist. The most comprehensive directory of trade and professional associations is *The Encyclopedia of Associations* (published annually). Also useful is *National Trade & Professional Associations of the United States* (published annually). The most comprehensive directory of trade and professional publications is *Business Publication Rates and Data*, published annually by Standard Rate & Data Services, Inc.

Other sources of industry information are government publications, such as the *U.S. Industrial Outlook* (published annually) and investment publications such as Standard & Poor's *Industry Surveys*. Several of the most useful of these sources are found in the section on Sources of Information in the bibliography included in the book as Appendix C. There are also a number of indexing services that can be used to find industry information. We have also selected what we consider the most useful of these indexing services for inclusion in the bibliography.

# Competition

It would seem to go without saying that a buyer trying to place a value on a prospective acquisition would want to check out the existing and potential competition, but this important qualitative factor is often neglected.

## Existing Competition

Analysis of the competition takes different forms in different lines of business or professional practice, so I can offer only broad suggestions. In general, it is desirable to know the number of competitors, their names, their locations, the sizes of their respective operations, and how long they have been in business. One or more significant *new* competitors could be an important factor, since the full effects of their competition probably would not be reflected in the historical financial statements of the entity being valued. It is also desirable to know in what ways the competition is similar or differentiated along product or service lines, pricing policy, marketing methods, and other factors.

The statement "We have no competition" simply is not adequate. Everyone has competition. The world has finite buying power and infinite demands. There are very few products or services for which there is absolutely no substitute. The appraiser should probe the question of competition until a satisfactory picture is developed.

Of course, a certain amount of competition can be healthy. A cluster of related retailers, though competitors, often are successful because they collectively draw a good flow of traffic interested in their line of wares. Wineries have found it profitable to be located among groups that collectively promote tours and local wines. And we have all heard the old saw that an attorney in a town with no competition will starve to death, but when a second attorney comes to town they will both prosper.

## Potential Competition

From the point of view of the person trying to value an operation, the most dangerous competition is the competition that isn't there yet, because its effect on the subject entity's earning power is a matter of guesswork. A unit of a large retail chain opening near a small or medium-sized independent store can sometimes put the independent out of business completely. Introduction of a technically superior or lower-cost competitive product may damage or even destroy some manufacturers and their distributors. A manufacturer may authorize an additional distributor in the same territory, or even open a company store in competition with its distributor. The easier the entry into the line of business, the more likely that new competition may be lurking just around the corner. It is never possible to know all the competitive problems that the future will bring, but an effort should be made to avoid being blindsided by new competition that might have been foreseen.

# Regulation

Various industries and professional practices are subject to greater or lesser degrees of regulation, mostly from government agencies, but sometimes from their own professional associations. From a valuation viewpoint, the regulation can have either positive or negative implications. In any case, it is desirable to understand the regulatory situation.

## Present Regulations

The gamut of existing regulations that affect the values of businesses and professional practices defies comprehensive categorization, but a few general groupings deserve special note.

**Compliance Requirements.** Two major government bodies administering regulations that cost the private sector hundreds of millions of dollars are the Occupational Safety and Health Administration (OSHA) and the Environmental Protection Agency (EPA). The appraiser should inquire whether there are any OSHA, EPA, or other compliance requirements that may cost some money to satisfy.

**Restrictions on Entry.** Some protection from excessive competition may be provided by restrictions on others entering the field. These restrictions range from the monopoly status of most utilities (gas, electric, water, local telephone, cable TV, and so on) to merely the requirements of passing certain competency tests in order to obtain licensing.

Licenses for many activities, such as paging systems, taxicabs, and (in most states) liquor outlets, are available only in limited numbers. Wherever there are regulatory restrictions on entry, there is likely to be some intangible value to the existing entities.

## Potential Changes in Regulatory Environment

The political and social moods of the country and its leaders have been changing rapidly in recent years, causing dramatic changes in regulations affecting businesses and professions, which in turn have had dramatic impacts on the values of businesses and practices in many lines. Generally, the widespread move toward deregulation allows new competition and reduces the premium values that entrenched entities may formerly have commanded. At this writing, for example, in the banking industry, interstate barriers are gradually crumbling, while travel agencies wait apprehensively to assess the impact of deregulation of airplane ticket issuance.

Costs of regulatory compliance are driving the values of many businesses to zero, as they shut down because the costs of compliance are too great. Others sell far below book value because the economic return possible under current conditions is not enough to justify the amount of investment made at an earlier time.

On the other hand, changes in regulatory requirements can create bonanzas for entities in a position to provide products or services to assist companies in meeting newly mandated requirements.

Another area of government regulation that undergoes constant review and change is the amount of federal and state subsidies and reimbursements available for various activities, as well as import restrictions and tariffs. With the present mood against subsidies and restrictions, businesses dependent on them face considerable risk, and their values are likely to be discounted considerably. Import firms, on the other hand, may enjoy substantial windfall increments in their values from the relaxing of import restrictions. The values of nursing homes and other health care facilities, for another example, are very sensitive to changes in the programs of cost reimbursements available for their patients.

The foregoing comments and examples just scratch the surface of the major problem of anticipating and assessing the effect of a myriad of potential regulatory changes on the values of existing businesses and professional practices.

# Product or Service Lines

The product or service lines being offered is another qualitative factor that will have different degrees of impact on value in different situations.

## Existing Lines

The appraiser can get an understanding of the product or service lines being offered through sales literature, a visit to the premises, and/or interviews with an owner or manager. The appraiser should inquire about the relative size of each major product line and how long the company has offered it. He should also ask about any prior lines that may have been discontinued. This information should help him judge the extent to which historical operating information for the company represents a reasonable basis for extrapolating the future.

The more the market demand that already exists for the particular product or service, as opposed to others that are merely comparable, the more valuable is the entity that sells or distributes it. Good examples of this principle are found in the pricing of soft drink bottlers and beer distributorships, where almost all of the goodwill value is associated with the volume of the leading brands that are sold.

## Opportunities for Related Lines

From the buyer's point of view, there could be value in the opportunity to add related lines. For example, there may be a perfect opportunity for a professional practice to enhance its position by bringing in someone with a related specialty not adequately represented in the market. A small food packer may have established a strong local brand recognition and a route distribution system for a specialty line, which may provide an opportunity to sell related specialty items under the same brand name through the existing distribution system.

Related lines may be either developed internally or brought in from outside. Even though a buyer may recognize opportunities, however, he will be reluctant to pay for opportunities that have not been seized and developed.

## Patents, Copyrights, Trademarks

Like any intangible asset, the value of patents, copyrights, and trademarks lies in their ability to contribute to profits. Specific methods for placing values on each of these items are discussed in Chapter 32. In many valuations of businesses and professional practices, however, no attempt is made to value each item individually; rather, the items are considered qualitative factors in the valuation of the overall entity.

The importance of patents, copyrights, and trademarks lies in their ability to contribute to continuity of revenues, hopefully at higher margins of profit than would be possible if such legal protections did not exist. It is only to the extent that they fulfill this function that they genuinely contribute to the value of the enterprise, and their contributions should be reflected in the income approaches to value. To the extent that patents, copyrights, and trademarks are well protected or have been tested in court, and long-lived, the appraiser can have more confidence in the continuity of the income stream associated with them.

If the value of the total entity is determined to be greater than its net tangible asset value, then it may be desirable for tax purposes to allocate the value above the tangible asset value to specific intangible assets. As noted earlier, that is the subject of a later chapter.

## Relative Profitability of Lines

Sometimes it is revealing to inquire into the relative profitability of different lines. It is not unusual for a business to have one or more lines that generate impressive gross volume, but on examination are found to be marginal or even negative in contributing to profitability. That may explain why an operation produces profit margins below industry averages. If the business is being valued on an income capitalization basis, the low level of profitability will be reflected in the income stream being capitalized. However, if the business is being valued by some other method, the negative impact of low-margin lines needs somehow to be reflected in the value. For example, if some version of a multiple of gross revenues method is being used in the valuation, the revenues from the substandard lines should not be included in the revenues to be capitalized, or they should be capitalized at a lower multiplier than other lines.

## Service or Warranty Obligations

Obligations to service products sold can be either a positive or a negative influence on value, depending on the situation. If the company is a manufacturer with off-balance sheet warranty liability, this factor should be recognized, either as a lump-sum deduction from the enterprise value or as an expense deduction from the income stream being capitalized. On the other hand, if a company is a distributor that performs warranty service work, and adequate reimbursements come from the manufacturer for such work, the customer traffic generated by warranty service can be a very positive factor in assuring continuity of revenues and profits.

# Supplier Relationships

If supplier relationships are important to the entity, then this subject should be investigated carefully.

## Continuity

The continuity of a supplier relationship is of considerable importance to many businesses. The ultimate disaster would be the single-product distributor facing the loss of his supplier. Often, there are strong personal relationships between an owner and one or more key suppliers; the new owner will need to ascertain whether he can maintain a business relationship with this supplier now that the personal relationship is gone, or, if that is not possible, can he find another supplier. It is important to determine the extent to which continuity of supplier relationships can be assured or are at risk under new ownership.

The issue of prices may be important, as well as merely keeping the supplier relationship. The existing owner may have favorable pricing because of existing relationships, either contractual or noncontractual, which may be amended in a relationship with a new buyer. If the buyer faces this possibility, the effect on profit margins obviously must be assessed.

## Degree of Exclusivity

An exclusive relationship for a market generally is more valuable than a nonexclusive relationship, because it is more conducive to continuity of revenues and maintenance of profit margins. There has been a considerable movement away from exclusive arrangements in recent years, partly because of suppliers' policies, but largely because of legal mandates to avoid limiting competition. If the degree of exclusivity is threatened, that must be regarded as a negative factor in the valuation picture. Of course, if the transfer of an exclusive distributorship is contemplated, the willingness of the supplier to maintain the arrangement under new ownership must be ascertained.

## Contractual Relationships

As a general rule, the strongest type of contractual relationship with a supplier is a franchise, which usually is transferable. Most distributorship agreements are not actually franchises and are not transferable without the supplier's consent. That may pose a perplexing valuation problem, since considerable value may depend on whether or not a new owner could take over the distributorship agreement, a decision which may be entirely up to the supplier.

For tax purposes, case history has not included any value dependent on a relationship that the owner does not have the legal right to transfer. When selling a business, however, intangible value relating to the relationship usually is included in the price; but the deal is subject to the supplier's approval of the new owner. The arguments that go on over this issue in divorces, damage cases, dissenting stockholder suits, and other valuation disputes are voluminous enough to fill a book by themselves.

# Market Position

Whether the entity is a professional practice, a service business, a retailer, a manufacturer, or any other kind of business, its market position has an important bearing on the amount and certainty of its ability to generate earnings, and thus on its value.

## Reputation

Reputation is critically important to a professional practice, while it would be less important to a retailer of standard merchandise selling primarily on a price basis. As with many factors, the degree of importance should help to determine how much investigation is warranted. Sources of information can include customers, suppliers, competitors, current and/or former employees, outside consultants of various kinds who may be familiar with the business or practice, and creditors.

# Geographic Scope

An understanding of the entity should include the geographic scope of the markets it serves. The company's geographic scope can be either a positive or negative factor, depending on costs involved in doing business in the area, competitive factors, opportunities to increase market penetration, and other characteristics of the market.

# Method of Marketing and Distribution

The appraiser should understand the company's methods of marketing and distribution. If revenues are generated primarily because of referrals or location, then the appraiser should assess the potential continuity of the referral sources and the continued availability of the location. If revenues depend on continuous advertising, the business may not be able to continue without the advertising. If marketing is based heavily on personal sales efforts, will existing sales people or adequate replacements be available?

Another factor is whether the distribution system will continue to be available at a reasonable cost. If distribution is by mail, contract delivery service, or freight, will there be significant changes in costs?

In summary, it is important to understand how the revenues are generated, what brings the buyers to the entity, and how the goods and services are delivered, in order to assess the potential continuity of revenues and profit margins.

# Pricing Policies

**Commodity versus Specialized Products.** In general, on the bottom of the value scale is a company that prices on a commodity basis, that sells on a price basis alone, without differentiating between its products or services and those offered by several direct competitors in the market. Such companies' pricing policies are totally subject to the external forces of the marketplace; they have no control over their own destiny in that respect. Their profit depends on their ability to operate more efficiently than their competitors. These companies include those that distribute branded merchandise but compete primarily on a price basis. Most such companies change hands at or below their tangible net asset value.

At the other end of the spectrum is the company whose product or service is so unique or so superior that it is insulated from direct competition; such a company has a high degree of discretion over its own pricing policies. Such companies usually are able to maintain consistently high profit margins and returns on investment and usually sell at a premium price over their net tangible asset value, in some cases very handsome premiums.

Most companies and practitioners are, of course, somewhere between these extremes, and the appraiser must use his judgment to assess how the entity's pricing situation bears on the level and reliability of its earning power.

**Bid versus Negotiated Contract Prices.** For companies that do a large portion of their business on fixed-price contracts (or fixed prices, subject to certain variables), it is desirable to ascertain how much is done on a bid basis instead of on a negotiated basis. As a generality, companies that have a large portion of their contracts strictly on a bid basis are considered to be in the category of commodity firms in terms of pricing, while those with more contracts on a negotiated basis are considered to be in the category of specialty firms. However, in some lines of business, buyers exercise considerable discretion in accepting bids, with quality and service considered as well as price. In those cases, bidder firms are considered a step removed from commodity firms in pricing.

## Customer Base

Several aspects of the customer base are important, including diversification, persistence, and quality.

**Diversification.** For some companies, diversification or concentration of the customer base is a major factor. The low-value end of the spectrum would be represented by a company performing a single government contract that will be completed soon with no follow-up business presently in sight. (One might even question whether that situation should be classified as a going concern.) At the high-value end of the spectrum is a customer base so broad that losing a few customers would have no perceptible impact on the entity's revenues or profits.

Small businesses, and certain types of professional practices, commonly have one or a few large customers whose loss would deal a serious blow to the entity's earning capacity, or even to its viability. In these cases, the continuity of the key customers' business must be analyzed carefully and the risk assessed accordingly. Companies with very concentrated customer bases usually sell at discounts compared with other companies of comparable revenues and earnings but having more diversified customer bases, all other things being equal.

**Persistence.** Another aspect of the customer base is *persistence,* the extent to which the same customers tend to repeat. This characteristic has the dimensions of both longevity and frequency. In businesses such as insurance agencies and periodical publications, for example, first-year customers are not considered as valuable as longer-term customers, because statistics have shown a positive correlation between longevity and propensity to renew. A service business that provides its services regularly to the same clientele, such as annual audits provided by a CPA firm, is generally worth more per dollar of historical revenues and earnings than the kind of service business in which each service performed is a new piece of business, even though some of the customers may have patronized the firm previously.

**Quality.** Appraising the quality of the customer base certainly is a very subjective judgment, but nevertheless important. Some of the measures of quality are the customers' ability and willingness to pay their bills on time, their ability to pay the kind of prices the operation would like to charge, their ability to increase their purchases over time, and their ability and propensity to refer other customers of comparable quality.

## Customer Relationships

Closely akin to the analysis of the customer base is the analysis of customer relationships. If one or several major customers are relatives, or have close personal or other business ties with the owner or a key person, then the appraiser should candidly assess the ability to retain those customers under new ownership.

Another aspect of customer relationships is customer satisfaction. Talks with some customers and former customers can help shed some light on this factor.

## Market Continuity, Growth Opportunities, and Weaknesses

The point of this whole analysis of market position is to assess both the level and the degree of certainty of future revenues, along with the level and degree of certainty of the margins that those revenues will be able to generate in light of the pricing forces to which the company is subject. The greater the degree of continuity promised by the market position, the lower the risk. Growth opportunities are more valuable to the extent that they seem likely to evolve naturally from forces already in place than from large doses of entrepreneurial effort and expenditures. Weaknesses should be listed, evaluated, and reflected in the earnings stream and/or capitalization rates used in the valuation.

# Management and Employees

The people factor certainly is a key qualitative element in most businesses and professional practices; this is especially true in small businesses, where there typically is substantial owner involvement in management, or the business focuses around one or a few key people.

## Size and Composition of Work Force

A basic factor that influences the health of a business is the size and composition of the work force: the number of employees, their functions, their general backgrounds, qualifications, and levels of competence, and their basis and level of compensation. Whether the company is adequately staffed, understaffed, or overstaffed will have a bearing on the extent to which the company's long-term earning capacity will conform to its recent history.

# Key Employees

The importance of the owner or other key employees to the success of the business is a matter that must be given the utmost attention in valuing small businesses and professional practices. Information should be acquired as to age, length of service, education, and prior experience of each key employee, whether he works full-time or part-time, whether he has outside work or financial interests that may dilute his efforts or cause any conflict of interest, his level of compensation, including all fringe benefits and discretionary expenses, and how long he intends to stay with the entity.

If key employees' expertise and customer relationships would take some time to transfer to a new owner, then the value of the business or practice probably depends on their willingness to enter into an employment contract for the transitional period. Furthermore, if customers would follow them if they left and opened a new shop or joined a competitor, then the value of the business probably also depends on a noncompete agreement. Employment agreements and noncompete agreements, if applicable, usually are assumed to be included in the total value arrived at for the business or practice. However, in negotiating the actual deal, they often are separated and the total value allocated among purchase price, employment agreements, and covenants not to compete. This matter is discussed further in Chapter 28.

# Other Employees

It is helpful to have an idea of the nature of the work force, the extent to which it is unionized, or may be unionized, the history of any strikes or work stoppages, and its general adequacy for the tasks at hand. This analysis may give some indication of necessary or possible changes that may affect profitability.

# Compensation

**Nonowner Employees.** The main consideration with respect to nonowner employees is whether the compensation is adequate, inadequate, or too high. If inadequate, some additional costs should be allowed when estimating earning power. If compensation is too high, there should be room for savings, but perhaps not immediately.

**Owner Employees.** If an owner is going to stay on as an employee, his value in his employment role should be estimated. If he wants to take out more than the value of his employment in direct compensation and benefits, the purchase price can be adjusted downward accordingly.

## Personnel Policies, Satisfaction, Conflict, and Turnover

A prospective owner should know the main features of past personnel policies. Only a small percentage of small businesses and professional practices have personnel policies in writing, and those that do may or may not follow them closely. Consequently, such information usually needs to be gleaned through interviews. This study may also uncover some additional cost requirements or some possible savings.

Informal discussions with employees should give clues as to whether they are satisfied or dissatisfied and steps that might be necessary to correct existing problems. If there are internal conflicts, it may be possible to bring them to light during the valuation process. People do like to talk, especially about things that are bothering them. Interviews can bring many problems to light, enabling their impact on the value of the entity to be assessed. Sometimes the problems are frustrations over being unable to pursue opportunities an employee envisions—they may be true opportunities for the enterprise, as well.

A personnel turnover rate below the average for the kind of business usually is regarded as a plus, and a high turnover rate usually is considered a negative. Some businesses, however, intentionally have a high turnover rate in order to avoid the higher direct compensation and benefits that tend to accrue with seniority.

# Adequacy of Physical Facility

The physical facility may allow for considerable expansion; it may be just about adequate for current operations, it may require capital expenditures, or it may be so inadequate that a move is imminent. If the physical facility is important, its adequacy or lack of it obviously has a bearing on value.

## Condition

As discussed in Chapter 5, an important concern in the valuation of facilities is deferred maintenance, which can include such items as needed painting, repair of leaks, repair of broken or cracked windows, doors, and walls, equipment maintenance, and anything necessary to put the facility in good operating condition. For retail outlets or service establishments with considerable foot traffic, maintenance can also include modernizing, even though existing equipment and decor are not necessarily in bad condition, in order to keep up with current trends and upscale consumer expectations.

## Heat, Light, Plumbing, and Other Systems

Special attention should be paid to the adequacy of all operating systems, including all utility hookups, heating and air conditioning, all electrical systems, burglar alarms, sprinkler system, and plumbing, including the adequacy of rest rooms. There may be deferred maintenance, but more importantly, certain systems may be antiquated in their abilities to serve current needs, especially electrical systems, because commercial electrical appliances have come to be used far more extensively since most electrical systems were installed. These factors need to be assessed and any cost implications reflected in value.

## Size

The size of the facility should be considered not only in relation to current needs, but also in relation to needs in the foreseeable future. If a move appears to be in prospect, its cost and the likely changes in occupancy cost should be taken into consideration.

## Continuity of Occupancy

If it seems preferable to continue occupying the present location, then it is important to determine the length of time that the premises will be assured to be available, and at what cost. Any increased costs should be reflected in the valuation.

A friend of mine offers a good example of how the inadequacy of the physical facility affected the value of one business:

> A manufacturing company with a long history of steady earnings was initially valued at $1.1 million on a federal estate tax return. Based on history, the valuation made sense. Inspection of the plant, however, revealed severe physical deterioration–not to mention the fact that the building was condemned. Remaining management had already made plans to acquire a new building elsewhere, but the cost of the new plant, the cost of the move, and the salvage value of the old plant had not been factored into the value of the company. An estimate of $500,000 in net costs to the business as a result of the move led to a reduced valuation of $600,000 ($1.1 million minus the $500,000). The logic was simple: No buyer would pay the full value knowing that an additional $500,000 had to be invested immediately for the company to keep earning at historic rates.[2]

# Operating Efficiencies and Inefficiencies

Any special efficiencies or inefficiencies that may be identified should be helpful in assessing ongoing earning power and future costs. By

---

[2] Irving Blackman, "Valuing a Business: More than Numbers Alone," *Inc.*, November 1981, p. 153.

*efficiency* in this context, I mean getting the job done at the lowest possible cost, and by *inefficiency* I mean any circumstance that would cause higher-than-necessary costs.

## Physical Plant

Plant-related efficiency, or lack of it, generally arises from location, size, and layout, and the extent to which the equipment is or is not state-of-the-art. Some causes of plant inefficiency are easily correctable, some may be difficult or costly to correct, and some may be impossible to change. The valuation must consider the impact on earning power of any inefficiencies not correctable, such as extra transportation costs because of remote location, functional obsolescence of equipment, or extra labor costs because of inefficient layout, as well as the costs of correcting any existing inefficiencies that will be worthwhile to correct. It is also possible that correction of inefficiencies will result in some profitability gains that should be reflected.

## Accounting and Other Controls

Accounting systems can be adapted to be very useful tools of management control, but few small businesses and professional practices even approach getting maximum management benefit out of their accounting systems. The extent of controls implemented should be investigated. To the extent that good controls are in place and being utilized effectively, the risk of an unexpected earnings decline is reduced, although most of the upside profit potential from efficiency may already have been achieved. To the extent that controls are poor, of course, the risk of an unanticipated drop in earnings is increased.

# Reason for Sale

It is always desirable to know why the business is being offered for sale. If the sale is under pressure, the price is likely to be less than if there is no pressure to sell. If the business is in an estate, in most cases it is worth less than if the former owner/manager were still living; usually some value is lost due to the lack of an orderly transition period. This factor varies considerably, depending on the role of the former owner/manager in the operations of the business and his relationships with its public. The value implications of all the many reasons to sell vary greatly, but it is another qualitative item to take into consideration.

# Summary

This chapter covered a wide variety of qualitative factors that most frequently have a bearing on the value of a business or professional practice; it has not covered all the vast number of possible factors that might be encountered in any specific case.

It should be clear that it is impossible to create any quick fix or formula valuation models or methods that can fully reflect and evaluate all the subjective factors that bear on value. In most individual cases, one or a few subjective or qualitative factors really have a significant influence on value; a dozen or more others may have a minor influence. While the chapter has suggested factors to look for, the appraiser will require considerable experience and judgment to put them in perspective and to determine how they will influence his ultimate opinion of value, or the price that a buyer would be willing to pay, or that a seller should be willing to accept.

# Chapter 9

## The Buyer's Perspective–Pro Forma Statements

*Some successful small-company owners see the operation in terms of what the buyer could do with it, given an infusion of capital, while the buyer wants to buy what's already there.*[1]

Up until this point, we have been looking at the financial statements of the business in question under its current operations and as it stands. However, from the viewpoint of a prospective buyer, some changes may be necessary or desirable. The thrust of this chapter is to step into the buyer's shoes, to consider the financial statements and possible changes from the viewpoint of a knowledgeable buyer. Before coming to grips with the question of how much to offer, there are a number of factors a buyer should take into consideration.

The buyer must look at his total investment in the business, not just what he pays the seller. Apart from how much the buyer pays the seller for the business or practice, how much additional financing will be necessary, what will be its source, and what will it cost? Or will the business itself be a source of financing for the purchase?

# Analysis of Working Capital Requirements

If it will be necessary to provide additional working capital, the buyer's pro forma balance sheet should reflect the amount needed and the source. If the buyer will be providing extra dollars for working capital, that amount should be reflected in the pro forma balance sheet and recognized as part of the buyer's total investment in the business when deciding how much to offer the seller. If the buyer plans to borrow from a bank to finance working capital needs, the pro forma balance sheet should reflect the average amount of borrowing expected, and the interest should be reflected on the buyer's pro forma income statement. For definitions and examples of working capital and its components, see Exhibit 9–1.

## Steps in Analyzing Working Capital

If the prospective buyer doesn't know how much working capital it will take to operate the business, he can get some guidance from the industry average data discussed in Chapter 7. For example, Exhibit 7–1 shows that the average ratio of sales to working capital for women's ready-to-wear stores of all sizes is 7.0:1. Therefore, among those in the RMA sample the average women's ready-to-wear store expecting to do $1 million in sales would have about $143,000 in working capital.

Note, however, that in Exhibit 7–1 the range is quite wide. The upper quartile figure is 4.5 ($222,000 working capital to support $1 million sales), and the lower quartile is 12.3 ($81,000 working capital to support $1 million). One of the biggest variables, of course, would be

---

[1] Bradley Hitchings, "Selling Your Small Company," *Business Week*, February 4, 1985, p. 101.

Exhibit 9–1

## ANALYSIS OF WORKING CAPITAL
## AND ITS MAJOR COMPONENTS

### Definitions

**Working Capital** = Current Assets — Current Liabilities

**Current Assets.** Cash and items expected to be converted to cash or used up in the business within one year. Major items are cash, marketable securities, accounts receivable, notes receivable within a year, and prepaid expenses.

**Current Liabilities.** Items expected to be paid within one year. Major items are accounts payable, notes payable within a year (including any portion of longer-term debt that is due within a year), and accrued expenses.

$$\textbf{Current Ratio} = \frac{\text{Current Assets}}{\text{Current Liabilities}}$$

$$\textbf{Quick Ratio} = \frac{\text{Cash \& Equivalents} + \text{Receivables}}{\text{Current Liabilities}}$$

$$\textbf{Working Capital Turnover} = \frac{\text{Sales}}{\text{Working Capital}}$$

Preferably, this ratio is computed using *average* working capital as the denominator. However, as a matter of expedience, it often is computed using working capital at the end of the period as the denominator.

$$\textbf{Accounts Receivable Turnover} = \frac{\text{Sales}}{\text{Accounts Receivable}}$$

Preferably computed using *average* accounts receivable; for expedience, often computed using ending accounts receivable.

$$\textbf{Average Collection Period (Days)} = \frac{365}{\text{Accounts Receivable Turnover}}$$

$$\textbf{Inventory Turnover} = \frac{\text{Cost of Goods Sold}}{\text{Inventory}}$$

Preferably computed using *average* inventory; for expedience, often computed using ending inventory. Many companies have unusually low inventories at the end of their fiscal periods because they let the inventories run down to make it easier to taking the physical inventory count and/or because they set the end of the fiscal year to coincide with a seasonally slow time, when inventories would normally be low. In such cases, doing the computation on the basis of ending inventory will overstate the true inventory turnover.

$$\textbf{Average Days' Inventory} = \frac{365}{\text{Inventory Turnover}}$$

whether or not the store has a policy of selling on credit. The other major variables on the asset side are how often the inventory turns over (average length of time the merchandise stays in inventory) and, if the company sells on credit, the average length of time it takes to collect accounts receivable. On the liability side, the two main variables are the trade terms available from suppliers and the terms under which other financing (usually bank borrowing) can be arranged.

Exhibit 9–1 (*concluded*)

**Example of Working Capital Analysis**

| Sales | $100,000 | Cost of Goods Sold | $60,000 |
|---|---|---|---|

| Current Assets: | | Current Liabilities: | |
|---|---|---|---|
| Cash | $ 1,000 | Accounts Payable | $ 8,000 |
| Accounts Receivable | 10,000 | Bank Note Payable | 12,000 |
| Inventory | 15,000 | | |
| Prepaid Expenses | 2,000 | | |
| Total Current Assets | $28,000 | Total Current Liabilities | $20,000 |

**Working Capital** = $28,000 − $20,000 = $8,000

$$\text{Current Ratio} = \frac{\$28,000}{\$20,000} = 1.4$$

$$\text{Quick Ratio} = \frac{\$11,000}{\$20,000} = .55$$

$$\text{Working Capital Turnover} = \frac{\$100,000}{\$8,000} = 12.5$$

$$\text{Accounts Receivable Turnover} = \frac{\$100,000}{\$10,000} = 10$$

$$\text{Average Collection Period} = \frac{365}{10} = 36.5 \text{ Days}$$

$$\text{Inventory Turnover} = \frac{\$60,000}{\$15,000} = 4.0 \text{ times per year}$$

$$\text{Average Days' Inventory} = \frac{365}{4.0} = 91 \text{ days}$$

To summarize, the buyer's analysis of his working capital needs consists of the following steps:

1. Estimate sales volume.
2. Decide on credit policy, and estimate the average amount of accounts receivable on the basis of the average estimated collection period.
3. Estimate the amount of inventory needed on the basis of estimated average inventory turnover.
4. Estimate the amount of prepaid expenses needed.
5. Estimate the average amount of accounts payable on the basis of trade terms available from suppliers.
6. Estimate the average amount of bank financing on the basis of the terms of the bank financing available.
7. Allow for some extra cash, because the steps above are estimates and averages; there may not be enough cash at peak periods. (If the business is highly seasonal, this analysis should be done on the basis of the high seasonal requirements rather than on averages.)
8. From the steps above, compute the amount of working capital that will be necessary.
9. As a check, compute the current ratio, quick ratio, and working capital turnover based on the results of steps 1 through 8, and compare them with industry averages.

# An Example of Working Capital Analysis

1. Annie's Apparel has been doing $1 million volume. Industry sources expect retail selling prices to go up by about 5 percent this year. The shopping center's consultant has predicted a 4 percent increase in foot traffic. Considering these factors, and assuming no major changes in the operation, an estimated sales volume of approximately $1.1 million seems reasonable.
2. Annie's accounts receivable turnover has been 33 times per year, because she has extended only very limited credit. If the new buyer follows the same policy, on $1.1 million sales, we would estimate average accounts receivable at about $35,000.
3. Using the adjusted balance sheet (Exhibit 5–2), we see that the inventory value at current prices is $220,000. Using the adjusted income statement (Exhibit 6–1), we see that the cost of goods sold was $560,000. If the buyer can maintain the same gross margin, the cost of goods sold will be about $616,000 (.56 × $1,100,000 = $616,000). Inventory turnover last year was 2.6 times. If we maintain the same inventory turnover, we will need about $237,000 average inventory.
4. Annie's $3,000 of prepaid expenses includes a rental deposit only. The new buyer will need to pay a rent advance of $5,000 immediately. Also, as noted in Exhibit 6–2, Annie has not been carrying any fire, theft, or liability insurance. The buyer will need to take out a policy with a $2,000 premium, bringing total prepaid expenses to $10,000.
5. Trade credit is on a 30-day basis. With estimated purchases of $616,000 (from step 3 above), average estimated trade accounts payable would be about $51,000.
6. We find that we can get a bank line of credit of $200,000 based on 60 percent of inventory and accounts receivable under 90 days old. If we assume $237,000 average inventory and an average of $30,000 eligible accounts receivable (under 90 days old), average bank financing would be about $160,000 (.6 × $267,000 = $160,000).
7. There is not a great deal of seasonality to the business, and some flexibility is available in suppliers' trade terms at peak periods, so we will assume that $10,000 extra cash will cover fluctuations and contingencies.
8. On the basis of steps 1 through 7, working capital can be estimated as follows:

| Current Assets: | | Current Liabilities: | |
|---|---|---|---|
| Cash | $ 10,000 | Accounts Payable | $ 51,000 |
| Accounts Receivable | 33,000 | Bank Note Payable | 160,000 |
| Inventory | 237,000 | | |
| Prepaid Expenses | 10,000 | | |
| Total Current Assets | $290,000 | Total Current Liabilities | $211,000 |

Working Capital: $290,000 - $211,000 = $79,000.

$$\text{Current ratio} = \frac{\$290,000}{\$211,000} = 1.4$$

$$\text{Quick ratio} = \frac{\$10,000 + \$33,000}{\$211,000} = .2$$

$$\text{Working capital turnover} = \frac{\$1,100,000}{\$79,000} = 13.9$$

9. Exhibit 7–1 shows that the average current ratio for women's ready-to-wear stores of all sizes is 2.1, but the lower quartile is 1.5, approximately equal to our estimate. The average quick ratio is .7, with a lower quartile of .3, also fairly close to our estimate. The median sales/working capital (working capital turnover) ratio is 7.0, with a lower quartile of 12.3, again just a little above our estimate. The result is that the new owner's Annie's would be in the bottom 25 percent of similar companies in short-term liquidity, but probably can survive if our estimates are reasonably accurate.

In summary, the above analysis suggests a balance sheet that will include $290,000 of current assets, of which $51,000 will be financed by trade payables, $160,000 by short-term bank borrowings, and $79,000 by long-term debt and/or owner's equity.

This analysis of Annie's assumes business to be pretty much as usual, based on recent history. It should be noted that the inventory turnover of 2.6 times per year is near the bottom quartile of the industry average (from Exhibit 7–1), considerably below the median of 3.5. It would appear that there might be room for improvement in inventory turnover. On the other hand, Annie's gross margin of 44 percent is well above the industry average of 39.5 percent, which may be partly due to a merchandise mix inherently slower in turnover than the industry's average merchandise mix.

# Analysis of Fixed Assets

The buyer should analyze the fixed assets to determine whether an additional investment in fixed assets will be necessary, or whether any existing assets are above the needs of the business and could be sold without affecting the entity's earning power.

## Deferred Maintenance and Replacement Requirements

It is not at all uncommon to find that physical premises and equipment have not been kept up to the standard necessary to continue to perform their jobs effectively. Owners may have deferred normal maintenance and equipment for a wide variety of reasons, anything from inadequate capital to just plain apathy.

When such conditions are present, the buyer should estimate the cost of the deferred maintenance and replacements and consider that cost as part of the investment in the business. As a generality, if a buyer would pay $100,000 for a business with equipment in average condition, but it will cost $20,000 in repairs and replacements to bring the equipment in the subject business to normal condition, he might be willing to pay $80,000 for the business "as is."

## Compliance Requirements

As noted in Chapter 5, there may be some off-balance-sheet liabilities, such as costs of equipment to comply with OSHA, pollution control, zoning standards, building codes, or other governmental requirements. A buyer should make provision for any such costs as part of his investment.

## Other Asset Inadequacies

Sometimes a company has simply outgrown its physical capacity to do its job, because of inadequate space and/or equipment. Costs of moving, or any capital additions necessary to maintain the level of revenues on which the valuation analysis is based, should be provided for as part of the buyer's investment.

## Excess Assets

In some cases, businesses have assets that are not really needed in the operations, usually excess equipment and/or real estate. Any net proceeds a buyer could expect to receive from disposals of such assets could be used to reduce the amount of permanent investment he might otherwise require. If disposal of excess assets is contemplated, any revenues and/or expenses associated with such assets should be removed when compiling the buyer's pro forma income statement.

# Contingent Liabilities

It is important that the buyer analyze any contingent liabilities that may carry forward into new ownership and determine what provision needs to be made for them. As noted in Chapter 5, they may be recognized on the balance sheet by either a line item in the liability section or a footnote.

# Structure of Long-Term Liabilities

At the time he is preparing to offer to buy a business or practice, the buyer should take into consideration the likely structure of his long-term liabilities. The structure of the buyer's financing has a bearing on the cost of capital, which in turn may influence the price offered for a business. This interrelationship is discussed in Chapter 10. The structure of the long-term liabilities also affects the buyer's ability to service the debt, as discussed in Chapter 18.

A buyer may elect to pay off some existing long-term liabilities because he considers the financing cost high, and either doesn't need it or can get it cheaper elsewhere. The buyer may be forced to pay off certain long-term liabilities because they are not assumable, a matter which must be checked in each case if a buyer is considering assuming any existing liabilities.

A buyer who has the desire and ability to obtain long-term financing for the purchase should investigate the probable amount and terms and reflect them in his pro forma balance sheet and income statement.

One option, which is very popular in sales of small businesses and professional practices, is to have the seller carry a long-term contract for a significant portion of the transaction price. Whether this contract will be technically the obligation of the business under the new owner, or a personal obligation of the new owner, putting the obligation on pro forma financial statements of the business makes clear the amounts that will have to be paid, one way or another, relative to the other financial variables of the business. As a practical matter, if it is technically a personal obligation of the buyer, the resources of the business probably will be pledged to secure its payment anyway.

# The Buyer's Income Statement

A sophisticated buyer will make a pro forma income statement for an entity he is considering purchasing, based on how he thinks he will operate the business.

Broadly speaking, a buyer's income statement might differ from the adjusted (normalized) income statements, as developed in Chapter 6, for three reasons:

1. Changes the buyer contemplates while still viewing the operation as a stand-alone, independent entity, with no basic changes in its business.
2. Changes the buyer contemplates as a result of effecting some changes in the nature of the business, but still viewing it as an independent entity.
3. Synergies and efficiencies that arise as a result of combining the entity in some way with other entities.

This categorization of possible changes is somewhat arbitrary, and the categories are not mutually exclusive. In most cases, the changes would sooner or later make the business worth more to the buyer than it would be worth if the business were assumed to continue to operate as it has in the past. Obviously, such considerations have a bearing on how much any "particular" buyer might be willing and able to pay. Since these items are predicated on the buyer's perception of his ability to change things to his advantage, he wants as little as possible of the potential benefit of such changes reflected in the transaction price. Consequently, in most cases, the seller and his representative never see the buyer's pro forma income statement.

# Changes in Existing Operations

**Revenues.** The buyer may believe that revenues can be increased, perhaps significantly, without major changes in the basic nature of the business. These improvements could result from a number of things, such as changes in the promotional theme, changes in the merchandise mix, or improved service to increase repeat business. Obviously, the buyer's pro forma statement must reflect any increased costs associated with the hypothetical increases in revenues.

**Operating Expenses.** The buyer should analyze all the operating expenses to determine whether he would anticipate their being higher or lower than in the past. His analysis may be based on his own experience or on industry averages, as developed in Chapter 7. Some of the items most likely to be adjusted might be wage costs and promotional expense items.

At this point in the analysis, the new owner/manager should set his own salary at something approximating a market rate for his services, regardless of what he actually thinks he may or may not take out of the business in salary and perks.

**Interest Expense.** Since the buyer probably would finance the operation somewhat differently from how it was financed in the past, there may be a difference in interest cost. The buyer's pro forma income statement should reflect interest based on how the buyer contemplates financing the business.

# New Business Directions

The potential for this category of change is so vast that it almost defies any comprehensive discussion of the many possibilities. The buyer may plan to turn a conventional retailer into a discounter. He may add entire new product lines. He may eliminate or implement a credit policy. He may discontinue a losing or marginal aspect of the operation. In any case, the buyer's income statement should reflect the anticipated consequences of the contemplated changes.

# Synergies and Efficiencies

A particular buyer may be in a unique position to effect changes because of other related operations under his control. He may benefit from eliminating a competitor, controlling a source of supply, controlling a distribution outlet, or reducing costs by combining activities. No two potential buyers' pro forma statements will be alike, but it is in the category of synergies where they are likely to differ the most. From the buyer's perspective, the most important aspects of the potential acquisition might be the synergies, without which he might have little or no interest in the seller's operation. The buyer will want to see what the income statement would look like when the benefits of the available synergies appear.

# Samples of Buyer's Pro Forma Statements

The following are hypothetical examples of buyers' pro forma income statements that illustrate the considerations from the buyer's perspective discussed in this chapter. The two examples continue the same two hypothetical companies used in the last three chapters.

## Purchase of a Sole Proprietorship

Exhibit 9–2 is a buyer's pro forma income statement for Annie's Apparel Store from the perspective of one hypothetical buyer. The prospec-

Exhibit 9–2

### ANNIE'S APPAREL STORE
### BUYER'S PRO FORMA INCOME STATEMENT

|  | Income Statement As Reported 1984 | | Adjusted Income Statement 1984 | | Pro Forma Income Statement | |
|---|---|---|---|---|---|---|
|  | $ | % | $ | % | $ | % |
| Sales | 1,000,000 | 100.0 | 1,000,000 | 100.0 | 1,100,000 | 100.0 |
| Cost of Goods Sold: |  |  |  |  |  |  |
| Beginning Inventory | 170,000 |  | 185,000 |  | 185,000 |  |
| Plus: Purchases | 570,000 |  | 570,000 |  | 695,000 |  |
|  | 740,000 |  | 755,000 |  | 880,000 |  |
| Less: Ending Inventory | 180,000 |  | 220,000 |  | 220,000 |  |
| Cost of Goods Sold | 560,000 | 56.0 | 535,000 | 53.5 | 660,000 | 60.0 |
| Gross Margin | 440,000 | 44.0 | 465,000 | 46.5 | 440,000 | 40.0 |
| Expenses: |  |  |  |  |  |  |
| Owner's Salary | 70,000 | 7.0 | 50,000 | 5.0 | 50,000 | 4.5 |
| Other Salaries | 150,000 | 15.0 | 150,000 | 15.0 | 150,000 | 13.6 |
| Payroll Taxes | 30,000 | 3.0 | 30,000 | 3.0 | 30,000 | 2.7 |
| Employee Benefits | 23,000 | 2.3 | 23,000 | 2.3 | 20,000 | 1.8 |
| Rent | 65,000 | 6.5 | 65,000 | 6.5 | 65,000 | 5.9 |
| Utilities | 3,000 | 0.3 | 3,000 | 0.3 | 3,000 | 0.3 |
| Telephone | 3,000 | 0.3 | 3,000 | 0.3 | 3,000 | 0.3 |
| Insurance | — | — | 2,000 | 0.2 | 1,000 | 0.1 |
| Supplies | 5,000 | 0.5 | 5,000 | 0.5 | 4,000 | 0.4 |
| Advertising | 25,000 | 2.5 | 25,000 | 2.5 | 20,000 | 1.8 |
| Travel & Entertainment | 25,000 | 2.5 | 5,000 | 0.5 | 3,000 | 0.3 |
| Automobile Expense | 5,000 | 0.5 | 5,000 | 0.5 | 3,000 | 0.3 |
| Outside Accountants | 5,000 | 0.5 | 5,000 | 0.5 | 3,000 | 0.3 |
| Legal | 3,000 | 0.3 | 3,000 | 0.3 | 1,500 | 0.1 |
| License, Registrations, etc. | 2,000 | 0.2 | 2,000 | 0.2 | 2,000 | 0.2 |
| Dues & Subscriptions | 1,000 | 0.1 | 1,000 | 0.1 | 1,000 | 0.1 |
| Allow. for Doubtful Accts. | — | — | 2,400 | 0.2 | 3,500 | 0.3 |
| Depreciation | 13,000 | 1.3 | 13,000 | 1.3 | 13,000 | 1.2 |
| Interest | 7,000 | 0.7 | 7,000 | 0.7 | 7,000 | 0.6 |
| Total Expenses | 435,000 | 43.5 | 399,400 | 39.9 | 383,000 | 34.8 |
| Pretax Income | 5,000 | 0.5 | 65,600 | 6.6 | 57,000 | 5.2 |

NOTE: Figures may not total due to rounding.

tive buyer of Annie's Apparel Store is Rags, Inc. Rags operates a chain of 10 women's ready-to-wear stores. Rags plans to continue to operate the new store as Annie's Apparel Store, although the merchandising mix will change somewhat, and thus the gross margins will probably be more in line with the 40 percent experienced by most of the Rags Stores. However, Rags does expect operating expenses to be less, due to efficiencies effected through combining the stores. Such expenses as legal, accounting, insurance, automobile, travel and entertainment, and supplies should be lower. Rags projects that Annie's sales will increase 10 percent due to a more effective advertising campaign, which will be less expensive than what Annie used. Rags' employee

Exhibit 9–3

### MARY'S MACHINERY & EQUIPMENT, INC.
### BUYER'S PRO FORMA INCOME STATEMENT

| | Income Statement As Reported 1984 | | Adjusted Income Statement 1984 | | Pro Forma Income Statement | |
|---|---|---|---|---|---|---|
| | $ | % | $ | % | $ | % |
| Sales | 2,400,000 | 100.0 | 2,400,000 | 100.0 | 2,400,000 | 100.0 |
| **Cost of Goods Sold:** | | | | | | |
| Beginning Inventory | 300,000 | | 400,000 | | 400,000 | |
| Plus: Purchases | 1,620,000 | | 1,620,000 | | 1,590,000 | |
| | 1,920,000 | | 2,020,000 | | 1,990,000 | |
| Less: Ending Inventory | 320,000 | | 430,000 | | 430,000 | |
| Cost of Goods Sold | 1,600,000 | 66.7 | 1,590,000 | 66.2 | 1,560,000 | 65.0 |
| Gross Margin | 800,000 | 33.3 | 810,000 | 33.8 | 840,000 | 35.0 |
| **Expenses:** | | | | | | |
| Officers' Compensation | 120,000 | 5.0 | 120,000 | 5.0 | 110,000 | 4.6 |
| Salaries & Wages | 230,000 | 9.6 | 230,000 | 9.6 | 230,000 | 9.6 |
| Employee Benefits | 50,000 | 2.1 | 50,000 | 2.1 | 50,000 | 2.1 |
| Payroll Taxes | 50,000 | 2.1 | 50,000 | 2.1 | 50,000 | 2.1 |
| Rent | 24,000 | 1.0 | 24,000 | 1.0 | 24,000 | 1.0 |
| Depreciation | 33,000 | 1.4 | 33,000 | 1.4 | 33,000 | 1.4 |
| Insurance | 20,000 | 0.8 | 20,000 | 0.8 | 20,000 | 0.8 |
| Travel & Entertainment | 30,000 | 1.3 | 30,000 | 1.3 | 25,000 | 1.0 |
| Maintenance & Repair | — | — | — | — | 20,000 | 0.8 |
| Policy Adjustments | 26,000 | 1.1 | 26,000 | 1.1 | 26,000 | 1.1 |
| Transportation Vehicles | 24,000 | 1.0 | 24,000 | 1.0 | 29,000 | 1.2 |
| Prov. for Bad Debt | 13,000 | 0.5 | 13,000 | 0.5 | 13,000 | 0.5 |
| Other | 90,000 | 3.8 | 90,000 | 3.8 | 90,000 | 3.8 |
| Total Expenses | 710,000 | 29.6 | 710,000 | 29.6 | 720,000 | 30.0 |
| Operating Income | 90,000 | 3.3 | 100,000 | 4.2 | 120,000 | 5.0 |
| **Other Income (Expense):** | | | | | | |
| Interest Expense | (15,000) | (0.6) | (15,000) | (0.6) | (20,000) | (0.8) |
| Dividend Income | 1,000 | Nil | 1,000 | Nil | — | — |
| Total Other Inc. (Exp.) | (14,000) | (0.6) | (14,000) | (0.6) | (20,000) | (0.8) |
| Income Before Taxes | 76,000 | 3.2 | 86,000 | 3.6 | 100,000 | 4.2 |
| Income Taxes | 16,000 | 0.7 | 20,000 | 0.8 | 25,750 | 1.1 |
| Net Income | 60,000 | 2.5 | 66,000 | 2.8 | 74,250 | 3.1 |

**NOTE:** Figures may not total due to rounding.
Nil = Inconsequential amount, greater (or less) than zero.

benefit program is not as generous as Annie's and will be less expensive.

# Purchase of Corporate Stock

Exhibit 9–3 is a buyer's pro forma income statement for Mary's Machinery & Equipment, Inc., from the perspective of Barney Backhoe, who has been working as general manager for Mary's. Mr. Backhoe and two associates want to purchase Mary's.

Mr. Backhoe plans to keep the name of the business as it is because Mary's has a reputation for good quality and service. He expects to be able to maintain sales at their current level. Mr. Backhoe does want to emphasize the service end of the business more, because Mary's has an excellent team of mechanics and service people. That should cause margins to improve slightly.

# Part III

Reaching the Value Conclusion

# Chapter 10

## Understanding Capitalization Rates

>*Capitalize.* To calculate the present value of future returns from a business.[1]
>
>*Capitalization.* The conversion of income into value.[2]
>
>*Capitalized value.* The asset value (principal) of a given number of income dollars determined on the basis of an assumed rate of return.[3]

This is one of the most vital chapters in the book.

The most important approach, or set of approaches, to valuing a going business or practice is to capitalize some measure of its earning power. The value of a business or professional practice is the price that will allow the investor an adequate return on the amount invested. In Part II we discuss the subject of determining the amount of earning power. The next step in valuation after determining the earnings base is to determine the applicable rate at which to capitalize the company's earning power, as measured in various ways.

*An understanding of the nature of capitalization rates and the selection of the applicable rate for a given situation is probably the most difficult problem in the entire process of business valuation.*

Perfectly valid methods of valuation will produce perfectly meaningless results, unless you use valid numbers. The ability to select applicable capitalization rates in a wide variety of situations is an indispensible skill of the expert business appraiser. It is also one of the most difficult skills to understand and implement thoroughly. Mistakes and poor judgment in the selection of capitalization rates probably are the most common sources of error in business valuation.

# Defining *Capitalization Rate*

The term *capitalization rate* is used, in different contexts, to mean many different specific concepts. Consequently, I think that it is most constructive first to approach the concept of a capitalization rate in the broadest terms. In 1984, the American Institute of Real Estate Appraisers recognized the many different usages of the term by using the following definition: "**Capitalization rate.** Any rate used to capitalize income."[4] This definition can be rephrased to say that a capitalization rate is a divisor or multiplier used to convert a stream of income to an indicated value.

The term *capitalization rate* is used most commonly to mean a percentage rate by which a constant income stream is divided in order to indicate a value. For example, if an income stream of $10,000 were to be capitalized at 25 percent, the calculation would be $10,000 divided by .25, which equals a capitalized value of $40,000. If the stream of income being capitalized is considered a constant stream over time,

[1] John J. Hampton, *Handbook for Financial Decision Makers* (Reston, Virginia: Reston Publishing Company, Inc., 1979), p. 341.

[2] *Dictionary of Real Estate Appraisal* (Chicago: American Institute of Real Estate Appraisers, 1984), p. 45.

[3] Jerry M. Rosenberg, *Dictionary of Banking and Finance* (New York: John Wiley & Sons, 1982), p. 88.

[4] *Dictionary of Real Estate Appraisal*, p. 46.

then the multiple is the reciprocal of the capitalization rate. For example, if the capitalization rate applicable to a constant income stream is 20 percent, the equivalent multiple is 5 $(1 \div .20 = 5)$.[5]

When a capitalization rate is used to discount a projected future income stream back to a present value, as in the discounted future earnings method, discussed in Chapter 13, the rate sometimes is referred to as a *discount rate*. In that context, the rate used usually reflects the cost of capital for the category of investment, as discussed later.

## Capitalization Rates Are Market-Determined

*Capitalization rates are determined by the market.* When expressed as a percentage return on an expected stream of income, *the capitalization rate represents the rate of return available in the market on investments expected to produce similar streams of income*; by "similar streams of income" I mean other streams of income defined the same way and with comparable risk and other characteristics.

In the terminology of economists, the capitalization rate can be thought of as an *opportunity cost*, the value of the return that could be obtained by investing the same amount of money in something else.

In the terminology of real estate appraisal, the capitalization rate can be thought of in terms of the *principle of substitution*; this principle states that a prudent purchaser would pay no more than the cost of acquiring an equally desirable substitute on the open market. As expressed in Real Estate Appraisal Terminology:

> The Principle of Substitution presumes that the purchaser will consider the alternatives available and will act rationally or prudently on the basis of the information about those alternatives, and that reasonable time is available for the decision. Substitution may assume the form of the purchase of an existing property, with the same utility, or of acquiring an investment which will produce an income stream of the same size with the same risk as that involved in the property in question.[6]

## Relating Capitalization Rate to Income Stream

Income streams can be defined in many ways. It is essential to understand the nature of the income stream being capitalized and to select a capitalization rate that is applicable to that particular income stream.

To appreciate this problem, consider the simple example of Sally's Salons, a small chain of hairdressing shops, well established in upscale

---

[5] For a more extensive discussion of the relationship between capitalization rates and price/earnings ratios, see *Valuing a Business*, pp. 62–64.

[6] Byrl N. Boyce, ed., *Real Estate Appraisal Terminology*, 4th ed. (Cambridge, Mass.: Ballinger Publishing Company, 1982), p. 234.

Exhibit 10–1

**SALLY'S SALONS, INC.**
**INCOME STATEMENT**

| | |
|---|---:|
| Sales | $1,000,000 |
| Operating Expenses (Excluding Owner's Compensation) | 730,000 |
| Owner's Discretionary Cash | $ 270,000 |
| Owner's Compensation | 150,000 |
| Earnings before Depreciation, Interest & Taxes | $ 120,000 |
| Depreciation | 40,000 |
| Earnings before Interest & Taxes | $ 80,000 |
| Interest | 50,000 |
| Earnings before Taxes | $ 30,000 |
| Income Taxes | 5,000 |
| Net Income | $ 25,000 |

apartment and hotel locations. As illustrated in Exhibit 10–1, several common ways of defining earnings are the following:

1. *Owner's discretionary cash.* Earnings before owner's compensation (as discussed in Chapter 6), depreciation, interest, and taxes.
2. *EBDIT.* Earnings before depreciation, interest, and taxes (but after owner's compensation).
3. *EBIT.* Earnings before interest and taxes (but after owner's compensation and depreciation).
4. *EBT.* Earnings before taxes (but after owner's compensation, depreciation, and interest).
5. *Net income.* The bottom line, earnings after all expenses, including income taxes if incorporated.

Sally asks a business broker what she can get for her business, and he replies: "Businesses like yours in this metropolis usually sell for net assets at market value plus one year's earnings." What does he mean by *earnings?* He may be referring to any of the five definitions above, or any of many possible variations. For example, as discussed in Chapter 6, depreciation may be included in expenses, but at an adjusted amount; or earnings may be stated before depreciation, but after an allowance for replacements. Similarly, owner's compensation may be deducted from sales as an expense, but at an adjusted amount.

Another variation sometimes encountered is the treatment of principal repayments on borrowed funds as an expense in determining the earnings variable to capitalize. That is done in order to get a capitalization rate in the form of a return on a cash-on-cash basis. A *cash-on-cash* return is the amount of cash per year expected to be available to the investor, divided by the amount of cash invested. In real estate appraisal, this concept is called the *equity dividend rate.*

In summary, there are many ways to define the income stream, none of which is right or wrong. No matter how the income stream is defined, it is essential that the capitalization rate selected be the rate that is appropriate to the particular definition of the income stream being capitalized.

# Return *on* Investment versus Return *on and of* Investment

In business appraisal, capitalization rates usually are stated in the form of some variation of return on investment. For example, if an investor were willing to invest $100,000 to receive an annual return of $25,000, we would say that the *return on investment* is 25 percent ($25,000 ÷ $100,000 = .25). In reverse, we would say that the $25,000 income stream was capitalized at a rate of 25 percent, meaning that the income stream was valued at $100,000 ($25,000 ÷ .25 = $100,000).

In some cases, however, (more often in real estate appraisal, but occasionally in business appraisal) a capitalization rate is stated in a form that represents a return *on and of* investment. I found an example of this approach in a business appraisal in which a broker was valuing a restaurant by a variation of the excess earnings method (described in Chapter 12). He capitalized earnings before depreciation. However, he assumed that the used restaurant equipment would have an average remaining life of five years. He accounted for this finite life by using a capitalization rate that gave him an 18 percent return on his investment in the equipment plus enough additional to amortize his investment completely in five years. In other words, he used a rate that got him an 18 percent return on his investment plus the return of his investment in five years.[7]

In the example above, the capitalization rate worked out to be 30.5 percent, or 12.5 percent over that investor's required return on capital. The additional amount was built into the capitalization rate instead of recognizing either depreciation or a reserve for replacements as an expense. This form of capitalization rate, in lieu of depreciation expense, is used quite commonly in the appraisal of buildings, but is not found frequently in business appraisals.

# Distinguishing between *Return on Equity* (ROE) and *Return on Investment* (ROI)

Much confusion arises among different people involved in valuing businesses because of failure to distinguish between return on equity and return on investment. *Equity* is the ownership interest. If the business is financed entirely by equity, then equity and investment are one and the same. However, *investment* is a broader term, including debt as well as equity. Therefore, if the business is financed by debt as well as equity, then equity is a subset, or only a portion, of the total investment.

---

[7] Dick Fraser, "How Much Is Your Business Worth?" *Restaurant Business*, August 1, 1981, pp. 85–88.

# Return on Equity

Return on equity (ROE) is defined as follows:

$$\frac{\text{Earnings}}{\text{Equity}}$$

For example, if a company had earnings of $10,000 and equity of $50,000, the return on equity would be computed as:

$$\frac{\$10,000}{\$50,000} = .20$$

If the company is a sole proprietorship or a partnership, earnings are on a pretax basis. If the company is a corporation, earnings in this formula conventionally are stated on an after-tax basis, unless otherwise specified. Therefore, if the appraiser desires to compute a pretax return on equity for a corporation, it should be specified that pretax earnings are to be used in the numerator, and the expression should be called *pretax return on equity* in order to avoid confusion.

An ambiguity that arises with respect to the equity in the formula is whether it refers to beginning equity, ending equity, or average equity. In the example above, consider the following conditions: the equity at the beginning of the year was $40,000; there were no additions to, nor withdrawals from, equity during the year; earnings of $10,000 were left in the business at the end of the year, making the ending equity $50,000. These conditions lead to the following conclusions: the return on equity figured on beginning equity would be .25 ($10,000 ÷ $40,000 = .25); the return on average equity would be .225 ($10,000 ÷ $45,000 = .225); and the return on ending equity would be .20, as computed above. As noted in Chapter 7, the preferred method from an analytical viewpoint is to compute the return on average equity, but, for expedience, many sources of comparative data compute it on ending equity. It makes a lot of sense to me, especially from a valuation viewpoint, to compute it on beginning equity; that tells me how much the company earned (or expects to earn, in the case of a projection or estimate) on the amount of equity it started with at the beginning of the period. Also, small businesses are less likely than large businesses to make productive reinvestments of earnings throughout the year.

# Return on Investment

*Return on investment* (ROI) is a term used more ambiguously than *return on equity*. As with return on equity, earnings can be computed variously on a pretax or after-tax basis, and the investment in the denominator can be a beginning, average, or ending amount. However, there is also ambiguity in the definition of *investment* itself. In some contexts, *investment* is defined to be synonymous with *capital*, that is, all equity plus long-term debt.[8] In other contexts, *investment* is defined

---

[8] If the balance sheet also has deferred items in the long-term liability section, such as deferred taxes or unearned subscription revenues, such items sometimes are included in "capital" and sometimes not.

to include all equity and interest-bearing debt, including short-term debt.

None of these ways of defining return on equity or return on investment is necessarily right or wrong. The point of all this discussion is that it is necessary to be explicit about the exact meaning of these expressions in any given context.

A typical formula for return on investment is:

$$\frac{\text{Earnings before interest and taxes (EBIT)}}{\text{Investment}}$$

For example, if a company had $75,000 worth of interest-bearing debt and $50,000 equity, and it paid $7,500 in interest on the debt and had $10,000 worth of pretax earnings, the return on investment would be computed as:

$$\frac{\$7,500 + \$10,000}{\$75,000 + \$50,000} = \frac{\$17,500}{\$125,000} = .14$$

# Required Total Rate of Return

The *total return* includes all the financial benefit the investor expects to receive from the investment. The total return includes both income and capital appreciation, if any is expected. The *total rate of return* is the total return expressed as a percentage of the amount invested to produce that return. The *required total rate of return* is the cost of capital for a particular category of investment. It is the expected total rate of return that the market requires in order to attract money to any category of investment, considering the risks and other characteristics of the investment. In other words, the required total rate of return is the rate of return that is available in the market on other investments comparable in risk, liquidity, and other characteristics of importance to investors.

A simple example of the total rate of return available in the market on one category of investment would be a bond that was only one year away from maturity, at which time the issuer would pay back the face value (usually $1,000 per bond) to the holder, along with any interest due. If the bond carried an interest rate of 10 percent, the interest would be $100 per year, because interest is computed on the face value of the bond ($1,000 × .10 = $100). If an investor bought the bond for $950, he would also expect to earn $50 in capital appreciation ($1,000 − $950 = $50), which would also be part of his total expected return. These two components of expected return would be expressed as a total expected rate of return by dividing the total expected return by the amount invested, as follows:

$$\frac{\$100 \text{ (interest)} + \$50 \text{ (capital appreciation)}}{\$950 \text{ (amount paid for bond)}}$$

In the example above, the total expected rate of return is 15.8 percent. (In bond terminology, the total expected rate of return is called the *yield to maturity*.)

The required total rate of return for an investment in the ownership of a closely held busines or professional practice can be thought of as being comprised of the following four components:

1. The rate of return available in the market on investments that are essentially free of risk, highly liquid, and virtually free of any administrative costs associated with ownership.
2. The premium that is required to compensate the investor for risk.
3. The premium that is required to compensate the investor for illiquidity.
4. The premium that is required to compensate the investor for administrative costs.

These four components of the required rate of return are discussed in the following four subsections.

## Risk-Free Rate of Return

The concept of the risk-free investment is that the investor can be sure to get back the exact amount of money promised, exactly when it is promised. The investor can count on receiving the principal at a certain time, along with a stated amount of interest. To make it even sweeter, if he decides he wants his money before the principal is due, there is a ready market in which he can instantly sell the investment to someone else, paying only a nominal commission cost.

The *risk-free rate* is the rate of return available to an investor at any given time on such an investment, such as U.S. Treasury bills or the highest quality money market funds. The rates of return available on such investments usually cover the expected rate of inflation plus something for renting out the money for a period of time. For example, if U.S. Treasury bills yielded 10 percent, and economists' expectations were that inflation was running at an annual rate of about 7 percent, the investor in T-bills would get enough interest to keep up with inflation, plus a real rate of return of about 3 percent for loaning the money on a risk-free basis.

For reasons discussed in a later section, the total rate of return available on long-term U.S. Government bonds frequently is used as a proxy for the risk-free rate when developing a required total rate of return for an equity investment.

## Premium for Risk

Risk is the uncertainty as to exactly when or how much return an investor will receive on a given investment. In order to induce an investor to put his money into something with risk, he must have a reasonable expectation that he will earn a higher rate of return than that available on a risk-free basis.

There are two categories of risks inherent in investing in a small business or professional practice: (1) risk factors peculiar to the specific business or practice, including those peculiar to the particular industry or profession within which it operates; (2) risk factors arising from general economic conditions, such as interest rates, availability of credit, and expansionary or recessionary conditions.

## Premium for Illiquidity

In contrast to the ready marketability noted as a hallmark of the risk-free investment, small businesses and professional practices are relatively illiquid. A sale usually requires a few months to accomplish, during which time the seller usually expends considerable time and effort on the sale. The seller will either pay a brokerage commission or incur other direct selling costs. It is hard to predict how long it will take to sell, or what the price will be relative to either what the owner paid for it or what his notion of its intrinsic value may be. When he does sell the business, more often than not, he will receive only part of the price in cash and the balance on a contract over some extended period of time.

In the practice of valuing businesses and business interests, there are two procedures in common usage for dealing with the adverse characteristic of illiquidity. Either procedure can be acceptable, if properly applied; but the procedures typically used for large businesses differ from those typically used for small businesses. In valuing interests in large businesses, for which a liquid public trading market is not readily available, the typical procedure is to reach a value as if a public trading market existed and then take a percentage discount for the lack of ready marketability. This procedure is attractive in valuing illiquid interests in large companies because there is considerable market evidence available to help you quantify the discount for illiquidity (lack of immediate marketability).[9]

In valuing small businesses and professional practices, however, the common procedure is to build the adverse characteristic of illiquidity into the capitalization rate. The relative impact of this factor is largely subjective, since little empirical evidence has been developed up to this point to quantify this factor as it applies to small businesses and professional practices.

In any case, it obviously requires a fairly high expected rate of return to induce investors to accept the risks and illiquidity of small businesses compared with available risk-free investments.

## Premium for Administrative Costs

Some analysts also recognize that the total required rate of return contains a component for the cost of administering the investment

---

[9] For a discussion of this procedure and related market data, see Pratt, "Data on Discounts for Lack of Marketability" *Valuing a Business*, p. 147.

which is separate from any compensation for services in managing the
business. This component would be analogous to a bank's custodial fee
for collecting, depositing, disbursing, and accounting for receipts and
expenditures from a client's investments. Such administrative costs
tend to be higher for direct proprietary investments in small businesses
or practices, even if the investment is made as a silent partner, than for
passive holdings in such things as publicly traded securities. There
usually is time spent communicating with people active in the business, and the tax aspects usually are more complicated than they are
for a securities investment.

# Relationship between *Required Total Rate of Return* and *Capitalization Rate*

As noted at the beginning of the chapter, a capitalization rate can be
any divisor or multiplier used to convert an income stream to a present
value, the process called capitalizing. The income stream may be defined in many ways. While the income stream to be capitalized usually
represents a return on capital (under the assumption that the capital
remains invested), the income stream may represent a return both on
and of capital (an amount that includes the recovery of the capital
invested). Thus *capitalization rate* is a broad, generic term; a more
specific definition of the capitalization rate applicable in any particular
case depends on the exact definition of the income stream to which it is
to be applied.

The *required total rate of return,* as the expression is used in finance,
is much more specifically defined. As noted in the prior section, it is
almost self-explanatory; it is the total expected rate of return required
by participants in the market to induce them to put their money in a
certain investment or class of investments. As such, it is a certain type
of capitalization rate, and is the applicable rate for capitalizing certain
types of streams of income. Specifically, the required total rate of return
should be applied as the capitalization rate when the income stream
being capitalized represents all the income the investor expects to get
from the investment. That is the situation, for example, in the discounted future earnings method of valuation, which is the subject of
Chapter 13.

If the income stream to be capitalized does not include all of the
total return expected on the investment, then the rate of return expected from some source other than the current income stream must be
subtracted from the required total rate of return, in order to get an
applicable rate at which to capitalize the current income stream. For
example, suppose that the required total rate of return on an equity
investment has been estimated to be 30 percent, that the investment
currently is expected to produce an annual income stream of $10,000,
and that the value of the investment is expected to increase at a rate of
3 percent per year. In that case, the 3 percent rate of return expected in
the form of capital appreciation can be subtracted from the 30 percent

total required rate of return in determining the applicable rate at which to capitalize the $10,000 expected current annual income stream. In this case, the capitalized value would be computed as follows:

$$\frac{\$10,000}{(.30 - .03)} = \frac{\$10,000}{.27} = \$37,037$$

Regardless of whether the appraiser plans to use the required total rate of return as a capitalization rate in one of his valuation methods, it is important that he have a pretty good idea of what the required total rate of return should be for the specific type of investment. Knowledge of the required total rate of return enables one to judge reasonably whether the capitalization rates used for certain streams of income, plus other elements of the total expected rate of return not reflected in the income stream, will actually sum up to the required total rate of return for the type of investment.

Some guidance as to required total rates of return, as well as other capitalization rates and component elements of capitalization rates, is presented in a later section on benchmarks for developing capitalization rates.

# Relationship between *Payback Period* and *Capitalization Rate*

Some purchasers of businesses use the *payback period* as a criterion to determine the maximum amount they will be willing to pay. The payback period is based on cash flow and can be defined as follows:

> The time required (usually in years) for estimated future net cash receipts to equal the initial cash outlay for a project. If the estimated receipts are the same amount each year, the payback period is equal to the investment outlay divided by this annual amount.[10]

Since the payback period is a cash flow concept, income before depreciation expense but after allowance for replacements should be used to compute the payback period. If the expected cash flow thus defined was $30,000 each year, and the asking price for the business was $120,000, the payback period could be computed as follows:

$$\frac{\$120,000}{\$30,000} = 4 \text{ years}$$

If a buyer sets a maximum payback period as a limit to the amount he would consider paying, and the expected cash flow is an even amount each year, the maximum price becomes the payback period times the expected annual cash flow. In the example with the $30,000 expected cash flow each year, if the buyer set a maximum payback period of

---

[10] W. W. Cooper and Yuji Ijiri, eds. *Kohler's Dictionary for Accountants*, 6th ed. (Englewood Cliffs, N. J.: Prentice-Hall, 1983), p. 375.

three years, the maximum price he would pay would be computed as follows:

$$\$30,000 \times 3 \text{ years} = \$90,000$$

When the expected cash flow is an even amount each year, the reciprocal of the payback period could be regarded as the capitalization rate applicable to cash flow. In other words, a three-year payback period would be equivalent to a 33.33 percent capitalization rate applicable to cash flow ($1 \div 3 = .3333$), in the same manner that the reciprocal of the price/earnings ratio is a capitalization rate for the earnings stream on which the price/earnings ratio is based.

One leading authority reports that maximum payback periods of two to five years are frequently used.[11]

A current text on financial decision-making offers the following comments:

> The payback method is the easiest and least precise of the cash-flow methods and has been widely used for a long time. Its primary role is as a supplemental tool in the evaluation of capital investments. Although it should not be used alone, it has the distinct benefit of highlighting the liquidity aspects of a proposal. It shows, in effect, how quickly cash will return . . . if the firm is operating in a highly uncertain environment, early cash return can be important.[12]

The payback period becomes most relevant when returns beyond a relatively short time horizon are highly uncertain. For example, during the housing boom of the 1970s, I recall a company buying small sawmills on the basis of a maximum payback period of three years, recognizing that the industry was highly cyclical and its future very uncertain.

The primary disadvantage of the payback period is that it gives no recognition whatsoever to expected returns beyond the payback period. Another, less important, criticism of the payback period is that it gives no recognition to the timing of the cash flows within the payback period. I concur that the payback period can be a useful supplemental tool, but it should not be used alone.

# How Expected Growth Affects Capitalization Rates

When a stock is selling at 12 times earnings, its *earnings yield* is 8.3 percent. (The *earnings yield* is the reciprocal of the P/E ratio; thus, $1 \div 12 = .083$.) The fact that a stock is selling at 12 times earnings should not be interpreted to mean that investors are satisfied with a total return of 8.3 percent on their investment. What it means is that the investors will accept a current earnings yield of 8.3 percent because they expect the earnings stream to grow in the future. The consensus of investors' expectations about the future rate of earnings growth is in-

[11] Harold Bierman, Jr., and Seymour Smidt, *The Capital Budgeting Decision*, 5th ed. (New York: MacMillan, 1980), p. 34.

[12] John J. Hampton, *Financial Decision Making*, 3d ed. (Reston, Va.: Reston Publishing Company, Inc., 1983), p. 377.

corporated into the rate at which they are willing to capitalize current earnings.

If an analyst can project into the future a specific amount of expected earnings for each of several years, then the discounted future earnings method (Chapter 13) is an appropriate method to use. More commonly, however, specific projections would be little more than mere guesses; but it is, nonetheless, intuitively reasonable to expect at least some growth in earnings. That expectation definitely has a bearing on value, so it needs somehow to be reflected in the valuation procedure.

The simplest way to look at expectations regarding future earnings growth is to assume some constant rate of growth in perpetuity. For the practical purpose of this analysis, 15 or 20 years is almost as good as perpetuity, since earnings expected to be generated after that length of time would have only a very minor effect on the value of the business today.

Consider, for example, a business operating in an environment with a 20-year forecast of 5 percent annually compounded inflation and two percent annually compounded population growth. Couple these assumptions with the expectations that the profit margins will keep up with inflation and that the business will maintain its share of the market; now there is a basis for a reasonable expectation of a 7 percent annually compounded rate of earnings growth as a result of the forces in place. How does the appraiser reflect these assumptions in determining the proper rate at which to capitalize current earnings?

Under the assumption of a constant annually compounded rate of growth in the earnings or cash flow stream in perpetuity, the correct rate at which to capitalize the current level of earnings or cash flow is the required total rate of return less the assumed growth rate.[13] If analysis leads to the conclusion that the required total rate of return should be 32 percent and the expected growth rate is 7 percent, the current earnings stream should be capitalized at 25 percent (.32 − .07 = .25).

Obviously, a seller would like to convince a buyer to expect a high growth rate. From the buyer's viewpoint, however, only growth that is virtually assured as a result of forces already in place should be reflected in deciding on a rate at which to capitalize current earnings or cash flow. The buyer would not expect to pay for potential future growth that may result from his own successful entrepreneurial efforts.

# Methods of Developing Capitalization Rates

If the applicable standard of value is fair market value, then the applicable capitalization rates are determined by the market. Therefore, they are a matter of fact; they are the rates acceptable to the market for comparable income streams at the time of the valuation.

---

[13] For a step-by-step mathematical proof of this relationship, see Professor Philip L. Cooley, *How to Value an Oil Jobbership for Purchase or Sale* (Bethesda, Md.: Petroleum Marketing Education Foundation, 1982), pp. 7-34–7-37.

From an analytical viewpoint, there are three methods of developing the applicable capitalization rate for any given situation. We will call these methods (1) the direct market comparison method, (2) the summation method, and (3) the weighted average method.[14]

# Direct Market Comparison Method

The direct market comparison method of developing a capitalization rate consists of finding transactions in the market involving the sale of entities with comparable income streams and computing the capitalization rates implied in the prices at which the transactions took place. The example most familiar to people is price/earnings ratios in the public stock market.

For example, if a small restaurant chain wants to value shares of its stock for the purpose of selling shares to the public (going public), the valuator will look at the prices at which similar small restaurant chain stocks are selling in the public market in relation to various measures of earning power, one of which will be the latest 12 months' earnings per share. The price/earnings ratio reported in daily newspapers is the current market price of a stock, divided by the latest reported 12 months' earnings per share. In the public market, price/earnings ratios are quoted on the basis of after-tax earnings. If the valuator finds that most similar stocks are selling between six and nine times their latest 12 months' earnings, that provides a ballpark within which to capitalize the subject company's latest 12 months' earnings to determine a public offering price. The analyst then will examine very carefully all the comparative companies' characteristics relative to the subject company and make an estimate of just where within that ballpark the subject company belongs. The analyst, then, using the comparative companies' financial statements, will do the same exercise to develop market-indicated capitalization rates for several other measures of earning power. Such measures could include, for example, the last three and five years' straight and/or weighted average earnings, projected next year's earnings, and perhaps one or several measures of cash flow. In other words, for each of several measures of earning power, the market will provide a range of capitalization rates for various comparative companies, and the analyst will have to exercise his judgment to determine where in each range the subject company best fits.

The most important thing about the above example is that the analyst derived a different applicable capitalization rate from the public market for each different measure of earning power considered for the subject company. Capitalization rates derived directly from transaction data should be based on the same measure of earning power as the measure of the subject company's earning power to which that

---

[14] This classification of methods of developing capitalization rates was suggested by Ronald W. Welch in connection with valuations for ad valorem taxes and quoted in Arlo Woolery, ed., *The Art of Valuation* (Lexington, Mass.: Lexington Books, 1978), pp. 19–20. Welch called the three methods the "market-determined rate," the "summation approach," and the "band of investment approach."

capitalization rate will be applied. Otherwise, adjustments must be made; and such adjustments may be difficult to support.

It is obvious from the above example that the analyst conceivably could have developed quite a wide array of capitalization rates. These capitalization rates could include those based on each of several different definitions of earnings, each involving several different historical and/or projected time periods. The analyst must judge which measure or measures of earning power, along with the respective indicated capitalization rate(s), most realistically indicate value in each case. Any capitalization rate found in a market transaction reflects expectations of the level and risk of future earnings. In order for capitalization rates found in the market to be realistic guides for valuing the subject company, there must be a reasonable basis for expecting the subject company's earnings stream to be at least approximately parallel to what was expected from the earnings streams from which the capitalization rates were derived.

Returning to the small restaurant chain example, if the average stock was selling at eight times last year's earnings, the market is capitalizing *last year's earnings* at 12.5 percent ($1 \div 8 = .125$). The market certainly is not buying those stocks because it expects their future earnings to be only 12.5 percent of the current stock price; the market obviously expects earnings growth, since earnings of 12.5 percent are available on much safer investments. For you to realistically capitalize the subject company's latest year's earnings at the market-derived capitalization rate of 12.5 percent, you must reasonably expect the growth and risk characteristics of the subject company's future earnings to be somewhat similar to the industry, or, more specifically, to that subset of the industry from which the capitalization rate was derived.

The point of the example above is to stress the need for comparability between the subject company and the companies from which the capitalization rate is derived; the comparability should be reflected in the definition of the earnings base being capitalized and also in the assumptions regarding it.

Also, note that the purpose of the valuation clearly influenced the valuator's choice of data. Since the purpose was a public offering, public market data were used for comparison. That is not to say that public market data cannot be used at all for other purposes for which small business valuations may be undertaken but, as discussed in Chapter 4 and elsewhere in this book, it is much more difficult to make useful comparisons between public companies and small private companies than between public companies and medium-sized to larger private companies.

The same kind of exercise can be used to derive capitalization rates from closely held company market transaction data. The problem is that the data themselves are much harder to obtain, because there is no requirement for public reporting of most private transaction data. Sources of such data that do exist are discussed in other parts of this book.

The direct market comparison method generally is considered the best method, if a sufficient number of directly comparable transactions are available for comparison; but that is a big "if." As noted above, comparative data are not always readily available. Moreover, because of the unique nature of each business, the appraiser must exercise a great deal of analytical judgment to ascertain the degree of comparability between the subject company and the comparative transactions found in the market.

# Summation Method

In the *summation method*, a capitalization rate is developed by adding up the rates applicable to each of its conceptual components. In other words, the appraiser starts with a safe interest rate (the risk-free rate), and adds other factors that cause the rate applicable to the income stream being capitalized to be different from the risk-free rate. The two most important factors, as discussed earlier, are risk and lack of liquidity.

In using the summation method, at least one, and possibly all, of the components may have been developed by observing data directly in the market. Factors involved in the summation method were discussed in more detail in the section on elements of the investor's required total rate of return. Some sources of market data that might be used are discussed in a section later in this chapter, "Benchmarks for Developing Capitalization Rates." The advantage of the summation method is that it consciously encompasses all the conceptual elements of the capitalization rate that should be considered. The disadvantage is that, in some cases, the appraiser may have little or no market data available to help him quantify the number of percentage points of capitalization rate that should be attributed to each factor, so that the resultant rate may be largely subjective.

The summation method is also sometimes referred to as the *built-up method* of developing a capitalization rate.

# Weighted Average Method

The *weighted average method* is not really a separate method; it merely blends two or more capitalization rates to get one. Each of the capitalization rates used to get the weighted average rate may be developed by either the direct market comparison method or the summation method.

The most common form of the weighted average method is to assume that the purchase of a business can be financed partly with debt and partly with equity. For example, if we assume that Millicent Milliner can buy Harry's Haberdashery with a bank loan at 14 percent for 40 percent of the purchase price, and, based on a study of alternative opportunities, she wants at least a 25 percent return on the other 60 percent of the money that she will be investing as equity funds, the weighted average capitalization rate based on those two component rates can be computed as follows:

|            | Proportion |          | Rate |          |
|------------|------------|----------|------|----------|
| Debt       | .40        | $\times$ | .14  | = .056   |
| Equity     | .60        | $\times$ | .25  | = .150   |
| Weighted Average |      |          |      | .206     |

In valuations for ad valorem taxation and some other contexts, this method has come to be known as the *band-of-investment method*.[15] It is also sometimes called the *blended capitalization rate method* or the *stock and debt method*. When a weighted average approach is used to develop a capitalization rate applicable to total capital (debt and equity capital combined), the method sometimes is referred to as the *overall capitalization rate method*.

When determining rates to use in the weighted average capitalization rate method, current market rates should be used for each component. As one appraiser explains it:

> All elements of the cost of capital are in terms of current market yields, not historic relationships. The rate of return on debt capital is the current rate the prudent investor would pay for long-term debt capital to finance his purchase of the business. The proportion of debt capital to total capital can be reasonably estimated by examining the proportions of debt to total capital (based on market values) of comparable companies. The proportion used should represent the long-term expected leverage position the prudent investor would expect to maintain.[16]

Data on industry-average leverage (proportions of debt and equity) for 330 small business industry groups are contained in Robert Morris Associates' *Annual Statement Studies*.

At the outset of this section, I injected the condition that the foregoing methods of developing capitalization rates are applicable if the applicable standard of value is fair market value. If the standard of value is intrinsic value (as defined and discussed in Chapter 2), the same general methodology may be used, but the rates should be suitably modified to conform to rates that are acceptable to a particular investor rather than to those that are characteristic of the market in general.

# Benchmarks for Developing Capitalization Rates

Although determining the appropriate rate at which to capitalize an expected level of earnings is not an exact science, neither is it a guessing game without guidance. There is, in fact, considerable information available to help you arrive at an informed judgment about the capital-

---

[15] See, for example, *Industrial Real Estate*, 4th ed. (Washington, D.C.: National Association of Realtors, 1984), pp. 473–5.

[16] Roger J. Grabowski and Steven C. Dilley, *Closely Held Corporations: Valuation* (East Lansing, Mich.: Federal Tax Workshops, Inc., 1984), p. 80.

ization rate that should be applied to a particular expected stream of earnings at any particular time.

One of the reasons why rules of thumb do not work very well for valuing businesses and professional practices is that the economic forces that combine to determine capitalization rates at any time are constantly changing, and rules of thumb fail to take account of these changes.

It is my personal opinion, based on hundreds of observations, that participants involved in the purchase and sale of small businesses and professional practices (buyers, sellers, brokers) tend to underestimate the appropriate capitalization rate more often than they overestimate it. Underestimating the appropriate capitalization rate (expressed as a percentage rate of return) leads to overvaluing the business or practice, and vice versa. In many instances, the underestimation of the appropriate capitalization rate and consequent overvaluation of the business or practice results in the business or practice not being sold, or being sold only after a very long time (and then at a large discount from the asking price), or being sold on a contract that eventually defaults because the price is unaffordable.

The benchmarks discussed in the following sections represent the world of reality and should be taken into consideration when determining the applicable capitalization rate for a particular stream of income.

# Treasury Bill Rates

The investment that generally is considered most risk-free is U.S. Treasury bills, which are obligations of the U.S. government, usually issued with maturities of 90 to 180 days. The disadvantage of using the Treasury bill rate as the bellwether risk-free rate is that short-term interest rates fluctuate a great deal more than long-term rates, and capitalization rates applicable to the earnings of businesses or professional practices fluctuate more closely in line with longer-term than with short-term rates.

# Long-Term Government Bond Rates

Long-term U.S. Government bonds generally are considered risk-free, as far as certainty of payment of principal and interest when due; they also are readily marketable at any time, with a very small commission cost. They do carry the risk, however, that the owner may not be able to get the full face value if the bonds are sold before maturity, because of fluctuations in the general level of interest rates. If a person holds a bond bearing a 10 percent interest rate at a time when rates available on new bonds have gone up to 12 percent, the holder would have to discount the price enough to provide a buyer a 12 percent yield to maturity on the price the buyer would pay.

In spite of this risk factor, the long-term U.S. Government bond yield is a very useful benchmark to consider as a virtually risk-free alternative available when determining the capitalization rate for the earnings of a business or practice. Because of its long-term nature and greater stability, compared with the Treasury bill rate, I find that most valuation practitioners prefer to use the long-term Government bond, rather than the Treasury bill rate, as a base rate.

## Corporate Bond Rates

Corporate bonds carry varying degrees of default risk and are graded accordingly by rating services such as Standard & Poor's and Moody's. Publicly traded corporate bonds have a ready market, but are not quite as liquid as U.S. Government bonds. Corporate bonds offer higher rates of return than U.S. Government bonds, with the rates of return increasing with the higher-risk, lower-grade bonds.

## Bank Loan Rates

Small businesses and professional practices with good credit ratings usually can borrow on a short-term basis, and sometimes on an intermediate-term basis, at two to three percentage points above banks' *prime lending rate*, which is sometimes defined as the rate banks typically charge their largest and most creditworthy customers. This rate understates the total cost of the borrowing, however. There may be loan fees. Some time usually elapses between the time the borrower receives and deposits money and the time the money is credited to the borrower's loan account. Some banks require or expect that some balances (called *compensating balances*) be kept in the borrower's checking account instead of being credited to the loan balance. Most small business borrowing is on a secured basis, with accounts receivable, inventory, equipment, and/or the owner's personal assets pledged as collateral, resulting in varying degrees of administrative personnel cost to the borrower. It is not unreasonable to estimate that the typical total cost of borrowing for a small firm would run five percentage points above the banks' prime rate.

Keep in mind, too, that a firm usually cannot borrow all of its capital from a bank. The bank expects the owners of the firm to have some of their own capital committed, the equity cushion that bears all the residual risk.

## Mortgage Rates

Data are readily available on prevailing mortgage rates for various classes of commercial properties. When you consider such rates as guides for developing capitalization rates to apply to small business and professional practice earnings, you must remember that such loans are of relatively low risk to the lender; they are secured by real estate, which the lender can sell in case of default, and usually are for only about 80 percent of the property value, with the owner holding the more risky equity portion of the total property investment.

# Rates of Return on Publicly Traded Stocks

Over long periods of time, common stocks on the New York Stock Exchange have provided their investors with a total rate of return that has averaged 8.2 percent more than the average rate of return on short-term U.S. Treasury bills, and 7.8 percent more than the average rate of return on long-term U.S. Government bonds.[17] The stocks of the smaller (generally more risky) New York Stock Exchange companies have provided higher rates of return, averaging 14.3 percent more than long-term U.S. Government bonds.[18]

Investments in most small businesses and professional practices would be considered more risky than investment in even the smallest companies on the New York Stock Exchange. Also, the listed stocks are readily marketable. Therefore, it would seem that the required rate of return for equity investments in small businesses and professional practices would be at a somewhat higher premium over U.S. Government bond rates than the rates of return on NYSE stocks, even the smallest ones.

# Allowed Rates of Return for Public Utilities

Each state has a Public Utilities Commission (PUC) which determines the rates that the utilities are allowed to charge. The rates allowed are those that would be expected to result in a fair rate of return on invested capital. Consequently, as part of the rate-making process, each PUC determines the allowed rate of return on each class of capital (debt, preferred stock, and common stock), as well as an overall (weighted average) rate of return for each public utility within its jurisdiction. The rates allowed are those which the respective PUCs determine are required by the market for investments of comparable risk and other characteristics in light of prevailing economic conditions. Such allowed rates of return are reviewed periodically, usually when utilities request permission to increase the rates they charge customers for their services.

Based on an overall average of electric utility company rate decisions from 1981 through 1984, the average allowed return on equity for such companies ranged between roughly 15 percent and 16 percent. For the full year 1984, the average rate of return on equity calculated from electric utility rate cases was estimated at 15.3 percent.[19] Rates of return on equity allowed to gas, telephone, and other regulated industries tend to be greater than the rates granted to electric utilities.

Investments in most small, closely held companies certainly have considerably more risk, and are less liquid, than investments in the

---

[17] *Stocks, Bonds, Bills, and Inflation: 1985 Yearbook* (Chicago: Ibbotson Associates, Inc., 1985), pp. 23, 42.
[18] Ibid.

[19] *Regulatory Study* (Regulatory Research Associates, January 11, 1985), quoted in *Electric Utility Week*, January 21, 1985.

stocks and bonds of most public utilities; therefore, they should command considerably higher expected rates of return.

## Sources of Information for Benchmark Rates

Current rates on the various categories of investment discussed in the preceding sections can be found in *Barron's*, *The Wall Street Journal*, the *Federal Reserve Bulletin*, and a wide assortment of other business and financial publications. More and more business sections of metropolitan daily newspapers recently have started reporting such data. Yields on specific corporate bonds, along with their quality ratings, can be found in Standard & Poor's *Bond Guide* and *Moody's Bond Record*.

Actual pretax rates of return on tangible net worth (book value of tangible equity) for small businesses in 330 industry groups is shown in Robert Morris Associates' *Annual Statement Studies*. It must be kept in mind, however, that those rates of return are on the book value at historical costs not adjusted to current market value. Furthermore, they represent only what returns actually were achieved in the respective years, which were not necessarily what investors expected to achieve.

## Different Rates for Different Buyers

The cost of capital, either debt or equity, is different from one potential buyer to another. For an individual buying a sole proprietorship from another individual, the cost of capital probably would be about the same for the buyer as for the seller. On the other hand, the cost of capital to a sizable public company probably is somewhat less than the cost of capital to the typical small entrepreneur.

The buyer usually will use a capitalization rate based on that buyer's own cost of capital. The seller should consider the cost of capital to the likely classes of buyers, and estimate the capitalization rates that they are likely to use.

A pair of small business consultants offers this explanation:

> The appropriate discount rate is defined as the required rate of return of the investor. Thus, when valuing a business, the buyer and seller will almost always have different required rates of return, as each individual will have different investment opportunities available, each of which has a different return and a different risk. Risk and return are directly related—if one opportunity poses a riskier situation than another it must consequently promise a higher return to compensate the investor for taking the additional risk. Therefore, if one investor perceives an investment opportunity as being riskier than does a second investor considering the same opportunity, the former will require a higher rate of return on that investment than the latter.[20]

---

[20] James W. Carland, Jr., and Larry R. White, "Valuing the Small Business," *Journal of Small Business Management*, October 1980, p. 44.

As discussed earlier, when fair market value is the applicable standard of value, capitalization rates used should be representative of a market consensus. However, when determining intrinsic value to a particular party, the applicable capitalization rates are those based on that party's cost of capital, risk perceptions, and other relevant factors.

# What the Players Are Saying

The consensus among participants in the marketplace (buyers and sellers, brokers, appraisers, and others) seems to be that the required total rate of return on an equity investment in a small business is in the range of 20 to 40 percent; this depends on the degree of risk, and is higher for unusually risky situations. Following are a few representative quotes:

> An estimated capitalization rate of 20 percent would seem to be a minimum rate in today's economy, assuming that the business in question had stable growth and good market position and was relatively free from excessive competition. (This means that the product is protected in some way from someone starting a similar business in direct competition. This protection might include a franchise, exclusive distributorship, geographical location, or the unique knowledge of the owner.) Businesses being evaluated without one of these 'edges' would require a higher risk premium and, therefore, a higher capitalization rate.[21]

> As a broad gauge, most buyers will want a return of at least 25 percent on the investment.[22]

> If I were to invest in a business as a passive investor looking only to the return on investment element, I'd set my minimum goal at 25-30 percent–and this presumes a fair degree of safety.[23]

Venture capitalists look for 25 to 50 percent (or sometimes more) compounded annual rates of return, depending on the stage of development of the company and the degree of risk.[24] One business broker says that 30 percent to 40 percent is a typically required discount rate for a service business in his area of the country, and a slightly lower rate applies to the manufacturing, wholesaling and product distribution businesses.[25]

---

[21] Harold S. Olafson, "How to Valuate a Small Business," *Real Estate Today*, March/April 1984, p. 55.

[22] Bradley Hitchings, "Selling Your Business," *Business Week*, February 4, 1985, p. 101.

[23] Arnold S. Goldstein, *The Complete Guide to Buying and Selling a Business* (New York: New American Library, 1983), p. 110.

[24] See for example, Arthur Lipper III, *Venture's Guide to Investing in Private Companies* (Homewood, Ill.: Dow Jones-Irwin, 1984), p. 155.

[25] Glen Cooper, "How Much Is Your Business Worth?" *In Business*, September-October 1984, p. 51.

# Chapter 11

## Basic Capitalized Earnings Approaches

A basic capitalization of earnings approach means the application of one divisor or multiplier to one earnings figure; the result is an indication of value derived from that single multiplication or division. In real estate terminology, this process is called *direct capitalization*, defined as follows:

> The capitalization method used to convert an estimate of a single year's income expectancy or annual average of several years' income expectancies into an indication of value in one step, either by dividing the income estimate by an appropriate rate or by multiplying the income estimate by an appropriate factor.[1]

The income stream to be capitalized can be the latest year's, a straight or weighted average of past years', a normalized income stream, a forecast of the coming year's, or some other variation. The income stream can be either before or after any or all of several items, such as interest, depreciation, allowance for replacements, owner's compensation, taxes, principal payments on debt, and many more.

The key is that the income stream being capitalized must be clearly defined, and the capitalization rate chosen must be a rate that is appropriate for the particular income stream, as defined. In order to avoid being encyclopedic, this chapter discusses only the most common few among the many possible variations.

# Deciding on the Earnings Base to be Capitalized

It is obvious from the foregoing discussion that there are many possible earnings bases to capitalize to derive indications of the value of a business or practice. The appropriate choices depend on many factors; perhaps the most important of these are (1) the purpose of the appraisal, (2) the availability of reliable and valid data, and (3) the ability to develop a realistic capitalization rate that would be applicable to the earnings base chosen.

## How the Purpose Affects the Selection of the Earnings Base

An owner who wants to sell his business or practice obviously wishes to present as optimistic an earnings base as possible. If the latest year is the best year, he is likely to want to rely on that. If the latest year was not the best year, he probably will point to the average of whatever number of years it takes to show the best results. Alternatively, he may adjust his historical results to his concept of a normalized earnings base, or he may forecast earnings for the year ahead. If he has a large amount of depreciation, he may choose to focus on cash flow rather than earnings. If interest was high, he may want to focus on operating in-

---

[1] *The Dictionary of Real Estate Appraisal* (Chicago: American Institute of Real Estate Appraisers, 1984), p. 93.

come (earnings before interest). There certainly is nothing wrong with a seller putting his best foot forward, as long as the information is accurate and complete enough not to mislead. As long as the information is clearly labeled as to exactly what it represents, a buyer can judge for himself how he will use it in deciding what he is willing to pay.

On the other hand, the same owner who will be paying gift, estate, inheritance, or ad valorem taxes on the basis of the valuation will be inclined to be conservative when selecting an earnings base to be capitalized. He will not want to pay taxes on the basis of future earnings increases that may or may not materialize. When it comes to paying taxes based on the value of the business, he is not likely to believe that the highest level of earnings he has ever achieved is the best basis for the valuation of the business.

As a generalization, valuations for taxes and many other legal purposes should be based as far as possible on the actual historical record, whereas valuations for transactions, damage cases, and other purposes that tend to look to future results may rely more on estimates. Business executives are accustomed to making decisions on the basis of estimates. Except in certain types of damage cases and certain other instances, courts generally prefer to rely on an actual historical record, if that record is meaningful.

## Availability of Reliable and Valid Earnings Data

By *reliable* earnings data, I mean dependable and accurate data. For many small businesses, obtaining reliable earnings data on which to base a valuation is a major problem. In many cases, the problem arises from inadequate recordkeeping. In other cases, discretionary expenses that some people might regard as part of owner's compensation are so intertwined with essential expenses that it is virtually impossible to separate them. In some cases, it is necessary to work with only a single year's earnings or even an estimate, simply for lack of any other reliable data.

By *valid* earnings data, I mean data that are relevant to the current circumstances as of the valuation date. When a fire closes down a business for months, or when a major product line is discontinued, there may be perfectly reliable records of earnings for last year, but the difference in circumstances may render such historical data inapplicable to the situation at hand.

In summary, the earnings base or bases chosen to be capitalized should be both reliable and relevant to the current circumstances.

## Ability to Develop an Applicable Capitalization Rate

It usually is easier to develop an applicable capitalization rate for certain earnings bases than for others, especially if the rate is to be developed by the direct market comparison method. There simply may be no market capitalization rate data available for many definitions of an earnings base, which otherwise are acceptable for valuation. Consequently, the appraiser may believe that one definition of earnings is best for conceptual reasons but may have to rely on an earnings base defined some other way just because of the availability of comparative market data from which to develop a capitalization rate.

# Capitalizing Earnings Available to Equity

In direct capitalization of earnings, there are only two variables: (1) the definition of the income stream to be capitalized, and (2) the capitalization rate. The capitalization rate may be expressed either as a divisor or as a multiplier. As discussed earlier, the key is to select a capitalization rate applicable to the particular earnings base.

## Defining the Earnings Base

In the typical small business or professional practice, I prefer to use the normalized earnings base, as developed in Chapter 6, if sufficient data are available. To summarize, the normalized earnings base represents as accurate a picture as possible of true economic earnings on the equity investment:

1. After interest payments, but before any principal payments.
2. After depreciation, adjusted to a best estimate of actual reduction in value due to wearing out and/or obsolescence; or before depreciation but after an allowance for the asset replacements necessary to maintain the income stream.
3. After reasonable compensation for owner's services in the business.

Income taxes are a genuine economic cost. However, for reasons already discussed (lack of availability of data and different tax rates among various parties), most capitalizations of small business and professional practice earnings are done on a pretax basis. That is not extremely important, as a practical matter in most cases, since most small businesses and professional practices are positioned so that the income tax on the business is very low or nonexistent.

## Capitalization Rate by Summation Method

Having developed a normalized level of economic earnings available to equity, the next step is to develop the capitalization rate applicable to the earnings stream. If the standard of value is fair market value, the correct capitalization rate is the rate available on the most comparable investments for which data are available, adjusted for differences in risk and other characteristics between the subject investment and the nearest comparable investments for which data are available. As discussed in the previous chapter, the two primary methods for developing a capitalization rate applicable to earnings available to equity are (1) the summation method, and (2) the direct market comparison method.

In the summation method, the first step is to develop a required total rate of return; the second step is to adjust that rate for any portion of the expected return that may not be reflected in the earnings stream being capitalized. One good starting place for the summation method is the rate of return available on long-term U.S. Government bonds, a rate readily available in *The Wall Street Journal* and many metropolitan daily newspapers. To that rate can be added the long-term historical average difference in rate of return on small stocks over long-term U.S. Government bonds; through 1984, this was 14.3 percent, as discussed in the last chapter.[2] That total can be adjusted upward or downward for differences in perceived risk between the average small NYSE stock (comprising 20 percent of the smallest companies on the NYSE) and the subject company. Adjustment can also be made for the fact that the small NYSE stocks are readily marketable, while a closely held business is less liquid. It is not uncommon to adjust the required rate of return upward, up to 10 percentage points, to reflect these factors, or sometimes even more, but there is little empirical evidence available for guidance in quantifying this adjustment. On the other hand, the investments in publicly traded stocks are minority interests, but we are discussing a controlling interest in the closely held business. Some investors would be willing to trade off the advantage of liquidity of investment, as found in a public company stock, for control of a small business, thus partially or even fully offsetting the upward adjustment to the capitalization rate for risk and lack of liquidity.

As discussed in the previous chapter, the total required rate of return *includes*, as a component, the expected rate of inflation. If we can assume that the earnings stream will grow in perpetuity at the rate of inflation, we can subtract the expected inflation rate from the total required rate of return in order to get a capitalization rate to apply to the current level of normalized economic earnings.

An example of the development of a capitalization rate, as described above, is as follows:

| | |
|---|---|
| Long-Term U.S. Government Bond Rate | 12% |
| Plus: Average Premium Return on Small Stocks over U.S. Government Bonds | 14 |
| Expected Total Rate of Return on Small Public Stocks | 26 |
| Plus: Premium for Greater Risk and Illiquidity | 4 |
| Total Required Expected Rate of Return for Subject Company, Including Inflation Component | 30 |
| Less: Consensus Long-Term Inflation Expectation | 5 |
| Capitalization Rate to Apply to Current Earnings | 25% |

[2] Ibbotson Associates, *1985 Yearbook*, p. 23.

# Capitalization Rate by Direct Market Comparison Method

If pertinent data are available, it is also desirable to develop a capitalization rate, or range of capitalization rates, by the direct market comparison method. The best opportunity for using this method is when the appraiser has data available on the sales of other comparable closely held companies. For example, if data indicated that several comparable companies had sold for prices ranging from 3.2 to 5 times earnings, with earnings defined the same way as for the subject company, that data would imply a range of capitalization rates from .313 to .200 (1 ÷ 3.2 = .313; 1 ÷ 5 = .200). This range would suggest some upper and lower boundaries for the capitalization rate suggested by the summation method. The valuator should take into consideration the qualitative factors discussed in Chapter 8 in deciding where within the indicated range the capitalization rate applicable to the subject company should fall.

Keep in mind that published price/earnings ratios on publicly traded stocks are based on after-tax earnings. For reasons discussed elsewhere, the smaller the business, the less likely that public stock information will be useful for the purpose of valuing the business. However, if the analyst decides that the subject company's stock is such that capitalization rates for earnings of public companies are relevant, he can compute price/pretax earnings ratios for the public companies by using current stock prices and earnings data from the companies' annual and interim reports.

# Applying the Rate to Determine the Value

If a 25 percent capitalization rate were selected and applied to expected annual earnings available to equity of $10,000, the value of the equity in the business would be computed as follows:

$$\frac{\$10,000}{.25} = \$40,000$$

In other words, if a buyer requires a 25 percent return on equity for an investment to be attractive to him, he would capitalize the $10,000 expected earnings at 25 percent; that is, he would be willing to pay $40,000 for the $10,000 expected earnings stream because the *earnings yield* would be 25 percent ($10,000 ÷ $40,000 = .25).

# Adjusting for Excess Assets or Capital Deficiency

The $40,000 value developed in the previous section represents the total value of the investment on a going-concern basis. If assets not needed in the operation of the business are to be included in the transaction, the buyer could add to the $40,000 his estimate of the net proceeds that would be available from selling those excess assets.

On the other hand, if additional investment would be necessary to sustain the $10,000 earnings stream (for working capital, deferred maintenance, or anything else), such additional investment should be subtracted from the amount to be paid.

# Capitalizing Earnings Available to Overall Investment

The difference between overall investment and equity in this context is that overall investment includes interest-bearing debt as well as equity. This approach is appropriate when a portion of total investment may be financed with borrowed funds. This approach is also called the *debt-free approach.*

In some versions, the approach includes all interest-bearing debt; in other versions it includes only long-term debt. As noted elsewhere, many small businesses use short-term debt as if it were long-term debt. Neither version is necessarily right or wrong, but much confusion arises when an appraiser fails to specify whether or not short-term borrowing is included in his definition of overall investment.

## Defining the Earnings Base

The earnings base should be the amount that is available to whatever has been defined as the overall investment. Except for interest, my preference is to define earnings as in the previous section. If overall investment means equity and long-term debt only, then the earnings should be after any interest on short-term debt, and before interest on long-term debt.

If overall investment includes all interest-bearing debt, then the earnings base should be earnings before any interest. The earnings base thus defined is sometimes referred to as *EBIT* (earnings before interest and taxes), and also as *net operating income.*[3]

## Capitalization Rate by the Weighted Average Method

When capitalizing earnings available to overall investment, it is appropriate to use a weighted average capitalization rate, consisting of one capitalization rate for the portion of the investment to be financed by

---

[3] *Net operating income* is the income remaining after all expenses except interest, income taxes, and items not directly related to the company's operations. In accounting terminology, it is after depreciation. In real estate terminology, it is before depreciation, but in some usages it is after allowance for replacement expenditures.

equity, and one or more other rate(s) for the portion(s) of the investment to be financed by debt, as discussed in the previous chapter. (There may be more than one rate for debt, because there may be different portions of the debt at different rates.)

**Capitalization Rate for Equity Portion.**   The procedure for developing the capitalization rate applicable to the equity portion of the investment is the same as outlined in the previous section. When deciding what rate to use, within a reasonable range, you should consider that the higher the leverage (the amount of debt capital compared to the amount of equity capital), the higher the capitalization rate applicable to the equity capital portion, because increasing the amount of leverage increases the risk of the equity ownership.

**Capitalization Rate for Debt Portion.**   The capitalization rate for the debt portion is basically the cost of the borrowed funds. As discussed in the previous chapter, the total cost should be included; this means not just the interest rate, but also all the associated costs, such as loan fees, compensating balance requirements, and administrative costs.

**Weighted Average Capitalization Rate.**   Once the capitalization rate has been determined for each of the components of the total investment, the next step is to weight them on the basis of the proportion each is of the total investment.

For example, let's say it has been determined that the capitalization rate for the portion to be financed by debt should be 15 percent, and the capitalization rate for the portion to be financed by equity should be 25 percent. Let's also say that the debt portion will carry 50 percent of the total investment, leaving 50 percent to be financed by equity. The weighted average capitalization rate can be computed as follows:

|        | Cost |   | Proportion |   |      |
|--------|------|---|------------|---|------|
| Debt   | .15  | x | .5         | = | .075 |
| Equity | .25  | x | .5         | = | .125 |
| Weighted Average Capitalization Rate |   |   |   |   | .200 |

The above capitalization rate is also sometimes referred to as an *overall capitalization rate* or a *blended capitalization rate*.

# Applying the Rate to Determine the Value

If an overall capitalization rate of 20 percent were applied to earnings of $20,000 before interest charges, the value of the total investment would be computed as follows:

$$\frac{\$20,000}{.20} = \$100,000$$

In other words, if $50,000 debt were available, at a cost of 15 percent, the interest cost would be $7,500 per year (.15 × $50,000 = $7,500).

Subtracting the $7,500 in interest from the $20,000 of earnings would leave $12,500 available for earnings on the equity portion, or 25 percent ($12,500 ÷ $50,000 = .25).

Of course, if there were excess assets or capital deficiencies, appropriate adjustments should be made in reaching the final value conclusion.

# Examples of Valuations by the Capitalized Earnings Approach

The following are hypothetical examples to illustrate the procedures discussed in this chapter. The two examples continue to use the same two hypothetical companies used in Part II on analyzing the company.

## Sole Proprietorship Example

Annual pretax income available to the owner of Annie's Apparel, according to the adjusted income statement (Exhibit 6–1), is $65,600. This figure allows for a normal salary for the owner/manager and for interest on a long-term contract payable, to be assumed by the buyer.

In the previous chapter, we discussed required total rates of return for equity investments in small businesses and practices ranging from 20 to 40 percent, with most falling in the 25–35 percent range. If we assume that about 5 percent of the total required rate of return will come more or less automatically as a result of the profits of the business keeping up with inflation, capitalization rates for current earnings will range from about 20 to about 30 percent.

When you are deciding where in the range the appropriate capitalization rate falls for Annie's earnings available to the owner (after a reasonable salary), you should recognize at least two risk factors. First, leverage is present because of the $100,000 contract being assumed. Second, the $65,600 earnings represents 6.6 percent return on sales, considerably above the industry average, as shown in Exhibits 7–1, 7–2, and 7–3; this would lead one to question whether that level of earnings can be sustained for the long run.

If we decide that the upper end of the range, 30 percent, is the appropriate rate, then a valuation calculation can be made as follows:

$$\frac{\$65,600}{.30} = \$218,669$$

From the buyer's perspective, if Rags were to capitalize the pro forma earnings of $57,000 at 25 percent, reflecting a lower degree of risk inherent in the lower pro forma earnings estimate, then a valuation calculation can be made as follows:

$$\frac{\$57,000}{.25} = \$228,000$$

# Corporation Example

Since Mary was leaving the business, one of her key employees, Barney Backhoe, and two of his associates decided that they would like to try to buy Mary's Machinery and Equipment, Inc., through a leveraged buy-out. That is, they would use borrowed funds whose collateral would be the company's assets. Based on the financial statements and adjusted balance sheets and income statements, the bank indicated interest in making a term loan of approximately 60 percent of the purchase price at 12 percent interest. The term loan will have monthly interest payments and annual principal reductions, with the note personally guaranteed by each of the three parties involved in the purchase. There are no significant extra costs associated with the loan.

Because the business has been well established for several years, the buyers feel that a 25 percent total pretax rate of return on equity would be satisfactory in order to make the deal attractive. They also believe that the combination of inflation and population growth in their area will bring a 5 percent annual growth in earnings, so they are willing to accept a 20 percent return on the first year (.25 − .05 = .20). On this basis, they would capitalize the first year's expected earnings as follows:

|  | Capitalization Rate | | Proportion | |
|---|---|---|---|---|
| Debt | .12 | × | .60 | = .072 |
| Equity | .20 | × | .40 | = .080 |
| Weighted Average Capitalization Rate | | | | .152 |

$$\text{Pretax income (from Exhibit 6–3)} \quad \frac{\$86,000}{.152} = \$565,790$$
Capitalization rate

It is easy to capitalize the income stream using any proportion of leverage the buyer considers reasonable. For example, if a buyer believed that only 40 percent of the purchase price could be financed with debt, with the same costs of the debt and equity components of the capital structure, he could calculate the capitalized value of the income stream as follows:

|  | Capitalization Rate | | Proportion | |
|---|---|---|---|---|
| Debt | .12 | × | .40 | = .048 |
| Equity | .20 | × | .60 | = .120 |
| Weighted Average Capitalization Rate | | | | .168 |

$$\text{Pretax income (from Exhibit 6–3)} \quad \frac{\$86,000}{.168} = \$511,905$$
Capitalization rate

As can be seen in the example above, an increase of 1.6 percent in the assumed weighted average capitalization rate makes a difference of over $50,000 in the amount that the buyer would be willing to pay. The lesson should be clear. As the cost of capital goes up, the values of existing businesses come down, and vice versa. To the extent that low-cost debt financing is available to a buyer to finance a purchase, the weighted average cost of capital for that buyer is lower than it would be if such financing were less available or not available at all. As economic conditions change, the cost and availability of financing changes. These changes have an important impact on the values of businesses.

# Chapter 12

## The Excess Earnings Method

The *excess earnings method* of valuation actually is another version of a capitalized earnings approach. We devote a separate chapter to it because it is the most widely used and misused of all methods for valuing small businesses and professional practices.

It is widely written about, and more than half the business and professional practice brokers that I know use some version of it. It is widely used by courts in divorce proceedings for determining the value of goodwill in professional practices. Yet the Internal Revenue Service, which spawned the method back in 1920, now roundly denounces it.

# History of the Excess Earnings Method

The excess earnings method is sometimes called the *Treasury Method* because the method originally appeared in a 1920 publication by the U.S. Treasury Department, ARM 34, which stood for Appeals and Review Memorandum Number 34. It was adopted to compute the value of goodwill that breweries and distilleries lost because of prohibition.

Since then, both taxpayers and IRS agents have widely used (and misused) it in connection with valuations of businesses for gift and estate taxes. Also, perhaps partly because of its wide publicity and partly because its apparently simplistic nature is appealing, it has been widely adopted in one form or another for pricing small businesses and professional practices.

In 1968, the Internal Revenue Service updated and restated the ARM 34 method, with the publication of Revenue Ruling 68–609, which is reproduced here as Exhibit 12–1. Revenue Ruling 68–609 is still in effect.

### Exhibit 12–1

REVENUE ruling 68–609 (formula method)

The "formula" approach may be used in determining the fair market value of intangible assets of a business only if there is no better basis available for making the determination; A.R.M. 34, A.R.M. 68, O.D. 937, and Revenue Ruling 65-192 superseded. (1968-2, C.B., 327).

#### REVENUE RULING 68-609

The purpose of this Revenue Ruling is to update and restate, under the current statute and regulations, the currently outstanding portions of A.R.M. 34, C.B. 2, 31 (1920), A.R.M. 68, C.B. 3,43 (1920), and O.D. 937, C.B. 4, 43 (1921).

The question presented is whether the "formula" approach, the capitalization of earnings in excess of a fair rate of return on net tangible assets, may be used to determine the fair market value of the intangible assets of a business.

The "formula" approach may be stated as follows:

A percentage return on the average annual value of the tangible assets used in a business is determined, using a period of years (preferably not less than five) immediately prior to the valuation date. The amount of the percentage return on tangible assets, thus determined, is deducted from the average earnings of the business for such period and the remainder, if any, is considered to be the amount of the average annual earnings from the intangible assets of the business for the period. This amount (considered as the average annual earnings from intangibles), capitalized at a percentage of, say 15 to 20 percent, is the value of the intangible assets of the business determined under the "formula" approach.

Exhibit 12–1 (*concluded*)

The percentage of return on the average annual value of the tangible assets used should be the percentage prevailing in the industry involved at the date of valuation, or (when the industry percentage is not available) a percentage of 8 to 10 percent may be used.

The 8 percent rate of return and the 15 percent rate of capitalization are applied to tangibles and intangibles, respectively, of businesses with a small risk factor and stable and regular earnings; the 10 percent rate of return and 20 percent rate of capitalization are applied to businesses in which the hazards of business are relatively high.

The above rates are used as examples and are not appropriate in all cases. In applying the "formula" approach, the average earnings period and the capitalization rates are dependent upon the facts pertinent thereto in each case.

The past earnings to which the formula is applied should fairly reflect the probable future earnings. Ordinarily, the period should not be less than five years, and abnormal years, whether above or below the average, should be eliminated. If the business is a sole proprietorship or partnership, there should be deducted from the earnings of the business a reasonable amount for services performed by the owner or partners engaged in the business. See **Lloyd B. Sanderson Estate v. Commissioner,** 42 F 2d 160 (1930). Further, only the tangible assets entering into net worth, including accounts and bills receivable in excess of accounts and bills payable, are used for determining earnings on the tangible assets. Factors that influence the capitalization rate include (1) the nature of the business, (2) the risk involved, and (3) the stability or irregularity of earnings.

The "formula" approach should not be used if there is better evidence available from which the value of intangibles can be determined. If the assets of a going business are sold upon the basis of a rate of capitalization that can be substantiated as being realistic, though it is not within the range of figures indicated here as the ones ordinarily to be adopted, the same rate of capitalization should be used in determining the value of the intangibles.

Accordingly, the "formula" approach may be used for determining the fair market value of intangible assets of a business only if there is no better basis therefor available.

See also Revenue Ruling 59-60, C.B. 1959-1, 237, as modified by Revenue Ruling 65-193, C.B. 1965-2, 370, which sets forth the proper approach to use in the valuation of closely-held corporate stocks for estate and gift tax purposes. The general approach, methods, and factors, outlined in Revenue Ruling 59-60, as modified, are equally applicable to valuations of corporate stocks for income and other tax purposes as well as for estate and gift tax purposes. They apply also to problems involving the determination of the fair market value of business interests of any type, including partnerships and proprietorships, and of intangible assets for all tax purposes.

A.R.M. 34, A.R.M. 68, and O.D. 937 are superseded, since the positions set forth therein are restated to the extent applicable under current law in this Revenue Ruling. Revenue Ruling 65-192, C.B. 1965-2, 259, which contained restatements of A.R.M. 34 and A.R.M. 68, is also superseded.

Source: 1968-2, C.B. 327.

# How It Works

## A Step-by-Step Explanation

The steps in the excess earnings method can be summarized as follows:

1. Determine a net tangible asset value, as in Chapter 5. (Note that this value is for net tangible assets only and would not include intangible items such as leaseholds, patents, copyrights, and so on.)
2. Determine a normalized level of earnings, as in Chapter 6.
3. Determine an appropriate percentage rate of return, or, in the parlance of this book, a capitalization rate on the net tangible asset value. Multiply the net tangible asset value from Step 1 by that rate to determine the amount of earnings attributable to the tangible assets. Subtract that amount from the normalized earnings developed in Step 2. The result of this step is called the *excess earnings*, that is, the amount of earnings above a fair return on the net tangible asset value.
4. Determine an appropriate capitalization rate to apply to the excess

earnings, which are presumably the earnings attributable to good-will or other intangible assets, as opposed to tangible assets. Capitalize the excess earnings at that rate.

**5.** Add the values from Steps 1 and 4.[1]

# An Example

Let's suppose that Flora's Flower Shop has a net tangible asset value of $20,000. Let's also suppose that, after allowance for a reasonable salary for Flora, the shop earns about $8,000 per year. For the purpose of this example, we will use a rate of return of 15 percent on the tangible assets, and will capitalize the excess earnings at 33 1/3 percent. (The matter of determining applicable rates is discussed later in the chapter.) In this scenario, the value of Flora's Flower Shop would be computed as follows:

| | | |
|---|---|---|
| Net Tangible Asset Value | | $20,000 |
| Normalized Earnings | $8,000 | |
| Earnings Attributable to Tangible Assets ($20,000 x .15) = | 3,000 | |
| "Excess" Earnings | $5,000 | |
| Value of Excess Earnings ($5,000 ÷ .333) = | | 15,000 |
| Total Value | | $35,000 |

# A Popular Version

Exhibit 12–2 is typical of the summaries of the excess earnings method in popular usage. The text accompanying the formula offers the following comments:

> The buyer looks at the business for its ability to earn a fair return on investment, after deducting his or her salary. The present and future earning power of the business is of prime importance. If the business is not at least equal in earning power to an outside investment in a comparable business or in securities, the buyer usually will not be willing to pay more than the price of tangibles. In fact, the buyer may not want to buy the tangible assets—even at bargain prices—if the business is not profitable. . . .
>
> Goodwill can be thought of as the difference between an established successful business and one that has yet to establish itself and achieve success. The price the buyer should be willing to pay for goodwill depends on the earning power and potential of the business.
>
> The price the seller should be content with is the amount considered as compensation for the transfer of intangible values and for the surrender of the expected earning power of the business. The seller should base the value of goodwill on the actual condition and earning power of the business. If past efforts and capital were used effectively, the current earning power of the business should be above average. If earnings are

---

[1] As an alternative to using the present net tangible asset value and normalized earnings, some appraisers base the computations of the value of excess earnings on average net tangible assets and average earnings for some period of time, usually five years. This procedure is satisfactory if the period used is representative of reasonable future expectations. If this procedure is used, the value of excess earnings still is added to the present net tangible asset value to arrive at the value for the total entity.

Exhibit 12-2
A Popular Version of the Excess Earnings Method

| The Pricing Formula | Example: | Business A | Business B |
|---|---|---|---|
| **Step 1.** Determine the adjusted tangible net worth of the business. (The total market value of all current and long-term assets less liabilities.) | **1.** Adjusted value of tangible net worth (assets less liabilities). | $100,000 | $100,000 |
| **Step 2.** Estimate how much the buyer could earn annually with an amount equal to the value of the tangible net worth invested elsewhere. | **2.** Earning power at 10%* of an amount equal to the adjusted tangible net worth, if invested in a comparable risk business. | 10,000 | 10,000 |
| **Step 3.** Add to this a salary normal for an owner-operator of the business. This combined figure provides a reasonable estimate of the income the buyer can earn elsewhere with the investment and effort involved in working in the business. | **3.** Reasonable salary for owner-operator in the business. | 18,000 | 18,000 |
| **Step 4.** Determine the average annual net earnings of the business (net profit before subtracting owner's salary) over the past few years.<br><br>This is before income taxes, to make it comparable with earnings from other sources or by individuals in different tax brackets. (The tax implications of alternate investments should be carefully considered.)<br><br>The trend of earnings is a key factor. Have they been rising steadily, falling steadily, remaining constant, or fluctuating widely? The earnings figure should be adjusted to reflect these trends. | **4.** Net earnings of the business over recent years (net profit before subtracting owner's salary). | 30,000 | 23,350 |
| **Step 5.** Subtract the total of earning power (2) and reasonable salary (3) from this average net earnings figure (4). This gives the extra earning power of the business. | **5.** Extra earning power of the business (line 4 minus lines 2 and 3). | 2,000 | (4,650) |
| **Step 6.** Use this extra, or excess, earning figure to estimate the value of the intangibles. This is done by multiplying the extra earnings by what is termed the "years-of-profit" figure.<br><br>This "years-of-profit" multiplier pivots on these points. How unique are the intangibles offered by the firm? How long would it take to set up a similar business and bring it to this stage of development? What expenses and risks would be involved? What is the price of goodwill in similar firms? Will the seller be signing an agreement with a covenant not to compete?<br><br>If the business is well established, a factor of five or more might be used, especially if the firm has a valuable name, patent, or location. A multiplier of three might be reasonable for a moderately seasoned firm. A younger, but profitable, firm might merely have a one-year profit figure. | **6.** Value of intangibles —using three-year profit figure for moderately well-established firm (3 times line 5). | 6,000 | None |
| **Step 7.** Final Price equals Adjusted Tangible Net Worth plus Value of Intangibles. (Extra Earnings times "Years of Profit.") | **7.** Final price (lines 1 and 6). | $106,000 | $100,000 (or less) |

**In example A,** the seller receives a value for goodwill because the business is moderately well established and earning more than the buyer could earn elsewhere with similar risks and effort. Within three years, the buyer should have recovered the amount paid for goodwill in this example.

**In example B,** the seller receives no value for goodwill because the business, even though it may have existed for a considerable time, is not earning as much as the buyer could through outside investment and effort. In fact, the buyer may feel that even an investment of $100,000—the current appraised value of net assets—is too much because it cannot earn sufficient return.

* *This is an arbitrary figure, used for illustration. A reasonable figure depends on the stability and relative risks of the business and the investment picture generally. The rate of return should be similar to that which could be earned elsewhere with the same approximate risk.*

Source: Reprinted with permission from Bank of America, NT&SA, "How to Buy or Sell a Business," *Small Business Reporter*, copyright 1982.

low, the buyer probably will resist paying any amount for intangibles.
. . .

Because each business and sales transaction is different, the formula should be used only to indicate some of the major considerations in pricing a business.[2]

# Denunciation by the IRS

The IRS Appellate Conferee Valuation Training Program uses colorful language to denounce the use of ARM 34 or the excess earnings method of valuation. Following are some pertinent excerpts:

---

[2] *How to Buy or Sell a Business*, Small Business Reporter series (San Francisco: Bank of America, 1982), p. 8.

One of the most frequently encountered errors in appraisal is the use of a formula to determine a question of fact, which on a reasonable basis must be resolved in view of all pertinent circumstances. . . . ARM 34 has been applied indiscriminately by tax practitioners and by members of the Internal Revenue Service since it was published. On occasion the Tax Court has recognized ARM 34 as a means of arriving at a fair market value. The latest and most controlling decisions on valuation, however, relegate the use of a formula to a position of being a last resort. ARM 34 was published in 1920, but since that time it has continually appeared in the annals of tax valuation and resulted in many improper appraisals.

By such a formula the same value would be found in 1960 as in 1933, although values per dollar of earnings actually were very different in those two years. The basic defect is apparent; the rates of return which are applied to tangibles and to intangibles are completely arbitrary and have no foundation in fact. . . .

The 8 percent rate, or any other arbitrary rate of earnings as a normal return on tangible assets, cannot be demonstrated to have a reasonable basis. Similarly, the 15 percent rate or any specific rate on intangible assets is not in itself a supportable figure. If there were a somewhat comparable business which had earned $50,000 per year as an average for five years and which had been sold for $400,000 cash it could be said that there was a 12½ percent indicated rate of return on total investment but no one could ascertain what has been the rates of return on the tangible and intangible assets. All that can be said for ARM 34, or a similar formula method of capitalization using two rates of interest, is that you hope to get a good answer based upon two bad guesses. It is difficult enough to get one reasonably accurate rate of capitalization using normal appraisal methods. . . . To get two fairly accurate rates, one for tangibles and the other for intangibles, other than by the use of pure guesswork, is impossible. . . .

Any capitalization of earnings must take into consideration the economic conditions prevailing at the specific date of appraisal, including those conditions controlling in the industry in this particular company's area, and even in the national economy.

If we assume that a fair rate of return for this type of business is 8 percent, the better procedure is to capitalize a representative earnings figure (in this instance 1953 income) at that rate. To attempt to segregate value based on earnings as between normal income and that induced by whatever goodwill or other intangible assets the business may possess, is to aspire to a higher degree of clairvoyance than has yet been demonstrated as obtainable by mere man.[3]

# Analysis of the Method

A method that has been so thoroughly denounced by its own promulgators, and yet is one of the most widely used methods in existence today, certainly deserves some analysis.

First of all, the Treasury Department did not initiate the method to value the total entity by the method, but specifically to value the good-

---

[3] U.S. Internal Revenue Service. *IRS Apellate Conferee Valuation Training Program*. Chicago: Commerce Clearing House, 1978, pp. 82–86. The section was repeated with no substantive changes in the 1980 revision.

will or other intangible value, if any, above the tangible asset values. However, since it seems logical that any intangible value identified by the method must be added to tangible value to get a total value, the method has attained popularity for valuing the total entity.

# Appropriate Rate of Return on Tangible Assets

No one has totally and convincingly refuted the position stated by the IRS that any arbitrary rate of earnings as a normal return on tangible assets cannot be demonstrated to have a reasonable basis. Nevertheless, there are some ways to look at the problem of determining a fair rate of return on tangible assets that could be helpful. For one thing, commercial bank loan officers tend to look at the value of tangible assets as collateral in determining how much they will lend. Therefore, the asset values that can be used as collateral have a bearing on the company's cost of capital, because they influence how much capital will be available at bank loan rates. Since banks usually will not make loans to 100 percent of the assets used as collateral, and since there are some costs to bank borrowing that are in addition to the basic interest rate, it is reasonable to suggest that businesses need to earn a rate of return on their investment in tangible assets that is at least a few points above the rate at which bank loan money is available to them.

# Appropriate Capitalization Rate for Excess Earnings

Tangible assets provide at least a modicum of safety in that, if earnings fail to materialize as expected, the assets usually can be liquidated for something. Goodwill, on the other hand, (as well as most other intangible assets) has no liquidation value in the absence of earnings, since its very value depends on its ability to generate earnings. Therefore, the risk attached to the intangible portion of the assets would seem to be greater and demand a higher rate of return.

Furthermore, a good case can be made that the tangible assets have a much more persistent and predictable life than goodwill or other intangible assets in many, if not most, cases. Despite the IRS fiction that purchased goodwill cannot be amortized because its value does not diminish, in most cases goodwill values do diminish over time, and the rate of diminution in value is often much greater than the rate of economic depreciation of tangible assets.[4] One might say that goodwill, if not nourished, will perish. In general, investors are not willing to pay

---

[4] For an interesting discussion of the diminution of the value of goodwill, see Jerald H. Udinsky, "Goodwill Depreciation: A New Method for Valuing Professional Practices in a Marital Dissolution," *Community Property Journal*, Fall 1982, pp. 307–22.

cash up front for more than one to five years' worth of earnings from commercial goodwill, implying a range of capitalization rates from 20 percent to 100 percent to be applied to such earnings, depending on the perceived persistence of those earnings in the future, independent of further investment of time and effort to perpetuate them.

## Summary: Conceptual Basis for the Two Capitalization Rates

In light of the foregoing discussion, it is reasonable, conceptually, to determine appropriate capitalization rates to apply to earnings generated both from a base of tangible assets and from intangible factors over and above an acceptable return on the investment in tangible assets. The conceptual basis is that the difference in the cost of capital depends on the presence or lack of tangible assets. Generally, the greater the value of the tangible assets the buyer receives for his investment, the less risky the buyer perceives the investment to be, thus the lower his required rate of return. Furthermore, the assets support borrowing, thus reducing the weighted average cost of capital.

I suggest, therefore, that the rate to be applied as a return on tangibles be a weighted average of the cost of borrowing and the cost of equity. The weighting logically would depend on what percentage of the assets could be financed by borrowing.

I suggest that the capitalization rate for the excess earnings be at the high end of a range of reasonable required rates of return on equity, because the risk would be perceived to be greater with no tangible asset backing. The determination of the rate in each case should depend on the expected duration and the perceived risk of the excess earnings. The capitalization rates applied to current earnings can be adjusted to reflect how much the earnings stream is expected to grow as a result of the forces in place, as discussed in Chapter 10.

# Negative Goodwill

The excess earnings method deals with how to value the earnings, if any, over and above a reasonable rate of return on the tangible assets. What if the earning power is less than a reasonable rate of return on the tangible assets? Such a circumstance could indicate negative goodwill; it could be an indication that the value of the total entity would be less than the value of its tangible assets (on a replacement value basis, as discussed in Chapter 5).

In such a situation, earnings are insufficient to justify buying the business on the basis of the replacement value of its assets, and the lower value indicated by the capitalized earnings should predominate over the adjusted tangible asset value as developed in Chapter 5. Should the value indicated by the earning power fall below the liquidation value of the assets, one could conclude that the business would be worth more dead than alive, and liquidation would be a rational economic choice.

# Common Errors in Applying the Excess Earnings Method

The excess earnings method is widely misused in valuing small businesses and professional practices. Some of the errors most commonly encountered are discussed in the following sections.

## Failure to Allow for Owner's Salary

As noted in Revenue Ruling 68–609 (Exhibit 12–1), "If the business is a sole proprietorship or partnership, there should be deducted from the earnings of the business a reasonable amount for services performed by the owner or partners engaged in the business." This point is also covered in Chapter 6.

I have often seen valuations done by the excess earnings method that did not include a reasonable allowance for compensation to the owner or owners for services performed. This error results in an overstatement of the true economic earnings, which in turn leads to an overstatement of the value of the business.

## Failure to Use Realistic Normalized Earnings

To the extent that the method is valid, it depends on a reasonable estimate of normalized earnings, developed as discussed in Chapter 6. As noted in Revenue Ruling 68–609, "The past earnings to which the formula is applied should fairly reflect the probable future earnings."

I frequently have seen the method applied blindly to the latest year's earnings, or to some simple or weighted average of recent years' earnings, without regard to whether or not the earnings base used reflects fairly the probable future earnings. Such completely uninformed use of some historical earnings base usually results in an undervaluation or overvaluation.

## Using Book Values of Assets without Adjustment

As noted in Chapter 2, book value is something of a misnomer, since it is not a value at all, but rather an accounting term meaning the dollar amount at which the item is carried on the company's financial records. The book value of assets usually represents the cost of assets less any depreciation recorded for financial accounting and/or tax purposes. The longer the company has held the assets, the less likely it is that their book value will be a reasonable approximation of any kind of economic value, such as replacement or liquidation value.

Net tangible asset value used in the excess earnings approach should reflect an informed judgment about the value of the tangible assets, as discussed in Chapter 5. Understatement of the value of the tangible assets results in a high capitalization rate being applied to too large a portion of the total earnings, which leads to an undervaluation of the total entity, or vice versa if the tangible asset value is overstated.

# Errors in Choosing Appropriate Rates

The choice of the two capitalization rates is critical to the validity of the result of the excess earnings method. A conceptual approach to the determination of the rates to use was suggested in an earlier section. However, there is one clearly erroneous practice that recurs in the selection of the rates. That error is using the rates suggested in the Ruling itself.

The Ruling, written in 1968, suggests rates of 8 to 10 percent on tangible assets, with 15 to 20 percent applied to the excess earnings. However, the Ruling states that "The percentage of return . . . should be the percentage prevailing in the industry involved at the date of the valuation. . . . The above rates are used as examples and are not appropriate in all cases. . . . The capitalization rates are dependent upon the facts pertinent thereto in each case."[5]

Both the wording of the Ruling and common sense indicate that the specific rates mentioned in the Ruling are examples, and the actual rates to use depend on the facts at the time. In spite of that, even in 1985, we find people using the rates for the excess earnings method suggested in 1968, when prevailing rates were much lower. Using capitalization rates that are too low inevitably results in overstating of the value of the entity.

The average yield on long-term government bonds in 1968 was about 5 percent, and in 1985 it was about 12 percent. If we do no more than use this seven-point differential as a guide to updating the rates suggested in the Ruling, the indicated range would be 15 to 17 percent return on tangible assets, and a 22 to 27 capitalization rate for excess earnings under 1985 conditions. These rates are at least somewhere within the realm of reasonableness.

---

[5] Revenue Ruling 68–609, 1968-2 C.B. 327.

# Chapter 13

## The Discounted Future Earnings Method

*The valuation of an ongoing business is the present worth of the future stream of net income.*[1]

*The real value of any going business is its future earnings power. Accordingly, the discounted cash flow approach, more than any other, determines the true value of your business.*[2]

This chapter is short, because the discounted future earnings (DFE) method and its close variant, the discounted cash flow (DCF) method, are not often used in the valuation of small businesses and professional practices. They are used more often in the valuation of medium-sized and large businesses. Nevertheless, in spite of their practical difficulties, they are conceptually excellent methods and at least deserve to be discussed here.[3]

# Pros and Cons of the Discounted Future Earnings Method

The discounted future earnings (DFE) method of valuation is based on the almost universally accepted theory that the value of the business depends on the future benefits it will produce (denominated in terms of earnings or cash flow), discounted back to a present value at some appropriate discount (capitalization) rate. This method is another version of a capitalized earnings approach, in this case relying on specific projections of earnings (or cash flow) for several years into the future.

The method is not used widely in the valuation of small businesses and professional practices, partly because it requires projections of earnings or cash flow for several years into the future. Many owners or prospective buyers of small businesses and professional practices would consider such projections too speculative to be useful.

Another reason why the method is not used more in small businesses and professional practices is that what will happen in the future is more a function of the personal efforts of the owner/operator than of forces that will carry forward with the business itself, independent of the owner's personal contributions. Consequently, buyers are naturally reluctant to include in the present value any future benefits that really depend on their own efforts rather than automatically resulting from forces already in place.

A buyer may, however, wish to do a discounted future earnings exercise for his own analysis. There certainly are some small business and professional practice valuations to which the discounted future earnings method of valuation would apply; those would be businesses and practices whose earnings could be predicted with enough reliability

---

[1] Walter Jurek, *How to Determine the Value of a Business* (Stow, Ohio: Quality Services, Inc., 1977), p. 28.

[2] Thomas J. Martin, and Mark R. Gustafson, *Valuing Your Business* (New York: Holt, Rinehart & Winston, 1980), p. 14.

[3] For a more complete exposition of the discounted future earnings method, see Chapter 4 in Pratt, *Valuing a Business*.

to make the exercise useful and whose earnings result largely from forces already in place.

# The Discounted Future Earnings (Discounted Cash Flow) Formula

The basic formula for valuing an entity by the DFE method is as follows:

$$PV = \sum \frac{E_i}{(1 + r)^i}$$

Where:

$PV$ = Present value of the entity
$E_i$ = Earnings in the $i^{\text{th}}$ year
$r$ = Discount rate (required rate of return or capitalization rate)

# Quantifying the Variables

There are only two variables that need to be quantified:

1. The expected earnings for each future year.
2. The applicable capitalization rate by which to discount those projected future earnings back to a present value.

## Projecting the Future Earnings

Projecting the earnings is really a matter of carrying out for several years the adjusted income statement exercises discussed in Chapter 6 and Chapter 9. The projection can be done either on the basis of earnings available to equity or earnings available to overall investment (including borrowed funds as well as equity).

There is no *right* answer to the question of how far into the future one should try to carry the earnings projections. Theoretically, the further the better. As a practical matter, for most small operations, it is not possible to project earnings very far before the projections become so unreliable that they are useless. The best guidance I can offer is that the appraiser should project as many years into the future as he has a realistic basis for predicting. At the end of that period, it might be reasonable to assume either some constant growth rate or a given level of sustainable earnings, either for a limited period or into infinity.

One question that frequently arises is whether the projections should be done on the basis of constant dollars (1986 dollars, for example, if the projection is being done in 1986), or whether an estimate of the effects of inflation should be included in the projected earnings figures. The answer is that the projection can be based on either assumption, but the choice of constant or inflation-adjusted dollars affects the choice of capitalization rate, as discussed in the next section.

## Selecting the Discount Rate

The appropriate discount rate to use in the denominator is the rate of return that the market requires for comparable investments, as discussed in Chapter 10. If the future earnings projection is the earnings available to equity, then use the capitalization rate that applies to an equity investment. If the projection is for the earnings available to a total investment that includes borrowed funds, then a capitalization rate applicable to the overall investment (weighted average cost of capital) should be used.

Recall that Chapter 10 pointed out that one component of the capitalization rate is inflation, which is intended to compensate the investor for the decreased buying power of future dollars, when he receives them. If the earnings projections are in dollars that include the effects of inflation, then a capitalization rate that includes the inflation component (as developed in Chapter 10) should be used as the discount rate. If the earnings projections are in constant dollars, then the inflation component should be subtracted out of the total required rate of return to arrive at the appropriate capitalization rate. Economic forecasts available from banks or government agencies can be used to obtain a consensus forecast of the long-term inflation rate.

## An Example

Ace Widget Company has developed an outstanding patented widget, and its market acceptance has grown steadily over the last few years. The market potential for continued growth in sales and earnings seems assured, but Ace himself has decided to sell out and seek new challenges.

We carefully prepared a set of pro forma adjusted income statements for the next five years (prepared in accordance with Chapters 6 and 9), which indicate the following projected earnings:

| Year 1 | Year 2 | Year 3 | Year 4 | Year 5 |
|--------|--------|--------|--------|--------|
| $20,000 | $30,000 | $40,000 | $50,000 | $60,000 |

For years 6 and beyond, it appears that the market will have reached saturation and that earnings will level off at around $65,000 per year.

We have great confidence in the future of Ace's widgets. We have decided that it would be worthwhile for us to buy the business from Ace at a price that would provide us a rate of return on our investment of 20 percent or more (our estimate of our weighted average cost of capital developed in accordance with Chapter 10).

Using the discounted future earnings formula presented earlier, the present value of the earnings for the first five years can be computed as follows:

$$\frac{\$20{,}000}{(1 + .20)} + \frac{\$30{,}000}{(1 + .20)^2} + \frac{\$40{,}000}{(1 + .20)^3} + \frac{\$50{,}000}{(1 + .20)^4} + \frac{\$60{,}000}{(1 + .20)^5}$$

At the end of five years, we project a business whose earnings are $65,000 per year. If we capitalize $65,000 per year at 20 percent, the value of that projected earnings stream starting at the end of the fifth year can be computed as follows:

$$\frac{\$65{,}000}{.20} = \$325{,}000$$

However, that value is five years away and has to be discounted back to a present value. The present value of the earnings stream starting five years from now can be computed as follows:

$$\frac{\$325{,}000}{(1 + .20)^5}$$

Putting the whole thing together, we can compute the value of Ace Widget Company as follows:

$$\frac{\$20{,}000}{(1 + .20)} + \frac{\$30{,}000}{(1 + .20)^2} + \frac{\$40{,}000}{(1 + .20)^3} + \frac{\$50{,}000}{(1 + .20)^4} + \frac{\$60{,}000}{(1 + .20)^5} + \frac{(\$60{,}000 \div .20)}{(1 + .20)^5}$$

$$= \$16{,}667 + \$20{,}833 + \$23{,}148 + \$24{,}113 + \$24{,}113 + \$130{,}610$$

$$= \$239{,}484 \text{ (or } \$240{,}000, \text{ rounded)}$$

On the basis of this analysis, we would decide to purchase Ace Widget if we can negotiate a deal with Ace at less than $240,000, cash or cash equivalent. (As we will see in Chapter 17, we can afford to pay Ace as much as $300,000 or more, if he is willing to take a substantial portion of it in a long-term contract at a low interest rate; but that is another story.)

The calculations above can be done using present value tables, or they may be done easily on an inexpensive pocket calculator such as the Texas Instruments Business Analyst II. For example, computing the present value of $325,000 five years from now, discounted at 20 percent compounded annually, simply requires putting the TI II in the *finance* mode and entering the following:

$$
\begin{array}{rl}
325{,}000 & FV \\
5 & N \\
20 & \%i \\
& 2^{nd} \\
& PV
\end{array}
$$

The answer should show as $130,610.

Values calculated by the DFE method can cover a wide range, depending on the earnings projections used and the discount rate selected. Exhibit 13–1 shows how the indicated value can vary using pessimistic, most likely, and optimistic earnings forecasts, and varying the discount rate from 16 to 24 percent. By varying the earnings forecasts up or down by 20 percent, and the discount rates up or down by 4 percent,

Exhibit 13–1

## PRESENT VALUE OF ACE WIDGET COMPANY
## BY THE DISCOUNTED FUTURE EARNINGS METHOD

### OPTIMISTIC EARNINGS FORECAST

| Year | Projected Earnings | Present Value Discounted at | | | | |
|---|---|---|---|---|---|---|
| | | 16% | 18% | 20% | 22% | 24% |
| 1 | $24,000 | $ 20,690 | $ 20,339 | $ 20,000 | $ 19,672 | $ 19,355 |
| 2 | 36,000 | 26,754 | 25,855 | 25,000 | 24,187 | 23,413 |
| 3 | 48,000 | 30,752 | 29,214 | 27,778 | 26,434 | 25,175 |
| 4 | 60,000 | 33,137 | 30,947 | 28,935 | 27,084 | 25,378 |
| 5 | 72,000 | 34,280 | 31,472 | 28,935 | 26,640 | 24,560 |
| 6 on | 78,000 | 232,105 | 189,414 | 156,732 | 131,182 | 110,860 |
| Total Value | | $377,718 | $327,241 | $287,380 | $255,199 | $228,741 |

### MOST LIKELY EARNINGS FORECAST

| Year | Projected Earnings | Present Value Discounted at | | | | |
|---|---|---|---|---|---|---|
| | | 16% | 18% | 20% | 22% | 24% |
| 1 | $20,000 | $ 17,241 | $ 16,949 | $ 16,667 | $ 16,393 | $ 16,129 |
| 2 | 30,000 | 22,295 | 21,546 | 20,833 | 20,156 | 19,511 |
| 3 | 40,000 | 25,626 | 24,345 | 23,148 | 22,028 | 20,979 |
| 4 | 50,000 | 27,615 | 25,789 | 24,113 | 22,570 | 21,149 |
| 5 | 60,000 | 28,567 | 26,227 | 24,113 | 22,200 | 20,466 |
| 6 on | 65,000 | 193,421 | 157,845 | 130,610 | 109,318 | 92,383 |
| Total Value | | $314,765 | $272,701 | $239,484 | $212,665 | $190,617 |

### PESSIMISTIC EARNINGS FORECAST

| Year | Projected Earnings | Present Value Discounted at | | | | |
|---|---|---|---|---|---|---|
| | | 16% | 18% | 20% | 22% | 24% |
| 1 | $16,000 | $ 13,793 | $ 13,559 | $ 13,333 | $ 13,115 | $ 12,903 |
| 2 | 24,000 | 17,836 | 17,236 | 16,667 | 16,125 | 15,609 |
| 3 | 32,000 | 20,501 | 19,476 | 18,519 | 17,623 | 16,784 |
| 4 | 40,000 | 22,092 | 20,632 | 19,290 | 18,056 | 16,919 |
| 5 | 48,000 | 22,853 | 20,981 | 19,290 | 17,760 | 16,373 |
| 6 on | 52,000 | 154,737 | 126,276 | 104,488 | 87,454 | 73,907 |
| Total Value | | $251,812 | $218,160 | $191,587 | $170,133 | $152,495 |

we get a range of values from a high of $380,000 to a low of $150,000, a differential of well over 2 to 1 on the indicated value of the business.

No wonder different people can have wide disagreements about the value of any particular business!

Exhibit 13–2 is an excellent article presenting a real-life example of pricing a small business by the discounted cash flow method.

Exhibit 13–2

# How Much Is Your Business Worth?

**Whether you're a seller, buyer or investor, you need to know how to calculate the value of a business.**

## Glen Cooper

As a business broker, I'm frequently asked to estimate the dollar value of a business at my first meeting with the seller. While I do have an abbreviated method for arriving at a range of values which I'll explain, there are a few concepts that need to be understood.

**1. Rules of Thumb Are Dumb.**

The conventional rules you will hear in a particular industry sound sensible, but they're greatly oversimplified. If I tell you that your business is worth "three times net," it really doesn't mean much if you've structured it to have a low, or even negative, reported net income. And if you're not running your business that way, you're . . . well, unusual.

Most owners have recorded figures which understate the volume and profitability of their business in ways which are unique to them. This makes multipliers, ratios and rules of thumb highly unreliable for valuing these businesses.

**2. Only Future Benefits Create Value.**

The value of a business is based on the value of *believable* future projections of earnings or other benefits. Most buyers want to buy themselves a job and a future.

A business is a money machine which sometimes generates other benefits. The first benefit is a full time job and desired lifestyle; the second is often no more than a vague notion that the future of the business is bright. A smart seller will help the prospective buyer envision both *job* and *future,* while avoiding undue emphasis on the past and showing the prospect how to quantify "return on labor" and "return on investment." The value will depend upon how the buyer will quantify these future benefits and calculate their present value.

**3. Nobody Really Knows Exactly What Your Business Is Worth.**

Business valuation is not a science. At best, an appraisal is a rational exercise in estimating future values that reasonable people can agree upon. Even the most experienced appraiser makes a professional "guesstimate," usually qualified by many assumptions, some quite arbitrary. The reasonable value range can be very broad, so don't be intimidated by the experts.

**4. You Can Control the Process.**

You can set the tone of negotiations that will determine the ultimate price and terms. The valuation and sale is on a human scale you can handle if you try. But a word of caution: Don't try to "rip-off" the buyer. Overpricing beyond the limits of reason and common sense will result in a lengthy time on the market. Like other merchandise, it can become shopworn and decline sharply in value.

## So What's The Formula?

With the above concepts in mind, let's get into my "short formula" for arriving at a range of values. It's basically an abbreviated approach of the detailed method used for a full-scale appraisal.

Exhibit 13–2 (*continued*)

Step 1 Project Next Year

| Your Income Expenses | As Reported | As Adjusted* | As Projected† |
|---|---|---|---|
| Gross sales | $279,623 | $279,623 | $305,000 |
| | (100%) | (100%) | (100%) |
| (−) Cost of goods | 125,727 | 125,727 | 130,000 |
| | (45%) | (45%) | (43%) |
| (−) All expenses | 131,058 | 94,258 | 148,000 |
| | (47%) | (34%) | (48%) |
| (=) Pretax net | 22,838 | 59,638 | 27,000 |
| | (8%) | (21%) | (9%) |

* Adjust Expenses by subtracting your depreciation, interest and personal expenses. In measuring 'cash flow', depreciation is not an actual out-of-pocket expense; your interest and personal expenses will, most likely, be completely different for the new owner (who is now your prospective buyer).
† Project income and expenses for the new owner's first year. Close examination of the Cost of Goods, for example, might indicate that the industry average differs from your actual figures. In this case, you are then safe to go with industry averages if that is realistically attainable by the new owner.

*Expense projections need to include a fair market wage for the new owner's management responsibilities, as well as realistic reserves for replacement of worn out equipment and buildings.*

## Step 1. Project Next Year

Using the past as a guideline, develop an adjusted income and expense statement for your business for the next year. Estimate next year's gross sales, cost of goods (if appropriate), and operating expenses.

When it comes to depreciation, interest (debt service) and personal expenses charged to the business, estimate the figures that will be appropriate for the new owner. At this point, assume a cash sale for simplicity.

If there are new income or expense items that a prospective owner will encounter, use estimated figures for the new owner instead of your own figures. Budget a reasonable wage for the new owner, as well as realistic reserves for replacement of worn-out equipment and buildings. Remember, this future projection will have to be believable to a prospective buyer if it is to be used to arrive at an asking price for the business.

The result of this first step will be a new net profit before debt service and before income taxes. Since you have already included a budgeted wage rate for the new owner (a "return on labor"), the net operating income you have come up with will roughly represent the new owner's "return on investment" for the first year.

## Step 2. Project Future Years.

Project this net profit before debt service and taxes into the future at least five years.

Allow for changes in sales which can be defended as logical. Keep costs of goods and other expenses in line with sales. Check to see how closely these match those which are typical for your particular business, as well as for your type of industry. If you differ too much from your own historical pattern, or that of your general industry, be prepared to explain why.

In the first two steps, you can get as detailed as you like, if that really increases your accuracy. However, my experience is that precision is illusive. In many cases, errors made on the small items tend to offset each other. Concentrate on the larger items and trends.

The result of this second step should be a series of cash flows that a new owner could expect over the next five years, and beyond, as an "income stream" before debt service and taxes.

Exhibit 13–2 (*continued*)

Step 2 Your Projection of New Owner's Future Cash Flows

|  | Year 1 | Year 2 | Year 3 | Year 4 | Year 5 | Year 6+ |
|---|---|---|---|---|---|---|
| Gross sales* | $305,000 | $329,400 | $352,500 | $373,650 | $392,350 | |
|  | (100%) | (100%) | (100%) | (100%) | (100%) | |
| (−) Cost of goods† | 130,000 | 138,000 | 144,525 | 149,500 | 156,900 | |
|  | (43%) | (42%) | (41%) | (40%) | (40%) | |
| (−) All expenses‡ | 148,000 | 161,400 | 172,750 | 183,100 | 192,250 | |
|  | (48%) | (49%) | (49%) | (49%) | (49%) | |
| (=) Pretax cash flow | 27,000 | 30,000 | 35,225 | 41,050 | 43,200 | $45,000§ |
|  | (9%) | (9%) | (10%) | (11%) | (11%) | |

\* Gross sales in this example have been predicted to stabilize at a long-term growth rate of 5 percent annually.
† Cost of goods have been predicted as stabilizing at 40 percent, the industry average.
‡ Expenses have been predicted as stabilizing at 49 percent, the industry average.
§ Net pretax cash flow has been stabilized at $45,000 annually for years 6 and beyond for the sake of simplicity only. The actual effect of precise estimates beyond the sixth year, even if possible, would probably be minimal in their impact on present value. An alternative to this approach would be to assume a sixth year sale of the business to measure the owner's equity build-up, or the salvage value of the business.

## Step 3.   Discount to Present Cash Value.

Calculate the present value of these cash flows at various interest rates that you estimate might represent a reasonable rate of future "return on investment" for the buyer prospect you have in mind. This procedure is known as the "discounting" of future cash flows at an appropriate discount rate.

Just which rate of return is appropriate will vary. But, generally, unless there is a compelling reason why your business has an unusually attractive market position, *30 percent to 40 percent is a typically required discount rate for a service business in my area of the country, and a slightly lower rate applies to the manufacturing, wholesaling, and product distribution businesses.*

Using this discount rate to calculate the present value of cash flows on a

Step 3 Discount Future Cash Flows to a Present Value

|  |  | Discounted Present Values of Future Annual Cash Flows at 40 percent and 30 percent Desired Return on Investment* | |
|---|---|---|---|
| Net Pretax Annual Flows† |  | At 40% | At 30% |
| End of Year 1 | $27,000 | $19,286 | $20,769 |
| End of Year 2 | 30,000 | 15,306 | 17,751 |
| End of Year 3 | 35,225 | 12,837 | 16,033 |
| End of Year 4 | 41,050 | 10,686 | 14,373 |
| End of Year 5 | 43,200 | 8,032 | 11,635 |
| End of Year 6 | 45,000‡ | 14,941 | 31,076 |
| Value range for total investment | | $81,088 | $111,637 |
| (−) Less amount needed for working capital | | (15,000) | (15,000) |
| (=) Expected cash sales price range§ | | $66,088 | to $96,637 |

\* We find 30–40 percent projected before-tax return on cash invested to be a typically accepted range for small service businesses we sell.
† Net Pretax Annual Cash Flows were taken from Step 2.
‡ See footnote (4) of Step 2.
§ This is the amount of cash a buyer would reasonably pay for your business, assuming (1) agreement with your projections, including your budgeted salary for the owner/manager; and (2) that the buyer desired a predictable annual rate of return of between 30–40 percent on his cash invested as net pretax cash flow from the business. This range of value is arrived at by adding the present values of predictable future cash flows less the amount of cash needed for working capital.

Exhibit 13–2 (*continued*)

financial calculator is simple, if you know how. Or, there are special discount tables that you can buy in your local bookstore. But, if this is unfamiliar to you, then you will need to consult with someone who knows how.

The result is a present cash value range for your business. This cash value represents the total cash investment a buyer can afford to make, unless financing is available.

**Step 4.  Adjust to Terms Value.**

Almost all businesses are sold on terms. The buyer usually doesn't risk all of his/her own cash. Loans are typically available to leverage the buyer's personal funds.

Just like in a real estate purchase, the less of the buyer's cash that is needed, the better the value to the buyer, as long as the payments are affordable. The better the terms, or borrowing conditions, the higher the price the buyer can afford to pay.

To derive a "terms" value, estimate the maximum amount of financing that might be available for your business. You can either base this estimate upon the amount you know a bank would loan, or you might even want to estimate what you, as the seller, would be willing to loan. Whatever the source, calculate the annual debt service that this financing will require. Then, subtract this amount from each year's cash flow, as calculated in Step 2.

This will lower the present value of the cash flows as derived in Step 3. But, because the buyer is now using other people's money, the rate of return on the buyer's cash, as separated from the lender's cash, is usually increased. This increase in the rate of return on the buyer's cash investment is what allows the seller to raise the selling price and still provide the buyer with a fair return.

This is a process of working, and reworking, the numbers until the right balance is achieved. You can, in fact, come up with a different "terms" value for each set of assumed terms.

At this point, you may now be very close to the actual value of your business. At least, this derived value can be used as a starting point for any further refinements you choose to make. This four step process also offers an excellent and logical framework for negotiations with potential buyers.

## Refinements You Can Make

As with any formula, this one I have just outlined will prove to be too simple for some situations. Below are the areas of refinement that I normally have to consider when performing a thorough business appraisal.

**Separate Asset Valuation.**  An on-going business should not be valued by adding up separate asset values. But, the formula above assumes that all current assets owned by the business are needed in the business, which is not always a good assumption.

If there are extra assets (like extra real estate or equipment) which are not needed to produce the predicted cash flows, the value of these extra assets would have to be added to the final value estimate, on the theory that they can be sold separately. By the same token, we would have to subtract from the final value estimate the cost of items which would be needed to produce the predicted future cash flows, but which are not now present in the business, unless purchase of these need items has been considered in the reserves for replacement. The only other reasons assets need to be valued are for financing and tax allocation purposes.

**Different Rate of Return Measures.**  People measure rates of return in different ways. Even people who measure it the same way have different ideas on its appropriate level and use.

Exhibit 13–2 (*continued*)

### Step 4 Adjust to 'Terms' Value

The "terms" you offer a buyer will dramatically affect the actual value of your business to the buyer. The more generous the terms of your financing arrangement, the more the buyer can leverage cash invested, the higher the price which can be justified.

To illustrate how the "terms" value can be significantly higher than the "cash" value, let's assume that the expected cash sales price range of between $66,000 and $97,000 is accurate. To get more, you decide to offer generous terms.

You, as seller, will agree to carry a $135,000 loan at 12 percent with a 15-year amortization, secured by business and personal assets of the buyer, as long as you can get $30,000 cash downpayment. This would result in a total purchase price of $165,000 ($135,000 loan plus $30,000 down), with monthly payments to you totaling $19,443 per year. So far, so good. But, is it reasonable for the buyer?

To test these terms, we have to subtract the new debt service from the predicted cash flows, and recalculate present values of these cash flows. We are looking to see if the buyer's cash investment that this plan calls for ($30,000 down with $15,000 in working capital) is within the range of the resulting present value totals. If this $45,000 cash needed is within the resulting range of present value totals, we will have a logical argument that the terms offered actually could increase the value of the business, making $165,000 within the resulting "terms" price range.

From the buyer's point of view, this new arrangement is justified, and may actually be better, even though the price is higher. Now, instead of up to $111,637 in cash, the buyer only needs $45,000 ($30,000 as a down payment and $15,000 as working capital) to buy the business at the "terms" price.

The chart indicates that the buyer can afford to purchase the business at a price which ranges from just over $155,000 to slightly more than $170,000, under the terms you might be willing to offer, yet still may yield between 30 percent and 40 percent before-tax return on cash invested.

| Net Pretax Annual Cash Flows (Assuming a $135,000 loan at 12 percent, payable monthly, for 15 years, with annual debt service at $19,443 per year.) | Discounted Present Values of Future Annual Cash Flows at 40 percent and 30 percent Desired Return on Investment (Terms value) | |
|---|---|---|
| | At 40 percent | At 30 percent |
| EOY 1    $27,000 (−) $19,443 (=) $7,557 | $5,398 | $5,813 |
| EOY 2    30,000 (−) $19,443 (=) 10,557 | 5,386 | 6,247 |
| EOY 3    35,225 (−) $19,443 (=) 15,782 | 5,751 | 7,183 |
| EOY 4    41,050 (−) $19,443 (=) 21,607 | 5,624 | 7,565 |
| EOY 5    43,200 (−) $19,443 (=) 23,757 | 4,417 | 6,398 |
| EOY 6+   45,000 (−) $19,443 (=) 25,557 | 8,486 | 17,649 |
| Value range for cash investment | $35,062 | $50,855 |
| (−) Less amount needed for working capital | (15,000) | (15,000) |
| (=) Justified cash down payment range | $20,062 | to $35,855 |
| (+) Proposed loan amount | 135,000 | 135,000 |
| (=) Expected "terms" sales price range | $155,062 | to $170,855 |

Exhibit 13–2 (*continued*)

*In the professional literature on the subject, most analysts assume that, in today's economy, we can achieve a 10 percent before-tax rate of return without significant risk. With a little more risk, but without the demands of management, we can often achieve a 15–20 percent rate. If that sounds reasonable to you, then chances are a 30–40 percent rate might seem logical as the basis for an investment in a small, closely held business. At least, that's what I see in the marketplace. Many buyers and sellers seem to end up in that range, even if they don't calculate it the same way.*

*Whatever the rate used, it should be applied in relationship to the cash required from the potential buyer, including the amount of working capital that needs to be tied up in the business. If it's going to be a cash purchase, then the full purchase price is added to the amount of working capital needed. If it's going to be a leveraged purchase, then only that amount of cash provided by the buyer is added to the working capital figure.*

**Tax Consequence Analysis.** The effects of tax laws governing tax credits, asset depreciation, and taxes due on the sale of a business are important, even though I believe their impact on small business values is overemphasized.

When a business is sold, the price must be allocated specifically to the assets being acquired. Whether it's a corporate stock sale, or an asset sale, the resulting tax consequences are almost always significant. Analyzing these consequences is usually a matter for your accountant, unless you are knowledgeable in this area. It is, however, a necessary area of refinement for a complete business appraisal. It is also something that must be worked out at the time of sale, and not later.

The complicated and ever-changing nature of tax laws, however, limits the real influence of tax consequences on values paid for small businesses. Despite the best efforts of business brokers and accountants to educate their clients in this area, tax analysis remains too complicated for most buyers and sellers to understand.

**Projecting Long-Term Cash Flows.** Instead of projecting a stable cash flow indefinitely into the future after the fifth year, as we have done above, we might estimate a salvage value or equity buildup. If we can estimate a salvage value at the end of a definite ownership period, then this may be more accurate. If we're trying to measure the equity buildup of the owner, then projecting a future sale can also be an acceptable method.

In actual practice, I most often project a sale at the end of the fifth year to measure equity buildup and to show the prospective new owner the benefits of possible appreciation. Whatever the case, you must realize that calculating the present value of the cash flows for only the next five years is not enough, even if that's all you can reasonably predict. A business usually has benefits which last longer and which must be measured in some reasonable manner.

**Alternative Analyses.** If you are trying to define the value of the business to yourself, rather than to a buyer prospect, then substitute your own figures for those of the hypothetical buyer. If you're looking for an investor, you'll have to do some reading on the value of partial interests or stock offerings, both of which would represent variations of the above methods.

## Would You Buy Your Own Business?

After making all of these projections, performing the calculations, and refining your figures, there may still be that buyer who walks through your door and offers you "three times net" for your business. Now, however, you will have different "nets" to choose from; you will have a greater appreciation for

Exhibit 13–2 (*concluded*)

the dramatic effect of "terms"; and you will have some idea of other areas
which you need to consider, even if the buyer doesn't.

Most buyers don't have complicated formulas or methods for buying a business. Many don't have any formulas or methods at all! Common sense is not an
unusual trait, however. We all have some of it, and the true entrepreneur
usually has a lot.

The best advice I can give is to use common sense when applying any valuation method. A good question to ask yourself is: "If I were the buyer, would I
buy this business at this price on these terms?"

Source: This article was reprinted with permission from the September-October 1984 issue of *In Business* magazine, a national small business magazine published by the J.G. Press, Box 323, Emmaus, PA 18049. The author,
Glen Cooper, is currently writing a book entitled "How to Price a Business: A Handbook for Sellers and Buyers and
Their Accountants, Appraisers, Attorneys, Bankers, and Brokers," to be published by John Wiley & Sons in the fall
of 1986.

# Chapter 14

## Gross Revenue Multipliers

One of the most widely used and abused approaches to the valuation of small businesses and professional practices is gross revenue multipliers. They can be useful, but their usefulness has severe limitations. When gross revenue multipliers are used for valuation without completely understanding the limitations that apply to each case, the result can be an extremely misleading estimate of value.

# The Basic Concept

Another, and perhaps more descriptive, name for the gross revenue multiplier is the *price-to-sales ratio*. In other words, the basic concept is that the value is some multiple of the amount of revenue that the entity generates.

For example, if data on sales of a certain type of business or practice indicated that they almost always sell in a range of .40 to .75 times revenue, and we are interested in a business or practice that generates $200,000 in annual revenues, the range of multiples of sales would indicate that the entity should be worth $80,000 to $150,000 (.40 × $200,000 = $80,000 and .75 × $200,000 = $150,000). Where our subject entity should fall within that range would depend on its profitability, if that information is available, and on a variety of other factors. Some of the other relevant general factors are discussed in Chapter 8.

The concept of the gross revenue multiplier, as an approach to the valuation of the business or practice, assumes that there is some relatively consistent relationship between revenues and profits for the particular type of business or practice. The usefulness of the approach obviously varies from one type of business or practice to another, to the extent that that assumption holds true.

# When Gross Revenue Multipliers May be Useful

As a broad generalization, gross revenue multipliers may be useful for the following objectives:

1. To get a very rough range of possible values with a minimum of time and effort.
2. To get an estimate of value when other data are unavailable or inadequate.
3. As one indicator of a value or a range of values, used in conjunction with other valuation approaches.

The following sections discuss some of the situations in which gross revenue multipliers may be useful.

# When Gross Sales Are the Only Reliable Income Data Available

For many entities, especially small sole proprietorships, a record of profitability may be impossible, or nearly impossible, to construct, either because there have never been complete records or because personal and business receipts and expenditures are difficult to clearly separate from each other.

# For Companies with Losses or Erratic Earnings

For many reasons, a company may not have demonstrable earnings to capitalize, even though it has considerable potential; this may be because of adverse economic conditions that are expected to improve, because the company is in a start-up or research and development stage, or because of significant nonrecurring factors. In cases such as these, most buyers would construct a pro forma income statement for one or several years into the future. However, ratios of price to revenues at which sales of comparative companies took place can offer one indication of value.

Earnings of some companies may be highly erratic, either because of economic factors affecting the industry or because of special factors affecting the particular company. Attempts to normalize the earnings may require a great deal of subjective judgment about what level of past earnings best suggests future earnings expectations. Gross revenue multipliers derived from recent sales of comparable companies or practices may give some indication of how others assess the future of the industry or profession.

Finally, recent earnings may have experienced a "spike," an unprecedented upward thrust, which may or may not be sustainable. In this case, analysis of the gross revenue multipliers of other recent sales of comparable companies may prevent a buyer paying too much, based on an unsustainable earnings level.

# For Highly Homogeneous Industries and Professions

The more similar many businesses or practices within an identifiable industry are, the more valid the indication of value provided by the gross revenue multiplier approach. If an industry or profession tends to have a fairly standard cost structure, then a given level of revenue should be expected to produce a somewhat predictable amount of profit. In the limited number of industry or professional segments for which this homogeneity is characteristic, entities may sell within a fairly tight range of each other in terms of multipliers of revenue.

Even for relatively homogeneous industry or professional practice segments, gross revenue multipliers usually can be expected to vary quite a bit at any given time from one geographical region to another.

# Problems in Using Gross Revenue Multipliers

Anyone using gross revenue multipliers as indicators of value should do so with eyes wide open. Everything possible should be done to assess the impact on value of whatever differences there may be between the subject entity and the population from which the range of gross revenue multipliers was drawn. Even after being as thorough as possible, the appraiser should realize that there still may be considerable latitude in the resultant range of reasonable values. Following are some of the problems with using gross revenue multipliers as indicators of value.

## Ambiguity as to Exactly What Was Sold

As noted in Chapter 1, value is meaningless until it is clear what is being valued. Some people tend to bandy about figures purported to be representative gross revenue multipliers, without making it clear just what they supposedly represent. Does the multiplier value only the intangibles? Intangibles and fixed assets? Inventory? Other assets? Liabilities? When a gross revenue multiplier is quoted, one should take care to understand what the multiplier is supposed to represent before judging its meaningfulness.

## Ambiguity as to Terms of Sale

Is the gross revenue multiplier at issue supposed to represent a cash value, or does it relate to a price on some noncash terms that may be typical for sales of entities in the particular business or profession? A price on long, easy terms may be half again as much as a value in cash, as discussed in Chapter 17.

When gross revenue multipliers are discussed, they more often than not relate to terms of sale typical in the business or profession rather than to cash values for the business or practice.

## A Profit Factor Usually Comes into Play

As noted earlier, for most kinds of businesses or industries for which gross revenue multipliers are commonly used, the assumption of some level of profitability is inherent in the range of multipliers generally quoted. To apply the gross multiplier approach intelligently, the appraiser should have some idea what level of profitability is implicit in the multiplier and what the chances are that the subject entity will achieve the implied level of profitability.

# Differences in Persistence of Revenues

Another factor implied in any industry average gross revenue multiplier is some industry average persistence of the revenues to which it is applied. In other words, if a buyer thinks of the value of an entity in terms of a multiple of its revenues, he is thinking in terms of "buying a book of business" (as insurance people put it). He must have some idea about how much of that business is likely to stay with the entity after he buys it, and for how long.

In order to use gross revenue multipliers intelligently, the appraiser must have some idea of the degree of expected persistence on which the industry average multiplier is based and the likelihood that the persistence for the subject entity will be better or worse than the industry standard expectation.

# Uniqueness of Each Entity

As noted earlier, the validity of gross revenue multipliers as indicators of value depends on some degree of homogeneity among a class, which, typically, is not characteristic among diverse entrepreneurs and professional practitioners. The historical developments of different entities, as well as the unique personalities and preferences of the personally managed operations, may create a uniqueness not characteristic of real estate or other commercial investments. The appraiser may have great difficulty adjusting data for any group of entities, for which a range of multipliers supposedly is representative, so that it can be usefully applied to any particular entity.

# Multipliers Change Considerably over Time

A business broker recently told me that the multipliers of revenue at which sales of businesses through his office were being consummated were running 30 percent lower than a year earlier. In other words, at the time of our conversation, he would have expected to sell at 70 percent of a year's revenues a business that would have sold for 100 percent of a year's revenues a year earlier.

Even when gross revenue multipliers may be useful, it must be recognized that they are volatile, and change over time for several reasons.

**Ease of Entry.** The degree to which it is easy, or even feasible, to start one's own operation may vary over time, either because of supply and demand in the business or practice category or because of changes in the regulatory environment, such as the amount or method of allocating licenses for a certain activity. These factors obviously influence what people will pay to get into an established business or practice.

**Fashions, Fads, and Fantasies.** Certain types of businesses and practices may be in or out of fashion in the market at any given time, just as certain groups of stocks can be the darlings of the market one year and the dogs the next. Innovative ideas and scarce opportunities are the kinds of things that drive multipliers up; fading glitter and a glut of participants can move multipliers down.

**Economic and Industry Conditions.** Economic and industry conditions can considerably influence the outlook for persistence of revenues for both the near-term and long-term future; they can also affect the profit margins that those revenues can generate. Obviously, these factors will have an impact on what a buyer will be willing to pay per dollar of revenues currently being attained.

**Interest Rates.** Interest rates change constantly; they change the cost of capital, and therefore how much buyers are willing to pay per dollar of expected profits. Since the real point of buying revenue-generating capability is to buy its attendant profit-making capability, changes in the cost of capital also influence gross revenue multipliers.

In summary, reliance on gross revenue multipliers based on outdated data without adequate adjustments for changing conditions can be worse than useless—it can be downright misleading.

## Even Gross Revenue Data May Not Be Reliable

For some businesses, it is not even possible to get reliable data on the amount of gross revenues being generated. That is especially true of cash businesses, including many types of retail and service establishments. This fact poses a dilemma. Will the buyer rely on somebody's oral estimate of revenues, or will he consider only data that can be verified? There is no right answer to that question. Different buyers have different criteria by which they judge the reliability of the data they may be willing to accept.

## Multiples of Some Measure of Physical Volume

In a few industries, some buyers look at some measure of physical volume in determining how much they are willing to pay. For example, the cable TV industry looks at the number of subscribers. Funeral homes are priced partly on the basis of the average number of services per year, although that pricing approach is less dominant today than it used to be. Buyers of soft drink bottlers and beer distributors look at the number of cases sold, with most of the value related to the premium brands. Taverns sometimes are priced on the basis of the monthly volume of draft beer purchased from the distributor.

But even gross physical volume measures are not always reliable. A business broker told me of an owner who bought and sold taverns frequently and usually owned two or more at any one time. When he planned to sell a tavern, the purchase invoices showed that the tavern bought a lot of kegs of beer from the distributor during the months prior to his offering the tavern for sale. What the prospective buyer, inspecting the records, didn't know was that some of the kegs went out the back door and were actually sold through one of the owner's other taverns.

Once, when I thought I might use the quantity of liquor purchased to help estimate the true sales volume of a cocktail lounge, the owner told me that he was pretty sure that a recently terminated employee had been bringing in significant amounts of liquor on his own so that his skimming would go undetected.

# Using Industry Earnings Data to Check Gross Revenue Multipliers

Logically, the multiplier of revenue at which a company should sell would be the company's profits, expressed as a percentage of sales, divided by the applicable rate at which its earnings should be capitalized. For example, suppose that a manufacturing company earned an average of 5 percent on its sales, and buyers of companies in that industry demanded a 20 percent return on their investment. The buyers would be willing to pay:

$$\frac{.05}{.20} = .25, \text{ or 25 percent of sales}$$

If someone proposes to price a company or group of companies in an industry on the basis of a gross revenue multiplier, the average return on sales for the industry can be looked up in any of the sources discussed in Chapter 7 or from trade association statistics, if they are available. If the average profit on sales, divided by a satisfactory capitalization rate, comes out somewhere near the proferred gross revenue multiplier, then the multiplier would appear to be fairly accurate.

Some data on gross revenue multipliers for specific types of businesses and practices are presented in Chapter 29.

# Chapter 15

## Asset-Related Approaches

Even though earnings approaches are accorded the most weight in the valuation of most businesses and professional practices, buyers want to know what tangible assets they are getting and what the assets might be worth. The relative importance of the tangible asset values varies considerably from one kind of business to another and from one situation to another. This chapter deals with some of the uses of asset value approaches in the valuation process, and Chapter 16 discusses how much weight is appropriate for asset approaches under various circumstances.

Chapter 5 discussed adjusting the asset values to fair market value on the balance sheet, so that topic is not discussed at any length in this chapter. Also, Chapter 24 discusses aspects of adjusting balance sheets for tangible assets of professional practices. That chapter also discusses adjusting a balance sheet from a cash basis to an accrual basis, a topic that is not limited to professional practices but applies in the valuation of any business that uses a cash instead of an accrual basis of accounting. The fact that this chapter is brief does not mean that valuation of assets is trivial—it is just that a considerable part of the discussion of the valuation of assets and their role in the overall entity valuation is contained elsewhere in the book.

# Book Value

As noted earlier, *book value* is really a misnomer, since it is not a value at all, but actually an accounting concept. The book value of an asset is the historical cost less any depreciation or amortization that has been charged against it.

Considering the definition of book value, it is obvious that the shorter the time the company has owned any particular asset, the closer the book value is likely to be to the current market value of the asset. A company whose total assets are largely current will tend to have a book value close to market value, with exceptions as discussed in Chapter 5. For a company with a large amount of fixed assets, book value will not normally represent a reasonable approximation of market value, unless a large proportion of the assets have been acquired quite recently.

The main advantage of book value is that virtually every business has the information fairly readily available, and the appraiser can use it as a starting place.

# Adjusted Book Value

Adjusted book value, as discussed in Chapter 5, is asset values adjusted to an approximation of their replacement cost in their current condition; it is generally considered the best representation of the fair market value of the assets. For some kinds of businesses which seem to have no intangible value, such as basic machine job shops and some kinds of retailers, adjusted book value may represent the most accurate approach to the valuation of the entire entity.

# Price/Book Value Ratio

In many industries, companies tend to sell consistently at prices above their book values. In a few, especially certain types of basic manufacturing industries, companies tend to sell consistently below their book values. A study of sales prices of comparable companies relative to their respective book values may provide some guidance to a range of reasonable values for a business entity.

The extent to which the price/book value ratio can be useful as a guide to value depends a great deal on the extent to which the subject company is comparable to the other companies from which the price/book value market transaction data were derived. Comparability can be measured in terms of many criteria. For the purpose of judging whether the price/book value ratios that were found in other transactions may be useful indicators of value for the subject company, the following are five of the most important comparability criteria:

1. Asset mix.
2. Age of assets.
3. Accounting policies.
4. Comparative capital structures.
5. Return on equity.

## Comparative Asset Mix

If the appraiser has common-size balance sheets, as shown in Exhibits 5–2 and 7–1 (which express each asset category as a percentage of total assets), the proportions of various categories of the subject company's assets on its balance sheet can be compared readily to industry averages and to individual comparative companies. The more similar the proportions of asset categories between the subject company and the comparative companies, the more useful will be the price/book value ratios for the comparative company transactions as an indicator of value.

Also, as a generality, the more the subject and comparative companies' assets tend to be current, the more the price/book value ratios are likely to be useful indicators of value, since that ratio gives some indication of the intangible values that tend to be present in the industry.

## Relative Age of Assets

To the extent that the subject company has owned its assets for approximately the same average length of time as the comparative companies, the price/book value ratios for the comparative transactions will more likely provide useful indicators of value for the subject company. If the subject and comparative companies have held their assets for comparable lengths of time, then changes in market values and the amount of depreciation charged off are also likely to be relatively comparable.

## Comparative Accounting Policies

In order for price/book value ratios to be meaningful, the accounting policies for the subject company and the companies from which the market data were derived should be comparable, especially for inventory and depreciation accounting methods. If some companies use FIFO inventory accounting and others use LIFO, it is relatively simple to make them comparable by adjusting all the LIFO companies to a FIFO basis, using the procedures described in Chapter 5. If some of the companies use accelerated depreciation and others use straight-line depreciation, the adjustments necessary to make them comparable involve more work, and the necessary data may not be available.

## Comparative Capital Structures

Price/book value ratios are much more meaningful as indicators of the value of a company to the extent that the capital structures found in the comparative companies are similar to the subject company. If the subject company's ratio of equity to total assets deviates significantly from industry norms, price/book value ratios are less meaningful as a value indicator.

## Effect of Return on Equity

In all industries for which my staff and I have studied the relationship between the sales price/book value ratios and return on equity, we have found a positive correlation. That certainly is what one would expect to find. It demonstrates that the market is willing to pay more for a dollar's worth of book value with a higher demonstrated earning power than for a dollar's worth of book value with a lower demonstrated earning power. For some industries, the correlation between these two variables is stronger than for others.

If there are enough comparative companies for which the sales price/book value ratio and the return on equity are available, the analyst can do a linear regression on the two variables and, from that, determine a price/book value ratio that market data would indicate is compatible with the subject company's return on equity.

# Price/Adjusted Book Value Ratio

Perhaps the ideal asset-related approach is to use the prices at which comparative companies have sold in relation to their respective adjusted net asset values—that is, their asset values adjusted to market value, as discussed in Chapter 5. Unfortunately, such data rarely are available for the comparative companies. Pretty good data are available fairly consistently for real estate holding companies and forest products companies with standing timber.

# Role of Intangible Assets

In the vast majority of business appraisals, the appraiser does not attempt to identify the values attributable to individual intangible assets. This practice is colloquially called the "big pot" approach, since any value attributed to the total entity over and above net tangible asset value is considered to be in one big pot, frequently called goodwill.

Goodwill, as discussed elsewhere in the book, really means those factors that tend to bring customers back to the business. A business may have many other intangible assets that could be identified and appraised individually if it were important to do so, such as subscriber lists, customer lists, trade names, copyrights, patents, benefits arising from any of a wide variety of possible contractual relationships, and many others.

If the amount of intangible value in the total business is substantial, it is to the buyer's advantage to identify and value the specific individual elements of intangible value and allocate the purchase price accordingly. The amortization of goodwill cannot be deducted from taxable income as a business expense, but amortization of almost all other intangible assets is deductible from taxable income over their respective remaining economic lives. The techniques for valuation of specific intangible assets are the subject of Chapter 32.

# Typical "Assets Plus . . ." Rules of Thumb

The following are typical of many rules of thumb used by business brokers in the pricing of small businesses for sale.

Kenneth Perry of Business Opportunity Counselors, Inc., in Auburn, Maine, reports that businesses commonly are sold at net worth, adjusted to fair market value plus a negotiated factor for goodwill.

Gregory Swirtz, of Professional Investments in Minneapolis, Minnesota, suggests pricing businesses at the market value of their furniture, fixtures, and leasehold, the cost value of inventory, plus one year's adjusted annual net income before taxes, including depreciation and the owner's salary, fringes, and perks.

Nick Clark, of ANI Business Brokers in Jackson, Mississippi, suggests that the value of "all assets, plus one year's net, plus the owner's salary and perks, equals the asking price." He says the selling price usually ranges from 10 to 20 percent below the asking price.

These brokers fully recognize of course, that every business is different, and the foregoing ideas are merely very broad suggestions that may provide a simplified starting point for negotiations. Like all rules of thumb, they do not apply in all cases, and should not be used by themselves to reach a conclusion as to value, but only in conjunction with other valuation approaches.

# Liquidation Value

Liquidation value is generally defined to mean the net proceeds that could be realized if the assets of the business were sold off piecemeal and the business terminated. If the going-concern value, as indicated by capitalization of the company's earning capability as an operating entity, is less than the liquidation value, this indicates that the business is worth more dead than alive, as noted in an earlier chapter. The rational economic decision in such a case would be to liquidate the business and reinvest any proceeds in something else. Not all small businessmen are prone to making decisions that are rational on economic grounds alone, and many businesses whose liquidation value is greater than their going concern value still operate.

# Chapter 16

## Choosing and Balancing the Approach or Approaches

No individual approach or combination of approaches is necessarily right or wrong in any specific case; the approaches used should make sense in relation to the entity at hand, be based on reliable data, and be carried out properly. I do make the point repeatedly, however, that for operating companies, asset approaches alone do not make economic sense unless it can be demonstrated that sufficient earning power can be generated to justify the amount of the investment. Valuations of holding companies tend to focus primarily on assets, with earnings and/or cash flow accorded secondary consideration; valuations of operating companies focus primarily on their ability to generate earnings and/or cash flow.

This chapter deals primarily with generalizations about selecting an approach or approaches.

# Conceptual Superiority versus Reliability of Data

One of the frustrations in appraising small businesses and professional practices is a pragmatic problem: There is a trade-off between some approaches that are conceptually superior and others that are conceptually inferior, but for which more reliable data are available.

As noted in Chapter 13, the discounted future earnings or discounted cash flow approach is conceptually the best approach, in most instances; but it is used very infrequently to appraise small businesses and professional practices because it is difficult to develop reliable earnings and cash flow forecasts, and there is the problem of choosing an applicable discount rate.

After the discounted future earnings approach, the most conceptually desirable approach, in most cases, would be the capitalization of normalized earnings, preferably after reasonable compensation to the owner and either normal depreciation or an allowance for replacement expenditures. This approach has the same basic problems as the discounted future earnings approach, which include estimating the normalized earnings base and choosing the applicable capitalization rate. Current normalized earnings usually can be estimated with greater reliability than future earnings; so this approach is used more frequently than the discounted future earnings approach. Nevertheless, the degree of reliability of the normalized earnings estimate varies greatly from one situation to another. The two variables for which the most reliable data are available in most cases are gross revenues and the value of the inventory. This is one reason why inventory plus "x" times gross revenues is a fairly commonly-used approach for retailers.

The goal should be to use the best conceptual approaches for which reliable data can be developed; the appraiser can rely on conceptually preferable approaches as long as the underlying data can be considered reliable, but go to other approaches, if necessary, in order to base the analysis on the most reliable available data.

# Concentration or Dispersion of Market Parameters

*Parameters* can be thought of as the variables, and sometimes as the boundaries of the variables, used in mathematical equations. In business valuations, the parameters with which we are concerned are the various capitalization rates (multipliers or divisors) to be applied to the data for the subject company. They can be gross revenue multipliers, price/earnings ratios, price/cash flow ratios, expected rates of return at which to capitalize various levels of earnings, price/book value ratios, or price/adjusted net asset value ratios.

When looking at market sales data for several comparative companies, we usually find that certain market parameters tend to fall in a fairly tight cluster, while others will vary widely. Generally speaking, it is desirable to rely most heavily on approaches using the parameters that are found to be most consistent in the pricing of sales of comparable companies or practices.

# Industry Pricing Formulas

In certain lines of business, there are more or less widely accepted approaches to valuation. When such widely used approaches exist, they should not be ignored. They should be tested as one or more of the approaches taken into consideration in reaching the value conclusion.

There are both positive and negative factors to consider in using approaches thought acceptable within an industry group. On the positive side, if they really are accepted and used in the industry, then they exert a major influence on the pricing of companies in that industry. Secondly, if they are used consistently, they must have been found to work; they must tend to produce indicated values close to what buyers and sellers are able to agree on. On the negative side, they usually are extremely simplistic, and their accuracy usually has not been well verified. Industry formulas are gross approximations in most cases, as discussed in the chapter on gross revenue multipliers, and do not reflect all of the many differences from one company to another. A lot of subjective judgment is required in order to arrive at parameters that are useful in an industry pricing formula and that reflect fairly all the unique facets of the subject entity.

The other main negative factor is that most industry pricing formulas come from articles or word-of-mouth sources and have not been tested in the marketplace under current conditions. People think that businesses are priced that way because they heard it someplace, but in most cases nobody has done a study of recent sales to be sure that it really is so.

Although I do not like to ignore existing industry formula approaches, I also do not like to use them solely.

# When Asset Value Approaches Are Most Useful

Asset approaches are useful when start-up is a viable alternative to buying an existing business, for certain kinds of businesses that typically sell on an asset basis, and when a sale of assets is likely.

## When Start-Up Is a Viable Alternative

If a reasonable alternative to buying an existing business is to start one like it from scratch, then the assets play a major role in the valuation. In businesses that are relatively easy to start up, the costs of getting into business and getting a satisfactory amount of revenue coming in would not be a great deal more than the basic cost of buying the necessary assets. Such businesses would include, for example, many types of retail stores, job machine shops, auto body repair shops, and small construction subcontractors operating entirely, or largely, on a competitive bid basis.

## Businesses that Sell Largely on an Asset Basis

In addition to the types of companies that are very easy to start up, as described in the section immediately above, the main types of businesses that sell largely on an asset basis are those deriving income mainly from the assets themselves, rather than from the personal efforts of the owners and employees. These companies would include real estate holding companies, equipment leasing companies, and investment companies owning a portfolio of securities or other investments.

## When Sale of Assets Is Likely

If the assets themselves are likely to be sold off by the buyer, rather than retained for operations, then, of course, the potential sale value of the assets is quite important to the valuation. If certain assets may be sold, then those assets should be valued separately and added to the value of the business as an operating entity.

# Weighted Average of Approaches

If one approach stands out as clearly superior, or if two or more relevant approaches indicate values within a close range, the decision of how much weight to accord to any particular approach is not a problem. Sometimes, however, different approaches lead to significantly different results. When that occurs, an intuitively appealing method of dealing with the dilemma is to use the appraiser's subjective but informed judgment: Decide on a percentage weight to be assigned to the results of each relevant valuation approach used, and base the final valuation on the weighted average of the results of the various approaches. An example of the weighted average method is given in the following section.

The main weakness of the weighted average method is that there is no mathematical model available to use in deriving the weights to be assigned to the results of each of the different valuation approaches. The relative weights assigned to each approach depend on the judgment of the appraiser; however, it forces the appraiser to present his thinking in clearly quantified terms. The method also has the appeal of being simple to understand. If someone evaluating the results disagrees with some aspect of the appraiser's judgment, the point of departure is readily identifiable, and it is easy to apply an alternate set of weights and quickly recompute the result.

Court cases in which values of stocks have to be determined under dissenting stockholders' appraisal rights have tended to rely on this method.

# Examples of Choosing and Balancing Approaches

The following hypothetical examples illustrate the procedures discussed in this chapter. The two examples continue to use the two hypothetical companies, Annie's Apparel Store and Mary's Machinery and Equipment, from the previous chapters.

## An Asset Sale Example

As discussed in earlier chapters, the owner of Annie's Apparel Store (Annie's) wants to retire and sell her store. Rags, Inc., is interested in buying Annie's and wants a business appraiser to give it an idea of what it should pay for the business. Annie's income statement, adjusted to reflect the way Rags, Inc., would operate, appears in Exhibit 9–2. Annie's adjusted balance sheet appears in Exhibit 5–2. From the balance sheet, it can be seen that Annie plans to retain the cash and to pay off the current liabilities from the proceeds of the sale.

The purpose of this example is to illustrate how different valuation approaches are chosen and weighted in determining the market value of the company. Therefore, in this example and the next, we will not go into much detail on how the value is determined from each approach, since that has been discussed in other chapters and will be explained in more detail in connection with the sample case in Chapters 21 and 22.

**Capitalizing Normalized Earnings.** From Exhibit 9–2 it can be seen that Annie's normalized earnings, from the perspective of Rags, Inc., are $57,000. In choosing a capitalization rate for these earnings, we looked at a number of comparative transactions (from the data base described in Chapter 29). These companies sold at an average of about 4.0 times pretax earnings. In our opinion, that is a reasonable capitalization rate for Annie's earnings, and it results in the following value:

| *Earnings* | | *P/E Ratio* | | *Indicated Value* |
|---|---|---|---|---|
| $57,000 | × | 4.0 | = | $228,000 |

**Excess Earnings Method.** The reader can refer to Chapter 12 for a detailed explanation of this method. From Exhibit 5–2 it can be seen that Annie's adjusted net tangible asset value is $190,984. As discussed above, the company's normalized earnings are $57,000. What needs to be determined next is an appropriate percentage rate of return on the net tangible asset value, which should be equal to, or possibly somewhat less than, the company's overall weighted average cost of capital. We assumed that Rags could finance 50 percent of the tangible assets with bank financing at a total cost of 15 percent interest, and the balance with equity capital requiring a 25 percent return. This calculation results in a weighted cost of capital of about 20 percent, determined as follows:

| | *Percent of Capital Structure* | *Required Rate of Return* | |
|---|---|---|---|
| Debt | .50 | .15 | .075 |
| Equity | .50 | .25 | .125 |
| Weighted Average | | | .200 |

Finally, we chose a capitalization rate of 33 percent on the excess earnings. Under this scenario, the indicated value of Annie's would be computed as follows:

| | | |
|---|---|---|
| Net Tangible Asset Value | | $190,984 |
| Normalized Earnings | $57,000 | |
| Earnings Attributable to Tangible Assets ($190,984 x .20) = | 38,197 | |
| Excess Earnings | $18,803 | |
| Value of Excess Earnings ($18,803 ÷ .33) = | | 56,979 |
| Indicated Value | | $247,963 |

**The Discounted Future Earnings Method.** Since we do not have projections of Annie's earnings for several years into the future, we cannot use this approach.

**Gross Revenue Multipliers.** We looked at the price/sales ratios of the comparative transactions discussed in the capitalization of normalized earnings section above. Because the range of price/sales ratios was extremely wide (27 percent to 86 percent), we did not consider the data to be reliable enough to justify use of this approach.

**Price/Book Value.** Annie's adjusted book value is $190,984. The comparative companies were selling at an average of 110 percent of book value, which we believe would not be an unreasonable multiplier for Annie. This calculation results in the following indicated value:

*Book Value*     *P/BV Ratio*     *Indicated Value*
$190,984     ×          1.1          =          $210,082

**Summary.**  When valuing an operating company, the most weight should be placed on the earnings approaches and less on the asset approaches. In keeping with this thinking, we placed 65 percent weight on the two earnings approaches and 35 percent on the price/book value approach. Within these two earnings approaches, we placed more weight on the capitalization of normalized earnings (50 percent) in this case, partly because of the buyer's assumption of Annie's long-term debt. The excess earnings method does not fully account for variations in capital structure; therefore, we gave this approach only 15 percent weight. The approaches, weighting, and resulting value are summarized below:

| Approach | Value | | Weight | | Wtd. Value |
|---|---|---|---|---|---|
| Capitalization of | | | | | |
| Normalized Earnings | $228,000 | x | .50 | = | $114,000 |
| Excess Earnings | $247,963 | x | .15 | = | 37,194 |
| Price/Book Value | $210,082 | x | .35 | = | 73,529 |
| | | | | | $224,723 |
| | | | Rounded to | | $225,000 |

In our opinion the market value of Annie's Apparel Store is approximately $225,000.

# A Stock Sale Example

The owner of Mary's Machinery and Equipment (Mary's) wants to sell the business and retire to Hawaii. Barney Backhoe and two partners are interested in purchasing the business. They have retained a business appraiser to give them an idea of what they should pay for the company. Mary's adjusted income statement and Mary's pro forma income statement, adjusted to reflect the way Mr. Backhoe and his associates would operate the company, appears as Exhibit 9–3. Mary's adjusted balance sheet is shown as Exhibit 5–3. Mary intends to sell her 100 shares of Mary's common stock, which is 100 percent of the outstanding shares.

**Capitalizing Normalized Earnings.**  Mary's normalized pretax earnings from Exhibit 9–3 are $86,000. They were the company's adjusted earnings in 1984. Although it is often appropriate to capitalize five-year average earnings, in this case the company lost money in 1982 and 1983, and these losses are not expected to be repeated in future years. Therefore, average earnings are an unreasonably low earnings base to capitalize.

Based on the comparative transactions analyzed and other valuations we have done of wholesale machinery distributors, we believe a multiple of 6.5 is appropriate for Mary's earnings. Note that the reciprocal of 6.5 would be a capitalization rate of 15.4 percent ($1 \div 6.5 =$

.154), which is very close to the capitalization rate of 15.2 percent developed for Mary's in Chapter 11. The multiple of 6.5 results in the following indicated value:

| Earnings | P/E Ratio | | Indicated Value |
|---|---|---|---|
| $86,000 | × 6.5 | = | $559,000 |

It should be noted that with Mr. Backhoe operating the company, the normalized pretax earnings should be $100,000 (Exhibit 9–3); however, he will not be willing to pay 6.5 times these earnings because that incremental value will result from his input. However, he may be willing to pay somewhere between the $559,000 and $650,000.

**Excess Earnings Method.**   Mary's tangible book value is $578,635 ($586,835 less the leasehold interest of $8,200). If we assume that the buying group could borrow 60 percent of the value of the tangible assets at 12 percent and finance the balance with equity at a required return of 20 percent, then the weighted average capitalization rate that applies to the tangible book value would be 15.2 percent, as developed in Chapter 11. Applying that rate to Mary's tangible book value of $578,635 would indicate that Mary's should be earning $87,952 on its tangible assets, which is approximately the company's current level of earnings. This exercise indicates that Mary's currently has no excess earnings and therefore should not be worth more than the tangible book value of $578,635.

**The Discounted Future Earnings Method.**   Mary's has no projections of future earnings, so this approach cannot be used.

**Gross Revenue Multipliers.**   Mary's normalized sales are $2,400,000. The comparative companies were selling at an average of 30 percent of sales; however, they were more profitable than Mary's, which should therefore have a lower multiple. We chose 25 percent as appropriate.

| Sales | P/Sales Ratio | | Indicated Value |
|---|---|---|---|
| $2,400,000 × | .25 | = | $600,000 |

Because of lack of comparability between the profitability of the comparative companies and Mary's, this approach should not be relied upon very heavily.

**Price/Book Value Approach.**   As already stated, Mary's tangible book value is $578,635. The comparative companies were selling at an average of 1.4 times book value, but, again, they were more profitable than Mary's, as exhibited by their higher return on equity. In general, the higher (lower) a company's return on equity the higher (lower) a multiple of book value an investor will pay. Accordingly, in our opinion, a multiple of about 1.0 times book value is appropriate, indicating a value of $578,635.

**Summary of Approaches.**   The four approaches just described produced values ranging from $559,000 to $600,000, summarized as follows:

| Approach | Indicated Value | |
|---|---|---|
| Capitalization of Normalized Earnings | $559,000 | |
| Excess Earnings | 578,635 | (maximum) |
| Gross Revenue Multiplier | 600,000 | |
| Price/Book Value | 578,635 | |

Since these values are clustered fairly close together, they would seem to indicate a value of about $575,000, which is close to the company's tangible book value.

## Summary

I like to use as many approaches as possible, taking into consideration the reliability of the available data and the reasonableness of the approaches as they apply to the entity at hand. The weighting, or final conclusion, must then be decided in light of the perceived reliability of the data underlying each approach and the conceptual applicability of each approach to the type of business or practice being valued, and any special circumstances that should be reflected.

# Chapter 17

## Tradeoff between Cash and Terms

*I'll let you name any price you want if you'll let me name the terms.*
Deal-Makers' Credo

As noted in the previous chapter, most sales of small businesses and professional practices are done on some kind of terms rather than for cash. In most cases, the seller "carries the paper," that is, the seller accepts an installment payment contract for the balance of the purchase price over and above the down payment.

The main reason for this arrangement is that the typical buyer of a small business or professional practice does not have the personal resources to pay the full purchase price in cash, and most lending institutions would not regard the business or practice being purchased as adequate collateral to support a term loan for the balance of the purchase price. In no other broad category of transactions is it nearly as commonplace for the seller to take an installment contract for a significant portion of the selling price. Larger businesses usually sell to larger corporations, which pay in cash or possibly in stock, if the buyer is a publicly traded company. Buyers of real estate usually can obtain debt financing for a substantial portion of the total purchase price by using the real estate as collateral, thus cashing out the seller.

In a sale of a business or professional practice on terms, the seller is, in effect, making a loan to the buyer to finance the purchase. It is, therefore, of the utmost importance to the seller to have a good contract on the sale, with adequate protective covenants.

The purpose of this chapter is to explain the difference between the face value of a transaction on terms and the equivalent cash value of that transaction. This difference usually is quite significant in the sale of small businesses and professional practices, because the rate of interest on contracts carried by the seller usually is *far below* a market rate of interest for any other comparable contract. I think it fair to say that the typical small business sale at a face value of $100,000 probably has a cash equivalent value somewhere around $80,000, a difference considerably greater than most people realize. Therefore, it is worthwhile for people dealing with small business and professional practice transactions to be able to convert the price of a deal on terms to an equivalent cash value or vice versa. It is also worthwhile to be able to assess the differences in impact (in terms of cash equivalent value) between one set of terms and some alternative set of terms.

# Converting a Price on Terms to an Equivalent Cash Value

## A Typical Example

Let's start right off with an example. John owns a small marina, which he sells on terms for a face amount of $100,000. The terms are as follows:

John's Marina

| | |
|---|---|
| Sale price | $100,000 |
| Down payment | 20% |

Balance in equal monthly installments including principal and interest at the rate of 9 percent per annum over a period of 10 years.

Let's assume that the prime commercial bank lending rate is 12 percent, the average interest rate on 10-year prime commercial mortgages is 13 percent, and the average yield on 10-year high-grade corporate bonds is 13.5 percent. The buyer's installment note, secured by the small marina, is not as high-quality a debt instrument as any of the foregoing, so a reasonable market rate of interest for a note of such characteristics would have to be higher, let's say 15 percent. (We will discuss how to determine an applicable market rate in a subsequent section.)

What is the cash equivalent value of this transaction? The first step is to compute the amount of the monthly payments that John will receive. You can do this with a set of annuity or present value tables, but the easiest way is to use a simple pocket calculator such as the Texas Instruments Business Analyst II. The annual interest rate of 9 percent is equal to .75 percent per month ($9.00 \div 12 = .75$). So the buyer will be paying John 120 monthly payments of principal plus interest at .75 percent per month on a contract balance of $80,000. This schedule works out to monthly payments of $1,013.41. Exhibit 17–1 shows the exact steps to make this calculation on the TI II calculator.

Exhibit 17–1

**CALCULATING THE AMOUNT OF A PAYMENT
USING TEXAS INSTRUMENTS BUSINESS ANALYST II**

Have calculator in "FIN" mode

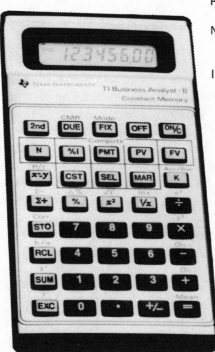

Present Value: $80,000

Number of Payments: 120
  (Monthly Payments for 10 Years)

Interest Rate Per Period: .75%
  (9.00% Annual Rate ÷ 12)

Enter: $80,000

Press: PV (Present Value)

Enter: 120

Press: N (Number of Payments)

Enter: .75

Press: % i (Percent Interest per Period)

Press: 2nd (This Tells the Calculator
  to Compute.)

Press: PMT (Payment)

Answer: $1,013.41.

The other step is to convert this stream of 120 monthly payments to a cash equivalent value using a market rate of interest. The question here is, how much cash would a lender pay for this installment contract in order for it to provide him a rate of return of 15 percent per year (1.25 percent per month), which is slightly more than prime commercial loans, prime mortgages, or high-grade corporate bonds. The formula for this is:

$$PV = \sum_{1}^{n} \frac{PMTi}{(1 + r)^i}$$

Where:

$PV$ = Present value
$n$ = Number of payments
$PMT$ = Amount in monthly payment in dollars
$i$ = The $i$th payment

Substituting values into this formula would give us a calculation as follows:

$$PV = \sum_{1}^{120} \frac{\$1,013.41}{(1 + .0125)^i}$$

$$= \frac{\$1,013.41}{1.0125} + \frac{\$1,013.41}{1.0125^2} + \cdots + \frac{\$1,013.41}{1.0125^{120}}$$

Exhibit 17–2 shows the exact steps to make this calculation on a TI II calculator.

In this example, John sold his marina for $20,000 cash, plus a note with a present value of $62,814, for a total of $82,814 cash equivalent value.

## Some Variations

**Extending the Contract.**  Suppose John has accepted a note under the same terms and conditions but with the payments spread out over 15 years instead of 10. In this case, using the same calculations, he would receive monthly payments of $811.41 for 180 months. Also using the same calculations, the present value of his contract at a 15 percent annual market rate would be $57,975.19, or a total present value of $20,000 + $57,975.19 = $77,975. In this variation, the cash equivalent value is $4,839 less than in the 10-year example.

**Accepting a Lower Contract Interest Rate.**  Let's suppose that John had accepted a contract with an interest rate of 7.2 percent (.6 percent per month), instead of 9 percent. Using the same calculations, on a 10-year contract, he would receive payments of $927.16 per month for 120 months. At a 15 percent market rate of interest, the present value of his contract balance would be $58,087.84. Adding this amount to his $20,000 down payment would indicate a cash equivalent value for the deal of $78,088, or $4,726 less than the value with a 9 percent interest rate.

Exhibit 17–2

**CALCULATING THE PRESENT (CASH EQUIVALENT) VALUE**
**OF A SERIES OF PAYMENTS**
**USING TEXAS INSTRUMENTS BUSINESS ANALYST II**

Have calculator in "FIN" mode

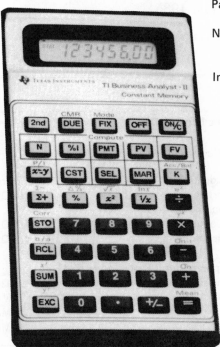

Payment: $1,013.41

Number of Payments: 120
(Monthly Payments for 10 Years)

Interest Rate Per Period: 1.25%

Enter: $1,013.41

Press: PMT (Payment)

Enter: 120

Press: N (Number of Payments)

Enter: 1.25

Press: %*i* (Percent Interest per Period)

Press: 2nd (This Tells the Calculator
to Compute.)

Press: PV (Present Value)

Answer: $62,814.

**Variations in Market Rate of Interest.** Suppose that John made the same deal when the market rate of interest on his contract was about 18 percent. He would receive $1,013.41 per months for 120 months, as in the original example. However, the present value of his contract would have to be figured by discounting his payments back to the present time at 1.5 percent per month (18.00 ÷ 12 = 1.5). Using the same calculations, the present value of his contract would be $56,243. Adding this amount to the down payment of $20,000 would indicate a cash equivalent value for the deal of $76,243, or $6,571 less than if the market rate of interest were 15 percent.

**Combining the Variations.** For our last variation in this series, we'll assume that John took his $80,000 balance in the form of an installment note with equal monthly payments of principal plus a 7.2 percent annual rate of interest for 15 years (180 months), at a time when a market rate of interest on an installment note such as this would be 18 percent. In this case, he would receive 180 monthly payments of $728.04. The present value of these payments at an 18 percent annual market rate of interest would be $45,208. Adding the $20,000 down payment gives a cash equivalent value for the deal of $65,208, or about 35 percent less than the $100,000 price or face amount of the deal.

# Determining the Applicable Market Interest Rate

All of the foregoing is simple mechanical arithmetic, done on an inexpensive pocket calculator in a few seconds. However, determining the applicable market interest rate requires a little bit of data and a little bit of judgment. Exhibit 17–3 offers a quick listing of lending rates current in mid-1985.

Exhibit 17–3

## LENDING RATES

|   |                                        | Date             | Rate % |
|---|----------------------------------------|------------------|--------|
| a | **Prime Lending Rate**                 | Week of 6/26/85  | 9.50   |
|   | **Mortgage Lending Rates** (Average)   |                  |        |
| b | Residential                            | March 1985       | 13.26  |
| c | Apartments                             | 4th Qtr. 1984    | 12.94  |
| c | Shopping Centers (Commercial Retail)   | 4th Qtr. 1984    | 12.90  |
| c | Office Buildings                       | 4th Qtr. 1984    | 12.91  |
|   | **Corporate Bond Rates** (Average)     |                  |        |
| d | New Issues                             | 1st Qtr. 1985    | 11.90  |
| e | Aaa                                    | May 1985         | 11.72  |
| e | Baa                                    | May 1985         | 13.15  |
| f | Caa                                    | May 1985         | 16.57  |

## CURRENT YIELDS[g]

|                             |       |
|-----------------------------|-------|
| Certificates of Deposit     | 9.2%  |
| Money Market Funds          | 7.8   |
| Prime Lending Rate          | 10.5  |
| Three-Month Treasury Bills  | 8.3   |
| Long-Term Government Bonds  | 11.5  |
| BBB Corporate Bonds         | 12.7  |

a  *Standard & Poor's Outlook*, June 26, 1985.
b  *Federal Reserve Bulletin*, June 1985—Average contract rates on new commitments for conventional first mortgages; from Department of Housing and Urban Development.
c  *The Appraiser*, June 1985.
d  *Standard & Poor's Trends & Projections*, May 16, 1985—seasonally adjusted annual rate.
e  *Moody's Bond Record*, June 1985.
f  Median calculation from *Moody's Bond Record*, June 1985.
g  Standard & Poor's *Outlook*, February 27, 1985: Standard & Poor's *Statistical Service*, January 1985.

# Data on Market Interest Rates

**Bank Lending Rates.**  Bank prime lending rates (the rates banks charge large borrowers with high credit ratings) are published regularly in newspapers and business magazines; or, by a telephone call to any bank, one can learn its current prime lending rate. Banks usually lend to small businesses at about 2-1/2 to 3 percentage points above their prime lending rates, if the business is sound and the loan is well secured, usually by current accounts receivable or inventory.

**Mortgage Rates.**   General business and real estate publications publish rates for residential mortgages and for various classes of commercial mortgages, such as apartment houses, shopping centers, office buildings, and so forth. These mortgages are usually well secured by good-quality, marketable property, so that the lending institution can foreclose and resell the property fairly readily in case of the borrower's default.

**Corporate Bond Rates.**   Corporate bonds are rated in terms of their quality (degree of certainty that the corporation will be able to pay the bonds' interest and principal on time) by various rating services such as Standard & Poor's and Moody's. Moody's ratings, for example, start with Aaa as the highest and go down through a grade of C, which is very speculative. *Barron's* and other publications show average yields for high-grade corporate bonds down through Baa. For medium-grade and lower-grade corporate bonds, reliable averages are not published, but yields for individual bonds can be found in publications such as the Standard & Poor's *Bond Guide* and *Moody's Bond Record*.

# Using an Ounce of Judgment

An installment note receivable, secured by the stock and/or assets of a small business or professional practice, is almost always riskier than any of the foregoing debt instruments and, therefore, must have a higher market interest rate. It is unlikely that an installment contract receivable on a small business sale would have a quality rating any better than grade Caa to C for corporate bonds, if that high.

Furthermore, all the foregoing debt instruments are readily marketable, which an installment contract receivable on a small business is not. Banks sell good-quality loans to other banks. Mortgage lenders sell mortgages to other mortgage lenders. Corporate bonds are traded on the public market (both the New York Stock Exchange and the over-the-counter market). There is no such ready market for installment contracts receivable on small businesses and professional practices.

The number of percentage points that needs to be added to the benchmark rates discussed above, in order to determine an appropriate market rate for a small business installment contract, depends on the degree of risk. If there is a substantial down payment, if the note is relatively short in duration (perhaps three to five years), and it is well secured and well protected by covenants in the purchase agreement, only a few percentage points need be added. If the down payment is small, the length of the term long, and protective covenants poor or absent, no rate may be high enough.

# Converting a Cash Value to a Price on Terms

Let's say that Dusty Trail has concluded that the value of his Paperback Western Bookstore on a cash basis is $150,000, but he expects to sell the business on terms, probably one third ($50,000) down and the balance ($100,000 cash equivalent) on a contract, with interest at something less than a market rate. He now wants to determine the price and terms that would give him his $150,000 cash equivalent value.

The first step is to figure out a market rate of interest for the contract, probably by using one or more of the benchmark rates discussed in the previous section for guidance. Let's say that the bank prime rate is 12 percent and the high-grade corporate bond yield is 13.5 percent, and he thinks that the present contract should cost about prime plus three points and about 1.5 percent over the high-grade corporate bond rate (or about 15 percent), to obtain the credit on an arm's-length basis in the open market. (That is not a very high premium over the rate for top-quality credit; it implies that he believes there will not be a very high degree of risk associated with the credit.)

The second step is to determine what the monthly payments on the contract will be at a market rate of interest. This calculation can be done with a pocket calculator such as the TI II. If he assumes that the contract will run for seven years (84 months), the net level payments of principal and interest on $100,000, at a 15 percent annual rate (1.25 percent per month), are $1,929.68 per month. The steps to do this calculation on the TI II are the same as those in Exhibit 17–1. The monthly payments per $100 of contract balance for various rates of interest, for various lengths of time, are shown in Exhibit 17–4.

Exhibit 17–4

**MONTHLY PAYMENT REQUIRED PER $100 OF CONTRACT BALANCE**

| Contract Int. Rate | Number of Payments | | | | | | | | | | | | |
|---|---|---|---|---|---|---|---|---|---|---|---|---|---|
| | 12 | 18 | 24 | 30 | 36 | 48 | 60 | 72 | 84 | 96 | 120 | 144 | 180 |
| 12% | 8.88 | 6.10 | 4.71 | 3.87 | 3.32 | 2.63 | 2.22 | 1.96 | 1.77 | 1.63 | 1.43 | 1.31 | 1.20 |
| 13% | 8.93 | 6.14 | 4.75 | 3.92 | 3.37 | 2.68 | 2.28 | 2.01 | 1.82 | 1.68 | 1.49 | 1.37 | 1.27 |
| 14% | 8.98 | 6.19 | 4.80 | 3.97 | 3.42 | 2.73 | 2.33 | 2.06 | 1.87 | 1.74 | 1.55 | 1.44 | 1.33 |
| 15% | 9.03 | 6.24 | 4.85 | 4.02 | 3.47 | 2.78 | 2.38 | 2.11 | 1.93 | 1.79 | 1.61 | 1.50 | 1.40 |
| 16% | 9.07 | 6.29 | 4.90 | 4.07 | 3.52 | 2.83 | 2.43 | 2.17 | 1.99 | 1.85 | 1.68 | 1.57 | 1.47 |
| 17% | 9.12 | 6.33 | 4.94 | 4.11 | 3.57 | 2.89 | 2.49 | 2.22 | 2.04 | 1.91 | 1.74 | 1.63 | 1.54 |
| 18% | 9.17 | 6.38 | 4.99 | 4.16 | 3.62 | 2.94 | 2.54 | 2.28 | 2.10 | 1.97 | 1.80 | 1.70 | 1.61 |
| 19% | 9.22 | 6.43 | 5.04 | 4.21 | 3.67 | 2.99 | 2.59 | 2.34 | 2.16 | 2.03 | 1.87 | 1.77 | 1.68 |
| 20% | 9.26 | 6.48 | 5.09 | 4.26 | 3.72 | 3.04 | 2.65 | 2.40 | 2.22 | 2.10 | 1.93 | 1.84 | 1.76 |

The third and final step is to convert this stream of monthly payments back to a contract face value on the basis of the rate of interest that will be shown on the contract. Let's say that Dusty thinks the rate of interest shown on the contract will be 10 percent per annum, or the equivalent of .83333 percent per month. On that basis, the face value of the contract balance should be $116,238.94. The steps to arrive at this amount using the TI calculator are the same as those in Exhibits 17–1 and 17–2.

In other words, if the rate of interest on the contract is 10 percent, it takes about $116,000 of face value to have a cash equivalent value of $100,000, if the market rate of interest on such a contract is 15 percent and the term of the contract is seven years. The business could be offered for sale at $166,000, with $50,000 down and a contract balance of $116,000; the monthly payments would include interest at a 10 percent annual rate for 84 months, and the deal would have a cash equivalent value of about $150,000. Exhibit 17–5 shows the effect of different market rates on various contract terms.

Exhibit 17–5

**PRESENT VALUE OF A $1,000 CONTRACT
AT VARIOUS MARKET RATES**

**"Market Rate" 15%**

Number of Months

| Contract Int. Rate | 24 | 30 | 36 | 48 | 60 | 72 | 84 | 96 | 120 | 144 | 180 | 240 |
|---|---|---|---|---|---|---|---|---|---|---|---|---|
| 15% | 1000 | 1000 | 1000 | 1000 | 1000 | 1000 | 1000 | 1000 | 1000 | 1000 | 1000 | 1000 |
| 14% | 990 | 988 | 986 | 982 | 978 | 974 | 971 | 968 | 962 | 958 | 952 | 944 |
| 13% | 981 | 976 | 972 | 964 | 956 | 949 | 943 | 937 | 925 | 916 | 904 | 890 |
| 12% | 971 | 964 | 958 | 946 | 935 | 925 | 915 | 906 | 889 | 875 | 858 | 836 |
| 11% | 961 | 953 | 944 | 929 | 914 | 900 | 887 | 875 | 854 | 835 | 812 | 784 |
| 10% | 952 | 941 | 931 | 911 | 893 | 876 | 860 | 846 | 819 | 796 | 768 | 733 |
| 9% | 942 | 930 | 917 | 894 | 873 | 852 | 834 | 816 | 785 | 758 | 725 | 683 |
| 8% | 933 | 918 | 904 | 877 | 852 | 829 | 808 | 788 | 752 | 721 | 683 | 635 |
| 7% | 923 | 907 | 891 | 860 | 832 | 806 | 782 | 760 | 720 | 685 | 642 | 589 |
| 6% | 914 | 895 | 876 | 844 | 813 | 784 | 757 | 732 | 688 | 650 | 603 | 544 |

**"Market Rate" 16%**

Number of Months

| Contract Int. Rate | 24 | 30 | 36 | 48 | 60 | 72 | 84 | 96 | 120 | 144 | 180 | 240 |
|---|---|---|---|---|---|---|---|---|---|---|---|---|
| 15% | 991 | 989 | 987 | 983 | 979 | 976 | 973 | 970 | 965 | 960 | 955 | 949 |
| 14% | 981 | 977 | 973 | 965 | 958 | 951 | 945 | 939 | 928 | 919 | 908 | 896 |
| 13% | 971 | 965 | 959 | 947 | 936 | 926 | 917 | 908 | 893 | 879 | 863 | 844 |
| 12% | 962 | 953 | 945 | 930 | 916 | 902 | 890 | 878 | 858 | 840 | 819 | 793 |
| 11% | 952 | 942 | 932 | 913 | 895 | 878 | 863 | 849 | 824 | 802 | 775 | 744 |
| 10% | 943 | 930 | 918 | 896 | 874 | 855 | 837 | 820 | 790 | 765 | 733 | 695 |
| 9% | 933 | 919 | 905 | 879 | 854 | 832 | 811 | 792 | 757 | 728 | 692 | 648 |
| 8% | 924 | 908 | 892 | 862 | 835 | 809 | 786 | 764 | 725 | 692 | 652 | 603 |
| 7% | 915 | 896 | 879 | 846 | 815 | 787 | 761 | 737 | 694 | 658 | 613 | 558 |
| 6% | 906 | 885 | 866 | 829 | 796 | 765 | 736 | 710 | 644 | 624 | 576 | 516 |

**"Market Rate" 17%**

Number of Months

| Contract Int. Rate | 24 | 30 | 36 | 48 | 60 | 72 | 84 | 96 | 120 | 144 | 180 | 240 |
|---|---|---|---|---|---|---|---|---|---|---|---|---|
| 15% | 981 | 976 | 972 | 965 | 957 | 951 | 944 | 938 | 928 | 920 | 909 | 898 |
| 14% | 971 | 965 | 959 | 947 | 936 | 926 | 917 | 908 | 893 | 881 | 865 | 848 |
| 13% | 962 | 953 | 945 | 930 | 916 | 902 | 890 | 879 | 859 | 842 | 822 | 799 |
| 12% | 952 | 942 | 932 | 913 | 895 | 879 | 864 | 850 | 826 | 805 | 780 | 751 |
| 11% | 943 | 930 | 918 | 896 | 875 | 856 | 838 | 822 | 793 | 768 | 739 | 704 |
| 10% | 933 | 919 | 905 | 879 | 855 | 833 | 812 | 794 | 760 | 732 | 698 | 658 |
| 9% | 924 | 908 | 892 | 862 | 835 | 810 | 787 | 766 | 729 | 697 | 659 | 613 |
| 8% | 915 | 896 | 879 | 846 | 816 | 788 | 763 | 739 | 698 | 663 | 621 | 570 |
| 7% | 906 | 885 | 866 | 830 | 797 | 766 | 739 | 713 | 668 | 630 | 584 | 529 |
| 6% | 896 | 874 | 853 | 812 | 778 | 745 | 715 | 687 | 639 | 598 | 548 | 488 |

Exhibit 17–5 (*concluded*)

## PRESENT VALUE OF A $1,000 CONTRACT
## AT VARIOUS MARKET RATES

### "Market Rate" 18%

**Number of Months**

| Contract Int. Rate | 24 | 30 | 36 | 48 | 60 | 72 | 84 | 96 | 120 | 144 | 180 | 240 |
|---|---|---|---|---|---|---|---|---|---|---|---|---|
| 15% | 971 | 965 | 959 | 947 | 937 | 927 | 918 | 910 | 895 | 883 | 869 | 853 |
| 14% | 962 | 953 | 945 | 930 | 916 | 903 | 892 | 881 | 862 | 846 | 827 | 806 |
| 13% | 952 | 942 | 932 | 913 | 896 | 880 | 866 | 852 | 829 | 809 | 786 | 759 |
| 12% | 943 | 931 | 919 | 896 | 876 | 857 | 840 | 824 | 796 | 773 | 745 | 713 |
| 11% | 934 | 919 | 906 | 880 | 856 | 835 | 815 | 796 | 764 | 738 | 706 | 669 |
| 10% | 924 | 908 | 893 | 863 | 837 | 812 | 790 | 769 | 733 | 703 | 667 | 625 |
| 9% | 915 | 897 | 880 | 847 | 817 | 790 | 765 | 743 | 703 | 670 | 630 | 583 |
| 8% | 906 | 886 | 867 | 831 | 798 | 769 | 742 | 717 | 673 | 637 | 593 | 542 |
| 7% | 897 | 875 | 854 | 815 | 785 | 748 | 718 | 691 | 644 | 605 | 558 | 502 |
| 6% | 888 | 864 | 841 | 799 | 761 | 727 | 695 | 666 | 616 | 574 | 524 | 464 |

### "Market Rate" 19%

**Number of Months**

| Contract Int. Rate | 24 | 30 | 36 | 48 | 60 | 72 | 84 | 96 | 120 | 144 | 180 | 240 |
|---|---|---|---|---|---|---|---|---|---|---|---|---|
| 15% | 962 | 954 | 946 | 931 | 917 | 905 | 893 | 883 | 864 | 849 | 832 | 812 |
| 14% | 952 | 942 | 932 | 914 | 897 | 881 | 867 | 854 | 832 | 813 | 791 | 767 |
| 13% | 943 | 931 | 919 | 897 | 877 | 859 | 842 | 827 | 800 | 778 | 752 | 723 |
| 12% | 934 | 920 | 906 | 881 | 858 | 836 | 817 | 799 | 767 | 743 | 713 | 679 |
| 11% | 925 | 909 | 893 | 864 | 838 | 814 | 792 | 773 | 738 | 709 | 675 | 637 |
| 10% | 915 | 897 | 880 | 848 | 819 | 792 | 768 | 746 | 708 | 676 | 639 | 595 |
| 9% | 906 | 886 | 868 | 832 | 800 | 771 | 745 | 720 | 679 | 644 | 603 | 555 |
| 8% | 897 | 876 | 855 | 816 | 782 | 750 | 721 | 695 | 650 | 612 | 568 | 516 |
| 7% | 888 | 865 | 842 | 801 | 763 | 729 | 698 | 670 | 622 | 582 | 534 | 478 |
| 6% | 879 | 854 | 830 | 785 | 745 | 709 | 676 | 646 | 595 | 552 | 501 | 442 |

### "Market Rate" 20%

**Number of Months**

| Contract Int. Rate | 24 | 30 | 36 | 48 | 60 | 72 | 84 | 96 | 120 | 144 | 180 | 240 |
|---|---|---|---|---|---|---|---|---|---|---|---|---|
| 15% | 953 | 943 | 933 | 915 | 898 | 883 | 869 | 856 | 835 | 817 | 797 | 775 |
| 14% | 943 | 931 | 920 | 898 | 878 | 860 | 844 | 829 | 803 | 782 | 758 | 732 |
| 13% | 934 | 920 | 907 | 882 | 859 | 838 | 819 | 802 | 773 | 748 | 720 | 690 |
| 12% | 925 | 909 | 894 | 865 | 840 | 816 | 795 | 776 | 742 | 715 | 683 | 648 |
| 11% | 916 | 898 | 881 | 849 | 821 | 795 | 771 | 750 | 713 | 683 | 647 | 608 |
| 10% | 907 | 887 | 868 | 833 | 802 | 773 | 748 | 724 | 684 | 651 | 612 | 568 |
| 9% | 898 | 876 | 856 | 818 | 784 | 753 | 725 | 699 | 655 | 620 | 578 | 530 |
| 8% | 889 | 865 | 843 | 802 | 765 | 732 | 702 | 675 | 628 | 589 | 544 | 492 |
| 7% | 880 | 855 | 831 | 787 | 747 | 712 | 680 | 651 | 601 | 560 | 512 | 456 |
| 6% | 871 | 844 | 819 | 772 | 730 | 692 | 658 | 627 | 574 | 531 | 480 | 422 |

# Chapter 18

## Making a Sanity Check: Is It Affordable?

As noted in earlier chapters, the large majority of sales of small businesses and professional practices are financed, most often by the seller, sometimes by an outside lender. It is in the interest of both the buyer and the lender (whether the lender is the seller or an outside lender) to make every effort to be sure that the deal is structured so that the debt service (principal and interest payments) can be met. Lack of adequate capital is very high on the list of the most frequent causes of business failure.

One experienced authority, already quoted elsewhere in the book, discusses the propensity for extended financing terms as follows:

> *Down Payment.* Buyers are worried about how much cash they need to invest. Price resistance goes down as the down payment goes down. Our firm has been able to rapidly sell many businesses with such attractive terms that price becomes a secondary consideration. Of course, a reduced down payment adds risk in the form of other required financing. However, lowering the down payment demand makes the business accessible to more buyers, and many buyers with high aspirations but little cash will pay a premium for the opportunity to get into their own businesses.
>
> Many sellers have reported that they had little trouble selling their businesses for the top price once creative financing and a low down payment requirement was available. I share that experience. Many buyers literally ignore price itself once they're satisfied that they can raise the few dollars to buy the business, and that the business can pay off the loans.[1]

# Cash Available for Debt Service

Of course, the key phrase in the quotation above is "satisfied . . . that the business can pay off the loans." In most cases, the source of debt repayment will be cash generated by the business or practice. To measure the ability to cover the debt service, we need a variable not previously defined or discussed in the book, which we will call *cash available for debt service.* This phrase is just basic and descriptive, rather than being a term with very specific meaning that is universally accepted in the annals of finance and appraisal, so we can be somewhat creative in how we define it. Determining the amount of cash available for debt service is a matter of using practical common sense, in light of the basic facts of each case.

As a generalized framework to measure affordability, I would suggest defining the cash available for debt service as follows. It is income:

1. Before interest and principal payments (since we are measuring the coverage of those items).
2. Before depreciation and amortization (or other noncash charges).
3. After reasonable compensation for services of owner.
4. After capital expenditures, including both replacements and additions.

---

[1] Arnold S. Goldstein, *The Complete Guide to Buying and Selling a Business* (New York: New American Library, 1984), p. 102.

**5.** After federal and state income taxes (based on taxable income per IRS code).

The above list assumes that the business or practice itself will be the source of the funds to cover each item on the list. To the extent that funds are available from other sources for one or more of the requirements, the list may be modified.

# Amount of Coverage Needed

The amount of coverage of the debt service that should be required depends largely on the degree of risk in the expected cash flow. To the extent that the expected cash flow is highly uncertain or volatile from year to year, the amount of coverage in an average year should be higher.

Paul Baron, a veteran business broker, also quoted elsewhere in this book, suggests that debt service should not be more than 35 to 50 percent of after-tax cash flow. (He defines after-tax cash flow in approximately the same way that we have defined cash available for debt service, except that Baron does not deduct from cash flow additions to working capital and capital expenditures for additions.)[2]

Walter Jurek advocates allocating 50 percent of the net cash flow to the servicing of the acquisition debt:

> The entire income stream that is available should not be used for debt service. Any company needs a cushion between its debt service retirement schedule and its net available income for debt service. Normally, only 50 percent of the net available cashflow after taxes and reasonable capital expenditures should be used for debt service or debt retirement.[3]

# Possible Adjustments to the Contract

If the terms being considered on the first pass do not seem affordable by a comfortable margin, then several adjustments to the contemplated terms may be considered. The length of the contract may be extended, the payments may be varied (perhaps interest only for a time, or an increasing payment schedule, if the cash available is expected to be low at first but increasing); some payments may be contingent on some level of cash flow, or there may be a longer-term amortization with a balloon payment.

Contracts with contingencies in the payment schedule are not unusual for businesses that are known to be cyclical. The principal portion of the payment, or even the entire principal and interest payment, may be suspended for a year if cash flow is negative, extending the length of

[2] Paul B. Baron, *When You Buy or Sell a Company*, rev. ed. (Meriden, Conn.: The Center for Business Information, Inc., 1983), p.7–26.

[3] Walter Jurek, *How to Determine the Value of a Business* (Stow, Oh.: Quality Services, Inc., 1977), p. 29.

the contract if that occurs. There may be a range of minimum and maximum payments per year depending on the amount of available cash flow.

A 10-year amortization with a 5-year balloon means that the periodic payments are of a principal and interest amount that would pay off the contract in 10 years, but that at the end of the fifth year the remaining contract balance becomes payable all at once. Longer-term amortizations with balloon payments are sometimes used, but I always wonder where the money is going to come from for the balloon payment.

If reasonable alternatives have been considered and do not seem affordable, then, just possibly, in spite of all the valiant valuation exercises done (supposedly in accordance with the previous chapters), the price is simply too high. Back to the drawing board.

# Protective Covenants

From the viewpoint of a lender or a seller selling on a contract, it obviously is important to have covenants in the contract that will protect the ability of the business or practice to generate adequate cash flow to cover the debt service. Such covenants usually restrict such items as owner's compensation, capital expenditures, any investments outside of the normal course of the business, and assumption of other indebtedness.

# An Example

The following example uses the Mary's Machinery and Equipment case, as in prior chapters.

In Chapter 16, we estimated a value of $575,000 for Mary's common stock. Mary requires a $200,000 down payment and is willing to extend to the buyer a five-year contract to cover the balance of $375,000 at 12 percent interest. There would be equal annual payments of principal and interest.

The first step in analyzing whether the company can cover this debt service is to calculate the cash available for debt service. The company's pretax income under the new owner, Barney Backhoe, is estimated at $100,000, as shown in Exhibit 9–3. To calculate the company's taxes, we need to take into consideration that Mary's will receive a tax savings from the increased interest expense, if the $375,000 is financed on a contract. The first year's interest expense on the contract will be $45,000 (.12 × $375,000 = $45,000), which will reduce Mary's taxable income to $55,000 ($100,000 − $45,000 = $55,000). Statutory taxes on this amount would be $9,750, resulting in a net income of $45,250.

Cash available for debt service equals net income before depreciation and interest related to the contract. That is computed as follows:

| Net income | $ 45,250 |
|---|---|
| Depreciation | 33,000 |
| Interest | 45,000 |
| Cash available for debt | $123,250 |

The next step is to determine the debt service requirements which this contract creates. A five-year contract for $375,000 bearing 12 percent interest results in annual principal and interest payments of $104,029.

Therefore, the anticipated cash available for debt is less than 1.2 times the projected debt ($123,250 ÷ $104,029 = 1.18). This level of available cash relative to the requirement for debt service is very low, and a prospective buyer probably would not want to enter into the agreement under these terms. The question about the buyer's ability to pay would make the contract risky from the seller's viewpoint as well.

It is unlikely that Mary will accept less than the $575,000 for her company, since she is not in a real rush to sell. However, if she is going to realize that price, she probably will have to extend more favorable terms. If she extends the length of the contract to 10 years, the annual debt service becomes $66,369. Under this scenario, the cash available to service the debt is almost twice the amount of the debt ($123,250 ÷ $66,369 = 1.86), a much more comfortable level and probably something the buyer could live with. Another alternative, if Mary wanted to keep the contract length to five years, would be to accept a lower interest rate on the debt. Also, since earnings are expected to go up by about 5 percent a year, contract payments could escalate by a similar percentage.

What this example points out is that, while a cash value of $575,000 was indicated for the common stock of Mary's, based on our valuation approaches, the sanity check shows that the company could just barely afford the debt service relating to the purchase of the company if the terms are $200,000 down with the balance payable over 5 years at 12 percent interest. The purchase of the company becomes more affordable if the contract is extended for 10 years or if a lower interest rate is charged. Therefore, the sanity check indicates that a cash equivalent price of $575,000 may be on the high side when affordability is taken into consideration, as the debt service of the company to either the seller or the bank will be a strain unless the terms are spread out over 10 years or a low interest rate is accepted.

The foregoing example was based on normalized earnings, assuming no significant fluctuations from year to year. If cash available for debt service is likely to fluctuate significantly over the years, then it would be desirable to make a forecast for several years, perhaps for the full length of the contract.

# Chapter 19

## Comparison between Business Appraisal Practices and Real Estate Appraisal Practices

Appraisal of a business differs from appraisal of real estate in several respects. The most important difference, of course, is the nature of what is being appraised. A business is a complex and dynamic entity, involving the interaction of many resources. Real estate, by definition, is physical property, which may be one part of a total business. The valuation of a business integrates the total entity: real estate, machinery and equipment, current assets, and intangible assets.

Other differences have arisen from the historical development of the two appraisal disciplines and the backgrounds of the people involved. Great confusion exists because some of the terminology overlaps, while some of the same terms in the two disciplines have widely divergent meanings.

There are also many similarities between business appraisal and real estate appraisal. The purpose of this chapter is to provide the reader with some perspective by highlighting some of the differences and similarities between business and real estate appraisal.

# Nature of Property Being Appraised

Real estate, by definition, is static property. The leading authority in the field of real estate defines real estate as "Physical land and appurtenances affixed to the land, e.g., structures."[1]

A business, by contrast, is a complex and dynamic organization of interrelated resources, including people, capital, and a wide variety of tangible and intangible assets, one of which may be real estate. In other words, real estate may be one component of a business.

The major categories of rights that need to be appraised in conjunction with real property are interests in the fee estate (ownership of the property itself) and the leasehold estate (rights of a lessee). Other rights may include items such as underground rights, air rights, and easements.

By contrast, the appraisal of a business involves an almost limitless amalgam of rights and opportunities, some contractual and others not, including any or all of the bundle of rights that may be associated with a parcel of real estate or, in some cases, many different parcels of real estate.

In most cases, especially with respect to properties utilized by small businesses and professional practices, the real estate is separable from the business. In such cases, as I have suggested in earlier chapters, the real estate and the business should be appraised separately, with the income stream to the business charged with an appropriate rent expense.

When the business and the real estate it occupies are virtually inseparable, as in the case of a single-use property, I suggest that the intertwined business/real estate entity will have more of the economic characteristics of a business entity than the economic characteristics

---

[1] *The Dictionary of Real Estate Appraisal* (Chicago: American Institute of Real Estate Appraisers, 1984), p. 249.

normally associated with real estate. When that is true, approaches normally associated with business appraisal are likely to lead to a more reliable appraisal result than approaches normally associated with real estate appraisal. Thus concluded a recent landmark court case involving the appraisal of an industrial property for the purpose of assessing ad valorem taxes.[2]

# Relative Development of the Disciplines

The discipline of business appraisal has been neglected compared with the discipline of real estate appraisal.

One of the most striking differences between the two appraisal fields is the dearth of authoritative writings and teachings about business appraisal compared with the plethora of writings and teachings about real estate appraisal. Definitive books and articles on business appraisal are relatively scarce, and only a handful of business schools offer even a single course on business appraisal. Books and articles on real estate appraisal abound, and virtually every business school offers a course or a series of courses on real estate appraisal.

The body that provides leadership in the discipline of business appraisal is the American Society of Appraisers, a multidisciplinary appraisal society conferring professional certification in several fields. Its members certified in business appraisal number in the hundreds, while its members certified in one or more aspects of real estate appraisal number in the thousands. In addition, in the field of real estate appraisal, the American Institute of Real Estate Appraisers and the Society of Real Estate Appraisers offer an extensive array of publications and course offerings.

Most of the organized development of business appraisal theory and practice has taken place since 1980, and has been spearheaded by the Business Valuation Committee of the American Society of Appraisers. More information on the A.S.A and the current state of the art of the business appraisal discipline is included in Chapter 34.

The development of the business appraisal discipline has drawn heavily on the theory and practice of corporate finance and security analysis. The use of the theory and knowledge of corporate finance and security analysis is eminently reasonable, since the umbrella labeled *corporate finance* really covers the financing of all kinds of business entities, regardless of whether they happen to be corporations, partnerships, or sole proprietorships. The basic thrust of security analysis is the appraisal of an interest in an operating entity; the discipline of security analysis, therefore, is really a specialized variation of business appraisal. The business appraisal discipline combines the relevant elements of these fields of expertise, along with the requisite understanding of economics, business management, and accounting; it formulates an appraisal process that incorporates and focuses the considerations necessary to estimate the value of an operating entity within the economic and industry environment prevalent at any given time.

---

[2] *General Dynamics* v. *Board of Assessors of Quincy, et al.*, 388 Mass. 24 (Jan. 21, 1983).

# Language Similarities and Differences

A term may have a certain well-accepted definition in the language of finance and security analysis and a different and equally well-accepted definition in the language of real estate. Similarly, practitioners in business finance and security analysis may label a concept with one name, and practitioners in real estate appraisal may identify the same concept by some other name. The language of business appraisal logically follows the language of finance and security analysis, since the subject matter is operating businesses.

Under generally accepted accounting principles (GAAP), the term *net operating income* is unequivocally defined to be income after the deduction of depreciation and amortization, and the literature of finance follows the accounting definition.[3] By contrast, real estate terminology does not include noncash items such as depreciation or amortization within its definition of operating expenses, and therefore the definition of net income as used in real estate terminology is before deduction of depreciation or amortization expense.

In business finance and security analysis terminology, the term *cash flow* (or *cash throwoff*) is most commonly (although not universally) used to mean net income after all cash expenses, which means after interest costs but before noncash items such as depreciation and amortization.[4] However, in real estate terminology, cash flow is defined to mean "income remaining from net operating income after debt service is paid,"[5] which means after principal payments as well as interest payments.

It is beyond the scope of this book to provide a comparative lexicon of terminology used in the fields of real estate and business appraisal. Hopefully, the foregoing examples will alert the reader to the problem, so that he will be aware of which definition is intended when he encounters one of the many terms which have ambiguous usage. The ambiguities prevalent in current usage are responsible for enormous miscommunications, and many erroneous appraisal results.

# Differences in Appraisal Approaches

As a generalization, I would say that approaches to business appraisals are less rigidly structured than approaches to real estate appraisal. That is not to say that any approach used in business appraisal can or should be any less rigorously carried out; however, the variations and

---

[3] For example, a typical finance text defines net operating income as "Income before interest and income taxes but after depreciation produced by operating assets." Charles O. Kroncke, et al., *Managerial Finance: Essentials* (St. Paul: West Publishing Company, 1976), p. 479. The business appraisers regard a property the company utilizes in its operations as an operating asset.

[4] For example, the *Dictionary of Banking and Finance* defines cash flow as "the reported net income of a corporation, plus amounts charged off for depreciation, depletion, amortization, and extraordinary charges to reserves which are bookkeeping deductions and not actually paid out in cash" (New York: John Wiley & Sons, 1982), p. 92.

[5] *The Dictionary of Real Estate Appraisal*, p. 237.

complexities of business appraisal require more flexibility in the choice and design of appraisal methodology.

## Real Estate Appraisal Approaches

In the field of real estate appraisal, it is almost universally accepted that there are three approaches:

1. *Income approach (income capitalization approach):* "A set of procedures in which an appraiser derives a value indication for income-producing property by converting anticipated benefits into property value. This conversion is accomplished either by (1) capitalizing a single year's income expectancy or an annual average of several years' income expectancies at a market-derived capitalization rate or a capitalization rate that reflects a specified income pattern, return on investment, and change in the value of the investment; or (2) discounting the annual cash flows for the holding period and the reversion at a specified yield rate."[6]
2. *Cost approach:* "A set of procedures in which an appraiser derives a value-indication by estimating the current cost to reproduce or replace the existing structure, deducting for all accrued depreciation in the property, and adding the estimated land value."[7]
3. *Market approach (sales comparison approach):* "A set of procedures in which an appraiser derives a value indication by comparing the property being appraised to similar properties that have been sold recently, applying appropriate units of comparison, and making adjustments, based on the elements of comparison, to the sales prices of the comparables."[8]

## Business Appraisal Approaches

In business appraisal, there is no universal acceptance of any specific number of approaches. Individual writers sometimes make such categorical statements as "There are five approaches for valuing a business" or "Seven approaches are acceptable," but there is no consensus that the discipline of business appraisal should be practiced according to some specific number of structured approaches.

The value of an operating business stems almost entirely from its ability to generate earnings. Therefore, the business appraiser is concerned primarily with developing one or more measures of the subject company's demonstrated or potential earning power and an appropriate rate of return that an investor should expect in light of the risks involved. In this sense, the basic thrust of business appraisal is akin to the income capitalization approach in real estate appraisal.

Within the income capitalization approach, the real estate ap-

---

[6] Ibid., p. 159.

[7] Ibid., p. 75.

[8] Ibid., p. 268.

praisal profession recognizes certain variations that are closely parallel to variations of earning power capitalization approaches used in business appraisal. For example, what real estate appraisers call "direct capitalization"[9] is essentially the same procedure as I have described as capitalizing normalized earnings in Chapter 11. Within the category of direct capitalization, the real estate profession includes gross income multipliers, recognizing, as we do in Chapter 14, that the assumption underlying their validity is that a given level of gross income generated by a certain type of property or business should be able to generate a certain level of net income. What real estate appraisers call "yield capitalization"[10] is essentially the same procedure I have described as "The Discounted Future Earnings Method" in Chapter 12.

Income capitalization approaches are conceptually similar in business appraisal and real estate appraisal. However, in most cases, estimating an income stream for an operating business is much more difficult than estimating an income stream for an apartment or office building or some similar income-producing property. Furthermore, the risks of an operating business are more complex to assess and quantify, and therefore the selection of appropriate capitalization rates is more difficult in the context of business appraisal. To cope with these challenges adequately, the business appraiser needs a broad understanding of relevant economic and industry factors, capital market conditions, business management, and accounting.

As a generality, the business appraiser's asset approaches are somewhat akin to the real estate appraiser's cost approach, but in most cases the business appraiser would accord less weight to asset-related approaches. Except for assets that may be liquidated, the business appraiser is not interested in the assets per se, but rather in assets that contribute to the total entity. The business appraiser focuses on determining the extent to which the assets included with the business are adequate to generate the income stream being capitalized; he may, in some instances, be interested in the liquidation value of the assets as a measure of the downside risk. The business appraiser is interested in inventory value, of course, because it is expected to be sold in a relatively short time. To carry out a complete cost approach, however, which would be parallel to the real estate appraiser's cost approach, the business appraiser would have to estimate the cost to create not only the tangible assets, but also the intangible values, such as goodwill. He would also have to calculate appropriate deductions for both functional and economic obsolescence. The asset approaches used by the business appraiser only occasionally entail estimating values for specific tangible assets.

As for the market or sales comparison approach, the business appraiser normally does not think of that as an approach; rather he believes that market data should be the basis of every indicator of value. As the real estate appraiser will seek data on sales of comparable properties, the business appraiser will seek data on transactions in comparable businesses. The business appraiser will interpret the comparable

[9] *Appraisal of Real Estate* (Chicago: American Institute of Real Estate Appraisers, 1983), Chapter 16.
[10] Ibid., Chapter 17.

transaction data for guidance in determining applicable valuation parameters—such as capitalization rates for earnings or cash flow, and gross revenue multipliers—and ratios of the entity's market value to asset value measures such as book value or adjusted net tangible asset value. Sometimes the business appraiser will set out a separate valuation approach, using the market value indicators based on some specific transaction data; but more often the business appraiser will consider each relevant market value parameter as an approach, with each approach drawing to the fullest possible extent on available comparative sales data.

# Differences in Capitalization Rates

Pretax income streams from direct investment in real estate tend to be capitalized at lower rates of return than comparably defined pretax income streams from investments in non real estate oriented businesses. The primary reason for this is the tax advantages of real estate, which usually result in a comparably defined pretax income stream translating into a higher after-tax income stream. Another reason may be a lower perceived level of risk in direct real estate investment compared with the typical investment in a small business.

Furthermore, real estate investors may accept a lower rate of return from their cash flow stream because they expect extra return in the form of capital appreciation on the property. This is in sharp contrast to a business investment that includes machinery and equipment that eventually will become worthless through wear and tear and/or obsolescence.

# Availability of Comparable Sales Data

Useful comparable sales data are much harder to obtain for sales of businesses than for sales of real estate. The problem of obtaining comparable transaction data is greater for small businesses and professional practices than for large businesses.

Real estate transaction data are readily available in county courthouses, and sales of public companies are reported in great detail. However, there is no requirement for public reporting of data on sales of closely held companies. As a consequence, unless the appraiser has access to a private data source, there may be no comparative transaction data available for guidance.

Another problem with the use of comparable sales data for business appraisers is the uniqueness of every business. Each parcel of real estate is also unique, of course; but the large number of variables, many of which are impossible to measure numerically, usually make the matter of comparability a greater problem when using comparative business sale transaction data than when using comparative real estate transaction data.

# Summary

When done correctly, real estate appraisal practices and business appraisal practices are totally compatible with each other. In fact, logically, valuation of income-producing real estate may be viewed as a special case of business valuation, in the sense that income-producing real estate is logically equivalent to a business that has very limited assets. When each is done properly, the significant differences in approaches and emphases emerge logically from the basic differences in the nature and scope of the property being appraised. It is unfortunate, however, that the terminology used by the two disciplines is not interchangeable. The differences in usage of certain important terms are so ingrained that I see no realistic prospect for developing a set of mutually compatible terms.

# Chapter 20

## Common Errors

*It is better to know that we do not know than to know not that we know not.*

Old Wise Man's Saying

This is a long chapter. It is long because so many different people frequently perpetrate so many common errors in their attempts to determine values of small businesses and professional practices.

I hope that this chapter will assist those who are not professional appraisers to be able to make a reasonably critical review of someone else's appraisal of a business or practice, and to be able to correct, or at least call attention to, some of the errors that seem to recur most frequently. I hope also that the chapter will help the novice appraiser to avoid such pitfalls. Possibly, it will even help one or two veteran but misguided appraisers to mend a few of their wayward ways.

# Rigid Categorization of Business Valuation Methods

Watch out when you hear, "There are currently five accepted methods for valuing a business," or "Three methods exist for valuing a small business," and so on. There is no finite number of commonly accepted methods for valuing small businesses and professional practices. One author references 32 valuation methods.[1]

There are three sources from which a business or practice can generate money for its owners: (1) earnings, (2) sale of assets, and (3) sale of the business or practice. All valuation methods attempt to measure one or a combination of these three factors, directly or indirectly, and translate them into a present value. The various methods by which different appraisers approach the problem are not discrete, but rather variations of each other, with considerable overlap.

In my experience, viewing the problem of estimating value in terms of a finite number of specific methods tends to go hand in hand with implementing each of the methods by using some specific formula; more often than not, the formula is applied without the benefit of experienced judgment as to whether or not it conforms to the economic realities of the situation. Estimating the value of a business or professional practice is much more than a mechanical exercise—it requires large doses of informed judgment, distilled out of years of experience and extensive continuing education on developments in the field of business and practice valuation.

# Reliance on Real Estate Appraisal Methods

As noted in the previous chapter, the traditional world of real estate appraisal has categorized the problem of valuation into three approaches: (1) the cost approach, (2) the market approach, and (3) the

[1] Thomas J. Martin and Mark Gustafson, *Valuing Your Business* (New York: Holt, Rinehart & Winston), 1980, p. 23.

income approach. Elements of these approaches are found in generally accepted business appraisal practices. However, some people with a real estate background tend to try to force business appraisal into those three categories as they are applied to real estate, without a full understanding of how the dynamics and personal characteristics of operating businesses and professional practices differentiate such entities from inanimate pieces of property.

Chapter 4 deals with differences between valuation of large businesses (some of which may be publicly traded) and valuation of small businesses and professional practices. Chapter 19 deals with differences between appraising real estate and appraising small businesses and professional practices. Between the two, it is my opinion that small businesses and professional practices, with their dynamics of people and operations, have more in common from a valuation viewpoint with their larger brethren than with inanimate real estate. I believe that a person schooled in the techniques of security analysis, but without schooling in real estate, can adapt more adequately to the demands of small business and professional practice appraisal than can a real estate appraiser without schooling in security analysis.

# Reliance on Rules of Thumb

The following are a few representative quotes from business and professional practice brokers and appraisers on the subject of rules of thumb:

> There seem to be norms for the worth of every imaginable business. My advice: Ignore them. Buying a business is too important for Kentucky windage.[2]

> Rules of thumb are dumb . . . greatly oversimplified . . . highly unreliable.[3]

> They are dangerous and full of pitfalls.[4]

> Simplicity is often achieved at the considerable loss of realism.[5]

> Over the past five years inflation has affected the pricing of business and thrown traditional "rule of thumb" methods out of whack.[6]

Some of the problems with rules of thumb were discussed in the section on "Problems with Gross Revenue Multipliers," in Chapter 12. Other problems are discussed in the accompanying article (Exhibit 20–1) by Jay Fishman, an active business appraiser and a member of the American Society of Appraisers Business Valuation Committee.

For industries in which a valuation rule of thumb is widely recognized, the appraiser should consider it, but certainly not accept it at face value.

---

[2] Thomas P. Murphy, "What Price Independence?" *Forbes*, September 27, 1982, p. 209. Murphy is the head of a venture capital firm.

[3] Glen Cooper, "How Much Is Your Business Worth?" *In Business*, September–October 1984, p. 50.

[4] Alan Johnson, "Figuring the Worth of a Firm." *Computer Systems News*, February 13, 1984, p. 24.

[5] Harry Weber, "An Evaluation of Business Valuation Techniques." *Valuation*, November 1982, p. 104.

[6] *The Business Broker*, February 1985, p. 1.

Exhibit 20–1

## THE PROBLEM WITH RULES OF THUMB
## IN THE VALUATION OF CLOSELY-HELD ENTITIES

### by Jay E. Fishman, A.S.A.*

Recently we completed the valuation of a pharmacy in a matrimonial matter. Our search for comparable transactions yielded insufficient information to make a direct Market Data Approach useable. Accordingly, we relied on the other traditional methods used in the valuation of closely held businesses, including a Capitalization of Income Approach. Our client reviewed the report and quickly pointed out that we failed to consider the industry rule of thumb for the valuation of pharmacies, as discussed in various pharmacy journals and trade publications. Application of that formula would have produced a negative value for the common stock of the pharmacy and was not used by our client when he purchased the pharmacy three years before. The pharmacist thought that the negative value aspect was perfectly acceptable for matrimonial purposes, but showed great reluctance to use the formula to sell his store.

The pharmacy episode was followed by our involvement in a court case relating to the valuation of a new car dealership. In this matter, the wife's expert determined goodwill grounded on a so-called industry practice which estimated goodwill based on $1,500 for new cars sold on an annual basis. Cross-examination revealed that the so-called industry practice was not derived from actual sales of automobile dealerships, but was based on yet another expert's verbal representation to this witness. Interestingly, the subject new car dealership had an average gross profit margin on the sale of new cars of approximately $500 per car.

The search for a "quick-fix" to the complex problems surrounding the valuation of a closely held enterprise has led many to rely on rules of thumb or industry formulas. The above examples illustrate the enormous potential for abuse in applying these standards to the valuation of a closely held entity.

**What are the rules of thumb?** Rules of thumb or industry formulas are supposedly market derived units of comparison. The multiple or percentage contained in the formula is an expression of the relationship between gross purchase price and some indicator of the operating results of an enterprise. Accordingly, the sale of casualty insurance brokerage concern is discussed in terms of a commission multiple, the goodwill of a retail fuel oil business is discussed in terms of cents per retained gallon and the sale of a medical practice is referred to in terms of a multiple or percentage of the gross revenue or of the net disposable income.

The use of a rule of thumb in the valuation of a closely held entity is actually a variation of the Market Comparison Approach. The Market Comparison Approach attempts to establish value via direct comparison with exchanges of similar assets in the marketplace. The use of direct Market Comparison is contingent on the availability of sales involving reasonably comparable businesses in a free and active marketplace. Adjustments for differences between the acquired businesses and the subject entity are then calculated. Examples of adjustments include differences in market share, profitability, capital structure and management depth. These adjustments result in the production of a multiple, usually related to earnings, cash flow or equity which is applied to the subject entity resulting in an expression of value.

Since rules of thumb or industry formulas are a variation of the direct Market Comparison Approach, certain minimum criteria must exist prior to their use in the valuation process. These criteria include the following:

● The single multiple or percentage must be derived from an adequate information base.

● The expert must understand the terms and conditions of each transaction in the information base.

● The transactions should involve reasonably similar businesses.

● Adjustments should be made for differences between the acquired companies and the entity under appraisement.

**Problems with industry formulas.** We have found that most industry formulas or rules of thumb are not derived from actual transactions in the marketplace. Industry formulas are commonly derived from textbooks, trade publications, verbal representations or other similar sources of information. Clearly, these sources of information will not provide the expert with sufficient information to render a meaningful opinion of value for the enterprise using these formulas. There are at least three fundamental problems associated with the industry formula "quick fix" approach. All of these fundamental problems are a result of their failure to meet the above minimum criteria.

*First,* the lack of knowledge concerning the actual transactions that comprise the industry formulas will lead to confusion concerning the property acquired by a buyer during a particular transaction. Buyers will commonly purchase the assets or the equity of an entity. Since the objective of an appraisal for matrimonial purposes is usually the common stock or equity portion of an enterprise, reliance on an industry formula that produces a value for the assets of an entity can fundamentally misstate the value of the equity for the subject firm.

*Second,* the lack of an adequate data base can lead to considerable confusion over the actual purchase price paid for a comparable entity. An opinion of Market Value presumes a 100 percent cash price at the valuation date. Without knowledge of the actual transactions underlying a given group of comparables, the experts would be unable to determine the real purchase price paid for the comparable enterprises.

For example, a gross price of $100,000 could be listed as the purchase price for a comparable entity, but this purchase price could be paid over ten years with no interest. This would further reduce the Market Value paid by the buyer due to the time value of money. If the expert is unaware of the terms of the transaction, he or she would be unable to make such a time value of money adjustment. Therefore, the gross consideration would be confused with a 100 percent cash price at the valuation date and result in a distortion in the opinion of value using the industry formula.

Alternatively, the purchase price could be augmented by a convenant not to compete given to the seller over a period of years. This covenant not to compete could actually be part of the purchase price paid for the business, but was structured in this way for tax purposes. Again, without knowledge of the actual terms of the transaction, a misstatement of value relying on formulas derived from these types of transactions would occur.

*Thirdly,* most industry formulas in textbooks, trade publications and other sources presume a typical or average entity. Lacking knowledge of actual transactions results in distortions due to differences in profitability, capital structure, management and other important considerations inherent in what a buyer would offer for a business entity. The insufficient information base would result in the expert's inability to make these types of adjustments. The insufficient information base would make it impossible to gauge whether the subject enterprise is typical or atypical, and accordingly, would command a price superior or inferior to the typical multiple displayed in the industry formula.

For example, an accounting firm which could be valued on a one times gross basis would have the same value whether it was profitable or unprofitable. The same would apply as to whether it had a long term lease or short term lease, whether the gross revenue was generated by 100 small clients or 3 large clients. This hypothetical situation indicates the flaws inherent in using industry formulas without sufficient information.

**Summary.** There are no "quick fixes" to the valuation of closely held entities. It is essential to remember that industry formulas or rules of thumb are commonly not market derived representations of actual transactions. Since most industry formulas or rules of thumb are derived from textbooks, trade publications, verbal representations, or other similar sources of information, they are poor substitutes for the Direct Market Comparison Approach.

---

\*  Mr. Fishman is President, Financial Research, Inc., Narberth, Pennsylvania.

Source: *Fairshare,* Vol. 4, No. 12, p. 13 (Dec. 1984); reprinted with the permission of Law & Business, Inc.

# The "Assets Plus . . ." Approach

Some business brokers and others seem to think that every business and practice in existence is worth at least its net tangible asset value (used replacement cost basis, as discussed in Chapter 5), plus some amount for goodwill and/or whatever other intangible factors may be presumed to exist.

That simply is not always true. Many businesses cannot even generate enough earnings to justify their purchase at net tangible asset value. If the earning power justifies a price less than the adjusted net tangible asset value but more than the liquidation value, it is rational to expect the value determined by the earning power to predominate. If the value on a capitalized earnings basis is less than liquidation value, then it would seem that the rational choice is to liquidate.

Some owners who wish to sell cannot accept the notion that the economic value of the entity could be less than the replacement cost of its assets. The fact is, however, that there are many such businesses that would never be worth replacing if they did not already exist. They are worth only their economic value based on what they can earn, not what it would cost to replace a business that nobody would choose to replace in its existing form and location.

Most owners who delude themselves into overvaluing their businesses on the basis of an asset value approach without regard to earning power eventually just go quietly out of business, some via bankruptcy.

# Indiscriminate Use of Price/Earnings Ratios

Valuation by the good old price/earnings (P/E) ratio has broad appeal. It seems so natural, because everyone has heard of it and it is apparently so simple. Just take the earnings, apply a multiplier, and you have a value. P/E ratios for thousands of publicly traded stocks are published daily. By simply picking a P/E ratio and deciding what level of earnings for the subject company to apply it to, you can come up with almost any value you might like. What could be better? It is a valuation method that is simple, widely used, and easily manipulated (albeit more frequently out of ignorance than malice aforethought), and it seems to support almost any desired answer.

One must understand the following characteristics of publicly traded stocks in order to use their P/E ratios for guidance in valuing closely held businesses and professional practices:

1. The publicly traded market prices of the stock represent minority interests, not controlling interests.
2. The stocks are highly liquid—they can almost always be sold in a matter of minutes with cash delivered to the seller within a week.
3. The prices are for stock in a corporation and do not represent a direct purchase of any combination of assets.

4. The P/E ratios apply to earnings after depreciation and amortization, after interest on all short-term and long-term debt, after compensation to all employees in the business, including stockholder/employees, and after all federal and state corporate income taxes.
5. The earnings are from audited statements prepared in accordance with generally accepted accounting principles (GAAP).
6. The price in the P/E ratio usually is the price of the last transaction on the day before the quotation was published.
7. The earnings in the P/E ratio are what are called "latest 12 months' trailing earnings," that is, the earnings for the 12 months ending with the latest quarter for which the company has reported earnings.

Most common errors in the use of P/E ratios stem from failure to recognize one or a combination of the above seven characteristics of public company P/E ratios.

## Failure to Identify What One Gets for the Price

For the price that becomes the numerator in the P/E ratio, the buyer receives a share of stock representing a proportionate equity interest in a total corporate enterprise; it is an indirect, residual, proportionate interest in all assets, subject to all liabilities, and with no direct claim on any assets. A common error is to use such a P/E ratio to price an asset purchase of a private business or practice without recognizing the fact that the combination of assets actually being transferred may be quite different from the stock being bought for the price in the P/E ratio.

## Applying P/E Ratios to Earnings that Are Not Comparable

Following are a few examples of applying public company P/E multiples to private company earnings that are not comparable:

1. Applying the P/E ratio (based on after-tax earnings) to a private company's pretax earnings.
2. Applying the P/E ratio to a private company's net operating profit (earnings before interest and taxes).
3. Applying the P/E ratio to a private company's operating cash flow (earnings before interest and taxes plus depreciation).
4. Applying the P/E ratio to a private company's seller's discretionary cash (operating cash flow before allowance for compensation to owner).

The potential effects of the four errors above can be illustrated by Exhibit 20–2, which starts with identical income statements and balance sheets for Public Corporation X and Private Corporation Y. Ex-

## Exhibit 20–2

### PUBLIC CORPORATION X

| | | |
|---|---:|---:|
| Sales | | 10,000 |
| Operating Expenses: | | |
|   Salaries | 5,500 | |
|   Other Operating Exp. | 2,900 | |
|   Depreciation | 400 | |
| Total Oper. Expenses | | 8,800 |
| Net Operating Profit (EBIT) | | 1,200 |
| Interest Expense | | 200 |
| Net Income before Taxes | | 1,000 |
| Federal and State Income Taxes | | 400 |
| Net Income | | 600 |
| Shares Outstanding | | 300 |
| Net Income per Share | | 2 | ($600 ÷ 300 = $2) |
| Market Price per Share | | 12 |
| Price/Earnings Ratio | | 6x | ($12 ÷ 2 = 6x) |
| Current Assets | 2,000 | |
| Fixed Assets | 3,000 | |
| Total Assets | 5,000 | |
| Current Liabilities | 1,000 | |
| Long-Term Liabilities (10%) | 2,000 | |
| Stockholders' Equity | 2,000 | |
| Total Liabilities & Equity | 5,000 | |

### PRIVATE CORPORATION Y

| | | | "Adjustments" | "Adjusted" Income Statement |
|---|---:|---:|---:|---:|
| Sales | | 10,000 | | 10,000 |
| Operating Expenses: | | | | |
|   Owner's Salary | 500 | | (500) | |
|   Other Salaries | 5,000 | | | |
|   Other Oper. Exp. | 2,900 | | | |
|   Depreciation | 400 | | (400) | |
| Total Oper. Expenses | | 8,800 | | 7,900 |
| Net Operating Profit (EBIT) | | 1,200 | | |
| Interest Expense | | 200 | (200) | |
| Net Income before Taxes | | 1,000 | | |
| Federal and State Income Taxes | | 400 | (400) | |
| Net Income | | 600 | | |
| "Earnings Available to Owner" or "Seller's Discretionary Cash" | | | | 2,100 |
| Current Assets | 2,000 | | | |
| Fixed Assets | 3,000 | | | |
| Total Assets | 5,000 | | | |
| Current Liabilities | 1,000 | | | |
| Long-Term Liabilities (10%) | 2,000 | | | |
| Owner's Equity | 2,000 | | | |
| Total Liabilities & Equity | 5,000 | | | |

hibit 20–2 also shows market data for the stock of Public Corporation X and several adjustments to the income statement of Private Corporation Y.

It can readily be seen that the aggregate market value of the outstanding shares of Public Corporation X is $3,600 (300 shares × $12 per share). If one applies the P/E ratio of 6 from Public Company X to the comparable net earnings of Private Company Y, the implied value of Private Company Y's stock is $3,600 (6 × $600 = $3,600). That is a reasonable comparative indication of value before any adjustments for differences in liquidity, for minority or controlling interests, and for any other differences.

However, the following calculations illustrate the potential effects of the four common errors listed above:

1. *P/E applied to pretax earnings:*
   6 × $1,000 = $6,000.
2. *P/E applied to net operating profit:*
   6 × $1,200 = $7,200.
3. *P/E applied to operating cash flow:*
   6 × $1,600 = $9,600.
4. *P/E applied to seller's discretionary cash:*
   6 × $2,100 = $12,600.

Nobody could be that far misguided, could he? WAIT! How about combining the above with the "assets plus . . ." syndrome discussed earlier? Suppose the "six times seller's-discretionary cash flow" is interpreted to represent only the goodwill or intangible value. As noted on the balance sheets in Exhibit 20–2, the company has a net asset value of $2,000. Adding that to the value derived from number 4 above would give an indicated value of $14,600!

## Applying P/E Ratios When Time Periods Are Not Comparable

We noted that the P/E ratios published in daily newspapers are based on the current stock prices divided by the companies' latest 12 months' actual reported earnings. Using such a P/E ratio, but applying it to *any other* earnings base for the subject company, can produce significantly misleading results. Following are a few examples of a public company's P/E ratio from one time period being applied to the subject company's earnings for a different time period.

**P/E Ratio Applied to a Forecast.**   Vassar Video, a publicly traded marketer of video cassettes, had 1984 earnings of $4 per share; and early in 1985 the stock traded at $36 per share, for a P/E ratio of 9 ($36 ÷ $4 = 9). Alan Analyst, who has been retained to value the stock of Yale Yuppies, a privately owned company marketing a competitive line of video cassettes, forecasts that Yale will earn $3 per share in 1985. Applying the comparative publicly traded company's P/E of 9 to

Alan's forecast of $3 per share for Yale gives Yale stock an indicated value of $27 per share (9 × $3 = $27), on a publicly traded equivalent basis, before adjustments for liquidity and so on.

What Alan overlooked was that analysts following Vassar stock were predicting that Vassar would earn $6 per share in 1985. Therefore, if one divided the *current stock price* by the *forecasted earnings*, the P/E ratio so derived would be 6 ($36 ÷ $6 = 6), rather than 9. Applying the P/E ratio of 6 on Vassar's forecasted earnings to Yale's forecasted earnings of $3 would give a publicly traded equivalent indication of value for Yale stock of $18 per share (6 × $3 = $18). Alan erred by applying a P/E ratio based on historical earnings to forecasted earnings in an industry experiencing steep earnings growth at the time.

**Failure to Match Historical Time Periods.**    Alan was called on to value the stock as of December 31, 1983, of Audrey's Automotive Corp., a small subcontractor to the highly cyclical automotive industry. The most comparable publicly traded company was Buddy's, another automotive subcontractor, which earned $5 per share for its latest fiscal year, ended September 30, 1983. Buddy's stock traded at $40 per share on December 31, 1983, so the *Daily Bugle* showed a P/E ratio of 8 ($40 ÷ $5 = 8). Alan applied the P/E multiple of 8 to Audrey's earnings of $4 per share for calendar 1983, resulting in a publicly traded equivalent indicated value of $32 per share for Audrey's stock.

What Alan overlooked was that the fourth quarter of 1983 was a big recovery quarter for the industry, during which Buddy earned $2 per share, compared to a loss of $1 per share in the fourth quarter of 1982 (results not dissimilar to Audrey's). Therefore, for the calendar year 1983, Buddy's stock actually earned $8 per share, and its P/E ratio at December 31, based on 1983 calendar year actual results, was really 5 ($40 ÷ $8 = 5). Applying the P/E ratio of 5, based on Buddy's calendar year 1983 earnings (instead of Buddy's fiscal year earnings), to Audrey's calendar year earnings of $4 would give a publicly traded equivalent indication of value for Audrey's stock of $20 per share (5 × $4 = $20). Alan erred by applying a P/E ratio based on earnings for an earlier time period to actual earnings for a later time period in an industry experiencing a sharp cyclical recovery.

Examples of the application of a P/E ratio derived from earnings of one time period to an earnings base of another time period are endless.

**Averaging P/E Ratios over Time.**    If Alan didn't like the result he got using a current P/E ratio, he had a handy solution: Just use the average of the P/E ratios for the last five years. That way, he applied P/E ratios born out of one set of economic conditions to earnings generated under current economic conditions. About half the time, that variation on the P/E ratio approach helped his case. Alan found that he was only rarely challenged on this anomaly. Alan did a lot of testimony on values of small businesses and professional practices in divorce cases, and he felt that he needed to be flexible in his approaches. Alan was not a member of any professional appraisal association (all of which have codes of ethics).

# Using the Reciprocal of the P/E Ratio as the Required Rate of Return

How often we all have heard that the reciprocal of the P/E ratio is the capitalization rate! For example, if a stock is selling at a P/E ratio of 12, the reciprocal would be 8.3 percent ($1 \div 12 = .083$). It is not reasonable to expect anyone to buy a stock for an 8.3 percent total rate of return when he could get more on government bonds and money market funds. The reason the P/E is 12 on historical earnings is that the market expects future earnings to be higher.

The capitalization rate applicable to *expected* earnings is the reciprocal of the public market P/E ratio *only* in the rare case when the earnings, on which the P/E ratio is based, are expected to be constant over time.[7]

# Failure to Make Appropriate Adjustments

Public companies and transactions in publicly traded stocks differ in many ways from exchanges of interests in privately held businesses and professional practices, as discussed in Chapter 4. It is unfortunately common to find uninformed people attempting to practice the art of business appraisal by using P/E ratios to value small businesses and professional practices without taking account of such important factors as size or capital structure of the entity, the degree of liquidity, and the relative proportion of the total company represented by the interest being valued.

# Other Errors in Deriving Capitalization Rates

The capitalization rate must be the one applicable to the earnings base being capitalized, both in terms of definition of the earnings base and in terms of the rate applicable at the particular time. Most errors involve some failure in matching the applicable capitalization rate with the earnings being capitalized.

## Using Rates from an Earlier Time Period

The cost of capital varies considerably over time. As the cost of capital goes up, the value of an existing business or practice goes down, and vice versa. Therefore, if capitalization rates used are other than the ones actually prevalent at the time of the valuation, the result will be an overstatement or understatement of value.

Incredibly, some people still use the rates given as illustrative at the time in Revenue Ruling 68–609 (Exhibit 12–1), when using the

---

[7] For a more complete discussion of this relationship, see Pratt, *Valuing a Business*, pp. 62–64.

excess earnings method. Rates have not been that low in many years, so the inevitable result of using those rates is overvaluation. This common error is discussed in some detail in the chapter on the excess earnings method.

## Applying Rates on "Safe" Investments to Small Business Investments

As discussed in Chapter 10, the biggest variable influencing the capitalization rate is the degree of risk. Many people, however, have never been exposed to this basic economic truth and use some virtually riskless rate, such as the prevailing money market fund or certificate of deposit rate, as a capitalization rate for valuing the expected earnings of small businesses and professional practices. Using too low a capitalization rate results, of course, in an overvaluation.

The rationale for that error is "That is what I can get on my money in an alternative investment." The correct rationale is "What I can get on my money in an alternative investment of equal risk, liquidity, and other characteristics." The lowest rate that is reasonable to use is the rate at which the business or practice can borrow the money. However, the total investment cannot be financed at that low a rate, as discussed in Chapter 5 and the following section.

## Failure to Match the Capitalization Rate with the Earnings Base

It is common to find people applying a capitalization rate appropriate to bottom-line net income to other levels of earnings, such as pretax earnings, earnings before depreciation (often called cash flow), earnings before interest, and even earnings before compensation to owners. Most of these errors seem to occur from applying too low a capitalization rate to too high an earnings base, resulting in an overvaluation.

A related common error is applying the company's borrowing rate to the entire equity investment. For example, if the investor thinks he can borrow from the bank for 15 percent, using accounts receivable as collateral, he uses 15 percent as the rate at which to capitalize his entire equity investment. As discussed in Chapter 5, the equity level is where most of the risk is, and an equity investment, therefore, should command a much higher rate of return. The borrowing rate should be used only as a capitalization rate for the percentage of the total investment that actually can be borrowed at that rate.

## Mistaking Historical Results for Required Rates of Return

A common fallacy among the uninformed is to use a recent historical average rate of return on equity capital for an industry as a proxy for that industry's cost of equity capital. The following illustrates just how ridiculous that approach really is.

Suppose, for example, a representative group of publicly traded forest products companies earned an average rate of return of 6 percent per year on their equity capital from 1980 through 1984. Does that mean that the appraiser developing an appropriate rate of return by which to discount a projected income stream in 1985 should use 6 percent for the equity portion of the cost of capital? Of course not! To do so would imply that investors in 1985 would be willing to invest in stocks of that industry for a 6 percent expected return, which is far less than the return available on savings bonds or money market funds!

All that the 6 percent historical return means is that the forest products industry did not do well in the 1980–84 period. The recession was longer and deeper and affected the industry far more than was anticipated.

The required rate of return is based on investor expectations. To use historical results as a proxy for expectations can be very misleading, especially when the historical results are for a single industry and for a relatively short time period.

# Failure to Estimate a Realistic Normalized Earnings Base

The name of the game is to buy earning power. If that earning power is not correctly assessed, the result will be an overvaluation or undervaluation of the entity.

## Reliance on Past Results without Judgment

There is a mind set that I think of as the "mechanistic mentality," for lack of a better expression. It mechanistically relies on past data, without considering whether adjustments should be made or whether it is reasonable to expect future results to conform to past results.

Analysis of the earnings patterns of thousands of companies has shown that a pure extrapolation of recent past results more often leads to a poor forecast than to a good forecast. We do not analyze past results for their own sake, but only as a guide to future expectations. The mechanistic mentality may be an excellent tabulator of the past; it fails the test of usefulness for appraisal purposes, however, because it lacks the essential perspective to judge how representative past results are of reasonable future expectations.

## Failure to Recognize Any Depreciation

It is common simply to add back all depreciation to get a cash earnings figure, because depreciation is an accounting charge not requiring any cash outlay. Except in the unusual occasion when the property is not wearing out or growing obsolete at all, this practice overstates the true earnings. As discussed in Chapter 5, the correct procedure is to adjust the depreciation charges to an amount that genuinely estimates the degree of wear and tear and/or obsolescence, or else make a separate deduction for the cash outlays that will be required for the average amount of replacements necessary to maintain the income stream.

## Not Allowing Compensation to Owner/Operator

Another common practice is to add back to the earnings all compensation to the owner(s), which results in a figure often called owner's discretionary cash, or some such appellation. My own thinking is that the cash really isn't discretionary until the owner has at least enough to live on, if it is assumed that he will work full-time in the business or practice. As discussed in Chapter 6, the preferred procedure is to consider the value of the owner's services (how much it would cost to hire a comparable worker) as a normal expense of the business in arriving at the earnings base to capitalize.

Any amount that a buyer pays for so-called earnings, which actually includes his own reasonable compensation for his services, can be thought of as an employment fee. There is nothing wrong with a person buying himself a job, as long as he recognizes that that is what he is doing.

# Failure to Consider the Full Cost of the Purchase

All too often, a prospective buyer capitalizes the alleged earning power to decide what to offer the seller, only to find that additional investment will be required in order to achieve that earning power. Any additional investment needed to get the earnings should be deducted from the total capitalized earning power value, in determining how much should be paid for whatever is being purchased.

## Working Capital Requirements

The need for additional investment for working capital frequently is overlooked. Analysis of working capital requirements is covered in Chapter 9.

## Deferred Maintenance

Property, leasehold improvements, and equipment should be inspected to determine how well they have been kept up and whether additional investment is needed to bring them up to standards. If so, that amount should be deducted from the purchase price.

## Other Investment Needed

It would be an error in valuation to fail to deduct the cost of any investment needed to maintain the earnings stream. Such items could include the cost of relocation, the cost of replacing personnel lost in the transition, the cost of meeting various governmental compliance requirements, and a host of other things. Failure to foresee and adjust the valuation for such expenditures is an extremely common error.

# Assuming that the Buyer Will Pay for the Now and the Hereafter

The seller would like to be paid today for what the business could be worth in five years, if a buyer brings in additional capital, manages well, and is very lucky. Some owners seriously entertain that pipe dream.

The buyer, of course, does not see it that way. He wants to pay only for ongoing earnings that the business has already proved it can produce with a high degree of certainty.

With respect to the two positions above, the real world leans much more toward the buyer's perspective than the seller's. Value is based largely on what is there now, as opposed to what might be there sometime. Would-be sellers are misled when they think they should be paid now what the business may be worth after the buyer brings his own magic show to the party.

However, note that in almost every newspaper classified section in the country, the relevant classification does not read "Businesses for Sale," but "Business Opportunities." A genuine opportunity should be worth something—certainly more to one buyer than another, depending on how good the buyer perceives the opportunity to be.

# Chapter 21

## A Sample Case: John Dough Bakery, Inc.

John Dough Bakery is a case contrived to illustrate the application of many of the principles and procedures discussed in this book for use in valuing a small business. The hypothetical company is not intended to be patterned after any real-world company, and the reader should not be concerned with whether any of the assumptions bear resemblance to the reader's perception of reality in the bakery industry. In this chapter, we describe the business, its operations, and its financial condition. In the next chapter, we illustrate by example the application of a variety of valuation methods used in arriving at the value of the business.

# Background of John Dough Bakery, Inc.

John Dough Bakery is located in a suburban neighborhood of Tucson, Arizona. John Dough and his wife, Muffin, run the business, which was founded by John Dough, Sr., in 1935. John and Muffin are in their 60s now and wish to retire. Their only child, Cupcake, has no interest in running the business; therefore, the Doughs have decided to sell the bakery. They have asked us to express an opinion about the market value of 100 percent of the common stock of John Dough Bakery, Inc., as of February 28, 1985. On a field trip, and through interviews with Muffin and John Dough, the following information has been gathered.

# Economic Data

The suburb of Tucson in which the bakery is located is a growing area. The population is expected to increase 20 percent over the next five years. Plans are presently on the drawing board for the construction of a new hotel, shopping center, and school within the next three years. Several high-tech companies have announced plans to move into the area. Due to this growth, local wages are expected to increase at a slightly faster pace than the national average.

# Operations

John Dough makes doughnuts, sweet rolls, cakes, pies, and cookies, which it sells primarily to institutions. It also operates a retail store at its manufacturing facility. About 75 percent of the company's sales are to various institutions, and the rest are made through the retail store. The company has three large customers—Community College, Memorial Hospital, and West Medical Center—which accounted for 10 percent, 15 percent, and 12 percent of sales, respectively, in 1984. The rest of the sales to individual institutional customers accounts for less than 5 percent of John Dough's sales.

The company sells its products locally. Bakery goods are delivered to customers daily by two route truck drivers.

John Dough has no brand name associated with its products, as does one of its major competitors, Hostess, but it does have an excellent reputation for quality and service. Competition is keen, especially in price, but John Dough believes the company has a slight competitive edge due to its excellent quality and service. John Dough has had long relationships with many of its customers, who also bought from John's father.

# Management and Employees

John Dough has 20 full-time employees, including the following in management positions:

| | |
|---|---|
| John Dough | President |
| Muffin Dough | Bookkeeper |
| Sam Jones | Sales Manager |
| Glenda Brown | Production Manager |
| Eileen Hudson | Retail Store Manager |

John Dough is responsible for the overall operation of the company. He participates in important sales calls, is in charge of purchasing (primarily the raw materials), decides what products to sell and at what price, and supervises the management staff. Muffin Dough does all the bookkeeping for the bakery and assists John with purchasing, primarily office supplies and packaging materials. She is also the employee relations specialist; all the employees go to her with any problems. She is quite adept at soothing people's feelings and solving any problems.

Sam Jones and Glenda Brown have been with the company for years. Sam is responsible for servicing current accounts, as well as calling on new accounts. He also supervises the two route truck drivers. Glenda Brown is responsible for scheduling and supervising production workers and for quality control. Eileen Hudson has been with the company for one year. Previously, she managed a Dunkin Donut Shop. She is responsible for supervising and scheduling the retail employees, as well as opening and closing the retail store.

The bakery has eleven production workers, two route truck drivers, and two retail clerks. None of the employees is unionized.

Many of the employees have been with the company for some time and there is a sense of camaraderie among the employees. All the employees like and respect John and Muffin, and a happy work atmosphere can be sensed as one walks around the plant. Personnel policies are relaxed and, in fact, no strict rules exist.

# Facilities and Product Lines

When John Dough, Sr. picked the location for the bakery 50 years ago, he had expansion in mind. In 1935, he leased a retail bakery, but also took an option on a large adjoining vacant warehouse. Five years later, when John Dough, Sr. saw interest in his product from institutional customers, he exercised his option and converted the warehouse into a production facility.

# Lease

In 1980, a 10-year lease was signed to cover both the retail and production facilities. In the lease, John has the right of first refusal if the property is sold. The present lease expires February 28, 1990. While the

Exhibit 21–1

**JOHN DOUGH BAKERY, INC.**
**BALANCE SHEET**
**AS OF DECEMBER 31, 1984**

|  | $ | % |
|---|---|---|
| TOTAL ASSETS |  |  |
| Current Assets: |  |  |
| Cash | 10,000 | 3.3 |
| Accounts Receivable | 38,000 | 12.7 |
| Inventory | 45,000 | 15.0 |
| Other | 2,000 | 0.7 |
| Total Current Assets | 95,000 | 31.7 |
| Fixed Assets: |  |  |
| Machinery & Equipment | 268,000 |  |
| Leasehold Improvements | 10,000 |  |
| Autos & Trucks | 80,000 |  |
|  | 358,000 |  |
| Less: Accum. Depreciation | 153,000 |  |
| Net Fixed Assets | 205,000 | 68.3 |
| TOTAL ASSETS | 300,000 | 100.0 |
|  |  |  |
| TOTAL LIABILITIES & STOCKHOLDERS' EQUITY |  |  |
| Current Liabilities: |  |  |
| Notes Payable | 15,000 | 5.0 |
| Current Mat. Long-Term Debt | 25,000 | 8.3 |
| Accounts Payable | 45,000 | 15.0 |
| Accrued Expenses | 10,000 | 3.3 |
| Other | 5,000 | 1.7 |
| Total Current Liabilities | 100,000 | 33.3 |
| Long-Term Debt | 80,000 | 26.7 |
| Stockholders' Equity: |  |  |
| Common Stock | 20,000 | 6.7 |
| Retained Earnings | 100,000 | 33.3 |
| Total Stockholders' Equity | 120,000 | 40.0 |
| TOTAL LIABILITIES & STOCKHOLDERS' EQUITY | 300,000 | 100.0 |

**SOURCE:** Company financial statements, 1984.

amount of rent has been increased every time the lease has been renewed, it has not kept up with fair market rents in the neighborhood. The Doughs have become personal friends with the owners, who are glad to have such a good tenant. The bakery pays $1,000 per month in rent, although the fair market rate is more like $1,500 per month. Five years remain on the lease, and if the business is sold, the lease would be assumable.

## Description of Facilities and Product Lines

The size of the plant is adequate for its current operations, but there is no room for an additional product line to be added. John considered adding croissants to the product line a few years ago, but there was not room for the operation. John Dough modernized the plant about five years ago, and everything now is almost completely automated. The plant is laid out efficiently, and work flows smoothly. The doughnut and cookie operations are the most fully automated. These products account for about 60 percent of sales and require only four employees to operate. Sweet rolls account for about 20 percent of sales and require three employees. Cakes and pies account for the remaining 20 percent of sales. These product lines are the least automated and require four employees to operate. Given this information, it would seem that

Exhibit 21–2

### JOHN DOUGH BAKERY, INC.
### AGED ACCOUNTS RECEIVABLE
### AS OF DECEMBER 31, 1984

| Account Name | Total $ | Current $ | 31-60 Days $ | 61-90 Days $ | 91-120 Days $ | Over 120 Days $ |
|---|---|---|---|---|---|---|
| ABC Elementary | 1,000 | | | | 1,000 | |
| Bee's Cafe | 1,500 | | 1,500 | | | |
| Community College | 4,000 | 4,000 | | | | |
| Dixie Hotel | 2,500 | | | | | 2,500 |
| Glendale Retire. Home | 2,000 | | | 2,000 | | |
| Harrison High School | 1,500 | 1,500 | | | | |
| Jack's Eating Establish. | 2,000 | | | | | 2,000 |
| Memorial Hospital | 6,000 | 6,000 | | | | |
| Porter Junior High | 3,500 | 3,500 | | | | |
| The Pancake Palace | 2,500 | | 2,500 | | | |
| Ridge Nursing Home | 2,500 | | | | 2,500 | |
| Sally's Coffee House | 1,500 | | 1,500 | | | |
| Vic's Family Restaurant | 2,000 | | | 2,000 | | |
| West Medical Center | 5,500 | | 5,500 | | | |
| | 38,000 | 15,000 | 11,000 | 4,000 | 3,500 | 4,500 |
| | 100.0% | 39.5% | 28.9% | 10.5% | 9.2% | 11.8% |

**SOURCE:** John Dough Bakery.

Exhibit 21-3

## JOHN DOUGH BAKERY, INC.
## INCOME STATEMENTS
### Years Ended January 31

| | 1984 $ | 1984 % | 1983 $ | 1983 % | 1982 $ | 1982 % | 1981 $ | 1981 % | 1980 $ | 1980 % |
|---|---|---|---|---|---|---|---|---|---|---|
| Sales | 1,000,000 | 100.0 | 950,000 | 100.0 | 900,000 | 100.0 | 825,000 | 100.0 | 750,000 | 100.0 |
| Cost of Sales | 600,000 | 60.0 | 579,500 | 61.0 | 540,000 | 60.0 | 511,500 | 62.0 | 457,500 | 61.0 |
| Gross Profit | 400,000 | 40.0 | 370,500 | 39.0 | 360,000 | 40.0 | 313,500 | 38.0 | 292,500 | 39.0 |
| Operating Expenses: | | | | | | | | | | |
| Owner's Comp. | 100,000 | 10.0 | 90,000 | 9.5 | 80,000 | 8.9 | 70,000 | 8.5 | 60,000 | 8.0 |
| Salaries & Wages | 150,000 | 15.0 | 140,000 | 14.7 | 130,000 | 14.4 | 120,000 | 14.5 | 110,000 | 14.7 |
| Payroll Taxes | 25,000 | 2.5 | 23,000 | 2.4 | 21,000 | 2.3 | 19,000 | 2.3 | 17,000 | 2.3 |
| Employee Benefits | 15,000 | 1.5 | 14,000 | 1.5 | 13,000 | 1.4 | 12,000 | 1.5 | 11,000 | 1.5 |
| Rent | 12,000 | 1.2 | 12,000 | 1.3 | 12,000 | 1.3 | 12,000 | 1.5 | 12,000 | 1.6 |
| Depreciation | 23,000 | 2.3 | 20,000 | 2.1 | 20,000 | 2.2 | 17,000 | 2.1 | 17,000 | 2.3 |
| Repairs | 10,000 | 1.0 | 10,000 | 1.1 | 10,000 | 1.1 | 10,000 | 1.2 | 10,000 | 1.3 |
| Utilities | 9,000 | 0.9 | 9,000 | 0.9 | 9,000 | 1.0 | 9,000 | 1.1 | 9,000 | 1.2 |
| Accounting & Legal | 7,000 | 0.7 | 6,000 | 0.6 | 6,000 | 0.7 | 4,000 | 0.5 | 4,000 | 0.5 |
| Licenses & Taxes | 3,000 | 0.3 | 3,000 | 0.3 | 3,000 | 0.3 | 3,000 | 0.4 | 3,000 | 0.4 |
| Insurance | 5,000 | 0.5 | 5,000 | 0.5 | 5,000 | 0.6 | 5,000 | 0.6 | 5,000 | 0.7 |
| Autos & Trucks | 10,000 | 1.0 | 10,000 | 1.1 | 10,000 | 1.1 | 10,000 | 1.2 | 10,000 | 1.3 |
| Other | 20,000 | 2.0 | 15,000 | 1.6 | 15,000 | 1.7 | 10,000 | 1.2 | 15,000 | 2.0 |
| Total Oper. Expenses | 389,000 | 38.9 | 357,000 | 37.6 | 334,000 | 37.1 | 301,000 | 36.5 | 283,000 | 37.7 |
| Operating Profit | 11,000 | 1.1 | 13,500 | 1.4 | 26,000 | 2.7 | 12,500 | 1.5 | 9,500 | 1.3 |
| Other Income (Expenses): | | | | | | | | | | |
| Gain (Loss) on Sale of Assets | (10,000) | (1.0) | (9,000) | (0.9) | (10,000) | (1.1) | (11,000) | (1.3) | (12,000) | (1.6) |
| Business Interrupt. | (5,000) | (0.5) | — | — | — | — | — | — | 8,000 | 1.1 |
| Discont. Oper. | — | — | — | — | (12,000) | (1.3) | — | — | (10,000) | (1.3) |
| Total Other Income (Expense) | (15,000) | (1.5) | (9,000) | (0.9) | (22,000) | (2.4) | (7,000) | (0.8) | (14,000) | (1.9) |
| Pretax Income | (4,000) | (0.4) | 4,500 | 0.5 | 4,000 | 0.4 | 5,500 | 0.7 | (4,500) | (0.6) |

**SOURCE:** Company financial statements, 1980-1984.

Exhibit 21–4

## MANUFACTURERS - BREAD & OTHER BAKERY PRODUCTS  SIC# 2051

| | Current Data 38(6/30-9/30/83) 0-1MM (23) | 1-10MM (38) | 10-50MM (23) | 50-100MM (5) | 51(10/1/83-3/31/84) ALL (89) | ASSET SIZE / NUMBER OF STATEMENTS | Comparative Historical Data 6/30/79-3/31/80 ALL (85) | 6/30/80-3/31/81 ALL (100) | 6/30/81-3/31/82 ALL (105) | 6/30/82-3/31/83 ALL (108) | 6/30/83-3/31/84 ALL (89) |
|---|---|---|---|---|---|---|---|---|---|---|---|
| | % | % | % | % | % | **ASSETS** | % | % | % | % | % |
| | 7.6 | 9.6 | 9.9 | | 9.0 | Cash & Equivalents | 8.1 | 6.3 | 7.6 | 8.3 | 9.0 |
| | 15.9 | 20.9 | 16.4 | | 18.3 | Accts. & Notes Rec. - Trade(net) | 22.0 | 20.9 | 20.0 | 18.6 | 18.3 |
| | 13.4 | 13.2 | 7.1 | | 11.6 | Inventory | 13.7 | 15.9 | 12.8 | 12.9 | 11.6 |
| | .7 | 2.5 | 4.5 | | 2.8 | All Other Current | 3.1 | 2.5 | 1.7 | 1.9 | 2.8 |
| | 37.6 | 46.2 | 37.9 | | 41.8 | Total Current | 46.8 | 45.6 | 42.0 | 41.7 | 41.8 |
| | 54.0 | 42.6 | 54.6 | | 48.7 | Fixed Assets (net) | 44.0 | 45.0 | 50.3 | 48.8 | 48.7 |
| | 2.7 | .5 | 1.2 | | 1.3 | Intangibles (net) | 2.4 | 1.5 | .8 | 1.5 | 1.3 |
| | 5.8 | 10.7 | 6.4 | | 8.3 | All Other Non-Current | 6.8 | 8.0 | 6.9 | 8.0 | 8.3 |
| | 100.0 | 100.0 | 100.0 | | 100.0 | Total | 100.0 | 100.0 | 100.0 | 100.0 | 100.0 |
| | | | | | | **LIABILITIES** | | | | | |
| | 4.2 | 3.2 | 2.6 | | 3.2 | Notes Payable-Short Term | 5.2 | 5.3 | 4.4 | 4.4 | 3.2 |
| | 9.3 | 4.1 | 3.1 | | 5.0 | Cur. Mat-L/T/D | 3.5 | 5.1 | 4.4 | 4.8 | 5.0 |
| | 14.2 | 17.0 | 14.9 | | 15.2 | Accts. & Notes Payable - Trade | 16.1 | 17.8 | 16.0 | 15.8 | 15.2 |
| | 4.7 | 7.5 | 9.4 | | 7.1 | Accrued Expenses | 7.0 | 7.2 | 6.2 | 7.3 | 7.1 |
| | 4.3 | 2.9 | 2.2 | | 3.4 | All Other Current | 3.8 | 3.5 | 4.4 | 2.3 | 3.4 |
| | 36.7 | 34.7 | 32.2 | | 33.9 | Total Current | 35.5 | 39.0 | 35.4 | 34.6 | 33.9 |
| | 30.4 | 20.2 | 26.5 | | 23.8 | Long Term Debt | 19.3 | 20.3 | 22.1 | 24.8 | 23.8 |
| | .8 | 3.7 | 4.0 | | 3.3 | All Other Non-Current | 3.8 | 3.7 | 2.6 | 2.9 | 3.3 |
| | 32.0 | 41.5 | 37.3 | | 38.9 | Net Worth | 41.5 | 37.1 | 39.9 | 37.8 | 38.9 |
| | 100.0 | 100.0 | 100.0 | | 100.0 | Total Liabilities & Net Worth | 100.0 | 100.0 | 100.0 | 100.0 | 100.0 |
| | | | | | | **INCOME DATA** | | | | | |
| | 100.0 | 100.0 | 100.0 | | 100.0 | Net Sales | 100.0 | 100.0 | 100.0 | 100.0 | 100.0 |
| | 64.9 | 63.1 | 63.0 | | 64.0 | Cost Of Sales | 65.1 | 64.6 | 63.4 | 61.0 | 64.0 |
| | 35.1 | 36.9 | 37.0 | | 36.0 | Gross Profit | 34.9 | 35.4 | 36.6 | 39.0 | 36.0 |
| | 31.4 | 31.8 | 32.0 | | 31.2 | Operating Expenses | 31.6 | 31.0 | 32.9 | 33.8 | 31.2 |
| | 3.6 | 5.1 | 5.0 | | 4.8 | Operating Profit | 3.3 | 4.4 | 3.7 | 5.2 | 4.8 |
| | 2.0 | .4 | .7 | | .9 | All Other Expenses (net) | 1.3 | 1.6 | 1.1 | 1.1 | .9 |
| | 1.6 | 4.6 | 4.3 | | 3.9 | Profit Before Taxes | 2.0 | 2.8 | 2.6 | 4.1 | 3.9 |
| | | | | | | **RATIOS** | | | | | |
| | 1.7 | 1.9 | 1.9 | | 1.9 | Current | 2.2 | 1.7 | 1.8 | 2.0 | 1.9 |
| | 1.3 | 1.2 | 1.1 | | 1.2 | | 1.4 | 1.2 | 1.3 | 1.3 | 1.2 |
| | .7 | .9 | .8 | | .8 | | .9 | .8 | .8 | .9 | .8 |
| | 1.2 | 1.3 | 1.0 | | 1.3 | Quick | 1.3 | 1.1 | 1.3 | 1.3 | 1.3 |
| | (22) 1.0 | .9 | .8 | (88) .9 | | | .9 | .7 (103) .9 | | .8 (88) .9 | |
| | .3 | .5 | .6 | | .5 | | .6 | .5 | .5 | .5 | .5 |
| | 3 130.0 | 16 22.2 | 16 22.5 | | 16 22.5 | Sales/Receivables | 18 20.0 | 15 24.7 | 15 25.1 | 14 27.0 | 16 22.5 |
| | 20 18.3 | 24 15.2 | 23 15.7 | | 23 15.7 | | 24 15.3 | 22 16.8 | 22 16.7 | 21 17.0 | 23 15.7 |
| | 28 13.0 | 35 10.3 | 27 13.6 | | 30 12.2 | | 33 11.1 | 31 11.7 | 30 12.2 | 28 13.1 | 30 12.2 |
| | 11 34.0 | 10 36.5 | 9 39.4 | | 10 37.0 | Cost of Sales/Inventory | 10 36.8 | 12 29.4 | 11 34.6 | 11 33.6 | 10 37.0 |
| | 19 19.7 | 18 20.1 | 11 31.8 | | 17 21.1 | | 18 20.8 | 22 16.5 | 16 22.4 | 17 21.4 | 17 21.1 |
| | 33 10.9 | 48 7.6 | 21 17.6 | | 35 10.4 | | 39 9.3 | 42 8.6 | 33 11.1 | 33 11.1 | 35 10.4 |
| | 12 31.0 | 22 16.8 | 25 14.4 | | 18 19.9 | Cost of Sales/Payables | 15 23.9 | 18 19.8 | 17 21.4 | 14 25.8 | 18 19.9 |
| | 20 18.2 | 30 12.1 | 26 13.8 | | 26 13.8 | | 24 15.0 | 28 13.2 | 25 14.7 | 26 13.8 | 26 13.8 |
| | 33 11.2 | 45 8.1 | 49 7.5 | | 41 8.9 | | 45 8.2 | 38 9.6 | 39 9.4 | 43 8.4 | 41 8.9 |
| | 14.0 | 10.9 | 10.7 | | 11.1 | Sales/Working Capital | 11.7 | 15.3 | 14.5 | 13.4 | 11.1 |
| | 42.1 | 38.6 | 59.5 | | 42.1 | | 33.7 | 45.4 | 45.5 | 35.7 | 42.1 |
| | -45.3 | -158.1 | -29.7 | | -50.9 | | -98.4 | -37.3 | -35.7 | -137.4 | -50.9 |
| | 6.2 | 8.9 | 8.6 | | 8.0 | EBIT/Interest | 9.6 | 5.2 | 4.6 | 6.5 | 8.0 |
| | (20) 2.5 | (34) 4.2 | (19) 4.0 | (76) 4.0 | | | (72) 2.1 | (83) 2.6 | (83) 2.2 | (94) 3.2 | (76) 4.0 |
| | 1.0 | 1.9 | 2.4 | | 1.7 | | 1.0 | 1.1 | 1.0 | 1.6 | 1.7 |
| | 4.5 | 5.4 | 7.3 | | 5.7 | Cash Flow/Cur. Mat. L/T/D | 6.2 | 6.5 | 7.0 | 8.0 | 5.7 |
| | (11) 2.0 | (26) 3.7 | (15) 4.5 | (55) 3.8 | | | (48) 2.7 | (63) 2.9 | (65) 2.8 | (69) 4.1 | (55) 3.8 |
| | .6 | 1.8 | 2.5 | | 1.8 | | 1.2 | 1.4 | 1.6 | 2.4 | 1.8 |
| | .9 | .4 | 1.1 | | .8 | Fixed/Worth | .6 | .8 | .8 | .8 | .8 |
| | 1.4 | 1.1 | 1.7 | | 1.3 | | 1.2 | 1.3 | 1.3 | 1.2 | 1.3 |
| | 5.5 | 1.7 | 2.3 | | 2.2 | | 2.0 | 2.2 | 2.3 | 2.2 | 2.2 |
| | .9 | .8 | .9 | | .8 | Debt/Worth | .6 | .9 | .8 | .8 | .8 |
| | 1.9 | 1.4 | 2.0 | | 1.6 | | 1.4 | 1.9 | 1.5 | 1.5 | 1.6 |
| | 8.3 | 2.1 | 2.9 | | 3.1 | | 3.3 | 3.6 | 2.9 | 2.8 | 3.1 |
| | 53.7 | 38.7 | 46.8 | | 45.5 | % Profit Before Taxes/Tangible Net Worth | 31.0 | 37.6 | 28.7 | 47.3 | 45.5 |
| | (20) 28.2 | (36) 21.9 | 24.8 | (84) 22.6 | | | (79) 17.5 | (95) 16.7 | (100) 13.0 | (96) 22.1 | (84) 22.6 |
| | 7.5 | 11.6 | 16.1 | | 13.2 | | 2.0 | 4.7 | 2.8 | 8.0 | 13.2 |
| | 21.0 | 20.9 | 17.2 | | 17.9 | % Profit Before Taxes/Total Assets | 16.1 | 12.9 | 12.1 | 17.3 | 17.9 |
| | 6.7 | 9.1 | 8.7 | | 8.7 | | 5.1 | 6.1 | 5.8 | 9.1 | 8.7 |
| | 1.3 | 4.0 | 6.0 | | 4.5 | | .2 | .8 | .5 | 3.5 | 4.5 |
| | 10.6 | 11.2 | 5.8 | | 10.0 | Sales/Net Fixed Assets | 12.1 | 12.0 | 9.6 | 9.9 | 10.0 |
| | 7.0 | 6.7 | 4.7 | | 5.8 | | 6.9 | 6.9 | 6.7 | 6.3 | 5.8 |
| | 4.3 | 4.5 | 3.3 | | 4.0 | | 4.3 | 4.5 | 4.1 | 4.0 | 4.0 |
| | 5.0 | 3.3 | 3.4 | | 3.8 | Sales/Total Assets | 3.9 | 4.0 | 4.0 | 4.1 | 3.8 |
| | 3.5 | 2.8 | 2.4 | | 2.8 | | 3.0 | 2.9 | 2.9 | 3.0 | 2.8 |
| | 2.4 | 2.1 | 1.9 | | 2.0 | | 2.1 | 2.3 | 2.4 | 2.3 | 2.0 |
| | 2.3 | 2.2 | 2.4 | | 2.2 | % Depr., Dep., Amort./Sales | 1.4 | 1.5 | 1.7 | 1.8 | 2.2 |
| | (22) 3.2 | (35) 2.5 | (19) 2.9 | (80) 2.7 | | | (78) 2.3 | (95) 2.5 | (95) 2.4 | (103) 2.7 | (80) 2.7 |
| | 4.5 | 3.3 | 3.5 | | 3.6 | | 3.4 | 3.0 | 3.3 | 3.5 | 3.6 |
| | 1.2 | .8 | | | 1.0 | % Lease & Rental Exp/Sales | .7 | .7 | .6 | .7 | 1.0 |
| | (17) 1.8 | (15) 2.0 | | (38) 1.5 | | | (45) 1.3 | (62) 1.5 | (51) 1.2 | (56) 2.5 | (38) 1.5 |
| | 3.6 | 3.5 | | | 3.4 | | 2.8 | 2.7 | 3.2 | 4.2 | 3.4 |
| | 2.7 | 1.4 | | | 1.5 | % Officers' Comp/Sales | 1.6 | 1.9 | 1.5 | 1.6 | 1.5 |
| | (13) 5.1 | (15) 2.4 | | (31) 3.1 | | | (41) 2.6 | (45) 2.8 | (39) 2.6 | (38) 3.1 | (31) 3.1 |
| | 7.6 | 4.9 | | | 7.4 | | 4.1 | 6.2 | 5.3 | 5.3 | 7.4 |
| | 30824M | 477184M | 1143706M | 860043M | 2511757M | Net Sales ($) | 1323978M | 1936459M | 2108353M | 2129136M | 2511757M |
| | 9595M | 165438M | 453228M | 331996M | 960257M | Total Assets ($) | 420732M | 733161M | 697764M | 790733M | 960257M |

* Robert Morris Associates 1984     M = $thousand   MM = $million

See Pages 1 through 13 for Explanation of Ratios and Data

SOURCE: *Annual Statement Studies*, 1984 edition (Philadelphia, PA: Robert Morris Associates, 1984) (1616 Philadelphia National Bank Building, Philadelphia, PA 19107).

Exhibit 21–5

TABLE I: CORPORATIONS WITH AND WITHOUT NET INCOME, 1983 EDITION

MANUFACTURING: FOOD AND KINDRED PRODUCTS:

## Bakery products

| Item Description For Accounting Period 7/78 Through 6/79 | A Total | B Zero Assets | C Under 100 | D 100 to 250 | E 250 to 500 | F 500 to 1,000 | G 1000 to 5,000 | H 5,000 to 10,000 | I 10,000 to 25,000 | J 25,000 to 50,000 | K 50,000 to 100,000 | L 100,000 to 250,000 | M 250,000 and over |
|---|---|---|---|---|---|---|---|---|---|---|---|---|---|
| | | | | | | | SIZE OF ASSETS IN THOUSANDS OF DOLLARS (000 OMITTED) | | | | | | |
| 1. Number of Enterprises | 2935 | 3 | 1914 | 157 | 335 | 267 | 180 | 48 | ••• | ••• | ••• | 6 | 3 |
| 2. Total receipts (in millions of dollars) | 10124.1 | 18.0 | 312.4 | 82.4 | 305.2 | 590.6 | 1217.6 | 1001.0 | ••• | ••• | ••• | 2238.6 | 3021.2 |
| Selected Operating Factors in Percent of Net Sales | | | | | | | | | | | | | |
| 3. Cost of operations | 60.2 | 65.1 | 62.3 | 66.5 | 66.6 | 62.9 | 65.8 | 58.8 | ••• | ••• | ••• | 64.1 | 51.1 |
| 4. Compensation of officers | 1.5 | 2.9 | 8.6 | 9.0 | 6.1 | 4.1 | 2.1 | 1.3 | ••• | ••• | ••• | 0.4 | 0.5 |
| 5. Repairs | 1.1 | 0.7 | 1.3 | 0.3 | 1.0 | 1.4 | 0.7 | 0.9 | ••• | ••• | ••• | 1.5 | 0.8 |
| 6. Bad debts | 0.4 | - | - | 1.3 | 0.1 | 0.1 | 0.2 | 0.3 | ••• | ••• | ••• | 0.2 | 0.8 |
| 7. Rent on business property | 1.0 | 1.0 | 3.9 | 1.6 | 1.8 | 1.2 | 1.0 | 0.5 | ••• | ••• | ••• | 1.2 | 0.9 |
| 8. Taxes (excl Federal tax) | 2.8 | 2.4 | 3.9 | 2.8 | 3.0 | 3.1 | 2.6 | 3.1 | ••• | ••• | ••• | 2.5 | 2.9 |
| 9. Interest | 1.0 | 0.1 | 0.2 | 0.5 | 1.0 | 1.3 | 0.6 | 1.1 | ••• | ••• | ••• | 1.0 | 1.3 |
| 10. Deprec/Deplet/Amortiz† | 2.6 | 1.7 | 2.8 | 2.2 | 2.3 | 3.3 | 2.1 | 2.8 | ••• | ••• | ••• | 2.1 | 3.0 |
| 11. Advertising | 2.5 | 1.5 | 0.4 | 0.4 | 0.4 | 0.3 | 1.3 | 2.0 | ••• | ••• | ••• | 2.4 | 4.6 |
| 12. Pensions & other benef plans | 2.4 | 0.3 | 0.9 | - | 1.5 | 1.2 | 1.9 | 2.1 | ••• | ••• | ••• | 3.3 | 2.2 |
| 13. Other expenses | 21.5 | 24.2 | 17.2 | 12.7 | 13.9 | 20.5 | 17.4 | 24.5 | ••• | ••• | ••• | 20.1 | 27.8 |
| 14. Net profit before tax | 3.0 | 0.1 | * | 2.7 | 2.3 | 0.6 | 4.3 | 2.6 | ••• | ••• | ••• | 1.2 | 4.1 |
| Selected Financial Ratios (number of times ratio is to one) | | | | | | | | | | | | | |
| 15. Current ratio | 1.8 | - | 0.9 | 4.3 | 1.4 | 1.6 | 2.0 | 1.4 | ••• | ••• | ••• | 1.4 | 2.2 |
| 16. Quick ratio | 1.1 | - | 0.7 | 3.1 | 1.0 | 1.0 | 1.3 | 1.0 | ••• | ••• | ••• | 0.7 | 1.2 |
| 17. Net sls to net wkg capital | 12.1 | - | - | 5.5 | 16.3 | 18.2 | 11.8 | 20.6 | ••• | ••• | ••• | 22.2 | 7.4 |
| 18. Net sales to net worth | 4.4 | - | 15.2 | 4.5 | 7.1 | 8.5 | 5.6 | 6.1 | ••• | ••• | ••• | 4.5 | 3.2 |
| 19. Inventory turnover | 10.1 | - | 33.0 | 6.0 | 22.2 | 20.2 | 14.5 | 16.3 | ••• | ••• | ••• | 10.4 | 5.6 |
| 20. Total liab to net worth | 1.0 | - | 3.4 | 0.4 | 1.9 | 2.0 | 0.9 | 1.2 | ••• | ••• | ••• | 1.1 | 1.1 |
| Selected Financial Factors in Percentages | | | | | | | | | | | | | |
| 21. Current liab to net worth | 46.2 | - | 158.7 | 24.9 | 107.8 | 85.6 | 46.7 | 67.7 | ••• | ••• | ••• | 48.3 | 36.8 |
| 22. Inventory to curr assets | 33.8 | - | 18.8 | 22.8 | 20.2 | 28.4 | 28.6 | 21.4 | ••• | ••• | ••• | 42.8 | 38.5 |
| 23. Net income to net worth | 10.0 | - | - | 13.3 | 15.2 | 5.4 | 17.9 | 9.2 | ••• | ••• | ••• | 6.2 | 9.8 |
| 24. Retained earn to net inc | 57.6 | - | 100.0 | 100.0 | 98.5 | 41.6 | 67.8 | 83.6 | ••• | ••• | ••• | 59.7 | 42.4 |

†Depreciation largest factor

SOURCE: Leo Troy, *Almanac of Business and Industrial Financial Ratios*, 1983 edition (Englewood Cliffs, N.J.: Prentice-Hall, 1983, p. 42.

Exhibit 21–6

## COMPARATIVE MARKET VALUE DATA
## SALES OF BAKERY COMPANIES
## INCOME STATEMENTS

| | Bakery 1 $ | Bakery 2 $ | Bakery 3 $ |
|---|---|---|---|
| Sales | 770,000 | 1,200,000 | 485,000 |
| Operating Expenses (Excluding Owner's Compensation, Depreciation, & Interest) | 670,000 | 1,045,000 | 430,000 |
| Seller's Discretionary Cash | 100,000 | 155,000 | 55,000 |
| Owner's Compensation | 40,000 | 75,000 | 25,000 |
| Earnings before Depreciation, Interest, & Taxes | 60,000 | 80,000 | 30,000 |
| Depreciation | 20,000 | 32,000 | 12,000 |
| Earnings before Interest & Taxes | 40,000 | 48,000 | 18,000 |
| Interest | 12,000 | 3,000 | 5,000 |
| Earnings before Taxes | 28,000 | 45,000 | 13,000 |
| Price of Transaction: | | | |
| Face Amount | 120,000 | 300,000 | 87,500 |
| Terms: Amount of Down Payment | Cash | 75,000 | Cash |
| Interest Rate on Balance | N/A | 10% | NA |
| Payment Terms on Balance | N/A | * | N/A |

* Equal monthly payments of interest and principal over five years.

**SOURCE:** Willamette Business Sale Data Base.

Exhibit 21–6 (*concluded*)

**COMPARATIVE MARKET VALUE DATA**
**SALES OF BAKERY COMPANIES**
**BALANCE SHEETS**

| | Bakery 1 $ | Bakery 2 $ | Bakery 3 $ |
|---|---:|---:|---:|
| **ASSETS** | | | |
| **Current Assets:** | | | |
| Cash | 16,000 | 25,000 | 2,000 |
| Accounts Receivable | 40,000 | 75,000 | 38,000 |
| Inventory | 60,000 | 70,000 | 34,000 |
| Prepaid Expenses | 4,000 | 5,000 | 1,000 |
| Other | — | — | — |
| Total Current Assets | 120,000 | 175,000 | 75,000 |
| | | | |
| **Fixed Assets:** | | | |
| Equipment | 270,000 | 240,000 | 167,000 |
| Furniture | 15,000 | 10,000 | 8,000 |
| Vehicles | 60,000 | 50,000 | 35,000 |
| Leasehold Improvements | 5,000 | — | 5,000 |
| Other | — | — | — |
| Total Fixed Assets | 350,000 | 300,000 | 215,000 |
| Less: Accumulated Depreciation | 170,000 | 175,000 | 100,000 |
| Net Fixed Assets Other than Real Estate | 180,000 | 125,000 | 115,000 |
| Other Assets—Deferred Charges | — | — | 10,000 |
| **TOTAL ASSETS** | 300,000 | 300,000 | 200,000 |
| | | | |
| **TOTAL LIABILITIES & OWNER'S EQUITY** | | | |
| **Current Liabilities:** | | | |
| Accounts Payable | 35,000 | 40,000 | 45,000 |
| Accrued Expenses | 10,000 | 15,000 | 10,000 |
| Current Portion Long-Term Debt | 20,000 | 5,000 | — |
| Notes Payable | 15,000 | — | 35,000 |
| Other—Federal and State Taxes | — | 10,000 | — |
| Total Current Liabilities | 80,000 | 70,000 | 100,000 |
| | | | |
| Long-Term Debt | 100,000 | 20,000 | — |
| | | | |
| Other Liabilities—Deferred Taxes | — | — | 10,000 |
| Total Liabilities | 180,000 | 90,000 | 100,000 |
| Owner's Equity | 120,000 | 210,000 | 100,000 |
| **TOTAL LIABILITIES & OWNER'S EQUITY** | 300,000 | 300,000 | 200,000 |

**SOURCE:** Willamette Business Sale Data Base.

doughnuts and cookies would probably be the most profitable product lines, and that is, in fact, the case. The cakes and pies are the least profitable, but they are necessary because customers want a full line of baked goods, not just doughnuts and cookies.

# Financial Statements

Exhibit 21–1 shows the bakery balance sheet as of December 31, 1984. John plans to withdraw the $10,000 cash before selling the stock. Exhibit 21–2 shows the accounts receivable aging as of that date. John estimated that the net depreciated book value of the fixtures and equipment is less than it would cost to replace them but more than the amount for which they probably could be liquidated.

Exhibit 21–3 illustrates the bakery's income statements for the years ended December 31, 1980 through 1984. Muffin Dough's salary is $20,000 per year and has been included in salaries and wages, not owners' compensation. The $20,000 is fair compensation for the services she provides.

John Dough expects earnings before taxes and owner's compensation for the next three years to be $100,000 in 1985, $110,000 in 1986, and $120,000 in 1987, with the $120,000 level sustainable through 1988 and thereafter.

# Related Financial Data

Exhibits 21–4 through 21–6 provide information that may be used to determine the market value of John Dough Bakery. Exhibit 21–4 shows financial ratios of bakeries as compiled by Robert Morris Associates. Exhibit 21–5 also illustrates financial ratios for bakeries, but these ratios are from the *Almanac of Business and Industrial Financial Ratios*. Exhibit 21–6 provides income statement and balance sheet data on sales of three similar bakeries that were sold recently, along with sale prices and terms.

# Chapter 22

## Suggested Solution to the Sample Case

In this chapter, we present an analysis of the market value of 100 percent of the common stock of John Dough Bakery, Inc., as of February 28, 1985. This chapter represents the analysis that the appraiser goes through to arrive at a value, but we have assumed that the Doughs will not require a formal, written appraisal report.[1]

# Adjusting the Balance Sheet

The adjusted balance sheet is shown in Exhibit 22–1. Since John Dough is taking the cash out of the business when he sells it, we need to reduce the current assets by $10,000. Two other adjustments are indicated as well: one to accounts receivable, and one for the value of the leasehold interest. Although it is desirable to adjust the balance sheet to reflect the market value of the fixtures and equipment, we have not been provided with information necessary to make that adjustment. However, based on the opinion expressed by John, such an adjustment would not appear to be significant.

## Adjustment to Accounts Receivable

The adjustment to accounts receivable is based on Exhibit 21–2 in the previous chapter, the aged accounts receivable schedule. Two accounts are over 120 days old, and it is unlikely that they will be collected; therefore, accounts receivable need to be reduced by $4,500.

## Valuation of Leasehold Interest

Since the buyer can assume the bakery's lease, which is at a below-market rate, a leasehold interest exists. (An explanation of how to calculate the value of the leasehold interest is in Chapter 5.) The difference between the rent under the lease and the market rate is $500 per month, and 60 months remain on the lease. We choose to discount this savings at a 20 percent annual discount rate, to arrive at a leasehold interest of $18,872.

In choosing a discount rate for the rent advantage, to determine the present value of the leasehold interest, we estimated John Dough's weighted average cost of capital. We estimated the cost of debt at 15 percent (approximately two percentage points higher than the BBB corporate bond rate). We estimated the cost of equity capital at 25 percent, as discussed elsewhere in this chapter. From Exhibit 21–4, we see that the typical capital structure for bakeries of this size is approxi-

---

[1] The reader can refer to Chapter 15 in Pratt, *Valuing a Business*, for an example of a formal written appraisal report.

Exhibit 22–1

## JOHN DOUGH BAKERY, INC.
## ADJUSTED BALANCE SHEET

| | As of December 31, 1984 | | | |
|---|---|---|---|---|
| | Balance Sheet as Reported $ | Adjustments $ | Balance Sheet as Adjusted $ | % |
| **ASSETS** | | | | |
| Current Assets: | | | | |
| Cash | 10,000 | (10,000) | — | — |
| Accounts Receivable | 38,000 | (4,500) | 33,500 | 11.0 |
| Inventory | 45,000 | | 45,000 | 14.8 |
| Other | 2,000 | | 2,000 | 0.7 |
| Total Current Assets | 95,000 | (14,500) | 80,500 | 26.4 |
| Fixed Assets: | | | | |
| Machinery & Equipment | 268,000 | | 268,000 | |
| Leasehold Improvements | 10,000 | | 10,000 | |
| Autos & Trucks | 80,000 | | 80,000 | |
| | 358,000 | | 358,000 | |
| Less: Accumulated Dep. | 153,000 | | 153,000 | |
| Net Fixed Assets | 205,000 | | 205,000 | 67.4 |
| Leasehold Interest | — | 18,872 | 18,872 | 6.2 |
| TOTAL ASSETS | 300,000 | 4,372 | 304,372 | 100.0 |
| **LIABILITIES & STOCKHOLDERS' EQUITY** | | | | |
| Current Liabilities: | | | | |
| Accounts Payable | 45,000 | | 45,000 | 14.8 |
| Accrued Expenses | 10,000 | | 10,000 | 3.3 |
| Current Portion LTD | 25,000 | | 25,000 | 8.2 |
| Notes Payable | 15,000 | | 15,000 | 4.9 |
| Other | 5,000 | | 5,000 | 1.6 |
| Total Current Liabilities | 100,000 | | 100,000 | 32.9 |
| Long-Term Debt | 80,000 | | 80,000 | 26.3 |
| Stockholders' Equity: | | | | |
| Common Stock | 20,000 | | 20,000 | 6.6 |
| Retained Earnings | 100,000 | 4,372 | 104,372 | 34.3 |
| Total Stockholders' Equity | 120,000 | 4,372 | 124,372 | 40.9 |
| TOTAL LIABILITIES & STOCKHOLDERS' EQUITY | 300,000 | 4,372 | 304,372 | 100.0 |

LTD = Long-term debt.
**SOURCE:** Company financial statements, 1984; Willamette Management Associates, Inc.

mately 50 percent debt and 50 percent equity. On this basis, John Dough's weighted average cost of capital is as follows:

| | Percent of Capital Structure | Required Rate of Return | |
|---|---|---|---|
| Debt | .50 | .15 | .075 |
| Equity | .50 | .25 | .125 |
| Weighted Average | | | .200 |

As a result of the computation above, we discounted the annual rent advantage at a rate of 20 percent to determine the present value of the leasehold interest.

# Adjusting the Income Statement

In arriving at the normalized income statement, shown in Exhibit 22–2, three adjustments needed to be made: owner's compensation to a level closer to the industry average; an allowance for bad debts; and the removal of several nonrecurring items. It should be noted that we have investigated the amount of depreciation expensed by the bakery, and in our opinion, it represents the genuine economic depreciation of the fixtures and equipment.

## Owner's Compensation Adjustment

As can be seen in Exhibit 21–3, John Dough's actual compensation in 1984 was $100,000, or 10.0 percent of sales. To determine whether that is similar to the amount of compensation typically paid in the industry, we looked at two industry sources.

According to Robert Morris Associates (RMA), the median percentage of owner's compensation/sales for bakeries with an asset size of $0 to $1 million was 5.1 percent, and the upper quartile was 7.6 percent (see Exhibit 21–4). According to the *Almanac of Business and Industrial Financial Ratios*, the average was 6.1 percent (see Exhibit 21–5). In our opinion, owner's compensation of $65,000, or 6.5 percent of sales, is reasonable. That is above the RMA median but below the upper quartile; consequently, we used an owner's compensation/sales ratio of 6.5 percent (6.4 percent in 1982 due to rounding) in the adjusted income statements for 1980 through 1984.

## Recognition of Bad Debt Expense

As can be seen from Exhibits 21–1, 21–2, and 21–3, the bakery had been making no allowance for doubtful accounts, and the accounts receivable balance was not net of such an amount. According to the *Almanac of Business and Industrial Financial Ratios* (Exhibit 20–4), the average bad debt expense for a company the size of John Dough Bakery was .1 percent of sales. Accordingly, in our normalized income statements, we made an allowance of $1,000, or .1 percent of sales, each year for bad debts.

## Removal of Nonrecurring Items

The final adjustment we made was to remove the nonrecurring items that appeared under Other Income in the income statement. Since we

Exhlbit 22-2

**JOHN DOUGH BAKERY**
**ADJUSTED INCOME STATEMENTS**
Years Ended December 31

| | 1984 $ | 1984 % | 1983 $ | 1983 % | 1982 $ | 1982 % | 1981 $ | 1981 % | 1980 $ | 1980 % |
|---|---|---|---|---|---|---|---|---|---|---|
| Sales | 1,000,000 | 100.0 | 950,000 | 100.0 | 900,000 | 100.0 | 825,000 | 100.0 | 750,000 | 100.0 |
| Cost of Sales | 600,000 | 60.0 | 579,500 | 61.0 | 540,000 | 60.0 | 511,500 | 62.0 | 457,500 | 61.0 |
| Gross Profit | 400,000 | 40.0 | 370,500 | 39.0 | 360,000 | 40.0 | 313,500 | 38.0 | 292,500 | 39.0 |
| Operating Expenses: | | | | | | | | | | |
| Owners' Comp. | 65,000 | 6.5 | 62,000 | 6.5 | 58,000 | 6.4 | 54,000 | 6.5 | 49,000 | 6.5 |
| Salaries & Wages | 150,000 | 15.0 | 140,000 | 14.7 | 130,000 | 14.4 | 120,000 | 14.5 | 110,000 | 14.7 |
| Payroll Taxes | 25,000 | 2.5 | 23,000 | 2.4 | 21,000 | 2.3 | 19,000 | 2.3 | 17,000 | 2.3 |
| Employee Benefits | 15,000 | 1.5 | 14,000 | 1.5 | 13,000 | 1.4 | 12,000 | 1.5 | 11,000 | 1.5 |
| Rent | 12,000 | 1.2 | 12,000 | 1.3 | 12,000 | 1.3 | 12,000 | 1.5 | 12,000 | 1.6 |
| Depreciation | 23,000 | 2.3 | 20,000 | 2.1 | 20,000 | 2.2 | 17,000 | 2.1 | 17,000 | 2.3 |
| Repairs | 10,000 | 1.0 | 10,000 | 1.1 | 10,000 | 1.1 | 10,000 | 1.2 | 10,000 | 1.3 |
| Utilities | 9,000 | 0.9 | 9,000 | 0.9 | 9,000 | 1.0 | 9,000 | 1.1 | 9,000 | 1.2 |
| Accounting & Legal | 7,000 | 0.7 | 6,000 | 0.6 | 6,000 | 0.7 | 4,000 | 0.5 | 4,000 | 0.5 |
| Licenses & Taxes | 3,000 | 0.3 | 3,000 | 0.3 | 3,000 | 0.3 | 3,000 | 0.4 | 3,000 | 0.4 |
| Insurance | 5,000 | 0.5 | 5,000 | 0.5 | 5,000 | 0.6 | 5,000 | 0.6 | 5,000 | 0.7 |
| Autos & Trucks | 10,000 | 1.0 | 10,000 | 1.1 | 10,000 | 1.1 | 10,000 | 1.2 | 10,000 | 1.3 |
| Other | 20,000 | 2.0 | 15,000 | 1.6 | 15,000 | 1.7 | 10,000 | 1.2 | 15,000 | 2.0 |
| Allowance for Doubtful Accts. | 1,000 | 0.1 | 1,000 | 0.1 | 1,000 | 0.1 | 1,000 | 0.1 | 1,000 | 0.1 |
| Total Oper. Expenses | 355,000 | 35.5 | 330,000 | 34.7 | 313,000 | 34.8 | 286,000 | 34.7 | 273,000 | 36.4 |
| Operating Profit | 45,000 | 4.5 | 40,500 | 4.3 | 47,000 | 5.2 | 27,500 | 3.3 | 19,500 | 2.6 |
| Other Income (Expense): | | | | | | | | | | |
| Interest Expense | (10,000) | (1.0) | (9,000) | (0.9) | (10,000) | (1.1) | (11,000) | (1.1) | (12,000) | (1.6) |
| Pretax Income | 35,000 | 3.5 | 31,500 | 3.3 | 37,000 | 4.1 | 16,500 | 2.0 | 7,500 | 1.0 |

**SOURCE:** Company financial statements, 1980-1984.

are interested in the sustainable earning power of the company, and it is unlikely that these events will occur again, their effect needs to be eliminated from the income statement. These items included a loss on sale of assets in 1984, a gain from the sale of assets in 1980, a business interruption due to construction in front of the bakery in 1982, and income or losses from discontinued operations in 1979 and 1980.

# Analysis of Adjusted Financial Statements

## Balance Sheets

Exhibit 22–1 presents the bakery's adjusted balance sheet as of December 31, 1984. Current assets totaled $80,500, consisting primarily of accounts receivable and inventory. Fixed assets accounted for 67.4 percent of total assets. The cost of fixed assets was $358,000, and they were depreciated 42.7 percent, resulting in net fixed assets of $205,000. The estimated value of the leasehold interest, as computed earlier, was $18,872.

Current liabilities totaled $100,000, resulting in negative working capital (a working capital deficit) of $19,500, as of December 31, 1984. The largest liability was accounts payable ($45,000), accounting for nearly half of current liabilities. Long-term debt was $80,000, or 26.3 percent of total assets. Total liabilities accounted for 59.1 percent of total assets.

Stockholders' equity was $124,372 as of December 31, 1984, or 40.9 percent of total assets.

## Income Statements

The adjusted income statements shown in Exhibit 22–2 show that John Dough's sales have increased every year from $750,000 in 1980 to $1 million in 1984, for a five-year compound growth rate of 7.5 percent. Gross profit margins have remained stable at around 40 percent, and operating expenses have also been rather stable, ranging from 34.7 percent to 36.4 percent over the five-year period. Interest expense has been lower in recent years due to declining interest rates. Pretax profit margins have ranged from 1.0 percent to 4.1 percent, although they have been around 3.5 percent for the past two years. Pretax income has averaged around $35,000 the past three years, and that would appear to be a sustainable level of earnings.

## Comparison with Industry Averages

Exhibit 22–3 shows a comparison of John Dough's ratios with those of Robert Morris Associates (RMA). John Dough's gross margin is nearly

Exhibit 22-3

### JOHN DOUGH BAKERY, INC.
### COMPARISONS WITH INDUSTRY AVERAGES

| Asset Size:<br>No. Statements: | RMA[1]<br>$0 - $1mm<br>23 | John<br>Dough<br>Bakery[1] |
|---|---|---|
| **COMPOSITION OF INCOME STATEMENTS** | | |
| Net Sales | 100.0% | 100.0% |
| Cost of Sales | 64.9 | 60.0 |
| Gross Profit | 35.1 | 40.0 |
| Operating Expenses | 31.4 | 35.5 |
| Operating Profit | 3.6 | 4.5 |
| All Other Expenses (Net) | 2.0 | 1.0 |
| Profit Before Taxes | 1.6 | 3.5 |
| **RATIOS** | | |
| Current Ratio | 1.7<br>1.3<br>0.7 | 0.8 |
| Quick Ratio | 1.2<br>1.0<br>0.3 | 0.3 |
| Sales/Working Capital | 14.0<br>42.1<br>* | * |
| EBIT/Interest | 6.2<br>2.5<br>1.0 | 4.5 |
| Debt/Worth | 0.9<br>1.9<br>8.3 | 1.7 |
| % Pretax Income/Tangible Net Worth | 53.7<br>28.2<br>7.5 | 33.2 |
| % Pretax Income/Total Assets | 21.0<br>6.7<br>1.3 | 12.1 |
| Sales/Total Assets | 5.0<br>3.5<br>2.4 | 3.5 |
| % Officers' Comp./Sales | 2.7<br>5.1<br>7.6 | 6.5 |

[1] Based on adjusted statements.
* No meaningful ratio due to deficit working capital.
EBIT = Earnings before interest and taxes.
**SOURCE:** Company financial statements, 1984. Robert Morris Associates, *Annual Statement Studies*, 1984 Edition.

5 percentage points higher than RMA, which would be expected, since 25 percent of John Dough's sales came from the retail operation, which has a higher margin than the production of bakery products. The RMA category is for bakery manufacturers, not retailers.

John Dough's operating expenses are slightly higher than RMA, but its other expenses are lower, allowing John Dough's pretax profit margin of 3.5 percent to remain above the industry average of 1.6 percent. Again, part of this above-average profitability is to be expected, due to the retail operation.

John Dough has below-average liquidity ratios, as can be seen by the current, quick, and sales/working capital ratios, which were all close to lower-quartile figures for the industry.

The company's debt ratio (debt/worth) is slightly lower than the industry average, indicating a relatively strong equity position. Its interest expense coverage ratio (EBIT/interest) is well above the industry average. Therefore, on the whole, the company is less leveraged than the industry as a whole.

John Dough's pretax return on tangible net worth and assets were both above average, while asset turnover was exactly equal to the RMA median.

The company's officers' compensation/sales ratio, as adjusted earlier, is above the median but below the upper quartile.

Overall, John Dough has below-average liquidity ratios, an average asset utilization ratio (sales/total assets), and above-average debt and profitability ratios.

# Analysis of Qualitative Factors

At this point, it is important to summarize the important qualitative factors in order to judge whether they should positively or negatively affect the valuation.

## Positive Factors

1. Population and economic growth of the area in which the bakery is located.
2. Excellent reputation due to high quality and good service.
3. Loyal customer base.
4. Experienced management and good employee relations.
5. Production facility is laid out efficiently and work flows smoothly. Plant has been modernized.
6. Based on adjusted financial statements, the bakery has exhibited above-average profitability, although that is partly due to the retail operation. John Dough's bakery is somewhat less leveraged than the average bakery.

# Negative Factors

1. Wage increases will probably be above-average due to the economic growth expected in the area.
2. Three customers account for 37 percent of sales. The loss of one or more of these accounts would hurt profitability.
3. Competition is keen, especially from the bakery's major competitor, Hostess, which can rely on its brand name to a large extent.
4. The loss of John and Muffin Dough could negatively affect customer loyalty and employee loyalty.
5. The current production facility has no room for expansion.

# Deriving Capitalization Rates from Transaction Data

In the previous chapter, information was provided on three bakery transactions (Exhibit 21–6). The various price/earnings, price/sales, and price/book value multiples at which these transactions occurred can provide guidance in valuing John Dough Bakery. A summary of these multiples and how they were computed appears in Exhibit 22–4.

## Adjusting Transaction Data to Cash Equivalent Value

The transaction involving Bakery 2 was not a cash transaction, and accordingly we need to convert it to a cash price so that it is comparable to the other two transactions.

The terms of the transaction were $75,000 down and the balance ($225,000) paid in equal monthly installments of principal and interest for five years at 10 percent interest. In general, a bakery could probably borrow money from the bank at 2½ points above the prime rate of 10½ percent, or about 13 percent. Since a seller's contract is normally not secured by specific collateral, as a bank loan is, there is more risk involved. Assuming that the contract is fairly well secured and is protected by covenants in the purchase agreement, a market rate of 15 percent is probably appropriate.

Assuming a market rate of 15 percent, the previously described contract has a cash value of $275,950. Refer to Chapter 17 for an explanation of how to make this calculation.

## Price/Earnings before Taxes (EBT)

The price/EBT multiples of the three comparative transactions ranged from 4.3 to 6.7, with a mean of 5.7 and a median of 6.1 (see Exhibit 22–4). If we assume that the information provided to us represents what

Exhibit 22–4

### JOHN DOUGH BAKERY, INC.
### DERIVATION OF COMPARATIVE COMPANY
### MARKET VALUE INDICATORS

|  | Bakery 1 $ | Bakery 2 $ | Bakery 3 $ | John Dough Bakery |
|---|---|---|---|---|
| Cash Price (1) | 120,000 | 275,950 | 87,500 | (a) |
|  |  |  |  |  |
| EBT (2) | 28,000 | 45,000 | 13,000 | 35,000 |
| + Depreciation | 20,000 | 32,000 | 12,000 | 23,000 |
| = EBDT (3) | 48,000 | 77,000 | 25,000 | 58,000 |
|  |  |  |  |  |
| Cash Price | 120,000 | 275,950 | 87,500 | (a) |
| + Long-Term Debt | 100,000 | 20,000 | – | 80,000 |
| + Current Mat. LTD | 20,000 | 5,000 | – | 25,000 |
| + Notes Payable | 15,000 | – | 35,000 | 15,000 |
| = Price of Invested Capital (4) | 255,000 | 300,950 | 122,500 | (a) |
|  |  |  |  |  |
| EBT | 28,000 | 45,000 | 13,000 | 35,000 |
| + Interest | 12,000 | 3,000 | 5,000 | 10,000 |
| = EBIT (5) | 40,000 | 48,000 | 18,000 | 45,000 |
| + Depreciation | 20,000 | 32,000 | 12,000 | 23,000 |
| = EBDIT (6) | 60,000 | 80,000 | 30,000 | 68,000 |
|  |  |  |  |  |
| Sales (7) | 770,000 | 1,200,000 | 485,000 | 1,000,000 |
| Tangible Book Value (8) | 120,000 | 210,000 | 100,000 | 105,500 |

| Ratios: |  |  |  | Mean | Median |
|---|---|---|---|---|---|
| Price/EBT [(1) ÷ (2)] | 4.3 | 6.1 | 6.7 | 5.7 | 6.1 |
| Price/EBDT [(1) ÷ (3)] | 2.5 | 3.6 | 3.5 | 3.2 | 3.5 |
| Price of Invested Capital/ EBIT [(4) ÷ (5)] | 6.4 | 6.3 | 6.8 | 6.5 | 6.4 |
| Price of Invested Capital/ EBDIT [(4) ÷ (6)] | 4.3 | 3.8 | 4.1 | 4.1 | 4.1 |
| Price/Sales [(1) ÷ (7)] | 0.16 | 0.23 | 0.18 | 0.19 | 0.18 |
| Price/Book Value [(1) ÷ (8)] | 1.0 | 1.31 | 0.88 | 1.06 | 1.00 |
| Return on Equity [(2) ÷ (8)] | 0.23 | 0.21 | 0.13 | 0.19 | 0.21 |

E = Earnings   B = Before   D = Depreciation   I = Interest   T = Taxes
LTD = Long-term Debt
(a) To Be determined
**SOURCE:** Willamette Business Sale Data Base.

could be considered a sustainable level of earnings, then the reciprocals of the mean and median multiple would indicate what the current capitalization rates are. The reciprocal of the mean and median ratios produce capitalization rates of 17.5 percent and 16.4 percent, respectively.

# Price/Earnings before Depreciation and Taxes (EBDT)

The price/EBDT or price/pretax cash flow multiples ranged from 2.5 to 3.6, with a mean of 3.2 and a median of 3.6. We believe, although we do not know for a fact, that the depreciation of the comparative companies is comparable to that of John Dough Bakery. Again, assuming that the earnings bases are sustainable, the mean and median multiples indicate capitalization rates of 27.8 and 31.3 percent, respectively. These capitalization rates are higher than the rates applicable to EBT because in this calculation we are using cash flow as our earnings base.

# Price/Earnings before Interest and Taxes (EBIT)

This approach is often referred to as a debt-free approach, because in using it we remove the interest expense from the earnings base. When we take out the interest expense from the earnings, however, we also need to add to the transaction price the interest-bearing debt that was assumed. In other words, if no debt was assumed, an investor would have paid a higher price and there would have been no interest expense in the earnings. We have assumed that the debt is at current market rates. If that was not the case, then it would have to be adjusted to reflect the current market rates. We also assumed that the amount of notes payable shown on the balance sheet was close to the average amount of notes payable throughout the year. The price (including interest-bearing debt)/EBIT ratios for the comparative companies ranged from 6.3 to 6.8, with a mean of 6.5 and a median of 6.4 (Exhibit 22–4). Again, if we assume that the earnings bases of the comparative companies are sustainable, the indicated mean capitalization rate is 15.4 percent and the median capitalization rate is 15.6 percent.

# Price/Earnings before Depreciation, Interest, and Taxes (EBDIT)

Price/EBDIT is also a debt-free ratio; it is based on debt-free cash flow. Again, the price used in computing the ratio must include the transaction price plus the amount of the company's interest-bearing debt assumed by the buyer. As computed in Exhibit 22–4, the price/EBDIT ratios ranged from 3.8 to 4.3, with a mean and median of 4.1, indicating a capitalization rate of 24.4 percent, based on the previously mentioned assumptions.

## Price/Sales

The price/sales ratios of the comparative transactions ranged from 16 percent to 23 percent, with a mean of 19 percent and a median of 18 percent (see Exhibit 22–4).

## Price/Book Value

The price/book value ratios ranged from 88 percent to 131 percent, with a mean and median of 106 percent and 100 percent, respectively.

---

# Capitalization of Normalized Earnings

There are a number of earnings bases that can be capitalized. We chose to look at the following four earnings bases: pretax earnings (EBT), pretax cash flow (EBDT), debt-free pretax earnings (EBIT), and debt-free pretax cash flow (EBDIT). The debt-free approaches remove the effect of different debt structures on comparative company data. The pretax cash flow method removes the effect of different depreciation methods, while the debt-free pretax cash flow method removes the effects of *both* different debt structures *and* depreciation methods.

In determining the four earnings bases to capitalize, one can look at current or average earnings. In our opinion, John Dough's earnings in 1980 and 1981 do not reflect its current earning power. Since the average of earnings for the past three years has been nearly equal to current earnings, we chose to look at current earnings in computing the four earnings bases.

In choosing capitalization rates for these various earnings bases, we looked at the comparative company data just discussed. Since the spread between the multipliers of each earnings base was not very wide, in our opinion, they provided a pretty good indication of what current multipliers are in the industry. In choosing which rate to apply to John Dough's earnings, we looked at the positive and negative factors relative to John Dough Bakery, discussed earlier. In our opinion, the positive and negative factors tend to neutralize each other, so a ratio in the middle of the comparative company ratios is appropriate. For each of the following approaches, we chose a ratio between the mean and median ratios.

## Price/EBT

As can be seen in Exhibits 22–2 and 22–4, John Dough's EBT in 1984 was $35,000. We chose a ratio of 6.0 (between the mean of 5.7 and median of 6.1) to apply to these earnings, resulting in the following indication of value:

| EBT | | P/E Ratio | | Indicated Value |
|---|---|---|---|---|
| $35,000 | × | 6.0 | = | $210,000 |

# Price/EBDT

John Dough's EBDT in 1984 was $58,000 (see Exhibit 22–4). We chose a multiple of 3.4 (between the mean of 3.2 and median of 3.5) to apply to these earnings, resulting in the following indication of value:

| *EBDT* | | *P/E Ratio* | | *Indicated Value* |
|--------|--|-------------|--|-------------------|
| $58,000 | × | 3.4 | = | $197,200 |

# Price/EBIT

John Dough's EBIT in 1984 was $45,000 (see Exhibit 22–4). We chose a ratio of 6.5 (the mean was 6.5 and the median 6.4) to apply to these earnings. When we apply this multiple to the EBIT, the resulting value includes the value of the interest-bearing debt. Therefore, to arrive at an indicated value for the equity (stock) of John Dough Bakery, we need to subtract from that value $120,000, which is the total amount of John Dough's interest-bearing debt. The following steps summarize the computation described.

| | |
|---|---:|
| EBIT | $ 45,000 |
| P/E Ratio | x   6.5 |
| | $292,500 |
| Less: Interest-Bearing Debt | (120,000) |
| Indicated Value | $172,500 |

# Price/EBDIT

John Dough's EBDIT in 1984 was $68,000 (see Exhibit 22–4). We chose a ratio of 4.1 (which was both the mean and the median) to apply to these earnings. Again, the amount of interest-bearing debt must be subtracted to arrive at the indicated value, which is derived as follows:

| | |
|---|---:|
| EBDIT | $ 68,000 |
| P/E Ratio | x   4.1 |
| | $278,800 |
| Less: Interest-Bearing Debt | (120,000) |
| Indicated Value | $158,800 |

# Summary

The four capitalization of normalized earnings approaches can be summarized as follows:

| | Earnings Base | | Capitalization Ratio | | | Less: Interest-Bearing Debt | Indicated Value |
|------|---------------|--|----------------------|--|-----------|-----------------------------|-----------------|
| EBT | $35,000 | x | 6.0 | = | $210,000 | N/A | $210,000 |
| EBDT | 58,000 | x | 3.4 | = | 197,200 | N/A | 197,200 |
| EBIT | 45,000 | x | 6.5 | = | 292,500 | $120,000 | 172,500 |
| EBDIT | 68,000 | x | 4.1 | = | 278,800 | 120,000 | 158,800 |

The mean of these four approaches is $184,625, while the median is $184,850. The two debt free approaches indicate values below the median. In our opinion, since these approaches adjust for differences in capital structures, we would lean slightly more toward these values, although all four approaches are valid. In our opinion, based on these four approaches, a value of approximately $180,000 for the stock of John Dough Bakery, Inc. is indicated by the capitalization of normalized earnings.

# Excess Earnings Method

The reader should refer to Chapter 12 ("The Excess Earnings Method") for a step-by-step explanation of how the method works. As discussed in that chapter, a normalized level of earnings and a net tangible asset value need to be determined. For John Dough Bakery, the normalized earnings are $35,000, the company's earnings in 1984, and, we believe, a sustainable level of earnings in the future. The net tangible asset value is $105,500, which is the company's adjusted book value less the value of the leasehold interest ($124,372 − $18,872 = $105,500.)

Next, an appropriate percentage rate of return on the net tangible assets needs to be determined. The rate of return on the tangible assets should be at, or slightly below, the company's overall weighted average cost of capital. We made this analysis earlier in the chapter when we chose a rate at which to discount the savings in rent from the favorable lease. We estimated the cost of debt at 15 percent and the cost of equity at 25 percent. Furthermore, we assumed a capital structure consisting of 50 percent debt and 50 percent equity. This calculation resulted in a weighted average cost of capital of 20 percent. For the rate of return in tangible assets we believe a slightly lower rate of 18 percent is reasonable. (This would imply the ability to borrow 70 percent of the value of the tangible assets at 15 percent, leaving 30 percent of the value of the tangible assets to be financed with equity at a cost of 25 percent; the result is a weighted average capitalization rate of 18 percent applicable to the tangible assets.)

Finally, it is necessary to determine an appropriate rate to apply to the excess earnings (the earnings attributable to intangible assets rather than tangible assets). As discussed in Chapter 12, since the risk attached to the intangible portion of the assets is greater, and since goodwill is in many cases perishable, a higher capitalization rate than the rate applicable to total equity is required on the excess earnings. We chose a rate of 30 percent as appropriate.

Based on the above information, the value of John Dough Bakery derived from the excess earnings method can be computed as follows:

| | | |
|---|---|---|
| Net Tangible Asset Value | | $105,500 |
| Normalized Earnings | $35,000 | |
| Earnings Attributable to Tangible Assets ($105,500 x .18) = | 18,990 | |
| Excess Earnings | $16,010 | |
| Value of Excess Earnings ($16,010 ÷ .3) = | | 53,367 |
| Total Value | | $158,867 |

It should be noted that we did not adjust the fixed assets to reflect their replacement cost; rather, they are simply stated at their depreciated book value. While, as we stated earlier, we believe that the current depreciation expense represents the amount of deterioration occurring on the equipment, we believe that the book value of the fixed assets is probably less than the used replacement cost due to the high inflation in the late 1970's and accelerated depreciation methods the company used at that time. For that reason, the figure we used for the company's tangible net asset value does not, in all probability, approximate economic reality; therefore, the indicated value of the bakery determined from this approach should not be relied upon heavily.

# Discounted Future Earnings Method

As already discussed in Chapter 13, the discounted future earnings approach is conceptually the best valuation approach in most instances. John Dough's earnings before taxes and owner's compensation for the next three years have been projected as follows:

|      |           |
|------|-----------|
| 1985 | $100,000  |
| 1986 | $110,000  |
| 1987 | $120,000  |

Mr. Dough has informed us that he expects earnings to level off after 1987. Also, his projections are in dollars that include the expected effects of inflation.

To arrive at normalized earnings figures to discount, we need to make the same adjustments we did for the historical statements. Mr. Dough has told us that his estimates do not include any nonrecurring items. Therefore, we need to deduct from these forecasts a reasonable salary for Mr. Dough and an allowance for doubtful accounts. Mr. Dough's normalized salary in 1984 was $65,000. We assumed that he would maintain this salary in 1985, but then raise it to $70,000 in 1986 and $75,000 in 1987. An annual allowance of $1,000 for doubtful accounts also needs to be expected in 1985, 1986, and 1987.

These adjustments result in the following normalized future earnings for John Dough Bakery:

|                                | 1985      | 1986      | 1987      |
|--------------------------------|-----------|-----------|-----------|
| Estimated Earnings per John Dough | $100,000  | $110,000  | $120,000  |
| Normalized Owner's Compensation   | (65,000)  | (70,000)  | (75,000)  |
| Allowance for Doubtful Accounts   | 1,000     | 1,000     | 1,000     |
| Normalized Pretax Earnings        | 34,000    | 39,000    | 44,000    |

The next variable that needs to be determined is the appropriate discount rate. Since the future earnings projection is the amount of earnings available to equity, a capitalization rate applicable to an equity investment should be used.

As discussed in Chapter 10, it is necessary to choose a capitalization rate, at which to discount future earnings, that reflects returns available on investments without significant risk, plus an adequate premium for the risk and illiquidity of investing in a private company. As discussed in Chapter 10, the market seems to require an expected return of about 25 percent to 30 percent on equity investments in privately held companies. Because of the long-established nature of John Dough Bakery, we will use a discount rate of 25 percent.

Discounting these earnings at 25 percent results in an indicated value of $164,800 for the John Dough Bakery, Inc. stock, derived as follows (see Chapter 13 for a detailed explanation):

Present value of earnings from 1985 to 1987:

$$\frac{\$34,000}{(1 + .25)} + \frac{\$39,000}{(1 + .25)^2} + \frac{\$44,000}{(1 + .25)^3} = \quad \$ \ 74,688$$

Present value of earnings for 1988 and thereafter:

$44,000 \div .25 = \$176,000$

$$\frac{\$176,000}{(1 + .25)^3} = \qquad\qquad\qquad \underline{90,112}$$

Indicated value                                                          $\underline{\$164,800}$

# Multiplier of Gross Revenues

The capitalization of sales approach is often considered an appropriate approach to valuation, especially when it is used in conjunction with several other valuation approaches. In a way, it can be considered a shortcut to a capitalization of earnings approach, since generally there is an implicit assumption that a certain level of sales should be able to generate a certain level of earnings in a given type of business. This approach is reasonable to use for John Dough Bakery because there has been a fairly consistent relationship between sales and profits over the years (especially in the last three years). Guidance in arriving at an appropriate multiplier of sales can again be found in the multipliers at which the comparative bakery transactions occurred.

The price/sales (P/S) multipliers for the comparative transactions ranged from 16 percent to 23 percent, with a mean of 19 percent and a median of 18 percent. For the same reasons that have been mentioned, we chose a multiplier of 19 percent, which is equal to the mean and slightly higher than the median. Before applying this multiplier to sales, it is important to note that the pretax profit margins of the three bakeries involved in the transactions ranged from 2.7 percent to 3.8 percent, very similar to John Dough's margin of 3.5 percent in 1984. This analysis helps to confirm the use of this approach as being appropriate in this case.

Applying the previously determined multiplier of 19 percent to John Dough's 1984 sales results in the following indication of value:

| Sales | P/S Ratio | | Indicated Value |
|---|---|---|---|
| $1,000,000 $\times$ | .19 | = | $190,000 |

# Price/Book Value Approach

In trying to determine what multiplier of book value John Dough Bakery might be worth, we again looked for guidance from the comparative transactions. The price/book value (P/BV) multipliers ranged from 88 percent to 131 percent, with a mean of 106 percent and a median of 100 percent. Whereas in our other approaches, we have chosen a multiplier close to the mean and median, for this approach, we believe an above-average multiplier is appropriate. As discussed in Chapter 15, generally the higher a company's return on equity, the higher its price/book value multiplier should be. John Dough's pretax return on equity in 1984 was 33.2 percent, higher than any of the comparative companies', which ranged from 13.0 percent to 23.3 percent. Accordingly, we chose a multiplier of 1.5 as appropriate for John Dough Bakery. This multiplier of 1.5 is 15 percent above the highest P/BV multiplier among the three comparative transactions for which data were available, and this is reasonable, given the company's high return on equity. That resulted in the following indication of value:

| Book Value | | P/BV Ratio | | Indicated Value |
|---|---|---|---|---|
| $105,500 | × | 1.5 | = | $158,250 |

# Valuation Summary

The five valuation approaches we have discussed produced indicated values ranging from $158,250 to $190,000. They are summarized below:

| Approach | Indicated Value |
|---|---|
| Capitalization of normalized earnings | $180,000 |
| Excess earnings method | 158,867 |
| Discounted future earnings method | 164,800 |
| Multiple at gross revenues | 190,000 |
| Price/book value approach | 158,250 |

Since we are valuing an operating company, more consideration should be given to the earnings approaches than to the asset approach (price/book value). Of the four earnings approaches, the least weight should be given to the excess earnings approach, for reasons discussed earlier. The remaining three approaches range in value from $164,800 to $190,000, with an average of about $180,000. This value is 1.7 times the company's adjusted tangible book value, which is not unreasonable, given the company's high return on equity.

# Requirements for Working Capital

Although we have determined the total value of the equity in the company based on certain assumptions as to its earning power, a prospective buyer would probably pay somewhat less for the business because it has a working capital deficiency. We did not include this factor among the negative factors we considered when choosing our earnings and book value multipliers, because we chose to consider it separately at this time.

When we did the ratio analysis as part of our financial statement analysis, John Dough's and RMA's liquidity ratios were as follows:

|  | John Dough | RMA |
|---|---|---|
| Current Ratio | 0.8 | 1.7<br>1.3<br>0.7 |
| Quick Ratio | 0.3 | 1.2<br>1.0<br>0.3 |
| Sales/Working Capital | * | 14.0<br>42.1<br>* |

*No meaningful ratio due to deficit working capital.

As can be seen, the bakery's ratios are near the bottom-quartile figures for the industry. To get an idea of the amount of working capital that will be needed, we can apply the RMA median figures to John Dough's current liabilities and sales. This exercise produces the following working capital requirements:

| RMA Ratio | Indicated Amount | | | Indicated Cash Infusion |
|---|---|---|---|---|
| Current Ratio | $130,000 | in | Current Assets | $49,500 |
| Quick Ratio | $100,000 | in | Cash & Receivables | $66,500 |
| Sales/Working Capital | $123,753 | in | Current Assets | $43,253 |

Therefore, to be operated according to industry averages, John Dough Bakery would need $43,253 to $66,500 of additional working capital. However, the bakery could be operated with liquidity ratios below the industry averages. In our opinion, $35,000 of additional capital is probably sufficient. This additional capital would produce a current ratio of 1.2, a quick ratio of .7 (assuming that the $35,000 was in cash), and a sales/working capital ratio of 64.5. Those are below the RMA median but above the lower-quartile figures. We will assume that the potential buyer has $35,000 of cash to put into the business.

# Valuation Conclusion

In our opinion, the market value of 100 percent of the common stock of John Dough Bakery, Inc., as of February 28, 1985, was $145,000 ($180,000 less the $35,000 of additional working capital needed).

# Chapter 23

## Valuing Minority Interests

*The value of a partial interest in a business or practice may be equal to, more than, or less than a proportionate share of the value of a 100 percent interest in the business or practice.*

This revelation comes as a shock to many people, who may have always assumed that a partial interest would be worth a pro rata portion of the value of the total enterprise. To compound the frustration of the uninitiated, it is also true that the sum of the values of the individual parts does not necessarily equal the value of the whole.

How can this be? As the King mused, " 'Tis a puzzlement."[1]

# Elements of Control

The following is a list of some of the more common prerogatives of control:

1. Appoint management.
2. Determine management compensation and perquisites.
3. Set policy and change the course of business.
4. Acquire or liquidate assets.
5. Select people with whom to do business and award contracts.
6. Make acquisitions.
7. Liquidate, dissolve, sell out, or recapitalize the company.
8. Sell or acquire treasury shares.
9. Register the company's stock for a public offering.
10. Declare and pay dividends.
11. Change the articles of incorporation or bylaws.

From the above list, it is apparent that the owner of a controlling interest in an enterprise enjoys some very valuable rights that an owner not in a controlling position does not.

# Degree of Control

The matter of a control position versus a minority position is not an either/or proposition. Relevant state statutes and the way the overall ownership of the entity is distributed have a bearing on the relative rights of minority and controlling stockholders.

## Effect of State Statutes

Statutes affecting the relative rights of controlling versus minority stockholders vary from state to state. In some states, a simple majority can approve major actions such as a merger or sale of the company. Other states require a two-thirds majority to approve such actions,

---

[1] Oscar Hammerstein II, *The King and I* (New York: Random House, 1951).

which means that a minority of just over one third has the power to block such actions. Under California statutes, minority stockholders enjoy certain rights under some circumstances that minority stockholders in other states do not. The variations in state law concerning what rights are given to what proportion of ownership can have an important bearing on the valuation of certain percentage interests in some cases.

## Effect of Distribution of Ownership

If one person owns 49 percent of the stock and another owns 51 percent, the 49 percent holder has little or no control of any kind; however, if two stockholders own 49 percent each and a third owns 2 percent, the 49 percent stockholders may be on a par with each other, depending on who owns the other 2 percent. The 2 percent stockholder may be able to command a considerable premium over the pro rata value for that particular block of stock because of its swing vote power.

If each of three stockholders or partners owns a one-third interest, no one has complete control, but no one is in a relatively inferior position, unless two of the three have close ties with each other, which are not shared by the third. Equal individual interests normally are each worth less than a pro rata portion of what the total enterprise would be worth, so that the sum of the values of the individual interests normally is less than what the total enterprise could be sold for to a single buyer. However, the percentage discount from pro rata value for each of such equal interests normally would not be as great as for a minority interest which had no control whatsoever.

Each situation has to be analyzed individually with respect to the degree of control, or lack of it, and the implications for the value of the minority interest.

# Distinction between Discount for Minority Interest and Discount for Lack of Marketability

Much confusion exists because some writers and appraisers fail to distinguish between a minority interest discount and a discount for lack of marketability. These are two separate concepts, although there is some interrelationship between them.

The concept of *minority interest* deals with the relationship between the interest being valued and the total enterprise, based on the factors discussed in the first two sections of this chapter. The primary factor bearing on the value of the minority interest in relation to the value of the total entity is how much control the minority interest does have over the particular entity.

The concept of *marketability* deals with the liquidity of the interest, how quickly and certainly it can be converted to cash at the owner's discretion.

People sometimes overlook the fact that discounts are meaningless until the base from which the discount is to be taken has been defined.

Since a minority interest discount reflects lack of control, the base from which the minority interest discount is subtracted is its proportionate share in the total entity value, including all rights of control. Since a discount for lack of marketability reflects lack of liquidity, the base from which the discount is subtracted is the value of an entity or interest that is otherwise comparable but enjoys higher liquidity.

Even controlling interests suffer to some extent from lack of marketability. It usually takes a few months to sell a company. The relationship between the discount for lack of marketability and for minority interest lies in the fact that, even after discounting a minority interest for its lack of control, it still is usually much harder to sell a minority interest than to sell a controlling interest in a closely held business.

If one is valuing a minority interest in a closely held company by comparing it with values of publicly held stocks, one must discount only for lack of marketability, because a minority interest discount is already reflected in the public stock's trading price.

# How the Applicable Standard of Value Affects Minority Interests

As discussed in Chapter 2, the applicable standard of value for the vast majority of valuation situations will fall into one of three categories: (1) fair market value, (2) intrinsic value, or (3) fair value. The applicable standard of value is determined primarily by the purpose and circumstances of the valuation. In some situations, the applicable standard of value is mandated by law. In other situations, the choice of the standard of value lies within the discretion of the parties involved.

## Fair Market Value

Recall from Chapter 2 that the fair market value standard implies a price at which an arm's-length transaction would be expected to take place between normally motivated investors under open market conditions, without considering any special benefits that might be related to the transaction for any particular buyer or seller. Considering the unattractiveness of minority interests in closely held companies to investors at large, the discount from a proportionate share of enterprise value under the fair market value standard normally would be quite large.

## Intrinsic Value

In Chapter 2, the intrinsic value standard (also called *fundamental value* or *investment value*) was defined as the value to a particular investor, taking into consideration that investor's cost of capital, perception of risk, and other characteristics unique to him. Because of the particular attributes of ownership to any specific investor, the intrinsic value of a minority interest in a particular enterprise may be equal to, greater than, or less than fair market value, and also may be equal to, greater than, or less than a pro rata portion of the total enterprise value.

# Fair Value

As noted in Chapter 2, the fair value standard suffers from lack of consistent definition from one context to another. It crops up most often as the statutory standard of value applicable to appraisals under dissenting stockholders' rights. Such valuations, by their nature, are valuations of minority interests. The need to interpret the meaning of this standard of value from a study of the legal precedents in dissenting stockholder actions in each of the 50 states and Canada poses a continuing challenge to the appraisal profession. Certain precedents have suggested that fair value be interpreted to mean fair market value without a minority interest discount (a proportionate share of enterprise value). However, I cannot emphasize enough that research of the specifically applicable legal precedents is very important in each context to which the fair value standard is determined to apply.

# Approaches to Valuation of Minority Interests

There are two basic ways of approaching the valuation of minority interests: (1) a proportionate share of the total enterprise value, or a discount from this value, and (2) a direct comparison with values of other minority interests.

## Proportion of the Enterprise Value Less a Discount

One way to approach the valuation of a minority interest is the following three-step process:

1. Determine the value of the total enterprise.
2. Compute the minority owner's pro rata interest in the total.
3. Determine the amount of discount, if any, applicable to the pro rata value of the total enterprise to reflect properly the value of the minority interest.

The value of the total enterprise should be determined as discussed in the earlier part of this book, with certain possible variations noted in a later section. The proportionate value normally is a straightforward computation, although occasionally there may be complications due to special rights of different classes of partners or stockholders.

The amount of discount to reflect the minority interest can be a matter of great controversy. The degree of control or lack of it, as discussed in an earlier section, definitely has a bearing on the applicable discount, but there is no magic formula for quantifying this factor. Also, the discount generally is lower for stocks that pay cash dividends, or partnerships that distribute considerable cash flow, than for those that do not, but there is no formula to quantify that factor, either. Some guidance to typical discounts and ranges of discounts found in actual transactions is included in later sections of this chapter.

# Valuation by Comparison with Other Minority Interests

If the appraiser can find data on actual sales of other comparable minority interests, he might be able to reach a conclusion of value by direct comparison to such transactions, without ever going through the step of estimating a value for the total enterprise. The appraiser can value the subject minority interest using parameters similar to those used for valuing a total company. Such parameters would include, for example, capitalization of earnings, capitalization of cash flow, a ratio of price to book value or adjusted net asset value, and so on. Guidance for the quantification of the market value parameters would be taken from the comparative minority interest transaction data.

**Sources of Comparative Data.**  One source of comparative data could be prior arm's-length transactions involving minority interests in the same company.

There is no generally available source of data on any broad group of minority interest transactions in closely held companies, but there is, of course, a readily available data base on daily transactions in minority interests in thousands of publicly traded companies. Subject to several limitations discussed earlier in the book, guidance for parameters for the valuation of minority interests might be drawn from the prices of publicly traded stocks.

**Adjustments for Risk and Marketability.**  As discussed earlier in this book, if the comparison with public stock prices approach is taken, adjustments need to be made for differences in risk and other factors. The most important of these factors is the lack of liquidity (lack of marketability) of the minority interest in the closely held company, compared with the virtually instant marketability of a publicly traded stock.

This difference in marketability is a more important factor with respect to value than most people who have not had experience in dealing with it usually realize. The fair market values of minority interests in closely held companies average about 35 to 50 percent less than prices of comparable minority interests in very liquid, publicly traded companies, all other things being equal.[2]

---

[2] For a detailed discussion of the impact of marketability, or lack of it, see Pratt, Chapter 10, "Data on Discounts for Lack of Marketability," in *Valuing a Business*, pp. 147–56.

# Errors to Avoid

The following points should help the reader avoid certain common errors in the valuation of minority interests and to identify such errors when they appear in someone else's minority interest valuation analysis.

## The Public Offering Myth

Incredibly, I frequently have seen authors and analysts use the estimated cost of a public offering as a method for quantifying the discount for lack of marketability for a minority interest in a closely held company. The rationale for such an approach is that if the difference in value compared to a publicly traded minority interest is lack of marketability, the discount should be no more than the cost of overcoming that deficiency. The fallacy in that approach is the basic fact that a minority stockholder does not have the legal right to register the company's stock for a public offering. Since registration for a public offering is not an alternative available to a minority stockholder, the matter of what it would cost him to do so is not pertinent.

## Irrelevant Financial Statement Adjustments

In Part II, "Analyzing the Company," we suggested that in developing the company's earnings capacity, the appraiser might want to remove from expenses such items as Uncle Rusty's consulting fees and the cost of Grandpa's chauffeured Cadillac. At that time, we were contemplating valuation of the entire company, and we were assuming that it was within the controlling owner's discretion to remove such expenses with no significant impairment to revenues. The minority stockholder, however, has no such power, so these adjustments may not be relevant in estimating an earnings base for the valuation of minority interests, unless there is reason to believe that the changes actually are going to be made.

The same general concept applies to adjustments to the balance sheet to reflect the values of excess assets. Unless the controlling person or group is expected to take action to liquidate such assets, their values to the minority stockholders are remote.

## Comparison with Real Estate Minority Discounts

Discounts for minority interests in direct investment in real estate, when taken at all, usually are only about 10 to 20 percent below a pro rata proportion of the value of the total parcel. Sometimes people more familiar with direct investments in real estate than with investments in businesses impute similarly low minority interest discounts to investments in business interests. Perhaps because of the extremely wide diversity of options available to the controlling owner of a business enterprise, or for whatever other reasons, the average of actual minority interest discounts in transactions involving business interests is much greater than the average of minority interest discounts in transactions involving direct investment in real estate.

# Data on Sales of Minority Interests

Very few reliable data exist on sales of minority interests in closely held businesses. The market for publicly traded stocks, on the other hand, provides thousands of reported transactions every day.

## Trust and Estate Sales

Some of the most convincing data I have found on actual sales prices of minority interests in closely held businesses were compiled by a bank trust officer responsible for administering estates that owned all or portions of closely held businesses. For openers, he offers the following generalities:

> A number of years of experience has demonstrated that it is extremely difficult to find any market for minority interests . . . , despite efforts to do so. . . . On the relatively rare occasions when an offer is made to buy a minority interest, it is almost always for an amount far less than the fiduciary and the beneficiary expect to get.[3]

The trust officer compiled data on 30 actual sales of minority interests. He found that the average transaction price was 36 percent below book value, and he concludes with the following observations:

> Only 20 percent of the sales were made at discounts less than 20 percent. A little more than half the sales (53⅓ percent) were made at discounts that ranged from 22 percent to 48 percent, and 23⅓ percent of the sales were made at discounts of from 54.4 percent to 78 percent.
> It would be dangerous to draw too many generalizations from the survey, but those sales where the discounts were below 20 percent involved, with one exception, purchases from close relatives where friendly relations existed. The exception was the sale by a holder of swing shares who used his leverage well, but still took a 4.3 percent discount. At the other end of the spectrum was the settlement of a three year bitter dispute between two families; the majority family raised its token offer only after threat of a lawsuit, but the price the minority interest took nonetheless represented a 78 percent discount.[4]

Note that the discounts in the foregoing surveys were from book value, not from the value of the enterprise as a whole. Book value, of course, recognizes no appreciation in assets above depreciated net asset value, although, in a very few cases in the survey referenced above, the dis-

---

[3] H. Calvin Coolidge, "Fixing Value of Minority Interest in a Business; Actual Sales Suggest Discount as High as 70 Percent," *Estate Planning*, Spring 1975, p. 141.

[4] Ibid., p. 141.

counts were computed from an adjusted book value reflecting appreciation in real estate values. I would expect that the total enterprise value would be above the book value in most cases; if that was true in the survey, then the discounts from the owners' proportionate shares of the total enterprise values were even greater than the discounts as shown in the survey, which were from book value.

An update published in 1983 indicates a trend toward even higher discounts when disposing of minority interests in closely held corporations. In the update, there was a much higher concentration of discounts from book value at the high end of the range, and the average discount for the two studies combined was approximately 40 percent. The updated study concludes as follows:

> Each of the sales used in the survey involved a combination of factors that made it somewhat unique. To use any of the data, or any classification of the data, as definitive proof of the discount to be applied in a prospective valuation would be dangerous. This should not, however, obscure the true significance of the data, which is that in the actual marketplace, the typical discount is not of token size, but of substantial magnitude.[5]

## Public Stock Market Data

The thousands of daily stock transactions on stock exchanges and in the over-the-counter market are, of course, minority interest transactions. The prices per share at which these transactions take place usually are significantly below the prices stockholders receive when an entire company or a controlling interest is purchased.

The following are some examples involving companies which probably are familiar names to many readers.

| Name of Company Acquired | Date of Buyout | Premium Paid over Market[a] % | Implied Minority Int. Discount[b] % |
|---|---|---|---|
| Atlantic Oil Co. | 2/24/83 | 71.4 | 41.7 |
| Dan River, Inc. | 5/25/83 | 56.5 | 36.1 |
| Scripto, Inc. | 6/21/83 | 28.5 | 22.2 |
| Bekins Company | 7/5/83 | 23.5 | 19.0 |
| Lenox, Inc. | 8/2/83 | 59.3 | 37.2 |
| Mirro Corp. | 9/19/83 | 20.0 | 16.7 |
| Stokely-Van Camp | 11/7/83 | 91.3 | 47.7 |
| Kaiser Steel Corp. | 1/19/84 | 36.8 | 26.9 |

a   The premium paid over market is a percentage based on the buyout price over the market price of the seller's stock five business days prior to the announcement date.

b   Formula: 1 − (1 ÷ (1 + Premium Paid)), for example, 1 − (1 ÷ 1.714) = 1 - .583 = .417.

**SOURCE:** W.T. Grimm's *Mergerstat Review 1983* and Willamette Management Associates, Inc.'s calculations.

---

[5] H. Calvin Coolidge, "Survey Shows Trend towards Larger Minority Discounts," *Estate Planning*, September 1983, p. 282.

The average percentage discount from the buyout price at which stocks were selling immediately prior to announcements of acquisitions for the years 1980–84 were as follows:

| | |
|---|---|
| 1980 | 33.3% |
| 1981 | 32.4% |
| 1982 | 32.2% |
| 1983 | 27.4% |
| 1984 | 27.5% |

**SOURCE:** *Mergerstat Review 1984* (Chicago: W.T. Grimm & Co., 1985). Discount calculated by Willamette Management Associates, Inc.

---

# A Few Personal Experiences

The following anecdotes from my own experience should cast some light on the realities of the values of minority interests.

## Split-Up of the Brothers-in-Law

Two brothers-in-law owned a small service business, which was incorporated. One brother-in-law owned two thirds of the stock and the other one third. There was no buy/sell agreement. The brother-in-law who owned one third left the company and requested that the two-thirds owner buy his stock at book value, either personally or through the corporation. The two-thirds owner declined, but offered to buy at a lower price. The one-third owner, believing that he should receive book value, declined the counter offer. Ten years went by, during which time the business prospered and grew greatly. The two-thirds owner kept increasing his salary, and the retained earnings built up mountainously. No dividends were ever paid on the stock. At the end of the 10 years, the two-thirds owner offered to buy the stock at what the book value had been 10 years earlier (the price the one-third stockholder had originally asked), and the one third stockholder accepted.

## The Lost Sheep Out in the Cold

One stockholder in a family-controlled corporation has wanted to sell his stock for years. The business is successful, but the stock pays no dividends, and the family member who wants to sell receives no benefit from owning the stock. He lives hundreds of miles from the location of the business operation, and there is little or no social or other communication among the family members. He would accept 10 percent of book value. In spite of repeated efforts, he has been unable to get an offer from anyone to buy his stock at any price.

# When the Controlling Interest Is Sold

One corporation had two stockholders, one owning 70 percent of the stock and the other owning 30 percent. The 70 percent stockholder sold his stock for $50 per share. The buyer had no obligation to purchase the minority owner's stock at $50 per share or at any price. The minority owner agreed to accept an offer of $20 per share from the new controlling owner for the remaining 30 percent of the stock.

The foregoing example is representative of several that I know. Many people assume that minority stockholders automatically will receive the same treatment as a controlling stockholder, if a controlling interest is sold. However, unless minority stockholders are protected either by statute or agreement, they do not necessarily receive equal treatment when a controlling interest is sold. This startling revelation has been the genesis of many lawsuits.

# Conventional Valuation Practices

Our firm frequently is engaged to value minority interests in corporations or partnerships for the purpose of buying out a minority stockholder or partner. From time to time in such cases, we have been specifically instructed to value a minority interest as a pro rata portion of the total enterprise value, with no discount, even though the controlling stockholders or partners had no legal obligation to make the buyout on that basis. However, such instructions to value a minority interest at a pro rata portion of enterprise value, while perhaps not rare, could not be regarded as typical. If the specified standard of value is fair market value, as is sometimes found in a buy/sell agreement, we normally would expect to value a minority interest at a discount from a pro rata portion of the total enterprise value. If the parties do not intend any discount from a pro rata portion of the enterprise value, then their intentions should be made clear in the buy/sell agreement, or in whatever document governs the valuation.

Further discussions of the circumstances under which minority interests may be valued at a pro rata proportion of the total enterprise value, or at some discount therefrom, are included in later chapters on litigation and estate planning.

# Part IV

Valuing Professional Practices

# Chapter 24

## Adjusting the Professional Practice Balance Sheet

Assets
    Cash
    Accounts Receivable
    Work-in-Process Inventory
    Inventory of Supplies
    Prepaid Expenses
    Equipment
    Leasehold Improvements
Liabilities
    Accounts Payable
    Accrued Liabilities
    Deferred Liabilities
    Long-Term Debt
    Lease Obligations
    Contingent Liabilities
Summary

When valuing professional practices, as when valuing small businesses, it is important to analyze and make appropriate adjustments to
the entity's tangible and intangible assets and liabilities. Valuation of
the professional practice differs from that of the small business, however, because the types of assets possessed by a professional practice are
very different from those used by a small business. Perhaps the most
important difference is that goodwill plays a much more important part
in the professional practice than in the typical small business. The
whole process of valuing tangible and intangible assets of the professional practice is further complicated by the cash basis accounting used
by most professional practices.

There may be a good deal of value in assets not recorded on the
balance sheets of a cash basis entity, such as accounts receivable, work-
in-process inventory, and prepaid expenses. Furthermore, fully depreciated equipment still being used by the practice may have been removed
from the balance sheet, and leasehold improvements that would be
irrelevant to the typical business may form an integral part of the
operation of the professional practice. By the same token, such liabilities as accounts payable, accrued vacation time for employees, and
accrued taxes may not be recorded on the balance sheet. The appraiser
must use his judgment to determine whether these assets and liabilities are necessary to the practice operations and how they affect its
income.

## Assets

Below is a discussion of the most common types of assets that the
appraiser can find in professional practices. The list is not all-inclusive,
and the appraiser should give specific recognition to the type of practice
being appraised in order to develop a list of potential assets the practice
may possess.

For a discussion of intangible assets that may be held by a professional practice, see Chapter 32.

## Cash

The reliability of the cash figure on the balance sheet may depend on
whether the statements were audited by an independent accountant or
merely compiled by the office manager or a bookkeeping service. If
there is reason to believe that the recorded cash balance may be incorrect, the appraiser should request copies of bank statements and statement reconciliations, and should review the deposit activity for a period
just following the valuation date. We have found on occasion that
checks received in payment were not recorded until they were deposited
in the bank the following day. Some practices use a system of tax
deferral not authorized by the IRS—for a certain amount of time preceding the fiscal yearend, they hold all incoming checks; they then

deposit them at the beginning of the next fiscal year, enabling them to include the income on the following year's tax returns. At the other end of the spectrum of error, petty cash may be shown incorrectly on the books, not to save taxes, but because of poor recordkeeping.

Cash generally is considered an operating asset, but if it becomes apparent that a reduction in cash would not affect the operation of the practice, then the practice has excess cash, and the appraiser should adjust the balance sheet to reflect it. The appraiser should not neglect to adjust interest income accordingly.

## Accounts Receivable

Accounts receivable often are not shown on the balance sheets of professional practices, because they generally operate on a cash basis of accounting. It is therefore necessary to determine the value of accounts receivable in order to include them in the value of the professional practice. There are several ways of keeping records of accounts receivable. Gross receivables at any given date are easily determined from the day sheets or accounts receivable journals of most practices.

One system that may cause more difficulty than the normal accounts receivable journal is based on a card file. Under a card system, client charges are recorded on a card that is kept in a file with accounts showing a debit or credit balance. Payments are recorded on the card, and when the account is paid, the card is returned to the client's file. To determine the gross value of outstanding accounts receivable at the current date, the appraiser merely sums the debit and credit amounts on the cards in the "accounts receivable drawer."

If the valuation date precedes the appraiser's field work, however, it can be difficult to reconstruct the accounts receivable due at the valuation date, because accounts with zero balances are simply filed away, and there is no record of former balances. The appraiser could extrapolate from current accounts receivable to estimate accounts receivable at the valuation date; or he could analyze the relationship between current and past collection amounts to value the level of receivables at the valuation date. On the other hand, such an estimate can be rendered unusable because the amount of accounts receivable is crucial to the valuation, or because some change in the operation has made a reliable estimate impossible; then the appraiser might request all cards (both in the accounts receivable drawer and in the client files) and use them to recalculate the actual balances that existed at the valuation date. He may also need to request appointment books and collection records for the relevant period of time to verify all cards have been provided. Obviously, that can be a time-consuming task. Alternatively, he might examine cash deposit records following the valuation date to identify specific payments received.

Another type of receivable often overlooked is accounts that have been turned over to a collection agency, because they are often written off the accounts receivable balance when they are turned over to the agency. Although the value of these accounts is usually small (because the collection agency deducts its fee of as much as 50 percent of amounts collected off the top), the appraiser should be aware of the value and include it in the overall accounts receivable amount.

Having determined the gross value of the accounts receivable, the appraiser must adjust for uncollectible and slow-pay accounts. The two most common methods for estimating uncollectible accounts are:

1. Accounts receivable aging—discounting the accounts on the basis of how long past due they are.
2. Actual payment history—analyzing the payment trends of the specific practice and whether the trend is for more or fewer write-offs.

Both of these methods have positive and negative characteristics, however, and the appraiser should determine which is appropriate for the practice at hand.

**Aging of Receivables.**   The appraiser must either acquire or create an accounts receivable aging schedule, such as the one illustrated in Exhibit 5–1. The time periods outstanding generally run in 30-day increments, with the last category including accounts more than 180 days old. After totaling each category, the appraiser applies a discount factor to each, with the further past-due balances receiving higher discounts.

This method of determining uncollectible accounts receivable does not recognize individual payment histories or the payment procedures of the specific practice. For example, to discount by 50 percent all accounts over 180 days past due would cause an underestimation of the value if there were many accounts for which small monthly payments had been arranged and were being paid. In addition, the discount amounts are necessarily subjective, and the average may not reflect the particular payment procedures of the clients whose practice is being appraised. If the practice does work for any of various federal agencies, it will be paid for its work eventually, but dependable private clients pay sooner. A 60-day past-due billing for the government should not be discounted as much as a 60-day past-due billing for a private client.

**Actual Payment History.**   The second method of estimating the reserve for uncollectible accounts receivable analyzes the practice's individual collection history. It compares the accounts receivable write-offs from one period to the billings generated during the same period. The appraiser requests a payment history for a 36-month to 60-month period. This history would take the form of a schedule showing monthly charges, collections, credit adjustments, debit adjustments, and month-end receivable balances. From these data, the charges, collections, and net adjustments would be totaled for the entire period and for each fiscal year. The appraiser would then calculate the percentage of net adjustments to billings in order to establish an average for the period and for each fiscal year. In this way, the appraiser determines the actual percentage of charges that are never collected and, by analyzing trends for the fiscal years, he can determine if a pattern of higher or lower write-offs is forming.

The problem with computing the percentage of historical net adjustments to the billings is that, if the practice has a significant number of patients who pay immediately and are not billed for services, the total charges would reflect not only accounts receivable, but also cash transactions. Including accounts that were paid when incurred would tend to reduce artificially the percentage of historical write-offs; in that case, the percentage of immediate cash payments on account would need to be considered in the calculation of historic write-offs.

Many practices house clean their accounts at the end of the fiscal year, writing off the ones they consider uncollectible. The appraiser should be aware if his work follows a house cleaning, so that he does not inadvertently overadjust for uncollectible accounts and so that he can examine the practice's write-off method and adjust for too much or not enough estimation of uncollectible accounts.

As mentioned previously, slow-pay accounts may need to be discounted to allow for the time value of money (see Chapter 17). If the practice collects receivables fairly rapidly, the discount may be very small. However, if collections tend to take a long time, the accounts should be discounted accordingly, netted against any interest the practice charges on past-due amounts.

# Work-in-Process Inventory

Many professional practices have unrecorded assets for work they have performed but not yet billed. Typically, work-in-process is an asset found in practices that charge hourly for professional or staff time, such as CPA firms, consulting practices, and law firms, or practices that charge on a percentage of completion basis, such as engineering and appraisal firms. This asset might be called *unbilled accounts receivable*.

Since work-in-process is based on time spent by the professional practice's staff, there are usually time records available from which to determine the amount of services that are unbilled. However, it has been our firm's experience that most practices can estimate unbilled receivables only at the current date; they cannot reconstruct the work-in-process inventory at any prior date. Therefore, to make a reasonable estimate of the work-in-process inventory at a prior date, the appraiser must understand the billing procedures of the practice—how often the work-in-process is billed and on what day(s) of the month, what procedures are used to compile and bill work-in-process, by what criteria the accounts are determined billable, and what records show work-in-process that has been written off.

It is important to remember that practices using cash basis accounting probably have already recorded all expenses associated with the work-in-process inventory; for that reason, it is unnecessary to calculate the gross or net margins on their work-in-process inventory. For practices accounting on an accrual basis, work-in-process should be listed as an asset on the practice's financial statements and, except for minor adjustments, the appraiser can use the figures shown on the financial statements for the value of the work-in-process. However, under a *modified accrual system,* accounts receivable are included in revenues, but work-in-process is not recognized. In that case, goods and/ or margins may become important to the appraiser.

Exhibit 24–1 shows a typical method of calculating the value of work-in-process inventory for a firm using cash basis or modified ac-

Exhibit 24–1

**SMITH & WILSON CONSULTING, INC.**
**CALCULATION OF VALUE OF WORK-IN-PROCESS INVENTORY**
**AS OF SEPTEMBER 30, 1985**

|  | J. Smith | K. Wilson | Total |
|---|---|---|---|
| Hours in Unbilled Inventory | 130 | 210 | |
| Hourly Billing Rate | X  $125 | $75 | |
| Gross Value of Unbilled Inventory | $16,250 | $15,750 | |
| Total Gross Value of Unbilled Inventory | | | 32,000 |
| Less:   3-Year Historical Adjustment to Work-in-Process (Amount Not Billed Is Equal to 7% of Total) | | | (2,240) |
| Estimated Work-in-Process Inventory that Will Be Billed | | | $29,760 |
| Less:   3-Year Historical Write-Off on Accounts Receivable (Amount of Charges Not Collected Is Equal to 9% of Total Charges) | | | (2,678) |
| Estimated Cash Value of Work-in-Process before Calculation of Discount for Time to Collect | | | $27,082 |

crual basis accounting. It is apparent in this exhibit that $32,000 worth of unbilled consulting is not equal to $32,000 of collections. Hours are often written down or written up for a variety of reasons, and the appraiser should calculate an historical percentage to determine how much of the firm's billable time is actually billed. Then the amount is discounted for uncollectible receivables, as discussed above, to determine how much is likely finally to be collected. If there are fixed-fee contracts, the appraiser should calculate their value on the basis of the estimated percentage of completion at the valuation date.

One final adjustment may be necessary. The appraiser who finds a significant number of old unbilled hours still in inventory should determine how diligently the firm has house-cleaned its inventory. If there has been only haphazard house cleaning, or none at all, the appraiser probably needs to age the work-in-process inventory and discount significantly (or even eliminate) the old unbilled hours.

# Inventory of Supplies

The value of the supplies inventory depends on the type of practice. The office supplies of a CPA firm will have a small value compared, for instance, to the inventory of glasses frames in an optometric practice of comparable size. Without a detailed cataloging of inventory items, the appraiser usually can estimate the amount of inventory on hand for practices that do not have substantial value in inventory. Nevertheless, the appraiser ought to tour the practice offices and at least check the level of supplies kept.

A review of the prior year's history of supply purchases can aid the appraiser in estimating the value of supplies on hand. If the practice generally orders supplies once a month, the total supply expense for the prior year could be divided by 12 for an estimate of the value of supplies on hand at any particular time. However, if the practice keeps a 90-day supply on hand, this method would underestimate the value of the supply inventory.

## Prepaid Expenses

Two specific expenses are often prepaid—rent and insurance. These two expenses (including insurance policies for errors and omissions and for malpractice) are almost always prepaid, but because they are continuing, their amounts are not necessarily allocated to the periods when they are used. If they do not fluctuate significantly, the IRS will ignore the fact that they are improperly classified in one period, because over several periods, the tax effect will net to zero. The appraiser, on the other hand, generally is concerned with a specific valuation date, and for that reason, prepaid expenses must be classified properly on the balance sheet to recognize the fact that future expenses have already been paid. For example, if the appraiser finds that a physician has paid $5,000 on December 30 for the next year's professional liability insurance, approximately three fourths of the premium is actually prepaid, and therefore an asset, as of the March 30 valuation date.

## Equipment

As was true of supplies, the amount and value of equipment necessary to operate any given practice depends very much on what type of practice it is. A general dentistry practice will require significantly more valuable equipment than a psychiatric practice. The appraiser must judge whether the equipment should be appraised by a professional equipment appraiser; for example, if there is a great deal of equipment, if it is highly specialized, or if there are antiques among the practice's assets. If there is very little equipment, or if it consists primarily of automobiles, the business appraiser could estimate the value himself (for example, using the *Kelly Blue Book*).

An equipment appraiser should be chosen carefully. A qualified equipment appraiser understands *standards of value* and can appraise the equipment using the same standards as the business appraiser, but a used equipment dealer may give as a value only the amount he would pay for it under liquidation conditions.

Several rule-of-thumb valuation methods discussed in Chapter 26 include the value of the equipment. If one of these methods is used to value a professional practice, the appraiser still needs to consider the value of the equipment. It may be old, unnecessary to the practice operation, or extremely specialized; any of these characteristics alter the multiples in the rule-of-thumb method or make them useless for the specific valuation.

Finally, the appraiser may examine the equipment listed on the practice's depreciation schedule. That procedure is wise, but the list should be verified, because assets owned by the practice may have been removed or may never have been listed on the schedule.

## Leasehold Improvements

Another important asset is the leasehold improvements of the practice. During the appraiser's tour of the practice office, he should pay attention to the condition of the improvements—in other words, how well the office is packaged. If the leasehold improvements are in good condition and have been fully depreciated on the balance sheet, he may want to adjust their value upward, considering both their life expectancy and the term of the current lease.

In his overall analysis of the practice's assets, the appraiser should continually ask if the asset is necessary to the practice operation. Assets that are unnecessary for the practice's success should be treated as excess to the total practice value, and any income or expenses resulting from these assets should be removed from the income statements.

# Liabilities

There may be several categories of liabilities not reflected on the books of the average professional practice. On the other hand, from a valuation standpoint some may appear there (and even be required by GAAP) that are not real debts (such as deferred rent).

## Accounts Payable

Cash basis financial statements typically do not show accounts payable. Since most professional practices sell services, their accounts payable usually relate to continuing bills, such as supplies, telephone, utilities, taxes, and so forth, rather than materials for manufacturing or sale.

There are two basic methods for estimating accounts payable. Under the first method, the appraiser reviews all unpaid invoices at the valuation date. If field work is done substantially after the appraisal date, the appraiser should request all canceled checks written during a reasonable period of time after the valuation date, along with the corresponding invoices. With this information, the appraiser can determine how much money the practice owed as of the appraisal date.

The second method is less accurate, but it can give a reasonable estimate with less effort. The appraiser begins with the total expenses shown on the practice's income statement. From that amount he subtracts expenses that do not belong with accounts payable—those payable immediately, those that were paid in advance, those not requiring cash, and those shown elsewhere on the balance sheet as payables (e.g., payroll taxes payable). The appraiser considers the practice's regular bill-paying procedures, such as how often all invoices are paid and how long the practice holds them before payment, to calculate the estimated accounts payable at the valuation date. Exhibit 24–2 illustrates this computation.

Exhibit 24–2

### SMITH & WILSON CONSULTING, INC.
### CALCULATION OF ESTIMATED AMOUNT OF ACCOUNTS PAYABLE
### AS OF SEPTEMBER 30, 1985

| | | |
|---|---:|---:|
| Total Expenses Shown on Fiscal Year-End September 30, 1985, Income Statement | | $175,000 |
| Less: | | |
| Those Expenses Paid Immediately When Due: | | |
| Salaries (Officers and Employees) | 105,000 | |
| Interest | 500 | |
| Those Expenses Paid in Advance: | | |
| Rent | 12,000 | |
| Insurance | 2,500 | |
| Dues and Subscriptions | 200 | |
| Those Expenses Not Requiring Cash: | | |
| Amortization | 20 | |
| Depreciation | 1,250 | |
| Those Expenses Already Shown as Payables on Financials: | | |
| Pension Plan | 20,000 | |
| Payroll Taxes | 4,500 | |
| Total of Expenses Not Part of Accounts Payable | | (145,970) |
| Total of Expenses that Can Be Part of Accounts Payable | | 29,030 |
| Practice Normally Pays Bills after 30 Days, Once per Month | | ÷ 12 |
| Estimated Accounts Payable at September 30, 1985 | | $2,419 |

# Accrued Liabilities

Accrued liabilities are expenses, such as payroll, payroll taxes, or interest, that are allocated to a prior period but not yet due. If a note payable calls for interest payments at the end of the year and the appraisal date is at midyear, the appraiser should adjust for accrued interest (unless it is already shown on the financial statements), even though it is not payable for another six months.

Many firms pay employees one to five days after a payroll cycle; if the appraisal takes place at the end of a payroll cycle, there could be a large payable for salaries.

One liability often overlooked is accrued employee vacation time. The appraiser should consider the company's vacation policy and verify the amounts of accrued vacation held by employees. If there is a significant amount of vacation time pending, this liability should be reflected on the balance sheet, or at least disclosed in the appraisal report.

# Deferred Liabilities

Deferred liabilities fall into three categories: deferred revenues, deferred expenses, and deferred taxes.

Deferred revenues are amounts that have been received for services not yet performed. An obstetrician-gynecologist (OB–G) medical practice is likely to have this type of liability, although it may not be shown on the balance sheet. OB–G specialists often receive from expectant mothers their entire fees for prenatal care and delivery. If the specialist is on cash basis accounting, he is likely to report this prepayment as current income, although from an accounting viewpoint, there is a liability for services yet to be performed. Deferred revenues may also need to be considered in law firms and consulting firms that receive retainers before beginning work on the case.

Deferred expenses are relatively unusual. One example might be deferred rent. A landlord may offer several months of free rent in return for a tenant's signing of a long-term lease. This situation would warrant a liability account for deferred rent, because the tenant could theoretically have negotiated a lease for the same period of time at a lower monthly rent, had he opted not to accept the free rent, even though the total payments under each option would be equal. Exhibit 24–3 shows entries to account for a deferred rent liability.

As Exhibit 24–3 illustrates, even though the company paid only $1,000 cash toward rent during the first seven months, the financial statements show rental expense of $6,363.63; the difference between the expense and the cash paid was allocated to Deferred Rent. From the appraiser's point of view, this deferral is not a real liability and should be removed; however, when calculating the expected future income, the rent expense should be adjusted upward by $90.91 per month.

Deferred income tax is the third type of deferred liability. The purpose of deferred income taxes appearing on financial statements is to match income tax expense with the related financial accounting income for the appropriate accounting period.

Deferred income taxes usually occur because of the difference in timing between recognition of income or expense for two different accounting systems of the same practice. For example, the practice may use straight-line depreciation on its own financial statements to reflect more accurately economic depreciation, but it might use accelerated depreciation on tax returns. The result of using these two procedures would be to show more income on the financial statements and less on the tax returns. The amount of deferred income taxes on the financial statements is equal to the difference between income taxes actually

Exhibit 24–3

**SMITH & WILSON CONSULTING, INC.**
**ACCOUNTING ENTRIES FOR "DEFERRED RENT" ACCOUNT**

Assumption: For the signing of a 60-month lease for offices, Smith & Wilson received an additional six months' free rent—the total rent over the term of the lease would total $60,000, or $1,000.00 per month over 60 months. Generally accepted accounting principles would require that the rent be charged against income over the 66-month term, or $909.09 per month.

| | | | |
|---|---|---|---|
| Month 1: | Debit, Rent Expense | 909.09 | |
| | Credit, Deferred Rent | | 909.09 |
| | | | |
| Months 2-6 Totals: | Debit, Rent Expense | 4,545.45 | |
| | Credit, Deferred Rent | | 4,545.45 |
| | | | |
| Month 7: | Debit, Rent Expense | 909.09 | |
| | Debit, Deferred Rent | 90.91 | |
| | Credit, Cash | | 1,000.00 |

Therefore: At the end of seven months, rent expense totaled $6,363.63, cash was decreased by $1,000, and Deferred Rent Expense equaled $5,363.63.

paid and what they would have been if based on the higher income as shown on the financial statements.

For the appraiser, this account may or may not reflect a true liability. If the practice rarely purchases new equipment, the depreciation for tax purposes will ultimately be less than for financial statement purposes, consequently showing more income on the tax returns than on the financial statements. In that case, the taxes actually paid will be higher than taxes shown due on the financial statements, which means that the deferred taxes are an actual liability.

On the other hand, if the practice continually buys new equipment, the financial statements could always show greater profits than the tax returns. In that case, the appraiser could conclude that deferred taxes will never be paid in the foreseeable future and remove them from the balance sheet liabilities.

# Long-Term Debt

Long-term debt in professional practices is usually associated with equipment purchases. However, in some instances, it represents amounts due to the former owner of the practice who sold it to the current owner. These situations should alert the appraiser to investigate the past sale. If the appraiser has reason to believe that the amounts listed in long-term debt are incorrect, copies of the debt instrument(s) and payment records should be obtained. Also, the debt instrument will disclose if the practice has an accrued interest liability that is not shown on the balance sheet.

# Lease Obligations

The appraiser should always obtain copies of all leases of the practice whether the practice is a lessor or a lessee. The financial statements usually show capital lease obligations, under which the practice will ultimately be obliged to purchase the leased equipment. These future lease payments should be treated as long-term debt, after separating imputed interest payable.

# Contingent Liabilities

Contingent obligations, as discussed in Chapter 5, are liabilities (or assets) for which there is insufficient information about the outcome to know how to account for them on the financial statements. The professional may be a defendant or plaintiff in a malpractice suit or there may be disputed billings, and these facts may not be disclosed on the financial statement. The appraiser should investigate these types of liabilities (or assets).

# Summary

Although there has been a great deal of literature written on the subject of professional goodwill and other intangible assets, there has been very little on the valuation of tangible assets of professional practices. These assets may have substantial value, and the appraiser should not overlook them when concentrating on valuing the practice's goodwill. Goodwill usually cannot exist by itself, but is frequently supported by tangible assets of some kind.

# Chapter 25

## Elements That Create Professional and Practice Goodwill

Simply stated, goodwill is the amount of the purchase price for a business or professional practice that is over and above the value of its identifiable assets and net of the liabilities assumed. It is treated as an asset on the balance sheet of the acquiror, and, because it does not have a determinable life, it generally cannot be amortized against income for income tax purposes. This definition is helpful, however, only to accountants balancing the books. It does not explain goodwill—why it exists, how much of it there is in any given business, or even how it can be built up or dissipated. In professional practices, goodwill is even more difficult to define, because it usually is strongly tied to the individual practitioners.

Appraisers often hear professionals say that the practice can't have any goodwill value because "without me, it's worthless." Others believe that there is no way to transfer their professional goodwill because it is so personal. These ideas seem plausible, but they are not necessarily true. With careful planning and cooperation between seller and buyer, at least some portion of the professional goodwill that has been built up usually can be transferred to the new owner.

# Reasons to Value a Professional Practice

Unlike other businesses, professional practices generally require an appraiser to be retained for only two purposes: (1) various buy/sell situations and (2) marital dissolutions. Appraisals of professional practices for estate tax situations are rare, because the practice left by a decedent sole practitioner usually loses its value very rapidly after his death. If the decedent practitioner is a member of a multipractitioner entity, there are usually buy/sell agreements to set a binding value that will be paid to the estate. If the buy/sell agreement is properly drafted, the value set by that agreement may also be used in the estate tax return. Dissenting stockholder suits in professional practices are also rare, but they may become necessary when partners or shareholders disagree over how to run the practice. ESOPs, estate planning recapitalizations, and damage suits (involving the value of the practice) are all extremely rare and possibly nonexistent for professional practices.

For these reasons, the focus of this chapter will be a discussion of the elements that cause professional goodwill to exist in buy/sell and divorce situations. Because the factors involved in the sale of a practice are different from those involved in valuation for a divorce, the elements creating goodwill can be different. Therefore, this chapter discusses what elements are important for each valuation purpose.

# Characteristics of a Professional Practice

As the title of this book implies, there are both similarities and differences between a small business and a professional practice. There are several characteristics of a professional practice that, when taken together, distinguish it from other small businesses. These characteristics can be broken down into five categories.

1. The practice is primarily a service business.
2. There is necessarily a relationship of trust and respect between the client and the professional or employee of the practice because the client must rely on professional expertise which the client himself is not fully capable of understanding or evaluating.
3. The practice or the practitioner relies upon a referral source or sources.
4. A specific college degree is usually required for the professional to practice in his chosen field.
5. The practitioner is licensed by a government agency and/or certified by a recognized professional organization.

It is apparent from the list above that the distinction between professional practices and certain kinds of service businesses may be a fine line, at least for some of the characteristics.

## Service Business Characteristics

Professional practices provide services of various kinds, from giving tax advice to treating Fido's illnesses. The nature of these services, in light of the professional's specialized training and the client's dependence on the professional's expertise, causes price to be a less important consideration than in the purchase of goods or less-specialized services.

If an individual wants to buy a refrigerator, for example, he will generally shop several appliance stores to find the best price available. However, he is likely to be far less price-conscious in choosing a cardiologist or a defense attorney. Pricing will be important if the particular need is not critical or as an upper limit of the client's ability to pay, but more important is the expertise that the client or patient needs in his situation. A person with only wage and interest income will probably be completely satisfied with a bookkeeping service preparing his tax return, but a person with complicated investments, capital gains income, and so forth, will want a higher-priced CPA or attorney to complete his returns. Both these people may purchase refrigerators from the same store on the basis of price, but price is not the determining factor for either in choosing his tax preparer.

## Client Trust and Respect

The trust and respect that clients hold for the members of the practice are crucial to its success. As long as his trust is maintained, the client generally will return to the practitioner. This characteristic is the chief reason that the goodwill is so strongly related to the practitioner.

## Dependence on Referral Sources

New clients choose a professional practice primarily on the basis of referral from another source. They generally do not choose their doctors, lawyers, or accountants from ads in the Yellow Pages, but on the recommendation of someone they know. Some types of practices, however, such as optometrists, dentists, veterinarians, and chiropractors, may get a substantial portion of their new patients by means of their location or by advertisements. At the other extreme, some practices depend totally on new referrals to generate patient visits. An oral surgeon, for example, does not have continuing relationships with his patients, so he must maintain relationships, through professional societies, social clubs, and promotional activities, with the general dentists who can refer patients to him.

## Education

The people who make up a professional practice have graduated from institutions offering some kind of specialized education. Although some professions require a bachelor's degree or a certain number of years in a special course of study, others demand a master's or a doctor's degree, plus extensive on-the-job training. This requirement for extensive training affects professional goodwill in two ways: (1) the client's trust and respect is increased or generated by the long years of study involved; (2) the long years of study represent an investment in time and money on the part of the professional, who expects a monetary return on his investment.

## Licensing and Certification

Generally, the professional must be licensed by a government agency or admitted to a professional organization before he can practice his specialty. This factor has the effect of limiting the number of individuals who can practice that profession.

# Distinction between Practice Goodwill and Professional Goodwill

In a professional practice, there are generally two types of goodwill: *practice goodwill* (sometimes referred to as *business goodwill*) and *professional goodwill* (sometimes referred to as *personal goodwill*). *Practice goodwill* is the goodwill associated primarily with the entity, while *personal goodwill* is the goodwill associated primarily with the individual.

# Practice Goodwill

Practice goodwill is specifically an asset of the practice entity and therefore not really different from the goodwill that can be held by any other small business. A professional obviously cannot sell his reputation, skills, or knowledge. However, he may use these attributes to establish a successful practice and generate large earnings. In doing so, he has started a business, and through it will acquire many of the elements, such as location, operating systems, staff, and a patient or client base, which are common to both a small business and a professional practice and which make up business (practice) goodwill. These elements and others like them can generate value over and above the entity's net asset value, thus producing goodwill (or going-concern) value.[1] A professional practice that has these elements has a certain amount of practice goodwill, which can be significant in value.

# Professional Goodwill

While a professional practice does not possess personal goodwill, the practitioner(s) may have personal goodwill. A certain portion of the practitioner's clients or patients may come to him because of his personal reputation, thereby causing earnings for the practice. If the practitioner suddenly left the practice, a large majority of the income generated from these personal clients and patients would be likely to leave as well.

A common misconception is that personal goodwill is not marketable because it is never transferable. Although the transfer of personal goodwill is more difficult than the transfer of practice goodwill, there are methods by which the practitioner can facilitate the transfer of his goodwill or at least a portion of his goodwill to another well-qualified practitioner.

The transfer of client trust and respect from seller to buyer requires the cooperation of both parties. Their efforts would include at least a letter of announcement from the seller to current clients, informing them that the buyer is taking over their cases and that the buyer has the qualifications and expertise to handle their needs. In this way, the selling professional uses his reputation to transfer his goodwill to the buyer. Another means of ensuring the transfer of personal goodwill would be for the seller to stay with the practice during a transition period so that clients can become familiar and comfortable with the new practitioner. It requires the seller's best efforts to transfer his goodwill to the new practitioner. Frequently, the clients will not be made aware that the "buyer" is other than an "associate." This means often proves effective in increasing client retention.

---

[1] Some writers have made a distinction between *goodwill* and *going-concern value*. When this distinction is made, the term *goodwill* refers to those factors that generate repeat business, whereas the term *going-concern value* is more of an operations concept, that is, the value of having all the work force and physical elements such as equipment and inventory in place, in balance, and working well together. For the purpose of this chapter, we lump these elements of going-concern value under the general heading of goodwill.

It is more difficult to transfer goodwill if the seller depends upon professional or personal contacts to refer clients. The seller cannot so easily write a letter to his friends at the country club and convince them that the person buying his practice should, from now on, get their referrals. Similarly, if an oral surgeon has persuaded general dentists of his expertise through presentations at professional seminars, the oral surgeon buying his practice will not necessarily have an easy time persuading them that his expertise is comparable. On the other hand, the sole cardiac surgeon in a community can relatively easily transfer his referral base to the cardiac surgeon buying the practice. Personal goodwill is hardly ever so personal that none of it can be transferred.

# Buying and Selling a Practice—Elements of Goodwill

In order for goodwill to have value transcending a transfer of ownership of the practice, the goodwill must be transferable along with the ownership. There are many elements in a professional practice that can cause transferable goodwill to exist. As mentioned at the beginning of this chapter, the elements that create goodwill in a buy/sell situation are somewhat different from those considered in a divorce valuation. For example, one element that is very important in a buy/sell situation is the marketability of the practice—although that factor is irrelevant under many states' divorce guidelines.

Goodwill is elusive and hard to define, generated by so many different factors and combinations of factors that it is impossible to list them all. However, several factors are dominant in determining the existence and value of practice and personal goodwill for professional practices:

1. Earnings levels that can be expected in the future.
2. The level of competition.
3. The referral base.
4. The types of patients or clients the practice serves.
5. Work habits of the practitioner.
6. The fees charged (compared to others in the same specialty).
7. Where the practice is located.
8. The practice's employees.
9. The general marketability of the type of practice being sold.

## Expected Future Earnings

Like other business enterprises, one of the biggest factors contributing to goodwill value in a professional practice is the level of earnings. Although, generally, the higher the earnings, the more goodwill in the enterprise, an abundance of earnings does not inherently indicate an abundance of goodwill, nor does a dearth of earnings inherently indicate its lack. In judging the existence and value of goodwill based on the level of earnings, the appraiser should be sure to know the causes for the earnings levels before concluding a value. High earnings may result from the professional's skills, reputation, and efficiencies, or from his working longer hours and seeing more clients per day. Like goodwill itself, earnings do not occur by themselves, but because of other factors.

The term *earnings* does not refer to the practice's net income, because real earnings are usually given out to principals in the form of salaries, perquisites, and benefits; the net income as shown on the books of an incorporated practice is usually close to zero.

To determine the true earnings of the practice, the appraiser should analyze five years' worth of financial statements and tax returns, with each account on the income statements and balance sheets compared to the other years and set out in percentages of the relevant figures (on the income statements, all accounts expressed as a percent of revenues; on the balance sheets, all accounts expressed as a percent of total assets). For comparative purposes, earnings usually are measured on a cash basis, because professionals generally use that accounting for tax purposes, and because earnings surveys are generally on a cash basis.

Trended income statements are also helpful. In our firm, we calculate two types of trended statements—expressing each account as a percentage of the same account in the first year considered, and expressing each account as a percentage of the same account in the year immediately prior. From this information, the appraiser can discover unusual year-to-year activity in specific income accounts (owner's salaries, retirement benefits, and directors' fees are among the possibilities). The appraiser then requests support documents (retirement plan payment allocations, the general ledger, various journals, check registers, invoices, etc.) in order to calculate accurately the practice's available income.

## Level of Competition

Approximately 20 to 30 years ago, because of the shortage of physicians in this country, a physician who had met his educational requirements and received his license could hang up his shingle and begin seeing patients during his first week of practice. Because it was so easy to start medical practices, there was little market for their sale. Medical schools responded to the shortage by graduating more physicians, and the shortage was eliminated in most parts of the country, followed by an oversupply of physicians in many places.

It is not as easy now to start a successful practice as it was at that time, and, in fact, it is impossible in many areas. For that reason, established medical practices in some areas of the country are selling at prices more attractive to the seller (compared to several years ago), because new physicians are seeking to associate with established practices or to buy them outright. Obviously, as the demand for established practices has increased, so too has their value.

When appraising a professional practice, the appraiser should take into account the number of other practitioners in the same profession in the area, and what proportion they bear to the population at large. The census of supply of professionals has a marked bearing on the value of the professional practice.

## Referral Base

Since the sources of referrals are a key characteristic of a professional practice, it is natural that they should also have a profound effect on the value of goodwill. A practice whose referrals come from a large number of current patients and clients will generally have more goodwill value than one that relies on referrals from a relatively small client base or from other professionals. Because of the variations in difficulty of transferring the goodwill associated with a base of referrals, as discussed earlier in this chapter, this element is more important in the sale of an entire practice than when a new associate joins the practice or in a valuation for a divorce.

## Types of Patients and Clients

The appraiser should know the types of clients who patronize the practice and why. He should estimate how many are seen each day, how many new clients seek the practice's services for the first time during a time period and how many cease to do so, and whether the practice depends on any particular client or specific group of clients for a significant portion of its income. Especially in medical and dental practices, the appraiser should learn the percentage of patients who have private insurance, who are part of the medicare program, and who qualify for the government's medicaid program. The practice with a large percentage of patients who either pay their bills themselves or who have private insurance will have a higher value than one with a preponderance of medicare and medicaid patients, because these government insurance programs generally pay less per procedure than the usual fee charged by the practitioner.

## Work Habits of the Practitioner

It's almost a cliche that professionals work long hours. However, some are willing to work longer hours than others. A practice that requires 80 hours a week of a practitioner's time will not be worth as much per dollar of income to a purchaser as one that requires only 50 hours per week. Different work habits may also affect the intrinsic value of a practice. Some dentists like to spend time with each patient, while others prefer to schedule several patients at a time and delegate more of the procedures to dental assistants or technicians. Obviously, a dentist of the more "personal" type considering purchasing a practice owned by one of the "mass production" type needs to consider how his work habits will alter the earning capacity of that practice. On the other hand, a potential purchaser may find that the selling practitioner liked to spend time on administrative duties that could have been handled by an office manager, and thus that there would be time to generate more revenue or play more golf.

## Fee Schedules

It is important that the appraiser understand the practice's fee schedule. Does it charge by procedure, time spent, or some other measure? How do this practitioner's fees compare with those of others of comparable qualifications? The appraiser should know how often the fees are adjusted and when the last fee adjustment occurred. If fees fall below the community's standard rate, what would happen to the income if the fees were raised, and how many patients or clients would be lost because of a fee increase? All these questions should be considered in the course of examining the practice's earnings.

The fee schedule also provides an index to the skill and reputation of the practitioner. A practitioner with above-average fees and a large client base could be assumed to have above-average expertise or at least a better reputation.

## Practice Location

The location of a practice has a substantial impact on its value. Some areas are perceived to be more desirable than others. Some communities are good "family" towns, while others provide a fast-track lifestyle. Like anyone else, professionals like to practice in the kind of communities they like to live in. Therefore, areas that provide a comfortable lifestyle for the practitioner and his family, with a growing population or a strong and vibrant economy, will generally have more expensive professional practices than will areas that are personally unattractive and/or economically depressed. The appraiser should investigate local demographics, the economic health of the area, and the overall quality of life in the community.

## Employees of the Practice

The employees of a professional practice can be very important to its value. They know the procedures, they know the clients, and the expense of training them has already been incurred. When patients come in for their first visit with the new practitioner, the familiar faces of the support personnel will help relieve their anxieties.

The appraiser should learn the number of employees and their names, their job titles and job descriptions, their pay scales, and the length of time they have been with the practice. He should inquire whether they plan to stay under the new management.

Particularly important are the nonowner professionals employed by the practice. They may actually hold the goodwill of some clients, and if they chose to leave the practice, their clients might go with them. The appraiser should determine to what extent that is the case in the practice at hand. The buyer does not want to pay for goodwill value that is ultimately not the seller's to sell, because it is owned by an employee who may or may not stay with the practice. In such a situation, an employment contract and a covenant not to compete should be negotiated with that employee, so that, in effect, the buyer purchases his goodwill as well.

## Marketability of the Practice

The marketability of the practice depends on a number of factors, some of which have been discussed throughout this chapter. Demand for the practice obviously determines marketability, but often for reasons not directly related to the specific practice itself. If there is a glut of accountants seeking to purchase accounting practices, then the demand for established accounting practices is likely to rise, thus raising their goodwill value. If it is relatively easy to enter the specific profession, goodwill value will be lower. In many parts of the country, professional practices do not sell at all because the economy is so weak. On the other hand, some professions are inherently unmarketable, such as a psychiatric practice in which the trust between patient and doctor is so crucial that it is, for all practical purposes, not transferable. The appraiser should examine these circumstances and use his judgment in determining the market value of professional practices.

## Divorce Valuation—Elements of Goodwill

Valuations for divorces are among the most common professional engagements the appraiser of professional practices encounters. Most of the states whose appellate courts have ruled on whether professional goodwill is a marital asset, subject to valuation and division, have held that it is indeed an asset and should be valued and accounted for in the division of property. Only one state (Texas) has consistently held that professional goodwill is not subject to division,[2] but it has held that practice goodwill can be valued.[3]

Even though all the elements that create goodwill discussed in the preceding section should be considered in valuing professional goodwill for divorce purposes, some are not necessarily as important in that context as in valuation for a sale of the practice. In a divorce valuation, the marketability of the practice generally does not determine the existence or value of professional goodwill. In a California appellate court ruling, the court was quite specific:

> The value of community goodwill is not necessarily the specified amount of money that a willing buyer would pay for such goodwill. In view of exigencies that are ordinarily attendant on a marriage dissolution, the amount obtainable in the market place may well be less than the true

---

[2] *Nail* versus *Nail* 486 S.W.2d 761 (Texas Supreme Court 1972).
[3] *Geesbreght* versus *Geesbreght* 570 S.W.2d 427 (Texas Civil Appeals Court 1978).

value of the goodwill, and the community goodwill is a portion of the community value of the professional practice as a going concern on the date of dissolution of the marriage.[4]

Courts in California and other states have taken a similar position.

The difficulty of transferring referral sources is not a consideration for value in divorce cases, primarily because there is no transfer of the professional goodwill occurring. It is more as if the "silent partner" (nonpracticing spouse) is retiring and the practicing spouse is continuing in practice; for that reason, no diminution in professional goodwill will necessarily occur.

The various state courts have been helpful in establishing some fairly uniform guidelines to the factors that must be considered in appraising professional goodwill. The genesis of these factors is the California case, *Lopez* versus *Lopez* (38 Cal. App. 3d 93). The *Lopez* decision is a good treatise on the valuation of professional goodwill for marital dissolutions. It has been widely quoted in many other states in supporting the establishment of value for professional goodwill in divorce cases.

One of the primary sections of the *Lopez* case deals with what elements the appraiser should consider before expressing an opinion of professional goodwill value. The factors it determined to be appropriate included the following:

1. The age and health of the professional.
2. The professional's demonstrated past earning power.
3. His reputation in the community for judgment, skill, and knowledge.
4. His comparative professional success.
5. The nature and duration of his practice, either as a sole proprietor or as a contributing member of a partnership or professional corporation.[5]

As comprehensive as they seem, these factors have been the source of some confusion among appraisers, attorneys, and the trial courts to determine how they should be measured.

## Practitioner's Age and Health

It is far easier to determine the practitioner's age and health than to know how these factors affect professional goodwill value. Naturally, the practitioner's age is important. One close to retirement generally does not have a high professional goodwill value, even though his historical earnings may have been good, because those earnings cannot be expected to continue very far into the future. For example, if the practitioner were going to retire and close his practice two years after the valuation date, any multiple of his earnings (or excess earnings) over two would significantly overvalue his professional goodwill. On the other hand, a fairly young practitioner who had only recently started

---

[4] *In re Marriage of Foster*, 117 Cal. Rptr. 49; (42 Cal. App. 3d 93 [1974]).

[5] *In re Marriage of Lopez*, 113 Cal. Rptr. 58; (38 Cal. App. 3d 1044 [1974]).

practice would necessarily have a lower earning potential than the "average" practitioner; therefore, adjustments should be made before comparing those earnings to the average practitioner.

Health is another important factor. In one case, the appraiser retained by the nonprofessional spouse reached the opinion that the professional goodwill of the practitioner—a heart surgeon—was very high because of his past earning power. If that appraiser had inquired as to the doctor's health, he would have learned that the surgeon recently had been diagnosed as having a degenerative disease in his joints, which in a very short period would cause him to curtail his surgical practice. Since the practice was not readily salable and the practitioner could not expect continued earnings from his practice, the court dismissed the appraiser's determination of value and ruled that only a nominal amount of goodwill existed.

# Demonstrated Past Earning Power

As is true in virtually all kinds of business appraisals, earnings are a very important consideration in determining a value. Because of the peculiar circumstances of property divisions in a divorce, future earnings potential generally cannot be measured by projecting those earnings, because they will result from the practitioner's efforts after the marriage is terminated; future earnings are, therefore, not a marital asset. However, the courts have recognized that goodwill value is merely an expression of the value of expected future income, and the best estimate of future income is what has happened in the past. Generally, in our valuations, we consider the past five years of earnings of the practitioner, as of the valuation date.

# Reputation for Judgment, Skill, and Knowledge

The practitioner's reputation for judgment, skill, and knowledge is one of most abstract factors in the measurement of goodwill. After many professional practice valuations, the appraiser begins to get a "feel" for how these elements affect value, but it is difficult to quantify.

The appraiser should request a copy of the practitioner's curriculum vitae and inquire if he has received any special certifications, written any articles, taught classes, received any professional awards, or if he is a member in any professional societies. Any of these credits might help quantify these elements. On the other hand, if the professional has been judged by a court to have committed malpractice (or even publicly accused), that would also have a bearing on the value of his professional goodwill. An interview form listing the specific questions the appraiser needs to ask can be helpful in discovering information relating to the practitioner's reputation. Experienced appraisers usually have developed proprietary interview forms and valuation worksheets that can be of great assistance to the valuation process.

# Comparative Professional Success

Comparative professional success is a crucial factor in establishing professional goodwill. "Success" is usually measured by earnings, but other factors, such as the number of patients seen, hours generally spent working, community standards of living, and so forth, must also be considered.

It is very important to compare professionals with like professionals. If the appraiser is valuing the professional goodwill of a corporate attorney, he should compare his earnings to other attorneys in corporate law. There are many earnings surveys, and they should be consulted, but to whatever extent is possible the earnings considered should be on a Golden Delicious-to-Golden Delicious basis, not Golden Delicious-to-crab apples.

# Nature and Duration of Practice

Goodwill is built up over time, so the length of time the practice has been in existence will have a bearing on goodwill. A long-established law firm will attract more and higher-paying clients than one with wet paint on the shingle. The nature of the practice should also be considered. The following information about it can be relevant in determining goodwill:

Type of service offered.

Type of client served.

Length of time at the current location.

Length of time remaining on the lease.

How the fees are billed.

Source of new clients.

The individual practitioner's amount of production.

The number of employees and their length of service.

Economic and demographic information on the community where the practice is located.

The number of other professionals in the community offering the same service or specialty.

# Summary

Divorce valuation is different from valuation for the sale of a practice, and the appraiser needs to understand the differences. In the discussion of various valuation methods included in the next chapter, methods used primarily in divorce situations are specifically identified. Each state has slightly different case law concerning the valuation of professional goodwill, and any appraisal of goodwill for divorce purposes should recognize that state's particular statutes and case law in arriving at a conclusion.

# Chapter 26

## Determining the Value of the Practice

Standard Methods of Professional Practice Valuation
>   Excess Earnings
>   Capitalization of Earnings
>   Multiple of Revenues
>   Cash Flow Measurement
>   Depreciating Goodwill Method
>   Comparative Transactions and Buy-Ins
>   Punitive and Retirement Formulas

Rule-of-Thumb Methods for Various Types of Practices
>   Accounting Practices
>   Dental Practices
>   Engineering/Architecture Practices
>   Law Practices
>   Medical Practices
>   Optometric Practices
>   Medical Laboratories
>   Veterinary Practices

The Complete Value

There is no single correct method of valuing professional practices, any more than there is a single correct method of valuing small businesses. Several methods do predominate, however, depending on the type of practice. This chapter examines several methods of valuing professional practices, along with rules of thumb used by some brokers and appraisers. The last section of this chapter considers the complete value from the seller's point of view.

# Standard Methods of Professional Practice Valuation

Over the years, many methods have been devised to appraise professional practices, most of them ultimately discarded as redundant, invalid, or too complex. Several methods, though, when properly used, have withstood the tests of time and reasonableness and are now the primary methods for valuing professional practices:

1. Excess earnings.
2. Capitalization of earnings.
3. Multiple of revenues.
4. Cash flow measurement.
5. Depreciating goodwill.
6. Comparative transactions and buy-ins.
7. Punitive and retirement formulas.

Each method has good and bad points, and not every one will be appropriate to every specific type of practice or valuation assignment.

## Excess Earnings

The excess earnings method has already been described in detail in Chapter 12, so we do not need to repeat its history or how it is calculated. The excess earnings method is used quite frequently in divorce proceedings—probably more so than in actual transactions. Although most courts have held that there is no single method of valuing professional goodwill, in one case, the court held that this method was the only one appropriate for doing so.[1]

Generally, for a professional practice, *total earnings* are defined as all earnings available to the practitioner, and are computed as follows:

1. The net income of the practice, including salary and benefits to the practitioner(s) or owner(s).
2. Plus nonrecurring expenses less nonrecurring income.
3. Plus excessive expenses (expenses not related to the generation of practice income).

---

[1] *Levy* v. *Levy*, 397 A 2d 374 (N.J. Sup. Ct., 1978).

It was pointed out that a fair salary for the owner/manager should be deducted from earnings in most business valuations. In professional practices, however, earnings are counted before the owner's salary, benefits, and perquisites in most earnings surveys, because, as discussed in Chapter 25, professionals usually pay out most of the practice earnings in salaries, perquisites, and benefits.[2] In comparing the practice earnings to the industry level, it obviously is important to be consistent between the practice being appraised and the survey data being used.

**Determination of Net Asset Value for Return on Investment Calculation.** Chapter 24 discusses methods of valuing net assets for professional practices. The appraiser valuing a practice may wonder how to treat items such as art work owned by the practice, whether a monetary return should be calculated on this kind of asset. Even though it is arguable that the asset is not essential to the practice operations and that operating earnings should therefore not be charged for a return on nonoperating assets, others would argue that the money for this art work could have been invested in operating equipment; therefore the total investment in the practice, no matter what type of asset is involved, should realize a return on investment.

Both arguments have merit, and the answer is, as usual, found somewhere between the two extremes. In general, return on net asset value is calculated on operating assets less operating liabilities, but it should give recognition to a certain portion of assets (and/or liabilities) that might not be considered operating, but that are not unusual in the type of practice being appraised. As an example, the value of moderately priced office lithographs would probably be included in net asset value, because the practice's offices need a pleasant atmosphere for its clients. However, if the office contained 50 original M. C. Escher woodcut prints, the fair market value of these prints would be most appropriately removed from the net asset value (along with any associated debt) before calculating a return on capital, because they go far beyond the general requirements of office furnishings.

There are instances when, using the excess earnings method on professional practices, no return on capital is calculated. Sometimes earnings surveys for self-employed professionals include earnings that represent a return on capital to those practitioners. If earnings from such a survey are being used for comparison with earnings of a self-employed professional, it would be improper to remove from that professional's earnings an amount for a return on his capital. On the other hand, if the self-employed professional is being compared against salaries for nonowner professional employees, it is necessary to figure his return on capital because nonowner professionals have no investment at risk.

---

[2] The two most widely used surveys for medical practice earning data are *Medical Economics*, a semimonthly periodical that contains an earnings survey each September (along with specific practice specialty surveys throughout the year), and the American Medical Association's *Socioeconomic Characteristics of Medical Practice* (published annually), previously known as *Profile of Medical Practice*.

For law practices, two annual surveys are generally used: Altman-Weil Management Consultants, Inc., "Corporate Law Department Surveys" and "Survey of Law Firm Economics"; and Steven Langer & Associates "Compensation of Attorneys."

**Earnings Levels.** In determining the earnings level of the practice, the appraiser should consider at least five years of earnings data, if they are available. A careful analysis of the practice's earning history will provide a basis for estimating the practice's future earning capacity. A five-year average figure may or may not reflect the future earnings potential of the practice, but the five-year history will reveal trends and unusual occurrences that could be buried in an average.

Consider, for example, the partnership of Bean & Bacon, restaurant consultants. If an average earnings figure for the five-year period were routinely accepted by the appraiser as indicative of future earning capacity, then under the following earnings assumptions the appraiser would calculate the average earnings at $77,400 ($387,000 ÷ 5 = $77,400) for Bacon.

|  | Total Earnings of Bacon | Total Earnings of Bean & Bacon |
|---|---|---|
| Latest Year | $100,000 | $200,000 |
| Year 4 | 120,000 | 240,000 |
| Year 3 | 75,000 | 200,000 |
| Year 2 | 52,000 | 175,000 |
| Year 1 | 40,000 | 160,000 |
| Total | $387,000 | $975,000 |

Even though $77,400 is the mathematical average of Bacon's five-year earnings, the trend suggests that that does not represent his future earning capacity. In year 1, Bacon received 25 percent of the practice's total earnings; in year 2, the amount had risen to 30 percent; in year 3 to 37½ percent; and in years 4 and 5, Bacon received 50 percent of total practice earnings.

If the appraiser had investigated, he would have found that partners Bean and Bacon had agreed that Bacon would take a lower percentage of profits in the first three years, but would begin to receive 50 percent in year 4 and continue at that level of earnings from then on. Therefore, Bacon's current earning capacity is 50 percent of the practice's earning capacity; and it should be stated at 50 percent of the five-year average of the partnership's earnings, or $97,500 ($975,000 × 50 percent ÷ 5). The appraiser should consider all relevant facts before concluding on current or future earning capacity.

**Earnings Surveys.** A practitioner's earnings should be compared, as much as possible, to those of a like practitioner. The comparative practitioner should be in the same specific field, in the same geographic area, of approximately the same level of experience, and so on, as the professional whose practice is being valued. A psychiatrist, although an MD, should not be compared to a cardiologist, because each specialist has different earnings expectations.

**Capitalization Rates.** The return expected on the professional practice's net asset value should be neither more nor less than any other small business would expect to receive. Typically, the capitalization rate for the professional's excess earnings depends upon the positive and negative influences of the elements of value discussed in Chapter

25. Capitalization rates for the professional's excess earnings range from 20 to 100 percent (or multiples of five to one).

**Benefits and Drawbacks of the Excess Earnings Method.** The primary benefits of the excess earnings method are the following:

1. It is widely used, and therefore recognized and understood by many people.
2. Conceptually, it logically quantifies the value of intangible assets related to excess earnings.
3. It is codified (Rev. Rul. 68–609), and has been approved in many court rulings for valuation of professional practice goodwill.

The primary drawbacks of the excess earnings method are:

1. It is easily misapplied, because it requires so many subjective judgments on the part of the appraiser.
2. It can overstate the value of goodwill because it does not recognize the factor of marketability.
3. It can understate the value of goodwill because it does not always factor in the going concern elements of a practice already in place, even one that does not have excess earnings.

# Capitalization of Earnings

Chapter 10 presents a long description of capitalization rates and factors that need to be considered in their selection. In professional practices, two types of earnings are typically capitalized—pretax earnings after a fair salary to the owner or practitioner, and total earnings (including the owner's or practitioner's salary and benefits). Both definitions of earnings assume normalized earnings (having removed nonrecurring income and expenses and adjusting certain expenses to reflect more accurately economic reality).

**Choosing a Capitalization Rate.** In any given professional practice, the capitalization of each earnings base should produce fairly consistent values, even though the earnings figures (according to the different definitions) are considerably different. When using total earnings (pretax stated earnings plus owner salary and benefits), the capitalization rate should be much higher than when using only pretax earnings after reasonable owner's compensation. It is not unusual to see capitalization rates of 100 percent or more when using total earnings as a base, compared to a 20 to 35 percent capitalization rate for pretax earnings after owner's compensation.

**Benefits and Drawbacks of the Capitalization of Earnings Method.** The capitalization of earnings method is one of the best means of appraising an entity and one of the most abused. Besides the difficulty of selecting an appropriate capitalization rate, proper use of the method requires astute judgments concerning the real earning capacity of the practice and the expected growth in its earnings.

This value generally represents the value of the whole practice—not just the goodwill portion. If a practice has excess assets, or if the assets used in generating income could be replaced by less expensive items with the same function, the appraiser must add the excess asset value back to the calculated value.

# Multiple of Revenues

Revenue multiples have been discussed elsewhere in this book, primarily in the context of emphasizing that they should not be used alone. Revenue multiples serve as one of the primary rules of thumb for many industries, particularly professional practices. It is very common to see revenue multiples used in valuations for professional practices for divorces. The multiple of revenues can be a useful valuation approach used in conjunction with others, but it can be misleading if one relies on it solely. Several specific industry revenue multiples are discussed in the "Rule-of-Thumb Methods" section of this chapter.

Revenue multiples are popular in appraising professional practices for several reasons:

1. The method is simple to understand.
2. Revenues are often easier to determine than the economic earnings of the practice.
3. When looking for comparative transactions, sale price to revenues is often the only valuation ratio that can be calculated.

**Proper Use of the Multiple of Revenues.**  Revenue multiples are often used in setting prices for sales of professional practices. It is not wise to rely entirely upon them, however, because the specific practice may have certain positive and negative attributes that the multiple would not take into account. For example, if an accounting practice were appraised by the excess earnings method to be $100,000, the appraiser may want to state this value in terms of a multiple of revenue, in order to check it against the industry standard rule-of-thumb revenue multiple. If it seems out of line with the industry, the appraiser knows that he may have erred in calculating value using the excess earnings method (and needs to search for and correct his error), or that the particular practice is so different from the typical accounting practice that it does not fall in the standard revenue multiple range (and the appraiser should analyze such differences).

**Benefits and Drawbacks of the Multiple of Revenues Method.** The biggest benefit of this appraisal method is that, being relatively easy, it is a good way of making an educated guess at a practice's value. By itself, on the other hand, it does not consider the essence of value, which is the return necessary to justify the risk.

# Cash Flow Measurement

Cash flow measurement can be said to determine at what price a practice could afford to buy itself. There are compelling reasons to use this method, and it is used by many professional practice brokers. If a buyer is going to finance the purchase of the practice that will provide his main source of income, he obviously should pay no more than he can reasonably afford. Since the practice is intended to provide the purchasing power, its available cash flow must determine the size of loan that can be serviced—which, in essence, sets the value. However, this method can be subject to misuse, and it calls for the appraiser to make many subjective judgments. A wrong judgment on any assumption can lead to absurd results.

**Description of the Method.** Suppose that a dental practice has the following cash flow, before owner's salary and benefits and interest expense:

| | |
|---|---|
| Total Earnings | $ 98,000 |
| Depreciation Expense | 2,500 |
| Yearly Gross Cash Flow Available | $100,500 |
| Less: Yearly Estimate of Equipment Replacement | (1,000) |
| Yearly Net Cash Flow Available | $ 99,500 |

Now suppose that dental practices are currently selling on terms, with 25 to 35 percent of the purchase price down and the balance financed over a five-year period, with monthly payments to amortize the loan fully over the 60 months. The sale price does not include cash, accounts receivable, nonoperating assets, or any practice liabilities.

The buyer needs a yearly income so that he can live comfortably, but it does not have to be as high as the prevailing salary for employed dentists. Therefore, the appraiser assumes that a yearly $35,000 salary for the purchasing practitioner is adequate. Since the buyer has no immediate working capital, it is estimated that $45,000 of the loan proceeds will be needed for working capital requirements. Exhibit 26–1 shows the calculation of the value of this dental practice under the assumptions listed above. This method produces a value range of $241,000 to $278,000.

Many dentists could not afford to purchase this hypothetical practice at the value indicated because they do not have cash available for a down payment, or because they require a higher income from the practice for their personal needs. On the other hand, a dentist who has enough cash for a 50 percent down payment, under this formula, would pay considerably more for the practice; this is an assumption that has no rational merit. In other words, a change in assumptions can affect dramatically the value of the practice found under this method. Therefore, the appraiser cannot make arbitrary assumptions; he needs to investigate thoroughly what is happening in the real world.

**Benefits and Drawbacks of the Cash Flow Measurement Method.** The cash flow measurement method is best used to determine the value of a practice for a typical buyer, for example, and for a

Exhibit 26–1

**CASH FLOW MEASUREMENT**
**APPLIED TO A DENTAL PRACTICE**

| | |
|---|---:|
| Cash Flow Available | $ 99,500 |
| Less: Salary Requirement | (35,000) |
| Yearly Cash Flow Available for Debt Service | 64,500 |
| | ÷ 12 |
| Per Month | 5,375 |
| Factor for Determining Total Loan Proceeds Available for a 60-Month Fully Amortized Loan at 15% Annual Interest Rate (Market Rate) | x 42.03459 |
| Total Loan Proceeds Available (Rounded) | $226,000 |
| Less: Necessary Working Capital | (45,000) |
| Loan Proceeds Available for Financed Portion of Practice Purchase | 181,000 |
| Assuming a 25% Down Payment, Total Practice Value Equals (181,000 ÷ (1.0 - 0.25)) | 241,000 |
| Assuming a 35% Down Payment, Total Practice Value Equals (181,000 ÷ (1.0 - 0.35)) | 278,000 |

seller who wishes to gain a general notion of what is happening in the marketplace. An appraiser may be inclined to use this method as a check against other methods of valuation, to see if they produce values within the same ballpark.

The difficulty in using this valuation technique is caused by the definition of *typical* buyer. Used carefully, however, with real-world assumptions, the cash flow measurement method can be an aid in determining value.

# Depreciating Goodwill Method

As discussed in Chapter 25, goodwill is not constant, but, like most other assets, diminishes in value over time. Goodwill must be nurtured to maintain its value. That is why the accountant may treat his client to lunch once a year, and the dentist sends out holiday greetings to his patients.

Generally, the depreciating goodwill method uses a modified excess earnings formula.[3] The appraiser establishes a level of excess earnings, but instead of capitalizing those excess earnings at a constant rate, he treats them as a wasting asset, depreciating to zero after a certain period. He then calculates the present value of those depreciating excess earnings using a discount factor that reflects the risk associated with those earnings.

Even though we find the concept of depreciating goodwill soundly based and have no argument with the general approach of valuing

---

[3] See, for example, Tony Leung, "Professional Goodwill: A Management Perspective," *Washington State Bar News*, June 1984, pp. 39–41.

depreciating excess earnings, we have found some misuse of the approach by various appraisers.

**Common Errors in Depreciating Goodwill.** The first common error is that the depreciating excess earnings generally are capitalized at the same rate used in the capitalization of excess earnings method discussed earlier. Since risk is one of the determining factors in selecting capitalization rates, and since the recognition of the depreciation of goodwill reduces risk, the capitalization rate used in a valuation on the basis of the depreciation of excess earnings should be reduced to reflect the lowered risk, compared to an excess earnings approach that does not factor in depreciation.

The second common error is the assumption that it can be estimated at what date the goodwill will reach zero. A good analogy might be the purchase and nurturing of a houseplant. For the houseplant to live and grow, the weekend horticulturist must water and feed the plant. However, a person with a green thumb will prune the plant, find the most ideal location for it, and probably even mist it regularly, producing a healthy and beautiful plant. Even though both plants will grow, the latter plant will have much more expansive foliage.

The professional practitioner who merely performs services for his clients or patients will see his goodwill diminish, but, like the weekend horticulturist, probably will not see it depreciate to zero. In other words, goodwill, like most other assets, will generally have some salvage value.

**Benefits and Drawbacks of the Depreciating Goodwill Method.** The concept of depreciating goodwill is appealing because it makes economic sense. However, it is extremely difficult to measure how much depreciation has taken place, or will take place. The type of practice, location, types of clients or patients of the practice, and many other variables affect the rate at which goodwill depreciates. Considering that it is difficult to measure and value by itself, it is almost impossible to determine the life cycle of such an intangible and elusive asset.

# Comparative Transactions and Buy-Ins

The use of comparative transactions and buy-ins is not necessarily a set of formulas, such as have been previously discussed, but is a methodology by which various measurements of value can be computed and compared to the practice being appraised.

**Comparative Transactions.** For example, assume that a small veterinary practice were being appraised, and the appraiser found 15 comparative sales of similar practices in the same geographic area during the prior 12 months. The price of each practice probably was based on various formulas, several, or all, of which were different from the others. However, if it was found that all sales occurred at a revenue multiple of between 90 and 120 percent of the latest year's net revenue, or at a multiple of the latest year's total earnings of 1.75 to 2.00, these multiples could be applied to the practice under appraisal. The comparative transactions are not a formula in themselves for establishing value, but can be related to previously discussed methods (excess earnings or revenue multiples, for example), which can then be applied to the practice under appraisal.

**Buy-Ins.**  There is a situation, however, in which the comparative transaction may be based on a formula that the appraiser can rely upon to value the practice. Buy-in formulas may exist in the practice being appraised or in practices similar to it. Typically, they are designed so that a new partner or shareholder of an established practice can buy his interest in the partnership with before-tax dollars, offering only a small down payment, if any.

For example, suppose that Dr. Holladay's practice is expanding so rapidly that he anticipates reaching soon his maximum patient load. He therefore decides to bring in an associate who will be able to increase the number of patients the practice can handle, and ultimately make him a partner. Because of economies of scale, Dr. Holladay would enjoy a higher income with the associate than he would by remaining a sole practitioner. However, Dr. Holladay realizes that he has spent a long time building his practice and thinks that a new associate should be willing to purchase an interest in the practice.

Dr. Holladay could ask a new practitioner to buy a half interest in the practice immediately. However, because such a purchase would require after-tax dollars from the new associate, and would be likely to reduce Dr. Holladay's immediate income as this became shared, he decides to ask for a small down payment and arranges a vesting schedule for the allocation of income between himself and the new associate. According to this schedule, during the early years Dr. Holladay would receive over 50 percent of total practice earnings, even though both doctors spend approximately equal time seeing approximately the same number of patients. The sample appraisal report in the following chapter illustrates this method of valuation.

**Benefits and Drawbacks of the Use of Comparative Transactions and Buy-Ins.**  When the appraiser has comparative transaction data available, which provide relatively consistent measurements of value, this method is extremely helpful in establishing value. Buy-in transactions, especially in the practice under appraisal, are also very strong evidence of value. Unfortunately, the comparative data can be very sketchy and the prior buy-in may be too remote in time, or may involve unique circumstances, which cause the data to be incomplete or outdated for the current appraisal.

# Punitive and Retirement Formulas

Punitive and retirement valuation formulas are established by contract in the practice being appraised. They do not necessarily establish the market value of the practice or the interest in a practice, but they set forth a value for the practitioner's interest when he leaves or retires.

Therefore, if the standard of value calls for the appraiser to value goodwill on a going-concern basis, these contractual obligations may not necessarily aid in determining that going-concern value.

**Purpose of Punitive and Retirement Formulas.**   A punitive formula is sometimes written into a partnership agreement to discourage partners from leaving the firm. The punitive contract offers the exiting partner a prescribed buyout formula that is lower than the fair market value of his partnership interest. A retirement formula, which also is often included in partnership agreements, may attempt to value the partnership interest at its fair market value, or perhaps even above its fair market value, to reward the partner for many years of valuable service.

**Benefits and Drawbacks of the Use of Punitive and Retirement Formulas.**   Having a prescribed formula for the interest to be valued is helpful if the reason for the appraisal is the event that calls the formula into operation. However, these formulas are generally of little help if the purpose of the appraisal is some reason other than that which would cause the formula to be invoked.

# Rule-of-Thumb Methods for Various Types of Practices

> A rule of thumb is a homemade recipe for making a guess. It is an easy-to-remember guide that falls somewhere between a mathematical formula and a shot in the dark.[4]

The various methods already discussed can be applied to almost all types of professional practices. However, certain types of practices do have specific formulas (almost all based on revenue multiples) which tend to be commonly used in their respective valuations. Below is a listing of some types of professional practices that have a rule of thumb that can be applied to estimate the practice value.

The appraiser should be cautioned, however, that these are general rules that will be accurate only as averages, given a large number of observations. However, in any specific observation, the rule may need to be adjusted or even discarded, if it is not appropriate to the situation at hand.

## Accounting Practices

Small accounting firms tend to sell for their net asset value plus a goodwill value, that, when paid over time, is equal to 75 to 150 percent

---

[4] Tom Parker, *Rules of Thumb* (Boston: Houghton Mifflin, 1983), p. vii.

of the latest year's revenues. However, this very simple formula has some complicating adjustments.

The goodwill usually is purchased by the buyer's payment to the seller of a certain percentage of fees collected from clients who continue with the practice for a period of time. For example, at the date of sale, a list of past clients may be prepared, and buyer and seller agree that 20 percent of all fees charged to those clients (and paid by them) for the next five years will be transferred to the selling accountant immediately after those fees are paid. This agreement results in a revenue multiple of 1 (20 percent $\times$ 5 = 1). However, at the date of sale, in order to determine a value for the goodwill, the appraiser would need to investigate the attrition rates of clients and also apply a discount to the expected income stream for the time value of money.

Another method of valuing the goodwill of an accounting firm would be to apply a different multiple to each segment of revenue. Generally, an accountant would be willing to pay more for a continuing audit client or a write-up client than for numerous individual tax return clients.

# Dental Practices

The old rule was that general dental practices sold for the value of their equipment, furniture, and fixtures plus a value for goodwill of either 25 to 35 percent of revenues, or 50 to 100 percent of total earnings available to the doctor. Others have used factors of all the way from 35 to 75 percent of revenues to value the goodwill and the equipment, furniture, and fixtures.

# Engineering/Architecture Practices

Depending on the type of practice, these firms are valued at their net asset value plus 20 to 40 percent of the latest year's revenues. Practices with continuing clients would tend to sell at the high end of the multiple range. This formula should be used cautiously, because many of these firms possess little, if any, goodwill.

# Law Practices

A general law practice can be sold for its net asset value only, because legal ethics forbid the sale of clients' files or goodwill. However, some attorneys who wish to retire refer their cases to a new attorney and then split the fee paid by the referred client with the new attorney.

In divorces, many state courts have held that goodwill should be valued, even if it can't be sold. However, no standard rule of thumb method exists for this type of appraisal.

# Medical Practices

Ten years ago, medical practices were difficult to sell because the relative ease of entry into the market diminished their value. However, with the oversupply of physicians in many parts of the country, medical practices are selling, and they are commanding goodwill value. Generally, these practices sell in a range of 20 to 60 percent of revenues for the equipment, supplies, and goodwill. Obviously, the type of practice has a large influence on the multiple; referral practices are near the low end, and practices with a continuing patient base toward the high end, of the range.

There is no general rule of thumb for valuing goodwill only; however, a recent survey of prices paid for just goodwill in the sale of 100 percent interests in medical practices showed a range for goodwill value of 12 to 98 percent of the latest year's revenues; the mean multiple was 38 percent and the median was 25 percent.[5] The survey did not, however, disclose the terms of the transfer. A recent article stated that medical doctors are selling their goodwill at an average of 25 percent of the previous year's gross receipts.[6]

# Optometric Practices

These practices can be more like retail businesses than professional practices, because their location is more important than in other types of professional practices. Generally, the value of an optometric practice's equipment, supplies, patient eye prescriptions, and goodwill can range from 40 percent to 60 percent of the latest year's revenues.

# Medical Laboratories

There have been many acquisitions of local laboratories by publicly traded laboratory companies. Acquisition prices as a percent of latest year's revenues have had an extremely wide range, but the vast majority fall in the range of 50 to 80 percent of latest year's revenues for the goodwill and net asset value.

# Veterinary Practices

Small animal clinics in good locations can command premium prices. Generally, these practices sell for 75 to 125 percent of the latest year's revenues for the goodwill, equipment, and supplies.

---

[5] *Summary Report of the Goodwill Registry* (Bala Cynwyd, Pa.: The Health Care Group, 1984).

[6] Doane Harrison, "Pump Up and Preserve Your Practice Goodwill," *Medical Economics*, April 15, 1985, pp. 107–12.

# The Complete Value

As was mentioned at the beginning of this book, sales of small businesses and professional practices tend to be asset sales. When a practitioner says he sold his practice for 50 percent of revenues, that does not really inform his hearer of the total value he received, because, typically, cash, accounts receivable, owner's automobiles, and liabilities are not included in the sale. A rule-of-thumb multiple may value only goodwill, or it may value the goodwill plus supplies, furniture, and equipment. Therefore, to arrive at the complete value, the appraiser needs to consider not only the assets and liabilities that are sold, but the assets and liabilities that were retained.

We were once involved in a litigated valuation dispute in which the other side's appraiser used the prior purchase price of a retailing business (as a percent of revenues) to value the business as of the trial date. He correctly stated that the business sold at 10 percent of its revenues, and he therefore applied a 10 percent factor to the $4,000,000 current revenues and concluded with a value of $400,000 for the business assets, liabilities, and goodwill. However, this appraiser did not investigate this sale, so he did not realize that the seller assumed all liabilities. When that was pointed out to him, he recalculated his value and came up with $150,000 ($400,000 less liabilities of $250,000). Needless to say, if this appraiser had considered the complete value, the case would have settled and never gone to trial.

# Chapter 27

# Sample Professional Practice Valuation Report

# Introduction

## Description of the Assignment

Willamette Management Associates, Inc., has been requested by Robert A. Attorney, to appraise Dr. Stanley McNee's interest in the medical practice known as Internal Medicine Associates, Inc., located in Sacramento, California, and to appraise his professional goodwill. The valuations are as of February 1984, using information available at that time. The appraisal is being conducted for the marital dissolution of Dr. and Mrs. McNee.

In completing this appraisal, we have followed the standards and guidelines established by the California courts in regard to professional practice valuation.

## Summary Description of the Practice

Internal Medicine Associates, Inc., is a medical corporation located in Sacramento, California, with two shareholders, Dr. McNee and Dr. Leon Chandler. Each individual has a 50 percent ownership in the medical practice.

## Sources of Information

In preparing this appraisal report, we have reviewed the following documents:

1. Annual compiled financial statements prepared by the corporation's independent certified public accounting firm for the fiscal years ending January 31, 1980, through January 31, 1984.
2. U.S. corporate income tax returns for the corporation for the fiscal years ending January 31, 1980, through January 31, 1984.
3. U.S. individual income tax returns for Stanley and Kathleen McNee for the years 1979 through 1983.
4. A copy of the lease agreement between the corporation and Professional Medical Building, Inc., for the building that houses the practice.
5. The fee schedule in effect in February 1984 for the practice.
6. Depreciation schedules for furniture, fixtures, and equipment owned by the practice.
7. The Articles of Incorporation, By-Laws, and minutes of shareholders' and board of directors' meetings for the years 1982 through 1984.
8. Schedules of gross fees charged, gross fees charged that were attributable to Dr. McNee, gross fees charged that were attributable to Dr. Chandler, and adjustments to accounts receivable for the fiscal years 1980 through 1984.
9. The past three years' appointment books for Drs. McNee and Chandler.

Ralph Arnold toured the offices of the practice and interviewed Dr. McNee and Dr. Chandler, as well as the independent accountant for the practice.

For economic data we considered *Employment Data Research,* produced by the state of California; Sacramento area Council of Governments *1984 Sacramento Business Handbook*; and information from the Sacramento Metropolitan Chamber of Commerce, the California State Board of Quality Assurance, and the California Medical Association.

For industry data, we considered the American Medical Association's *Socioeconomic Characteristics of Medical Practice, 1983*, as well as various articles appearing in the periodical *Medical Economics.*

## Summary and Conclusion

Based upon the analysis completed and discussed in this report, it is our opinion that the current value of Dr. McNee's equity interest in the practice is equal to $70,500. It is also our opinion that the value of Dr. McNee's professional goodwill as of February 1984 was equal to $86,000. The total values of these two items are $156,500.

# Sacramento Economic Profile

## Overview

The four-county Sacramento region, one of California's interior economies, is slated for continued growth and prosperity. According to the Center for Continuing Study of the California Economy (CCSCE) and the Bank of America, inland regions will outpace coastal areas, traditionally California's major growth centers.

The CCSCE predicts that the Sacramento region will see a 24.0 percent growth in population and a 33.7 percent increase in households by 1991. Personal income will rise from 53.0 percent to 73.1 percent in the same period, according to the same source. These figures compare to a statewide average of 3.9 percent to 51.5 percent growth in personal income.

The per capita income of the four-county region—Sacramento, Yolo, Placer, and El Dorado—was $11,248 in 1981 and was estimated to be $13,336 to $15,089 in constant dollars by 1991. Average household income was expected to grow from $29,893 to between $33,026 and $37,365. Taxable sales were expected at least to double in constant dollars, from $6.75 billion in 1982 to a predicted $13.43 billion in 1991.

The short-range economy was also promising. James H. Pattersen, a private consultant and former economist for the state legislature, predicted employment to rise by 3.5 percent by 1985 with similar increases through 1998. Pattersen expected a growth rate of 6 percent in the manufacturing sector. His projections for other employment sectors were optimistic as well.

Government was the largest employment sector, with 149,200 workers, or 33.5 percent of nonagricultural workers. Not surprising for a state capital, more than 81 percent of those workers were involved with state or local government. Total nonagricultural employment in the Sacramento four-county metro area during 1983 was 445,000. The service sector accounted for 20.4 percent of the work force, retail trade 19.7 percent, wholesale trade 5.0 percent, and manufacturing 6.7 percent. Unemployment in the Sacramento metro area at the close of 1983 was 10.7 percent.

The population of Sacramento County was predicted by the Population Research Unit of the state Department of Finance to top 1 million by the mid-1990s. A population of 1.5 million was predicted by 2020. Those projections, based on 1980 U.S. census data, represented major increases over projections based on the prior census. The population for the metro area was projected to exceed 1.4 million by 1995 and reach 1.7 million by 2000. The 1985 population for Sacramento County was projected to reach 889,800, a 4.9 percent increase from the 1983 population of 848,400. The metro area population was estimated to be at 1.3 million by 1985.

# Health Care

As one of the fastest-growing areas in the state, medical services and health care were expanding in the Sacramento area. Current services and care were considered excellent. The area had 18 hospitals and an in-patient capacity of 2,663 licensed beds.

There are 2,799 licensed physicians in the four-county area, including approximately 160 internists, according to the state Board of Medical Quality Assurance and the area county Medical Societies. The ratio of 314.5 physicians per 100,000 civilian population was above the state average of 232.1 physicians per 100,000 civilian population.

Four health maintenance organizations (HMOs) offered services in the Sacramento area: Foundation Health Plan, Healthcare, Kaiser Foundation Health, and TakeCare.

Foundation offered medical and hospital services on a direct service basis. It had 111,000 members in February 1984 and was predicted to be at 150,000 by January 1986. It had 1,500 private practice physicians under contract. Foundation served a five-county area, including Sacramento, Yolo, El Dorado, Nevada, and Placer Counties.

Healthcare served 15,266 people and was a federally qualified HMO. It operated three primary care facilities and offered complete medical and hospital services through approximately 170 private practice physicians.

Kaiser Foundation Health was a direct services plan providing medical and hospital services through its exclusive physicians and facilities. Kaiser currently served three clinics in the Sacramento area, with 348 full-time and 40 part-time physicians under contract.

TakeCare was affiliated with Blue Cross of California. The HMO emphasized preventive care, as well as treatment for illness. The plan provided complete health care services to its members for a prepaid monthly fee. It served 11,000 members through six clinics and had 32 on-site and 100 off-site physicians under contract.

# Survey of the Medical Practice Field

The private medical practice field is in a period of relatively rapid change. Largely unaffected by the 1981–82 economic recession, which had profound effects on most segments of the United States industrial, business, and service sectors, private medical practice instead has been affected by a series of socioeconomic changes in the way the public approaches and receives medical services.

Among the forces cited as bringing about change in the medical practice environment are an increased surplus of doctors, relaxation of restrictions on physicians' advertising, the introduction of contract, prepaid health care delivery systems, a general crackdown on the high cost of health care, and provider arrogance in dealing with patients.

## Competition

Physicians are facing an increasingly competitive environment. Several factors have contributed to this trend. Patients and purchasers of health services are increasingly more cost-conscious due to the rise in health care costs. Medical costs are rising at a brisk 7 percent to 8 percent per year. That rate is projected to increase the nation's present health bill to $750 billion by 1990. For the average individual, health care costs per year will rise from $1,500 to $3,000 by 1990.

Secondly, the number of physicians has greatly increased in the last decade. Since 1970, the number of physicians has increased at a rate four times faster than the general population. During the same period, the cost of practicing medicine rose sharply, according to the American Medical Association.

These pressures have made it more difficult for some physicians to attract and retain patients. Physicians' concern over the cost-effectiveness of their practices is on the rise as a result of the more competitive environment within the medical profession.

Additionally, changes in practice services and the adoption of new marketing strategies by physicians have come about as a result of these competitive pressures.

## Changes in Practice Services

The most evident impact of competition on medical practice services is the increased use of nonphysician employees. Nonphysician personnel employed by physicians increased 22 percent in the two-year 1981–82 period. This trend in hiring nonphysician staff is stronger in younger physicians, whose less-developed practices are more vulnerable to competitive pressure. Physicians in practice for 10 years or less increased their nonphysician staff 34 percent in the same two-year period, compared to 18 percent for physicians in practice longer than 10 years. Physicians, in response to competition, have not significantly increased their house calls or weekend and evening office hours, according to 1982 data compiled by the American Medical Association. However, physicians have begun to use marketing strategies to identify patient needs and attract new patients. According to *Socioeconomic Characteristics of Medical Practice, 1983*, 40 percent of physicians surveyed have used at least one marketing strategy in the last five years. The most common strategy was a study of community demographics; 27 percent of physicians surveyed said they had employed such a marketing strategy.

The extent to which physicians adopt marketing strategies is affected by physician characteristics. Younger physicians and those in group practices were more likely to use marketing techniques than their older colleagues in solo practice (46 percent of those in practice 10 years or less compared to 38 percent with more than 10 years of practice; 53 percent of group practices in contrast to 32 percent of solo practices). Similar delineations are found by geographic region and specialty group. In the West, where competition is higher due to greater physician population ratios, 48 percent of physicians used marketing techniques, compared to 40 percent of physicians throughout the country. By specialty, 51 percent of medical specialists have used marketing strategies as compared to 38 percent of surgical and other specialists and 33 percent of general family practitioners.

## Prepaid Health Care

The delivery of health care services in the U.S. is changing. The evolution is away from a physician-dominated health care system to one geared toward consumer needs and preferences, operating as a business with full exposure to the competitive forces of the free marketplace.

Beginning in the 1970s, prepaid, contracted systems of health care emerged in contrast to the fee-for-service approach typified in the traditional private medical practice. Health Maintenance Organizations (HMOs) have led the prepaid care movement. With the dramatic increase in the 1970s in health care costs, HMOs and other prepaid services offered a method of containing price increases.

Health care analysts predict the trend toward prepaid health care to increase in the 1980s. In 1980, there were 235 HMOs in the country, serving four percent of the population, or 9 million patients. HMOs now serve 12 million patients, and that number is predicted to increase to 25–30 million patients by 1990.

Industry analysts also predict a trend toward fewer solo practices, with group practices growing (there were 88,000 group practices in the country in 1980) because of the complexity and cost of technology, the increasing necessity of expensive marketing programs, and stringent reimbursement systems which make solo practices less practical. More physicians are also expected to be employees by the end of the decade, working for contract health delivery systems instead of as solo or group practitioners.

# Personal Background

Dr. McNee is 54 years old and describes his health as good. In 1951, he received his Bachelor of Science degree from Holy Cross College in Worcester, Massachusetts. His medical school training was at the College of Medicine, University of Cincinnati, and was completed in 1954. He served his internship at St. Luke's Hospital in San Francisco and served his residency at the University of California Medical Center, San Francisco. In June 1960, he opened his medical practice in Sacramento, California. He was board-certified by the American Board of Internal Medicine in June 1965. He is also a member of the American Medical Association, American College of Physicians, and American Heart Association (Fellow).

Dr. McNee sees 10 to 15 patients per day in his office, in addition to patients he sees on daily hospital visits. His patients fall in all age ranges and he generally spends 10–15 minutes per patient, although at times as much as one hour.

Approximately 10 percent of the patients he sees are either on medicare or medicaid, with the balance generally having private medical insurance. Dr. McNee works from 8 A.M. to 6 P.M., Monday through Friday (except Wednesdays, when he finishes at 2 P.M.). He is on call every other weekend to the hospitals where his patients are staying. Dr. McNee estimates that he spends a total of 10–12 hours per day, four days a week, on practice-related activities and approximately six hours per day on Wednesdays. He works approximately three to four hours on the weekends when he is on call to the hospitals.

# Practice History

Dr. McNee owns a 50 percent interest in a professional corporation named The Internal Medicine Associates, Inc., with one other doctor, in Sacramento, California. The practice is located at 1501 A Street, across from one of Sacramento's main hospitals, Sacramento Memorial Hospital. The general area in which the practice is located has many other professional offices (medical, legal, accounting, and so on) in downtown Sacramento. The office was opened in 1960 by Dr. McNee.

In 1980, Dr. McNee was working nearly 60 to 70 hours per week because of a large increase in the number of patients he was seeing. Because he felt generally overworked, he decided to bring in an associate internist, Dr. Leon Chandler, who would purchase a 50 percent interest in his practice.

Dr. Chandler paid $100,000 for the net asset value and intangible value for the 50 percent interest in the practice. Based upon the sales agreement, $75,000 was attributable to the net assets of the practice and $25,000 attributable to the practice's goodwill.

Generally, the purchase price allocation between assets purchased and goodwill purchased is strongly influenced by income tax considerations rather than the actual fair market value of the various assets purchased. However, in this particular sale, our investigation revealed that the allocations were based on informed negotiations between Drs. McNee and Chandler and that the $75,000 allocated to 50 percent of the net tangible assets of the practice reasonably approximated the fair market value of those assets at that time.

Dr. Chandler signed an employment agreement in which it was agreed that during the fiscal years ended January 31, 1981, through January 31, 1983, he would take a lower salary than Dr. McNee. Of the total officers' salaries to be paid, Dr. Chandler would receive the following percentages for each of the fiscal years:

| 1981 | 32% |
| 1982 | 40% |
| 1983 | 45% |

Thereafter, the officers' salaries would be equally divided between Dr. McNee and Dr. Chandler.

The suite in which the practice is located is in a medical building in downtown Sacramento. It has approximately 2,500 square feet, including four examination rooms, a reception and office area, two doctor's offices, an employee lounge, and a storage area.

The practice has two full-time and one part-time nonowner employees. Edna Smith has been with Dr. McNee for 12 years as a receptionist/assistant. Janet Dollar has been with Dr. McNee for 10 years as the office bookkeeper. Donna Fisher works 16 hours per week as Dr. McNee's assistant.

# Financial Statement Analysis

Internal Medicine Associates, Inc., has a fiscal year ending January 31. The financial statements are compiled by the accounting firm of Wyckoff, Martin & Bear, Certified Public Accountants.

## Balance Sheets

Table I (Exhibit 27–1) is a schedule of cash basis balance sheets for the fiscal years ended January 31, 1980, through January 31, 1984. This schedule shows both dollar amounts and the amounts expressed as a percent of total assets.

In 1981, the amount of total assets of the practice decreased significantly from the fiscal year-end January 31, 1980. However, since that date, assets have continually increased. The primary reason for the decrease in 1981 was expenses associated with the expansion of the

Exhibit 27-1
Cash Basis Balance Sheets

TABLE I
INTERNAL MEDICINE ASSOCIATES, INC.
STATEMENT OF ASSETS, LIABILITIES, AND STOCKHOLDERS' EQUITY (CASH BASIS)

As of January 31

| | 1984 $ | 1984 % | 1983 $ | 1983 % | 1982 $ | 1982 % | 1981 $ | 1981 % | 1980 $ | 1980 % |
|---|---|---|---|---|---|---|---|---|---|---|
| **ASSETS** | | | | | | | | | | |
| Cash & Equiv. | 908 | 6.8 | 3,324 | 17.0 | 1,677 | 21.1 | (424) | (7.3) | 18,750 | 42.7 |
| Marketable Secs. (Cost) | – | – | – | – | – | – | – | – | 19,950 | 45.5 |
| | 908 | 6.8 | 3,324 | 17.0 | 1,677 | 21.1 | (424) | (7.3) | 38,700 | 88.2 |
| Furniture, Fixtures, and Equip. (Cost) | 44,390 | 330.1 | 44,390 | 226.7 | 31,168 | 391.8 | 27,560 | 476.3 | 21,168 | 48.3 |
| Accum. Deprec. | (31,850) | (236.8) | (28,135) | (143.7) | (24,890) | (312.9) | (21,350) | (369.0) | (16,002) | (36.5) |
| Net Fixed Assets | 12,540 | 93.3 | 16,255 | 83.0 | 6,278 | 78.9 | 6,210 | 107.3 | 5,166 | 11.8 |
| TOTAL ASSETS | 13,448 | 100.0 | 19,579 | 100.0 | 7,955 | 100.0 | 5,786 | 100.0 | 43,866 | 100.0 |
| **LIABILITIES** | | | | | | | | | | |
| Payroll Taxes Pay. | 445 | 3.3 | 211 | 1.1 | 295 | 3.7 | 350 | 6.1 | 413 | 0.9 |
| Note Payable | – | – | 7,500 | 38.3 | – | – | – | – | – | – |
| Pension Cont. Pay. | – | – | 5,000 | 25.5 | – | – | 15,600 | 269.6 | 59,000 | 134.5 |
| Shareholder Payable (Demand) | – | – | – | – | 5,789 | 72.8 | 12,354 | 213.5 | – | – |
| Total Liabilities | 445 | 3.3 | 12,711 | 64.9 | 6,084 | 76.5 | 28,304 | 489.2 | 59,413 | 135.4 |
| Shareholder's Eqty. | 13,003 | 96.7 | 6,868 | 35.1 | 1,871 | 23.5 | (22,518) | (389.2) | (15,547) | (35.4) |
| TOTAL LIABILITIES & EQUITY | 13,448 | 100.0 | 19,579 | 100.0 | 7,955 | 100.0 | 5,786 | 100.0 | 43,866 | 100.0 |

**SOURCE:** U.S. corporation tax returns.

offices and additional leasehold improvements and new equipment (some of which was not capitalized), which became necessary when Dr. Chandler joined the practice.

During the entire period considered, liabilities have continually decreased from a total of $59,400 in January 1980 to $445 in January 1984. The primary reason for the decrease has been a change in philosophy on the payment of bills. Dr. McNee stated that one of the agreements that he made with Dr. Chandler was to carry less debt on the books and to pay all bills on a timely basis. This philosophy is reflected primarily in the pension contributions, which are generally paid currently over the 12-month period instead of in one lump sum at the end or after the end of a fiscal year.

The cash basis financial statements show that shareholders' equity was in negative amounts during 1980 and 1981 fiscal years-end; however, it has increased each year since.

The cash and equivalents and marketable securities shown in 1980 were equal to almost 90 percent of total assets. However, the company has held a much lower value in current assets in the last four years. Conversely, the company also has a much lower value in current liabilities (total liabilities) than in 1980.

It should be noted that the balance sheet is on a cash basis and does not reflect such assets as accounts receivable or prepaid expenses, which in this particular case are quite meaningful. Also, the balance sheets as presented do not show accrued and unpaid bills.

## Income Statements

Table II (Exhibit 27–2) presents cash basis income statements for the practice for the fiscal years ended January 31, 1980, through January 31, 1984.

Total fees received have been increasing each year during the period considered. Also, there has been a continual increase in officers' salaries, although in 1984 officers' salaries dropped somewhat as a percent of total fees received.

Total operating expenses generally have averaged approximately 95 percent to 100 percent of total fees received; however, operating expenses include such items as officers' salaries, directors' fees, and other discretionary expenses.

In 1981, Dr. McNee sold marketable securities held by the corporation and realized a $32,500 gain on their sale. These securities were sold because of the large loss taken by the practice in that fiscal year and because of the expenditures for additional equipment and new leasehold improvements when Dr. Chandler joined the practice. Net income during the period fluctuated greatly, from the high in 1980 of $18,000 to a loss in 1981 of $7,000. During the past two years, the company has made nominal net income. This low or nonexistent net income is not unusual for a professional practice, because, generally, officers' salaries, perquisites, and benefits are calculated to an amount that will eliminate income from the corporation.

Exhibit 27–2
Cash Basis Income Statements

TABLE II
INTERNAL MEDICINE ASSOCIATES, INC.
STATEMENT OF CASH RECEIVED AND EXPENSES PAID

Years Ended January 31

| | 1984 $ | 1984 % | 1983 $ | 1983 % | 1982 $ | 1982 % | 1981 $ | 1981 % | 1980 $ | 1980 % |
|---|---|---|---|---|---|---|---|---|---|---|
| Fees Received | 483,818 | 100.0 | 442,069 | 100.0 | 422,789 | 100.0 | 375,447 | 100.0 | 298,894 | 100.0 |
| Operating Expenses: | | | | | | | | | | |
| Officers' Salaries | 310,500 | 64.2 | 292,500 | 66.2 | 258,000 | 61.0 | 230,000 | 61.3 | 126,679 | 42.4 |
| Other Salaries | 51,978 | 10.7 | 44,448 | 10.0 | 43,475 | 10.3 | 43,551 | 11.6 | 34,150 | 11.4 |
| Automobile | 2,258 | 0.5 | 4,565 | 1.0 | 2,898 | 0.7 | 1,778 | 0.5 | 1,324 | 0.4 |
| Travel | 610 | 0.1 | 1,131 | 0.3 | — | — | — | — | — | — |
| Promotion | 3,204 | 0.7 | 3,189 | 0.7 | 2,590 | 0.6 | — | — | — | — |
| Directors' Fees | 7,895 | 1.6 | 410 | 0.1 | — | — | — | — | — | — |
| Education | 1,439 | 0.3 | — | — | — | — | — | — | — | — |
| Accounting & Legal | 14,120 | 2.9 | 3,892 | 0.9 | 3,611 | 0.9 | 3,425 | 0.9 | 3,516 | 1.2 |
| Retire. Plan Contrib. | 38,209 | 7.9 | 46,009 | 10.4 | 46,912 | 11.1 | 96,289 | 25.7 | 78,921 | 26.4 |
| Other Expenses | 48,783 | 10.1 | 42,384 | 9.6 | 40,907 | 9.7 | 42,139 | 11.1 | 35,796 | 12.0 |
| Total Oper. Expenses | 478,996 | 99.0 | 438,528 | 99.2 | 398,393 | 94.2 | 417,182 | 111.1 | 280,386 | 93.8 |
| Operating Income | 4,822 | 1.0 | 3,541 | 0.8 | 24,396 | 5.8 | (41,735) | (11.1) | 18,508 | 6.2 |
| Other Income (Expense): | | | | | | | | | | |
| Interest Income | 2,361 | 0.5 | 2,192 | 0.5 | 2,113 | 0.5 | 1,875 | 0.5 | 768 | 0.3 |
| Interest Expense | (98) | (Nil) | — | — | — | — | — | — | — | — |
| Gain on Sale of Assets | — | — | — | — | — | — | 32,500 | 8.7 | — | — |
| Total Other Income | 2,263 | 0.5 | 2,192 | 0.5 | 2,113 | 0.5 | 34,375 | 9.2 | 768 | 0.3 |
| Pretax Income (Loss) (Cash Basis) | 7,085 | 1.5 | 5,733 | 1.3 | 26,509 | 6.3 | (7,360) | (2.0) | 19,276 | 6.5 |
| Income Tax Paid | (950) | (0.2) | (736) | (0.2) | (2,120) | (0.5) | 389 | 0.1 | (1,130) | (0.4) |
| Net Income | 6,135 | 1.3 | 4,997 | 1.1 | 24,389 | 5.8 | (6,971) | (1.9) | 18,146 | 6.1 |

Nil = Inconsequential amount, greater (or less) than zero.
SOURCE: U.S. corporations tax returns.

When considering the sum of officers' salaries, retirement plan contributions and pretax income, this practice's total earnings have fallen in a range of 73.6 percent to 85 percent of yearly revenues—an extremely high percentage compared to various medical surveys which show internists generally have total earnings of 50 percent to 60 percent of yearly revenues.

Since this practice has such a high percentage of total earnings to revenues, it may be at a greater risk of a loss of a portion of those earnings because of increased competition by others that want to participate in this large net profit margin. In fact, the practice has seen its total earnings, as a percent of revenues, drop during the past three years (in fiscal 1982 total earnings equaled 78.4 percent while in fiscal 1984 they fell to 73.6 percent).

Table III (Exhibit 27–3) is a statement of income as a percent of 1980. As can be seen, fees received in 1984 were 61.87 percent greater than in 1980. Generally, expenses have also increased over this period.

Exhibit 27–3
Statements of Income as a Percent of a Base Year

**TABLE III**
**INTERNAL MEDICINE ASSOCIATES, INC.**
**STATEMENT OF CASH RECEIVED AND EXPENSES PAID**
**AS PERCENT OF 1980 AMOUNTS**

| | Fiscal Years Ended January 31 | | | | |
|---|---|---|---|---|---|
| | 1984 % | 1983 % | 1982 % | 1981 % | 1980 % |
| Fees Received | 161.87 | 147.90 | 141.45 | 125.61 | 100.00 |
| Expenses of Operation: | | | | | |
| Officers' Salaries | 245.11 | 230.90 | 203.66 | 181.56 | 100.00 |
| Other Salaries | 152.20 | 130.16 | 127.31 | 127.53 | 100.00 |
| Automobile | 170.54 | 344.79 | 218.88 | 134.29 | 100.00 |
| Travel | NM | NM | NM | NM | NM |
| Promotion | NM | NM | NM | NM | NM |
| Directors' Fees | NM | NM | NM | NM | NM |
| Education | NM | NM | NM | NM | NM |
| Legal and Accounting | 401.59 | 110.69 | 102.70 | 97.41 | 100.00 |
| Retirement Plan Contrib. | 48.41 | 58.30 | 59.44 | 122.01 | 100.00 |
| Other Expenses | 136.28 | 118.40 | 114.28 | 117.72 | 100.00 |
| Total Operating Expenses | 170.83 | 156.40 | 142.09 | 148.79 | 100.00 |
| Operating Income | 26.05 | 19.13 | 131.81 | (255.50) | 100.00 |
| Other Income (Expense): | | | | | |
| Interest Income | 307.42 | 285.42 | 275.13 | 244.14 | 100.00 |
| Interest Expense | NM | NM | NM | NM | NM |
| Gain on Sale of Assets | NM | NM | NM | NM | NM |
| Total Other Income | 294.66 | 285.42 | 275.13 | 4,475.91 | 100.0 |
| Pretax Inc. (Loss) (Cash Basis) | 36.76 | 29.74 | 137.52 | (38.18) | 100.00 |
| Income Tax Paid | 84.07 | 65.13 | 187.61 | (34.42) | 100.00 |
| Net Income (Loss) | 33.81 | 27.54 | 134.40 | (38.42) | 100.00 |

NM = Not Meaningful
**SOURCE:** Table II.

Operating income has decreased as a percent of the 1980 operating income, while other income has increased. On a net income basis, 1984 income was approximately one third of the 1980 income.

Before one can conclude that this practice is making less money, the total earnings of the practice should be examined.

Table IV (Exhibit 27–4) calculates total compensation (earnings) of Internal Medicine Associates, Inc. This schedule, in calculating total

Exhibit 27–4

**TABLE IV**
**INTERNAL MEDICINE ASSOCIATES, INC.**
**SCHEDULE OF OWNERS' TOTAL COMPENSATION**

|  | Fiscal Years Ended January 31 | | | | |
|---|---|---|---|---|---|
|  | 1984 $ | 1983 $ | 1982 $ | 1981 $ | 1980 $ |
| Corporation's Net Income | 6,135 | 4,997 | 24,389 | (6,971) | 18,146 |
| Salaries to Officer(s) | 310,500 | 292,500 | 258,000 | 230,000 | 126,679 |
| Retirement Benefits for Officers' Benefit | 34,500 | 42,000 | 44,500 | 91,000 | 76,500 |
| Extraordinary Expenses (Income): |  |  |  |  |  |
| Directors' Fees | 7,895 |  |  |  |  |
| Excess Legal & Accounting | 10,000 |  |  |  |  |
| Excess Automobile |  | 3,500 |  |  |  |
| Gain on Sale of Securities |  |  |  | (32,500) |  |
| Total Practice Earnings | 369,030 | 342,997 | 326,889 | 281,529 | 221,325 |
| Less: Dr. Chandler's Portion of: |  |  |  |  |  |
| Officers' Salary | (155,250) | (131,625) | (103,200) | (73,500) | — |
| Directors' Fees | (3,948) | — | — | — | — |
| Retirement Benefits | (20,000) | (17,500) | (15,000) | (10,000) | — |
| Corporate Income | (3,068) | (2,499) | (12,195) | 3,486 | — |
| Excess (Expenses) & Income | (5,000) | (1,750) | — | 16,250 | — |
| Dr. McNee's Total Compensation | 181,764 | 189,623 | 196,494 | 217,765 | 221,325 |
| Less: Portion paid to Dr. McNee per Buy-In Agmt. | — | (14,625) | (25,800) | (41,500) | — |
| Dr. McNee's Normal Compensation | 181,764 | 174,998 | 170,694 | 176,265 | 221,325 |

SOURCE: U.S. corporate tax return; practice's books and records, retirement plan documents, and Dr. Chandler's Employment Agreement.

earnings, considers not only the corporation's net income, but also salaries paid to officers, officers' retirement benefits, and other extraordinary expenses and income that are not normal to the practice. As can be seen from this schedule, the extraordinary expenses included directors' fees of $7,895 paid in 1984. In essence, these fees, which were paid to the officers, are more accurately classified as officers' salary.

Our investigation also showed that there were excess legal and accounting expenses for the fiscal year ended January 31, 1984, for tax planning done for the personal benefit of each of the doctors.

In 1983, excess automobile expenses occurred. We learned that these expenses were accrued from prior years and did not necessarily represent the normal annual automobile expense for the practice.

Lastly, we removed the gain on the sale of securities that occurred in 1981, because that is not normal operating earnings of a medical practice. By means of these adjustments, we determined the total practice earnings. These earnings are discretionary and are the earnings a buyer of the practice would consider. Since we are valuing only a 50 percent interest in Internal Medicine Associates, Inc., we have removed the earnings and benefits received by the other shareholder, Dr. Chandler. As this schedule shows, we have removed the salary, fees, benefits, and income (including excess expenses and income) that Dr. Chandler received or that are attributable to his portion of the corporation. This computation gives us Dr. McNee's total compensation. However, Dr. McNee's total compensation includes excess payments made to him in accordance with the buy-in agreement with Dr. Chandler. We have calculated these payments and have deducted them from Dr. McNee's total compensation to make a determination of Dr. McNee's normal compensation over the past five years. In this way, we can gauge more accurately what Dr. McNee can expect to receive in the future.

As can be seen from this schedule, Dr. McNee's normal compensation dropped during fiscal years ended January 31, 1980 through 1982; it has increased from that time through January 31, 1984. Because of the changes in ownership and the compensation levels, which occurred in accordance with the employment agreement with Dr. Chandler, we decided that the last three years (fiscal years ended January 31, 1982, through January 31, 1984) are more representative of Dr. McNee's future compensation than the years that came before.

# Valuation of Medical Practice and Professional Goodwill

In the following sections, we calculate the value of Dr. McNee's equity in Internal Medicine Associates, Inc., and his professional goodwill.

## Medical Practice

Table V (Exhibit 27–5) is a statement of assets, liabilities, and shareholders' equity on both a cash basis and an adjusted accrual basis.

In calculating the net asset value of the company, it is inappropriate to use cash basis balance sheets, because they do not reflect various assets and liabilities that do, in fact, exist. Therefore, it is important that cash basis balance sheets be adjusted to an accrual basis and that assets not recorded at estimated market value be increased (or decreased) to reflect their current market value. Table V shows these calculations.

We adjusted the cash basis financial statements as of January 31, 1984, for the following purposes:

1. Our review indicated that there were checks worth $4,395 received by the practice on January 31, 1984, which were not deposited into the bank, although they had been adjusted out of accounts receivable. On the following day (February 1, 1984) these checks were deposited in the bank. Since the cash was in hand and in the doctors' office, we have reflected this sum as if it were cash already received.

Exhibit 27–5

**TABLE V**
**INTERNAL MEDICINE ASSOCIATES, INC.**
**ADJUSTED ACCRUAL BASIS BALANCE SHEET**
**AS OF JANUARY 31, 1984**

| | As Shown | Adjustments Dr | Adjustments Cr | Adjusted Balance Sheet |
|---|---|---|---|---|
| **ASSETS** | | | | |
| Current Assets: | | | | |
| Cash & Equivalents | 908 | 4,395[a] | | 5,303 |
| Accounts Receivable | — | 119,954[b] | 119,954 | |
| Reserve for Uncollectibles | — | | 10,196[c] | (10,196) | 109,758 |
| Supplies | — | 1,250[d] | | 1,250 |
| Prepaid Insurance | — | 3,650[e] | | 3,650 |
| Total Current Assets | 908 | 129,429 | 10,196 | 119,961 |
| Furniture, Fixtures & Equipment | 12,540 | 31,000[f] | 12,540[f] | 31,000 |
| Library | — | 500[g] | | 500 |
| **TOTAL ASSETS** | 13,448 | 160,749 | 22,736 | 151,461 |
| **LIABILITIES & SHAREHOLDERS' EQUITY** | | | | |
| Liabilities: | | | | |
| Accounts Payable | — | | 4,695[h] | 4,695 |
| Payroll Taxes Payable | 445 | | 500[i] | 945 |
| Payroll Payable | — | | 5,000[j] | 5,000 |
| Total Liabilities | 445 | | 10,195 | 10,640 |
| Shareholders' Equity | 13,003 | 32,931[k] | 160,749[k] | 140,821 |
| **TOTAL LIABILITIES & SHAREHOLDERS' EQTY.** | 13,448 | | 170,944 | 155,461 |

[a] To add to assets and cash in transit, not shown in either bank balance or accounts receivable.

[b] To add to assets the face value of accounts receivable, per accounts receivable journal.

[c] To reduce accounts receivable for estimated uncollectible accounts (based on 8.5% historical write-off of receivables by practice).

[d] To add to assets the estimated value of supply inventory (medical and office) on hand.

[e] To add to assets six-month prepaid malpractice insurance for Drs. McNee and Chandler.

[f] To increase the value of fixed assets to "depreciated replacement cost," per equipment appraisal completed by ABC Equipment Appraisers.

[g] To add to assets the value of the professional library (estimated).

[h] To add unrecorded unpaid bills to liabilities.

[i] To increase payroll taxes payable for taxes due for pay period from 1/16/84 to 1/31/84.

[j] To add to liabilities the payroll due on 2/5/84 for pay period from 1/16/84 to 1/31/84.

[k] Reversing entries.

SOURCE: U.S. Corporate tax returns, practice's books and records, equipment appraisal report, and interview with Dr. McNee.

2. We recorded accounts receivable for services performed but for which fees have not yet been collected, and we also estimated the reserve for uncollectible accounts receivable. This reserve for uncollectible accounts was based upon a review of the past three years' accounts receivable activity to determine the percentage of the accounts that have been written off compared to total charges made.

3. Based on discussions with Dr. McNee, we determined that approximately $1,250 worth of medical and office supplies were in inventory at January 31, 1984.

4. Based upon a review of the malpractice and other liability insurance policies carried by the practice, $3,650 of previous expense was actually a prepaid asset of the practice as of the valuation date.

**5.** After reviewing an appraisal completed by ABC Equipment Appraisers, we have adjusted the furniture, fixtures, equipment, and leasehold improvements to $31,000 from a stated net book value of $12,540 to reflect more accurately the depreciated replacement value of those assets.

**6.** The last asset adjustment was to reflect a nominal ($500) value for the professional library maintained by the practice.

**7.** Various liabilities were recognized which had not been recorded on the books, including unpaid bills (accounts payable), additional payroll taxes, and payroll payable, which represents payroll due to the three nonowner employees for the period January 16 through January 31, 1984. According to Dr. McNee, this payroll will be paid on February 5, 1984.

As can be seen on Table V, the total value of the shareholders' equity in the clinic is equal to $140,821. Dr. McNee's 50 percent interest in this equity is equal to $70,400 (rounded).

# Professional Goodwill

We have also calculated the value of Dr. McNee's professional goodwill as of January 31, 1984.

We have used two primary methods for calculating this goodwill. The first method is commonly known as the *excess earnings* method; the second method considers the value received by Dr. McNee in the sale of the 50 percent interest in this practice to Dr. Chandler in February 1980.

**Excess Earnings.** Table VI (Exhibit 27–6) is a schedule of various earnings (compensation) surveys conducted by the publication *Medical Economics* and by the American Medical Association. These earnings represent not only salaries paid to self-employed physicians, but the net income of the practice and benefits received by each physician.

As can be seen from this schedule, we have considered all the categories that could possibly include Dr. McNee. In 1982 the comparative earnings of physicians such as Dr. McNee ranged from $75,000 (all internists, median) to $113,550 (all incorporated multiphysician practices, median). In choosing an appropriate comparative earnings figure, it is our opinion that the earnings of incorporated multiphysician practices is the best comparative earnings amount to use. Our investigation has revealed that the primary reason for Dr. McNee's high earnings (giving consideration to the hours he spends on practice-related activities) is generally a result of the economies of scale achieved by associating with Dr. Chandler. Also, various earnings surveys indicate that multiphysician practices usually have much higher income per practitioner, compared to a solo practitioner. For these reasons, we believe the most comparative earnings figure to use is the figure for incorporated multiphysician practices.

Table VII (Exhibit 27–7) is a calculation of the value of goodwill using the excess earnings method. Of the past three years of Dr. McNee's income, we have weighted fiscal year January 31, 1984 (iden-

Exhibit 27–6

**TABLE VI**
**INTERNAL MEDICINE ASSOCIATES, INC.**
**SCHEDULE OF COMPARATIVE COMPENSATION**

| | Compounded Average Annual Increase % | 1982 $ | 1981 $ | 1980 $ | 1979 $ |
|---|---|---|---|---|---|
| Median Compensation, All Physicians (1) | 6.73% | 93,270 | 86,210 | 83,700 | 76,720 |
| Median Compensation, All Internists (1) | 4.52% | 85,910 | 79,710 | 74,310 | 75,230 |
| Median Compensation, Far Western State Physicians (1) | 5.49% | 87,220 | 80,630 | 81,610 | 74,290 |
| Median Compensation, Incorporated Internists (1) | 5.69% | NA | 89,120 | 80,630 | 79,790 |
| Median Compensation, All Incorporated Multi-Physician Practices (1) | 8.76% | 113,550 | 108,600 | 100,210 | 88,270 |
| Median Compensation, All Physicians (2) | 6.69% | 85,000 | 78,000 | NA | 70,000 |
| Median Compensation, All Internists (2) | 2.33% | 75,000 | 74,500 | NA | 70,000 |
| Median Compensation, Far Pacific State Physicians(2) | 4.55% | 80,000 | 80,000 | NA | 70,000 |
| Median Compensation, Non-Solo Practice Physicians (2) | 8.74% | 90,000 | 81,000 | NA | 70,000 |
| Median Compensation, All Physicians in Metro Areas of 1,000,000 or Greater(2) | 4.55% | 80,000 | 75,000 | NA | 70,000 |
| Median Compensation, All Physicians between the Ages of 46 Years to 55 Years (2) | 7.72% | 100,000 | 95,000 | NA | 80,000 |

NA = Not available
**SOURCE:** (1) Annual earnings surveys, *Medical Economics*; (2) *Socioeconomic Characteristics of Medical Practice, 1983*, American Medical Association.

tified as 1983) one half of the total, 1982 one third, and 1981 one sixth. Based on these calculations, Dr. McNee's three-year weighted average compensation was equal to $177,665.

As previously mentioned, in our opinion, the median compensation of all incorporated multiphysician practices (for each practicing physician) is the best indicator of comparative earnings in comparison to Dr. McNee. As shown in Table VI, the compound average annual increase

Exhibit 27–7

**TABLE VII**
**INTERNAL MEDICINE ASSOCIATES, INC.**
**CALCULATION OF GOODWILL**
**USING EXCESS EARNINGS METHOD**

| | Year | Normal Compensation | Weighting Factor | Weighted Compensation | |
|---|---|---|---|---|---|
| Calculation of Dr. McNee's Weighted Average Normal Compensation (see Table IV): | 1983 | 181,764 × | 3 | 545,292 | |
| | 1982 | 174,998 × | 2 | 349,996 | |
| | 1981 | 170,694 × | 1 | 170,694 | |
| Total | | | 6 | 1,065,982 | |
| Divided by Sum of Weighting Factors | | | | 6 | |
| Dr. McNee's 3-year Weighted Average Compensation | | | | | 177,664 |

| | Year | Comparative Compensation | Weighting Factor | Weighted Compensation | |
|---|---|---|---|---|---|
| Calculation of Comparative Weighted Average Compensation: | 1983 | 123,497 × | 3 | 370,491 | |
| | 1982 | 113,550 × | 2 | 227,100 | |
| | 1981 | 108,600 × | 1 | 108,600 | |
| Total | | | 6 | 706,191 | |
| Divided by Sum of Weighting Factors | | | | 6 | |
| Comparative 3-year Weighted Average Compensation | | | | | 117,698 |
| Dr. McNee's Excess Earnings | | | | | 59,966 |
| Capitalized at 50% (Equal to a Multiple of 2) | | | | | 50% |
| Indicated Value of Dr. McNee's Goodwill (Rounded) | | | | | 120,000 |

SOURCE: Tables IV & VI.

in compensation for this group of doctors from 1979 through 1982 has been 8.76 percent. As of this date, no data are available for 1983, so we have estimated 1983's total compensation in this category to be equal to an 8.76 percent increase over the 1982 level. That would indicate a comparative compensation for 1983 of $123,497. By weighting these earnings in the same way as we weighted Dr. McNee's, we have derived a comparative three-year weighted average compensation level of $117,698 for a comparable physician. That indicates that Dr. McNee's excess earnings are equal to $59,966.

In choosing an appropriate rate at which to capitalize these excess earnings, we have given specific recognition to the following factors:

1. Excess earnings are generally considered to have a higher risk of being maintained compared to earnings that are primarily generated by a return on a passive investment.
2. Dr. McNee is at the end of what is generally regarded as the high income-producing years of a physician (generally, high-income years fall between the ages of 45 to 55 years).
3. Major changes are now occurring in the health care industry which are being mandated by government, health insurance underwriters and private industry to control the growth in costs of providing health care.

Generally, excess earnings are capitalized at rates from 20 percent (equal to a multiple of 5) to 100 percent (equal to a multiple of 1). The median multiple, 3, is equal to a capitalization rate of 33⅓ percent.

Because of the factors listed above, we believe that Dr. McNee's excess earnings should be capitalized at an amount greater than the median rate, and therefore it is our opinion that a capitalization rate of 50 percent (equal to a multiple of 2) is appropriate. These computations produce an indicated value of $120,000 (rounded) for Dr. McNee's goodwill.

# Prior Transactions

One of the most reliable methods of valuing a practice, if the information is available, is a prior transaction in the practice being appraised. Fortunately, such a transaction is available for guidance in this valuation. As discussed earlier in this report, in 1981, Dr. Chandler purchased a 50 percent interest in the practice for $100,000. Of this amount, $25,000 was allocated to goodwill (in accordance with the buy-in agreement). As previously mentioned, our investigation revealed that this transaction was an arm's length sale of 50 percent of this practice and that the allocation of net tangible asset value and goodwill value appeared to be reasonable.

However, that $100,000 was not the only value received by Dr. McNee. A review of the appointment books revealed that Dr. McNee and Dr. Chandler have both worked an equal amount of time in the practice and have seen approximately the same number of patients per day. However, the employment agreement signed at the same time as the sale of the 50 percent interest indicated that Dr. McNee would receive a larger portion of the earnings of the practice for three years than would Dr. Chandler. The percentages were discussed earlier in this report. Therefore, Dr. McNee was receiving additional compensation, even though he was not seeing more patients or spending more time with the practice than was Dr. Chandler. Therefore, the difference between half of the officers' salaries and the amount received by Dr. McNee is an additional payment received by Dr. McNee for each of the three years that the employment agreement was in existence. Table VIII (Exhibit 27–8) shows the calculations of these excess payments. As this table discloses, Dr. McNee received the following excess payments:

| | |
|---|---|
| 1981 | $41,500 |
| 1982 | 25,800 |
| 1983 | 14,625 |

We have discounted the value of these payments to recognize that, as of the sale date, they were not worth their full face value. Because many uncertainties exist at the sale date for any enterprise, we believe that relatively high yield rates should be realized on these types of future payments and therefore have used a yield rate of 20 percent. Discounting these payments (as of the sale date) to give an annual yield of 20 percent produces the following present values for each of the future payments:

| | |
|---|---|
| 1981 | $34,583 |
| 1982 | 17,917 |
| 1983 | 8,463 |

Exhibit 27–8

### TABLE VIII
### INTERNAL MEDICINE ASSOCIATES, INC.
### CALCULATION OF GOODWILL
### USING PRIOR TRANSACTION

| | | | |
|---|---|---|---|
| Cash Payment Made by Dr. Chandler for 50% of Corporate stock | | 100,000 | |
| Less: Portion Attributable to Net Tangible Assets | | (75,000) | |
| Cash Payment Received for Goodwill Value | | | 25,000 |
| Calculation of Present Value (at Sale Date) of Deferred Payments (Agreed-Upon Reduction in Dr. Chandler's Salary and Increase in Dr. McNee's Salary): | | | |
| Dr. McNee's 1981 Officer Salary | | 156,500 | |
| 1981 Total Officer Salaries | 230,000 | | |
| 50% of 1981 Officer Salaries | x    50% | 115,000 | |
| Excess Payments Received by Dr. McNee | | 41,500 | |
| Present Value Factor—Payable at the End of 12 Months to Yield 20% | | 0.83333 | |
| Present Value of 1981 Deferred Payments | | | 34,583 |
| Dr. McNee's 1982 Officer Salary | | 154,800 | |
| 1982 Total Officer Salaries | 258,000 | | |
| 50% of 1982 Officer Salaries | x    50% | 129,000 | |
| Excess Payments Received by Dr. McNee | | 25,800 | |
| Present Value Factor—Payment at the End of 24 Months to Yield 20% | | 0.69444 | |
| Present Value of 1982 Deferred Payments | | | 17,917 |
| Dr. McNee's 1983 Officer Salary | | 160,875 | |
| 1983 Total Officer Salaries | 292,500 | | |
| 50% of 1983 Officer Salaries | x    50% | 146,250 | |
| Excess Payments Received by Dr. McNee | | 14,625 | |
| Present Value Factor—Payable at the End of 36 Months to Yield 20% | | 0.57870 | |
| Present Value of 1983 Deferred Payments | | | 8,463 |
| Present Value of Payments Received by Dr. McNee for Goodwill Value as of Sale Date | | | 85,963 |

**SOURCE:** Sale agreements and employment agreements between Drs. McNee and Chandler.

Adding these amounts to the original $25,000 received for goodwill value produces a total value for goodwill of $85,963.

**Goodwill Valuation Conclusion.**   Based upon the two methods for calculating the value of professional goodwill, considered in this report, we have a valuation range of $86,000 to $120,000. In testing these values, we have considered the results of a survey conducted by Management Consulting for Professionals, Inc. (Bala Cynwyd, Pennsylvania), which compares the goodwill value paid in sales of 100 percent of practices against that practice's latest year's fees. That survey showed that, in 1983, practices generally were selling with a goodwill value equal to 25 percent to 38 percent of the prior year's fees received.

Another rule of thumb for the valuation of a medical practice (besides goodwill plus equipment and supplies) is that the practice should sell for 20 percent to 60 percent of the latest year's revenues. Although Dr. McNee's practice has been established for over 24 years, the current economic and medical industry conditions would tend to dilute its value. For that reason, in our opinion, the appropriate percentage would be 33. Applying that percentage rate to the practice's last year's fees would produce a value of $160,000 (rounded). Dr. McNee's interest in that goodwill figure would equal $80,000.

Considering the excess earnings and actual transaction methods, it is our opinion that the actual transaction is a more appropriate method for this particular case, because we have an arm's-length sale between Dr. McNee and Dr. Chandler for a 50 percent interest in the practice we are appraising. Also, the value is relatively close to the range of goodwill values according to the Management Consulting Professionals, Inc., survey. Therefore, in our opinion, the value of Dr. McNee's professional goodwill is equal to $86,000.

## Valuation Conclusion

Based upon the analysis completed in this report and the conclusions reached, it is our opinion that the value for Dr. McNee's professional goodwill and his 50 percent interest in the corporation known as Internal Medicine Associates, Inc., is equal to:

| | |
|---|---:|
| One Half Equity in Practice (Rounded) | $ 70,500 |
| Professional Goodwill | 86,000 |
| Total Value | $156,500 |

# Part V

## Valuations for Specific Purposes

# Chapter 28

## Buying or Selling a Business or Practice

The ultimate objective of the buyer's and seller's valuation deliberations is to arrive at a *price* and a set of *terms* acceptable to both of them. Consequently, this chapter attempts to give equal consideration to the perspectives of both the buyer and the seller. Besides the entity's fair market value (as defined in Chapter 2), these factors bear on the price determined to be mutually acceptable:

1. Special circumstances of the particular buyer and seller.
2. Tradeoff between cash and terms (as discussed in Chapter 17).
3. Relative tax consequences for the buyer and seller, which depend on how the transaction is structured.

All too often, however, price negotiations become an exercise in futility because the prospective buyers and sellers never should have gotten that far in the first place. For that reason, we will step back from the price negotiations and consider briefly the decision to sell or buy that must precede the determination of the specific price.

# To Sell or Not to Sell

Ideally, the nonfinancial reasons for selling would become manifest at the same time that buyers would be willing to pay the seller an attractive price for the business. Unfortunately, it is usually true that the desire to sell does not coincide with the timing for the best price attainable. A prospective seller who considers in advance factors that affect the sell decision and factors that affect the price can synchronize his sell decision with conditions that bring a good price.

## Reasons to Sell

Common reasons to sell a business include the following:

1. Death of an owner.
2. Ill health.
3. Retirement.
4. Desire to start a new business or alternate career.
5. Boredom.
6. Frustration and/or disillusionment.
7. Disputes among owners.
8. Need for a parent company with the capital and resources necessary to perpetuate the business and realize its growth potential.
9. Poor financial condition and/or losing money.

Several of the reasons are so strong that they may be defined as *compulsion;* they are discussed under "Differing Perceptions and Circumstances of Sellers and Buyers," later in this chapter.

# Factors Affecting Price

Some of the most important factors affecting price are the following:

1. Recent profit history.
2. General condition of the company (such as condition of facilities, completeness and accuracy of books and records, morale, and so on).
3. Market demand for the particular type of business.
4. Economic conditions (especially cost and availability of capital and any economic factors that directly affect the business).
5. Ability to transfer goodwill or other intangible values to a new owner.
6. Future profit potential.

# Timing of the Sell Decision

When comparing these lists of reasons to sell and factors affecting price, it becomes obvious that the reasons to sell are not necessarily likely to surface at the same time that the business is most ripe for sale in terms of the factors affecting price. Owners who wish to sell their business at the best possible price should consider the following suggestions:

1. Anticipate the possibility of a sale, whether or not one is imminent, and prepare accordingly.
2. Make the sale when the timing is good from a financial standpoint, rather than holding back and risking a forced sale under less advantageous circumstances.
3. Hold off on selling when the seller is convinced that significantly higher profitability is on the immediate horizon, especially if the full potential of the increased profitability would not be immediately apparent to an outsider (which is almost always the case). If this realization does not materialize, however, especially if there is a downturn, it could be a significant loss to the seller.

In some respects, there is an inherent conflict between running the business the way an owner likes on an ongoing basis and preparing the business for sale. An owner typically makes a variety of discretionary expenditures that result in reduced reported profits. It may or may not be possible to convince a prospective buyer to adjust fully for these items when assessing profitability. An owner may do many things his own way when he is operating the business, but this may not make the business most attractive to the typical potential buyer. Ideally, the efforts to sell should be aimed at a time when the business can put its best foot forward.

Some owners find the decision to sell emotionally difficult to reach. Victor Niederhoffer, operating as a broker who finds small companies available to be purchased by larger companies, puts it this way:

It's very threatening to sell your company, perhaps harder than getting married. Some sellers get neurotic and kind of flip out. They let emotion get in the way of facts and analysis.

We're working with one guy who probably ruined his chances of selling his company. Two years ago, he was approached by a company that wanted to pick up his company at book value. Out of a fear of getting taken, he picked out a price out of the air, three times the company's worth. He's left for Germany. I don't think he'll ever sell his company.[1]

Sellers often procrastinate when the timing for the sale is financially opportune, and then they decide to sell later, after the economy, or other factors, have made it inopportune and it is impossible to find buyers willing to pay as much as they would when conditions were better. If an active owner dies, value almost always diminishes because the owner is no longer available to facilitate the transfer of goodwill to a new owner.

If the owner is confident of a sharp rise in profits, it will almost always be financially beneficial to keep the business until the increased profitability can be demonstrated to a buyer rather than just projected. Concerning the decision to keep or sell a small business, Stephen Einhorn, an acquisition specialist, has this to say:

> **Step I. Determine future profits: If I don't sell the business, what will be the most probable result?. . .**
>
> Step I is the key step in discussions with the potential seller. If his expectations and justifications for his future estimated results differ dramatically from most purchasers' perception of his potential, he probably is not truly prepared to sell his business. An owner who knows that his business is about to improve quickly and substantially, would not normally want to sell his temporarily undervalued business.[2]

Niederhoffer cites a case in point: "One company projected $800,000 in earnings for the year ahead, when it had three years of $100,000 earnings. A prospective buyer asked them why they didn't just wait a year to show the $800,000, and then sell. It was a reasonable question."[3]

A recent article in the *Harvard Business Review* makes the following points regarding picking the right time to sell:

> Timing is everything in selling a company. Here are a few suggestions regarding timing:
>
> Sell when business profits show a strong upward trend.
>
> Sell when the management team is complete and experienced.
>
> Sell when the business cycle is on the upswing, with potential buyers in the right mood and holding excess capital or credit for acquisitions.
>
> Sell when you are convinced that your company's future will be bright.
>
> Don't sell when the opposite of any of the previous suggestions holds.[4]

[1] "Getting Top Dollar for Your Company," *Inc.*, April 1980, p. 84.

[2] Stephen Einhorn, "Notes on the Decision to Keep or Sell a Small Business," *Mergers & Acquisitions*, Summer 1977, pp. 29–30.

[3] "Getting Top Dollar," p. 84.

[4] Charles W. O'Conor, "Packaging Your Business for Sale," *Harvard Business Review*, March-April, 1985, p. 56.

# Preparing the Business for Sale

One broker offers the following explanation of the need for long-term preparation for the sale of a business:

> In many cases, for reasons of age or health, the owner will find it necessary to sell his business.
>
> When he attempts to sell, his past use of accounting and financial management techniques for the primary purpose of tax avoidance produces the predictable result that he is either unable to sell the business or must sell it at a grossly understated value.
>
> **Reconstruction of records:** It is possible to reconstruct the financial statements of a small business to show the true net operating income and therefore give an accurate indication of the value of that business. However, such reconstruction aggravates the problem of selling the business at its true value because reconstruction may result in claims for back income taxes and penalties for the owner.
>
> Thus a small business owner must either sell at an understated value or plan a five- to seven-year preparation period for selling, based on accurate financial statements. This lead time is required so that accounting methods can be altered gradually over a three- to four-year period, thus avoiding IRS investigation and so that several years of accurate financial statements will be available to a prospective purchaser.[5]

The previously referenced *Harvard Business Review* article makes the following observation: "More often than not, the successful sale of smaller companies is the result of a carefully orchestrated long-term strategy. Making the strategy work are effective financial planning, internal organization, timing, and valuation analysis."[6]

The following are six suggestions for preparing the business for sale:

1. Have excellent records.
2. Clean up the balance sheet.
3. Have a good profit record.
4. Have the business in good general condition.
5. Have adequate personnel.
6. Do a valuation analysis.

## Have Excellent Records

Excellent records will help a seller to obtain the best possible price for his business, in most cases. The most credible statements are five or more years of financial statements audited by a CPA firm. The next best would be financial statements reviewed by a CPA firm. After that would be statements compiled by an outside CPA, including the footnoted disclosures that normally would be included in audited or reviewed statements. Internally prepared statements should be done as meticulously as possible and accord as closely as possible with proce-

---

[5] Robert F. Everett, "What is the Business Worth?" *Real Estate Today*, October 1978, p. 46.
[6] O'Conor, "Packaging Your Business," p. 52.

dures that would be used if an independent CPA were preparing them. If the company has only tax returns, good supporting documents should be readily available.

Good supporting schedules of the details contained within line items found on the statements are very helpful. Detailed schedules of expenses are especially useful if items are categorized so that they are comparable with industry averages. The list of property and equipment, and the related depreciation schedule, should be complete and up to date.

In general, the material listed in Exhibit 35–1, "Documents and Information Checklist for Valuation of Business or Professional Practice," should be as complete and accurate as possible.

## Clean Up the Balance Sheet

By "cleaning up the balance sheet," I mean removing items that a purchaser would consider undesirable. Such items would be most likely to include any nonoperating assets. If the business owns real estate, the seller may be wise to place the real estate in a separate corporation or partnership, charging rent at a market rate to the business or practice that is to be sold. In some cases, the same course might be advantageous for machinery and equipment. Depending on the nature of the business and the potential buyer, the seller may be able to get more for the business itself by keeping the hard assets and leasing them to a new owner than by selling them in a package with the business. (If there is any question about how to handle the fixed assets, the prudent owner will seek guidance from a business broker familiar with the particulars of selling his type of business.)

Many companies keep negative balances in their cash accounts, operating on the "float" provided by checks outstanding but not yet drawn from the account. This practice appears on the balance sheet either as a negative balance in the cash account on the asset side or as an overdraft on the liability side, neither of which looks very sound to readers of balance sheets. The seller should try to have a positive balance in the cash account as of the balance sheet date, even if it means delaying a few payables.

## Have a Good Profit Record

A good profit record probably is the single most important factor in preparing the business to sell for the best possible price. The best record is one of profits increasing steadily each year, with the profitability for the period immediately prior to the offer to sell at, or above, industry averages according to such measures as return on equity, return on assets, and return on sales. Establishing a good profit record may require careful management and relinquishing some hidden perks for a time, but it should be worthwhile to be able to produce a well-documented record of profitability at the time of the sale.

# Have the Business in Good General Condition

Like a house, car, or almost anything else, a business should fetch a better price if everything is clean, neat, and in good working order. Inventory should be current and well balanced. Promotional material should be attractive and up to date. Everything should work together efficiently and harmoniously.

# Have Adequate Personnel

A buyer is likely to look more favorably on a business if the personnel needed to perform the various tasks are in place, well trained, and working together with esprit. A buyer is likely to discount the price if he faces the chore of recruiting and training new personnel.

# Do a Valuation Analysis

A valuation analysis will help the seller determine a range of reasonable prices before exposing the business to the marketplace. He should find out at what prices similar businesses are selling currently and compare their prices to their revenues, earnings, assets, and other fundamental factors. A complete, written appraisal is not necessary for determining a range of acceptable prices. The seller should have in mind at least an objectively determined negotiating range before his first serious conversation with a potential buyer or broker about listing the business.

A written appraisal report, however, may be useful by providing more detailed information for the buyer, as well as for some potential sources of buyer financing, if the seller chooses not to carry a contract. The expense of a credible written appraisal report may be recovered many times over if the selling price increases over what might be achieved without such a report. Even if a lower price is indicated by the independent appraisal, it may make the seller more realistic about the selling price and therefore help facilitate the transaction.

# Deciding What to Buy

Some successful entrepreneurs will buy almost anything that comes along if they find it interesting and think the price is right—but not very many of them. Most who will buy almost anything eventually go broke because, sooner or later, they overextend themselves on what turns out to be a bad deal. This occasionally happens several times. (Entrepreneurs are very resilient.) Successful potpourri buyers succeed "on balance;" that is, they succeed because some good winners offset the losses from many mistakes.

I do not advocate that most potential buyers take a shotgun approach to potential acquisition targets. I suggest that a potential buyer carefully think out and write down his criteria for a business that he would consider buying, that he diligently pursue businesses worthy of consideration, and that he make an offer only for a business that meets the predetermined criteria. At a minimum, the list of criteria for a potential purchase should cover the following points:

1. The type of business or practice.
2. Acceptable geographic locations.
3. The minimum and maximum size the buyer considers worthwhile and that he is realistically capable of managing.
4. The amount of cash available for purchase. (If outside sources are to be used, the buyer should at least explore the availability of funds from such sources before he goes shopping for a business.)
5. Whether, and for how long, the buyer will need assistance from existing management, and/or the duration and structure of a management transition period.
6. Whether the buyer wants a smooth-running and profitable operation, or a "fixer-upper," an operation currently not doing so well.

With these and any other relevant criteria firmly in mind, the buyer should be ready to screen brokers' listings and companies advertised in newspapers and trade publications in order to develop a list of possibilities for purchase.

# Preparing to Make an Offer

Once the buyer has screened potential acquisitions and identified one or a few that meet his criteria, it is time for him to do his own valuation analysis. He may do one on his own or consult with a business appraiser, or he may have the appraiser prepare the whole analysis. His analysis should cover the elements discussed in this book, but usually will not require a formal written report.

In preparing to make an offer, the buyer and/or his appraiser should have available all the documents listed in Exhibit 35–1, "Documents and Information Checklist for Valuation of Business or Professional Practice." Moreover, they should have access to whatever records are necessary to verify any items that may be unclear or in question. If the seller is unwilling to supply enough documentation for the buyer to be totally comfortable with his offer, the buyer should walk away and consider something else. The financial and nonfinancial investment in a business is too high to buy a pig in a poke. Naturally, however, the buyer should be willing to sign a confidentiality agreement with respect to the seller's information.

A special problem arises when the seller and prospective buyer are competitors; should the deal fall through, the seller would be at a competitive disadvantage if the buyer had access to his financial information. I have seen the buyer handling this situation by engaging an independent appraiser to analyze the information, with the independent appraiser keeping most of the details confidential from the buyer until the negotiations appeared very likely to result in a completed transaction.

Buyers almost always expect to improve the profitability of the business they are considering buying. They should prepare pro forma statements, as discussed in Chapter 9, that reflect their expectations for the business under their ownership. The further into the future the buyer can prepare meaningful pro forma statements the better; but no benefit is derived from extending them to the point where they are completely speculative.

Arnold Goldstein, a veteran small business dealmaker, has this to say:

> When I counsel prospective buyers, I use a *pro forma* profit and loss statement. Before I even allow a buyer to think price, I put him through the exercise of planning his profit profile. Not only does this quantify earnings expectation, it forces the buyer to think through virtually every phase of the business as he would operate it.
>
> To get to that bottom line, the buyer starts at the top with sales and works his way down, through anticipated cost of goods and every last expense. Once he defines, justifies, and verifies each item on his projected P&L, he can measure forecasted earnings with some degree of confidence.[7]

The buyer's appraisal of the business as it stands (which may be somewhat less than the seller's appraisal of the business as it stands) probably represents the floor of a negotiating range, provided that the seller is under no compulsion to sell. A capitalization of earnings or discounted cash flow analysis, based on the buyer's pro forma statements (assuming that they are soundly conceived), should provide the absolute top of a negotiating range.

Conditions in the market for the particular kind of business or practice will determine where in the range an offer is likely to be successful without being too high. The buyer should investigate recent sales of comparative companies or practices and the supply and demand for the particular type of company, in order to assess how much, if any, premium should be offered over the value of the company as it stands, before considering any improvement to profits caused by the buyer's efforts. Comparative transactions are very difficult to find. A business broker may be able to be helpful in this regard, perhaps using transaction data such as described in the following chapter.

# Differing Perceptions and Circumstances of Sellers and Buyers

> Value is nothing more than perception, and we each bring to the valuation process our own ideas on what that "right" perception is. . . .
>
> That's what makes the process of placing a value on a business so interesting. So few buyers and sellers share that same perspective.[8]

[7] Arnold S. Goldstein, *The Complete Guide to Buying and Selling a Business* (New York: New American Library, 1983), p. 105.
[8] Ibid., p. 95.

Frequently, buyers and sellers use different criteria to reach conclusions about a particular business's value to them; each has his own reasons, which are valid under their respective circumstances. Obviously, both must be satisfied, whether or not for different reasons, in order for a transaction to be consummated. Goldstein's experience has led him to be somewhat caustic about the extent to which rationality influences many buyers' and sellers' assessments of their own situations.

> For every knowledgeable buyer or seller there are five others whose value system is on the blink. They invariably end up wondering about the deal that never was or worse—buying or selling at precisely the wrong price.[9]

> Having handled over 1500 transactions, I can assure you from first-hand experience that the rationality of the numbers seldom sells the buyer, but rather it's what the business does to the buyer's mind. For the small business buyer it's probably 80 percent psychological and 20 percent arithmetic. It may be an ego trip or a certain lifestyle. For the unemployed, the business may represent a tonic for anxiety and insecurity. A seller may simply be too tired or aggravated to continue, or perhaps his energies are directed to a new career.[10]

## Assessment of Future Profits and Risk

The overexuberance typical of sellers is exemplified by one more quote from Niederhoffer:

> A buyer is looking for a company that's going to keep growing, but I've never met a seller who doesn't think his business won't be three times bigger five years down the road. And they'll tell you that with unlimited capital their businesses would be tenfold larger. . . . Sellers always believe their companies will grow, but only half of them will. . . . All sellers believe their geese are swans.[11]

There is evidence, however, that buyers also tend to be overoptimistic:

> Statistics prove that past performance does not always hold up under new management. Buyers usually expect to equal past performance, but a study conducted by Northeastern University shows that 80 percent of the buyers surveyed responded that they thought they could *improve* profits by 50 percent or more. How accurate were they? Of the 80 percent who believed they would greatly increase profits "under *new* management":

> > 55 percent earned *less* money than their predecessors.

> > 25 percent only nominally increased profits, or continued to operate at the same level of profitability.

> > 15 percent increased profits by up to 49 percent.

> > Only 5 percent of the respondents fulfilled their prophecy by actually increasing profits by 50 percent or more.

---

[9] Ibid., pp. 95–96.
[10] Ibid., p.103.
[11] "Getting Top Dollar," p. 84.

I concluded that those interviewed didn't *project* profits, they only *predicted* them. There's a big difference. Most buyers look at the business through rose-colored glasses, assuming they can do better than the old management. As the survey showed, that's a dangerous assumption. Had new owners *projected* profits, they would have taken off the rose-colored glasses and realistically extrapolated the numbers.[12]

Obviously, different expectations of future profits logically would lead buyers and sellers to reach different conclusions of value. The foregoing quotes, however, suggest that both buyers and sellers tend to overestimate future profits. This condition can lead to transactions that are consummated at prices higher than the values that the parties would have estimated if their expectations of future profits had been accurate. I believe that the foregoing quotations do characterize the reality of the small business market and that more businesses sell above, than sell below, the values indicated if the prices were based on accurate projections of future profits.

The bias toward overpricing is further exacerbated by buyers, sellers, and small business brokers who tend to underestimate the risk, thus leading to unjustifiably low capitalization rates (that is, multiples that are too high).

# Opportunity

As I mentioned elsewhere in this book, it's interesting that the classified ads in most newspapers don't list businesses for sale, but rather business opportunities. I know business brokers who adhere to the philosophy that a buyer should never pay more than the value of the business as it stands (which may be less than the tangible asset value). The value of any opportunity would be part of the buyer's profits that result from a judicious entrepreneurial exploitation of the opportunity. I know other brokers who believe that a buyer should always pay more than the tangible asset value for the opportunity that comes with the business.

The value of opportunity per se is a matter for each individual to decide, not a matter that can be financially analyzed. I do not buy state lottery tickets because I am unwilling to accept a 40 cent average expected return for my dollar, in order to have the opportunity for the big win. However, I appreciate the fact that my taxes are lower than they otherwise might be because many other people do choose to buy them, thus contributing large sums of money to state treasuries. In other words, lottery tickets sell at a fair market value of $1 even though that price is about two and a half times their investment value (intrinsic or fundamental value) of $.40. Prices at which some businesses sell bear a similar relationship. I'm not sure how much of such premiums over investment value represent willingness to pay for opportunity and how much really represent failure to analyze investment value adequately.

---

[12] Goldstein, *Complete Guide*, pp. 104–5.

# Personal Rewards

A buyer may be willing to pay more than the value indicated by financial analysis because of personal rewards. He may fall in love with the physical location of an operation. The business may conduct an activity the buyer enjoys as a hobby. The buyer may desire the prestige associated with ownership of a certain business, or he may find the location and operating hours especially convenient. It certainly can be advantageous to a seller to find a buyer who perceives extra value in the business because of intangible personal benefits, whatever they may be.

# Synergism

One of the most important factors that may add to the transaction price in a sale, over and above its value on a stand-alone basis, is *synergism*, the concept that the value of the combined operations is greater than the sum of the values of the individual operations. An example would be two pickle packers, one with substantial excess production capacity and the other without nearly enough capacity to serve the demand created by its very successful marketing.

If there really is synergism, as there often may be between potential merger mates, how much of the value of the synergism will the seller be able to add into the selling price, and how much will be left to be reflected in the buyer's future returns? The answer, of course, is a matter of negotiation, but the respective parties' negotiating posture depends to a great extent on supply of, and demand for, the particular type of company. If many such companies are available for sale and there is only one buyer, or a few potential buyers, very little synergism is likely to be reflected in the transaction price. On the other hand, if there are only one or a few similar companies available for sale, and several active potential buyers, the seller is likely to be able to receive a premium for a significant portion of the synergism.

Obviously, it is in the seller's interest to seek out buyers who would have synergism with the selling company, because such buyers might well be able to afford to pay more than anybody else for the particular company.

# Compulsion

The definition of fair market value assumes that neither buyer nor seller is under any compulsion to buy or to sell. In many cases in the real world, that assumption is not met, and compulsion leads to the transfer of businesses at prices that are different from what reasonably might be considered to be fair market value.

The most common source of compulsion that drives owners to sell is probably foreclosure of credit, usually by banks. Other common sources of compulsion are illness, death of an owner or family member, and irreconcilable differences among present owners; these make it virtually impossible to operate the business effectively under current ownership.

Compulsion affecting buyers arises most often because of synergistic effects that might be lost if the deal falls through. For example, a buyer might feel compelled to buy the business of a key customer from the estate of a deceased owner in order to keep it from failing or falling into the hands of a competitor.

# Structuring a Deal

Tax and other consequences of the structure of a transaction can have a significant impact on the transaction price. The following points are broadly generalized simplifications, and I recommend that both seller and buyer consult a tax attorney and/or an accountant regarding tax and legal implications of the terms of the transaction.

## Stock versus Asset Sale

As noted elsewhere, the smaller the business the more likely is the transaction to involve a transfer of assets rather than of corporate stock, even if the selling company is a corporation.

Generally speaking, from a tax viewpoint, an asset transaction is more favorable to the buyer and a stock transaction more favorable to the seller. In a stock transaction, the seller receives capital gains treatment on the difference between his cost basis and the amount received, and the buyer's cost basis for the assets remains the same as the seller's cost basis. In an asset transaction, the buyer gets a new cost basis, as well as investment tax credits in some cases, for the assets purchased, but the seller is subject to ordinary income tax for any depreciation recapture and/or gain on inventory.

## Selling on an Installment Contract

Most sellers would prefer to sell for cash; usually, however, they ultimately sell for some combination of cash and a contract on the balance carried by the seller. This happens because most buyers of small businesses do not have the resources to pay the full purchase price in cash. See Chapter 17, "Tradeoff between Cash and Terms," for a discussion of how to price a sale on an installment contract to achieve the desired cash equivalent value.

A contract sale is automatically treated as an installment sale for tax purposes (regardless of the amount of the down payment or even if there is no down payment); this means that the seller pays taxes on the proceeds in the year he receives them. The seller, however, has the option of "electing" to include all the profit in the year of sale by reporting the transaction on IRS Form 4797.

When a seller accepts an installment contract, he is putting himself in the position of a lender; and the contract should contain the same kind of protective covenants that a bank or other lender would require. Such covenants usually cover such items as limiting salaries and withdrawals of the new owners, preventing pledging the assets as collateral for other debt, and maintaining certain financial ratios and levels of working capital and net worth. I can tell you a variety of horror stories involving contract sales without such covenants, in which the buyer soon got the company in such a position that he was unable to make the contract payments.

## Selling for Stock of the Buying Company

If a selling corporation receives the stock of the purchasing company, the transaction may be treated as a tax-free exchange, meaning that the seller does not pay taxes on the gain until he eventually sells the stock of the buying corporation. Of course, receiving stock in another company creates the whole problem of appraising the stock of the buying company, lest the seller find himself in the position of the little boy who sold his dog for $10,000, receiving two $5,000 cats as the consideration.

Also, stock of a publicly traded corporation received in exchange for another company normally is restricted from resale on the open market for a period of two years. Restricted stock usually is valued at a discount from freely tradable stock.[13]

## Leveraged Buyouts

The willingness of banks and other institutions to make loans for leveraged buyouts, including leveraged buyouts of small businesses, has made this form of transaction increasingly popular in recent years. The basic concept of the leveraged buyout is to use the assets of the selling company as collateral for a loan to buy the business. According to a recent *Business Week* article:

> Banks commonly lend up to 85 percent on accounts receivable and 40 percent to 60 percent on inventory, usually on a five-to-seven year payout at interest from 1 to 2½ percentage points above the prime rate, depending on the quality of the security. Leveraged buyouts can be the answer when the company is strong on assets, which will support bank loans, but not so strong on earnings, or when the new management thinks it can run the company on a leaner basis and thus squeeze out more earnings to service the new debt.[14]

The same article suggests that small businesses that do not have enough assets to secure a completely leveraged deal might be able to

---

[13] For data on discounts for restricted stock, see "Data on Discounts for Lack of Marketability," Chapter 10 in Pratt, *Valuing a Business.*

[14] Bradley Hitchings, "Selling Your Small Company," *Business Week,* February 4, 1985, p. 100.

sell on the basis of a partly leveraged buyout. The buyer could raise part of the purchase price by means of a bank loan secured by the company's assets and give the seller a contract for the balance secured by the company's stock. Naturally, it is in the interest of both the buyer and the seller to analyze carefully the company's ability to pay off both the bank loan and the seller's contract.

# Earn-Outs

If the buyer and seller would like to make a deal but can't get together on a cash price because of differing earnings expectations or different degrees of confidence in the projections, the answer is sometimes to structure the transaction with some amount of cash and a specified participation in earnings for a certain period of time, often three to five years. There is no limit to the variety of earn-out arrangements. For example, the *Business Week* article cited earlier suggests that if earnings before interest and taxes exceed 25 percent on the buyer's investment, the sellers might receive 40 percent of the excess for a specified period of time. In some cases, a minimum and/or maximum amount for the earn-out may be indicated.

My advice to sellers contemplating an earn-out arrangement is to be sure that they retain control of the operation for the full period of the earn-out, in order to protect themselves from changes in personnel and policies that might diminish or eliminate the value of the earn-out.

# Contingencies

Occasionally an unresolved contingency remains at the time a transaction is contemplated. The most common contingencies are the outcome of lawsuits, settlements of tax liabilities or refunds from past periods, and costs of compliance with regulatory requirements. In such cases, the problem of the uncertain effect of the contingency's outcome on the value of the entity can be solved by creating an escrow account. Any proceeds from collection of contingent amounts, or money left over after payment of contingent liabilities, can be distributed from the escrow account to the seller.

# Covenants Not to Compete

In approximately half of the sales of small businesses and professional practices, the seller provides the buyer with a covenant not to compete. The covenant usually covers certain activities within a specific geographical area for a specific period of time. It may be incorporated into the purchase agreement, or it may be a separate document. Payments over the life of a covenant not to compete are ordinary income to the seller and tax-deductible expenses to the buyer.

# Allocating the Purchase Price

From the buyer's viewpoint, the most desirable objective is to allocate as much of the purchase price as possible to assets that can be expensed, depreciated, or amortized most quickly. The seller normally would have an opposite viewpoint, since the kind of allocations that create the most write-offs for the buyer tend to create the most ordinary income, as opposed to capital gains, for the seller.

The buyer normally wants to see as much of the purchase price as possible allocated to such items as inventory and quickly depreciable fixed assets. The buyer normally would also like to have as much of the total price as possible allocated to the covenant not to compete, since such payments will be charged to expenses as paid. The buyer prefers to have little or none of the purchase price allocated to goodwill, because goodwill cannot be amortized for income tax purposes.

If the purchase price significantly exceeds the value of the tangible assets, many buyers examine the possibility of allocating some or all of the excess to specifically identifiable, intangible assets that can be amortized, such as customer lists. Chapter 32 deals with the subject of identifying and valuing specific intangible assets. The justification for the allocation to various depreciable and amortizable assets should be thoroughly documented in writing. If there is to be no allocation to a covenant not to compete, that should be specified in the purchase contract.

The relative tax circumstances of the buyer and seller usually have a major bearing on the eventual agreement about allocating the purchase price, and the agreement may have a measurable impact on the price finally agreed upon.

# Chapter 29

## Special Report: Survey of Small Business and Professional Practice Transaction Prices

By far the most important missing tool among those available to assist in valuing small businesses and professional practices is the lack of readily available data on prices of comparative transactions. This chapter presents the results of two sets of such data compiled during 1985. One compilation was done by Willamette Management Associates, Inc., a business appraisal firm; and the other by UBI Business Brokers, a franchise business brokerage chain.

# The Willamette Business Sale Data Base

The Willamette Management Associates, Inc., Business Sale Data Base is compiled from transactions submitted by business brokerages offices throughout the United States. The 78 brokerage offices participating in this program up to press time are listed in the acknowledgments at the beginning of this book. They represent 30 states and all regions of the country. Material from the Willamette data base is available to business brokers on a reciprocal basis and to others on a fee basis.

In order to maintain the confidentiality of the data, no company names are included, and the location of the business or practice is included only by state in most cases. If a business is fairly unusual, and thus easily identified by its location, only a broad geographical region is included instead of the specific state.

## Description of the Willamette Data Base

Exhibit 29–1 is the form used for the collection of the general data for each transaction. In addition, the following income and asset information is requested:

1. Sales.
2. Seller's discretionary cash (SDC) (income before owner's compensation, depreciation, interest, and taxes).
3. Owner's compensation.
4. Earnings before depreciation, interest, and taxes (EBDIT).
5. Earnings before interest and taxes (EBIT).
6. Earnings before taxes (EBT).
7. Net book value of tangible assets included in the sale.
8. Net value of assets included in the sale, adjusted to market value (defined as the current used cost to the buyer, including transportation and installation).

From the data above, it is possible to calculate the following ratios:

1. Price/sales.
2. Price/SDC.
3. Price/EBDIT.

**4.** Price/EBDT.

**5.** Price/EBIT.

**6.** Price/EBT.

**7.** Price/tangible book value.

**8.** Price/tangible net asset value at market.

# General Results of the Willamette Data Base

At press time, the Willamette data base included several hundred transactions, most of which took place in 1984 and 1985, scattered through about 60 industry groups. I found the following statistics from the overall data base especially interesting for typical small business and professional practice transaction characteristics.

Exhibit 29–1

BUSINESS VALUATION DATA BASE
TRANSACTION RECORD

1.   Type of Business
     Please give short description of business or major project line(s).

2.   Location of Business
     City and State—if multiple locations, please give headquarters location, followed by branch locations if readily available.

3.   Date of Transaction
     Closing Date or approximate closing date.

4.   Annual Sales Volume for the past five years, if available:

     _____

5.   Was Sale made under compulsion?      Yes _____ No _____
     Explain:
             _____

             _____

6.   Price:
     Face Amount

7.   Terms:                         Owner-Financed?    Yes _____ No _____

     Amount of Down Payment       _____

     Interest Rate on Balance     _____

     Payment Terms on Balance     _____

8.   Stock or Asset Sale?     (Please circle one)

9.   If Real Estate was not sold, was there a lease?

              Yes _____ No _____

     If there was a lease:
     (a)      How much time was remaining on the lease? _____

     (b)      Was lease transferrable to new owner?    Yes _____ No _____

10.  Was there an Employment Agreement and/or Covenant Not to Compete?  Yes _____ No _____

     If yes, were they included in the above transaction?  Yes _____ No _____

     Describe terms of these agreements: _____

     _____

***Stock versus Asset Sale.***  Approximately 94 percent of the transactions reported were asset sales, and approximately six percent were sales of corporate stock.

***Cash versus Terms.***  Of the transactions reported, about 22 percent were for cash, over 75 percent involved a down payment plus a contract carried by the seller, and the remaining three percent were on a contract with no down payment. The only industry groups that reported any preponderance of cash transactions were dental and optometric practices, whose buyers were able to obtain bank financing to cash out the sellers.

Of the 75-plus percent sold for a combination of cash and notes, the median down payment was 33.3 percent of the stated purchase price. The remaining time on the balance ranged from three months to 25 years, with a median contract duration of 4.7 years. Interest rates on the contract balances ranged from 8.0 to 15.0 percent, with a very large proportion of the total at 10.0 percent.

***Leases Assumed.***  Almost 60 percent of the transactions included a lease assumed by the buyer. The median time remaining on assumed leases was 3.0 years.

***Covenants not to Compete.***  Of the sales reported, 39.5 percent included covenants not to compete. However, of those that did include a covenant not to compete, less than 10 percent assigned a specific value to the covenant.

# Results of the Willamette Data Base by Industry and Professional Practice Category

Because the Willamette data base covers 60 categories of industries and professional practices, most specific categories contain only a handful of transactions at the time this book goes to press. Although careful analysis of those individual transactions can provide useful guidance for the valuation of other specific companies or practices in their category, they do not provide a basis for meaningful statistical generalizations. The five categories that contained enough transactions at press time to compute some general valuation parameters were restaurants, drinking places, motion picture rental stores, accounting practices, and dental practices.

***Restaurants.***  The median price of all of the restaurant sales reported was $120,000. In computing the price/sales ratio, we found that the median price was 46 percent of gross annual sales. Although there were some wide variations, the price/sales ratios clustered substantially within a range of 30 to 60 percent of gross sales.

Although restaurants were the largest category of all transactions reported, not many of the restaurant transactions reported included definitive earnings figures. Of the restaurant sales with earnings data reported, the median price was 2.9 times seller's discretionary cash and 3.8 times pretax earnings.

Almost all restaurant sales included a fairly large amount of "blue sky"; that is, almost all the sales of restaurants were at prices substantially above the value of the tangible net assets transferred. The ratios of prices to net book value and prices to net adjusted tangible asset value were so widely scattered that statistical averages were not very meaningful.

***Drinking Places.*** The "drinking places" in the Willamette data base include a few cocktail lounges, but most are taverns. The median price of the transactions reported was $105,000. On the average, they sold at higher ratios of price to both gross sales and seller's discretionary cash than did restaurants. The median price/sales ratio reported was .63, and the median price/SDC ratio reported was 3.7.

As with restaurants, prices tended to include substantial intangible value over and above net tangible asset values. In some states, the prices of licenses to sell alcoholic beverages seem to be pretty well defined, while in others any value attributable to a license tends not to be separately identified and quantified.

***Video Rental and Sales Stores.*** Transactions in the movie rental stores ranged from .31 to .83 times sales, with most of the transactions clustering in the upper end of the range, and a median of .72 times sales. Not enough data on other variables were reported to make meaningful average computations.

***Accounting, Bookkeeping, and Tax Preparation Practices.*** Sales of accounting practices ranged from .48 to 1.58 times gross revenue, with a very high concentration at 1.00 times gross revenue. However, in the majority of cases, the price was contingent on retaining the clients for some period of time, most typically one year, with the final price reduced by the amounts for any clients not retained. The median ratio of price/SDC was 1.64.

***Dental Practices.*** Sales of dental practices were reported at 35 to 81 percent of annual revenues collected, with the median average at 64 percent. Most of the practices sold between 83 and 163 percent of seller's discretionary cash (in professional practices sometimes called the *total practice net return*), with a median average of 133 percent. Most of the transactions were on the basis of cash to the seller, with the buyer able to obtain bank financing for the purchase.

# The UBI Business Sale Data Base

The UBI business sale data base, known as *Analyx*, is compiled from all the sales of businesses consummated by the 40 brokerage offices that are members of the UBI franchise business broker system. The material in the data base is available only to UBI franchisees.

# Description of the UBI Data Base

The following data are entered for each transaction:

1. Listing price.
2. Sale price.
3. Down payment.
4. Annual sales.

The listing and sale prices included in *Analyx* do not include either inventory or real property. From the data above, the following ratios are calculated for each transaction:

1. Sale price/listing price.
2. Down payment/listing price.
3. Sale price/annual sales.

UBI maintains its 1,000 most current transactions on-line so that member brokers may call up on display screens in their offices any transaction or group of transactions out of the last 1,000 at any time. Earlier transactions are maintained in file storage.

# Results of the UBI Data Base by Industry Category

UBI divides the transactions in its data base into 26 industry groups. Among their latest 1,000 transactions as of June 15, 1985, UBI president David Scribner considered that 21 of the 26 industry groups contained enough transactions among companies that were homogeneous enough to produce meaningful averages. Summary data for those 21 industry groups are shown in Exhibit 29–2.

# Observations and Comments

Reviewing data on hundreds of transactions from each of 78 business brokerage offices from all over the country confirmed something that I have always known in a general sense: there certainly is wide variation among brokers, both in their sophistication and in the general business practices they employ. Trade terminology is not standardized, especially as it relates to pricing or valuation of the businesses or professional practices they sell.

There also is little standardization in methods of arriving at prices, in the amount of information obtained from businesses or practices listed for sale, or in the records the brokers keep concerning past transactions. As a very broad generality, brokers who sell professional practices tend to be more thorough in these respects than brokers who sell most kinds of retailing and service businesses, even when comparing

Exhibit 29–2

**UBI BUSINESS BROKERS**
**SALES ANALYSIS BY INDUSTRY**

| Industry Group | Number of Transactions | Average Listing Price[1] | Average Sale Price[1] | Average Down Payment | Average Annual Sales | Sale Price/ Listing Price[2] | Down Payment/ Listing Price[2] | Sales Price/ Annual Sales[2] |
|---|---|---|---|---|---|---|---|---|
| Taverns | 31 | 54,096 | 48,548 | 20,846 | 93,833 | .884 | .312 | .549 |
| Cocktail Lounges | 22 | 81,636 | 70,500 | 28,750 | 121,047 | .886 | .330 | .569 |
| Dinner Houses | 14 | 156,071 | 124,066 | 52,714 | 285,846 | .832 | .360 | .489 |
| Coffee Shops | 104 | 86,201 | 73,134 | 33,409 | 175,701 | .850 | .339 | .448 |
| Fast Foods | 86 | 79,627 | 66,931 | 34,063 | 138,146 | .836 | .384 | .460 |
| Sandwich Shops/Delis | 92 | 75,467 | 62,293 | 31,015 | 155,000 | .827 | .272 | .500 |
| Ice Cream/Yogurt | 18 | 61,277 | 46,055 | 19,769 | 110,000 | .808 | .279 | .471 |
| Ethnic Foods/Pizza | 72 | 63,902 | 49,027 | 26,382 | 120,820 | .763 | .262 | .434 |
| Bakeries/Donut Shops | 18 | 90,166 | 78,222 | 37,357 | 139,588 | .866 | .294 | .591 |
| Convenience Markets/Dairies | 76 | 83,039 | 66,763 | 35,410 | 326,547 | .861 | .351 | .237 |
| Supermarkets | 3 | 300,000 | 187,666 | 100,000 | 2,700,000 | .742 | .273 | .072 |
| Liquor Stores | 60 | 128,533 | 116,716 | 58,596 | 339,067 | .909 | .372 | .366 |
| Dry Cleaners | 32 | 101,187 | 89,333 | 45,321 | 103,096 | .871 | .323 | .836 |
| Laundries/Vending Routes | 22 | 51,409 | 39,043 | 25,384 | 70,200 | .798 | .221 | .722 |
| Retail Clothing & Accessories | 10 | 66,600 | 44,600 | 26,500 | 180,700 | .703 | .482 | .261 |
| Florist Shops | 11 | 63,181 | 54,363 | 26,125 | 142,090 | .863 | .278 | .395 |
| Gift/Card Shops | 11 | 64,181 | 54,272 | 34,285 | 129,454 | .850 | .317 | .410 |
| General Retail & Auto Parts | 65 | 101,184 | 74,250 | 41,431 | 229,142 | .856 | .321 | .437 |
| Service Stations | 24 | 78,125 | 53,125 | 34,800 | 898,681 | .776 | .198 | .075 |
| Personal Services | 30 | 55,966 | 45,000 | 22,315 | 124,566 | .803 | .231 | .443 |
| Automotive Services | 26 | 69,807 | 57,269 | 44,166 | 135,375 | .765 | .289 | .337 |

**SOURCE:** UBI Business Brokers Analyx data base as of June 15, 1985.

[1] Listing and sales prices do not include either inventory or real property.

[2] Average ratios are computed by first computing the ratio for each individual transaction, and then computing an arithmetic average of those ratios.

data on transactions of approximately equal selling prices. As one would expect, brokers selling higher-priced retailing and service businesses tend to be more thorough than those selling lower-priced businesses.

Although the prices of individual businesses varied widely, the usefulness of the results reported in this chapter is bolstered by the fact that the averages indicated by the Willamette data base are reasonably consistent with those shown by the UBI data base in those categories that are comparable. For example, in Willamette's broad restaurant category, the average price/sales ratio was .46. The UBI data base breaks restaurants down into six categories, and the average price/sales ratios for each of the six categories were from .44 to .50, surrounding Willamette's broad average and remaining within a fairly narrow range. Willamette's average price/sales ratio for drinking places was .63, while UBI's was .55 for taverns and .57 for cocktail lounges, a reasonably close correlation. The data on average down payments were also reasonably consistent in Willamette's and UBI's studies.

Although the data presented in this chapter certainly are not as comprehensive as an appraiser would like, they do represent the first collection and public dissemination of any broad empirical study of the actual prices of sales of small businesses and professional practices. As these data bases become more comprehensive, they will become increasingly useful tools to assist in the valuation of small businesses and professional practices.

# Chapter 30

## Litigation: Divorce, Dissolution, Dissenting Stockholder Actions, and Damage Cases

The Legal Context
    Statutes
    Regulations and Administrative Rulings
    Case Law
    Court Directives and Preferences
Divorce
    Abstruse Legal Context
    Discovery
    Splitting Stock
Corporate and Partnership Dissolutions
Dissenting Stockholder Actions
    Reasons for Squeeze-Out Mergers
    Dissenting Stockholder Appraisal Rights
    Standard of Value
Damage Cases
    Breach of Contract
    Condemnation
    Lost Business Opportunity
    Antitrust Actions
    Personal Injury
    Insurance Casualty Claims

Frequently, litigation follows a dispute over the value of a business or professional practice (or an interest in one). The following are the most common reasons that owners of small businesses and professional practices become involved in litigation concerning the value of holdings: (1) divorces, (2) corporate or partnership dissolutions, (3) dissenting stockholder actions, and (4) damage suits.

Imminent or potential litigation requires that the appraiser understand the legal context within which the appraisal is being made. The appraiser must tailor his valuation methods and criteria to relevant statutory and case law, which often varies considerably from one valuation purpose to another, and from one jurisdiction to another. This chapter offers some general guidance regarding the most common situations in which the value of a business or practice (or a partial interest) is an issue in litigation.

# The Legal Context

Whenever a valuation involves litigation or potential litigation, a thorough understanding of the legal context is essential. The appraiser and the attorney must work very closely together so they both are fully cognizant of how the legal context may influence certain aspects of the valuation procedures and conclusion.

The primary aspects of the legal context are the following:

1. Statutes.
2. Regulations and administrative rulings.
3. Case law.
4. Court directives and preferences.

## Statutes

Federal law governs valuation issues in some types of cases, such as gift and estate tax matters and damages in antitrust actions. State statutes apply to many other valuation issues, such as divorces, damages resulting from condemnation, dissenting stockholder actions, and values for ad valorem taxation. Statutes governing these issues vary considerably from state to state, and states change their statutes from time to time. If there is a chance that litigation involving a valuation issue will arise, the appraiser should look into the legal jurisdiction and the relevant statutes.

## Regulations and Administrative Rulings

Statutes may be supplemented by regulations and administrative rulings, some of which have the force of law and some not. For example, to implement the federal tax laws, the U.S. Treasury Department issues regulations with the force of law. However, the Internal Revenue Service issues Revenue Rulings, representing the opinion of the Service on various issues, which do not have the force of law. The appraiser should know what regulations and rulings exist, and also what is their force and impact on the matter at hand.

## Case Law

*Case law* is defined as past judicial cases to which courts may look for established precedent on a particular issue. Since most courts follow precedents established by other cases within their jurisdictions, it behooves the appraiser to be familiar with the relevant case law. Courts may also consider precedents established in the decisions of courts in other jurisdictions, but they would not accept those decisions as binding.

Because courts rely heavily on case law, it plays an important part in valuations involving litigation. Some appraisers have studied case law in depth and maintain extensive files of court cases involving the valuation of businesses and professional practices. Others rely on the attorney involved in the case to research the case law and provide them with the relevant cases for their study. Either way, gaining the necessary understanding of relevant case law is an important area of cooperation between the appraiser and the attorney in any valuation situation involving litigation or potential litigation.

## Court Directives and Preferences

Most courts prefer not to hear valuation cases at all, and will try to encourage a settlement if possible. Some courts exercise considerable discretion in the handling of valuation cases, determining such matters as when or whether the retention of experts must be disclosed to the opposing side, rules for discovery, and whether or not written appraisal reports must be prepared and exchanged.

Some of the foregoing items are standing matters of law or policy in certain jurisdictions, and others are left to the discretion of the judge in the particular case. When litigation is involved, the appraiser should find out from the attorney at the outset what are the known ground rules and what are the court's preferences about the procedures of the case, so that the appraiser may plan accordingly.

# Divorce

Two of the most common problems in the valuation of businesses and professional practices for divorce settlements are the lack of clarity of valuation standards and the difficulty of discovery encountered by the appraiser retained by the spouse who is not active in the business or practice.

# Abstruse Legal Context

I believe that, in virtually all states, the legal context for valuations for divorces is more nebulous than the legal context for almost any other valuation purpose. For one thing, unlike valuations for taxes or dissenting stockholder actions, the various state statutes do not specify any particular standard of value to be applicable, such as fair market value, fair value, or intrinsic value. In many states, it is ambiguous whether the applicable valuation date is the date of separation, the date of filing for the divorce, the date of the divorce trial (which is the most commonly accepted date), or some other date.

Furthermore, the foregoing deficiencies in statutory law, in general, are not clearly addressed in the states' case law. Virtually no states have resolved the question of the standard of value. In fact, within one month, two districts of the California Appellate Court issued two conflicting decisions as to the standard of value to be used in a divorce situation. One court held that investment value was the standard of value, while another court held for market value![1]

In Hawaii, the applicable valuation date is at the court's discretion. In a valuation for a divorce following a four-year separation, I once went into court in Hawaii prepared to testify about the value of the business on each of four different dates!

With two of the key elements of the valuation problem—the standard of value and the valuation date—frequently left to the persuasion of the attorneys and the decision of the judge, it is no wonder that appraisers retained by opposing parties in divorce cases frequently come to court with vastly differing opinions about value!

Certain valuation issues do seem to have been resolved by the case law in certain states, sometimes with opposite results from one state to another. For example, courts in all of the West Coast states (Alaska, Washington, Oregon, and California), as well as several others, have held that goodwill, in professional practices and merchandise distributorships, for example, should be included in the value of the practice or business, whether or not the goodwill is transferable. In this sense, these states have departed from the standard of fair market value, under which goodwill would be included in the value of a practice or business only if it is transferable. Texas courts, on the other hand, have taken the opposite position from the West Coast states, determining that personal goodwill is not part of the marital assets.

Two oft-cited California divorce cases have been widely interpreted to say that it is improper to use publicly traded stocks for guidance in the development of capitalization rates for the valuation of closely held companies.[2] However, on careful reading of the cases, one finds that the court said that the appraisers made "improper" use of publicly traded

---

[1] On May 10, 1983, the California Court of Appeals, Second District, Division 7, held that the standard of valuation in a divorce proceeding should be the business's "investment value as distinguished from its market value." (*In re Marriage of Hewitson*, 142 Cal. App. 3d, 874). Less than one month later, the California Court of Appeals, Fourth District, Division 1, held that the proper standard of valuation in divorce proceedings should be the business's "market value" and not "going concern value" (*In re Marriage of Sharp*, 192 Cal. Rptr. 97).

[2] *In re Marriage of Lotz*, 120 Cal. App. 3d 379, 174 Cal Rptr. 168, and Hewitson.

stocks, not that the appraisers were required to ignore publicly traded stocks completely.

In some states, the division of marital assets may be based on the amount of increase in value during the marriage. This basis of value may require the appraiser to express an opinion as to the value of the business or practice both at the current time and also at the date of marriage, in order to compute an increase in value. Retrospective appraisals are much more difficult than current appraisals. Even appraisers who maintain extensive libraries of economic, industry, and company data do not retain everything in their files from 10 or 15 years ago.

# Discovery

Another major problem affecting valuations of businesses and professional practices for marital property settlements often is the intense animosity, distrust, and lack of cooperation between the parties. This antagonism frequently results in attempts to prevent the appraiser retained by the spouse not active in the business or practice from obtaining adequate information to make a thorough appraisal. Such attempts to block adequate discovery should not be allowed to succeed. The trend in the courts clearly is toward the enforcement of whatever is necessary to facilitate a thorough appraisal.[3]

In discussing the admissibility of financial projections as evidence of value of a business in a divorce proceeding, one court stated its position very succinctly: "Since valuation of securities is, in essence, a prophecy as to the future, . . . it is important that the prognostication be based on an examination of the appropriate financial tea leaves."[4]

In another case, the appeals court used the following language to explain its upholding a default judgment following one party's failure to file timely and complete answers to interrogatories:

> Both parties were fully aware of the consequences of failing to comply with the court's order calling for the filing of answers to interrogatories which went unanswered for over three and one-half months before imposition of the sanctions. The appellant's conduct, or lack of action, readily translates into a display of contumacious and deliberate disregard for the trial court's authority. The answers, when ultimately filed, were incomplete and interfered with scheduled deposition dates and trial settings. This disregard for authority served as a proper basis for the court imposed sanctions.[5]

---

[3] See especially *Merns* v. *Merns,* 185 N.J. Super. 529, 449 A2d 1337 (1982). The wife was granted discovery of all books and records of closely held corporations in which the husband had minority interests. See also *Gerson* versus *Gerson,* 148 N.J. Supr. 194, 372 A2d 374 (1977). The wife was granted discovery of the books and records of a closely held corporation in which the husband had a 50 percent interest, in spite of the objection of the other 50-percent stockholder.

[4] *Turgeon* v. *Turgeon,* 190 Conn. 269, 460 A2d 1260 (1983).

[5] *Portell* v. *Portell,* 643 S.W. 2d 18 (Mo. App. 1982).

# Splitting Stock

In my opinion, one of the outcomes to be avoided in almost all divorce cases is leaving both spouses with a continuing interest in the business or practice. Virtually all appraisers and attorneys who are experienced in divorces share this opinion. It generally is in the interest of both parties to make a clean break. As one author put it: "It is impossible to measure on the Richter Scale the seismic effect of a court order that awards the wife shares in a closely held corporation."[6] (Of course, by "wife," he means the spouse not operating the business.)

If the assets outside the business or practice are insufficient to offset the value of the business or practice in an equitable division of property, then the solution is to create the balance by fixed payments over a period of time in a total amount sufficient to make up the difference.

If the attorneys for the parties fail to present adequate expert testimony as to the value of the business, the court may elect to split the interest in the business between the parties. In divorce cases, as in all disputed valuation issues, the expert's opinion must be documented and supported, not simply presented as a conclusion that the court is expected to accept on faith. In one recent case, testimony at trial as to the value of the business ranged from $70,854 to $338,279. Experts chose various capitalization rates based on their opinions but unsupported by any objective evidence. The trial court held that it had inadequate proof of value, and ordered that the husband retain ownership of all the stock and awarded the wife an equitable one-half interest in the stock. In upholding the decision, the New Jersey Supreme Court held that expert witnesses should be able to document and support their findings and opinions[7].

# Corporate and Partnership Dissolutions

Corporate or partnership dissolutions have many characteristics in common with divorces. People are terminating a relationship, frequently under antagonistic circumstances. Generally speaking, there is little or no statutory or case law to provide any guidance for the issue of valuation.

In many instances, a buy/sell agreement exists that may specify a standard of value. (See the chapter entitled "Estate Planning, ESOPs, Buy/Sell Agreements, and Life Insurance" for a discussion of buy/sell agreements.) In other cases, the parties may draw a document specifically for the purpose of providing guidance on the valuation of the interest and other aspects of the dissolution. Arbitration can be a useful way to resolve valuation differences in conjunction with a corporate or

---

[6] Stephen A. Landsman, "Divorce Planning in the Closely-Held Business Context," *Trusts & Estates*, May 1984, p. 43.
[7] *Bowen* v. *Bowen*, 473 A2d 73 (N.J. Supreme Court, 1984).

partnership dissolution (see Chapter 36, "Arbitrating Disputed Valuations").

# Dissenting Stockholder Actions

In all states, stockholders controlling some percentage of the stock (ranging from 50 percent plus one share up to 90 percent, depending on the state) can force out minority stockholders by effecting a "statutory merger," often referred to colloquially as a "squeeze-out merger." The merger can be effected either with an already existing company or with a new company created by the controlling stockholders for the purpose of the merger. This and other corporate actions can give rise to dissenting stockholder actions requiring appraisal of, and cash payment for, shares held.

## Reasons for Squeeze-Out Mergers

Some common reasons for squeeze-out mergers include the cost or nuisance of having minority stockholders, disagreements with minority stockholders, and needs for additional capital infusion into a company which minority stockholders are not willing or able to share on a pro rata basis.

## Dissenting Stockholder Appraisal Rights

In all states except West Virginia, stockholders who dissent to certain corporate actions have the right to have their stock appraised and to be paid the value of the stock in cash. The corporate actions giving rise to the dissenting stockholders' appraisal rights vary from state to state. In general, though, events triggering dissenters' appraisal rights include a merger, the sale of the company, a sale of major corporate assets, or some other fundamental organizational change.

## Standard of Value

Statutes governing the value of stock pursuant to dissenting stockholders' appraisal rights in most states designate fair value as the standard of value. Only Hawaii and Florida now designate fair market value as the standard of value. California statutes, as well as certain others, specified fair market value as the applicable standard for many years, but a few years ago changed it to fair value.

None of the statutes defines fair value, so the appraiser must look to case law for interpretation of the concept in the context of dissenting stockholders' appraisal rights. Since so many companies are incorporated in Delaware, that state provides a significant portion of the case law regarding dissenting stockholders' appraisal rights. Traditionally, appraisals under the Delaware dissenting stockholder statutes have followed what some call the "Delaware Block Rule," which holds that various weightings should be given to each of four relevant factors: (1) earnings, (2) asset values, (3) dividends, and (4) market value. However, a landmark case in 1983 said that the traditional factors alone were not necessarily sufficient; all relevant factors must be taken into consideration. In the particular case, the court specifically made the point that projections of future earnings were available and should be considered. The court also made the point that not only did the conclusion as to value need to be fair, but the appraisal procedures needed to be fair as well.[8]

As a broad generality, the concept of fair value under dissenting stockholders' appraisal rights has been interpreted to mean a proportionate share of the value of the total enterprise, with no discount for the fact that the shares at issue represent a minority interest. This is opposed to the standard of fair market value, under which minority shares normally would be valued at something less than a proportionate share of the total enterprise value. However, two recent Canadian decisions have interpreted fair value to mean a proportionate share of enterprise value plus a premium for the taking![9]

# Damage Cases

The most common types of damage cases involving valuation of a business or practice are the following:

1. Breach of contract.
2. Condemnation.
3. Lost business opportunity.
4. Antitrust actions.
5. Personal injury.
6. Insurance casualty claims.

Except for a breach of contract that denies someone a right to a business interest, all of the above have at least one common characteristic: the result of the damage is that the business did not operate as it would have if the event had not caused the damage. This characteristic means that damage cases usually result in a hypothetical valuation, that is, a valuation of what would have been, had the damage not occurred. The loss may be either lost profits for some period of time or the total loss of the business.

One other factor that often differentiates damage cases from other litigation involving business valuations is that damage cases usually are tried before a jury, but most other valuation-related litigation, such as divorce cases, dissenting stockholder suits, and tax cases, usually are

---

[8] *Weinberger* v. *U.O.P. Inc.*, 457 A2d 701 (Del. Supr. 1983), rev. and remanding 426 A2d 1333.

[9] *Domglas Inc.* v. *Jarislowsky, Fraser & Co.*, [1980] C.S. 925, 13 BLR 135; Affirmed [1982] C.A. 377, 22 BLR 121, 138 DLR (3d) 521 (C.A.); *Les Investissements Mont Soleil Inc.* v. *National Drug*, [1982] C.S. 716: 22 BLR 139 at 176. Both cases added a 20 percent premium for the taking.

tried before a judge without a jury. Preparation for a jury trial requires every possible effort to simplify the presentation of the complex subject of business or professional practice valuation, along with graphic exhibits to illustrate major points.

# Breach of Contract

A variety of breach of contract actions can give rise to a lawsuit requiring a valuation of a business or a fractional interest in a business as a measure of damages. Perhaps a stockholder or partner was squeezed out in a manner that breached provisions of a contract between the parties, or perhaps a prospective stockholder or partner was denied stock or a partnership interest that the person had a contractual right to receive. In a totally different context, a supplier company could be injured or even destroyed if a customer canceled a major contract that it had awarded and that the supplier company had positioned itself to perform.

Denial of a right to a business interest usually is a normal, straightforward valuation problem involving the value of whatever interest in an entity was denied as a result of the breach of contract. When the business itself is damaged by a breach of contract, however, the valuation problem is determining the value of the lost profits, or, possibly, the total value of the business as it would have been, had the damage not occurred.

# Condemnation

A frequent cause of damages is the taking of business premises through eminent domain proceedings. Condemnation may result in the total loss of the business, if relocation is not feasible, or in a temporary loss of profits plus relocation costs. These temporary costs may also be combined with some permanent loss of locational goodwill, since it is unlikely that all patrons would follow a business or practice to a new location. Ideally, one would like to be able to document the loss of locational goodwill by the use of customer lists before and after the condemnation, but few businesses are likely to have such records.

# Lost Business Opportunity

The most common scenario leading to a damage claim for lost business opportunity is when an employee comes upon an opportunity through contacts made through the employer company, and then exploits the opportunity on his own, or through another company, without offering it to the initial employer. In this case, the measure of damages usually is the value lost to the initial employer as a result of not being offered the business opportunity.

# Antitrust Actions

Perhaps the most complicated of all categories of business damage cases is the antitrust area. The stakes can be very high, because damages resulting from antitrust violations can be trebled.

The valuation problem is difficult because the appraiser must develop evidence to demonstrate the difference in the profit the business would have made had it not been for the antitrust violations, compared with how much it actually made. Obviously, that requires hypothetical analysis.

Antitrust actions are tried in federal court, and each circuit of the federal court system develops its own case law. Courts usually take cognizance of case law developed in other circuits, but they are not bound by precedents from other circuits, some of which may conflict with the local circuit. Therefore, the appraiser should be aware of the local circuit case law as it affects the determination of damages in antitrust matters.

# Personal Injury

Sometimes a personal injury will impair a person's ability to carry on his business or practice. In such cases, the amount of the economic loss normally is the measure of damages, usually estimated by the discounted future earnings method, as discussed in Chapter 13. While the arithmetic is the same as presented in Chapter 13, the discount rate usually is the return that could reasonably be expected by investing the funds in securities.

# Insurance Casualty Claims

It is not uncommon to have a business interrupted or destroyed by a casualty loss, such as fire or storm. Again, the discounted future earnings method commonly comes into play to estimate the loss, offset by whatever value is salvaged.

# Chapter 31

## Estate Planning, ESOPs, Buy/Sell Agreements, and Life Insurance

Every business or practice should plan how it would cope with the eventualities of the owner's death, departure, or divorce. Also, an owner may wish to transfer all or part of his interest in the business to family members, employees, or charities, while still participating in the company. In all these cases, the fair and accurate valuation of the ownership interest is critical. Every owner should have a plan for determining the value and for providing any related funding that may be required.

# Estate and Gift Taxes

Estate and gift taxes can be minimized or avoided by several methods: a series of gifts within the gift tax exclusion limits; an estate-freezing recapitalization; reduction of the estate through charitable contributions; and establishment of a low value through a binding buy/sell agreement. Each of these means is explored briefly in this chapter. References for additional study on each topic are included in the bibliography.

## Estate and Gift Tax Rates and Exemptions

Owners of many small businesses and professional practices will never have to pay estate taxes, because the exemptions have been raised significantly in recent years. By 1987, the amount exempted from estate taxes will be $600,000 for a single person and $1.2 million for a married couple.

In addition, each person may give $10,000 per year to each of as many beneficiaries as he wants, totally free of any gift or estate tax consequences. For example, a husband and wife with four children could each give each child $10,000 per year, or a total of $80,000 per year, free of estate or gift tax consequences. Any value over $10,000 per year from any donor to any donee is charged against the $600,000 lifetime exemption.

Once the $600,000 per person ($1.2 million per married couple) exemption is exceeded, the rates in effect after 1987 are as follows:

| Amount Subject to Tax | Tax Rate |
|---|---|
| Over $600,000 to $750,000 | 37% |
| Over 750,000 to 1,000,000 | 39 |
| Over 1,000,000 to 1,250,000 | 41 |
| Over 1,250,000 to 1,500,000 | 43 |
| Over 1,500,000 to 2,000,000 | 45 |
| Over 2,000,000 to 2,500,000 | 49 |
| Over 2,500,000 to 3,000,000 | 53 |
| Over 3,000,000 | 55 |

In addition to the federal rates listed above, many states also impose inheritance taxes, which may not be subject to the same exemptions as the federal taxes.

# Rules for Valuation

The essential rules for valuation of closely held businesses and business interests for federal gift and estate taxes are contained in Revenue Ruling 59–60, which is included as Appendix B. States imposing inheritance taxes follow the same basic guidelines, although they may not follow exactly the same interpretations and are not bound by any federal determination of gift or estate tax.

Revenue Ruling 59–60 provides general guidelines for valuation. In the quarter century since the promulgation of Revenue Ruling 59–60, hundreds of gift and estate tax cases have been decided in the courts, giving rise to a body of case law concerning valuation of closely held businesses. If gift or estate tax consequences may be involved because of the materiality of the value, the taxpayer should have a written valuation report prepared by a person or firm thoroughly familiar with the case law relating to a gift or estate that involves an interest in a closely held business.

# Penalties for Undervaluation

The 1984 Tax Act imposed substantial penalties on taxpayers with closely held businesses who undervalue interests on their gift and estate tax returns. These penalties are as follows:

| Ratio or Claimed Valuation to Correct Valuation | Penalty % Applicable to Tax Underpayment |
|---|---|
| 50% or more, but not more than 66-2/3% | 10% |
| 40% or more, but not more than 50% | 20% |
| Less than 40%. | 30% |

# Estate-Freezing Recapitalizations

If the owner of a rapidly growing business wishes his children to receive the value of the business's future growth without estate tax consequences, one available estate planning device is the *estate-freezing recapitalization.*

In essence, the estate-freezing recapitalization involves dividing the ownership of the company into two or more classes of stock or partnership interests. Generally, one class will have a priority claim on assets and cash distributions up to a certain point, and another class will have the residual interest. Because the senior class of stock or partnership interest will have a ceiling on the payments it may receive, either in liquidation or in dividends or partnership distributions, its value will, in effect, be frozen, and the junior or residual class will receive any appreciation in the overall value. The junior class can be transferred to the younger generation of family members, thus removing the future appreciation from the older generation's taxable estate.

A corporation can be divided into one or more classes of common stock and one or more classes of preferred stock. A partnership can be divided into general partnership interests and one or more classes of limited partnership interests. All or part of the common stock or general partnership interests can be transferred to the next generation of family members. There is a wide variety of possible rights that may attach to any of the various classes of interests, so that they can be structured to meet the needs and desires of various family members or groups.

At the time of the recapitalization, the value(s) of the interest(s) being recapitalized must be established at fair market value. The fair market values of stock or partnership interests received in conjunction with the recapitalization must be equal to the fair market values of interests given up, according to the guidelines set forth in Revenue Rulings 59–60 and 83–120. (Revenue Ruling 83–120 deals with the valuation of preferred stock.)

In the most typical of the many estate freezing recapitalizations that I have seen, the older generation retains voting control while passing the growth in the value of the company along to the younger generation. If an estate-freezing recapitalization is contemplated, I recommend retaining at the outset a business appraiser who is experienced in recapitalizations to assist in designing the features of the classes of stock or partnership interests. Because the number of features available to each class is almost unlimited, each may have a positive or negative impact on the value of the units of that class of interest.[1]

# Charitable Contributions

The 1984 Tax Reform Act requires individuals, closely held corporations (other than Subchapter S corporations), and personal service corporations (not including Subchapter S service corporations) to obtain a qualified appraisal for noncash property contributions having a claimed value of more than $5,000. In the case of securities not traded publicly, a qualified appraisal is required if the claimed value of the securities donated to one or more donees is greater than $10,000. The statute stipulates that the appraisal must include a description of the property or security; a statement of its fair market value; the specific basis of the valuation; a statement that the appraisal was prepared for income tax purposes; and qualifications of the appraiser, his signature, and tax identification number. The following are some of the most salient points:

1. No appraisal will be accepted if all or part of the appraisal fee is based on a percentage of the appraised value of the property.
2. The appraisal must be made by a person qualified to appraise the donated property.

---

[1] For a more complete discussion of estate-freezing recapitalizations, see Pratt, *Valuing a Business*, pp. 288–90. See also bibliographical references contained in that book and in the bibliography published annually in the March issues of *Business Valuation News*.

**3.** The appraisal must be received by the donor before the due date (including extensions) of the return on which the deduction is claimed. The donor must attach to the return on which the deduction is claimed a summary of the written appraisal (in a form prescribed by the Treasury Department).

**4.** *Appraisers beware.* The new requirements include sanctions against appraisers submitting overstated valuations. Appraisers are subject to a civil tax penalty for aiding and abetting an understatement of tax liability (Section 6701). A $1,000 penalty can be imposed against the appraiser, and the appraiser may be barred from presenting evidence in administrative proceedings, causing the appraisal to be disregarded.

# Employee Stock Ownership Plans (ESOPs)

*Employee Stock Ownership Plans (ESOPs)* have become an increasingly advantageous and popular means of transferring all or any part of a company's ownership to employees. In a single transaction, an owner may sell all his stock to employees through an ESOP; or any proportion of ownership can be sold at any time through one or a series of transactions. An ESOP can be used effectively for financing, and can result in significant savings in both income taxes and estate taxes.

## The ESOP Concept

The concept of an ESOP is a plan to allow employees to have an ownership interest in the business. An ESOP is a form of employee benefit plan, subject to the Employee Retirement Income Securities Act, similar in many respects to a pension or profit-sharing plan. The corporation may contribute cash to the ESOP, and the ESOP may use the cash to buy stock from one or more current stockholders. Alternatively, the corporation may issue additional shares of stock and contribute such shares to the ESOP. The ESOP's ownership interests are allocated among employees on a basis similar to pension and profit-sharing fund ownership allocations.

## Leveraged ESOPs

A leveraged ESOP is one that borrows money, usually from a bank. The money may be used to buy stock from one or more existing owners or to buy stock from the corporation. In either case, the corporation guarantees the loan and makes annual cash contributions to the ESOP, which in turn are used to pay off the loan.

**The Leveraged Buyout.**  If the ESOP borrows money to buy all or part of the company's stock from the current owner or owners, and uses the company's assets as collateral, that is a perfect example of a leveraged buyout at work. This avenue is becoming increasingly open to small businesses, partly because of the banks' increasing willingness to make such loans, and partly because of the excellent tax advantages, as detailed in the next section.

**The ESOP as a Vehicle for Financing.**   The ESOP also can borrow money to buy newly issued stock or treasury stock from the corporation. In this situation, the ESOP is used as a vehicle to provide new equity financing to the corporation.

# Tax Advantages of ESOPs

Companies with ESOPs have enjoyed favorable income tax treatment since 1974, but legislation passed in 1984 offered new ways to use ESOPs that are attractive from both the income tax and estate planning viewpoints. The 1984 Tax Reform Act contained four major provisions that will encourage many companies to form new ESOPs, and also will help many existing ESOP companies.
  The four major provisions are:

1. Dividends are tax-deductible to the paying corporation.
2. Half of interest income is tax-free to lenders to ESOPs.
3. Sale of stock to an ESOP can be a tax-free exchange.
4. Estate taxes can be paid by the ESOP over an extended period and at very favorable interest rates.

**Tax-Deductible Dividends.**   Dividends paid to ESOP participants will be deducted from the paying corporation's taxable income. This provision is effective for tax years beginning after July 1984.

**Half of Interest Income Is Tax-Free to Lenders.**   A commercial lender, such as a bank or insurance company, can exclude from taxable income 50 percent of the interest it receives on the loan an ESOP uses to acquire employee securities. This stipulation is effective immediately for new loans. This provision certainly should make financing easier for ESOP companies to obtain and should make ESOPs a very attractive vehicle for leveraged buyouts.

**Tax-Free Rollover on Sale of Stock to ESOP.**   A sale of a company's stock to an ESOP will be treated as a tax-free exchange if the ESOP owns at least 30 percent of the total value of the employer's securities outstanding after the transaction and if the proceeds are reinvested in some other security of another domestic corporation. The seller must have held the stock at least one year, and the proceeds must be reinvested within one year in a corporation whose passive investment income is not more than 25 percent of its gross receipts. This provision is effective for ESOP companies beginning with tax years after July 1984.

**Extended Payment of Estate Taxes by the ESOP.**   Certain estates may transfer stock to an ESOP in return for the ESOP's obligation to pay estate taxes. The ESOP may pay interest only for four years, with the balance payable in equal installments over as many as ten succeeding years. A 4 percent rate applies to a portion of the payment, and the regular IRS rates based on the prime rate apply to the remainder. This provision is effective for estates required to file returns after July 18, 1984.

Consider, for example, an estate worth $1 million, of which $400,000 represents the value of a business. From Table 31–1 we can compute the amount of estate tax, which is $153,000 ($150,000 × 37% plus $250,000 × 39% = $153,000). The estate can take care of the estate taxes by selling anywhere from $153,000 worth of the company stock up to all of the company stock to the ESOP, giving the ESOP up to 14 years to pay the $153,000 estate taxes at a favorable rate of interest.

# Rules for Valuation of ESOP Shares

Valuation of ESOP shares in privately-held companies must meet the requirements of both the IRS and ERISA (Employee Retirement Income Securities Act). The IRS goes by Revenue Ruling 59–60, the general guidelines for gift and estate tax valuation and, as of this writing, has not issued any supplemental revenue ruling or other guidelines specifically applicable to ESOPs. Section 3(18) of ERISA refers to fair market value determined in good faith "and in accordance with regulations promulgated by the Secretary (of Labor)," which regulations have not been promulgated as of this writing.

In the absence of specific regulatory guidance, the appraiser of ESOP shares must rely on generally accepted appraisal practices and the case law that has developed to date. In any case, the appraiser appointed by the ESOP fiduciaries should meet two basic criteria:

1. The appraiser should be a company or person who regularly engages in the valuation of businesses or business interests.
2. The appraiser should be independent with respect to the issuing company and parties to an ESOP transaction.

Treasury Regulation Section 54.4975-11(d)(5) states: "An independent appraisal will not in itself be a good faith determination of value in the case of a transaction between a plan and a disqualified person. However, in other cases, a determination of fair market value based on at least an annual appraisal independently arrived at by a person who customarily makes such appraisals and who is independent of any party to a transaction under Section 54.4975(b)(9) and (12) will be deemed to be a good faith determination of value."[2]

I would encourage any company considering starting an ESOP to contact The ESOP Association, 1725 DeSales Street, N.W., Suite 400, Washington, D.C. 20036, telephone (202) 293–2971. The Association is

---

[2] *Valuing ESOP Shares* (Washington, D.C.: The ESOP Association, [1984]), pp. 3–4.

composed of companies that have ESOPs and can supply names of firms that specialize in installing and administering ESOPs, as well as firms that specialize in appraising ESOP shares. The ESOP Association also offers a variety of informative publications.

# Buy/Sell Agreements

A buy/sell agreement can effectively avoid many potential problems regarding disposition of stock or a partnership interest of a departing or deceased stockholder or partner. The buy/sell agreement can accomplish the following objectives:

1. Provide a mechanism for the departing owner or his estate to liquidate the ownership interest.
2. Set a price or provide a mechanism for determining a price for the ownership interest.
3. Under some circumstances, set a price that will determine a binding value for estate tax purposes.
4. Prevent the ownership interest from being sold to any party not acceptable to the other owners.
5. Provide a mechanism for pricing and liquidating the interest of a departing spouse in the event of a divorce.[3]

## Types of Agreements

The two basic types of buy/sell agreements are the *cross-purchase agreement* and the *entity purchase agreement* (also called a *repurchase agreement* or a *stock redemption agreement*). There may also be a combination of the two, usually called a *combination agreement* or a *hybrid agreement*.

In the cross-purchase agreement, the various stockholders buy the shares owned by the deceased or departed owner. In the entity purchase agreement, the corporation buys the shares of the deceased or departed owner. In a combination agreement, stockholders may be required or given the option to buy shares not redeemed by the corporation, either because the corporation elects not to exercise its option to redeem the shares or because it does not meet the requirements under state law to make such a redemption.

In deciding which type of buy/sell agreement to use, consideration should be given to the desires of the parties, the tax consequences, and the abilities of the parties to fund the possible transaction. An attorney experienced in buy/sell agreements should be consulted before finally deciding the type of agreement, as well as for drafting the agreement.

---

[3] For an interesting discussion of the use of buy/sell agreements for divorce planning, see Stephen A. Landsman, "Divorce Planning in the Closely-Held Business Context," *Trusts & Estates*, May 1984, pp. 41–6.

# Provisions for Valuation

The provision for valuation is a critical element of the buy/sell agreement. The parties have a great deal of flexibility in structuring this provision, but it is often neglected or done hastily, in a manner that eventually turns out to be unfair to one party or the other.

The valuation provision can be the same under all triggering events or it can differ in different circumstances, such as death of the owner, voluntary termination of employment, or involuntary termination. The most common valuation provisions establish a set price, a formula for determining a price, or a procedure for having the interest appraised at the date of the event that triggers the buy/sell agreement.

Unless the parties desire to make the buy/sell agreement price determine value for another purpose, such as estate taxes,[4] there is no requirement that the buy/sell agreement provide for a price that conforms to any particular standard of value, such as fair market value, fair value, or intrinsic value.

Even though the valuation provision of a buy/sell agreement can be as arbitrary as the parties may desire, most owners want the price to have some semblance of fairness to all concerned when the event that triggers the agreement occurs. If a price is fixed and not updated regularly, it usually becomes out of date quickly and gives an unfair value to one party or another when the event occurs that sets the agreement provisions in motion.

A common type of valuation provision, and one of the fairest, calls for the parties to update the valuation at least annually and provides for independent appraisal if the last agreement on price was dated more than a certain period of time, usually a year, prior to the event that causes change in ownership. The appraisal can be conducted by a person or firm specified in the buy/sell agreement, or the agreement can provide for a means to appoint an appraiser or panel of appraisers. Exhibit 31–1 is a sample buy/sell agreement valuation section providing for a panel of appraisers in case the pricing agreement has not been updated within a year of the triggering event.

If the buy/sell agreement provides for appraisal, the standard of value should be specified. The parties should keep in mind that fair market value normally implies that a minority interest would be valued at some discount from a proportionate share of the total enterprise value. If the parties desire the minority interests to be valued as proportionate shares of the fair market value of the total enterprise, the buy/sell agreement should specify that decision. Buy/sell agreements often state that minority interests will be valued at a certain percentage discount (usually 20 to 40 percent) from a proportionate share of the total enterprise value.

---

[4] In general, in order for a buy/sell agreement price to be determinative for estate tax purposes, the price must be fixed or determinable by formula, must be binding on the decedent during his lifetime, as well as on the estate at death, and must be a bona fide business arrangement. See the bibliography for references covering this and related points.

Exhibit 31–1

## SAMPLE VALUATION ARTICLE FOR BUY/SELL AGREEMENT
### (Corporation Stock Redemption Example)

As soon as practical after the end of each fiscal year, the stockholders shall agree on the value per share of the stock that is applicable to this agreement. Such value will be set forth in Schedule A, which shall be dated, signed by each stockholder, and attached hereto. Such value shall be binding on both the corporation and the estate of any deceased stockholder whose date of death is within one year of the last dated and signed Schedule A.

If more than a year has elapsed between the date when Schedule A was last signed and the date of death of a deceased stockholder, then the value per share shall be determined, as of the date of death of the stockholder, by mutual agreement between the surviving stockholder and the personal representative or administrator of the deceased stockholder's estate.

If the surviving stockholders and the personal representative of the deceased stockholder's estate are unable to agree upon such a value within 90 days after such personal representative or administrator has qualified to administer the estate of the deceased stockholder, then such value shall be determined by binding arbitration. Either party may give written notice of such binding arbitration pursuant to this agreement to the other party. Within 30 days of such notice of arbitration, each party shall appoint one arbitrator. Within 30 days of the appointment of the two arbitrators, the arbitrators so appointed will select a third arbitrator. The first two arbitrators will have sole discretion in the selection of the third arbitrator, except that he must be an individual or qualified representative of a firm that regularly engages, as a primary occupation, in the professional appraisal of businesses or business interests. In the event that the first two arbitrators are unable to agree on a third arbitrator within 30 days of their appointment, the Executive Director of the ABC Trade Association shall appoint the third arbitrator.

The standard of value to be used by the arbitrators shall be fair market value of the shares being valued as of the date of death, under the assumption that the stockholder is deceased and the corporation has collected the proceeds, if any, of insurance on the life of the deceased stockholder payable to the corporation.

Each arbitrator shall use his sole discretion in determining the amount of investigation he considers necessary in arriving at a determination of the value of the shares. The corporation shall make available on a timely basis all books and records requested by any arbitrator, and all material made available to any one arbitrator shall be made available to all arbitrators.

Concurrence by at leat two of the three arbitrators shall constitute a binding determination of value. The value concluded by the arbitrators shall be reported to the corporation and to the personal representative or adminstrator of the estate of the deceased in writing, signed by the arbitrators concurring as to the concluded value, within 90 days of the appointment of the third arbitrator unless an extension of time has been agreed upon between the corporation and the personal representative of the estate.

The corporation and the estate shall each be responsible for the fees and expenses of the arbitrators they appoint. The fees and expenses of the third arbitrator shall be divided equally between the corporation and the estate.

The terms of payment should also be specified in the buy/sell agreement. The payment terms may be different under different circumstances, and the agreement may allow the company some flexibility, making allowance for the company's ability to pay.

# Funding with Life Insurance

In general, three basic needs can be fulfilled through the use of life insurance:

1. Liquidation of the stock of a departed or disabled stockholder, either by the corporation or by other stockholders.
2. Payment of estate taxes.
3. Provision for continuity of the business after loss of a key person.

The owner should constantly monitor the value of the business in order to know how much life insurance is needed to fulfill these needs; he should update the life insurance coverage accordingly. The owner should seek out and consult periodically with a professional who knows how to apply life insurance to businesses, especially the tax implications of the many types of policies and the various configurations of ownership and beneficiaries. The bibliography (Appendix C) contains several references that deal with types of policies and their tax implications.

## Liquidation of Departed or Disabled Owner's Stock

The beneficiary of life insurance purchased for the purpose of purchasing a departed owner's stock logically is determined by the buy/sell agreement: the corporation is the beneficiary in connection with a repurchase agreement, and the various stockholders are the beneficiaries in connection with a cross-purchase agreement. The repurchase agreement, with the corporation as the beneficiary of the life insurance policies, usually is simpler administratively, if there are three or more stockholders involved, but tax and other considerations may outweigh administrative simplicity.

Funding of the purchase of a stockholder's interest, if the stockholder is terminated but not deceased, can be accomplished through an annuity or through life insurance with a cash value feature. The matter of insurance to cover needs in case of the permanent disability of a stockholder is often overlooked, but such needs arising from permanent disability are a common occurrence.

## Payment of Estate Taxes

Estate taxes become a problem only to the extent that the value of the estate exceeds the amounts excluded from estate taxes, as discussed earlier in this chapter. If the value exceeds the amount eligible for exclusion, the estate tax liability can be estimated from the table shown under "Estate and Gift Taxes" earlier in this chapter. Provision for payment of the estimated amount of estate tax can be covered by life insurance in that amount.

# Providing for Business Continuity

Life insurance payable to the corporation can also provide funding to assure continuity of the business following the loss of a key person. It is common to find a key person contributing far more to the annual cash flow of a business than he is taking out in salary and benefits. The company can be protected against the financial impact of the loss of such a valuable person by estimating the potential earnings or cash flow shortfall to be compensated for until the key person can be replaced and the replacement brought up to speed. The company can then cover the estimated amount of that risk with life insurance on the key person.

# Review of Prior Life Insurance Funding

If funding of the foregoing requirements has been provided for through life insurance taken out in prior years, that insurance should be reviewed as to both amount and type of insurance.

The amounts of insurance necessary can change for several reasons. One, of course, is general inflation. Another likely reason for needing more insurance is the increased value of the business due to its success. Another could be changes in the makeup of the ownership of the business. Finally, the value of a particular person in his role as a key person in the business can change over time due to a variety of circumstances.

There has rarely, if ever, been as much change in the variety and costs of life insurance products as there was during the first half of the 1980s, and important changes still are occurring at mid decade. A review of the life insurance funding may very well reveal new products that are better suited to the owner's objectives and/or are more cost efficient.

# Summary

The various owners of a business or professional practice can protect their interests and those of their families by keeping track of the value of their ownership of the business or practice and taking appropriate action, as discussed in this chapter. The general objectives are liquidation of the ownership interest in case of death, permanent disability, or departure from the company, avoidance or minimization of estate taxes, and continuity of the enterprise. These objectives can be accomplished on a basis that is fair to all concerned, and that will avoid unnecessary crises, by having the owners carefully consider a buy/sell agreement, do estate planning to the extent appropriate for the value of the interest, and provide for funds to cover eventualities.

# Part VI

## Topics Related to Valuation

# Chapter 32

## Valuing Intangible Assets

# Reasons to Value Intangible Assets

The two primary reasons to value specific intangible assets are (1) the allocation of the purchase price of an entity for tax purposes and (2) transfer of ownership of a specific intangible asset.

## Allocation of the Purchase Price

Often in the valuation process, the entire business is appraised, without separating out the intangible assets. In some instances, however, it is imperative that the individual intangible assets be identified and valued. These situations arise when the business is being purchased, and the buyer, having paid for the intangible assets, needs to know if they can be amortized against future income, and if so, at what rate. An intangible asset can be amortized for tax purposes only if it is specifically identifiable, if its value is based on reasonable valuation assumptions, and if it has a measurable life span.

## Transfer of Ownership

Besides allocation of the purchase price of a total entity for income tax purposes, the other primary reason to value intangible assets is the transfer of their ownership. Rights to individual intangible assets may either be sold or gifted, with either case requiring a determination of value.

# Types of Identifiable Intangible Assets

There never has been a complete listing of all conceivable intangible assets, nor is there ever likely to be one. Any given business may have some identifiable intangible assets that are utterly unique. Nevertheless, many identifiable intangibles are quite common.

## Proprietary Lists

Proprietary lists include customer, client, or patient lists. Proprietary lists can also include mailing lists, whether or not the names are customers or clients. They can be very valuable to a business or practice, particularly if customer relationships are ongoing. For example, consider an employment agency that has 25 companies as steady customers, regularly listing jobs with the agency and representing 75 percent of its total revenues. It is clear that if this agency has any goodwill value, a substantial portion of it, if not all, will lie in that customer list.

In order to amortize its customer list, the business could conduct an historical study of customer turnover and, by that means, estimate a reasonable annual attrition rate. Alternatively, it could assign a specific value to each of the 25 customers. If one of the companies terminated its relationship with the agency, it could write off that customer's assigned value against the value of the customer list. As a general rule, customers of longer standing are more valuable than more recent customers because of their demonstrated propensity toward repeat patronage.

## Beneficial Contracts

Companies often enter beneficial long-term contracts that add intangible value to the company. These contracts arise from two basic circumstances:

1. The company has arranged to sell a product or service at a higher mark-up than noncontract customers pay.
2. The company is purchasing (or leasing) a product or service at a rate below what it would pay if the contract did not exist.

Under either of these assumptions, the company is receiving more income than it would if the contract did not exist.

Generally, the value of a beneficial contract can be amortized over the length of the contract, or in a shorter time if it can be demonstrated that the economic benefit of the beneficial contract will disappear before the end of the contract period.

## Patents and Applications for Patents

Patents and applications for patents can be extremely valuable intangible assets. Patent valuation probably has received more attention in appraisal literature than any other type of intangible asset valuation.[1]

Generally patents have two life spans—a legal life span and an economic life span. The shorter of the two should be used to amortize the value of a patent. However, some patent attorneys feel that the effective legal life span actually ends several years before the 17th year of the patent. It is felt that enforcement of patent rights in the later years is generally not pursued because of the delays that can occur during the legal process. The most commonly used method of valuing patents is the discounted cash flow method based on the patent's economic contribution, as discussed in a later section.

In valuing patents, the strength of the patent claim should be taken into consideration if possible. However, strengths of patent claims are very difficult to assess, except in the small minority of cases in which the patent has successfully withstood the test of litigation. The appraiser may seek guidance about the strength of the patent from the client company's patent counsel.

---

[1] For an excellent article on patent valuation, see Scott G. McMullin, "The Valuation of Patents," *Business Valuation News*, September 1983, pp. 5–13.

# Copyrights

Copyrights tend to have very long legal life spans, although their economic life spans can be relatively short. A good example of this trait is a book, for which the copyright is valid for the lifetime of the author plus 50 years, but which may go out of print in five years.

The valuation of copyrights depends to an important extent on the track record of the author. Copyrights for the works of authors with a history of past successes generally are several times more valuable than copyrights for works of authors without such a record. The valuation of a particular copyright is easier, of course, if the specific work has been exposed to the market and developed its own sales record.

# Trademarks and Brand Names

If a trademark or brand name allows a company to sell its product at a higher price than similar products of its competitors, the trademark definitely has value. Since trademarks usually do not have a determinable life, they cannot be amortized for income tax purposes.

# Subscriptions and Service Contracts

In the valuation of a business, subscriptions and service contracts can be valuable assets. Newspapers and cable television stations, for example, can have substantial value built up in the number of subscriptions they hold. The longer the time the subscription has been in effect, the higher that subscription's value. Since subscriptions are for finite periods, tax laws permit them to be amortized against income for tax purposes.

# Franchises and Territorial Agreements

As the trend toward franchising increases, the appraiser will more and more find himself assigned to judge the value of franchise agreements. A franchise with a long track record and a well-known name will have a significantly higher value than one that is relatively new or not commonly recognized. Franchise agreements usually cannot be amortized against income because their lives are generally undeterminable.

Territorial agreements, being a form of monopoly, may have a value, depending on the length of the contract and the degree of exclusiveness. A territorial agreement with a short-term cancellation clause is not significantly valuable in itself (although its existence can add value to the business as a whole), but long-term agreements may be very valuable, especially if their benefits are quantifiable. Like franchises, territorial agreements usually are not capable of being amortized because of the uncertainty of the length of their lives; however, if there is a time period specified in the contract and the supplying party has a policy of not renewing such agreements, the value of the agreement may be amortized.

# Software

The advent of the inexpensive business microcomputer has made it possible for many businesses to develop software uniquely suited to their own operations. If this software is providing efficiencies and benefits to the business, it should be valued as a separate asset. If the software's life span can be determined, it can be amortized against income for tax purposes.

# Goodwill

Goodwill has been defined in many ways, but it is generally regarded as those factors that generate continued repeat patronage, such as reputation and location. As discussed elsewhere in this book, the term goodwill sometimes is used more broadly to mean "all" of the intangible values of a business, in which case it is called the "big pot" concept of goodwill. Since goodwill cannot be amortized for income tax purposes, it usually is in the interest of a buyer who pays more than tangible asset value for a business to have the individual intangible assets identified and appraised so that they may be amortized over their useful lives for income tax purposes.

If the "big pot" concept of goodwill is used, the value of the goodwill can be determined by the excess earnings method as discussed in Chapter 12.

# Intangible Asset Valuation Methods

There are three basic methods employed in the valuation of intangible assets: cost of creation, capitalization of income, and discounted cash flow. Rule of thumb methods sometimes are encountered for certain intangible assets in certain industries, but should be used only to provide ballpark estimates as to value and should never be used alone.

## Cost of Creation

The cost of creation method attempts to determine how much it would cost to duplicate a given asset at the present time. It does not measure the asset's future contribution to profits; that would fall under a capitalization of income or discounted future earnings method.

The cost of creation method can be used to value many types of intangible assets, particularly insofar as they are directly related to the operation of the business. For example, such assets as proprietary software can be valued by either a cost-to-create method or an income method. A company may have developed an inventory package that is utterly unique, which enables the company to operate much more efficiently than its competitors and to manage its cash flow better. Since the company is not in the business of selling computer software, it may never have income from its excellent inventory package, but its value is undeniable. In such a case, a cost-to-create approach should be considered an appropriate valuation technique. Other intangible assets that may be valued according to the cost of creation include patents, copyrights, subscriptions and customer lists, and service contracts.

## Capitalization of Income or Savings

The capitalization of income method, described in Chapter 11, is used to measure the value of expected future benefits when those benefits are expected to be generated over a long period of time or into perpetuity. The capitalization rate should reflect the risks associated with the particular intangible asset being appraised. If the intangible asset is employed as an integral part of the business, with little risk, the weighted average cost of capital for the business sometimes is used as the capitalization rate. A trade name could possibly be valued using this method, because the length of its life is undeterminable.

The employment agency's customer list, described under "Proprietary Lists" earlier in this chapter, probably would be most appropriately valued according to the capitalization of income method, because there is no basis on which to anticipate losing those customers' business. Trademarks, brand names, and territorial agreements might also be valued by this method. Copyrights and patents have limited legal lives. Copyrights are good for the life of the author plus 50 years, while patents have a 17-year legal life span. When these assets are new, the end of their economic benefit may be so far ahead that it is irrelevant. As they come closer to ending, the appropriate method of appraising them may change.

Sometimes the annual benefit to be capitalized will be in the form of savings to the company, as a result of owning the intangible asset, rather than income as a result of owning it. For example, as a result of owning a patent, a company may relieve itself from the cost of paying a royalty on some other patent that would otherwise be used to accomplish a similar result. In that case, the savings stream to be capitalized would be in the nature of relief from royalties. A company may own a patent that results in a more efficient production process than would be possible without the patent, in which case a capitalization of the annual savings would be a reasonable approach to the valuation of a patent.

## Discounted Cash Flow

The discounted cash flow (or discounted future earnings method), described in Chapter 13, is a method used extensively for the valuation of intangibles whose predictable life spans and future financial benefits can be reasonably anticipated. A beneficial contract would be valued by this method, because its termination date is known, and the savings the contract provides can be reasonably calculated. The appraiser must not only calculate the current extra profits that arise from such a contract, but also estimate the future yearly benefit for the length of its life. Subscriptions and service contracts, because they have definite ending points and easily definable values, should be valued according to the discounted future earnings approach. Since many companies holding patents derive royalty income from leasing out the right to use that patent, some patents should be valued using a discounted earnings method, based on projected future royalties.

The discounted cash flow valuation model can be applied to savings flows as well as income flows, as discussed in the previous section.

# Chapter 33

## Working with a Business Broker

The intermediaries who put together the large mergers and acquisitions in Corporate America are known as "investment bankers," while those that perform a similar service for small businesses and professional practices are known by the less elegant but much more descriptive designation of "business brokers."

According to Equitable Business Brokers, a franchised business brokerage chain, approximately 25 percent of all businesses that change hands today are sold through business brokers, compared with less than one percent only 10 years ago. Based on estimates that approximately 2.5 million small businesses change hands annually, brokers are selling over 600,000 businesses each year. Obviously, buyers and sellers are becoming increasingly aware of the business brokerage industry and the services it offers.

# The "State of the Art" of the Business Brokerage Industry

The business brokerage industry has been both growing and increasing its sophistication over the last few years. Although nobody knows the exact number, it is safe to say that there are well over 2,500 business brokerage offices in the United States, employing well over 15,000 people in the activity of selling businesses. Most brokered sales of businesses and professional practices are through brokers who specialize in selling businesses and/or practices, although some real estate brokers also sell businesses.

Business brokerage companies are themselves small businesses, typically employing one to 15 people. Until a few years ago, each brokerage office operated pretty much in a vacuum, with little communication among them. However, the industry has been evolving in the mid-1980s. This evolution is making business brokers, as a group, a much more effective and viable force in the sale of businesses and professional practices throughout the nation. As I view the industry, its transformation is characterized by three main developments:

**1.** National and regional professional associations.
**2.** Franchises.
**3.** Independent training and multiple listing services.

## Professional Associations

The Institute of Certified Business Counselors pioneered the idea of a national professional association among business brokers. This group offers several courses and seminars on various aspects of business brokerage, holds an annual convention, and publishes a newsletter for its members called the *Counselor*. Members meeting educational and experience criteria established by the association are awarded the professional designation of Certified Business Counselor (C.B.C.). A companion organization, the Center for Small Business Growth, offers courses for the business owner or prospective owner, such as "Starting, Buying, or Selling a Business." Although members of the Certified Business Counselors sell businesses of all sizes, many of them concentrate their activities among businesses selling in the $100,000 to $5 million range, some larger.

Another national association just getting under way in 1985 is the International Business Brokers Association, which plans to have regularly scheduled conventions and educational activities. There are also several regional associations and a couple of associations of brokers specializing in selling certain types of businesses. Exhibit 33–1 lists

Exhibit 33–1
National, Regional, and Specialized Organizations of Business Brokers

**Florida Association of Business Brokers, Inc.**
410 North Office Plaza Drive
Tallahassee, Florida  32301
(904) 656-1172

A not-for-profit corporation organized for a variety of purposes. Among these purposes are conducting meetings, seminars, and conferences for the mutual benefit and education of the members; serving as a clearinghouse for information relevant to business brokers in Florida; and cooperating with other state and national associations and trade groups in a common effort to protect and enhance the business brokerage business.

This association will be offering an eight-course sequence leading to the designation of Certified Business Broker, in conjunction with the Florida State University College of Business and the Florida State University Center for Professional Development and Public Service.

**Georgia Business Brokers Association**
c/o Associated Business Brokers
2167 N. Lake Parkway
Building Two, Suite 112
Tucker, Georgia  30084
(404) 548-2700

A state organization that dates back to 1973.

**Hotel & Motel Brokers of America (HMBA)**
10920 Ambassador Drive
Suite 520
Kansas City, Missouri  64153
(816) 891-7070

Formed to faciliate the exchange of hotel and motel listings among member brokers and to encourage cooperative selling on a national basis. Members are licensed real estate brokers specializing in hotel/motel sales.

**Independent Brokers Association of Arizona**
c/o American Award Real Estate
9402 N. Central Avenue
Phoenix, Arizona  85020
(602) 861-3201

A 40-member association of independent business brokers.

Exhibit 33–1 (*continued*)

**Institute of Certified Business Counselors (CBC)**
3301 Vincent Road
Pleasant Hill, California 94523
(415) 945-8440

A nonprofit trade association whose membership is composed of brokers/sales-persons, consultants, accountants, attorneys, appraisers, and business owners who are interested in the continuation, the valuation, or the buying and selling of businesses, either for their own account or for a fee.

As a source of education, evaluation, and consultation of small businesses, the Institute is dedicated to the professionalism of the business brokerage field and to working with state and national government agencies that regulate the community. Certification requires three basic courses which are offered regularly around the country; they must be completed within a two-year period of acceptance in the Institute and are required for certification.

**International Business Brokers Association (IBBA)**
Box 247
Concord, Massachusetts 01742
(617) 369-5254

Created to provide all business brokerage companies and individuals alike with education, political action, a national convention, publications, insurance, public relations, advertising, national recognition, professional standards, regional seminars, and an international directory, and to foster and encourage state associations.

**National Association of Business Brokers (NABB)**
P.O. Box 262
506 S. Edward Street
Mt. Prospect, Illinois 60056
(312) 870-7253

This association claims three key benefits: professionalism, new opportunities, and contacts made through membership and credibility.

**National Association of Independent Business Brokers (NAIBB)**
32 Elm Street
Hartford, Connecticut 06106
(203) 549-1894

The NAIBB was founded by the Structured Approach Corporation to allow for a systematic and timely registration of "Business for Sale Opportunities." This registration allows network management to gather and distribute business-for-sale data to NAIBB members. Members in good standing submit listings to the network center located in Hartford, Connecticut, and receive data on other member listings. The cycle for business lists occurs monthly. Membership in the NAIBB is currently limited to fully SAI-trained brokers.

**National Association of Media Brokers (NAMB)**
P.O. Box 11898
Atlanta, Georgia 30355
(404) 261-3000

The stated purpose of this organization is to be of service to buyers and sellers of media properties in their merger and acquisition activities.

Exhibit 33–1 (*concluded*)

**PROBUS of Winston-Salem**
Professional Business Brokers & Appraisers
Bethesda Oaks Office Condominium
Suite 606C
Winston-Salem, North Carolina  27103
(919) 765-7121

Once a franchising company, PROBUS now functions as an independent association of business brokerage offices serving the Southeastern states (mainly North
Carolina) with approximately 15 completely independent offices.

**Texas Association of Business Brokers**
2200 Post Oak Blvd.
Suite 418
Houston, Texas  77056
(713) 960-1046

A professional trade association whose members are actively involved in selling,
buying, and appraising business enterprises. The association was organized for
the following reasons: recognition of the specialized nature of the profession,
the need to educate the general public about business investments, and the need
to develop a code of ethics within the profession.

The Dallas/Ft. Worth chapter of the Texas Association of Business Brokers
has developed within its educational committee a list of approved subjects to be
offered to their members as well as to other interested parties who may be interested in buying, selling, or improving the overall operation on their own businesses. These courses either may be audited or will apply for credit towards certain professional business brokerage designations; they may be used for continuing
real estate education credit as related courses. These courses will be taught by
active professional business brokers and attorneys who are members of the Texas
Association of Business Brokers.

**West Michigan Association of Business Brokers (WMABB)**
c/o Investment Exchange Company
210 Ionia N.W.
Grand Rapids, Michigan  49503
(616) 454-9858

Meets monthly, offers its members an educational forum and an exclusive business multi-list, in addition to providing a professional public image.

the national, regional, and specialized organizations of business brokers active at the time this book went to press.

# Franchises

New organizations of franchised business brokerage offices are popping
up faster than I can keep track of them. Franchisers typically offer a
training program, standardized forms for all aspects of the business,
varying programs of ongoing management consulting, and a computer-
ized network through which to access business listings of all offices
throughout the franchise group. Exhibit 33–2 is a list of business brokerage franchisers as of mid-1985.

Exhibit 33–2
Business Brokerage Franchisers

**Allied Business Brokers of America**
100 Northcreek Office Park
Atlanta, Georgia 30327
(404) 262-1960

**ABBEX**
**American Business Brokers**
**and Exchange**
2650 S. Tamiami Trial
Sarasota, Florida 33579
(813) 957-0507

**Business Investment Group**
**of America, Inc. (BIG)**
1519 Killearn Center Blvd.
Suite C
Tallahassee, Florida 32308
(904) 893-4904

**Corporate Finance Associates (CFA)**
300 Embassy Row, Suite 670
6600 Peachtree Dunwoody Road
Atlanta, Georgia 30345
(404) 399-5633

**Corporate Investment Business**
**Brokers, Inc.**
1515 East Missouri Avenue
Phoenix, Arizona 85014
(602) 266-0100

**Equitable Business Brokers**
255 E. Hancock Avenue
Athens, Georgia 30601
(404 548-2700

**National Equipment & Business**
**Brokers, Inc. (NEBB)**
9103 West Central
Wichita, Kansas 67212
(316) 721-2542

**proVENTURE, Inc.**
79 Parkingway
Quincy, Massachusetts 02169
(617) 773-0530

**UBI Business Brokers**
11965 Venice Blvd.
Suite 204
Los Angeles, California 90066
(213) 390-8635

**VR Business Brokers, Inc.**
Executive Offices
197 First Avenue
Needham, Massachusetts 02194
(617) 444-3040

**Zarex Management**
**(Division of Ezzron Corp.)**
21 St. Clair Avenue East
Upper Penthouse
Toronto, Ontario M4T 1M1
CANADA
(416) 968-0339

# Independent Training and Multiple Listing Services

Several companies now offer training programs and/or multiple listing services for brokers who want those services but do not want to buy into a franchise chain. Exhibit 33–3 lists some firms providing such services and a brief description of their services. Most such groups limit membership to one brokerage firm in each geographical market.

# Trade Publication

In 1983, a former business broker, Tom West (cofounder and past president of VR Business Brokers), started a trade publication called *The*

Exhibit 33–3
Business Broker Information, Training, and Multiple Listing Services

**Business Brokerage Press**
Thomas L. West, Editor and Publisher
Business Brokerage Press
Box 247
Concord, Massachusetts 01742
(617) 369-5254

Publishes a newsletter, *The Business Broker*, for the business brokerage industry.
Also, publishes sourcebooks on various business brokerage subjects.

**Business Broker's Profit System**
James M. Hansen, Editor and Publisher
Grenadier Press
7900 East Mercer Way
Mercer Island, Washington 98040
(206) 232-8300

What is offered is a comprehensive course on business brokerage to be studied
and mastered at one's own pace. Included are a text on buying and selling a
business, a business broker's documents kit, a business broker's study program
(14 audio tapes), and a business broker's examination kit to test on all subjects
covered in the program.

**Nation-List Headquarters**
W.T. (Chip) Fuller
1660 South Albion St.
Suite 407
Denver, Colorado 80222
(303) 759-5267

This company is an independent association of business brokers that currently
has nearly 40 member brokers from all across the country. Nation-List is different from the franchising companies in that it does not provide start-up assistance. Among the features this company provides are a weekly Nation-List
display ad in the *Wall Street Journal* seeking sellers and buyers; a printout of
approximately 1,000 prospective buyers nationwide who have called their
toll-free number in the last 12 months; a confidential multi-list of member's
listings, and direct mail support for each member broker to help in obtaining
listings. Nation-List accepts as members only business brokers who also are real
estate-licensed.

**Nationwide Business Services**
Lorimar C. "Jerry" Hall
2141 East Highland, Suite 135
Phoenix, Arizona 85016
(602) 954-0774

One central office that has a computer databank of buyers and sellers that networks across the nation, very similar to a multiple listing service. Conducts frequent seminars for business buyers and sellers

Exhibit 33–3 (*concluded*)

**Structured Approaches, Inc. (SAI)**
Frank Covich, President
1225 River Rd.
Suite 2-d
Edgewater, New Jersey 07020
(201) 886-7345

A professional business start-up organization that offers an intensive formal program designed for the business person who wishes to establish a business brokerage consulting organization without the franchise alliance. The program trains
new brokers in business brokerage; they then join an affiliated association, the
NAIBB, for ongoing services.

*Business Broker.* It is published monthly by the Business Brokerage
Press, P.O. Box 247, Concord, Massachusetts 01742. *The Business Broker* does a nice job of keeping brokers up to date on developments in the
industry.

In recent years, these developments have facilitated increased competency, as basic training and professional contact with other brokers
now are readily available to those who are interested. At the same
time, the boom in the business brokerage industry has attracted many
new, inexperienced participants, some of whom undoubtedly believe
that brokering businesses is as simple as selling used cars.

# Services Offered by Business Brokers

The basic service of a business broker, of course, is bringing together a
buyer and a seller and negotiating the transaction. Some business brokers also offer appraisal services, and some serve to find financing for
the buyer. A few also offer financing services to existing small businesses, even though a sale of the business is not involved. For example,
Adam Commercial Funding of Dallas, Inc., (operated by Don McIver
and affiliated with First Main Capital Corporation) provides financing
to small businesses by buying their accounts receivable. At press time,
Adam operated in nine cities nationally.

Most business brokers have typically represented the seller of a
business through an agency relationship as the seller's sole and exclusive agent. More recently, however, some brokers are being asked to
represent buyers. This gives the buyer the advantage of the broker's
expertise and can save the buyer considerable time that might otherwise be wasted.

# Typical Fees

Brokers typically receive commissions of 10 to 12 percent of the face
amount of the transaction on sales up to about $500,000 and somewhat
lower percentages on higher amounts. Most brokers also have some

minimum commission, the amount of which varies considerably from one brokerage firm to another. The broker receives his commission in cash at closing. Thus, if the down payment is 30 percent of the face amount and the commission is 10 percent, the commission amounts to one third of the down payment.

Fees for finding financing usually are about 2.5 to 5 percent of the amount of money raised.

Business brokerage traditionally has been a strictly commission business. However, there has been a trend recently for some brokers to charge sellers nonrefundable retainers that usually are deducted from the commission if the business is sold. The services covered by such retainers vary considerably. In some cases, the retainer may entitle the seller to receive the broker's opinion as to an appropriate price for the business. However, brokers do not often provide appraisal services of the scope discussed in this book. The retainer may cover the development of a presentation package that highlights relevant information about the business or practice.

Some brokers' retainers run several thousand dollars. However, it is more typical for a retainer for a small business to be $1,000 to $2,000. The retainer helps to cover some of the broker's out-of-pocket expenses and to weed out sellers who are not serious and would merely waste the broker's time. From the seller's viewpoint, the retainer should help to get the broker's full attention and enhance at least his moral obligation to pursue rigorously the sale of the business.

# Finding the Right Broker

Unfortunately, business brokers in general are not as well oriented as real estate brokers to "co-oping" a listing, that is, having the listing commission go to one firm while the sales commission goes to another firm. There is virtually no co-oping of transactions among business brokers within most local markets, although some takes place between brokers in different cities. The main reason for lack of co-oping among business brokers, a Portland broker has noted, is that confidentiality is too easily lost. The impact can be devastating if rumor of an impending sale is leaked out before the right time, and it can be financially destructive to both the seller and the buyer. A seller should select a broker whose direct sales efforts, or whose particular listing network, will be likely to reach the potential buyers for that seller's business. A buyer would be wise to make his interests known to several different brokers who may have access to listings that would be of interest.

## Criteria for Selection

The following criteria deserve more or less weight in selecting a broker with whom to work, depending on the situation:

1. Types of businesses commonly brokered.
2. Size of businesses commonly brokered.

**3.** Geographical scope.
**4.** Overall competence of the broker.
**5.** Success ratio (percentage of listings actually sold).
**6.** Willingness of broker to spend money advertising the business for sale.

**Types of Businesses.** Certain brokers specialize in specific types of businesses and practices, such as radio and TV stations, magazines, beer distributorships, auto dealerships, funeral homes, hotels and motels, accounting practices, or medical practices. Others specialize in more general categories, such as wholesalers, retailers, or manufacturers. Many others do not necessarily specialize as a matter of policy, but they simply have considerable experience in transactions in one or a few industries. A broker experienced in an industry usually would have an advantage over a broker without such experience in finding buyers and sellers in that industry and in negotiating a mutually satisfactory transaction.

**Size of Businesses.** The statistics I have seen indicate that most businesses sold through business brokerage offices are priced in a range of roughly $25,000 to $150,000 (normally not including either receivables or real estate). Most brokers tend to concentrate their efforts within a certain price range. Some brokers may do very well with businesses priced under $100,000, while others find their level of comfort and success in the $100,000-to-$250,000 range, and still others do most of their business in the $250,000-and-up category. I suggest that buyers and sellers seek brokers who generally handle transactions in the appropriate size category.

**Geographical Scope.** Regional and national connections are not important to a seller whose business would appeal only to a local buyer, such as small retailers, taverns, and so on. However, if a buyer could conceivably come from elsewhere in the region or nation, the seller would want to contact a broker whose connections extend outside the local area. A seller should inquire whether the brokers' networks would facilitate the exposure of his listing in the various markets where buyers might be located.

A buyer seeking to locate in a particular city logically would talk to brokers in that city. If he thinks he might be interested in one of several cities, however, he should talk to brokers belonging to the multiple listing networks.

**General Competence.** Naturally, a broker's competence is an important consideration, but that is not easy to judge. A seller or buyer can inquire about the broker's educational and professional credentials (such as C.B.C.), how long he has been in the business, and what his experience has been with the type of company in mind. Beyond that, sellers or buyers should ask for and contact the broker's references. Some brokers may be reluctant to give out names and addresses of previous clients as references due to the confidentiality request of both buyers and sellers. Most brokers, however, can and freely will give out names of their banker, accountant, attorney, and other professional references which will satisfy the purchaser's or seller's need for some comfort level with references.

**Success Ratio.** Naturally, a buyer or seller will want to select a broker whose track record looks good. Find out the ratio of sales per listings.

**Willingness of a Broker to Spend Money on Advertising a Business for Sale.** Unless a brokerage firm is willing to spend some money on advertising, the chances for optimum exposure to the market diminish, possibly decreasing the likelihood of a timely sale.

## Locating the Broker

The *Yellow Pages* in every city offer many listings under the classification "Business Broker," but they give little or no information to assist a prospective buyer or seller in deciding which brokers would be most suitable for any particular situation. A better locally published source in most cases would be the Sunday "Business Opportunities" classified ads. They indicate which brokers are advertising businesses in which industries.

Of course, it would be ideal to locate a business broker by referral from someone who knows him first hand. In some cases, an attorney, accountant, banker, business appraiser, or insurance agent may be familiar with some of the local brokers either directly or through their clients. The headquarters offices of the various organizations of business brokers listed in Exhibit 33–1 can give names of member firms in the area, and in some cases can suggest which ones might be best suited to the buyer's or seller's particular needs. For example, Wally Stabbert, executive director of the Certified Business Counselors, is personally acquainted with most of the several hundred members of that group and their respective areas of specialization and strengths.

Buyers and sellers should not overlook the acknowledgments in the front of this book, listing brokerage firms that contributed data to the transaction study discussed in Chapter 29. This list cannot necessarily be construed as being my personal recommendations, because I have not even met many of the brokers who contributed to this study. I would, however, take their participation as a positive indication of their interest in the industry and in helping to improve its knowledge and professionalism.

## Pricing and Listing a Business or Practice for Sale

The essential elements of the listing agreement are:

1. The property being offered for sale.
2. The offering price and terms.

**3.** The commission.

**4.** The duration of the listing agreement.

The matter of defining what is being offered for sale was discussed in Chapter 1. Commissions were discussed earlier in this chapter. The duration of the agreement usually should be for six months on an exclusive basis, so that the broker has adequate opportunity to work the listing, because it usually takes several months to sell a business. Most brokers will not even accept nonexclusive listings.

How the buyer and the broker will set the price and terms of the listing varies a great deal from one type of business to another and, especially, from one broker to another. At the one extreme, some brokers insist on doing their own appraisal and accept the listing only if the price approximates their appraisal. At the other extreme, some brokers have nothing to do with the pricing and simply list a property at whatever price the seller designates. Most brokers will fall somewhere in between. They will offer some practical guidance if the buyer wants it, but normally will not do a complete appraisal.

In any case, a seller should have a pretty good idea of a reasonable price before contacting the broker. It is part of the purpose of this book to provide the seller the guidance to develop a reasonable range of possible values. If the seller wants objective guidance, he may seek a professional appraisal from an independent fee appraiser rather than a broker before offering the business for sale. It is a waste of both the seller's and the broker's time to start out by offering the business at a price inflated beyond a realistic range. On the other hand, a seller naturally should expect to get all he reasonably can, and not leave money on the table by underpricing the business.

Since most small businesses and professional practices are sold on terms rather than for cash, the listing price should be set to reflect just about the most generous terms the seller would be willing to accept. Chapter 17 shows how to convert a cash equivalent value to a higher price that appropriately reflects extended terms of sale. Then, if a deal looks possible on terms more favorable to the seller (or even better, if a cash deal looks possible), the seller can negotiate to a lower price that reflects the terms that are more favorable to the seller. It does not work psychologically to list the business priced on the basis of a cash deal, and then to raise the face amount to reflect the discount in value received as a result of extending terms to a buyer.

Statistics suggest that the average business sold closes at a price around 80 percent of its original listing price, but this average varies greatly from one brokerage office to another. The more sophisticated the seller and the broker are about realistic pricing, the higher the odds that the business actually will be sold, and the more likely that the price will be at or near the listing price.

Exhibit 33–4 is the Business Listing Contract approved by the Wisconsin Department of Regulation and Licensing. It is the most comprehensive listing contract form that I know; most brokers' listing contracts are on a single page. Some brokers who are aware of the Wisconsin forms use them, while others consider them too cumbersome.

## Exhibit 33–4

WB-6 Business Listing Contract - Exclusive Right To Sell
Approved by Wisconsin Department of Regulation and Licensing
11-1-83 (optional use date)
5-1-84 (mandatory use date)

Wisconsin Legal Blank Co., Inc.
Milwaukee, Wis.

Page 1 of 4 pages

### BUSINESS LISTING CONTRACT - EXCLUSIVE RIGHT TO SELL

1    AGREEMENT made between the undersigned real estate broker and the undersigned seller.

2    Seller gives Broker the sole and exclusive right to procure a purchaser for the business, including the stock-in-trade, good will, fixtures and
3    equipment thereof, and the real property (if included) described below at the price and on the terms set forth in this contract.

4    SELLER AGREES TO PAY BROKER A COMMISSION COMPUTED AS SET FORTH IN THIS CONTRACT:
5        a)   If a purchaser is procured for the business or the real property or any part thereof by Broker, by Seller, or by any other person, at the price
6    and upon the terms set forth in this contract, or at any other price, or upon any other terms accepted by Seller during the term of this contract, or
7        b)   If the business or real property or any part thereof is exchanged, leased, or optioned during the term of this contract, or
8        c)   If Seller enters into a management contract involving the business or real property or any part thereof during the terms of this contract, or
9        d)   If any other transaction occurs which causes an effective change of ownership and/or control of the business or real property or any part
10   thereof from Seller to a third party during the term of this contract, or
11       e)   If the business or the real property or any part thereof is sold, exchanged, leased, optioned, or a management contract is entered into
12   involving the business or real property or any part thereof or if any other transaction occurs which causes an effective change of ownership and control
13   of the business or real property or any part thereof from Seller to a third party within twelve (12) months after the expiration of this contract to or with
14   any person, firm, corporation or other entity or anyone acting for such person, firm, corporation or other entity to whom the business or property was
15   introduced by Seller, Broker or any of Broker's agents or by any other person, or with whom Seller, Broker or Broker's agents or any other person
16   negotiated prior to the expiration of this contract; however, as for those with whom Broker or Broker's agents negotiated or to whom Broker or
17   Broker's agents introduced the business or real property, Broker shall submit their names to Seller in writing by personal delivery or by depositing,
18   postage prepaid, in the United States mail, not later than twenty-four (24) hours after the expiration of this contract. A written offer to purchase
19   submitted to Seller during the term of this listing contract shall constitute the notice required by this paragraph without further notice to Seller.

20   Seller shall immediately notify Broker of the name of any person who contacts Seller directly and shows an interest in purchasing the business
21   or property during the term of this listing contract.

22   The submitting of the name of a person or entity in accordance with the terms stated herein shall constitute a submission and filing of not only
23   the name of the person or entity so named, but also the filing of names of the person's immediate family, the person's agents, servants and/or
24   employees, as well as the names of any and all corporations or other entity or entities controlled by or affiliated with or owned by said person or entity
25   in whole or in part.

26   If Seller of the business and/or real property described herein is a corporation, the officer or officers signing this listing contract thereby
27   represent that they have full authority to bind the corporation to this contract, and if the undersigned sells all or any part of the stock of the corporation
28   which owns the business and/or real property herein described, said sale shall be deemed to be a sale of the property in accordance with the
29   terms of this agreement.

30   SELLER AND BROKER AGREE THAT THEY WILL NOT DISCRIMINATE AGAINST ANY PROSPECTIVE PURCHASER
31   ON ACCOUNT OF RACE, COLOR, SEX, HANDICAP, RELIGION, NATIONAL ORIGIN, SEX OR MARITAL STATUS OF THE
32   PERSON MAINTAINING A HOUSEHOLD, LAWFUL SOURCE OF INCOME, AGE, ANCESTRY, OR IN ANY OTHER
33   UNLAWFUL MANNER.

34   If Buyer fails to carry out Buyer's agreement, and Seller elects to take as liquidated damages all money paid by Buyer, then such money shall be
35   applied first to reimburse Broker for cash advances made by Broker and one half of the balance, but not in excess of the agreed commission shall be
36   paid to Broker as Broker's full commission in connection with said transaction and the balance shall belong to Seller; this payment to Broker shall not,
37   however, terminate this listing contract.

38   Seller hereby agrees to hold Broker harmless of any losses suffered by Broker because of any breach of any contract by Seller where Broker
39   has acted as agent for Seller according to the terms and conditions set forth in this Agreement, including the payment of reasonable attorney fees
40   required to defend the Broker from claims by Buyer of the business or the property.

41   Should litigation arise between the parties in connection with this Agreement, the prevailing party shall have the right to reasonable attorney's
42   fees.

43   Seller warrants and represents that all written materials and/or information given the Broker in conjunction with the listing and/or sale of the
44   property and/or business described herein is true, accurate and correct, and that Seller agrees to hold Broker harmless from loss by reason of Broker's
45   use of said material or information, including the payment of reasonable attorney fees in the event of any suit against the Broker arising out of the use of
46   said information.

47   Seller warrants and represents to Broker and Buyer that Seller has no notice or knowledge of:

48   1.   As to the business and personal property,
49       a.   Any material defects in any of the equipment, appliances, fixtures, tools or furniture included in this transaction, and further warrants that
50            all will be in good working order on the day of closing.
51       b.   Any encumbrances on the business being sold, all integral parts thereof, or the personal property being conveyed in conjunction with the
52            business, except as stated in this contract and in any schedule attached to it.
53       c.   Any litigation, government proceeding or investigation being in progress or being threatened or in prospect against or relating to this
54            business.
55       d.   Any road change or road work which would materially affect the present use of the property.
56       e.   Any right granted to underlying lienholders to accelerate their obligation by reason of the transfer of ownership, or any permission to
57            transfer being required and not obtained.
58       f.   Any unpaid income taxes, sales taxes, payroll taxes, social security taxes, unemployment taxes, or any other employer/employee taxes
59            due and payable or accrued.
60       g.   Any failure of the financial statements and schedules to present the true and correct condition of the business as of the date on the
61            statements and schedules and that since the date of the last financial statements and schedules provided by Seller there has been no change
62            in the financial condition or operations of the business except changes in the ordinary course of business, which changes have not in the
63            aggregate been materially adverse.

64   2.   As to the real property,
65       a.   Any planned or commenced public improvements which may result in special assessments or otherwise materially affect the property.
66       b.   Any government agency or court order requiring repair, alteration or correction of any existing condition.
67       c.   Any structural or mechanical defect of material significance in property, including inadequacy for normal use of mechanical systems,
68            sanitary disposal systems and well, and unsafe well water according to state standards.

## Exhibit 33–4 (*continued*)

69      Seller further warrants and represents to Buyer that:

70   1.    The property is zoned for present use, or ...................................................

71      .........................................................................................

72   2.    The property is not located in a flood plain. as per ......................................

73      EXCEPTIONS TO WARRANTIES AND REPRESENTATIONS STATED IN LINES 48 TO 72 ..............

74      .........................................................................................

75      .........................................................................................

76      .........................................................................................

77      .........................................................................................

78      .........................................................................................

79      .........................................................................................

80      WARNING: IF SELLER'S WARRANTIES AND REPRESENTATIONS ARE NOT CORRECT, SELLER MAY BE LIABLE FOR
81   DAMAGES AND COSTS.

82      Any offer submitted by or through Broker shall be deemed to comply with the terms of this agreement if it substantially includes, in addition to
83   the terms herein contained, any or all of the provisions set forth in the last section of this contract, entitled GENERAL PROVISIONS OF
84   STANDARD BUSINESS OFFER TO PURCHASE.

85      In consideration for Seller's agreements herein, Broker agrees to list and use reasonable efforts to procure a purchaser for the business and/or
86   real property. including but not limited to the following: ...........................................

87      .........................................................................................

88      .........................................................................................

89      .........................................................................................

90      Seller agrees to furnish Broker and Buyer the information and schedules designated with an "X" in the space preceding lines 92 to 104 no
91   later than ...............................................................................

92      A.   An inventory of all furniture, fixtures and equipment included in this transaction.

93      B.   Copies of all leases affecting equipment, real estate or signs; and copies of all other leases pertaining to the business.

94      C.   Estimated principal balance of accounts receivable.

95      D.   Estimated principal balance of accounts payable.

96      E.   Copy of profit and loss statements, balance sheets, business books and records, and income tax returns for the following years:
97      ......................................., which Buyer may have examined by Buyer's agents or attorneys.

98      F.   Copies of latest real estate and personal property tax bills.

99      G.   Copies of franchise agreements, if any.

100      H.   Copy of corporate minutes approving or authorizing the sale, if Seller is a corporation.

101      I.   Copies of all licenses used in operating the business.

102      J.   An agreement regarding a restriction on Seller competing with Buyer after the closing of this transaction.

103      K.   Others: ..........................................................................

104      .........................................................................................

105      Included in the purchase price are the following:

106   1.    PERSONAL PROPERTY. All tangible and intangible personal property and rights in personal property owned by Seller and used in the
107   business, including furniture, trade fixtures and equipment, tools used in the business, telephone numbers and listings, customer lists, trade names,
108   business records. supplies, leases, advance lease deposits, customer deposits, signs, all other personal property used in said business, and. if
109   transferable. all permits. special licenses and franchises, except those assets disposed of in the ordinary course of business or as permitted by this
110   contract.

111   ADDITIONAL ITEMS INCLUDED IN SALE: ...............................................................

112      .........................................................................................

113      .........................................................................................

114      .........................................................................................

115      .........................................................................................

116   ITEMS NOT INCLUDED IN SALE: ......................................................................

117      .........................................................................................

118      .........................................................................................

119      .........................................................................................

120      .........................................................................................

121      Seller shall comply with the Wisconsin Bulk Transfers Law and shall convey the personal property by bill of sale or ...............
122   ......................................................... free and clear of all liens and encumbrances, except

123      .........................................................................................

124      .........................................................................................

125   NAME OF BUSINESS ..................................................................................

126   TYPE OF BUSINESS ..................................................................................

127   BUSINESS ADDRESS ..................................................................................

128      .........................................................................................

129   2.    REAL PROPERTY. Real Property described as: ..............................................

130      .........................................................................................

131      .........................................................................................

132      .........................................................................................

133      .........................................................................................

134      .........................................................................................

135      ......................................................., in the ........................ of

136      ........................................., County of ......................................, Wisconsin,

137   having a frontage of about ................... feet, with a depth of about ................... feet, and/or consisting of approximately

138   ............... acres or ............... square feet.

139   THIS CONTRACT. DATED ..................., 19 ......, INCLUDES THE BALANCE OF THE TERMS ON PAGES 3 AND 4.

## Exhibit 33–4 (*continued*)

**BUSINESS LISTING CONTRACT - EXCLUSIVE RIGHT TO SELL** (continued)                    Page 3

140  The following terms are part of the listing for business at ...................................................................
141        If real property is included in this agreement, included in the purchase price are all fixtures of a permanent nature as may be on the real
142  property, which will be delivered free and clear of encumbrances, EXCEPT THAT THE FOLLOWING ITEMS WILL NOT BE INCLUDED
143  IN SALE: .........................................................................................................................
144  ................................................................................................................................
145  ................................................................................................................................
146  ................................................................................................................................
147  LISTED PRICE ....................................................................................................................
148  ................................................................................. Dollars ($ ...........................................)
149  plus stock-in-trade based on the following cost: ..........................................................................................
150  ................................................................................................................................
151  ...............................................................................................................................,
152  .......................................................... and accounts receivable less ...... %, minus accounts payable, if assumed.
153  MINIMUM EARNEST MONEY $ ......................... WITHIN ........... DAYS OF ACCEPTANCE WHICH WILL
154  BE RETAINED BY BROKER IN BROKER'S TRUST ACCOUNT, UNLESS OTHERWISE AGREED BY SELLER AND BUYER.
155  TERMS: Cash: ...................................................................................................................
156  ................................................................................................................................
157  ................................................................................................................................
158  ................................................................................................................................
159  ................................................................................................................................
160  ................................................................................................................................
161  OCCUPANCY DATE ...............................................................................................................
162  OCCUPANCY CHARGE, If Seller occupies after closing $ .............................................................. per day.
163  ESCROW TO GUARANTEE OCCUPANCY TO BUYER (AND FOR NO OTHER PURPOSE) $...............................
164  CONVEYANCE OF THE REAL PROPERTY OTHER THAN WARRANTY DEED, IF ANY: ...............................
165  ................................................................................................................................
166  LEASE: If the real property occupied by the business is owned by Seller, but not sold or exchanged by this agreement, Seller agrees to lease the real
167  property to qualified Buyer on the following terms: ........................................................................................
168  ................................................................................................................................
169  ................................................................................................................................
170  ................................................................................................................................
171  ................................................................................................................................
172  ................................................................................................................................
173        Seller shall, upon payment of the purchase price, convey the real property by warranty deed, or other conveyance provided herein, free and
174  clear of all liens and encumbrances, excepting: municipal and zoning ordinances, recorded easements for public utilities, recorded building and use
175  restrictions and covenants, general taxes levied in year of closing and .................................................................
176  ................................................................................................................................
177  provided none of the foregoing prohibit present use.
178  THE BROKER'S COMMISSION SHALL BE ............ % of:
179      1.   The listed price (including) (excluding) (strike one) value of the stock-in-trade and net value of accounts receivable less any assumed
180           accounts payable,
181           (a)  if a purchaser is procured in accordance with the terms of this agreement, or
182           (b)  If the business and/or real property is exchanged or leased, or, if Seller enters into a management contract involving the business
183                and/or real property, or
184           (c)  If any other transaction occurs which causes an effective change of ownership and control of the business and/or real property from
185                Seller to a third party.
186      2.   The sales price, (including) (excluding) (strike one) value of the stock-in-trade and net value of accounts receivable less any assumed
187           accounts payable, if an offer is accepted for the sale of the business or real property or any part thereof.
188      3.   The sales price, (including) (excluding) (strike one) value of the stock-in-trade and net value of accounts receivable less any assumed
189           accounts payable, set forth in an option if the option granted is exercised.
190  OR BROKER'S COMMISSION SHALL BE A FLAT FEE OF $ ......................................................................
191  NAMED EXCEPTIONS TO CONTRACT: ............................................................................................
192  ..................................................... WHICH SHALL BE VALID UNTIL ....................................
193  SPECIAL PROVISIONS: ............................................................................................................
194  ................................................................................................................................
195  ................................................................................................................................
196  ................................................................................................................................
197  TERMS OF CONTRACT: FROM THE .................................... DAY OF ...................., 19 .....;
198  UP TO AND INCLUDING MIDNIGHT OF THE .......................... DAY OF ...................., 19 ......
199  but if an offer to purchase is procured prior to said expiration date at the price and upon the terms set forth herein but which provides for a closing
200  subsequent to said expiration date hereof, the term of this contract shall be extended as to such offer up to and including the date of such closing, but in
201  no event beyond ....................................... months from expiration date.
202        THIS CONTRACT INCLUDES THE BALANCE OF TERMS ON THE REVERSE SIDE AND ON PAGES 1 AND 2.

203  Dated this ................ day of ................., 19 .....    ...................................................
204                                                                 Seller

205  ..................................................               ...................................................
206  Broker                                                          Seller

207  ..................................................               ...................................................
208  By                                                              Seller

209  ..................................................               ...................................................
210  Broker's Address and Phone Number                               Seller's Address and Phone Number

Exhibit 33–4 (*concluded*)

211 PROVISIONS WHICH MAY BE ADDED IN SUBSTANCE TO ANY OFFER TO PURCHASE SUBMITTED BY OR THROUGH
212 BROKER IN PERFORMANCE BY BROKER WITH THE TERMS OF THIS LISTING CONTRACT.

213 　　　　　(GENERAL PROVISIONS OF STANDARD BUSINESS OFFER TO PURCHASE)

214 　　　If this offer is the result of a co-brokerage, then all money paid herewith shall be held in the selling broker's trust account until the acceptance of
215 this offer and shall be transmitted to the listing broker upon such acceptance.

216 　　　Buyer agrees that unless otherwise specified, Buyer will pay all costs of securing any financing to the extent permitted by law, and to perform all
217 acts necessary to expedite such financing and of obtaining any necessary license or permit.

218 　　　Legal possession of business and/or real property shall be delivered to Buyer on date of closing.

219 　　　Personal property tax, prepaid insurance (if assumed) and rents shall be prorated at the time of closing. Proration of personal property taxes
220 shall be based on the personal property taxes for the current year, if known, otherwise on the personal property taxes for the preceding year.

221 　　　Sales tax, if any, shall be paid by Seller. Seller agrees to surrender Seller's sales tax permit timely.

222 　　　Seller shall comply with the applicable Bulk Transfers Law. The execution and/or delivery of a fully executed copy of this contract to Seller
223 shall constitute a written demand for a list of creditors and for the preparation of a schedule of the property transferred, as required by the Bulk
224 Transfers Law.

225 　　　If this offer provides for a land contract, personal property transferred hereunder shall be subject to a security agreement under the Uniform
226 Commercial Code in favor of Seller and no bill of sale shall be given to Buyer until the land contract is paid in full.

227 　　　Seller shall continue to conduct the business in a regular and normal manner and shall use Seller's best efforts to keep available the services of
228 Seller's present employees and to preserve the good will of Seller's suppliers, customers and others having business relations with Seller.

229 　　　This offer is contingent upon the following: Buyer's ability to secure a license or permit of any kind, if the business being sold requires such
230 license or permit.

231 　　　Interest, rents, water and sewer use charges, other assessments, and unused fuels shall be prorated as of the date of closing. Accrued income
232 and expenses, including taxes for the day of closing, shall accrue to Seller.

233 　　　General taxes shall be prorated at the time of closing based on the net general taxes for the current year, if known, otherwise on the net general
234 taxes for the preceding year.

235 　　　CAUTION: If property has not been fully assessed for tax purposes, or reassessment is completed or pending, tax proration shall be on the basis of
236 $ . . . . . . . . . . . . . . . . . . . . . . . . . . . . . . . . . . . . . . estimated annual tax. Make special agreement if area assessment(s) is/are contemplated and/or
237 property owners association has assessed or may assess.

238 　　　Special assessments, if any, for work on site actually commenced or levied prior to date of this offer shall be paid by Seller. All other special
239 assessments, including any contemplated special assessments, shall be paid by Buyer.

240 　　　Seller shall furnish and deliver to Buyer for examination at least 15 days prior to date set for closing, Seller's choice of either:

241 1. 　A complete abstract of title made by an abstract company, extended to within 30 days of closing, said abstract to show Seller's title to be
242 　　　marketable and in the condition called for by this agreement, except for mortgages, judgments or other liens which will be satisfied out of the
243 　　　proceeds of the sale. Buyer shall notify Seller in writing of any valid objection to the title within 10 days after receipt of said abstract and Seller
244 　　　shall then have a reasonable time but not exceeding 60 days, within which to rectify the title (or furnish a title policy as hereinafter provided)
245 　　　and in such cases the time of closing shall be accordingly extended; or

246 2. 　An owner's policy of title insurance in the amount stated in the transfer tax return naming Buyer as the insured, as Buyer's interest may appear,
247 　　　written by a responsible title insurance company licensed by the State of Wisconsin, which policy shall guarantee Seller's title to be in condition
248 　　　called for by this agreement, except for mortgages, judgments, or other liens which will be satisfied out of the proceeds of the sale. A
249 　　　commitment by such a title company, agreeing to issue such a title policy upon the recording of the proper documents as agreed herein, shall be
250 　　　deemed sufficient performance.

251 　　　If this offer provides for a land contract, the same evidence of title shall be furnished prior to the execution of the land contract, and Seller shall
252 furnish written proof, at or before closing, that the total underlying indebtness, if any, is not in excess of the proposed balance of the land contract, and
253 that the payments on this land contract are sufficient to meet all of the obligations of Seller on the underlying indebtedness.

254 　　　Should Buyer fail to carry out this agreement, all money paid hereunder, including any additional earnest money, shall, at the option of Seller,
255 be paid to or retained by Seller as liquidated damages. If such money is held by Broker, Broker shall disburse such money as follows:

256 1. 　To Buyer, if Seller has not notified Buyer and Broker is writing of Seller's election to consider all money paid hereunder as liquidated damages
257 　　　or part payment for specific performance within 60 days of closing date set forth in this agreement; or

258 2. 　To Seller as liquidated damages, subject to deductions of Broker's commission and disbursements, if any, if neither party has commenced a
259 　　　lawsuit on this matter within 120 days of the closing date set forth in this agreement.

260 　　　Should Seller be unable to carry out this agreement by reason of a valid legal defect in title which Buyer is unwilling to waive, all money paid
261 hereunder shall be returned to Buyer forthwith and this contract shall be void.

262 　　　In the event the real property shall be damaged by fire or elements prior to time of closing in an amount of not more than five percent of the
263 selling price, Seller shall be obligated to repair the property and restore it to the same condition that it was on the date of this offer. In the event that
264 such damage shall exceed such sum, this contract may be cancelled at option of Buyer. Should Buyer elect to carry out this agreement despite such
265 damage, Buyer shall be entitled to the insurance proceeds relating to damage to property; however, if this sale is by land contract or a mortgage to
266 Seller, the insurance proceeds shall be held in trust for the sole purpose of restoring the property.

267 　　　All representations and warranties of Seller set forth in this agreement and in any written statements delivered to Buyer by Seller under this
268 agreement will also be true and correct as of the closing date as if made on that date. The representations, warranties and all provisions of this contract
269 shall survive the closing of this transaction.

# Working with the Broker

The more the seller or buyer understands the functions of brokers in general and the broker he is working with in particular, the smoother the relationship will be, and the more likely that it will be successful. Both sellers and buyers should respect the broker's time, and should try to accomplish maximum results with a minimum amount of the broker's time.

## The Seller's Role

The seller's main job is to provide the broker with business information that is as complete as possible, as discussed in Chapter 35, and updating it as necessary. The seller should encourage as many of the broker-age's representatives as possible to tour the place of business so that they will be familiar with it.

The seller should give the broker and other representatives of his firm a narrative account of the nature of the business and why it should be attractive to a buyer. He should make himself readily available to answer the broker's questions and to provide potential purchasers an opportunity to tour the premises and ask questions about the business. The information he provides should be complete, honest, and not exaggerated.

## The Buyer's Role

The buyer's first step is to make clear to the broker exactly what he is looking for—the type of business, acceptable price and size range, acceptable geographical area, the cash he has available for the down payment, and any other appropriate description of what is or is not acceptable. It is not fair for a buyer to waste a broker's time on "fishing expeditions" until he has thought these things through and answered these questions in his own mind. If he has not, he should be up-front and tell the broker so, seeking the broker's guidance, if appropriate.

A buyer who is serious about a business should be entitled to full disclosure of pertinent information. He should have access to all of the information necessary to complete all the steps in the valuation process discussed in this book. Obviously, such information is confidential, and the buyer should treat it that way. It is totally appropriate for the seller to require the buyer to sign a confidentiality agreement before releasing information.

Because of the lack of multiple listing cooperation among business brokers within virtually all cities, a buyer may need to review the listings of several brokers in order to find the business or practice most suitable for him.

## Closing the Deal

A problem constantly facing brokers is buyers and sellers trying to make a deal excluding the broker, so that he loses his commission. If a broker has introduced a buyer to a property, it is both unethical and illegal to avoid paying his commission if the deal is consummated. He is entitled to be paid for his services, and this obligation should be respected by both buyers and sellers.

The broker probably has offer-to-purchase and/or purchase agreement forms available. The comprehensiveness of these forms varies considerably from one brokerage firm to another, and the need for comprehensive forms varies considerably from one transaction to another. Exhibit 33–5 is the Business Offer to Purchase form approved by the Wisconsin Department of Regulation and Licensing.

## Exhibit 33–5

WB 16 Business Offer To Purchase
Approved by the Wisconsin Department of Regulation and Licensing
11-1-83 (optional use date)
5-1-84 (mandatory use date)

Wisconsin Legal Blank Co., Inc.
Milwaukee, Wis.

Page 1 of 3 pages

### BUSINESS OFFER TO PURCHASE
(Not to be used for the sale of corporate stock)

1 ............................................, Wisconsin, ..........................., 19 .....
2     The undersigned Buyer, ......................................................,
3 hereby offers to purchase the business described below, known as (name of business) ...................
4 (type of business) .....................................................................................
5 (street address) ................................. (city) ........................, (state) ...........
6 Included in the purchase price are the following:
7     1.   PERSONAL PROPERTY. All tangible and intangible personal property and rights in personal property owned by Seller and used in the
8 business, including furniture, trade fixtures and equipment, tools used in the business, telephone numbers and listings, customer lists, trade names,
9 business records, supplies, leases, advance lease deposits, customer deposits, signs, all other personal property used in said business, and,
10 if transferable, all permits, special licenses and franchises, except those assets disposed of in the ordinary course of business or as permitted by this
11 offer to purchase.
12     THE PURCHASE PRICE FURTHER INCLUDES (unless stricken):
13     a.   good will
14     b.   stock-in-trade (except that disposed of in the ordinary course of business prior to closing)
15     c.   accounts receivable
16     d.   other:
17     2.   REAL PROPERTY. Real property described as: ............................................
18 .................................................................................................
19 .................................................................................................
20 .................................................................................................
21 .................................................................................................
22 subject to municipal and zoning ordinances, recorded easements for public utilities, recorded building and use restrictions and convenants,
23 general taxes levied in the year of closing and .............................................,
24 in the .................. of ..................................................., County of
25 ........................................, Wisconsin, having a frontage of about ......... feet, with a depth of about
26 ......... feet, and/or consisting of approximately ......... acres or ......... square feet.
27     The purchase price shall be ..........................................................
28 ............................ dollars ($. .....................) and shall be paid on the terms and conditions as follows:
29 Earnest money of $........................ tendered herewith. Additional earnest money of $........................ in the form of
30 ................................................................. to be paid within ......... days of acceptance of offer or on
31 ................................................................. and the balance in cash at closing or as hereafter set forth.
32     The allocation of the purchase price between personal property, real property, good will and value of the lease or other valuation
33 shall be as follows:
34     a.   good will ........................................... $
35     b.   stock-in-trade ..................................... $
36     c.   accounts receivable ............................... $
37     d.   other personal property ........................... $
38     e.   real property ..................................... $
39     f.   other:   $
40     g.   $
41     TOTAL PURCHASE PRICE  $
42     If this offer is the result of a co-brokerage, then all money paid herewith shall be held in the selling broker's trust account until
43 the acceptance of this offer and shall be transmitted to the listing broker upon such acceptance.
44     Additional earnest money payments shall be made to the listing broker and held in the listing broker's trust account or
45 .................................................................................................
46 TIME IS OF THE ESSENCE AS TO: ADDITIONAL EARNEST MONEY PAYMENT, LEGAL POSSESSION, OCCUPANCY OF THE
47 REAL PROPERTY. POSSESSION AND RIGHT TO USE OF AND DISPOSITION OF THE PERSONAL PROPERTY, AND DATE
48 OF CLOSING. (Strike those not applicable.)
49 THE BUYER'S OBLIGATION TO CONCLUDE THIS TRANSACTION IS CONDITIONED UPON THE CONSUMMATION OF THE
50 CONTINGENCIES PROVIDED FOR ON LINES 122 TO 141 AND THE FOLLOWING:
51 (If this offer is subject to financing, or any additional contingency, it must be stated here. If none, so state.)
52 .................................................................................................
53 .................................................................................................
54 .................................................................................................
55 .................................................................................................
56 .................................................................................................
57 .................................................................................................
58 .................................................................................................
59 .................................................................................................
60 .................................................................................................
61 .................................................................................................
62 .................................................................................................
63 .................................................................................................
64 .................................................................................................
65 .................................................................................................
66 .................................................................................................
67 .................................................................................................
68 .................................................................................................
69 .................................................................................................
70 .................................................................................................
71     Buyer agrees that unless otherwise specified, Buyer will pay all costs of securing any financing to the extent permitted by law, and
72 to perform all acts necessary to expedite such financing and of obtaining any necessary license or permit.
73     Legal possession of business and/or real property shall be delivered to Buyer on date of closing.
74     It is understood the business and/or real property is now occupied by ...........................
75 under (oral lease) (written lease), which terms are: ............................................
76 .................................................................................................
77 .................................................................................................
78     Occupancy of ...................................................................................
79 ........................................ shall be given to Buyer on ...............................

## Exhibit 33–5 (*continued*)

Page 2

80  If Seller is permitted to occupy business and/or real property after closing, Seller shall prepay occupancy charge of
81  $ ............................... payable as follows: ...............................
82
83  In addition, the sum of $................................... shall be withheld from the purchase price to be escrowed with
84  ...............................
85  to guarantee delivery of occupancy of business and/or real property to Buyer AND FOR NO OTHER PURPOSE, which sum upon
86  Seller's failure to deliver occupancy shall be paid to Buyer as liquidated damages or returned to Seller if occupancy is delivered to Buyer
87  on the agreed date. This is not an exclusive remedy.
88  All earnest money paid shall be applied toward payment of the purchase price if this offer is accepted on or before
89  ..............................., 19 .....; otherwise, to be returned to the undersigned Buyer no later than
90  ..............................., 19 ..... and this offer shall become null and void.
91  If this offer is accepted, it shall not become binding upon Buyer until copy of accepted offer is deposited, postage prepaid, in the
92  United States mail, addressed to Buyer at ...............................
93  ..............................., or by personal delivery thereof.
94  This transaction is to be closed at the office of Buyer's mortgagee or at the office of ...............................
95  ............................... on or before ..................., 19 ....., or at such other time and place
96  as may be agreed in writing by Buyer and Seller.
97  AS TO THE BUSINESS OR ANY PERSONAL PROPERTY AFFECTED BY THIS AGREEMENT, THE FOLLOWING TERMS
98  SHALL APPLY UNLESS SPECIFICALLY PROVIDED TO THE CONTRARY HEREIN:
99  Personal property tax, prepaid insurance (if assumed) and rents shall be prorated at the time of closing. Proration of personal property taxes
100  shall be based on the personal property taxes for the current year, if known, otherwise on the personal property taxes for the preceding year.
101  Sales tax, if any, shall be paid by Seller. Seller agrees to surrender Seller's sales tax permit timely.
102  Seller shall deliver possession of the personal property on date of closing and shall convey the property by bill of sale or
103  ............................... free and clear of all liens and encumbrances, except
104  ...............................
105  Seller shall comply with the applicable Bulk Transfers Law. The execution and/or delivery of a fully executed copy of this contract to
106  Seller shall constitute a written demand for a list of creditors and for the preparation of a schedule of the property transferred, as required by the
107  Bulk Transfers Law.
108  If this offer provides for a land contract, personal property transferred hereunder shall be subject to a security agreement under the
109  Uniform Commercial Code in favor of Seller and no bill of sale shall be given to Buyer until the land contract is paid in full.
110  If the real property occupied by the business is owned by Seller, but not sold by this agreement, Seller agrees to lease the real property to
111  Buyer on the following terms: ...............................
112  ...............................
113  ...............................
114  ...............................
115  ...............................
116  Seller shall continue to conduct the business in a regular and normal manner and shall use Seller's best efforts to keep available the services
117  of Seller's present employees and to preserve the good will of Seller's suppliers, customers and others having business relations with Seller.
118  If stock-in-trade is purchased, its cost will not be in excess of $ ............................... and the purchase
119  will be based on the following cost: ...............................
120  ...............................
121  This offer is contingent upon the following:
122  1. Buyer's ability to secure a license or permit of any kind, if the business being sold requires such license or permit.
123  2. Buyer being able to obtain a transfer of an existing franchise or the issuance of a new franchise, if the business being sold is a
124  franchise business.
125  3. Seller furnishing Buyer within ...... days of the date of acceptance of this offer, and Buyers being satisfied with same, the
126  information and schedules designated with an "X" in the space preceding lines 129 to 141. IF BUYER FAILS TO REGISTER
127  DISAPPROVAL OF ANY OF THESE ITEMS IN WRITING WITHIN ......... DAYS OF RECEIVING THEM,
128  DISAPPROVAL SHALL BE WAIVED.
129  ____A. An inventory of all furniture, fixtures and equipment included in this transaction.
130  ____B. Copies of all leases affecting equipment, real estate or signs; and all copies of other leases pertaining to the business.
131  ____C. Estimated principal balance of accounts receivable.
132  ____D. Estimated principal balance of accounts payable.
133  ____E. Copy of profit and loss statements, balance sheets, business books and records, and income tax returns for the
134  following years: ..............................., which Buyer may have examined by Buyer's agents or attorneys.
135  ____F. Copies of latest real estate and personal property tax bills.
136  ____G. Copies of franchise agreements, if any.
137  ____H. Copy of corporate minutes approving or authorizing the sale, if Seller is a corporation.
138  ____I. Copies of all licenses used in operating the business.
139  ____J. An agreement regarding a restriction on Seller competing with Buyer after the closing of this transaction.
140  ____K. Others: ...............................
141  ...............................
142  AS TO ANY REAL PROPERTY AFFECTED BY THIS OFFER TO PURCHASE, THE FOLLOWING TERMS SHALL APPLY
143  UNLESS SPECIFICALLY PROVIDED TO THE CONTRARY HEREIN:
144  Real property transferred includes all fixtures on the property on the date of this offer, which will be delivered free and clear of
145  encumbrances, EXCEPT THAT THE FOLLOWING ITEMS WILL NOT BE INCLUDED IN SALE: ...............................
146  ...............................
147  ...............................
148  Interest, rents, water and sewer use charges, other assessments, and unused fuels shall be prorated as of the date of closing.
149  Accrued income and expenses, including taxes for the day of closing, shall accrue to the Seller.
150  General real property taxes shall be prorated at the time of closing based on the net general taxes for the current year, if known,
151  otherwise on the net general taxes for the preceding year.
152  CAUTION: If property has not been fully assessed for tax purposes, or reassessment is completed or pending, tax proration shall be
153  on the basis of $............................... estimated annual tax. Make special agreement if area assessment(s) is/are contemplated
154  and/or property owners association has assessed or may assess.
155  Special assessments, if any, for work on site actually commenced or levied prior to date of this offer shall be paid by Seller. All
156  other special assessments, including any contemplated special assessments, shall be paid by Buyer.
157  Seller shall furnish and deliver to Buyer for examination at least 15 days prior to the date set for closing, Seller's choice of either:
158  1. A complete abstract of title made by an abstract company, extended to within 30 days of the closing, said abstract to show Seller's title to
159  be marketable and in the condition called for by this agreement, except for mortgages, judgments or other liens which will be satisfied out
160  of the proceeds of the sale. Buyer shall notify Seller in writing of any valid objection to the title within 10 days after receipt of said abstract
161  and Seller shall then have a reasonable time, but not exceeding 60 days, within which to rectify the title (or furnish a title policy as
162  hereinafter provided) and in such cases the time of closing shall be accordingly extended; or
163  2. An owner's policy of title insurance in the amount stated in the transfer tax return, naming Buyer as the insured, as Buyer's interest may
164  appear, written by a responsible title insurance company licensed by the State of Wisconsin, which policy shall guarantee Seller's title to be
165  in condition called for by this agreement, except for mortgages, judgments, or other liens which will be satisfied out of the proceeds of the
166  sale. A commitment by such a title company, agreeing to issue such a title policy upon the recording of the proper documents as agreed
167  herein, shall be deemed sufficient performance.
168  THIS OFFER INCLUDES THE BALANCE OF TERMS ON PAGE 3

## Exhibit 33–5 (*concluded*)

**BUSINESS OFFER TO PURCHASE** (continued)                                                                    Page 3

169    The following terms are part of the offer to purchase dated . . . . . . . . . . . . . . . . . . . . . . . . . . . . . . . . . . . . . . . . , for business at
170
171    If this offer provides for a land contract, the same evidence of title shall be furnished prior to the execution of the land contract, and Seller
172    shall furnish written proof, at or before closing, that the total underlying indebtedness, if any, is not in excess of the proposed balance of the land
173    contract, and that the payments on this land contract are sufficient to meet all of the obligations of Seller on the underlying indebtedness.
174    Seller shall, upon payment of the purchase price, convey the real property by warranty deed, or other conveyance provided herein, free
175    and clear of all liens and encumbrances, except those stated on lines 22 to 23, provided none of the foregoing prohibit present use.

### SELLER'S WARRANTIES AND REPRESENTATIONS

176
177    Seller warrants and represents to Buyer that Seller has no notice or knowledge of:
178  1.  As to the business and personal property,
179       a) Any material defects in any of the equipment, appliances, fixtures, tools or furniture included in this transaction, and further warrants
180           that all will be in good working order on the day of closing.
181       b) Any encumbrances on the business being sold, all integral parts thereof, or the personal property being conveyed in conjunction
182           with the business, except as stated in this contract and in any schedule attached to it.
183       c) Any litigation, government proceeding or investigation being in progress or being threatened or in prospect against or relating to
184           this business.
185       d. Any road change or road work which would materially affect the present use of the property.
186       e) Any right granted to underlying lienholders to accelerate their obligation by reason of the transfer of ownership, or any permission to
187           transfer being required and not obtained.
188       f) Any unpaid income taxes, sales taxes, payroll taxes, social security taxes, unemployment taxes, or any other
189           employer/employee taxes due and payable or accrued.
190       g) Any failure of the financial statements and schedules to present the true and correct condition of the business as of the date
191           on the statements and schedules and that since the date of the last financial statements and schedules provided by Seller
192           there has been no change in the financial condition or operations of the business except changes in the ordinary course of
193           business, which changes have not in the aggregate been materially adverse.
194  2.  As to the real property,
195       a) Any planned or commenced public improvements which may result in special assessments or otherwise materially affect the property.
196       b) Any government agency or court order requiring repair, alteration or correction of any existing condition.
197       c) Any structural or mechanical defect of material significance in property, including inadequacy for normal use of mechanical
198           systems, sanitary disposal systems and well, and unsafe well water according to state standards.
199    Seller further warrants and represents to Buyer that:

200  1.  The property is zoned for present use, or . . . . . . . . . . . . . . . . . . . . . . . . . . . . . . . . . . . . . . . . . . . . . . . . . . . . . . . . . . . .
201    . . . . . . . . . . . . . . . . . . . . . . . . . . . . . . . . . . . . . . . . . . . . . . . . . . . . . . . . . . . . . . . . . . . . . . . . . . . . . . . . . . . .
202  2.  The property is not located in a flood plain, as per . . . . . . . . . . . . . . . . . . . . . . . . . . . . . . . . . . . . . . . . . . . . . . . . . . .
203    EXCEPTIONS TO WARRANTIES AND REPRESENTATIONS STATED IN LINES 177 TO 202 . . . . . . . . . . . . . . . . . . . . . . .
204    . . . . . . . . . . . . . . . . . . . . . . . . . . . . . . . . . . . . . . . . . . . . . . . . . . . . . . . . . . . . . . . . . . . . . . . . . . . . . . . . . . . .
205    . . . . . . . . . . . . . . . . . . . . . . . . . . . . . . . . . . . . . . . . . . . . . . . . . . . . . . . . . . . . . . . . . . . . . . . . . . . . . . . . . . . .
206    . . . . . . . . . . . . . . . . . . . . . . . . . . . . . . . . . . . . . . . . . . . . . . . . . . . . . . . . . . . . . . . . . . . . . . . . . . . . . . . . . . . .
207
208    All representations and warranties of Seller set forth in this agreement and in any written statements delivered to Buyer by Seller under
209    this agreement will also be true and correct as of the closing date as if made on that date. The representations, warranties and all provisions of
210    this contract shall survive the closing of this transaction.
211    Should Buyer fail to carry out this agreement, all money paid hereunder, including any additional earnest money, shall, at the option of
212    Seller, be paid to or retained by Seller as liquidated damages. If such money is held by Broker, Broker shall disburse such money as follows:
213  1.  To Buyer, if Seller has not notified Buyer and Broker in writing of Seller's election to consider all money paid hereunder as
214       liquidated damages or part payment for specific performance within 60 days of closing date set forth in this agreement; or
215  2.  To Seller as liquidated damages, subject to deductions of Broker's commission and disbursements, if any, if neither party has com-
216       menced a lawsuit on this matter within 120 days of the closing date set forth in this agreement.
217    Should Seller be unable to carry out this agreement by reason of a valid legal defect in title which Buyer is unwilling to waive, all
218    money paid hereunder shall be returned to Buyer forthwith, and this contract shall be void.
219    In the event the real property shall be damaged by fire or elements prior to time of closing in an amount of not more than five percent of
220    the selling price, Seller shall be obligated to repair the property and restore it to the same condition that it was on the date of this offer. In the
221    event that such damage shall exceed such sum, this contract may be cancelled at option of Buyer. Should Buyer elect to carry out this agreement
222    despite such damage, Buyer shall be entitled to the insurance proceeds relating to damage to property; however, if this sale is by land contract
223    or a mortgage to Seller, the insurance proceeds shall be held in trust for the sole purpose of restoring the property.
224    SPECIAL PROVISIONS: . . . . . . . . . . . . . . . . . . . . . . . . . . . . . . . . . . . . . . . . . . . . . . . . . . . . . . . . . . . . . . . . . .
225    . . . . . . . . . . . . . . . . . . . . . . . . . . . . . . . . . . . . . . . . . . . . . . . . . . . . . . . . . . . . . . . . . . . . . . . . . . . . . . . . . . . .
226    . . . . . . . . . . . . . . . . . . . . . . . . . . . . . . . . . . . . . . . . . . . . . . . . . . . . . . . . . . . . . . . . . . . . . . . . . . . . . . . . . . . .
227    . . . . . . . . . . . . . . . . . . . . . . . . . . . . . . . . . . . . . . . . . . . . . . . . . . . . . . . . . . . . . . . . . . . . . . . . . . . . . . . . . . . .
228    . . . . . . . . . . . . . . . . . . . . . . . . . . . . . . . . . . . . . . . . . . . . . . . . . . . . . . . . . . . . . . . . . . . . . . . . . . . . . . . . . . . .
229    . . . . . . . . . . . . . . . . . . . . . . . . . . . . . . . . . . . . . . . . . . . . . . . . . . . . . . . . . . . . . . . . . . . . . . . . . . . . . . . . . . . .
230    . . . . . . . . . . . . . . . . . . . . . . . . . . . . . . . . . . . . . . . . . . . . . . . . . . . . . . . . . . . . . . . . . . . . . . . . . . . . . . . . . . . .
231    . . . . . . . . . . . . . . . . . . . . . . . . . . . . . . . . . . . . . . . . . . . . . . . . . . . . . . . . . . . . . . . . . . . . . . . . . . . . . . . . . . . .
232    . . . . . . . . . . . . . . . . . . . . . . . . . . . . . . . . . . . . . . . . . . . . . . . . . . . . . . . . . . . . . . . . . . . . . . . . . . . . . . . . . . . .
233    . . . . . . . . . . . . . . . . . . . . . . . . . . . . . . . . . . . . . . . . . . . . . . . . . . . . . . . . . . . . . . . . . . . . . . . . . . . . . . . . . . . .
234    Buyer has read, fully understands and acknowledges receipt of a copy of this offer to purchase. BUYER IS ADVISED THAT
235    BROKER HAS AN AGENCY RELATIONSHIP WITH SELLER UNLESS BUYER HAS AN AGREEMENT WITH BROKER.

236    . . . . . . . . . . . . . . . . . . . . . . . . . . . . . . , 19 . . . . . .    . . . . . . . . . . . . . . . . . . . . . . . . . . . . . . . . . . . . . . . . .
237                                                                                                             (Buyer)
238    . . . . . . . . . . . . . . . . . . . . . . . . . . . . . . . . . . . . . . . . . .    . . . . . . . . . . . . . . . . . . . . . . . . . . . . . . . . . . . . . . . . .
239                    (Buyer)                                                                    (Buyer)
240    THIS OFFER IS HEREBY ACCEPTED. THE UNDERSIGNED HEREBY AGREES TO SELL AND CONVEY THE ABOVE-
241    MENTIONED PROPERTY ON THE TERMS AND CONDITIONS AS SET FORTH AND ACKNOWLEDGES RECEIPT OF A COPY
242    OF THIS AGREEMENT.

243    . . . . . . . . . . . . . . . . . . . . . . . . . . . . . . . , 19 . . . . . .    . . . . . . . . . . . . . . . . . . . . . . . . . . . . . . . . . . . . . . . . .
244                                                                                                             (Seller)

245    . . . . . . . . . . . . . . . . . . . . . . . . . . . . . . . . . . . . . . . . . .    . . . . . . . . . . . . . . . . . . . . . . . . . . . . . . . . . . . . . . . . .
246                    (Seller)                                                                   (Seller)
247                                             EARNEST MONEY RECEIPT
248    Earnest money in the amount of $. . . . . . . . . . . . . in form of . . . . . . . . . . . . . . . . . . . . . . . . . . . . . . . . . . . . . . . . . . .
249    received from . . . . . . . . . . . . . . . . . . . . . . . . . . . . . . . . . . . . . . . . . . . . . . . . . . . . . . . . . . . The undersigned hereby agrees
250    to hold same in an authorized real estate trust account in Wisconsin, or transmit the same in accordance with the terms of the above
251    offer.

252                                                                                    . . . . . . . . . . . . . . . . . . . . . . . . . . . . . . . . . . . . , Broker
253    . . . . . . . . . . . . . . . . . . . . . . . . . . . . . . , 19 . . . . . .
254                                                                           By . . . . . . . . . . . . . . . . . . . . . . . . . . . . . . . . . . . . . . . . .
255    Name of licensee who negotiated this offer with Buyer . . . . . . . . . . . . . . . . . . . . . . . . . . . . . . . . . . . . . . . . . . . . . . . . . .

Even if the parties choose to use the standard forms provided by the broker or obtained elsewhere, I recommend that both buyer and seller have their attorneys review the documents before finalizing the deal. However, both parties should expect their attorneys to be both expeditious and reasonable in the language they suggest in the purchase agreement. Too many deals have been killed unnecessarily by attorneys either failing to act on a timely basis or unreasonably demanding language that is unacceptable to the other party.

A significant proportion of the transactions put into escrow through some brokerage firms never close, and many that do close take an excruciatingly long time. I have heard of brokerage firms which, on the average, close less than half the transactions put into escrow. Firms that close over 90 percent of the transactions put into escrow tend to be very proud of that record. High closing records come with firms that have qualified buyers with cash available and sellers that provide full and timely disclosure of all information that a buyer needs and can verify. If these conditions are met, a transaction should clear escrow on a timely basis, to the satisfaction of both buyer and seller.

# Chapter 34

## An Inside Look at the Business Appraisal Profession

This chapter is primarily written to provide some insight into business appraisal for owners of businesses and professional practices and their professional advisors (e.g., attorneys, CPAs, financial planners, bankers, and other consultants and confidants) who are likely to be involved in using the services of a business appraiser. However, the perspective should also be of interest to those who may be considering the business appraisal profession as a career.

# Professionalism of the Business Appraisal Discipline

According to the U.S. Small Business Administration, there were over 17 million businesses in the United States in the 1980s:

Over 2.8 million corporations.

Almost 1.5 million partnerships.

Over 13 million sole proprietorships.

Every year millions of businesses and professional practices completely change ownership. There also are millions of partial changes of ownership. Moreover, hundreds of millions of dollars of payments are made every year based on decisions about the values of businesses. Such payments arise from gift, estate, and inheritance taxes, ad valorem (property) taxes, matrimonial property settlements, amounts of relief in damage cases, and many other matters. Considering the economic importance to millions of people of the proper appraisal of businesses and business interests, it seems almost incredible to me that it is only in the last few years that business appraisal has begun to emerge as a unified discipline in the United States.

## Default by the Business Schools

Economists and business school professors taught us in no uncertain terms that the most important objective of the owner, or head, of a business enterprise—who acts rationally as an "Adam Smith"-type, economically motivated person—should be to maximize the value of the firm. Yet, I did not know of a single business school, as late as the mid-1970s, that offered a single course in how to value a business, even as an elective, much less as a required course. In 1985, only about a dozen business schools offer such a course. The number appears to be growing, but slowly. (A few schools offer a multidisciplinary program in valuation sciences. Information about such programs is available from the American Society of Appraisers in Washington, D.C.)

Courses abound in the closely related subjects of security analysis and investment portfolio management, but such courses are narrowly focused, dealing almost entirely with minority interests in large corporations, in the form of publicly traded stocks and bonds. Such courses do not, for the most part, deal directly with the question of the value of the total firm. Furthermore, they do not deal at all with the values of either total or partial interests in closely held firms.

Business schools also offer courses in corporate finance, whose content tends to focus on obtaining and managing funds and making investment decisions in regard to capital budgeting. Capital budgeting decisions have much in common with decisions on how much it may be worth paying for an existing business. However, business schools, in general, fail to point out this important connection.

The analytical skills germane to the disciplines of security analysis and corporate finance are essential to the discipline of business appraisal. But the business schools have left a major gap by not undertaking the logical step of applying the skills of security analysis and corporate finance to the valuation of closely held companies and interests in them. The result is that the conceptual leadership in the development of the business appraisal discipline has resulted from collaborative efforts on the part of the community of professional practitioners, rather than from the academic community.

## Canadians Lead the Way

An organized effort toward conceptual development of the business appraisal discipline started in Canada earlier than in the United States. Not surprisingly, there was a specific catalyst that spurred the earlier organized development of the discipline in Canada. That catalyst was called Valuation Day, December 31, 1971 (Valuation Day for publicly traded companies was December 22, 1971).

The significance of Valuation Day was that it set a base valuation date from which all capital appreciation was measured for capital gains taxes and estate taxes. Consequently, the valuation of all property, including all businesses and business interests, as of that date became a matter of considerable significance. Since there were no market quotations for the values of closely held businesses and business interests, there suddenly was a need to develop values as of one specific date for a large number of entities.

The Canadian Institute of Business Valuators (CIBV, originally called the Canadian Association of Business Valuators) was born on January 6, 1971. Since then, it has held biennial meetings, with the proceedings published as *The Journal of Business Valuation*. The CIBV holds educational meetings for its members at various intervals.

The Canadian Institute of Business Valuators has developed a rigorous examination to test a candidate's professional skills in business valuation. The professional designation of CBV (certified business valuator) is awarded to those who demonstrate three years of full-time experience in business appraisal, or five years of part-time experience, or two years and a required course of study, who pass the exam, and meet certain other requirements. Information on CIBV may be obtained from The Canadian Institute of Business Valuators, 121 Bloor Street East, Third Floor, Toronto, Ontario M4W 3M5.

## The ESOP Association Valuation Advisory Committee

The first organized national effort in the United States toward some unification among leading business appraisers also came largely as a result of certain tax legislation. The relevant legislation was the portion of the 1974 Tax Act that granted especially favorable tax treatment to companies with Employee Stock Ownership Plans (ESOPs). This favorable tax treatment spurred the development of thousands of ESOPs, the large majority of which were in privately held companies.

Each private company with an ESOP must have its stock valued annually, and the nature of an ESOP poses certain unique valuation problems. In order to address these valuation problems in some unified manner, a group was formed consisting of business appraisers who were active in the valuation of ESOP shares in all parts of the country. This group became an advisory committee of The ESOP Association, an organization of companies that have ESOPs.

The ESOP Association Valuation Advisory Committee meets annually, in conjunction with The ESOP Association annual meeting, primarily to discuss issues concerning the valuation of ESOP shares in privately held companies. The Committee has worked toward the development of valuation guidelines, and in 1984 developed a 75-page booklet titled *Valuing ESOP Shares*.[1] Committee members also put on educational sessions for members of the ESOP Association and companies considering ESOPs.

Information on The ESOP Association may be obtained from The ESOP Association, 1725 DeSales Street, Washington, D.C. 20036.

## Business Valuation Committee of the American Society of Appraisers

The need for a broad program of education and professional accreditation in the discipline of business valuation finally was met with the formation in 1981 of the Business Valuation Committee of the American Society of Appraisers (A.S.A.). The A.S.A. is a long-standing, multidisciplinary organization, offering education and professional accreditation in many appraisal disciplines, including real property, machinery and equipment, personal property, and public utilities.

Prior to the formation of the Business Valuation Committee, the A.S.A. had for many years offered accreditation in "Intangible Property," which included stocks or other interests in businesses, as well as patents, copyrights, and other intangible property. However, there were not many candidates for accreditation under that designation. Under the auspices of the Business Valuation Committee, the name of the accreditation category was changed from "Intangible Property" to "Business Valuation," and the content of the examinations was revised to include a heavy emphasis on current techniques for appraising busi-

---

[1] *Valuing ESOP Shares* (Washington, D.C.: The ESOP Association, 1984).

nesses of all sizes, professional practices, and partial interests in them. The Business Valuation Committee now has the support of almost all the leading business appraisal firms in the United States, and in 1984 and 1985 the Business Valuation discipline was the fastest-growing category of accreditation in the American Society of Appraisers.

The professional designation *A.S.A.* stands for Senior Member of the American Society of Appraisers. For one to acquire it, the following are needed: five years of experience in the discipline in which the designation is granted, passing the relevant examination, and submitting two appraisal reports that meet the standards of the examining committee.

When an appraiser uses a professional grade of A.S.A. membership as a credential in connection with a valuation report, the Society's Code of Ethics requires that he set forth the discipline in which Member or Senior grade was achieved in his statement of qualifications and/or limiting conditions presented to, or received by, clients (e.g., "Peter Plausible, A.S.A., Business Valuation"). It would be a breach of ethics for someone who is accredited in Machinery and Equipment appraisal, for example, to write a Business Valuation report and be identified only as "Sandy Shoveler, A.S.A.," which might mislead the reader into thinking that the author was accredited in Business Valuation when in fact the accreditation was in a different appraisal discipline.

The American Society of Appraisers holds an annual meeting that includes members from all appraisal disciplines. In recent years, the annual meeting has included two days of educational meetings on business appraisal topics, with two days of basic sessions and two days of advanced sessions running concurrently. The Business Valuation Committee also sponsors a two-day Advanced Business Valuation Seminar each fall. In addition, local chapters of the A.S.A. sponsor educational programs from time to time.

Subcommittees of the Business Valuation Committee include Education, Examination Development, Board of Examiners, Bibliography, Relationships with Other Professionals, Directory, Publications, Theory and Techniques, and Public Relations.

The Business Valuation Committee also publishes a quarterly journal titled *Business Valuation News*, and the A.S.A. publishes a multidisciplinary appraisal journal titled *Valuation*.

Information on the American Society of Appraisers and a list of Senior Members accredited in Business Valuation may be obtained from the A.S.A. National Headquarters, P.O. Box 17265, Washington, D.C. 20041.

# Structure of the Business Appraisal Profession

The structure of the business appraisal profession can best be described as "fragmented." There are a few firms around the country that specialize in business valuation assignments of all kinds, maintaining a staff of full-time professional business appraisers. There also are appraisal firms that are primarily involved in other appraisal disciplines, such as real estate and/or machinery and equipment, which also have on staff a number of full-time professional business appraisers. There are a number of organizations in other industries, such as investment banking, public accounting, and commercial banking, that have small, specialized divisions that devote all, or some significant part, of their time to business appraisal work. There are also a number of small partnerships and sole practitioners specializing in business valuation. In addition, there are thousands who practice business valuation occasionally or part-time.

The structure of the business appraisal profession has changed greatly in the first half of the 1980s, and at middecade I see no sign of that transition ending. A significant portion of the larger appraisal firms has changed hands in the last five years, accompanied by a significant turnover in personnel. Several large organizations in other fields have started business appraisal divisions, as noted earlier, some of which have already been discontinued or sharply curtailed.

# Profile of a Business Appraiser

One of the questions I am most frequently asked is "What do you look for when you hire a business appraiser?" The following paragraphs attempt to answer that question.

## Academic Education

Almost all business appraisers have a college degree in some discipline, and a significant portion have one or more advanced degrees. Many have done a considerable amount of graduate study, even though it may not have been carried through to a master's or other higher level degree. Most have achieved above-average to excellent grades.

In general, I think that the most relevant academic degree is in business administration with a major in finance. There is no question about the fact that a broad understanding of how businesses operate is an important part of a business appraiser's education, and many believe that that can best be achieved academically through an M.B.A. program. I think that an M.B.A. is desirable. Nevertheless, I would rather hire someone who has top grades in an undergraduate concentration in finance from a school with a good finance department than someone with an M.B.A. but little concentration in finance or from a school with a weak finance department.

Accounting is an essential tool in business appraisal, and I encourage appraisers to have at least two years, preferably through the intermediate accounting (as opposed to cost, management, tax, or some other specialized aspect of accounting) series. That often means going back to school, since most nonaccounting majors did not choose to step up to intermediate accounting, which is one of the more challenging series of accounting courses in most business schools, as part of their undergraduate programs.

Mathematics, journalism, and many other undergraduate degrees may lead into a career in business appraisal, albeit many times by a circuitous route. A basic understanding of applied microeconomics and macroeconomics is also a necessary part of the business appraiser's tool kit, and virtually all business schools require a year or so of such courses. Watch out for degrees in economics, however. Most universities offer their degrees in economics through their schools of liberal arts rather than through their schools of business administration. Unlike the business schools, which require courses in economics, most liberal arts schools do not require their economics majors to take any courses in business administration. Therefore, if a person with an economics degree from a college of liberal arts were ever to learn anything about business administration, that education usually would have to come from outside his basic degree program.

## Professional Credentials

As discussed earlier, the basic professional credential in the field of business appraisal is the A.S.A.—that is, Senior Member of the American Society of Appraisers, with accreditation specifically in the Business Valuation discipline. (It is also possible to attain dual accreditation, that is, certification in more than one discipline in which the appraiser has demonstrated that he meets the requisite knowledge and experience requirements, such as both real estate and business valuation.)

However, I also expect most, or all, of the appraisers on my staff to have, or to attain, the professional designation of Chartered Financial Analyst (C.F.A.). That is a tough credential to attain, requiring demonstrated proficiency in seven areas: (1) accounting, (2) economics, (3) analysis of equity securities (mostly common stocks), (4) analysis of fixed income securities (bonds and notes), (5) quantitative analysis, (6) investment portfolio management, and (7) professional ethics. The candidate must pass three exams, each a year apart, and must pass each phase before being allowed to sit for the next phase.

As with business school classes in the field of investments, the C.F.A. program is narrowly focused on the analysis of minority interests in publicly traded corporations. Because of this focus, many business appraisers feel that the C.F.A. designation is not particularly important for the appraisal of closely held businesses, especially smaller ones. Nevertheless, I believe that the basic analytical skills involved are an essential part of the knowledge of a business appraiser. With the necessary additional knowledge and appropriate adaptation, most of these skills can be extended to the valuation of an interest of 100 percent, or any fraction, in a business or professional practice of any size and form of organization, whether closely held or publicly traded.

For several years, I have carried on a friendly running debate with an esteemed colleague, who recently retired from his position as head of another business appraisal firm, about the relative importance of the C.F.A. professional designation versus the M.B.A. academic degree. My position has been that if a business appraiser is going to have one or the other, I prefer the C.F.A. over the M.B.A., because of the direct relevance of much of the content of the C.F.A. program to business appraisal; the content of most M.B.A. programs, on the other hand, tends to be more general, and less specific in the field of financial analysis. My colleague feels that the broad understanding of business through an M.B.A. program is more important. Naturally, we would both like to be staffed completely with appraisers with both the M.B.A. and C.F.A. (as well as the A.S.A.), but we realize that this is unrealistic.

## Experience

Apart from hiring people with previous professional business appraisal experience, I have had both good and bad results both from hiring trainees straight out of school and from converting people with other experience and backgrounds to business appraisers. Generally, I have found that people with experience in securities analysis, portfolio management, and corporate finance seem to be more adaptable to business appraisal than most people with other kinds of backgrounds. Some people with accounting experience have succeeded as business appraisers, as have some with journalism and other varied types of experience.

In any case, I believe that the personal characteristics listed in the following section are much more important than the specific experience background in judging potential success as a business appraiser.

## Personal Characteristics

I look for the following characteristics:

1. High degree of honesty and ethics.
2. High degree of intelligence.
3. Analytical mind.
4. Intellectual curiosity and desire to learn.
5. Detail-oriented, but also having the ability to grasp the "big picture" and quickly identify the most significant factors.
6. Solid grounding in the field of finance.
7. Desire and ability to write well (most appraisal assignments result in a written report).
8. Propensity to work hard (like most professions, business appraisal is not a 9-to-5, 40-hour-per-week career).
9. Pleasant personality, ability to get along well with clients and other members of the staff.
10. Willingness to accept responsibility in a professional manner.
11. Ability to work efficiently, not easily distracted or a frequent visitor to the water cooler.
12. Professional appearance and demeanor.
13. Motivation to be a business appraiser as a career.

**14.** Willingness to travel (business appraisers help keep the airlines in business).

The above list represents my personal perspective, of course. Now that I reflect for a moment, though, on the members of the Business Valuation Committee of the American Society of Appraisers, I think that the above list represents a pretty good profile of the characteristics of the group as a whole.

# Chapter 35

## Working With a Business Appraiser

*In any transaction where "value" is the most important issue, a competent, experienced, and professional appraiser should be consulted on behalf of the client to determine the true value of an enterprise.*[1]

Situations that may call for a professional appraisal can include any of those listed in Chapter 3, as well as a few others. In addition to the basic service of appraising the business or practice, the professional appraiser may be able to provide related services.

# Services Typically Offered by Business Appraisers

Although not all business appraisers necessarily offer all services, the following are some services typically offered by business appraisers.

Preliminary appraisal opinions.

Complete appraisals, with oral reports only, brief letter reports, relatively short written reports, or comprehensive, fully documented appraisal reports.

Expert testimony.

Service as arbitrator in valuation disputes.

Assistance with purchase or sale negotiations.

Assistance in structuring purchase or sale terms.

Estate planning assistance.

Assistance in drafting of buy/sell agreement.

Assistance with public offerings.

Fairness opinion on a proposed transaction.

Assistance in designing classes of business interests in corporate or partnership reorganizations.

Litigation support research.

Allocation of purchase price among classes of assets.

# Finding and Engaging an Appraiser

The task of locating the right expert appraiser for the job at hand sometimes is undertaken by the owner(s) of the business or professional practice in question. More often, however, assistance in finding an appraiser is provided by the owner's attorney, CPA, insurance agent, or other professional advisor; these individuals are usually familiar with the qualifications of one or several business appraisers, some of whom they may have worked with on past occasions. If a referral is not available, a list of Senior Members of the American Society of Appraisers accredited in business valuation is available from the national headquarters of that organization, as noted in the previous chapter.

---

[1] John E. Moye, *Buying and Selling Businesses* (Minneapolis: National Practice Institute, 1983), p. 25.

# Selecting the Appraiser

The more the client or his advisors know about the qualifications of any business appraisal firm or individual being considered, the greater the likelihood of selecting the appraiser who is best suited for the particular assignment. An appraiser being considered usually will have available a brochure describing his firm and a resume of his own qualifications and will provide references on request. It is appropriate to interview a prospective appraiser, either on the telephone or in person; at that time, it is proper to inquire about his and/or his firm's specific experience relating directly to the assignment at hand. Alternatively, the appraisal firm or appraiser may be contacted in writing, with the assignment described and an inquiry made about the appraiser's qualifications to perform it.

The exact qualifications desired depend to some degree on the specific situation. Certainly, if there is litigation or potential litigation involved, experience with court testimony is an important factor. In any case, it is desirable that the appraiser be familiar with the law as it relates to the particular valuation situation. An article in *Inc.* magazine offered the following "Five tips on choosing a valuation expert:

1. Select someone with documented valuation experience, including a minimum of two years in the field and the references to prove it.
2. Choose an individual who is familiar with your industry.
3. Hire a professional who is willing to quote his rates in advance.
4. Pick a person who knows valuation law.
5. Find an expert with experience defending his valuations in court and before Internal Revenue Service agents."[2]

The article also adds:

> Seeking a valuator who is a member of the American Society of Appraisers (A.S.A.) is also a good idea. To become a member an individual must pass written and oral tests, have a minimum of two years' full-time experience as a professional appraiser, and abide by the organization's code of ethics. Distinctions are made by discipline and level of experience: Regular members have worked two to four years as professional appraisers, while senior members have five or more years of experience.[3]

When contacting a prospective appraiser, it is desirable to be as upfront and complete as possible about such matters as the identity, nature and size of the company, the purpose and scope of the appraisal assignment, and the desired schedule. Disclosure of confidential client information to unauthorized parties is prohibited, of course, by the Code of Ethics of the American Society of Appraisers. Confidentiality of client information should not be a problem when dealing with a reputable appraisal firm.

If there is any possible conflict of interest, this matter should be explored at the outset of the contract with the prospective appraiser. If the prospective appraiser contacted has any conflict of interest with

---

[2] Donna Sammons, "Evaluating the Valuators," *Inc.*, May 1983, p. 186. Reprinted with permission, Inc. magazine, (May, 1983). Copyright © (1983) by Inc. Publishing Company, 38 Commercial Wharf, Boston, MA 02110.

[3] Ibid.

respect to either the client or the assignment, he would be expected to disclose such conflict immediately.

# Fees and Scheduling

Besides determining that the prospective appraiser is properly qualified, the client and the appraiser should reach a mutual understanding about fees and schedule. Most appraisal firms base their fees on the amount of time that the engagement will require for one or several members of the appraisal staff, plus out-of-pocket expenses. Most appraisers have an hourly or daily billing rate, much as in a law practice. Some assignments, especially ones where the required time is difficult or impossible to estimate accurately, may be undertaken strictly on an hourly basis, usually with some estimated range of cost. If the appraiser has been furnished with sufficient information, and if the assignment can be well defined, most appraisers are willing to commit to a fixed fee for their services, plus out-of-pocket expenses. If court testimony or arbitration may be involved, the appraiser may quote a fixed fee for the basic appraisal, with the trial preparation, depositions, and court time charged on an hourly or daily basis, since the amount of such time required usually is out of the appraiser's control.

The following information about a prospective appraisal assignment would be helpful to an appraiser for quoting a fixed or estimated fee for an assignment, as well as for discussing scheduling:

1. Line(s) of business.
2. Locations(s) of operations.
3. Form of organization (corporation, Subchapter S corporation, general or limited partnerships, sole proprietorship).
4. Purpose of the appraisal.
5. Interest to be valued (100 percent or some partial interest).
6. Applicable valuation date or dates.
7. Status of financial statements (audited, reviewed, externally compiled, internally compiled, tax returns only, records in shoe boxes, and whether on cash or accrual basis).
8. Any subsidiaries or financial interest in other companies.
9. Annual revenues.
10. Annual profits.
11. Approximate book value.
12. Form and extent of appraisal report desired.
13. Desired schedule.

Some clients or their attorneys wait until the last minute to contact an appraiser, failing to allow a comfortable lead time to do the job thoroughly. In some cases, the client has received an unexpected offer for the purchase of his company, and he needs the opinion of the expert appraiser in only a few days in order to formulate his response. Most appraisal firms have enough flexibility in their staff scheduling to accommodate such urgent needs when necessary. Hopefully, however, those who have read this book have gained some appreciation of the complexities of business appraisal, and will give their appraisers as much lead time as possible to do the job properly. In most cases, that means a matter of weeks rather than days. If litigation is involved, lead time for adequate preparation—60 to 90 days in most cases—becomes even more important.

# Professional Services Agreement

Once the appraiser has been selected and the assignment and fee arrangements agreed upon, the engagement should be committed to writing, usually through the appraisal firm's standard professional services agreement, supplemented as necessary to provide complete details of the assignment. The professional services agreement basically should cover the definition of the valuation assignment, as discussed in some detail in Chapter 1. To summarize, the professional services agreement, engagement letter, or whatever form is used to formalize the engagement in writing, should cover the following points:

1. The property to be valued.
2. The purpose or purposes of the valuation.
3. The valuation date or dates.
4. The applicable standard of value.
5. The form and extent of the appraisal report.
6. The expected schedule.
7. Fee arrangements.

The engagement document should be signed by the appraiser and the client. It should be supplemented by written addenda if any of the factors are changed during the course of the engagement.

# Information to Provide the Appraiser

Exhibit 35–1 provides a generalized checklist of documents and other information that may be necessary or helpful for the appraisal. Naturally, not all of the listed items are applicable for every appraisal, and, for some situations, there will be relevant specialized information not included on the list. The list should be helpful to the client, however, in anticipating and preparing for the information requirements of the appraisal. The types of analysis to be done on the various data have already been discussed throughout the book, of course, so they will not be repeated in this chapter.

## Financial Statements

The key phrase about the length of time for which financial statements should be provided is the "relevant period." If operations have changed significantly, financial statements may be relevant only for the period

Exhibit 35–1

### DOCUMENTS AND INFORMATION CHECKLIST
### FOR VALUATION OF BUSINESS OR PROFESSIONAL PRACTICE

**Financial Statements**

Balance sheets, income statements, statements of changes in financial position, and statements of stockholders' equity or partners' capital accounts for up to the last five fiscal years, if available

Income tax returns for the same years

Latest interim statements if valuation date is 90 days or more beyond end of last fiscal year and interim statement for the comparable period the year before

List of subsidiaries and/or financial interests in other companies, with relevant financial statements

**Other Financial Data**

Equipment list and depreciation schedule

Aged accounts receivable list

Aged accounts payable list

List of prepaid expenses

Inventory list, with any necessary information on inventory accounting policies (including work in progress, if applicable)

Lease or leases (if lease does not exist or is not transferable, determine what new lease or rental terms will be)

Any other existing contracts (employment agreements, covenants not to compete, supplier and franchise agreements, customer agreements, royalty agreements, equipment lease or rental contracts, loan agreements, labor contracts, employee benefit plans, and so on)

List of stockholders or partners, with number of shares owned by each or percentage of each partner's interest in earnings and capital

Compensation schedule for owners, including all benefits and personal expenses

Schedule of insurance in force (key-man life, property and casualty, liability)

Budgets or projections, if available

**Company Documents**

If a corporation, articles of incorporation, by-laws, any amendments to either, and corporate minutes

If a partnership, articles of partnership, with any amendments

Any existing buy/sell agreements, options to purchase stock or partnership interest, or rights of first refusal

**Other Information**

Brief history, including how long in business and details of any changes in ownership and/or bona-fide offers received

Brief description of business, including position relative to competition and any factors that make the business unique

Marketing literature (catalogs, brochures, advertisements, and so on)

List of locations where company operates, with size, and whether owned or leased

List of states in which licensed to do business

If customer or supplier base concentrated, list of major accounts, with annual dollar volume for each

List of competitors, with location, relative size, any other relevant factors

Resumes of, or list of, key personnel, with age, position, compensation, length of service, education, and prior experience

Trade associations to which company belongs or would be eligible for membership

Relevant trade or government publications

Any existing indicators of asset values, including latest property tax assessments and any appraisals that have been done

List of patents, copyrights, trademarks, and other intangible assets

Any contingent or off-balance-sheet assets or liabilities (pending lawsuits, compliance requirements, warranty or other product liability, and so on)

Any filings or correspondence with regulatory agencies

Information on prior transactions

**SOURCE:** Willamette Management Associates, Inc.

since operations have been as they are now. On the other hand, for a very cyclical business, the appraiser may require statements for a long period of time to make an assessment of normalized earning power.

For many small businesses, financial statements may be somewhat incomplete or even nonexistent. If the appraiser has to try to create the necessary financial information from original source documents (invoices, check records, and so on), the process can be time-consuming and expensive. In any case, the appraiser has to do the best work he can with what is available, and his appraisal report will contain appropriate disclaimers regarding any information that is unavailable or unverifiable.

# Other Financial Data

The list on Exhibit 35–1 is pretty much self-explanatory and covers a wide spectrum of data. The relative importance of the items varies from case to case, of course, and common sense should suggest which ones are most important in any given situation. Documents that can be easily copied or prepared can be provided to the appraiser prior to his visit to the premises and interview(s) with owners and/or management. Those that are somewhat voluminous generally can be reviewed on-site by the appraiser during his visit to the company.

# Company Documents

Unless the company is a sole proprietorship, the appraiser usually will want to review the basic corporate or partnership documents and any special agreements among the parties. These documents contain information about the various rights and restrictions related to the interests, and thus can have an important bearing on value. These documents can be either provided to the appraiser separately from his field visit or inspected on the premises or at the offices of the client's legal adviser.

# Other Information

The "other information" category covers a universe of possibilities, and it is difficult to offer useful generalizations about it. The suggested list in Exhibit 35–1 should provide enough guidance to trigger the necessary thinking about the most important categories of relevant information. Again, the extent to which various materials are provided to the appraiser, prior to his on-site visit, is largely a matter of convenience and scheduling.

If the totality of Exhibit 35–1 and other aspects of client involvement in the appraisal process seems overwhelming, talk to the appraiser about what he really needs in light of the scope and purpose of the assignment. An experienced appraiser will get out his Ockham's razor to whittle away at multiplicity of data and effort, and get to what is specifically relevant to the appraisal issue at hand. Most appraisers will cooperate to the utmost to avoid making the process any more time-consuming or disruptive for the client than is absolutely necessary to get the job done properly.

# Field Visit

In the vast majority of appraisal assignments, it is desirable to have the appraiser visit the operating location(s). This first-hand visit to the operating premises usually can help the appraiser to gain an understanding of the operation beyond what is possible in an "armchair" appraisal (done entirely on the basis of interviews and a study of the documents, without a visit to the facilities).

## Preparation

To the extent possible, the appraiser usually wants to review and analyze financial statements and as many documents as conveniently possible before the field trip. This way, he can have an understanding of the business before arriving there and can be prepared with a list of general and specific questions that otherwise would have to be covered at some other time, or might even be overlooked.

## Mission

The kinds of information the appraiser will want to glean through his field visit have been discussed throughout the previous chapters. As discussed in the immediately previous section, the field trip can be a convenient time to review some of the documents that would be cumbersome or inconvenient to supply to the appraiser away from the premises.

The field trip usually is an excellent time to interview owners and/or managers. The appraiser's physical presence on the premises might help to trigger relevant questions that might not occur to him in the surroundings of the appraiser's own conference room or office. If interviews with several people are appropriate, it usually is more convenient to conduct them on the premises than away. Also, information usually is at hand for any questions management is unable to answer completely from memory.

Generally speaking, the mission of the field trip consists of gaining a good overview of operations, getting whatever specific information is needed that has not been obtained by other means, and assessing all the qualitative factors discussed in Chapter 8. As noted elsewhere, one of the main objectives is to assess factors that might cause the future to differ from what the past record might indicate.

## Confidentiality

Confidentiality is one problem with which the appraiser frequently has to deal carefully on field trips. If a business is being put up for sale, the owners frequently do not want the employees or other people to know about it; and there can be many other good reasons for confidentiality.

Experienced appraisers have learned to work around this problem. They can dress and act unobtrusively. If they have to be introduced or identified to someone who is not a confidant in the situation, they are "consultants," which is an accurate and adequately abstruse label.

As a last resort, the appraiser might visit the premises after working hours, when employees are not present. However, that will not give the appraiser as good a picture as he gets if he sees the facility in operation.

## Adversary Proceedings

Another problem that the appraiser sometimes faces is opposition to an adequate facilities visit (or sometimes any facilities visit at all), in the case of an adversary proceeding. Undoubtedly, this problem most commonly occurs in appraisals being made for the purpose of property settlements in divorces.

If that is a problem, it is the responsibility of the client's attorney to make the necessary arrangements for the appraiser to visit the facilities and interview the necessary people. The parties should understand that the field visit is a standard part of the appraiser's work. They should understand that the appraiser himself is not an adversary party and is not an advocate for either party, but has been retained to render an independent opinion about value, as discussed in the final section of this chapter. When using a reputable, professional appraiser, the parties should not have to be concerned with confidentiality, as discussed elsewhere in this chapter. Furthermore, the party who is in the adversary position to the appraiser's client should welcome the opportunity to tell his side of the story to the appraiser.

If all discovery has to proceed through interrogatories and court orders, the process will be much more time-consuming, costly, and disruptive to the business operation. It is usually a good business decision for parties on both sides of a dispute to cooperate with independent appraisers. More discussion on adversary proceedings is included in Chapter 30 on Litigation.

# The Appraisal Report

As noted earlier, the scope of the appraisal report should be addressed when the appraiser is engaged. The form, length, and content are dictated primarily by the purpose of the appraisal and the audience for the report. In some cases, the report format is mandated or heavily influenced by law or convention. In such cases, an experienced appraiser can give the client guidance as to the appropriate form and scope of the report. In other cases, the scope of the written report is largely or totally a matter of client preference.

In some cases, only an oral report is necessary. In such an instance, it usually is best if it can be done in a meeting, so that the appraiser can go over work papers and other materials to the extent necessary for the client to understand how the appraiser arrived at his opinion about the value. Sometimes, however, logistics dictate that a telephone conversation will have to suffice for the oral report.

In some cases, only a brief letter report is required, sometimes a single sentence. More commonly, a letter report is one or two pages, outlining concisely the assignment, the steps taken, the approaches used, and the conclusion.

The next level would be a slightly longer letter report, which would fill in more detail on steps taken and information sources utilized. It usually would give specific numbers, such as earnings, capitalization rates, and asset values used in the various approaches. It may include one or a few supporting tables.

A complete formal appraisal report could run from 15 pages to well over 100 pages, depending on the purpose of the report, how complex the appraisal was, and how great the need for a comprehensive and documented written report.

One example of a formal report is included as Chapter 27, "Sample Professional Practice Valuation Report." Since this book is primarily about small business and professional practice valuations, I have not included a sample of a longer, more comprehensive report, which normally would be used in conjunction with larger businesses. An entire chapter on written reports, plus an example of a longer, comprehensive written report are included in my earlier book.[4]

The purpose and intended (or possible) audience of the report are all-important. Reports that are strictly for a client's internal use usually do not need to include nearly so much detail as those intended for outside use. An appraisal report for a possible sale of a business or practice, for example, might be fairly brief if it is just for the guidance of the owner. If prospective purchasers will, or might, see it, however, considerably more detail usually is warranted.

Similarly, appraisal reports strictly for buy/sell agreements and to determine life insurance needs may be fairly brief. However, if the same report may also be used for gift or estate taxes, a longer report usually is necessary in order to encompass all the factors contained in Revenue Ruling 59–60.

If so desired by the client or his attorney or other representative, the appraiser can be quite helpful in making suggestions as to the appropriate format, content, and length of the report, once he has a good idea of the purpose of the appraisal assignment.

# Independence of Appraiser

In most situations, the appraiser is independent of the client who has retained him for the appraisal. That means the appraiser has no financial interest in the property being appraised, is not an employee or agent of the client, and neither has nor has had any financial or other dealing with the client that would prejudice his ability to render a fair

---

[4] Pratt, *Valuing a Business*, pp. 231–68.

and impartial opinion about the value of the subject property. Professional ethics require that disclosure be made to the extent that these conditions are not met.

Unless otherwise made clear, when a professional appraiser expresses his independent opinion about value, whether in a written report, court testimony, or some other context, he is acting neither as an agent nor as an advocate of the client, but he is an advocate of his own opinion. That does not mean that someone who has made an appraisal cannot assume a role that is not independent, such as that of a negotiator or agent for the client in effecting a transaction; but that role is different from that of an independent appraiser, and the relationship must be made clear to the parties involved. When an appraiser accepts an assignment as an "arbitrator," he maintains his role as an independent appraiser and is not an agent of any principal, as discussed more fully in the last chapter of this book.

# Chapter 36

## Arbitrating Disputed Valuations

Disputes over the values of businesses and professional practices arise from a variety of circumstances, such as divorces, corporate or partnership dissolutions, dissenting stockholder actions, and assorted damage cases. There has been a growing trend in recent years to resolve such disputes through arbitration rather than taking them through a court trial. I have been involved in many such arbitrations in the last few years, and frequently have found this to be a preferable alternative to a court trial.[1]

There can be much potential grief, however, for both the principals and the arbitrators, if all the essential elements of the arbitration process are not anticipated, understood, and agreed upon by all the parties involved. I hope that the following pages, which are based heavily on my experiences as an arbitrator and as a consultant in arbitration situations, will assist principals, their attorneys and other advisers, and those who may act as arbitrators to use the arbitration process efficiently and with results that are fair to all. Not all situations are suitable for arbitration, and a decision to arbitrate should be cleared by the principal's attorney in each case.

# Advantages of Arbitration versus Court Trial

The primary advantages of arbitration over a court trial are the following:

1. Usually takes less elapsed time from start to finish.
2. Usually costs less. Attorneys' time is reduced considerably, and experts' fees usually are less than for a court trial. The appraisal process itself may not be less expensive, but the time required to prepare for cross examination and to prepare to rebut an opposing expert in court can be very expensive.
3. Scheduling usually can be made more convenient for all parties involved.
4. Usually less formal and less taxing on all participants, especially the principals in the disputed issue.
5. Less likelihood of an outlandish result in favor of one side over the other, if the arbitrators are qualified, professional business appraisers.

# Independent Role of Arbitrators

The most important point to understand about the arbitration process is that, at least from the arbitrators' viewpoint, it is not an adversary proceeding, but a cooperative effort to reach a fair and equitable conclu-

---

[1] For discussions of preparation and presentation of expert testimony in court on disputed business valuations, see Chapter 16, "Court Testimony," in Pratt, *Valuing a Business*, pp. 269–82; and Brian P. Brinig and Michael W. Prairie, "Expert Testimony: The Business Appraiser as a Valuation Expert Witness," *Business Valuation News*, March 1985, pp. 8–23.

sion. All the parties should realize that each arbitrator, regardless of who appointed him, is not an agent of any principal (as might be the case in a negotiation for a sale); he is acting independently in using his expertise and judgment to reach a conclusion that is fair to all parties.

This attitude of cooperation is especially significant in the way expert appraisers appointed as arbitrators normally interact during the arbitration process, as opposed to their interaction when presenting expert testimony in a court proceeding. In a court proceeding, there normally is no direct communication whatsoever between experts. Expert testimony is limited to answering the questions posed by attorneys on direct or cross-examination, or to questions posed by the court. In an arbitration proceeding, on the other hand, maximum communication among arbitrators normally is expected from the outset; discussion is expected to cover all points thoroughly and impartially, and not be limited to answering questions posed by opposing attorneys, each acting from the perspective of advocacy.

# Situations Giving Rise to Arbitration

Almost any dispute over the value of a business or professional practice or a partial interest in one can lend itself to resolution by arbitration instead of trial. The following have been the major categories in my own experience.

In divorces and corporate or partnership dissolutions, a decision ahead of time to determine any matters of valuation by arbitration may prevent their ever reaching the point of dispute.

## Divorces

Of all situations involving disputed valuations of businesses or professional practices, I believe that those arising from divorces are the most difficult for the parties to resolve by amicable negotiation. Although divorces are only a small part of my staff's valuation practice, they account for a large proportion of the times that we prepare for, and appear on, the witness stand in court presenting expert testimony.

Disputed valuation issues can become a major element in the already intense emotional strain accompanying divorce proceedings. Frequently, the valuation for the property settlement is the major, if not the only, disputed issue. Besides the time and cost advantages, arbitration spares the parties the tension and added antagonism associated with fighting it out in court.

## Corporate and Partnership Dissolutions

Akin to a divorce situation is a corporate or partnership dissolution. I would also include in this general category the buyout of a minority stockholder or partner pursuant to a buy/sell agreement. By arbitrating the valuation issue, the principals can part on as friendly a basis as possible, whatever the circumstances of the dissolution may be.

## Dissenting Stockholder Actions

A merger, sale, or other major corporate action can give rise to dissenting stockholders' appraisal rights under the statutes of all states except West Virginia. The expediency and lower cost make the arbitration process an attractive alternative to a trial in such cases, especially smaller ones for which prolonged and expensive court proceedings can result in a no-win situation for everyone.

## Damage Cases

Damage cases, where the valuation of a business or practice often is the central issue in determining the amount of relief, include the following:

1. Breach of contract.
2. Condemnation.
3. Antitrust.
4. Lost profits.
5. Lost business opportunity.
6. Amount of casualty insurance proceeds or allocation of proceeds among parties at interest.

From my own experience and observation, I believe that the risk of an outlandish determination of value by a court is greater in damage cases, especially breach of contract and antitrust cases, than in any other major category of disputed valuation cases. This inclination toward an extreme decision one way or the other may result from a tendency of some juries or courts to allow the damage event to affect their objective view of the valuation issue; or perhaps some sentiment about the parties involved can affect them. This risk can be reduced significantly through the use of an arbitration process using qualified appraisers as arbitrators.

# Selection of Arbitrators

Two factors need to be delineated regarding the selection of arbitrators: the criteria and the procedure for selection.

## Criteria for Selection

The arbitration process produces the most equitable results for all parties if all the arbitrators (or the arbitrator) are experienced, qualified professional appraisers of businesses and/or professional practices. If there are three arbitrators, it is most desirable that all three should be full-time professional appraisers, but two out of three are better than only one or none at all.

In some cases, if the business or profession is highly specialized, it may be desirable to seek as arbitrators one or more appraisers who have experience in appraising the specific line of business or professional practice. It generally is not desirable to gain the desired industry expertise by utilizing as an arbitrator someone who is an active or retired participant in the industry or profession involved, or who has done ancillary functions such as accounting or economic analysis work in the industry or profession, but who is not experienced in matters related directly to valuation. Many of these people lack the requisite training to deal professionally with the specific issue of valuation, and there is also the risk that such people's biases toward the industry or profession could prevent objective valuation. Their expertise can be gained through informal discussion with the arbitrator(s) or by formal testimony presented to the arbitrator(s).

I have observed sound valuation conclusions reached by arbitration panels composed of industry people knowledgeable in finance, along with attorneys knowledgeable in both the industry and in valuation matters. However, in these instances, costs were incurred not only for the three arbitrators, but also for expert testimony to be presented to the arbitration panel by at least two appraisers in each case. I have also seen nonprofessional panels reach conclusions which I do not believe a consensus of responsible professional appraisers would consider to be supportable within a reasonable range of value.

Obviously, one criterion for selection is the availability of the desired arbitrator(s) within a reasonable time frame, so that the effectiveness of the arbitration is not significantly diminished.

## Procedure for Selection

The most typical procedure is that each party selects one arbitrator and the two arbitrators select the third. I think that it is preferable for the two arbitrators appointed by the parties to have complete authority to select the third, rather than having the selection of the third arbitrator subject to the approval of the principals. This avoids delays and dealing with pressures arising from the principals' biases, which are almost sure to be injected.

It is important that there be an alternative procedure for the selection of a third arbitrator in case of a deadlock. Plan this contingency procedure in advance, or in conjunction with entering into the arbitration agreement. The procedure in case of a deadlock should call for the appointment of the third arbitrator by some predetermined party, such as a court or a responsible (and totally neutral) official in the industry or profession. This procedure will almost assure that at least two of the three arbitrators will be professional appraisers, if one side has already chosen one. If one side insists that the third arbitrator be a qualified professional appraiser, and presents a list of such people who are totally independent of the principals involved, it is not likely that an independent party charged with making the appointment would select someone not so qualified over someone who was.[2]

There should be a deadline, at which time the alternate selection process takes effect if the first two arbitrators have failed to reach agreement on a third arbitrator.

Another possibility is to establish the procedure so that the two arbitrators attempt to reach agreement, bringing in the third arbitrator only if they are unable to do so. In that case, I recommend that the prospective third arbitrator be agreed upon between the first two at the outset, before they get involved in other aspects of interaction with each other in the arbitration process. This procedure could be established as part of the language in a buy/sell agreement.

If a court appoints an arbitrator, he may be an equal part of a three-member arbitration panel, or he may be a "special master," where the conclusion reached does not require the concurrence of any other arbitrator, although he normally would be expected to take their respective positions into consideration.

## American Arbitration Association Procedure

The American Arbitration Association (AAA) procedure for appointing arbitrators is different than that described in the foregoing section. When parties agree to submit a disputed matter to arbitration through the AAA, the association sends the parties a list of suggested arbitrators from the association's panel of arbitrators. Each party may veto nominees and make observations as to preferences, but the final decision is made by the AAA.

In a letter discussing an early draft of this chapter, Robert Coulson, president of the American Arbitration Association, makes the following observation:

> Although you encourage parties to use the party-appointed system, many arbitration experts have come to believe that using neutral arbitrators is more reliable and less subject to a concern that one of the party-appointed arbitrators might be prejudiced in favor of the party that appointed him.

Mr. Coulson also says, "I, too, believe that experts are the best arbitrators for such technical questions." However, there is no assurance that a panel appointed by the AAA will be composed of experts. Of three recent arbitration panels where my associates and I were not in the role of arbitrators but presented testimony on valuation issues to the panel, two panels included no valuation experts and one was composed of two attorneys and one business appraiser.

In the context of the AAA arbitration procedure, usually each party retains an expert who performs an appraisal and presents testimony before the arbitration panel, rather than having the expert actually participate as an arbitrator. In this sense, the preparation and presen-

---

[2] A list of senior members of the American Society of Appraisers who are certified in business valuation may be obtained from the American Society of Appraisers, Dulles International Airport, P.O. Box 17265, Washington, D.C. 20041.

tation of expert testimony is similar to a court testimony situation, although it is slightly less formal. For additional information, the address of the American Arbitration Association is 140 West 51st Street, New York, NY 10020.

The balance of this chapter discusses the type of situation where the appraiser is acting in the role of a member of the arbitration panel rather than a presenter of expert testimony.

# Engagement and Compensation of Arbitrators

Once the arbitrators have been appointed, the engagement should be committed to writing. The description of the engagement may take the form of an engagement letter initiated by one or more attorneys and/or principals, a standard professional services agreement initiated by an appraiser serving as arbitrator, or both. Either is satisfactory, as long as all aspects of the engagement are adequately covered. Sometimes, addenda to the initial engagement document(s) may be necessary, since decisions on some items, such as schedules and some expenses, may be made or changed as the engagement progresses.

The engagement document(s) should include by reference the document(s) giving rise to the arbitration (e.g., a buy/sell agreement) and should cover compensation of the arbitrator and all necessary instructions not addressed or not made clear in the arbitration document(s).

All documents relating to the engagement of an arbitrator should be signed by the arbitrator and whoever is responsible for compensating him for his services. The most common compensation arrangement is that each party assumes responsibility for the compensation and expenses of the arbitrator he has nominated or appointed, with the parties sharing equally the compensation and expenses of the third arbitrator. Such arrangements vary, however, from case to case.

The amount of compensation usually is based on each arbitrator's normal professional hourly or daily billing rate (or some mutually agreed-upon rate) plus out-of-pocket expenses. It is much less common for an arbitrator's compensation to be based on a fixed fee, because it is very difficult to determine in advance just how much time the total appraisal and arbitration process will require. However, it is reasonable to expect to discuss some estimate of probable fees and the daily rate or other basis for the fees.

# Establishing the Ground Rules for Arbitration

The ground rules by which the arbitration will proceed are of critical importance. They start with a document mandating certain elements of the arbitrators' assignment. This document may be, for example, a buy/sell agreement, a prenuptial agreement, or an agreement drawn up specifically for the purpose of the arbitration. Sometimes, an agreement such as a buy/sell agreement will be supplemented by written instructions agreed upon by the attorneys involved. It is important that the written agreement directing the arbitration specify what factors are mandated by the agreement and what factors are left to the discretion of the arbitrators.

# Factors Specified in the Arbitration Agreement

Factors that should be mandated by the agreement include the following:

1. Procedure for selection of arbitrators.
2. Definition of the property to be appraised.
3. The date as of which the property is to be valued.
4. The standard of value to be used (as discussed in Chapter 2 and elsewhere in the book).
5. What constitutes a conclusion by the arbitrators, such as:
    *a*. Agreement by at least two out of three.
    *b*. Average of the two closest to each other.
    *c*. The conclusion of the third (neutral) arbitrator, such as in a "special master" situation.
6. The format and procedure for the arbitrators to render their conclusion.
7. The terms of payment of the amount determined by the arbitrators, including interest, if any.
8. The time schedule for the various steps in the arbitration process, at least the selection of arbitrators and some outside time limit for the total process.

Failure to specify any of the matters above may leave the door open for costly and extensive legal battles. Most state statutes specify that the standard of value for dissenting stockholders' appraisal rights is fair value, although a minority of states specify fair market value. In other cases, the arbitrators usually must look to the arbitration document to establish the standard of value.

Some buy/sell agreements specify fair market value as the standard of value. In cases of minority interests, this standard of value, of course, implies a discount from a proportionate share of the fair market value of the total entity, a fact which many owners (and even some attorneys) may overlook when drafting the agreement. Some buy/sell agreements specify that the valuation is to be a proportionate share of the fair market value of the total enterprise, with no minority interest discount. I recommend that the drafter of the agreement discuss this with the parties to the agreement (see chapter on Estate Planning for sample wording).

A reporting deadline may be specified in the agreement or a reporting schedule may be worked out in conjunction with the process of engaging the arbitrators.

Because of the many ramifications inherent in the wording of the arbitration agreement, I recommend that an appraiser experienced in arbitration be consulted when drafting the agreement. This consultation will help to avoid both important omissions and unintentional implications of the wording discussing the valuation (such as the standard of value to be used).

# Factors Left to the Arbitrators' Discretion

Factors that can, and in most cases I believe should, be left to the discretion of the arbitrators include the following:

1. Whether or not each arbitrator is expected or required to make a complete, independent appraisal, or the extent to which each arbitrator considers it necessary to do independent work, as opposed to relying on certain data or analyses furnished by other arbitrators and/or appraisers.
2. The procedures for the arbitrators to communicate with each other (writing, telephone calls, personal meetings), and the rules for sharing information.
3. Scheduling of the arbitrators' work and meetings, within the constraint of the agreed-upon reporting schedule.
4. The valuation approaches and criteria to be taken into consideration, within the constraints of any legally mandated criteria.
5. The facts, documents, and other data on which to rely (although the principals may agree to stipulate certain facts or assumptions, which could make the arbitrators' job easier with respect to some matters of possible uncertainty).

# The Arbitration Process

One of the major variables in the arbitration process is the extent to which each arbitrator is expected or required to carry out independent appraisal work. Some arbitration documents specify that each expert on the arbitration panel do a complete, independent appraisal. More commonly, however (and I think preferably in most cases), the extent of independent appraisal work to be done is left to the judgment of each individual arbitrator, or to the arbitration panel as a group.

## Review of Arbitration Document

Each arbitrator should begin with a careful review of the document(s) giving rise to the arbitration. If there is any confusion or disagreement about any details of the assignment, such as the exact definition of the property, the effective date of the valuation, or the applicable standard of value, the arbitrators should seek clarification immediately. This should be done in writing to avoid any possible disputes later.

# Initial Communication among Arbitrators

I recommend that the arbitrators establish communication among themselves at the earliest possible time after their appointment. A face-to-face meeting is ideal, if geographic proximity to each other makes that feasible, but a conference call or a series of conference calls usually is sufficient, perhaps supplemented by correspondence. While each case is unique, the following is a generalized list of points to try to establish early:

1. Status of work already accomplished, if any (who has done what work up to that point).
2. An agreement as to sharing of information. (My preference is to agree that all information gathered or developed by one arbitrator will be shared with the other arbitrators as quickly as possible.)
3. An agreement, if possible, as to the relevant valuation approaches to consider.
4. A list of documents and data needed, and assignment of responsibility for obtaining each and seeing that the necessary distribution to other arbitrators is made.
5. Any other possible division of the research effort, such as searches for comparable transactions, development of economic and/or industry data, and routine financial statement analysis (spread sheets, ratio analysis, comparison with industry averages, and so on). Division of research effort, of course, must depend on each arbitrator's willingness to accept certain efforts of another, which must be based on a judgment of professional ability and unbiased presentation of data and analysis.
6. Scheduling.

# Field Visit

In most cases, arbitrators will want to visit the operating premises and interview relevant principals and/or management. I think that it works out best if the arbitrators can conduct this field trip together, if possible, rather than separately. That way, they all see the same things at the same time, and all can benefit from hearing first hand each other's questions and answers. A joint field trip also gives the arbitrators an opportunity to address any items not fully covered in their previous communications. Also, this gives arbitrators who did not know each other previously an opportunity to get to know each other and form a basis for working together.

# Hearings

The arbitrators should offer each party the opportunity to present oral and written information and opinions if they so desire. It frequently is convenient to hold a meeting to accommodate such input in conjunction with the field trip.

# The Valuation Meeting

Usually, the arbitrators will meet in person to reach the valuation conclusion. In some instances, this meeting may be replaced by a conference call. In either case, all should be as prepared as possible, having exchanged and assimilated as much information as possible prior to the meeting.

In the meeting, it usually is most productive to come to agreements issue by issue, identifying and keeping track of each point of agreement and disagreement. Good notes should be kept so that it is clear exactly what points have been agreed upon, and what the respective positions are on points which have been addressed but on which agreement has not been reached. Each arbitrator should be receptive to the others' information and viewpoints and attempt to reach compromises on points where reasonable judgments may differ.

It is most desirable to come to a conclusion that can be endorsed as fair by all members of the arbitration panel. In my experience, this agreement usually can be achieved if all of the arbitrators are qualified professional business appraisers. If unanimous agreement cannot be reached, the arbitrator in the minority position may render a dissenting opinion for the record, if he so desires.

# Reporting the Results of the Arbitration

The formal report of the valuation conclusion reached by the arbitrators usually is contained in a very brief letter which does no more than reference the arbitration agreement, state that the arbitrators have completed their assignment in accordance with the agreement, and state the conclusion reached. The letter is signed by the arbitrators concurring in the conclusion.

In a significant proportion of cases, the principals on both sides would like to have a brief report explaining how the valuation conclusion was reached. In such situations, I suggest that such an advisory report be the sole responsibility of the third appraiser. To make such a report a joint task of two or more arbitrators, each of whom probably judged various factors a little bit differently—though they were able to agree on a conclusion—usually would be an unnecessarily complicated and costly exercise.

If the valuation conclusion is reached unilaterally by a special master, normally he would be the only one to sign the report. An explanation of the procedures and criteria used is usually included.

# Summary: The Most Critical Elements

The two most critical elements for an expeditious and successful arbitration are (1) a definitive arbitration agreement that provides the arbitrators with unambiguous instructions on the key matters listed above and (2) the appointment of independent arbitrators who will be both fair and competent in reaching a conclusion about the value of the subject property. If these two elements are properly addressed, the arbitration process can be a very efficient and fair way of resolving business or professional practice valuation matters.

# Appendix A

## Present Value Tables

## APPENDIX TABLE A-1
### Present Value of One Dollar Due at the End of *n* Years

| n | 1% | 2% | 3% | 4% | 5% | 6% | 7% | 8% | 9% | 10% | n |
|---|----|----|----|----|----|----|----|----|----|-----|---|
| 1 | .99010 | .98039 | .97007 | .96154 | .95238 | .94340 | .93458 | .92593 | .91743 | .90909 | 1 |
| 2 | .98030 | .96117 | .94260 | .92456 | .90703 | .89000 | .87344 | .85734 | .84168 | .82645 | 2 |
| 3 | .97059 | .94232 | .91514 | .88900 | .86384 | .83962 | .81630 | .79383 | .77218 | .75131 | 3 |
| 4 | .96098 | .92385 | .88849 | .85480 | .82270 | .79209 | .76290 | .73503 | .70843 | .68301 | 4 |
| 5 | .95147 | .90573 | .86261 | .82193 | .78353 | .74726 | .71299 | .68058 | .64993 | .62092 | 5 |
| 6 | .94204 | .88797 | .83748 | .79031 | .74622 | .70496 | .66634 | .63017 | .59627 | .56447 | 6 |
| 7 | .93272 | .87056 | .81309 | .75992 | .71068 | .66506 | .62275 | .58349 | .54703 | .51316 | 7 |
| 8 | .92348 | .85349 | .78941 | .73069 | .67684 | .62741 | .58201 | .54027 | .50187 | .46651 | 8 |
| 9 | .91434 | .83675 | .76642 | .70259 | .64461 | .59190 | .54393 | .50025 | .46043 | .42410 | 9 |
| 10 | .90529 | .82035 | .74409 | .67556 | .61391 | .55839 | .50835 | .46319 | .42241 | .38554 | 10 |
| 11 | .89632 | .80426 | .72242 | .64958 | .58468 | .52679 | .47509 | .42888 | .38753 | .35049 | 11 |
| 12 | .88745 | .78849 | .70138 | .62460 | .55684 | .49697 | .44401 | .39711 | .35553 | .31863 | 12 |
| 13 | .87866 | .77303 | .68095 | .60057 | .53032 | .46884 | .41496 | .36770 | .32618 | .28966 | 13 |
| 14 | .86996 | .75787 | .66112 | .57747 | .50507 | .44230 | .38782 | .34046 | .29925 | .26333 | 14 |
| 15 | .86135 | .74301 | .64186 | .55526 | .48102 | .41726 | .36245 | .31524 | .27454 | .23939 | 15 |
| 16 | .85282 | .72845 | .62317 | .53391 | .45811 | .39365 | .33873 | .29189 | .25187 | .21763 | 16 |
| 17 | .84438 | .71416 | .60502 | .51337 | .43630 | .37136 | .31657 | .27027 | .23107 | .19784 | 17 |
| 18 | .83602 | .70016 | .58739 | .49363 | .41552 | .35034 | .29586 | .25025 | .21199 | .17986 | 18 |
| 19 | .82774 | .68643 | .57029 | .47464 | .39573 | .33051 | .27651 | .23171 | .19449 | .16351 | 19 |
| 20 | .81954 | .67297 | .55367 | .45639 | .37689 | .31180 | .25842 | .21455 | .17843 | .14864 | 20 |
| 21 | .81143 | .65978 | .53755 | .43883 | .35894 | .29415 | .24151 | .19866 | .16370 | .13513 | 21 |
| 22 | .80340 | .64684 | .52189 | .42195 | .34185 | .27750 | .22571 | .18394 | .15018 | .12285 | 22 |
| 23 | .79544 | .63414 | .50669 | .40573 | .32557 | .26180 | .21095 | .17031 | .13778 | .11168 | 23 |
| 24 | .78757 | .62172 | .49193 | .39012 | .31007 | .24698 | .19715 | .15770 | .12640 | .10153 | 24 |
| 25 | .77977 | .60953 | .47760 | .37512 | .29530 | .23300 | .18425 | .14602 | .11597 | .09230 | 25 |

## APPENDIX TABLE A-1 (Cont.)
### Present Value of One Dollar Due at the End of n Years

| n | 11% | 12% | 13% | 14% | 15% | 16% | 17% | 18% | 19% | 20% | n |
|---|---|---|---|---|---|---|---|---|---|---|---|
| 1 | .90090 | .89286 | .88496 | .87719 | .86957 | .86207 | .85470 | .84746 | .84034 | .83333 | 1 |
| 2 | .81162 | .79719 | .78315 | .76947 | .75614 | .74316 | .73051 | .71818 | .70616 | .69444 | 2 |
| 3 | .73119 | .71178 | .69305 | .67497 | .65752 | .64066 | .62437 | .60863 | .59342 | .57870 | 3 |
| 4 | .65873 | .63552 | .61332 | .59208 | .57175 | .55229 | .53365 | .51579 | .49867 | .48225 | 4 |
| 5 | .59345 | .56743 | .54276 | .51937 | .49718 | .47611 | .45611 | .43711 | .41905 | .40188 | 5 |
| 6 | .53464 | .50663 | .48032 | .45559 | .43233 | .41044 | .38984 | .37043 | .35214 | .33490 | 6 |
| 7 | .48166 | .45235 | .42506 | .39964 | .37594 | .35383 | .33320 | .31392 | .29592 | .27908 | 7 |
| 8 | .43393 | .40388 | .37616 | .35056 | .32690 | .30503 | .28478 | .26604 | .24867 | .23257 | 8 |
| 9 | .39092 | .36061 | .33288 | .30751 | .28426 | .26295 | .24340 | .22546 | .20897 | .19381 | 9 |
| 10 | .35218 | .32197 | .29459 | .26974 | .24718 | .22668 | .20804 | .19106 | .17560 | .16151 | 10 |
| 11 | .31728 | .28748 | .26070 | .23662 | .21494 | .19542 | .17781 | .16192 | .14756 | .13459 | 11 |
| 12 | .28584 | .25667 | .23071 | .20756 | .18691 | .16846 | .15197 | .13722 | .12400 | .11216 | 12 |
| 13 | .25751 | .22917 | .20416 | .18207 | .16253 | .14523 | .12989 | .11629 | .10420 | .09346 | 13 |
| 14 | .23199 | .20462 | .18068 | .15971 | .14133 | .12520 | .11102 | .09855 | .08757 | .07789 | 14 |
| 15 | .20900 | .18270 | .15989 | .14010 | .12289 | .10793 | .09489 | .08352 | .07359 | .06491 | 15 |
| 16 | .18829 | .16312 | .14150 | .12289 | .10686 | .09304 | .08110 | .07078 | .06184 | .05409 | 16 |
| 17 | .16963 | .14564 | .12522 | .10780 | .09293 | .08021 | .06932 | .05998 | .05196 | .04507 | 17 |
| 18 | .15282 | .13004 | .11081 | .09456 | .08080 | .06914 | .05925 | .05083 | .04367 | .03756 | 18 |
| 19 | .13768 | .11611 | .09806 | .08295 | .07026 | .05961 | .05064 | .04308 | .03669 | .03130 | 19 |
| 20 | .12403 | .10367 | .08678 | .07276 | .06110 | .05139 | .04328 | .03651 | .03084 | .02608 | 20 |
| 21 | .11174 | .09256 | .07680 | .06383 | .05313 | .04430 | .03699 | .03094 | .02591 | .02174 | 21 |
| 22 | .10067 | .08264 | .06796 | .05599 | .04620 | .03819 | .03162 | .02622 | .02178 | .01811 | 22 |
| 23 | .09069 | .07379 | .06014 | .04911 | .04017 | .03292 | .02702 | .02222 | .01830 | .01509 | 23 |
| 24 | .08170 | .06588 | .05322 | .04308 | .03493 | .02838 | .02310 | .01883 | .01538 | .01258 | 24 |
| 25 | .07361 | .05882 | .04710 | .03779 | .03038 | .02447 | .01974 | .01596 | .01292 | .01048 | 25 |

## APPENDIX TABLE A-1 (Cont.)
### Present Value of One Dollar Due at the End of n Years

| n | 21% | 22% | 23% | 24% | 25% | 26% | 27% | 28% | 29% | 30% | n |
|---|-----|-----|-----|-----|-----|-----|-----|-----|-----|-----|---|
| 1 | .82645 | .81967 | .81301 | .80645 | .80000 | .79365 | .78740 | .78125 | .77519 | .76923 | 1 |
| 2 | .68301 | .67186 | .66098 | .65036 | .64000 | .62988 | .62000 | .61035 | .60093 | .59172 | 2 |
| 3 | .56447 | .55071 | .53738 | .52449 | .51200 | .49991 | .48819 | .47684 | .46583 | .45517 | 3 |
| 4 | .46651 | .45140 | .43690 | .42297 | .40960 | .39675 | .38440 | .37253 | .36111 | .35013 | 4 |
| 5 | .38554 | .37000 | .35520 | .34111 | .32768 | .31488 | .30268 | .29104 | .27993 | .26933 | 5 |
| 6 | .31863 | .30328 | .28878 | .27509 | .26214 | .24991 | .23833 | .22737 | .21700 | .20718 | 6 |
| 7 | .26333 | .24859 | .23478 | .22184 | .20972 | .19834 | .18766 | .17764 | .16822 | .15937 | 7 |
| 8 | .21763 | .20376 | .19088 | .17891 | .16777 | .15741 | .14776 | .13878 | .13040 | .12259 | 8 |
| 9 | .17986 | .16702 | .15519 | .14428 | .13422 | .12493 | .11635 | .10842 | .10109 | .09430 | 9 |
| 10 | .14864 | .13690 | .12617 | .11635 | .10737 | .09915 | .09161 | .08470 | .07836 | .07254 | 10 |
| 11 | .12285 | .11221 | .10258 | .09383 | .08590 | .07869 | .07214 | .06617 | .06075 | .05580 | 11 |
| 12 | .10153 | .09198 | .08339 | .07567 | .06872 | .06245 | .05680 | .05170 | .04709 | .04292 | 12 |
| 13 | .08391 | .07539 | .06780 | .06103 | .05498 | .04957 | .04472 | .04039 | .03650 | .03302 | 13 |
| 14 | .06934 | .06180 | .05512 | .04921 | .04398 | .03934 | .03522 | .03155 | .02830 | .02540 | 14 |
| 15 | .05731 | .05065 | .04481 | .03969 | .03518 | .03122 | .02773 | .02465 | .02194 | .01954 | 15 |
| 16 | .04736 | .04152 | .03643 | .03201 | .02815 | .02478 | .02183 | .01926 | .01700 | .01503 | 16 |
| 17 | .03914 | .03403 | .02962 | .02581 | .02252 | .01967 | .01719 | .01505 | .01318 | .01156 | 17 |
| 18 | .03235 | .02789 | .02408 | .02082 | .01801 | .01561 | .01354 | .01175 | .01022 | .00889 | 18 |
| 19 | .02673 | .02286 | .01958 | .01679 | .01441 | .01239 | .01066 | .00918 | .00792 | .00684 | 19 |
| 20 | .02209 | .01874 | .01592 | .01354 | .01153 | .00983 | .00839 | .00717 | .00614 | .00526 | 20 |
| 21 | .01826 | .01536 | .01294 | .01092 | .00922 | .00780 | .00661 | .00561 | .00476 | .00405 | 21 |
| 22 | .01509 | .01259 | .01052 | .00880 | .00738 | .00619 | .00520 | .00438 | .00369 | .00311 | 22 |
| 23 | .01247 | .01032 | .00855 | .00710 | .00590 | .00491 | .00410 | .00342 | .00286 | .00239 | 23 |
| 24 | .01031 | .00846 | .00695 | .00573 | .00472 | .00390 | .00323 | .00267 | .00222 | .00184 | 24 |
| 25 | .00852 | .00693 | .00565 | .00462 | .00378 | .00310 | .00254 | .00209 | .00172 | .00142 | 25 |

## APPENDIX TABLE A-2

### Present Value of an Annuity of One Dollar for n Year

| n | 1% | 2% | 3% | 4% | 5% | 6% | 7% | 8% | 9% | 10% | n |
|---|---|---|---|---|---|---|---|---|---|---|---|
| 1 | .9901 | .9804 | .9709 | .9615 | .9524 | .9434 | .9346 | .9259 | .9174 | .9091 | 1 |
| 2 | 1.9704 | 1.9416 | 1.9135 | 1.8861 | 1.8594 | 1.8334 | 1.8080 | 1.7833 | 1.7591 | 1.7355 | 2 |
| 3 | 2.9410 | 2.8839 | 2.8286 | 2.7751 | 2.7232 | 2.6730 | 2.6243 | 2.5771 | 2.5313 | 2.4868 | 3 |
| 4 | 3.9020 | 3.8077 | 3.7171 | 3.6299 | 3.5459 | 3.4651 | 3.3872 | 3.3121 | 3.2397 | 3.1699 | 4 |
| 5 | 4.8535 | 4.7134 | 4.5797 | 4.4518 | 4.3295 | 4.2123 | 4.1002 | 3.9927 | 3.8896 | 3.7908 | 5 |
| 6 | 5.7955 | 5.6014 | 5.4172 | 5.2421 | 5.0757 | 4.9173 | 4.7665 | 4.6229 | 4.4859 | 4.3553 | 6 |
| 7 | 6.7282 | 6.4720 | 6.2302 | 6.0020 | 5.7863 | 5.5824 | 5.3893 | 5.2064 | 5.0329 | 4.8684 | 7 |
| 8 | 7.6517 | 7.3254 | 7.0196 | 6.7327 | 6.4632 | 6.2098 | 5.9713 | 5.7466 | 5.5348 | 5.3349 | 8 |
| 9 | 8.5661 | 8.1622 | 7.7861 | 7.4353 | 7.1078 | 6.8017 | 6.5152 | 6.2469 | 5.9852 | 5.7590 | 9 |
| 10 | 9.4714 | 8.9825 | 8.5302 | 8.1109 | 7.7217 | 7.3601 | 7.0236 | 6.7101 | 6.4176 | 6.1446 | 10 |
| 11 | 10.3677 | 9.7868 | 9.2526 | 8.7604 | 8.3064 | 7.8868 | 7.4987 | 7.1389 | 6.8052 | 6.4951 | 11 |
| 12 | 11.2552 | 10.5753 | 9.9539 | 9.3850 | 8.8632 | 8.3838 | 7.9427 | 7.5361 | 7.1607 | 6.8137 | 12 |
| 13 | 12.1338 | 11.3483 | 10.6349 | 9.9856 | 9.3935 | 8.8527 | 8.3576 | 7.9038 | 7.4869 | 7.1034 | 13 |
| 14 | 13.0038 | 12.1062 | 11.2960 | 10.5631 | 9.8986 | 9.2950 | 8.7454 | 8.2442 | 7.7861 | 7.3667 | 14 |
| 15 | 13.8651 | 12.8492 | 11.9379 | 11.1183 | 10.3796 | 9.7122 | 9.1079 | 8.5595 | 8.0607 | 7.6061 | 15 |
| 16 | 14.7180 | 13.5777 | 12.5610 | 11.6522 | 10.8377 | 10.1059 | 9.4466 | 8.8514 | 8.3125 | 7.8237 | 16 |
| 17 | 15.5624 | 14.2918 | 13.1660 | 12.1656 | 11.2740 | 10.4772 | 9.7632 | 9.1216 | 8.5436 | 8.0215 | 17 |
| 18 | 16.3984 | 14.9920 | 13.7534 | 12.6592 | 11.6895 | 10.8276 | 10.0591 | 9.3719 | 8.7556 | 8.2014 | 18 |
| 19 | 17.2261 | 15.6784 | 14.3237 | 13.1339 | 12.0853 | 11.1581 | 10.3356 | 9.6036 | 8.9501 | 8.3649 | 19 |
| 20 | 18.0457 | 16.3514 | 14.8774 | 13.5903 | 12.4622 | 11.4699 | 10.5940 | 9.8181 | 9.1285 | 8.5136 | 20 |
| 21 | 18.8571 | 17.0111 | 15.4149 | 14.0291 | 12.8211 | 11.7640 | 10.8355 | 10.0168 | 9.2922 | 8.6487 | 21 |
| 22 | 19.6605 | 17.6580 | 15.9368 | 14.4511 | 13.1630 | 12.0416 | 11.0612 | 10.2007 | 9.4424 | 8.7715 | 22 |
| 23 | 20.4559 | 18.2921 | 16.4435 | 14.8568 | 13.4885 | 12.3033 | 11.2722 | 10.3710 | 9.5802 | 8.8832 | 23 |
| 24 | 21.2435 | 18.9139 | 16.9355 | 15.2469 | 13.7986 | 12.5503 | 11.4693 | 10.5287 | 9.7066 | 8.9847 | 24 |
| 25 | 22.0233 | 19.5234 | 17.4131 | 15.6220 | 14.0939 | 12.7833 | 11.6536 | 10.6748 | 9.8226 | 9.0770 | 25 |

## Present Value of an Annuity of One Dollar for *n* Years

| n | 11% | 12% | 13% | 14% | 15% | 16% | 17% | 18% | 19% | 20% | n |
|---|------|------|------|------|------|------|------|------|------|------|---|
| 1 | .9009 | .8929 | .8850 | .3772 | .8696 | .8621 | .8547 | .8475 | .8403 | .8333 | 1 |
| 2 | 1.7125 | 1.6901 | 1.6681 | 1.6467 | 1.6257 | 1.6052 | 1.5852 | 1.5656 | 1.5465 | 1.5278 | 2 |
| 3 | 2.4437 | 2.4018 | 2.3612 | 2.3216 | 2.2832 | 2.2459 | 2.2096 | 2.1743 | 2.1399 | 2.1065 | 3 |
| 4 | 3.1024 | 3.0373 | 2.9745 | 2.9137 | 2.8550 | 2.7982 | 2.7432 | 2.6901 | 2.6386 | 2.5887 | 4 |
| 5 | 3.6959 | 3.6048 | 3.5172 | 3.4331 | 3.3522 | 3.2743 | 3.1993 | 3.1272 | 3.0576 | 2.9906 | 5 |
| 6 | 4.2305 | 4.1114 | 3.9976 | 3.8887 | 3.7845 | 3.6847 | 3.5892 | 3.4976 | 3.4098 | 3.3255 | 6 |
| 7 | 4.7122 | 3.5638 | 4.4226 | 4.2883 | 4.1604 | 4.0386 | 3.9224 | 3.8115 | 3.7057 | 3.6046 | 7 |
| 8 | 5.1461 | 4.9676 | 4.7988 | 4.6389 | 4.4873 | 4.3436 | 4.2072 | 4.0776 | 3.9544 | 3.8372 | 8 |
| 9 | 5.5370 | 5.3282 | 5.1317 | 4.9464 | 4.7716 | 4.6065 | 4.4506 | 4.3030 | 4.1633 | 4.0310 | 9 |
| 10 | 5.8892 | 5.6502 | 5.4262 | 5.2161 | 5.0188 | 4.8332 | 4.6586 | 4.4941 | 4.3389 | 4.1925 | 10 |
| 11 | 6.2065 | 5.9377 | 5.6869 | 5.4527 | 5.2337 | 5.0286 | 4.8364 | 4.6560 | 4.4865 | 4.3271 | 11 |
| 12 | 6.4924 | 6.1944 | 5.9176 | 5.6603 | 5.4206 | 5.1971 | 4.9884 | 4.7932 | 4.6105 | 4.4392 | 12 |
| 13 | 6.7499 | 6.4235 | 6.1218 | 5.8424 | 5.5831 | 5.3423 | 5.1183 | 4.9095 | 4.7147 | 4.5327 | 13 |
| 14 | 6.9819 | 6.6282 | 6.3025 | 6.0021 | 5.7245 | 5.4675 | 5.2293 | 5.0081 | 4.8023 | 4.6106 | 14 |
| 15 | 7.1909 | 6.8109 | 6.4624 | 6.1422 | 5.8474 | 5.5755 | 5.3242 | 5.0916 | 4.8759 | 4.6755 | 15 |
| 16 | 7.3792 | 6.9740 | 6.6039 | 6.2651 | 5.9542 | 5.6685 | 5.4053 | 5.1624 | 4.9377 | 4.7296 | 16 |
| 17 | 7.5488 | 7.1196 | 6.7291 | 6.3729 | 6.0472 | 5.7487 | 5.4746 | 5.2223 | 4.9897 | 4.7746 | 17 |
| 18 | 7.7016 | 7.2497 | 6.8399 | 6.4674 | 6.1280 | 5.8178 | 5.5339 | 5.2732 | 5.0333 | 4.8122 | 18 |
| 19 | 7.8393 | 7.3658 | 6.9380 | 6.5504 | 6.1982 | 5.8775 | 5.5845 | 5.3162 | 5.0700 | 4.8435 | 19 |
| 20 | 7.9633 | 7.4694 | 7.0248 | 6.6231 | 6.2593 | 5.9288 | 5.6278 | 5.3527 | 5.1009 | 4.8696 | 20 |
| 21 | 8.0751 | 7.5620 | 7.1016 | 6.6870 | 6.3125 | 5.9731 | 5.6648 | 5.3837 | 5.1268 | 4.8913 | 21 |
| 22 | 8.1757 | 7.6446 | 7.1695 | 6.7429 | 6.3587 | 6.0113 | 5.6964 | 5.4099 | 5.1486 | 4.9094 | 22 |
| 23 | 8.2664 | 7.7184 | 7.2297 | 6.7921 | 6.3988 | 6.0442 | 5.7234 | 5.4321 | 5.1668 | 4.9245 | 23 |
| 24 | 8.3481 | 7.7843 | 7.2829 | 6.8351 | 6.4338 | 6.0726 | 5.7465 | 5.4509 | 5.1822 | 4.9371 | 24 |
| 25 | 8.4217 | 7.8431 | 7.3300 | 6.8729 | 6.4641 | 6.0971 | 5.7662 | 5.4669 | 5.1951 | 4.9476 | 25 |

## APPENDIX TABLE A-2 (Cont.)
### Present Value of an Annuity of One Dollar for n Years

| n | 21% | 22% | 23% | 24% | 25% | 26% | 27% | 28% | 29% | 30% | n |
|---|-----|-----|-----|-----|-----|-----|-----|-----|-----|-----|---|
| 1 | .8264 | .8197 | .8130 | .8065 | .8000 | .7937 | .7874 | .7813 | .7752 | .7692 | 1 |
| 2 | 1.5095 | 1.4915 | 1.4740 | 1.4568 | 1.4400 | 1.4235 | 1.4074 | 1.3916 | 1.3761 | 1.3609 | 2 |
| 3 | 2.0739 | 2.0422 | 2.0114 | 1.9813 | 1.9520 | 1.9234 | 1.8956 | 1.8684 | 1.8420 | 1.8161 | 3 |
| 4 | 2.5404 | 2.4936 | 2.4483 | 2.4043 | 2.3616 | 2.3202 | 2.2800 | 2.2410 | 2.2031 | 2.1662 | 4 |
| 5 | 2.9260 | 2.8636 | 2.8035 | 2.7454 | 2.6893 | 2.6351 | 2.5827 | 2.5320 | 2.4830 | 2.4356 | 5 |
| 6 | 3.2446 | 3.1669 | 3.0923 | 3.0205 | 2.9514 | 2.8850 | 2.8210 | 2.7594 | 2.7000 | 2.6427 | 6 |
| 7 | 3.5079 | 3.4155 | 3.3270 | 3.2423 | 3.1611 | 3.0833 | 3.0087 | 2.9370 | 2.8682 | 2.8021 | 7 |
| 8 | 3.7256 | 3.6193 | 3.5179 | 3.4212 | 3.3289 | 3.2407 | 3.1564 | 3.0758 | 2.9986 | 2.9247 | 8 |
| 9 | 3.9054 | 3.7863 | 3.6731 | 3.5655 | 3.4631 | 3.3657 | 3.2728 | 3.1842 | 3.0997 | 3.0190 | 9 |
| 10 | 4.0541 | 3.9232 | 3.7993 | 3.6819 | 3.5705 | 3.4648 | 3.3644 | 3.2689 | 3.1781 | 3.0915 | 10 |
| 11 | 4.1769 | 4.0354 | 3.9018 | 3.7757 | 3.6564 | 3.5435 | 3.4365 | 3.3351 | 3.2388 | 3.1473 | 11 |
| 12 | 4.2785 | 4.1274 | 3.9852 | 3.8514 | 3.7251 | 3.6060 | 3.4933 | 3.3868 | 3.2859 | 3.1903 | 12 |
| 13 | 4.3624 | 4.2028 | 4.0530 | 3.9124 | 3.7801 | 3.6555 | 3.5381 | 3.4272 | 3.3224 | 3.2233 | 13 |
| 14 | 4.4317 | 4.2646 | 4.1082 | 3.9616 | 3.8241 | 3.6949 | 3.5733 | 3.4587 | 3.3507 | 3.2487 | 14 |
| 15 | 4.4890 | 4.3152 | 4.1530 | 4.0013 | 3.8593 | 3.7261 | 3.6010 | 3.4834 | 3.3726 | 3.2682 | 15 |
| 16 | 4.5364 | 4.3567 | 4.1894 | 4.0333 | 3.8874 | 3.7509 | 3.6228 | 3.5026 | 3.3896 | 3.2832 | 16 |
| 17 | 4.5755 | 4.3908 | 4.2190 | 4.0591 | 3.9099 | 3.7705 | 3.6400 | 3.5177 | 3.4028 | 3.2948 | 17 |
| 18 | 4.6079 | 4.4187 | 4.2431 | 4.0799 | 3.9279 | 3.7861 | 3.6536 | 3.5294 | 3.4130 | 3.3037 | 18 |
| 19 | 4.6346 | 4.4415 | 4.2627 | 4.0967 | 3.9424 | 3.7985 | 3.6642 | 3.5386 | 3.4210 | 3.3105 | 19 |
| 20 | 4.6567 | 4.4603 | 4.2786 | 4.1103 | 3.9539 | 3.8083 | 3.6726 | 3.5458 | 3.4271 | 3.3158 | 20 |
| 21 | 4.6750 | 4.4756 | 4.2916 | 4.1212 | 3.9631 | 3.8161 | 3.6792 | 3.5514 | 3.4319 | 3.3198 | 21 |
| 22 | 4.6900 | 4.4882 | 4.3021 | 4.1300 | 3.9705 | 3.8223 | 3.6844 | 3.5558 | 3.4356 | 3.3230 | 22 |
| 23 | 4.7025 | 4.4985 | 4.3106 | 4.1371 | 3.9764 | 3.8273 | 3.6885 | 3.5592 | 3.4384 | 3.3254 | 23 |
| 24 | 4.7128 | 4.5070 | 4.3176 | 4.1428 | 3.9811 | 3.8312 | 3.6918 | 3.5619 | 3.4406 | 3.3272 | 24 |
| 25 | 4.7213 | 4.5139 | 4.3232 | 4.1474 | 3.9849 | 3.8342 | 3.6943 | 3.5640 | 3.4423 | 3.3286 | 25 |

# Appendix B

## Revenue Ruling 59-60

## REVENUE RULING 59-60

In valuing the stock of closely-held corporations, or the stock of corporations where market quotations are not available, all other available financial data, as well as all relevant factors affecting the fair market value must be considered for estate tax and gift tax purposes. No general formula may be given that is applicable to the many different valuation situations arising in the valuation of such stock. However, the general approach, methods and factors which must be considered in valuing such securities are outlined.

### SECTION 1. PURPOSE.

The purpose of this Revenue Ruling is to outline and review in general the approach, methods and factors to be considered in valuing shares of the capital stock of closely-held corporations for estate tax and gift tax purposes. The methods discussed herein will apply likewise to the valuation of corporate stocks on which market quotations are either unavailable or are of such scarcity that they do not reflect the fair market value.

### SECTION 2. BACKGROUND AND DEFINITIONS.

.01 All valuations must be made in accordance with the applicable provisions of the Internal Revenue Code of 1954 and the Federal Estate Tax and Gift Tax Regulations. Sections 2031(a), 2032 and 2512(a) of the 1954 Code (sections 811 and 1005 of the 1939 Code) require that the property to be included in the gross estate, or made the subject of a gift, shall be taxed on the basis of the value of the property at the time of death of the decedent, the alternate date if so elected, or the date of gift.

.02 Section 20.2031-1(b) of the Estate Tax Regulations (section 81.10 of the Estate Tax Regulations 105) and section 25.2512-1 of the Gift Tax Regulations (section 86.19 of Gift Tax Regulations 108) define fair market value, in effect, as the price at which the property would change hands between a willing buyer and a willing seller when the former is not under any compulsion to buy and the latter is not under any compulsion to sell, both parties having reasonable knowledge of relevant facts. Court decisions frequently state in addition that the hypothetical buyer and seller are assumed to be able, as well as willing, to trade and to be well informed about the property and concerning the market for such property.

.03 Closely-held corporations are those corporations the shares of which are owned by a relatively limited number of stockholders. Often the entire stock issue is held by one family. The result of this situation is that little, if any, trading in the shares takes place. There is, therefore, no established market for the stock and such sales as occur at irregular intervals seldom reflect all of the elements of a representative transaction as defined by the term "fair market value."

### SECTION 3. APPROACH TO VALUATION.

.01 A determination of fair market value, being a question of fact, will depend upon the circumstances in each case. No formula can be devised that will be generally applicable to the multitude of different valuation issues arising in estate and gift tax cases. Often, an appraiser will find wide differences of opinion as to the fair market value of a particular stock. In resolving such differences, he should maintain a reasonable attitude in recognition of the fact that valuation is not an exact science. A sound valuation will be based upon all the relevant facts, but the elements of common sense, informed judgment and reasonableness must enter into the process of weighing those facts and determining their aggregate significance.

.02 The fair market value of specific shares of stock will vary as general economic conditions change from "normal" to "boom" or "depression," that is, according to the degree of optimism or pessimism with which the investing public regards the future at the required date of appraisal. Uncertainty as to the stability or continuity of the future income from a property decreases its value by increasing the risk of loss of earnings and value in the future. The value of shares of stock of a company with very uncertain future prospects is highly speculative. The appraiser must exercise his judgment as to the degree of risk attaching to the business of the corporation which issued the stock, but that judgment must be related to all of the other factors affecting value.

.03 Valuation of securities is, in essence, a prophesy as to the future and must be based on facts available at the required date of appraisal. As a generalization, the prices of stocks which are traded in volume in a free and active market by informed persons best reflect the

SOURCE: 1959-1 C.B. 237.

consensus of the investing public as to what the future holds for the corporations and industries represented. When a stock is closely held, is traded infrequently, or is traded in an erratic market, some other measure of value must be used. In many instances, the next best measure may be found in the prices at which the stocks of companies engaged in the same or similar line of business are selling in a free and open market.

## SECTION 4. FACTORS TO CONSIDER.

.01 It is advisable to emphasize that in the valuation of the stock of closely-held corporations or the stock of corporations where market quotations are either lacking or too scarce to be recognized, all available financial data, as well as all relevant factors affecting the fair market value, should be considered. The following factors, although not all-inclusive are fundamental and require careful analysis in each case:

(a) The nature of the business and the history of the enterprise from its inception.
(b) The economic outlook in general and the condition and outlook of the specific industry in particular.
(c) The book value of the stock and the financial condition of the business.
(d) The earning capacity of the company.
(e) The dividend-paying capacity.
(f) Whether or not the enterprise has goodwill or other intangible value.
(g) Sales of the stock and the size of the block of stock to be valued.
(h) The market price of stocks of corporations engaged in the same or a similar line of business having their stocks actively traded in a free and open market, either on an exchange or over-the-counter.

.02 The following is a brief discussion of each of the foregoing factors:

(a) The history of a corporate enterprise will show its past stability or instability, its growth or lack of growth, the diversity or lack of diversity of its operations, and other facts needed to form an opinion of the degree of risk involved in the business. For an enterprise which changed its form of organization but carried on the same or closely similar operations of its predecessor, the history of the former enterprise should be considered. The detail to be considered should increase with approach to the required date of appraisal, since recent events are of greatest help in predicting the future; but a study of gross and net income, and of dividends covering a long prior period, is highly desirable. The history to be studied should include, but need not be limited to, the nature of the business, its products or services, its operating and investment assets, capital structure, plant facilities, sales records and management, all of which should be considered as of the date of the appraisal, with due regard for recent significant changes. Events of the past that are unlikely to recur in the future should be discounted, since value has a close relation to future expectancy.

(b) A sound appraisal of a closely-held stock must consider current and prospective economic conditions as of the date of appraisal, both in the national economy and in the industry or industries with which the corporation is allied. It is important to know that the company is more or less successful than its competitors in the same industry, or that it is maintaining a stable position with respect to competitors. Equal or even greater significance may attach to the ability of the industry with which the company is allied to compete with other industries. Prospective competition which has not been a factor in prior years should be given careful attention. For example, high profits due to the novelty of its product and the lack of competition often lead to increasing competition. The public's appraisal of the future prospects of competitive industries or of competitors within an industry may be indicated by price trends in the markets for commodities and for securities. The loss of the manager of a so-called "one-man" business may have a depressing effect upon the value of the stock of such business, particularly if there is a lack of trained personnel capable of succeeding to the management of the enterprise. In valuing the stock of this type of business, therefore, the effect of the loss of the manager on the future expectancy of the business, and the absence of management-succession potentialities are pertinent factors to be taken into consideration. On the other hand, there may be factors which offset, in whole or in part, the loss of the manager's services. For instance, the nature of the business and of its assets may be such that they will not be impaired by the loss of the manager. Furthermore, the loss may be adequately covered by life insurance, or competent management might be employed on the basis of the consideration paid for the former manager's services. These, or other offsetting factors, if found to exist, should be carefully weighed against the loss of the manager's services in valuing the stock of the enterprise.

(c) Balance sheets should be obtained, preferably in the form of comparative annual statments for two or more years immediately preceding the date of appraisal, together with a balance sheet at the end of the month preceding that date, if corporate accounting will permit. Any balance sheet descriptions that are not self-explanatory, and balance sheet items comprehending diverse assets or liabilities, should be clarified in essential detail by supporting supplemental schedules. These statements usually will disclose to the appraiser (1) liquid position (ratio of current assets to current liabilities); (2) gross and net book value of principal classes of fixed assets; (3) working capital; (4) long-term indebtedness; (5) capital structure; and (6) net worth. Consideration also should be given to any assets not essential to the operation of the business, such as investments in securities, real estate, etc. In general, such nonoperating assets will command a lower rate of return than do the operating assets, although in exceptional cases the reverse may be true. In computing the book value per share of stock, assets of the investment type should be revalued on the basis of their market price and the book value adjusted accordingly. Comparison of the company's balance sheets over several years may reveal, among other facts, such developments as the acquisition of additional production facilities or subsidiary companies, improvement in financial position, and details as to recapitalizations and other changes in the capital structure of the corporation. If the corporation has more than one class of stock outstanding, the charter or certificate of incorporation should be examined to ascertain the explicit rights and privileges of the various stock issues including: (1) voting powers, (2) preference as to dividends, and (3) preference as to assets in the event of liquidation.

(d)  Detailed profit-and-loss statements should be obtained and considered for a representative period immediately prior to the required date of appraisal, preferably five or more years. Such statements should show (1) gross income by principal items; (2) principal deductions from gross income including major prior items of operating expenses, interest and other expense on each item of long-term debt, depreciation and depletion if such deductions are made, officers' salaries, in total if they appear to be reasonable or in detail if they seem to be excessive, contributions (whether or not deductible for tax purposes) that the nature of its business and its community position require the corporation to make, and taxes by principal items, including income and excess profits taxes; (3) net income available for dividends; (4) rates and amounts of dividends paid on each class of stock; (5) remaining amount carried to surplus; and (6) adjustments to, and reconciliation with, surplus as stated on the balance sheet. With profit and loss statements of this character available, the appraiser should be able to separate recurrent from nonrecurrent items of income and expense, to distinguish between operating income and investment income, and to ascertain whether or not any line of business in which the company is engaged is operated consistently at a loss and might be abandoned with benefit to the company. The percentage of earnings retained for business expansion should be noted when dividend-paying capacity is considered. Potential future income is a major factor in many valuations of closely-held stocks, and all information concerning past income which will be helpful in predicting the future should be secured. Prior earnings records usually are the most reliable guide as to the future expectancy, but resort to arbitrary five-or-ten-year averages without regard to current trends or future prospects will not produce a realistic valuation. If, for instance, a record of progressively increasing or decreasing net income is found, then greater weight may be accorded the most recent years' profits in estimating earning power. It will be helpful, in judging risk and the extent to which a business is a marginal operator, to consider deductions from income and net income in terms of percentage of sales. Major categories of cost and expense to be so analyzed include the consumption of raw materials and supplies in the case of manufacturers, processors and fabricators; the cost of purchased merchandise in the case of merchants; utility services; insurance; taxes; depletion or depreciation; and interest.

(e)  Primary consideration should be given to the dividend-paying capacity of the company rather than to dividends actually paid in the past. Recognition must be given to the necessity of retaining a reasonable portion of profits in a company to meet competition. Dividend-paying capacity is a factor that must be considered in an appraisal, but dividends actually paid in the past may not have any relation to dividend-paying capacity. Specifically, the dividends paid by a closely-held family company may be measured by the income needs of the stockholders or by their desire to avoid taxes on dividend receipts, instead of by the ability of the company to pay dividends. Where an actual or effective controlling interest in a corporation is to be valued, the dividend factor is not a material element, since the payment of such dividends is discretionary with the controlling stockholders. The individual or group in control can substitute salaries and bonuses for dividends, thus reducing net income and understating the dividend-paying capacity of the company. It follows, therefore, that dividends are less reliable criteria of fair market value than other applicable factors.

(f)  In the final analysis, goodwill is based upon earning capacity. The presence of goodwill and its value, therefore, rests upon the excess of net earnings over and above a fair return on the net tangible assets. While the element of goodwill may be based primarily on earnings, such factors as the prestige and renown of the business, the ownership of a trade or brand name, and a record of successful operation over a prolonged period in a particular locality, also may furnish support for the inclusion of intangible value. In some instances it may not be possible to make a separate appraisal of the tangible and intangible assets of the business. The enterprise has a value as an entity. Whatever intangible value there is, which is supportable by the facts, may be measured by the amount by which the appraised value of the tangible assets exceeds the net book value of such assets.

(g)  Sales of stock of a closely-held corporation should be carefully investigated to determine whether they represent transactions at arm's length. Forced or distress sales do not ordinarily reflect fair market value nor do isolated sales in small amounts necessarily control as the measure of value. This is especially true in the valuation of a controlling interest in a corporation. Since, in the case of closely-held stocks, no prevailing market prices are available, there is no basis for making an adjustment for blockage. It follows, therefore, that such stocks should be valued upon a consideration of all the evidence affecting the fair market value. The size of the block of stock itself is a relevant factor to be considered. Although it is true that a minority interest in an unlisted corporation's stock is more difficult to sell than a similar block of listed stock, it is equally true that control of a corporation, either actual or in effect, representing as it does an added element of value, may justify a higher value for a specific block of stock.

(h)  Section 2031(b) of the Code states, in effect, that in valuing unlisted securities the value of stock or securities of corporations engaged in the same or a similar line of business which are listed on an exchange should be taken into consideration along with all other factors. An important consideration is that the corporations to be used for comparisons have capital stocks which are actively traded by the public. In accordance with section 2031(b) of the Code, stocks listed on an exchange are to be considered first. However, if sufficient comparable companies whose stocks are listed on an exchange cannot be found, other comparable companies which have stocks actively traded on the over-the-counter market also may be used. The essential factor is that whether the stocks are sold on an exchange or over-the-counter there is evidence of an active, free public market for the stock as of the valuation date. In selecting corporations for comparative purposes, care should be taken to use only comparable companies. Although the only restrictive requirement as to comparable corporations specified in the statute is that their lines of business be the same or similar, yet it is obvious that consideration must be given to other relevant factors in order that the most valid comparison possible will be obtained. For illustration, a corporation having one or more issues of preferred stock, bonds or debentures in addition to its common stock should not be considered to be directly comparable to one having only common stock outstanding. In like manner, a company with a declining business and decreasing markets is not comparable to one with a record of current progress and market expansion.

## SECTION 5.  WEIGHT TO BE ACCORDED VARIOUS FACTORS.

The valuation of closely-held corporate stock entails the consideration of all relevant factors as stated in section 4. Depending upon the circumstances in each case, certain factors may carry more weight than others because of the nature of the company's business. To illustrate:

(a)  Earnings may be the most important criterion of value in some cases whereas asset value will receive primary consideration in others. In general, the appraiser will accord primary consideration to earnings when valuing stocks of companies which sell products or services to the public; conversely, in the investment or holding type of company, the appraiser may accord the greatest weight to the assets underlying the security to be valued.

(b)  The value of the stock of a closely-held investment or real estate holding company, whether or not family owned, is closely related to the value of the assets underlying the stock. For companies of this type the appraiser should determine the fair market values of the assets of the company. Operating expenses of such a company and the cost of liquidating it, if any, merit consideration when appraising the relative values of the stock and the underlying assets. The market values of the underlying assets give due weight to potential earnings and dividends of the particular items of property underlying the stock, capitalized at rates deemed proper by the investing public at the date of appraisal. A current appraisal by the investing public should be superior to the retrospective opinion of an individual. For these reasons, adjusted net worth should be accorded greater weight in valuing the stock of a closely-held investment or real estate holding company, whether or not family owned, than any of the other customary yardsticks of appraisal, such as earnings and dividend-paying capacity.

## SECTION 6.  CAPITALIZATION RATES.

In the application of certain fundamental valuation factors, such as earnings and dividends, it is necessary to capitalize the average or current results at some appropriate rate. A determination of the proper capitalization rate presents one of the most difficult problems in valuation. That there is no ready or simple solution will become apparent by a cursory check of the rates of return and dividend yields in terms of the selling prices of the corporate shares listed on the major exchanges of the country. Wide variations will be found even for companies in the same industry. Moreover, the ratio will fluctuate from year to year depending upon economic conditions. Thus, no standard tables of capitalization rates applicable to closely-held corporations can be formulated. Among the more important factors to be taken into consideration in deciding upon a capitalization rate in a particular case are: (1) the nature of the business; (2) the risk involved; and (3) the stability or irregularity of earnings.

### SECTION 7. AVERAGE OF FACTORS.

Because valuations cannot be made on the basis of a prescribed formula, there is no means whereby the various applicable factors in a particular case can be assigned mathematical weights in deriving the fair market value. For this reason, no useful purpose is served by taking an average of several factors (for example, book value, capitalized earnings and capitalized dividends) and basing the valuation on the result. Such a process excludes active consideration of other pertinent factors, and the end result cannot be supported by a realistic application of the significant facts in the case except by mere chance.

### SECTION 8. RESTRICTIVE AGREEMENTS.

Frequently, in the valuation of closely-held stock for estate and gift tax purposes, it will be found that the stock is subject to an agreement restricting its sale or transfer. Where shares of stock were acquired by a decedent subject to an option reserved by the issuing corporation to repurchase at a certain price, the option price is usually accepted as the fair market value for estate tax purposes. See Rev. Rul. 54-76, C.B. 1954-1, 194. However, in such case the option price is not determinative of fair market value for gift tax purposes. Where the option, or buy and sell agreement, is the result of voluntary action by the stockholders and is binding during the life as well as at the death of the stockholders, such agreement may or may not, depending upon the circumstances of each case, fix the value for estate tax purposes. However, such agreement is a factor to be considered, with other relevant factors, in determining fair market value. Where the stockholder is free to dispose of his shares during life and the option is to become effective only upon his death, the fair market value is not limited to the option price. It is always necessary to consider the relationship of the parties, the relative number of shares held by the decedent, and other material facts, to determine whether the agreement represents a bonafide business arrangement or is a device to pass the decedent's shares to the natural objects of his bounty for less than an adequate and full consideration in money or money's worth. In this connection see Rev. Rul. 157 C.B. 1953-2,255, and Rev. Rul. 189, C.B. 1953-2,294.

### SECTION 9. EFFECT ON OTHER DOCUMENTS.

Revenue Ruling 54-77, C.B. 1954-1,187, is hereby superseded.

_____

SOURCE: 1959-1, C.B. 237.

# Appendix C

## Bibliography

Books and Pamphlets
Articles
Sources of Information

# Books and Pamphlets

**American Collectors Association.** *Selling, Pricing or Buying an Agency.* Minneapolis: American Collectors Association Information Center (no date) (R − 1002).

**Babcock, Henry A.** *Appraisal Principles and Procedures.* Washington, D.C.: American Society of Appraisers, 1980.

**Baron, Paul B.** *When You Buy or Sell A Company.* Rev. ed. Meriden, Conn.: Center for Business Information, 1983.

**Bernstein, Leopold A.** *Financial Statement Analysis: Theory, Application and Interpretation.* Rev. ed. Homewood, Ill.: Richard D. Irwin, 1978.

**Bierman, Harold, Jr., and Smidt, Seymour.** *The Capital Budgeting Decision.* 5th ed. New York: Macmillan, 1980.

**Blackman, Irving L.** *How to Value Your Oil Jobbership for Tax Purposes.* Columbia, S.C.: Petroleum Marketing Education Foundation, 1981.

**Boyce, Byrl N.** *Real Estate Appraisal Terminology.* Rev. ed. Cambridge: Ballinger Publishing, 1982.

**Bunn, Vern A.** *Buying and Selling a Small Business.* 2d ed. Washington, D.C.: Small Business Administration, 1979 (Reprinted as *How to Buy & Sell a Small Business* in 1982).

*Business Insurance Agreements: A Guide For the Practicing Lawyer.* 5th ed. New York: Mutual Life Insurance Company of New York, 1980.

*Buying a Franchise.* San Francisco: Bank of America, 1981 (Small Business Reporter).

**Clatanoff, Robert M.** *The Valuation of Resort and Recreational Property: A Classified Annotated Bibliography.* Chicago: International Association of Assessing Officers, 1984.

**Coltman, Michael M.** *Buying (and Selling) a Small Business.* Seattle: Self-Counsel Press, 1983.

**Cooley, Philip L.** *How to Value an Oil Jobbership for Purchasing or Sale.* Bethesda, Md.: Petroleum Marketing Education Foundation, 1982.

**Desmond, Glenn M., and Kelley, Richard E.** *Business Valuation Handbook.* Marina del Rey, Calif.: Valuation Press, 1981.

———. *How to Value Professional Practices.* Marina del Rey, Calif.: Valuation Press, 1980.

*Determining the Going Concern Value of an Agency.* New York: Independent Insurance Agents of America, June 1979 (Agency Management Service).

*Determining the Market Value of an Agency.* New York: Independent Insurance Agents of America, August 1979 (Agency Management Service).

**Diamond, Stephen C., ed.** *Leveraged Buyouts.* Homewood, Ill.: Dow Jones-Irwin, 1985.

*The Dictionary of Real Estate Appraisal.* Chicago: American Institute of Real Estate Appraisers, 1984.

**Douglas, F. Gordon.** *How to Profitably Sell or Buy a Company or Business.* New York: Van Nostrand Reinhold, 1981.

**Dunn, Robert L.** *Recovery of Damages for Lost Profits.* 2d ed. Tiburon, Calif.: Lawpress Corp., 1981.

**Eskew, Robert K., and Jensen, Daniel L.** *Financial Accounting.* New York: Random House, 1983.

*Financing Small Business*. San Francisco: Bank of America, 1983 (Small Business Reporter).

**Fisher, Ken.** *Superstocks*. Homewood, Ill.: Dow Jones-Irwin, 1984.

*Franchise Register*. Bowling Green: Von-Vaughn Publications, 1984.

*Franchising*. San Francisco: Bank of America, 1977 (Small Business Reporter).

**Friedman, Edith J.** *Encyclopedia of Real Estate Appraising*. 3d ed. Englewood Cliffs, N.J.: Prentice-Hall, 1978.

**Gimmy, Arthur E.** *Tennis Clubs and Racquet Sports Projects: A Guide to Appraisal, Market Analysis, Development and Financing*. Chicago: American Institute of Real Estate Appraisers, 1978.

**Goldberg, Barth H.** *Valuation of Divorce Assets*. St. Paul: West Publishing, 1984.

**Goldstein, Arnold S.** *The Complete Guide to Buying and Selling a Business*. New York: New American Library, 1983.

**Graham, Benjamin, et al.** *Security Analysis: Principles and Technique*. 4th ed. New York: McGraw-Hill, 1962.

**Gumpert, David E., and Timmons, Jeffry A.** *The Insiders' Guide to Small Business Resources*. Garden City, N.Y.: Doubleday Publishing, 1982.

**Hansen, James M.** *Guide to Buying or Selling a Business*. Mercer Island, Wash.: Grenadier Press, 1979.

**Heuer, Karla L., and McKay, Cecil, Jr.** *Golf Courses: A Guide to Analysis and Valuation*. Chicago: American Institute of Real Estate Appraisers, 1980.

*How to Buy and Sell a Small Business*. Rev. ed. New York: Drake Publishers, Inc., 1982 (Reprint of Bunn's *Buying and Selling a Small Business*).

*How to Buy or Sell a Business*. San Francisco: Bank of America, 1982 (Small Business Reporter).

*How to Value a Restaurant Business*. Marina del Rey, Calif.: Valuation Press, 1980 (Business Valuation Monograph No. 4).

**Hull, Addis E.** *Stock Purchase Agreements in Estate Planning—With Forms*. 2d ed. Englewood Cliffs, N.J.: Prentice-Hall, 1979.

**Jones, Jeffrey D.** *Buying, Selling, and Evaluating the Small Business*. MBA Research Project, Pepperdine University, December 1979.

**Jurek, Walter.** *How to Determine the Value of a Business*. Stow, Ohio: Quality Services, Inc., 1977.

————. *How to Properly Finance a Business*. Stow, Ohio: Quality Services, Inc., 1976.

————. *A Reference Manual of Practical Information on Buying or Selling a Business*. Stow, Ohio: Quality Services, Inc., 1977.

**Kohler, Eric Louis.** *Kohler's Dictionary for Accountants*. Edited by W.W. Cooper and Yuji Ijiri. 6th ed. Englewood Cliffs, N.J.: Prentice-Hall, 1983.

**Kravitt, Gregory I.** *How to Raise Capital: Preparing and Presenting a Business Plan*. Homewood, Ill.: Dow Jones-Irwin, 1984.

**Kroeger, Herbert E.** *Using Discounted Cash Flow Effectively*. Homewood, Ill.: Dow Jones-Irwin, 1984.

**Lipper, Arthur, III.** *Venture's Guide to Investing in Private Companies*. Homewood, Ill.: Dow Jones-Irwin, 1984.

**Martin, Thomas J., and Gustafson, Mark R.** *Valuing Your Business*. New York: Holt Rinehart & Winston, 1980.

**McCullough, Rose.** *The ABC's of Agency Evaluation, Acquisition, and Merger.* Indianapolis: Rough Notes Co., April 1982.

*McGraw-Hill Dictionary of Modern Economics: A Handbook of Terms and Organizations.* 3d ed. New York: McGraw-Hill, 1983.

**Miles, Raymond C.** *Basic Business Appraisal.* New York: John Wiley & Sons, 1984.

**Moye, John E.** *Buying and Selling Businesses.* Minneapolis: National Practice Institute, 1983.

**Nelson, David M.** *The Valuation of Petroleum Jobberships In the United States, 1980 through 1983.* Bethesda: Petroleum Marketing Education Foundation, 1984.

**Pratt, Shannon.** *Valuing a Business: The Analysis and Appraisal of Closely Held Companies.* Homewood, Ill.: Dow Jones-Irwin, 1981.

**Rice, Michael Downey.** *Prentice-Hall Dictionary of Business, Finance and Law.* Englewood Cliffs, N.J.: Prentice-Hall, 1983.

**Rosenberg, Jerry M.** *Dictionary of Banking and Finance.* New York: John Wiley & Sons, 1982.

**Rushmore, Stephen.** *Hotels, Motels, and Restaurants: Valuation and Market Studies.* Chicago: American Institute of Real Estate Appraisers, 1983.

**Schnepper, Jeff A.** *The Professional Handbook of Business Valuation.* Reading, Mass.: Addison-Wesley Publishing, 1982.

**Schreiber, Irving, and Skiba, Jonathan.** *The Closely Held Corporation: Tax, Financial & Estate Planning.* Greenvale, N.Y.: Panel Publishers, 1983. See especially Ch. 705: "Buy-Sell Agreements."

**Shangold, Jules, and Greenberg, Frank.** *How to Buy, Sell and Share a Practice of Podiatric Medicine.* Mount Kisco, N.Y.: Futura Publishing Co., 1977.

**Siegel, Joel G.** *How to Analyze Businesses, Financial Statements, and the Quality of Earnings.* Englewood Cliffs, N.J.: Prentice-Hall, 1982.

*Small Business Acquisition Manual: The Right Way to Buy a Small Business.* Brattleboro, Vt.: Country Business Services, 1981.

**Smith, David C.** *Appraisal of Accounting/Tax Practices.* Mission Viejo, Calif.: Business Brokerage, Inc. (no date).

**Solomon, Jerome P.** *Financial and Accounting Handbook for Service Industries.* Boston: CBI Publishing Co., 1981.

*The State of Small Business: A Report to the President.* Washington, D.C.: U.S. Government Printing Office, 1984.

**Stefanelli, John.** *The Sale and Purchase of Restaurants.* New York: John Wiley & Sons, 1985.

**Stevens, Lawrence.** *Guide to Starting and Operating a Successful Travel Agency.* Wheaton, Ill.: Merton House Travel and Tourism Publishers, 1983.

**Tetreault, Wilfred F.** *Buying and Selling Business Opportunities: A Sales Transaction Handbook.* Reading, Mass.: Addison-Wesley Publishing, 1981.

*Understanding Financial Statements.* San Francisco: Bank of America, 1980 (Small Business Reporter).

**U.S. Department of Commerce. International Trade Administration and Minority Business Development Agency.** *Franchise Opportunities*

*Handbook.* Compiled by Andrew Kostecka. Washington, D.C.: U.S. Government Printing Office, 1984.

*Use of the Private Annuity in Transferring Agency Ownerships.* New York: Independent Insurance Agents of America, Summer 1977 (Agency Management Service).

*Valuation of a Dental Practice: A Brief Overview for Buyers and Sellers.* Chicago: American Dental Association (no date).

*Valuing a Medical Practice: A Short Guide for Buyers and Sellers.* Chicago: American Medical Association, 1982.

*Valuing ESOP Shares.* Washington, D.C.: The ESOP Association, 1984.

**Wert, James E., and Henderson, Glenn V., Jr.** *Financing Business Firms.* 6th ed. Homewood, Ill.: Richard D. Irwin, 1979.

**Woolery, Arlo, ed.** *The Art of Valuation.* Lexington, Mass.: Lexington Books, 1978.

# Articles

**Adams, P. E.** "It's Not Difficult to Put a Price Tag on a Pharmacy." *American Druggist* 185 (March 1982) pp. 77–8.

**"Agency Valuation."** *Hale's Reports,* November 1984, pp. 144–6.

**Antin, Michal.** "Economics of Buy-Sell Planning: Putting the Package Together." *Tax Institute, University of Southern California Law Center,* 1981, pp. 500–53.

**"The Appraisal Remedy in Corporate Freeze-Outs: Questions of Valuation and Exclusivity."** *Southwestern Law Journal* 38 (June 1984), pp. 775–98.

**Arnold, Ralph.** "P/E Ratios Held Inadequate as Sole Valuation Criterion *In Re Marriage of Hewitson.*" *Willamette Valuation News,* December 1983, p. 2.

————. "Putting a Value on Future Interests." *Family Advocate,* Summer 1984, pp. 32–6, 42.

————. "Valuation of Non-Marketable Goodwill for California Community Property Law Purposes." *Business Valuation News,* September 1982, pp. 5–10.

**Baker, G. A.** "Goodwill, Going Concern Become Harder to Avoid." *Mergers & Acquisitions* 19 (Summer 1984) pp. 58–62.

**Banks, Warren E.** "A Selective Inquiry into Judicial Stock Valuation." *Indiana Law Review* 6 (1972) pp. 19–44.

**Bannen, J. T.** "Valuation of Closely Held Corporations." *Wisconsin Bar Bulletin* 55 (February 1982) pp. 15–17.

**Basi, Bart A.** "Want Your Business to Go On? Try Using 'Buy-Sell' Agreements." *Industrial Distribution* 68 (May 1978) pp. 75–77.

**Bell, Lawrence.** "Valuation and the Probability of Bankruptcy in Chapter X." *American Bankruptcy Law Journal* 52 (Winter 1978) pp. 1–22.

**Bentley, Marvin J., and Lieberman, Jay.** "Goodwill—What Is It Worth In the Market?" *Journal of the American Dental Association* 101 (September 1980) pp. 459–63.

Bergman, Gregory M. "Valuation of Goodwill." *Los Angeles Bar Journal* 53 (August 1977) pp. 87–98.

Birk, David R. "Shareholders' Appraisal Process: Need for Reform." *New York State Bar Journal* 51 (June 1979) pp. 274–7, 314–21.

Blackman, Irving. "Taking Money Out of a Closely Held Company." *Inc.,* September 1982, pp. 108–10.

————. "Valuing a Business: More than Numbers Alone." *Inc.,* November 1981, pp. 153–4.

Blaine, Davis R. "Valuation of Goodwill and Going Concern Value." *Mergers & Acquisitions,* Spring 1979, pp. 4–11.

Boehm, Ted. "Hoskold's Formula for the Valuation of Intangibles." *Capital University Law Review* 10 (Winter 1980) pp. 293–307.

Brennecke, J. Nile. "The Valuation of a Closely Held Company: An Overview and Application." *Journal of the Institute of Certified Financial Planners,* Fall 1984, pp. 155–70.

Bucholtz, H. R. "Using Restrictive Sales Agreements to Fix a Low Estate Tax Value for a Business Interest." *Estate Planning,* May 1981, pp. 146–52.

Buono, Thomas J. "Valuations in Broadcasting." *Appraisal Journal,* July 1984, pp. 382–8.

"Buying or Selling a Business Usually a Major Undertaking." *Lawn Care Industry,* August 1984, pp. 11, 13.

"Buying or Selling a Company on the Installment Plan." *Business Owner,* May 1983, pp. 4–6.

Carland, James W., Jr., and White, Larry R. "Valuing the Small Business." Journal of Small Business Management, October 1980, pp. 40–8. (See also Lloyd and Hand).

Cheifetz, A. J. "A Practical Guide to Determining the Value of a Professional Practice." *Taxation for Accountants,* February 1982, pp. 102–5.

"Choosing the Best Buy-Sell Agreement For Your Business." *Tax, Financial, and Estate Planning for the Owner of a Closely Held Corporation,* July 1984 (Special Report).

Christiansen, Burke A. "Funding a Buy-Sell Agreement." *Trusts & Estates,* July 1984, pp. 57–8.

"Community Property—Valuation of Professional Goodwill." *New Mexico Law Review* 11 (Summer 1981) pp. 435–50.

Coolidge, H. Calvin. "Fixing Value of Minority Interest in a Business: Actual Sales Suggest Discount as High as 70 Percent." *Estate Planning,* Spring 1975, 138–40. (Data updated in "Survey Shows Trend . . ." *Estate Planning,* September 1983, pp. 281–2.)

Cooper, Glen. "How Much Is Your Business Worth?" *In Business* 6 (September–October 1984) pp. 50–4.

Curren, Joe. "100 Questions to Ask before You Buy a Rental Business." *Rental Equipment Register,* April 1978, pp. 46–52.

Danzig, L. H., and Robison, R. A. "Going Concern Value Reexamined." *Tax Adviser* 11 (January 1980) pp. 32–6.

"Dealing with Contract Complications When You Buy or Sell a Business." *Tax, Financial, and Estate Planning for the Owner of a Closely Held Corporation,* March 1984, (Special Report).

"Depreciability of Going Concern Value." *University of Pennsylvania Law Review* 122 (December 1973), pp. 484–97.

de Vries, Ted. "What Is Your Business Really Worth?" *Rental Age,* October 1982, p. 40.

Dickey, David H. "Buy-Sell Agreements Can Conclusively Limit Value without Recapitalization Problems." *Estate Planning* 11 (September 1984), pp. 268–73.

Dlugatch, Harvey E., and Olds, Harold D. "Determining Goodwill in a Professional Practice for Purposes of a Community Property Division in a Marital Dissolution." *Community Property Journal,* Spring 1982, pp. 120–30.

Drymalski, Raymond, Jr. "Valuation of Stock of a Subchapter S Corporation—A New Form of Business Organization." *Illinois Bar Journal* 56 (April 1968), pp. 672–89.

Dubin, Lawrence M. "Allocation of Costs to, and Amortization of Intangibles in Business Acquisitions." *Taxes,* December 1979, pp. 930–45.

Ducharme, Guy N. "To Sell or Not to Sell." *Best's Review (Life/Health)* 84 (June 1983), pp. 16, 18.

Eber, Victor I. "The Valuation of Closely Held Companies." *Journal of Accountancy,* June 1984, pp. 103–18.

Einhorn, Stephen. "Notes on the Decision to Keep or to Sell a Small Business." *Mergers & Acquisitions* 12 (Summer 1977), pp. 29–31.

Emshoff, Reginald A. "Valuation of a Professional Practice." *Wisconsin Bar Bulletin* 55 (May 1982), pp. 10–12.

Epstein, Seymour. "Buy-Sell Agreements and Corporate-Owned Life Insurance." *Financial Planning Today,* November 1979, pp. 286–90.

Everett, Robert F. "What Is Your Business Worth?" *Real Estate Today,* October 1978, pp. 46–50.

Faris, John P., Holman, Walter R., and Martinelli, Patrick A. "Valuing the Closely Held Business." *Mergers & Acquisitions,* Fall 1983, pp. 53–59.

Feeney, Charles F. "Buying or Selling an Accountant's Practice—The Reader's Response." *National Public Accountant,* July 1983, pp. 20–3.

———. "Current Practices When Selling an Accounting Firm." *National Public Accountant,* May 1982, pp. 16–22.

Fishman, Jay E. "The Problem with Rules of Thumb in the Valuation of Closely Held Entities." *Fairshare,* December 1984, pp. 13–5. (Reprinted here as Exhibit 20–1.)

Foonberg, Jay. "Checklist for Buying, Selling a Rental Business." *Rental Equipment Register,* November 1979, p. 59.

Forbes, Wallace F. "Putting a Value on a Closely Held Company." *Family Advocate,* Summer 1984, pp. 28–30.

Fox, Jeffrey D. "Closely Held Business Valuation: the Uninformed Use of the 'Excess Earnings Formula' Method." *Taxes,* November 1982, pp. 832–6.

Fraser, Dick. "How Much Is Your Business Worth?" *Restaurant Business,* August 1, 1981, pp. 85–8.

Friedlob, George Thomas. "What Are the Effects of Differing Types of Restrictions on Closely Held Stock?" *Journal of Taxation,* April 1983, pp. 240–3.

Frost, Ted S. "Estate Planning for the Small Business." *D&B Reports* 21 (November/December 1983), pp. 58–60.

Ganier, P. K. "Treatment of Goodwill: Allocating a Lump-Sum Purchase Price among Mixed Assets of a Going Business." *Journal of Corporate Taxation* 7 (Summer 1980), pp. 111–36.

Garrett, David J. "Transferring Control of a Closely-Held Corporation: How to Do It and What to Look Out for." *Practical Accountant* 14 (August 1981), pp. 41–8.

Garrity, Vincent F. "Buy-Sell Agreements." *Pennsylvania Bar Association* Quarterly 46 (March 1975), pp. 190–9.

Gerhardt, Charles D. "Putting a Value on a Medical Practice." *Family Advocate,* Summer 1984, pp. 10–13.

Gold, M. L. "Valuing a Life Insurance Agency." *Best's Review (Life/ Health)* 78 (November 1977), pp. 16, 56, 58, 60.

"Goodwill." 38 *American Jurisprudence* 2d. (1968), and Supplement with updated information.

Gray, Gerald. "When is Fair Market Value Unfair?" *Valuation,* June 1984, pp. 2–7.

Gross, Paul H. "Establishing Fair Market Value of Intangible Assets." *Journal of Business Valuation* 4 (July 1977), pp. 5–17.

Hagy, David W. "Valuation of Spousal Interest in a Professional Practice for Equitable Distribution: *Hirschfeld* versus *Hirschfeld*." *University of Richmond Law Review* 17 (1983), pp. 383–402.

Hand, John H., and Lloyd William P. "Determining the Value of a Small Business." *MSU Business Topics* 28 (Summer 1980), pp. 5–10.

Hardee, David W. "Valuation of a Closely Held Business (Part 1)." *ALI-ABA Course Materials Journal* 5 (June 1981), pp. 35–50.

———. "The Valuation of a Closely Held Business (Part 2)." *ALI-ABA Course Materials Journal* 6 (August 1981), pp. 79–92.

———. "The Valuation of a Closely Held Business (Part 3)." *ALI-ABA Course Materials Journal* 6 (October 1981), pp. 83–118.

Harrison, Doane. "Pump Up and Preserve Your Practice Good Will." *Medical Economics,* April 15, 1985, pp. 107–12.

Haynsworth, H. J., IV. "Valuation of Business Interests." *Mercer Law Review* 33 (Winter 1982), pp. 457–517.

Heath, John, Jr. "Appraisal Processes In Mergers and Acquisitions." *Mergers & Acquisitions,* Fall 1974, pp. 4–21.

Hempstead, John E. "Putting a Value on a Law Practice." *Family Advocate,* Summer 1984, pp. 15–9.

Hill, J. Jeptha. "Estate Planning for the Closely Held Corporation and Its Owner." *Alabama Lawyer* 40 (January 1979), pp. 122–48.

Hill, Michael. "How Much Is Your Practice Worth?" *Texas Dental Journal,* August 1978, pp. 34–5.

Hill, Norman E., et al. "Appraising a Life Insurer before and after the Acquisition." *Best's Review (Life/Health)* 81 (November 1980), pp. 84–7.

Hitchings, Bradley. "Selling Your Small Company." *Business Week,* February 4, 1985, p. 101.

"How to Value an Income Stream: Case Study on Buying a Business." *Business Owner* 7 (June 1983), pp. 7–13.

Howard, James. "Defuse the Hostility Factor in Acquisition Talks." *Harvard Business Review* 60 (July/August 1982), pp. 54–8.

———. "What's It Worth to You? A Step-by-Step Guide to Establishing an Accurate Valuation of Your Business." *Inc.*, July 1982, pp. 75–80.

Hubler, Richard S. "How to Buy (or Maybe Sell) an Optometric Practice." *Optometric Management*, May 1982, pp. 27–32.

Hunt, Lester K. "Your Closely Held Construction Company—How Much Is It Worth?" *Constructor*, February 1979, pp. 22—6.

"The Installment Sale—Still an Effective Business and Estate Planning Tool." *Tax, Financial, and Estate Planning for the Owner of a Closely Held Corporation,* May 1984 (Special Report).

Irving, Raymond N., "How Much Is Your Practice Worth?" *Dental Management,* October 1981, pp. 16–20.

Jackson, James B. "Determining the Value of Your Practice: A Realistic Approach." *Journal of the American Dental Association,* September 1984, pp. 402–12.

Jacques, John H. "Insurance Agency Worth?" *Professional Agent,* May 1980, pp. 45–8.

Jakobson, Cathryn. "Five Good Reasons to Sell Your Business–And How to Make the Most of It When You Do." *Working Woman,* September 1984, pp. 194–206.

Jensen, Susan A. "Valuing a Real Estate Brokerage." *Real Estate Today,* September 1978, pp. 41–6.

Johnson, Alan W. "How Much Is Your Company Worth?" *Apparel Industry Magazine,* November 1982, pp. 34–8.

Johnson, Bradford M. "Valuing Community Bank Stocks." *Magazine of Bank Administration,* September 1978, pp. 32–36.

Jones, Jeffrey D. "Rule of Thumb Formulas for Small Businesses." *Business Valuation News,* December 1982, pp. 7–18.

Joyce, Allyn A. "Valuation of Nonpublic Companies." In *Accountants Handbook.* 6th ed. New York: John Wiley & Sons, 1981, pp. 38-1–38-28.

Kain, Gary D. "Valuation of Small Retail Businesses." *Journal of Business Valuation* 4 (July 1977), pp. 39–45.

Keesey, R. L., "The Campground Resort—A Valuation Model." *Real Estate Appraiser & Analyst,* Spring 1984, pp. 8–13.

Kellogg, Douglas E. "How to Buy a Small Manufacturing Business." *Harvard Business Review,* September/October 1975, pp. 5–15.

King, Roger T. "The Valuation of Goodwill: An Approach for the Appraiser." *Appraisal Review Journal,* Summer 1984, pp. 77–79.

Kittredge, Ellen V. "Corporations—Mergers—Delaware Redefines 'Entire Fairness' Test for Cash-out Mergers and Suggests More Liberal Appraisal Remedy. *Weinberger* versus *U.O.P, Inc.* 426 A. 2d 1333 (Del.)." *Villanova Law Review* 28 (May 1983), pp. 1049–82.

Kopple, Robert C. "An Introduction to Buy-Sell Agreements for Closely Held Corporations." *ALI-ABA Course Material Journal* 4 (April 1980), pp. 5–24.

Kruger, D. F., and Wiseberg, S. C. "How to Sell a Closely Held Corporation." *Practical Accountant,* April 1981, pp. 15–23.

Kuntz, Joel D. "Stock Redemptions Following Stock Transfers—An Expanding Safe Harbor Under Section 302(c)(2)(B)." *Taxes* 58 (January 1980), pp. 29–42.

**471**

LaFlamme, Gerald T. "The Purchase of a Food Service Business—A Value Judgment." *California CPA Quarterly,* September 1979, pp. 17–22.

Landsman, Stephen A. "Divorce Planning in the Closely-Held Business Context." *Trusts & Estates* 123 (May 1984), pp. 41–46.

_____. "Handling the Control Problems When Close Corporation Stock Is Transferred in a Divorce." *Taxation for Accountants,* July 1983, pp. 26–31.

Lang, Stuart S. "Buying, Merging or Selling an Accounting Practice." *Practical Accountant,* November 1983, pp. 87–95.

Leffingwell, Douglas C. "Covenants Not to Compete: What Factors the Courts Consider in Valuing Them Today." *Journal of Taxation* 34 (January 1971), pp. 20–2.

Lefko, Orville B. "Buy-Sell Agreements and Appraisals." *Michigan State Bar Journal* 55 (February 1976), pp. 116–27.

Leung, T. S. Tony. "Valuation of Professional Goodwill." *Business Valuation News,* June 1983, pp. 11–18.

Leverett, E. J., et al. "Agency Valuation." *Best's Review (Property Edition)* 80 (October 1979), pp. 34, 36, 82.

Liddle, Jeffrey L., and Gray, William F., Jr. "Proof of Damages for Breach of a Restrictive Covenant or Noncompetition Agreement." *Employee Relations Law Journal,* Winter 1983–84, pp. 455–73.

Litvak, Lawrence. "The Use of Buy-Sell Agreements in Establishing the Value of Closely Held Businesses." *Business Valuation News,* March 1984, pp. 3–16.

Lloyd, William P., and Hand, John H. "Some Notes on Valuing the Small Business." *Journal of Small Business Management,* April 1982, pp. 70–72. (See also Carland and White.)

Longenecker, Ruth R. "A Practical Guide to Valuation of Closely Held Stock." *Trusts & Estates* 122 (January 1983), pp. 32–41.

Ludtke, David A. "Planning for Family Corporate Control." *Nebraska Law Review,* 1979, pp. 644–91.

Maddock, Thomas S. "Smoothing the Merger & Acquisition Route." *Consulting Engineer,* February 1979, pp. 82–89.

Maher, J. Michael. "Impact of Keyperson Insurance on the Valuation of Closely Held Business Interests." *Trusts & Estates* 118 (August 1979), pp. 39–40.

Manning, Jerome A. "The S Corporation: A Vehicle to Support the Entrepreneur's Family." *National Law Journal,* April 16, 1984, pp. 15–21.

Matsen, Jeffrey R. "Establishing the Price for Closely Held Business Buy-Sell Agreements." *Journal of Corporate Taxation,* Summer 1978, pp. 134–56.

_____. "A New Look at Business Buy-Out Agreements." *Practical Lawyer* 25 (July 1979), pp. 43–64.

McMullin, Scott G. "The Valuation of Patents." *Business Valuation News,* September 1983, pp. 5–13.

Megna, Michael S. "Appraising Closely Held Share Capital." *Trusts & Estates* 177 (September 1978), pp. 561–65.

Mesko, John J. "How We Valued Our Closely Held Corporation (Special Tools and Machinery)." *Management Accounting* 63 (February 1982), pp. 41–43.

Minard, Lawrence. "The Case Against Price/Earnings Ratios." *Forbes,* February 13, 1984, pp. 172–6.

Mininberg, Mark. "Achieving Fairness in Corporate Cash Mergers: *Weinberger* versus *U.O.P.*" *Connecticut Law Review* 16 (Fall 1983), pp. 95–119.

"Minority Shareholders and Cashout Mergers: the Delaware Court Offers Plaintiffs Greater Protection and Procedure Dilemma—*Weinberger* versus *U.O.P., Inc.* 457 A.2d 701 (Del.)" *Washington Law Review* 59, (1983/84), pp. 119–40.

Newton, Grant W., and Ward, James J., Jr. "Valuation of a Business in Bankruptcy." *CPA Journal* 46 (August 1976), pp. 26–32.

Ninker, Robert W. "Your Funeral Home's Worth: Do Your Job Now." *The Director,* May/June 1984, pp. 5, 12–13, 47–48.

O'Conor, Charles W. "Packaging Your Business For Sale." *Harvard Business Review,* March-April 1985, pp. 52, 56, 58.

Olafson, Harold S. "How to Valuate a Small Business." *Real Estate Today,* March/April 1984, pp. 53–56.

Olson, Irving J. "Valuation of a Closely Held Corporation." *Journal of Accountancy* 128 (August 1969), pp. 35–47.

Page, William H. "Antitrust Damages and Economic Efficiency: An Approach to Antitrust Injury." *University of Chicago Law Review,* 1979-80, pp. 467–504.

Park, William R. "How Much Is It Worth?" *Consulting Engineer,* July 1981, pp. 104–9.

Parkman, Allen. "The Treatment of Professional Goodwill in Divorce Proceedings." *Family Law Quarterly,* Summer 1984, pp. 213–23.

Patterson, R., and Albo, W. "What's It Worth? Business Valuation and the Banker (Canada)" *Canadian Banker* 91 June 1984, pp. 18–23.

Paulsen, James Walter. "Closely Held Corporations in the Wake of *Vallone*: Enhancement of Stock Value by Community Time, Talent, and Labor." *Baylor Law Review* 35 (1983), pp. 47–96.

Paulsen, Jon., "Measuring Rods for Intangible Assets." *Mergers & Acquisitions,* Spring 1984, pp. 45–9.

Payson, Robert K., and Inskip, Gregory A. "*Weinberger* v. *U.O.P. Inc.*: Its Practical Significance in the Planning and Defense of Cash-Out Mergers." *Delaware Journal of Corporate Law* 8 (1983), pp. 83–97.

Pine, Vanderlyn R. "A Method for Estimating Goodwill." *American Funeral Director,* February 1971, pp. 28–33.

Piontek, Stephen. "Selling Your Agency? Forget Two Times Commissions." *National Underwriter (Property & Casualty Insurance edition),* September 9, 1983, pp. 4, 16.

Popell, S. D. "Mediating the Value of Small Businesses and Professional Firms." *Community Property Journal,* Winter 1983, pp. 17–27.

Pratt, Shannon P., "Developing the Valuation Model: Comparisons, Approaches and Sources." *Journal of Business Valuation* (Proceedings of the Seventh Biennial Conference of the Canadian Association of Business Valuators 1984, published in 1985).

————. "1984 Tax Act Increases Attraction of ESOPs." *Willamette Valuation News,* December 1984, p. 1.

————. "Note on Developing a Capitalization Rate Using the Capital Asset Pricing Model." *Business Valuation News,* March 1985, p. 24.

_____. "Rates of Return as an Influence on Value." Institute on State and Local Taxation and Conference on Property Taxation, New York University, *Proceedings,* Third Annual, 1985.

Pratt, Shannon P., and Hugo Craig S. "Pricing a Company by the Discounted Future Earnings Method." *Mergers & Acquisitions* 7 (Spring 1972), pp. 18–32.

Prickett, W., and Hanrahan, M. "*Weinberger* v. *U.O.P.*: Delaware's Effort to Preserve a Level Playing Field for Cash-Out Mergers." *Delaware Journal of Corporate Law* 8 (1983), pp. 59–82.

"Private Treble Damage Antitrust Suits: Measure of Damages for Destruction of All or Part of a Business." *Harvard Law Review,* 1967, pp. 1566–87.

"Property Division-Goodwill in Law Practice . . . *Dugan* v. *Dugan* 457 A.2d 1 (N.J.)" *Journal of Family Law* 22 (January 1984), pp. 386–91.

"Putting a Value on Your Business." *Common Sense.* Worcester, Mass.: Guaranty Bank, February 1983.

Quinn, Jeff. "How to Get the Most Benefit from Buy-Sell Agreements in S Corporations." *Taxation for Accountants* 30 (June 1983), pp. 364–9.

Raggio, Grier H., Jr. "Professional Goodwill and Professional Licenses as Property Subject to Distribution upon Dissolution of Marriage." *Family Law Quarterly,* Summer 1982, pp. 147–60.

Rams, Edwin M. "Judicial Valuation of Dissenting Shareholder Interests." *Appraisal Journal,* January 1975, pp. 105–118.

"The Recognition and Valuation of Professional Goodwill in the Marital Estate." *Marquette Law Review,* Summer 1983, pp. 697–743.

Reed, Lawrence. "Agency Valuation—How Much Is Your Agency Worth?" *Iowa Insurance Interpreter* 39 (December 1982).

Rennie, R. E., et al. "Factors in the Determination of the Valuation of Private Business Interests." *Osgoode Hall Law Journal,* June 1982, pp. 261–73.

Rosenbloom, Arthur H., and Bishop, John A. "Application of Discoverability and Foreseeability Concepts to Federal Tax Valuations." *The Review of Taxation of Individuals,* Autumn 1980, pp. 344–51.

Rybka, L. "How Much Is a Successful Life Insurance Practice Worth?" *Best's Review (Life/Health)* 80 (March 1980), pp. 46–50.

Samuelson, Elliot D. "Putting a Value on a Professional Practice." *Family Advocate,* Summer 1984, pp. 4–7, 40.

Schilt, James H. "Challenging Standard Business Appraisal Methods." *Business Valuation News,* December 1984, pp. 4–14.

_____. "An Objection to the Excess Earnings Method of Business Appraisal." *Taxes,* February 1980, pp. 123–26.

_____. "Pitfalls in the Valuation of Closely Held Companies." *Trusts & Estates* 119 (June 1980), pp. 44–47.

_____. "A Rational Approach to Capitalization Rates for Discounting the Future Income Streams of a Closely Held Company." *Financial Planner,* January 1982, pp. 56–57.

_____. "A Review of the Standard Methods of Evaluating Closely Held Companies." *Valuation,* November 1981, pp. 2–9.

_____. "Selection of Capitalization Rates for Valuing a Closely Held Business." *Business Law News* 5 (Spring 1982), pp. 35–37.

———. "A Short Essay on Intrinsic Value." *Business Valuation News,* March 1984, pp. 23–26.

———. "*Weinberger* v. *U.O.P. Inc.*: Challenge for the Business Appraiser." *Trusts & Estates* 123 (August 1984), pp. 44–47.

Schnee, Edward J., and Cargile, Barney R. "Going Concern Value—A New Intangible?" *Tax Advisor,* July 1984, pp. 386–92.

Schultz, Bill. "Make Sure You Get the Right Price for Your Company." *Inc.,* October 1980, pp. 76–78.

Scott, R. C. "Pricing the Going Concern." *Journal of Small Business Management* 15 (July 1977), pp. 37–40.

Scribner, Tom. "Professional Goodwill in Dissolution Proceedings: The Personification of Property." *Gonzaga Law Review* 17 (1982), pp. 303–27.

"Setting a Buy or Sell Price on a Rental Business." *Rental Equipment Register,* October 1978, pp. 38–48.

Shulkin, Martin B., and Green, Richard A. "Purchase or Sale of a Closely Held Corporation—An Overview." *Massachusetts Law Review* 63 (October 1978), pp. 211–19.

Shultz, Clayton G. "What's a Professional Practice Really Worth?" *CA Magazine* 116 (June 1983), pp. 36–40.

———. "The Valuation of Professional Practices." *Journal of Business Valuation,* 1983, pp. 145–54.

Simon, David, and Novack, Gerald A. "Limiting the Buyer's Market Damages to Lost Profits: A Challenge to the Enforceability of Market Contracts." *Harvard Law Review* 7 (May 1979), pp. 1395–438.

Sledge, Jimmy R., Jr. "Eminent Domain . . ." *Mississippi Law Journal,* 1982, pp. 927–40.

Smiley, Robert W., Jr. "LBOs: A Promising Avenue for ESOPs." *Employee Ownership,* September 1984, p. 1.

Solberg, Thomas A. "Buy-Sell Agreements Can 'Freeze' Asset Values and in Some Cases Make Them Disappear." *Taxes* 59 (July 1981), pp. 437–42.

Steinmetz, Lawrence L. "How to Place a Value on Your Carwash Business." *Management Report,* Spring 1983, pp. 24–31.

"Survey Shows Trend toward Larger Minority Discounts." *Estate Planning,* September 1983, pp. 281–82 (Updates data from Coolidge article).

Swanson, Robert D. "Cross-Purchase, Stock Redemption or Hybrid: Which Type of Buy-Sell Agreement Is Best?" *Taxation for Accountants* 24 (January 1980), pp. 34–8.

Thomas, Richard L. "How to Use a Buy-Sell Agreement to Protect a Client's Business and to Save Estate Taxes." *Estate Planning,* September 1979, pp. 258–64.

Thompson, Gary W. "What's That Practice Really Worth?" *Medical Economics,* September 27, 1982, pp. 88–100.

Tibergien, Mark C., and Leung, T.S. Tony. "Pricing a Practice." *Financial Planning* 13 (October 1984), pp. 203–4.

Torres, Paul D. "The Valuation of Professional Accounting Practices—Guidelines for Buyers and Sellers." *National Public Accountant,* April 1978, pp. 24–32.

Treanor, Richard B. "Is the Eighth Circuit's St. Louis Bank Case the Death Knell for Restrictive Stock Agreements?" *Journal of Taxation,* October 1982, pp. 200–3.

"Two Capital Investment Decisions: Buying a Machine, Buying a Business." *Business Owner,* July 1984, pp. 4–7.

Udinsky, Jerald H. "Goodwill Depreciation: A New Method for Valuing Professional Practices in a Marital Dissolution." *Community Property Journal,* Fall 1982, pp. 307–22.

"Valuation of Dissenter's Stock Under Appraisal Statutes." *Harvard Law Review,* May 1966, pp. 1453–74.

"Valuing a Closely Held Business." *Small Business Report* 6 (July 1981), pp. 11–14.

Vassiliades, John. "Whether You're Buying or Selling, Consider the Return on Investment." *American Coinop,* January 1983, pp. 5–9.

Vaughn, Robert, Jr. "How to Acquire a Closely Held Business." *Practical Lawyer* 22 (January 1976), pp. 11–19.

Vinso, Joseph D. "Excess Earnings Estimation of Intangibles—A Note." *Business Valuation News,* December 1984, pp. 15–17.

Vogel, N. J., Jr., and Petrini, K. R. "New Considerations in Drafting Buy-Sell Agreements for Estate Valuation Purposes: The Impact of St. Louis County Bank." *Estate Planning Institute,* University of Notre Dame Law School, 1982, pp. 615–41.

Wall, Joseph R. "The Recognition and Valuation of Professional Goodwill in the Marital Estate." *Marquette Law Review,* Summer 1983, pp. 697–743.

Wallach, George I. "The Buyer's Right to Monetary Damages." *Uniform Commercial Code Law Journal,* Winter 1982, pp. 236–83.

Walker, Donna. "1984 Tax Reform Act Affects Appraisers." *Willamette Valuation News,* December 1984, p. 2.

Weber, Harry. "An Evaluation of Business Valuation Techniques." *Valuation,* November 1982, pp. 104–12.

Welch, Robert M., Jr. "Discovery and Valuation in a Divorce Division Involving a Closely Held Business or Professional Practice." *Community Property Journal* 7 (Spring 1980), pp. 103–22.

"What's Your Closely Held Corporation Really Worth?" *Rent All,* July 1979, pp. 28–30.

Willson, Prentiss, Jr., and Halverson, Lori. "Subchapter S Changes in the 1984 Act." *Journal of Partnership Taxation,* Winter 1985, pp. 363–71.

Wise, Richard M. "The CA's Role in Valuations: An Inside-Out Perspective." *CA Magazine* (Canada) 117 (September 1984), pp. 28–40.

————. "Determining 'Fair Value' under the Appraisal and Oppression Remedies—A Valuator's Perspective." In *Corporate Structure, Finance and Operations,* vol. 3. Edited by L. Sarna. Toronto: V. Carswell Co., 1984.

————. "Some Valuation Concerns in Buy-Sell Agreements." *CA Magazine,* February 1985, pp. 52–8.

Wright, Graham W. "Valuation of Construction and Real Estate Development Companies." *Journal of Business Valuation* 4 (July 1977), pp. 19–23.

Wright, Graham W., and Adelstein, A. Joel. "Valuing the Real Estate Company." *Journal of Business Valuation* 1 (March 1974), pp. 41–45.

# Sources of Information

**Akey, Denise S., ed.** *Encyclopedia of Associations.* 19th ed. Detroit: Gale Research Co., 1985. A guide to more than 18,000 national and international organizations.

*American Statistics Index.* Washington, D.C.: Congressional Information Service (annual, with monthly supplements). A comprehensive guide and index to the statistical publications of the U.S. government. Includes government reports on industries.

*Business Index.* Belmont, Calif.: Information Access Company. Microfilm format; Subject and author guide to articles in over 810 periodicals.

*Business Periodicals Index.* New York: H.W. Wilson Co. (monthly, with quarterly and annual cumulations). Indexes about 270 periodicals, covering a wide range of business topics, including industries, with indexing arranged alphabetically by subject and author.

*Business Week Magazine.* New York: McGraw-Hill (weekly). In January, industry outlooks for major categories of businesses are presented.

*Directory of Industry Data Sources: the United States and Canada.* 2d ed. Cambridge: Harfax, 1982. Organized by general reference sources, industry data sources, data publishers and producers, with subject indexes by SIC Code and by alphabetical subject, and with a title index.

**Federal Reserve Bank of Cleveland.** *Economic Trends.* Cleveland, Ohio (monthly). Discusses the economy in general, components of the economy, and the financial markets.

*Financial Studies of the Small Business.* Washington, D.C.: Financial Research Associates (annual). Presents financial ratios for firms under $250,000 in total assets, grouped by type of business, including professional services.

*Forbes Magazine.* New York: Forbes, Inc. (bi-weekly). Each January, a special issue reports on various industries.

*Fortune Magazine.* Los Angeles: Time, Inc. (bi-weekly). Each issue presents an economic analysis.

**Ganly, John, Diane Sciattara, and Andrea Pedolsky, eds.** *Small Business Sourcebook.* 1st ed. Detroit: Gale Research Co., 1983. Part 1 presents information sources for 100 types of small business; Part 2 lists information resources and services for small businesses, arranged by type of organization, such as state and local governments. Subject and title indexes are provided.

**Grant, Mary McNierney, and Becleant-Schiller, Riva.** *Directory of Business and Financial Services.* 8th ed. New York: Special Libraries Association, 1984. Covers sources for a broad range of service and manufacturing industries, as well as sources of information on legislation, government rulings, and taxation.

*National Trade and Professional Associations of the United States.* Washington, D.C.: Columbia Books, Inc. (annual). Excellent book to contact sources for industry information. Lists about 6,000 national trade associations, labor unions, professional, scientific, or technical societies, and other national organizations comprised of groups united for a common purpose.

*Predicasts F & S Index of United States.* Cleveland, Ohio: Predicasts, Inc. (weekly, monthly and annual cumulations). Index for current information on companies, products, and industries. Covers periodicals and a few brokerage house reports. Contains information on corporate acquisitions and mergers, new products, technological developments and sociopolitical factors. Includes sections arranged by SIC numbers and alphabetically by company name.

*Predicasts Forecasts.* Cleveland, Ohio: Predicasts, Inc. (quarterly). Economic and industry forecast index arranged by products, with published sources of forecasts cited.

*RMA Annual Statement Studies.* Philadelphia: Robert Morris Associates (annual). Includes comparative historical data and other sources of composite financial data. Composite balance sheets and income data with selected ratios for over 300 lines of business. Includes bibliography of sources for industry financial data. Issued annually in October, covering fiscal years-end 6/30 through 3/31.

*Standard & Poor's Industry Surveys.* New York: Standard & Poor's Corporation (monthly, quarterly and annual). Basic data and analysis on numerous industries with financial comparisons of the leading companies in each industry. Includes a "Basic Analysis" for each, revised annually. A "current analysis" is published quarterly for each industry. A monthly "Trends and Projections" includes tables of economic and industry indicators, as well as a discussion.

*Standard & Poor's Statistical Service.* New York: Standard & Poor's Corporation. Contains basic statistics on the economy and broad industry groups, supplemented monthly by current statistics. Includes security price index record by industry group.

**Standard Rate & Data Service.** *Business Publication Rates and Data.* Skokie, Ill. (monthly). Subject classification of those business magazines accepting advertising.

*Statistical Reference Index.* Washington, D.C.: Congressional Information Service (annual, with monthly supplements). A selective guide to American statistical publications from sources other than the U.S. government. Includes economic and industry materials from state and local governments, universities, associations, commercial publishers, and so on.

*Stocks, Bonds, Bills and Inflation: 1985 Yearbook.* Chicago: Ibbotson Associates, 1985.

*Tax, Financial, and Estate Planning for the Owner of a Closely Held Business.* Greenvale, N.Y.: Panel Publishers (monthly). Contains articles, tax planning pointers, tax news, special reports.

**Troy, Leo.** *Almanac of Business and Industrial Financial Ratios.* Englewood Cliffs, N.J.: Prentice-Hall (annual). Ratios arranged by industries. Data is from the IRS and is published four to five years late.

**U.S. Board of Governors of the Federal Reserve System.** *Federal Reserve Bulletin.* Washington, D.C. Current U.S. banking and monetary statistics, and such basic business statistics as employment, prices, national income, and construction. Includes articles on the economy and financial markets.

**U.S. Bureau of Economic Analysis.** *Business Conditions Digests.* Washington, D.C.: U.S. Government Printing Office (monthly). Includes charts and statistical titles for leading economic time series. Sections include cyclical indicators; composite indexes and their components; cyclical indicators by economic process; diffusion indexes and rates of change; national income and product; prices, wages and productivity; labor force, employment, and unemployment; government activities; U.S. international transactions and international comparisons.

**U.S. Bureau of Economic Analysis.** *Survey of Current Business.* Washington, D.C.: U.S. Government Printing Office (monthly). Some discussion with charts and statistical tables; as well as tables of statistics on general business indicators; commodity prices; construction and real estate; domestic trade; labor force employment and earnings; finance; foreign trade of U.S.; transportation and communication; chemicals and allied products; electric power and gas; food and kindred products; and so on. Special statistical reports appear such as the "National Income Issue," "Local Area Personal Income," Corporate Profits," "Plant and Equipment Expenditures," "State & Regional Income."

**U.S. Department of Commerce.** *U.S. Industrial Outlook.* Washington, D.C.: U.S. Government Printing Office (annual). Information on recent trends and outlook for about five years in over 350 individual industries. Narrative with statistics contains discussions of changes in supply and demand, development in domestic and overseas markets, price changes, employment trends, capital investment.

*U.S. Master Tax Guide.* Chicago: Commerce Clearing House (annual). Summarizes tax laws, presents tax tables, and discusses major tax law changes.

**Wasserman, Paul, et al.** *Encyclopedia of Business Information Sources.* 5th ed. Detroit: Gale Research Co., 1983. Listing of information sources arranged by subjects, including industries; sources include statistics, directories, almanacs, periodicals, associations, handbooks, bibliographies, dictionaries, and general works.

**Wasserman, Paul, managing ed.** *Statistics Sources.* 9th ed. Detroit: Gale Research Co., 1984. A subject guide to data on industrial, business, social, educational, financial, and other topics for the United States and internationally.

# Index

Rosenberg, Jerry M., 217
Royalties, relief from, 394
*Rules of thumb*, 170, 188–89, 224–26, 314–16

**S**

Sales comparison approach; *see* Market approach
Sammons, Donna, 428
Sandwich shops, 363
Scribner, David, 362
Seller's discretionary cash; *see* Owner's discretionary cash
Seller's market, 20
Selling price/listing price ratio, 363
Service businesses; specific businesses, such as *see* Automotive service businesses *and* Personal service businesses
Service contracts, 392
Service stations, 363
*Sharp, In re Marriage of* (divorce case), 367
*Small Business Acquisitions Manual*, 59
*Small Business Reporter*, 157–58
Smidt, Seymour, 132
Society of Real Estate Appraisers, 216
*Socioeconomic Characteristics of Medical Practice*, 306, 320, 323, 333–34
Soft drink bottlers, 96, 182
Software, 393
Special master, 442, 444, 447
Squeeze-out mergers, 25–26, 370–71
Stabbert, Wally, 406
Standard & Poor's
    *Bond Guide*, 204–5
    *Industry Surveys*, 93
    *Outlook*, 204
    *Statistical Service*, 204
    *Trends & Projections*, 204, 268–69, 367, 370–71, 444
Standards of value, 9
Statutory ("squeeze-out") mergers, 370–71
Steven Langer & Associates, 306
Stock versus asset sale, 34, 353, 359–60
Stock and debt method (of determining a capitalization rate), 137
Stock redemption agreement, 381, 384 *Stocks, Bonds, Bills, and Inflation: 1985 Yearbook*, 140
Straight-line (depreciation method), 61
Subscriptions, 392
Sum-of-the-years'-digits (depreciation method), 61
*Summary Report of the Goodwill Registry*, 316
Summation method (for developing capitalization rate), 134, 136, 146–47
Supermarkets, 363
*Survey of Current Business*, 89
*Survey of Law Firm Economics*, 306
S.W.A.G., 49–50
Swirtz, Gregory, 188
Synergism, 352–53

**T**

Taverns, 182–83, 361, 363
Tax-assessed value, 47
Taxes
    ad valorem, 23
    adjusting for, 45–46, 68–70
    ESOP provisions, 379–80
    estate, 375–76
    gift, 375–76
    income, 375–76
    inheritance, 375–76
    penalties for undervaluation, 376
    tax-free rollover, 379

Tender offer, 26
Terms of sale
    effect on price, 173–74, 199–208, 210–13, 353–55, 359–60
    typical transactions, 360, 363
Texas Instruments Business Analyst II calculator, how to use, 168, 201, 203, 206
Total practice net return, 361
Total return, 127–31
Trademarks, 96, 392
Transaction price, 13
Treasury bills, U.S., 128, 136
Treasury method; *see* Excess earnings (method of valuation)
Treasury stock, 31
Trust and estate sales, minority interests, 272–73
*Trusts & Estates*, 369, 381
*Turgeon* v. *Turgeon* (divorce case), 368

**U**

UBI Business Brokers, 361–63
Udinsky, Jerald H., 160
*United States Economic Indicators*, 89
Unrecognized costs, 67
Unrecorded obligations, 53

**V**

*Valuation* (journal of the American Society of Appraisals), 421
Valuation assignment checklist, 5
Valuation Day, 419
Value; *see specific entries*, such as Adjusted book value, Book value, Cash equivalent value, Cash value, Fair market value, Fair value, Fundamental value, Going concern value, Intrinsic value, Investment value, Liquidation value, Market value, Standards of value
*Valuing a Business: The Analysis and Appraisal of Closely Held Companies*, 22, 123, 129, 165, 232, 248, 270, 354, 377, 435, 438
*Valuing ESOP Shares*, 22, 380, 420
*Valuing Your Business*, 165, 223
Vending routes, 363
*Venture's Guide to Investing in Private Companies*, 142
Veterinary practices, 316
Video rental and sales stores, 361

**W–Y**

*Wall Street Journal, The*, 63, 147
Warranty obligations, 97
*Washington State Bar News*, 311
Weber, Harry, 224
Weighted average of valuation approaches, 193–94
Weighted average cost of capital, 134, 136–37, 150
*Weinberger* v. *UOP* (dissenting stockholder suit), 371
Welch, Ronald W., 134
West, Tom, 401
*When You Buy or Sell a Company*, 19, 54, 211
White, Larry R., 141
Wholesale price index, 88
Willamette Business Sale Data Base, 358–61, 363
Wisconsin Department of Regulation and Licensing
    Business Listing Contract, 408–11
    Business Offer to Purchase, 413–15
Wise, Richard M., 13
Woolery, Arlo, 134
Work-in-process, 283–84
Working capital, 34, 108–12, 263–64
Yield capitalization, 219
Yield to maturity, 127